D1599010

Amsterdamer Beiträge
zur neueren Germanistik

herausgegeben von

Gerd Labroisse
Gerhard P. Knapp
Anthonya Visser

Amsterdamer Beiträge
zur neueren Germanistik
Band 47 — 2000

Rereading Romanticism

830. 9
R 3 1

herausgegeben von

Martha B. Helfer

Amsterdam — Atlanta, GA 2000

Die 1972 gegründete Reihe erscheint seit 1977 in zwangloser Folge in der Form von Thema-Bänden mit jeweils verantwortlichem Herausgeber.

Reihen-Herausgeber:

Prof. Dr. Gerd Labroisse, Sylter Str. 13A, D – 14199 Berlin
Tel./Fax: (49)30 89724235
E-Mail: Gerd.Labroisse@t-online.de

Prof. Dr. Gerhard P. Knapp, University of Utah, Dept. of Languages and Literature, 255 S. Central Campus Dr. Rm. 1400, USA – Salt Lake City, UT 84112
Tel.: (1)801 581 7561, Fax (1)801 581 7581 (dienstl.)
bzw. Tel./Fax: (1)801 474 0869 (privat)
E-Mail: gerhard.knapp@m.cc.utah.edu

Prof. Dr. Anthonya Visser, Universiteit Leiden, Duitse taal en cultuur, Postbus 9515, NL – 2300 RA Leiden
Tel.: (31)71 5272071, Fax: (31)71 5273309 (dienstl.)
bzw. Tel.: (31)71 565 2156 (privat)
E-Mail: visser@rullet.leidenuniv.nl

Redaktion: Prof. Dr. Anthonya Visser

All titles in the Amsterdamer Beiträge zur neueren Germanistik (from 1999 onwards) are available to download and read from the CatchWord website: http://www.catchword.co.uk

♾ The paper on which this book is printed meets the requirements of "ISO 9706:1994, Information and documentation - Paper for documents - Requirements for permanence".

ISBN: 90-420-0739-7 (bound)
©Editions Rodopi B.V., Amsterdam-Atlanta, GA 1999
Printed in The Netherlands

Inhalt/Contents

Anschriften der Autorinnen und Autoren/List of Contributors

Professor Fritz Breithaupt
Indiana University
Dept. of Germanic Studies
USA – Bloomington, IN 47405-6601

Professor Jane K. Brown
University of Washington
Dept. of Germanics
USA – Seattle, WA 98195-3130

Professor Michel Chaouli
Harvard University
Dept. of Germanic Languages and Literature
USA – Cambridge, MA 02138-3879

Professor Angela Esterhammer
University of Western Ontario
Dept. of English
CA – London, ON N6A 3K7

Dr. Anke Gilleir
Katholieke Universiteit Leuven
Dept. Literatuurwetenschap
B – 3000 Leuven

Professor Martha B. Helfer
University of Utah
Dept. of Languages and Literature
USA – Salt Lake City, UT 84112

Professor Jonathan M. Hess
University of North Carolina
German Dept.
USA – Chapel Hill, NC 27599-3160

Professor Susan Kassouf
Vassar College
Dept. of German
USA – Poughkeepsie, NY 12601

Professor Claudia Brodsky Lacour
Princeton University
Dept. of Comparative Literature
USA – Princeton, NJ 08544

Prof. Dr. Winfried Menninghaus
Freie Universität Berlin
Inst. für Allg. und Vergl. Literaturwissenschaft
D – 14195 Berlin

Professor Helmut Mueller-Sievers
Northwestern University
German Dept.
USA – Evanston, IL 60602

Prof. Dr. Jürgen H. Petersen
Universität Osnabrück
FB Sprach- und Literaturwissenschaft
D – 4500 Osnabrück

Professor Marc Redfield
Claremont Graduate Center
Dept. of English
USA – Claremont, CA 91711

Prof. Dr. Helmut J. Schneider
Germanistisches Seminar der Universität Bonn
D – 53111 Bonn

Professor Karin Schutjer
University of Oklahoma
Modern Languages, Literatures, and Linguistics
USA – Norman, OK 73019

Professor Azade Seyhan
Bryn Mawr College
Dept. of German
USA – Bryn Mawr, PA 19010

Professor Carsten Strathausen
University of Missouri-Columbia
Dept. of German and Russian Studies
USA – Columbia, MO 6521

Preface

In the past two decades influential studies by Lacoue-Labarthe and Nancy, Kuzniar, Menninghaus, Seyhan, Ziolkowski, and others have cast early German Romanticism as the progenitor of our own critical consciousness. The present volume aims to extend this line of research by analyzing the structure of Romantic critical discourse, as well as its ties to twentieth-century discursive paradigms, in a series of case studies. In short, this project is part of the ongoing process of re-evaluating Romanticism inaugurated by Friedrich Schlegel in his famous dictum: "Die romantische Dichtart ist noch im Werden, ja das ist ihr eigentliches Wesen, daß sie ewig nur werden, nie vollendet sein kann" (*Athenäum* Fragment #116). Given its programmatic mutability, Romantic discourse demands to be continuously reread.

When I solicited contributions for the volume, I intentionally left the topic vague, since "progressive Universalpoesie" by definition is an all-inclusive, ever-evolving mix of genres, themes, and disciplines, a fusing of poesy and criticism. Accordingly, my call-for-papers specified only that the articles deal with topics relating to Romanticism and its critical aftermath. I was impressed by the breadth and sophistication of the essays I received. The present volume does not pretend to offer a comprehensive rereading of Romanticism in its entirety, but it does promise sixteen innovative, compelling contributions to this ongoing enterprise. While many different groupings would have been possible, I opted to arrange the essays in chronological order.

Ernst Behler had planned to contribute an essay to this volume before his untimely death. Any scholar working in Romanticism today owes a tremendous debt to Professor Behler for his editorial and critical contributions to the field, and I join many voices in celebrating his achievements and mourning his loss.

I am grateful to Gerhard Knapp, who encouraged me to take on this project, and to Gerd Labroisse for his kind support throughout. Thony Visser offered indispensable help in seeing the manuscript into and through production, and I am thankful for her cheerful, efficient assistance. I also am grateful to the University of Utah College of Humanities for both a sabbatical leave and a Career Development Grant, which helped made this volume possible.

Martha B. Helfer

Jane K. Brown

"Es singen wohl die Nixen":
Werther and the Romantic Tale[1]

The ambiguity in Schubert's song cycles as to whether the protagonist dies of thwarted love or for betraying his brook allows identification of two typical plots, "Werther (18th-century) paradigm" and "Undine (Romantic) paradigm". The implicit presence of the "Undine paradigm" is established in Werther. *The transition from the rational psychology of* Werther *to an allegorical Romantic depth psychology is traced in Goethe's poetry of the 1780s and 90s; the Romantic fairy-tale does not reverse 18th-century psychology, but develops patterns implicit in its most popular narrative.*

The pivotal importance of *Werther* is one of the most obvious cliches of German literary history. The novel became a European best-seller overnight, grounded Goethe's fame for the rest of his long life, and has remained the most typical and famous work of the age of sensibility. Few would disagree that it represents the high point of the epistolary novel in Europe. Yet despite its stature and European fame, *Werther* played little obvious role in the further development of the novel in Germany. Romantic theory and practice ignore it in favor of *Wilhelm Meister* and its only apparently fulfilling love relationships, in which the passion of Mignon is consigned to the Hall of the Past. Despite the popularity of *Werther* and Goethe's continuing fame as its author, hardly a German work still in the canon today from the succeeding four decades could readily be labeled "Wertherian". The single exception is Hölderlin's *Hyperion*, which is, however, much more an elegiac autobiography than a novel of thwarted love and thwarted subjectivity. When the plot of *Werther* reemerged in the Biedermeier, it was in cycles of poems, not primarily novels – Wilhelm Müller's "Die schöne Müllerin" and "Die Winterreise" of 1815 and 1817, and Heinrich

[1] This essay first appeared as: "Es singen wohl die Nixen": *Werther* und das Märchen der Romantik. In: Jane K. Brown: *Ironie und Objektivität: Aufsätze zu Goethe.* Würzburg 1998. It is reprinted here with the kind permission of the publisher. I am indebted to my colleague Brigitte Prutti for her thoughtful critique of an early version of this essay, in particular for her insistence of the miller's epistemological uncertainty and for calling my attention to the parallels between Werther's fixations on the well and on Lotte's mouth.

Heine's parodistic poems of the 1820s in *Das Buch der Lieder*. What does it mean that *Werther* had so little of the kind of resonance that generates new texts in its own genre? Some of the energy and skills developed to represent the modern subject in the epistolary tradition are reborn in romantic autobiographical and meditative poetry, represented in Germany by Goethe himself and again by Hölderlin, but otherwise at best fitfully in, say, Schiller and, much later, Mörike. How did so much energy dissipate so rapidly? And where, in particular, did the plot that evoked such a sensational response disappear to?

In the lyric cycles of Wilhelm Müller, where what I might call the "Werther plot" first resurfaces, it coexists with another paradigm of the period, familiar to us from Romantic fairy-tale. Indeed, it turns out that the Romantic paradigm is already implicit in *Werther,* and that the Romantic tale is the true heir of *Werther*'s plot and psychological insight. Once the connection is suggested, parallels spring to mind. *Werther* is not much longer than the longest of the Romantic tales; both involve lyrical and emotive prose otherwise foreign to German narrative; both are recognized milestones in the European depiction of the modern subject and of depth psychology.

While my argument turns on Wilhelm Müller's cycle of poems "Die schöne Müllerin", whose compelling interest for the age is best documented by Schubert's setting, its main focus is a twofold reinterpretation of *Werther*. First, I offer a reading that places the central focus not on the direct representation of the hero's subjectivity – whether exaggerated or triumphantly emergent – but on the disruption of the hero's connection to nature depicted in the novel. In this reading the novel suddenly looks much more like German Romantic tales such as Tieck's *Runenberg* or Fouqué's *Undine* than previously recognized. Hence, second, *Werther* then appears as the originary text of German Romanticism rather than the climax of sensibility. Romantic tales elaborate implications of *Werther* which Goethe himself might well not have been able or willing to articulate when he wrote the novel in the early 1770s, but that do seem to be emerging by 1778 in a poem like 'Der Fischer'. If the juxtaposition offered here is convincing, then *Werther* provides the previously missing link in the Romantics' transformation of fairy and folk tale material into their peculiarly Romantic form. This essay thus identifies a new and specific literary impact of *Werther* in Germany.

I

In the abstract, the plot of "Die Schöne Müllerin" is very close to
that of *Werther*. Werther's opening words, "Wie froh bin ich, daß
ich weg bin", could well be those of Schubert's miller, who begins by
singing "Das Wandern ist des Müllers Lust". Each hero puts his past
behind him as he enters an idyllic springtime world, inhabited by a
young woman with whom the hero falls in love. The woman actually
belongs to someone else – to an earlier betrothed in the case of
Werther's Lotte, to a hunter in Müller. While Werther has known
of Lotte's virtual engagement to Albert from day one, Müller's
miller feels betrayed by his beloved. But it is not explicit that the
girl was ever really in love with the miller, or that she did not have
some earlier relationship with the hunter, since everything is seen so
consistently through the eyes of the miller. About halfway through
each work the surrounding world begins to seem hostile to the hero,
and his alienation grows apace. Both end with suicide. This sequence,
which I am calling the "Werther-paradigm", can thus be readily
summarized: A nature enthusiast falls in love with a woman he
cannot marry. First he idealizes her, then interprets her inaccessibil-
ity as his complete alienation from nature. Confronted with the
prospect of eternal suffering caused by the indifference of a nature
beyond the control of his own subjectivity, he commits suicide.

Müller's later cycle, "Die Winterreise", also set by Schubert of
course, repeats the second half of this plot, for it begins after the
lover has lost his beloved, if he ever really had her. ("Das Mädchen
sprach von Liebe, die Mutter gar von Eh'" implies less commitment
than the traveler thought he had). The famous linden tree in the
fifth song ('Der Lindenbaum') alludes to a particularly sentimental
episode late in Goethe's novel in which Werther visits his childhood
home, a small town with a memory-laden linden tree before the
gates (Part II, letter of 9 May). As in "Winterreise", the tree is
associated with journeying and with failure in life. If Schubert's
traveler fails to commit suicide at the end of "Winterreise", it is
surely not for lack of longing for death, but because the brook,
which welcomes the unhappy miller, is now frozen solid.

Both cycles have in common with *Werther* copious projection of
the hero's emotions onto the landscape. It appears in imagery of
the seasons in all three works. More important, it appears in the
constant writing activity: *Werther* is a novel in letters, in which the
hero writes down his feelings and describes the world around him,
especially nature, in terms of his own feelings. In the two Schubert
cycles the heroes literally inscribe their emotions into the landscape

by cutting names and dates into trees or into the surface of frozen rivers, and they read the babbling of the brook and the falling of the last isolated leaf from a tree as messages to them alone. "War es also gemeint?" the miller keeps asking the brook. Like Werther, the heroes of Müller's cycle are solipsists. The only difference is that Goethe's novel inclines toward a critique of Werther's extreme subjectivity, while Müller and Schubert tend to romanticize it. This, then, is the "Werther-paradigm" as it appears in later German Romanticism.

But there is another way to read "Die schöne Müllerin", by focusing on the obvious importance of the water. In the second song, 'Wohin?', the wandering miller follows the sound of a little brook, which eventually leads him to the mill of the *schöne Müllerin*. He is attracted by the rushing sound ("Ich hört ein Bächlein rauschen"), which awakens incomprehensible longing ("Ich weiß nicht wie mir wurde [...]/ Ich mußte auch hinunter") to follow the brook, he knows not where. Uncertain of the brook's message ("Ist das denn meine Straße? [...] Du hast mit deinem Rauschen/ Mir ganz berauscht den Sinn") he nevertheless decides to follow what he takes to be the call of nature: "Was sag' ich denn vom Rauschen?/ Das kann kein Rauschen sein./ Es singen wohl die Nixen/ Tief unten ihren Reihn". He follows the sound of the nature spirits "hinunter und immer weiter", pursuing the voice of nature into the depths. The poem is titled with a question, punctuated with further questions, and turns on the miller's interpretation of his own description. One must read beneath the surface – of the water and of the text.

Small wonder the miller seems quite confused to arrive only at a new mill. "War es also gemeint?" he asks at the end of the third song and repeatedly in the fourth. When the brook does not answer his pressing questions as to what its call meant, he succumbs ("Nun wie es auch mag sein, ich gebe mich drein") and uncertainly transfers his affections from the mermaids of the brook to the miller's daughter who has unexpectedly turned up in their place. Indeed, millers' daughters have none too good a reputation in literature of the period: in Goethe they have a way of luring innocent young aristocrats into the mill of love and then betraying them. In his tempestuous passion for the girl Schubert's miller seems to drown out the music of the brook, though his questions periodically resurface (at the end of song 6, for example, or in 8). In his epistemological insecurity the young miller betrays the mermaids of the brook for the miller's daughter.

In this context the miller's death by water is more than suicide for unrequited love. After the girl abandons him (or whatever it is that happens) for the hunter, he returns to the brook, in which he ends up drowned. The mermaids have taken revenge for his betrayal, and now, in full possession, they rock him to sleep, much as Undine in Fouqué's famous tale of 1811, weeps her beloved to death. Had the miller not betrayed the mermaids, but surrendered to them directly he would still have drowned – but as the object of seduction, not revenge. All through the cycle the water attracts the miller downward, as if it represented some implicit death-wish. The mermaids' revenge and the miller's own inchoate longing for the Other combine to the same end. The young miller is destroyed by the conflicting attractions of the supernatural and the natural for his very soul.

This version of the plot may be called the "Undine-paradigm", and is common in shorter narratives in the Romantic period. Here the hero is pulled between two versions of the beloved, the one real and the other supernatural or uncannily demonic, often a mermaid. The moral or religious valence of each may be obvious or it may be unclear, and the hero may or may not commit himself to the nature spirit, but if he does, he disappears or goes mad (often the two are identical). If he commits to the mermaid and then abandons her he must either die, lose his sanity, or disappear, or all three. Thus in Fouqué's *Undine* of 1811 Huldbrand von Ringstetten encounters Undine in her isolated home, forgets the lovely Bertalda, whose service he had sought to enter, and marries the mermaid. Upon their return to the city they form a close friendship with Bertalda, who turns out to be the real but lost daughter of Undine's foster parents, hence a sort of double for Undine. The three maintain an uneasy love triangle (shades of *Werther!*), as Huldbrand wavers in his affection between the two women. Finally he leans definitively toward Bertalda and Undine must leave him; when he then marries Bertalda the unfortunate mermaid must (literally) weep him to death on his wedding night. In a final Ovidian gesture she turns into a weeping spring on his grave.

The paradigm occurs at its harshest in early Romanticism. In Tieck's *Der Runenberg* (1804) Christian is torn between the ambiguous *Waldweib*, incarnate both as hag of the forest and as the beautiful guardian of mountain crystals, and the gentle Elisabeth, through whom he is bound to the human community. After accepting the magic tablet of the beautiful *Waldweib*, Christian loses it and flees to the human world and Elisabeth. Drawn back to the mountains against his better judgment, he ends in apparently insane devotion to the now hideous *Waldweib*. Tieck's *Der blonde Eckbert*, (1797) perhaps the primal tale in this pattern, records the same basic plot. The apparent protagonist, Bertha, turns out to have been her husband Eckbert's sister and stand-in when he reenacts her marvelous journey to the wilderness paradise, and the gender distinction, like all other distinctions in the tale, has no apparent validity. In flight from the real world, Bertha has been sheltered and raised by a hideous but pious witch, but betrays her after some seven years of happiness by returning to the human world and marrying Eckbert. After Eckbert feels compelled to confess her crime Bertha dies, Eckbert's life collapses and he is drawn back to the witch, who reveals his life of incest to him as he collapses in madness. While neither of the supernatural women in these tales is a mermaid, it is striking that Eckbert's witch is located (on both Bertha's and his own journeys) by following the sound of a waterfall, and Christian's mountains are full of the mysterious sound of brooks murmuring in an incomprehensible language. Tieck's figures are sirens.

Other versions of the paradigm may also be a little vague about the specific status of the supernatural woman. Hoffmann, for example, makes his Serpentina in *Der goldene Topf* (1814) a salamander (spirit of fire) rather than an undine, but she and Anselmus do go off to live in Atlantis, presumably beneath the sea, at the end. In Eichendorff's *Das Marmorbild* (1819) the demonic female is Venus herself; nevertheless all of Florio's encounters with her take place by a mysterious pond ("Weiher"). And in his related poem, 'Frühlingsfahrt,' (1818) in which two youths go out into the world and succumb to the opposite kinds of love, the second falls victim to the sirens singing in the waves of the spring. But Hans Christian Andersen's "The little Mermaid" and all the Melusinas who spook though the German nineteenth century, even as late as Fontane's *Der Stechlin* (1899) make clear how persistent the underlying popularity of the mermaid motif for this figure was. The preference for mermaids over other nature spirits derives from the particular importance of flowing waters for the Romantics: they speak and one can drown in them and lose one's identity to nature. They image central concerns with the voice of nature and the threat of self-loss.

Hence the valence and import of the mermaid figure are vague. Sometimes the choice between the two women appears to have religious implications, as in Eichendorff, sometimes primarily aesthetic, as in Hoffmann, or psychological, as in Tieck. But which is good and which dangerous is neither clear nor consistent. If Hoffmann's Anselmus seems to find eternal happiness with his Serpentina and to be endangered by the real Veronika, Eichendorff's Florio has clearly done right in resisting Venus for the human Bianka. If Hoffmann associates the supernatural with the ideal, Eichendorff sees it as sin. But in Eichendorff's 'Frühlingsfahrt' both of his "rüst'ge Gesellen" seem to have made the wrong choice. The miller, we remember, keeps questioning the meaning of the brook's babble. If it were easy to choose between the two women, none of these tales would have to be written.

II

The fact that these two paradigms, "Werther" and "Undine", coexist so peacefully in "Die schöne Müllerin" raises the question of their relationship to one another. In fact, what I am calling the "Undine-paradigm" is already implicit in Goethe's first novel. My thesis must not be understood in too extreme terms. I really mean implicit, not fully worked out. Goethe and his Romantic successors only later solidified the paradigm and drew the full implications from it. Indeed, it is not important whether they even recognized its origins, though the case of Müller suggests they probably could have articulated them. In Goethe we have the inchoate underpinnings of the Romantic myth.

On the very first page Werther introduces himself as a seducer and abandoner, a trifler with the affection of innocent women. This seems at first an obvious quality inherited from the 18th-century epistolary novel. "Poor Leonore" apparently fell in love with him (and did we know not what to herself) while Werther trifled with her more outgoing and fascinating sister. Yet Werther did not ignore her; he admits to having nursed her emotions (letter of 4 May, 9).[2] When he and Lotte visit the country pastor Werther arouses the ire of the daughter Friedericke's fiancé by taking too much interest in the young lady (1 July, 36-37); and, of course, he does the same with Albert's fiancée Lotte as well. Yet Werther is no garden-variety gay Lothario, but a man of deep feeling whose sympathies and emotional relationships are very real to himself, at least during the moment of experience. In that respect Werther is a link between the rake of the eighteenth-century novel and the hero of the Romantic tale with a genuinely dual focus to his emotional life – a duality so strong that the two beloveds can appear as *Doppelgänger,* as they do in Eichendorff. Werther between Leonore and her sister on the first page of the novel anticipates a long line of Romantic heroes between their

---

[2] Citations to *Werther* are from *Goethes Poetische Werke. Vollständige Ausgabe.* 22 vols. Here, Vol. 6. Stuttgart 1958. I cite from the 1774 version of the novel. All of the passages cited or alluded to are essentially unchanged in the 1787 version.

two beloveds, right down to Fontane's Stechlin between the sisters Armgard and Melusine.

But Goethe does not develop the motif of paired but opposing women explicitly. Instead his version is more like that of Wilhelm Müller; hence the pivotal importance of "Die schöne Müllerin" for my argument. That is to say, Werther's first love in the novel is nature itself, which fills the first quarter of Book I before Lotte appears. As in the Romantic tales, the turn to nature is an escape – "Wie froh bin ich, daß ich weg bin!" the novel begins, and "Die Stadt selbst ist unangenehm, dagegen ringsumher eine unaussprechliche Schönheit der Natur" (10) still in the first letter. Werther flees society to recover the innocence he has lost in the affair with Leonore, if not earlier; thus the neighborhood is "paradiesisch" (10), and his initial description focuses for the entire last paragraph of the first letter on a garden of which Werther declares himself, like Adam, the master (10). Shortly after he compares his feelings for nature to those for the maternal friend of his childhood (17 May, 14). The second letter, the famous description of the cathedral of nature, seals the returned Werther's bond with the beloved – "wenns denn um meine Augen dämmert und die Welt um mich her und der Himmel ganz in meiner Seele ruht wie die Gestalt einer Geliebten" (11).

Such strong language of nature as the beloved is relatively rare in *Werther*. More commonly his devotion is expressed in three less poetic (but no less true) forms: in his love for common people (who normally shy away from members of the higher classes, but are ineluctably drawn to Werther [15 May, 13; 27 May, 20-21]), in children (also particularly drawn to Werther [e.g. 21]) and in his efforts to draw (26 May, 18). Werther draws successfully, however, only before he meets Lotte, mainly in the letter of 26 May, where he insists that he will henceforth cleave to nature alone (18). Within six weeks of meeting Lotte he confesses that he can no longer draw (24 July, 46), and we do not hear of him drawing until almost a year later, when he has been away from Lotte for nine months. He draws again only after a brief visit to the city of his birth, where he is greeted by the linden tree picked up by Wilhelm Müller, that is by the embodiment of the innocence of nature, the pre-Lotte life.

Werther's bond to nature centers on the well, first introduced as a place haunted by spirits:

Ich weiß nicht, ob so täuschende Geister um diese Gegend schweben oder ob es die warme, himmlische Phantasie in meinem Herzen ist, die mir alles ringsumher so paradiesisch macht. Da ist gleich vor dem Orte ein Brunn, ein Brunn, an den ich gebannt bin wie Melusine mit ihren Schwestern. –

Du gehst einen kleinen Hügel hinunter und findest dich vor einem Gewölbe, da wohl zwanzig Stufen hinabgehen, wo unten das klarste Wasser aus Marmorfelsen quillt. Das Mäuerchen, das oben umher die Einfassung macht, [...] die Kühle des Orts, das hat alles so was Anzügliches, was Schauerliches [...], so lebt die patriarchalische Idee so lebhaft um mich, [...] wie um die Brunnen und Quellen wohltätige Geister schweben. (12 May, 12)

Werther comes to sit here for an hour every day – at least until he meets Lotte, after which he neglects the beloved spot. The parallels to the wells and springs in *Undine* and to brooks in "Die schöne Müllerin", especially given the invocation of Melusine, Goethe's favorite water spirit, surely speak for themselves. But we might note also Werther's uncertainty: he cannot tell if the edenic feeling is natural (projected by his own phantasy) or the supernatural effect of deceptive spirits. Like the miller's brook the place invites one to descend down to the water, here to pass the explicit barrier of the small wall that presumably prevents accidental drownings. The effect upon him is ambiguous, both "anzüglich" and "schauerlich". By the end of the passage "täuschende Geister" have been replaced by "wohltätige Geister". The fairy-tale mood is gradually supplanted by allusions to the patriarchal idea of the Old Testament. Here is implicit the epistemological uncertainty that will be writ so large for Müller's miller or for Eichendorff's Florio.

The connection helps us to make sense out of two passing episodes associated with water in the novel. In the letter of July 6 Werther chances on his beloved well while walking with Lotte and realizes how he has neglected it. Overcome anew with its power he impulsively kisses Lotte's younger sister Malchen; the child immediately scrubs her face in the water. Lotte explains the act as offended innocence, but the rather mysterious occurrence makes more sense when we realize that the child, like the well, embodies the nature Werther now realizes he has neglected in favor of Lotte. His passing repentance, expressed in the kiss, is evidently rejected by the first beloved. Later, in the letter of 10 August, Werther gathers flowers while walking with Albert, binds them into a nosegay and tosses them into the brook (50). At the most obvious level the act signifies the recognition that his love for Lotte must pass with the flow of time. But given that water personifies the spirit of nature abandoned by Werther for Lotte, the sacrifice of the flowers to the brook foreshadows also the necessary sacrifice of his new love to the old – as it does more openly in "Die schöne Müllerin".

This reading makes us rethink the significance of Lotte herself. If Werther abandons nature for her, she occupies the place of the faithless miller's daughter in Wilhelm Müller, or worse of the fickle beloved in "Winterreise", or of selfish Bertalda in *Undine*. To be sure, this figure is occasionally positive, as in Tieck's *Runenberg*, in which motherly Elisabeth owes much to Lotte. As we have already seen, Lotte interferes with Werther's ability to draw and to focus on nature; furthermore the first result of his encounter with her is to be transported into a dream world – "ich stieg aus dem Wagen wie ein Träumender, als wir vor dem Lusthause stillhielten, und war so in Träumen rings in der dämmernden Welt verloren, daß ich auf die Musik kaum achtete, die uns von dem erleuchteten Saal herunter entgegenschallte" (16 June, 26), and in the next letter, "seit der Zeit können Sonne, Mond und Sterne geruhig ihre Wirtschaft treiben, ich weiß weder, daß Tag noch daß Nacht ist, und die ganze Welt verliert sich um mich her" (19 June, 31-32). Lotte is described virtually as a dangerous sorceress in the "Märchen vom Magnetenberg. Die Schiffe, die zu nahe kamen, wurden auf einmal alles Eisenwerks beraubt, die Nägel flogen dem Berge zu, und die armen Elenden scheiterten zwischen den übereinanderstürzenden Brettern" (26 July, 47). Remove the element of magnetism and we are left with Lotte as siren, the dangerous water nixie. In this reading Lotte is not the carrier of an ideal projected on her by Werther, but a dangerous distraction from the ideal of nature.

Interestingly enough, the mermaid image, in the reference to Melusine at the well and in the Romantic tales the embodiment of nature, here is extended to Lotte herself, the competitor to nature. Even where the portrayal of Lotte remains closest to the novel's roots in eighteenth-century sensibility, the image is crucially present. In one of the most famous moments of the novel, as Werther and Lotte stand at the window in the flush of their first evening together and watch the rain, Lotte invokes Klopstock. Werther immediately recalls the ode she has in mind as he sinks "in dem Strome von Empfindungen, den sie in dieser Losung über mich ausgoß" (16 June, 31). This central passage lays clear the nexus: the psychological issue, "Empfindung", is represented in the metaphor of the river in which Werther drowns. One has only to literalize the metaphor to arrive at the Romantic fairy tale, "Die schöne Müllerin", or to Eichendorff's dangerous "Frühlingswellen".

Lotte's association with nature is not a contradiction of the Undine paradigm, but a confirmation of it: she is the dangerous *Doppelgänger*. Like Venus and Bianka in Eichendorff's Das *Marmorbild* it is at first hard to distinguish the moral difference – harder really in *Werther* because the moral situation is so much more complex. Thus, Lotte is closely associated with nature, but not with the patriarchal calm of the well. In the wake of Klopstock in the scene above, or of Oliver Goldsmith in the scene beneath the walnut trees on the visit to the pastor, hers is the highly emotionalized nature of sensibility, like the moonlit garden in which Werther takes his farewell of her at the end of Part I, again replete with Klopstock allusions (to 'Die frühen Gräber'). In the second part of the novel her nature is dead – Werther can only write to Lotte in the countryside in the depths of winter (20 January, 74) – or artificial – as in her erotic parading with the tame canary that carries kisses from her lips to Werther's (15 September, 1787 version only). In the theme of kissing we can see her ultimate insidious displacement of the innocent Melusine of the well. In the letter of 24 November Werther barely controls his desire to kiss her; she flees to the piano and Werther continues:

Nie hab ich ihre Lippen so reizend gesehn; es war, als wenn sie sich lechzend öffneten, jene süße Töne in sich zu schlürfen, die aus dem Instrument hervorquollen, und nur der heimliche Widerschall aus dem süßen Munde zurückklänge – [...] Nie will ichs wagen, einen Kuß euch einzudrücken, Lippen, auf denen die Geister des Himmels schweben! – Und doch – ich will –. (24 November, 95-96)

As they provide a passage for the music that, like water, flows from the piano, Lotte's lips take the place of the small wall that surrounds the fountain of the letter of 12 May; and like the fountain they too are guarded by hovering spirits (cf. "wohltätige Geister schweben", 12). If the language is the same, the situation is not. We now realize in retrospect that kissing Malchen at the well was so appalling because it really anticipated the adulterous kisses he exchanges with Lotte less than a month after the scene just described. If Ossian has displaced Homer, as Werther asserts in a famous line (12 October, 89), Lotte has displaced the child Malchen and the Melusine of the well.

At the end nature turns on Werther and takes her revenge, as in the later Romantic tales. In the letter of 18 August a final detailed loving description of the landscape is transformed into a spectacle of horror (58-59). The letter begins with the assertion that Werther's initial love for nature has been transformed into an "unerträglichen Peiniger, zu einem quälenden Geiste, der mich auf allen Wegen verfolgt" (58), for all the world like Undine's angry uncle who torments Huldbrand. The same angry nature appears in the floods in which Werther madly triumphs toward the end of the novel (8 December, 101). Nature appears also as the mourner for her lost beloved in the pathos of the Ossian translations at the end of the novel, where Ossian's figures become the voices of the desolate landscapes they haunt, mourning their lost loved ones.

But Werther dies, it may be objected, by his own hand, not over-whelmed by angry or sorrowful waters. This important difference points to the underlying significance of the connection between "Werther" and the "Undine-paradigm". In *Werther* the vengeance and the mourning originate not with an independent external nature, but explicitly within his own psyche. In the passage cited above, it is his own love of nature that now torments him, not nature itself. And the floods at the end of the novel appeal to Werther because they seem to him to mirror his own disordered passions. Indeed, the novel depicts only a conflict in Werther's passions all along, not a conflict between some mermaid Melusine and the human Lotte. Both the nature and the Lotte of Werther's letters are clearly projections of his own ideals, views and longings. This phenomenon is guaranteed by the epistolary form. That Werther does not die by water like the miller or like Huldbrand, but shoots himself instead, shows that Goethe's novel still operates in terms of the explicit rationalist psychology of the eighteenth century, which at best finds objective correlatives in nature for its passions.

But the pervasive presence of the "Undine-paradigm" reveals the novel teetering on the brink of a different psychology. Romantic tales have third person narrators, or frames to objectify the first person narrations, instead of the radical subjectivity of Werther's epistolary mode. In the Romantic tales nature is not the objective correlative of human passion, but rather the carrier of a narrative that cannot be articulated in any other terms. The gain, of course, is access to the part of the psyche that does not operate in rational terms, what Freud, on the basis of the century's literary work of representing this new part of the self, would call the unconscious. Where *Werther* and the eighteenth-century tradition have simile and metaphor, Romantic depth psychology is driven to allegory.

III

But if *Werther* was teetering on the brink of a new mode of psycho-logical representation, Goethe himself was the first to enter the new territory, in the short ballad 'Der Fischer' of 1778. Here a fisherman sitting calmly in his boat is accosted by a mermaid who rises from the rushing and swelling water. Siren that she is, she tempts him to his death, or at least disappearance, in the waves by offering him access to his own inner self – "lockt dich dein eigen Angesicht" – a self that can no longer be described in terms of passions, but only in images, in this case the reflection of the fisherman's face on the surface of the water. The ballad addresses the whole gamut of typical Romantic dichotomies – human/natural, subject/object, natural/supernatural, rational/irrational, conscious/unconscious, order/disorder, temporal/eternal – but its extraordinary perfection hides the complexity of the transition to them, which Goethe explored repeatedly in the succeeding decades.[3]

His analysis of the representational issues can be observed in his own cycle of *Müllerin* poems, first published in 1799, to which Wilhelm Müller's cycle responds. It consists of three dialogue poems arranged around a ballad, 'Der Müllerin Verrat', that Goethe had translated from a French tale called "La folle en pèlerinage", (later included in *Wilhelm Meisters Wanderjahre* as "Die pilgernde Törin"). In that tale the ballad is sung by the mysterious young beloved of the narrator, who first met her sitting next to a well, like the mermaid Melusina. Of interest here are not the numerous verbal echoes in Wilhelm Müller's poems, but the plot of Goethe's cycle: an "Edelknabe" invites the pretty miller's daughter to dally with him in a bower in the fields, but she will not, because the flour dust would soil his beautiful coat and betray them. She will stick to young millers, she says. In the next poem a "Junggesell" (the youth in disguise? the young miller referred to by the girl?) discusses his love for the miller's daughter with the sympathetic (male) brook, who also loves her. The third poem is the French ballad; it narrates how the miller's family break in on the young nobleman's love tryst with the girl and try to make him marry her. He escapes with only his cloak to cover him. In the last poem the repentant girl comes to him disguised as a gypsy (painted black) to apologize for betraying him and ask for his love. Dismissed as a procuress, she reveals her identity and offers herself as his mistress; he forgives her and takes her to bed. Goethe's

---

[3] For a thorough discussion of the Romantic and modern depth-psychological qualities of this poem see David Wellbery's analysis in: *The Specular Moment: Goethe's Early Lyric and the Beginnings of Romanticism.* Stanford 1996. Pp. 246-84. Wellbery has also demonstrated amply just how responsive *Werther* is to Freudian reading in: Morphisms of the Phantasmatic Body: Goethe's *The Sorrows of Young Werther.* In: *Body and Text in the Eighteenth Century.* Ed. Veronica Kelly and Dorothea von Mücke. Stanford 1994. Pp. 181-208. His reading justifies my assertion that the beginnings of the Freudian unconscious can be documented in *Werther.* The focus on liquidity both in this essay and in *The Specular Moment* supports also the connection to the Romantic mermaids.

Müllerin is an ambiguous figure, both white and black, both scheming and loving (as is the pilgrim who sings the ballad in the French tale). The duality otherwise found between nature and human appears here within the girl, and it is hard for the youth to recognize (a central theme in the last two poems). With its two young lovers, the gentleman and the *Junggeselle,* the cycle stands exactly between *Werther* and Müller's "Die schöne Müllerin".

The cycle also straddles two kinds of representation. On the one hand the girl is a coquettish miller's daughter, an exaggerated version of the coquette Lotte perhaps, a figure that Wilhelm Müller could still sanitize for the Biedermeier drawing room. On the other hand, she is also, if not yet quite a mermaid, nevertheless as gypsy, over the boundary of domestic reality and into the realm of romance and fairy tale. Goethe originally characterized each of the poems in this group as "altenglisch", "altdeutsch", "altfranzösisch", and "altspanisch" respectively.[4] The move from north to south through the cycle corresponds to a shift from the normalcy of an eighteenth-century world in which wealthy young men seduce honest, or not so honest, working girls in bowers to the romanticism of Spanish romance. But the issue is not solely generic. In his collected poems Goethe included the group among his ballads, to which the epigraph reads: "Märchen noch so wunderbar,/ Dichterkünste machens wahr". Ballads are not only associated with fairy-tale, but with the realization of fairy-tale, or with the revelation of their truth. Through "poetic arts" they mediate the transition from rational or "Wertherian" to the magical narrative of the Romantic tale.

If "poetic arts" sounds pretentious, it shouldn't. It should rather be taken literally – as verse. The metrical form excuses or renders acceptable the fantastic content of the fairy-tale. Goethe had begun writing ballads even before he wrote *Werther,* but he returned to the ballad consciously as a form in 1797 and 1798, after two significant experiments at representing the irrational Other in prose: Mignon and the Harfner in *Wilhelm Meisters Lehrjahre* and the "Märchen" that concludes *Unterhaltungen deutscher Ausgewanderten.* The fairy-tale aspects of Mignon and the Harfner are both mystifying and, as the narrative penetrates further into their past, shocking. Indeed, so shocking is their history compared to the rational normalcy the cured Harfner had seemed to achieve, that when their past is narrated he commits suicide. The two modalities cannot exist side

---

[4] As subtitles in the original publication of 1799 in Schiller's *Musenalmanach* (except in the case of the third poem) and in a letter to Schiller included in *Reise in die Schweiz 1797* (WA 34.1, p. 341).

by side. The "Märchen" also contrasts strongly with the rational normality of the frame narrative in *Unterhaltungen;* the contrast is not shocking, as in *Wilhelm Meister,* but it is mystifying. Goethe moderates the shock into mystification by an elaborate introduction that defines the fairy-tale as by definition irrational and illogical. His turn to the ballad represents, then, a formal way to isolate and thereby control the shock of the new discourse of the unconscious. When the Romantics return from the literal poetry of ballads to the prose of *Werther* they complete the transition: without the mediation of poetic art, literally of meter, the irrational is exposed for all to see.

The "Werther-paradigm" is thus really the older, more rationalistic version of the "Undine-paradigm", and every once in a while it resurfaces, especially in the Biedermeier, as in "Die schöne Müllerin". The later versions of the paradigm from after the Restoration are a good deal tamer than Tieck's or even than Fouqué's. Tieck's hags claim the status of enforcers of divine justice and take their revenge with some gusto, while Fouqué's Undine already obeys this law with regret. In Eichendorff the considerable ambiguity as to which woman the hero ought to choose has mostly abated. In Eichendorff the question is only whether the hero will be able to distinguish the dangerous whiteness of the marble Venus from the Christian purity of the real Bianka, whether he will have the wit to trust the whiteness of the word over that of the image – or, in *Aus dem Leben eines Taugenichts,* whether the beloved is mistress or servant. The difference of course has to do with the different contexts and uses to which the paradigm is put. If Tieck addresses the horrors of a barely discovered subconscious, Eichendorff addresses the confused social and religious situation of the Restoration and Andersen, whose mermaid explicitly renounces revenge, has already repressed the confusions Eichendorff so honestly addresses. In this trend toward repression, we sense the developing awareness of the powers and dangers of the new depth psychology, dangers that would be confronted explicitly only at the end of the century.

I have shown, then, that the "Undine-paradigm" is in fact already implicit in *Werther,* waiting to be read out of it by a more self-consciously allegorical generation, hence the ambiguity of a text like "Die schöne Müllerin". From Goethe's elaborations of it in the 1790s it is but a small step indeed to the mystified heroes of Tieck's fairy tales, whose behavior is as incomprehensible to themselves as to those around them. The Romantic tale is not a sudden irruption into or reversal of 18th-century psychology, but rather the logical consequence of patterns implicit in its most popular narrative.

Winfried Menninghaus

Hummingbirds, Shells, Picture-Frames:
Kant's "Free Beauties" and the Romantic Arabesque

In the 1780s, following earlier discussions of the rocaille ornament, there is a widespread, though widely forgotten, debate on the arabesque in German aesthetics. This debate focuses on decorations of rooms and buildings, preeminently on those done by Raphael in the loges of the Vatican. Goethe's 1788 article On the Arabesque *responds to numerous treatises and reflections – among others by Karl Philipp Moritz and Heinse – which in part bore the same or very similar titles. In 1790, this discourse on the arabesque in architecture and in the fine arts enters tacitly – and, indeed, in such a discrete way as to escape attention – the stage of philosophy. From 1795 onwards, it becomes, all the more triumphantly and ostentatiously, the explicit centerpiece of Romantic poetics and literature. The question of this essay is why the multiplication, the spreading of the arabesque through various fields and disciplines, is both temporally and in essence coextensive with the foundation of modern aesthetics in Kant's* Critique of Judgment *and in early Romantic poetics. To start with, the author gives a brief overview of the 18th-century aesthetics of the arabesque before turning to its somewhat hidden transformation, in Kant, into the quintessential paradigm of what he calls "free beauty". The essay concludes with a discussion of Tieck's theory of the arabesque presented in* The Seven Wives of Bluebeard.

A *Lexicum Architectonicum* of 1744 gives the following definition: "Arabesques: floral lineaments are all and sundry sorts of composed leaf- and floral-work, such as the Arabs are wont to do for decoration, since otherwise they are forbidden to make any images of animals or people".[1] At about the same time, a new treatment of ornamental leaf- and shell-forms emerges that has become known as rocaille or Rococo. In this new type of ornament, shell- and leafwork is extended from the frame onto what is enframed until it largely comes to substitute for the image itself. From this, a hybrid emerges that is neither simply image nor ornament, but oscillates between the modes of ornament and im-

---

[1] Joh. Fr. Penther: *Ausführliche Anleitung zur bürgerlichen Bau-Kunst, Erster Theil, Enthaltend ein Lexicum Architectonicum oder Erklärung der üblichsten Deutschen, Französischen, Italienischen Kunstwörter.* Augsburg 1744. P. 6a.

agery.[2] This puzzling play exhibiting elements of beauty, eroticism, mortality, and also a chthonian threat has been designated by the art-historian Hermann Bauer as a "stage of transition to Romanticism"[3] – an insight that has received all too little attention in literary scholarship. The oscillation, in rocaille, between the modes of ornament and imagery calls into question the image's power of representation. It is indeed as a result of the ornament's invasion into the space of both object and image that some of the fundamental representational rules of what Foucault, in his book on Magritte's *Ceci n'est pas une pipe*, has called "classical painting", were being subverted first in the decorative arts and subsequently in literature and philosophy. Analogously, the conflation of the enframed and the frame, of the narrative core and the paranarra-tive framings is the most striking feature of both Lawrence Sterne's *Tristram Shandy* and Denis Diderot's *Jacques le Fataliste et son Mai-tre*, which therefore figure as the first examples of the Romantic theory of the literary arabesque. The Romantic literary arabesque, however, was soon refined to the point where an explicit intervention of a narrator was no longer the only and preeminent device for processing what, following Kant, I will henceforth call the diffence of ergon and parer-gon.

As to philosophy, I will try to show that Kant's third *Critique* and thus to some extent the foundation of modern aesthetics is precisely about phenomena like the puzzling shell-work or the structure of *Tris-tram Shandy*. Kant deals, so to speak, with the structure of the modern novel under a number of various disguises, among which one can find so seemingly diverse things as colonnades, hummingbirds, hems of clothing and wallpaper-decorations. All these examples, I hold, follow the pattern of privileging the parergon at the expense of the ergon. This discovery, in turn, leads to the question why the rather formal distinc-tion of ergon and parergon and the puzzling interplays between these poles could become such a powerful device for roughly one hundred years – from rocaille through E.T.A. Hoffmann to Poe, Gogol and others. In the first and most extensive part of my essay, I will elaborate on the significant role Kant's *Critique of Judgment* plays in this dis-course on ornament and the arabesque. Second, I will very briefly indicate to what extent Friedrich Schlegel's well-known theory of the arabesque can be read as following and radicalizing the line of the

---

[2] My presentation of rocaille follows completely the authoritative work by Hermann Bauer: *Rocaille. Zur Herkunft und zum Wesen eines Ornament-Motivs*. Berlin 1962. Here esp. pp. 8-9 and 19-22.
[3] Ibid. P. 70. Like Romantic literature, the rocaille ornament combines a movement of "idealization" and of the absorption of representation with an ironic distancing of art from itself (cf. ibid. P. 63 and 75).

Kantian argument. Only because Kant never speaks explicitly of "arabesque", could this Kantian heritage escape attention until now in the extensive research on the Romantic arabesque. Third, I will emphasize Ludwig Tieck's largely unknown contribution to this discourse. Three years before Schlegel's discussion of the arabesque in the 1799 *Letter on the Novel* [*Brief über den Roman*], Tieck's arabesque *The Seven Wives of Bluebeard* [*Die sieben Weiber des Blaubart*] not only outlines a new theory of the arabesque, it also already adheres to the genuine Romantic project that genre theory be pursued in the medium of the genres themselves.

The introduction of the new ornamental mode of rocaille met with considerable resistance; indeed it drew harsh polemics from the 1740s through the 1780s. It is perhaps in this resistance that one can best sense the dramatic shift in the laws of representation. Some Rationalist and Enlightenment authors experienced this shift as a vertiginous abyss and evidently felt threatened by it. The Rationalist polemic against the Rococo ornament[4] in the 1740s and 1750s seizes primarily upon the characteristics of semantic emptiness, non-representation, and the apparent ungroundedness of such play. To a great extent this critique is shared by Classicism and by Enlightenment authors in the 1780s. In 1755 Winckelmann, in his critique of the Rococo arabesque, had already set a criterion for the eventual rehabilitation of the arabesque. Only "by a more thorough study of allegory", according to Winckelmann, could the "meaningless paintings in our chambers [...] be purified and attain truth and understanding". Otherwise "the flourish [*Schnirkel*] and the much beloved shell-work [*das allerliebste Muschelwerk*]" are only "there to fill their space, and to cover the spaces that cannot be filled with gold-plate [...]. The aversion to empty space thus fills the walls; and paintings empty of thought are to replace the void".[5]

The Romantic arabesque from 1798 onwards[6] – in particular the paintings of Philipp Otto Runge – can be described as *one* way of

---

[4] Cf. the critique by Winckelmann's friend Reifstein (1746), by Cochin fils (1754), J. Gg. Fünck (1747), and Krubsacius (1759), which Bauer presents (ibid. Pp. 42-45 and 63-65).
[5] Johann Joachim Winckelmann: *Gedanken über die Nachahmung der griechischen Werke in der Malerei und Bildhauerkunst.* Ed. Ludwig Uhlig. Stuttgart 1969. Pp. 37-38.
[6] Cf. especially three excellent studies by Günter Oesterle: 'Vorbegriffe zu einer Theorie der Ornamente'. Kontroverse Formprobleme zwischen Aufklärung, Klassizismus und Romantik am Beispiel der Arabeske. In: *Ideal und Wirklichkeit der bildenden Kunst im späten 18. Jahrhundert.* Ed. Herbert Beck, Peter C. Bol, Eva Mack-Gérard. Berlin 1984. Pp. 119-139; Arabeske und Roman. Eine poetikgeschichtliche Rekonstruktion von Friedrich

fulfilling Winckelmann's requirement. For it ennobles the arabesque by giving it a new allegorical weight – even though the Romantic type of an enigmatic scripture [*Rätselschrift*] or "*Hieroglyphe*" surely goes beyond Winckelmann's concept of allegory. This first of several forms in which the arabesque "vacuum" is allegorically 'filled' is preceded, however, by attempts to liberate the arabesque from Winckelmann's imperatives of 'meaning' and 'truth'. The enlightenment critique considered the project of saving the arabesque by allegorizing it to be impossible, indeed wrong-headed. Rather, this critique tended to declare the arabesque unredeemable and hence to condemn it entirely. In a polemical text of 1788 that continues the older critique of the rocaille ornament, Adolf Riem calls arabesques "meaningless scribbling" ["*nichts bedeutende Sudeleyen*"] and "veritable monsters of the most unbridled imagination" ["*wahre Ungeheuer der zügellosesten Einbildungskraft*"]. As "senseless" and "most capricious serial patterns without purpose or intention",[7] he places them on the index of aesthetic criminality.[8]

In contrast, classicist, Kantian and earliest Romantic poetics attempt to legitimate the arabesque *without* relegating it to a mode requiring the infusion of an allegorical 'sense'. Instead of overcoming the vacuum – the lack of an object and therefore of meaning – the characteristics in question are rather submitted to a new theoretical elaboration. Precisely

---

Schlegels *Brief über den Roman.* In: *Studien zur Ästhetik und Literaturgeschichte der Kunstperiode.* Ed. Dirk Grathoff. Frankfurt a.M. 1985. Pp. 233-292; Arabeske, Schrift und Poesie in E.T.A. Hoffmanns Kunstmärchen *Der goldne Topf.* In: *Athenäum. Jahrbuch für Romantik* 1 (1991). Pp. 69-107. In the pages that follow I rely often on Oesterle's work; however, my treatment, taking its cue from Kant and Tieck's Blaubart tale, diverges principally in that it emphasizes a characteristic of the arabesque which is hardly mentioned by Oesterle: parergonality, the character of the frame. On the discussion of the arabesque before Oesterle see as well: Karl Konrad Pohlheim: *Die Arabeske. Ansichten und Ideen aus Schlegels Poetik.* Munich/Paderborn/Vienna 1966; Erwin Rotermund: Musikalische und dichterische 'Arabeske' bei E.T.A. Hoffmann. In: *Poetica* 2 (1968). Pp. 48-69; Raymond Immerwahr: Die symbolische Form des Briefs über den Roman. In: *Zeitschrift für deutsche Philologie* 88 (1969). Pp. 41-60; Gunnar Berefelt: Verzierungen mit Einsicht und Sinn – Notizen um Ph. O. Runge. In: *Kunsthistorisk Tidschrift* 41 (1972). Pp. 81-94; Jörg Traeger: *Philipp Otto Runge oder die Geburt einer neueren Kunst.* Munich 1977; Werner Busch: *Die notwendige Arabeske.* Pp. 13-55.
[7] A. Riem (ed.): Ueber die Arabeske. In: *Monatsschrift der Akademie der Künste und Wissenschaften zu Berlin* (1788). Part III. P. 128.
[8] Ibid. Part II. P. 28. Cf. Oesterle: 'Vorbegriffe zu einer Theorie der Ornamente.' P. 133.

the ornament's lack of purpose and significance suggested itself as a paradigm of aesthetic autonomy, and the difference between central and marginal, between frame and enframed, underwent several theoretical revaluations. Karl Philipp Moritz's classicist aesthetics of the ornament constitutes a compromise between the critique, which is still clearly perceptible, and an affirmative appreciation of the arabesque as both an autonomous play and a liminal art. On the one hand Moritz shared in the condemnation of the useless "games of chance"[9] and demanded that the "ornament" [*Zierath*] "contain nothing *foreign*, which could draw our attention away from the subject matter itself".[10] However, he legitimated the ornament by functionalizing it as an art of demarcation: "The ornament becomes the border guard of aesthetic autonomy internally and externally. It must redirect the surplus emanating outward from the artwork inwardly again[...and] it must outwardly protect the artwork against the tasteless and the uncultured".[11]

As an art of the border and a borderline art the arabesque frame is designed to confirm and to reinforce the identity of the artwork, and thus to demarcate the field of aesthetic autonomy.[12] As such it is a reaction to a new problem in aesthetics. For it is only with the emergence of the modern autonomous system of art that a precise demarcation between inside and outside becomes an urgent desideratum. The Kantian attempt to ground an absolutely "pure" and solely aesthetic judgment of beauty rigorously responds to this desideratum. The arabesque frame, now, provides the sought-for border demarcation: as a crossing between inside and outside at the outermost edge of the artwork, it expressly represents the difference between an inner and outer realm. Without directly using the concept, Kant's *Kritik der Urtheilskraft* (1790) formulates an elaborate philosopy of the arabesque which then serves as a major touchstone for for its reevaluation in early Romanticism:

> There are two kinds of beauty: free beauty (*pulchritudo vaga*) and merely adherent beauty (*pulchritudo adhaerens*). Free beauty does not presuppose a concept of what the object is [meant] to be [...]. Thus designs *à la grecque*, the foliage for frameworks or on wall-paper, etc., do not mean

[9] Karl Philipp Moritz: Einfachheit und Klarheit. In: K. Ph. Moritz: *Schriften zur Ästhetik und Poetik*. Ed. H. J. Schrimpf. Tübingen 1962. P. 149.
[10] Moritz: Die Säule. Sind die architektonischen Zierathen in den verschiedenen Säulenordnungen willkürlich oder wesentlich? In: *Schriften zur Ästhetik und Poetik*. P. 110.
[11] Cf. Oesterle: 'Vorbegriffe zu einer Theorie der Ornamente'. P. 126.
[12] On the dialectic of this function of framing see Karsten Harries: *The Broken Frame. Three Lectures*. Washington 1989. Pp. 64-89.

anything on their own; they represent nothing, no object under a determinate concept, and are free beauties. What we call fantasias in music (namely, music without a topic [*Thema*]), indeed all music not set to words may also be included in the same class.[13]

§4 had already struck a similar note: "Flowers, free designs, lineaments aimlessly intertwined – technically termed foliage, – have no significance [...] and yet please".[14] Kant's flowers and foliage directly correspond to the definition given above of arabesque ornamental decoration, and the "free designs *à la grecque*" present an analogy in contemporary fashion, where *à la grecque* indicated "the straight ornamental ribbon in Greek art which is called 'meander', which in the 18th century was once again applied particularly to knitting and other decorations, above all to the hems of clothing".[15]

Perhaps provocatively taking up Winckelmann's and Riem's earlier critique of arabesques as worthless and "meaning nothing" [*nichts bedeutend*], Kant emphasized two aspects that allowed for a positive evaluation of the incriminated insignificance. First, the arabesque represents "no object under a specific concept"; it "presupposes no concept of that which the object should be". Now, for Kant, an object-representation [*Objekt-Vorstellung*] without a specific concept *sensu stricto* represents nothing [*stellt nichts vor*]; as a representation of nothing it is also a non-representation. Precisely by virtue of this lack of concept and purpose does the arabesque permit a disinterested delight in the pure form, a delight "in the mere exhibition or faculty of exhibition" [*an der bloßen Darstellung oder dem Vermögen derselben*].[16] Second, Kant incessantly emphasizes the difference between minor and major

[13] Immanuel Kant: *Critique of Judgement*. Trans. Werner S. Pluhar, Indianapolis 1976-77. P. 72 (B 48-49, §16). Translation modified.
[14] Ibid. P. 49 (B 10-11, §4).
[15] Another meaning of *à la grecque* came into use only after the appearance of the *Critique of Judgement*: neo-classicist, free-flowing garments (Tunica) were termed 'republican' in opposition to the 'royalist' fashion. This application of the concept to designate the ornamental trim, however, maintained the criteria of freedom and frivolity which Kant emphasizes in the "free designs *à la grecque*", the arabesque decorations and the foliage for frameworks. For indeed the *à la grecque* fashion was distinguished from the previous fashion precisely by its "free and frivolous manner". Cf. on this Jacob Falke: *Die deutsche Trachten- und Modenwelt. Ein Beitrag zur deutschen Culturgeschichte*. 2. Teil. (*Die Neuzeit*). Leipzig 1858. Pp. 308-311; and Wolfgang Bruhn's article: "*à la grecque*". In *Reallexikon zur deutschen Kunstgeschichte*. Ed. Otto Schmitt. Vol. 1. Stuttgart 1937. Pp. 323-324. (The citation above comes from this article. P. 323.)
[16] Kant: *Critique of Judgement*. P. 97 (B 74; §23).

work, between frame and enframed – the fact that an ornament in essence is an accessory, an addition, a marginal decoration. The *Critique of Judgment* emphatically incorporates this quality of the ornament into the analytic of "pure" aesthetic judgments. With a remarkable and even puzzling consequence, an entire series of examples elaborates on the concept of a parergonal beauty:

> In painting, sculpture, indeed in all the visual arts, in architecture and horticulture insofar as they are fine arts, *design* is what is essential; in design the basis for any involvement of taste is not what gratifies us in sensation but merely what we like because of its form. [...] What we call *ornaments* (*parerga*), i.e. what does not belong to the complete representation of the object as an intrinsic constituent, but [is] only an extrinsic adjunct, does indeed increase our taste's liking, and yet it does so only by its form, as in the case of picture-frames or the garments on statues, or the colonnades around magnificent buildings.[17]

Certainly not every decorative adjunct or *parergon* named by Kant is an arabesque in the traditional sense. But the arabesques, which in the form of ornamental 'additions' establish a frame, clearly represent the most relevant paradigm of parergonality itself. Pursuing his interest in arabesques as parerga, Kant unhesitatingly equates the garments adorning statues with the frames of paintings; thus he conceives of them not as integral parts of the statues, but rather as an addition or ornamentation. As the parallel example of the colonnades around a magnificent building shows, Kant's interpretation of the statues' garments does not so much aim to take a stand vis-à-vis the question of whether such garments were in some cases posterior additions to the sculpture proper. Rather Kant is solely concerned with establishing a synchronic difference between ergon and parergon and with grounding the very definition of a "pure" beauty of art in this difference. The same holds for Kant's perspective on "ladies' attire" [*Putz der Damen*]: in its function as "ornaments[...] at a luxurious party", he without ado "comprises" this attire under the arabesque decorations of "rooms"[18] and thus equates it with ornamental wallpapers. Even the "free beauties of nature" – "wild flowers"[19] and animals like "the parrot, the hummingbird, the bird of paradise"[20] – are viewed as colorful dots added like ornaments to a nature which otherwise, and as a whole, is not supposed to be devoid of purpose. In a classically anthropocentric gesture, Kant holds that the

---

[17] Ibid. Pp. 71-72 (B 42-43, §14).
[18] Ibid. P. 193 (B 210, §56).
[19] Ibid. P. 77 (B 49, §16). P. 166 (B 166 §42).
[20] Ibid. P. 77. (B 49, §16).

human being is the only entity of nature that is a purpose in itself (*Selbstzweck*),[21] and that most other animals (like the horse) are subordinate to human purposes. For this reason he excludes all these natural beings – just like the artworks and man – from the ambit of purely aesthetic judgments.[22] The exoticism of many of the animals given as examples therefore serves the bewildering yet consistent construction of parergonal margins of nature, which Kant did not yet view as subjected to the central ergon of creation, namely European man. Even in Kant's time this task obviously required extended travels (of the imagination).

In a different way "shells" or "crustaceans of the sea" [*Schalthiere des Meeres*],[23] which Kant evokes several times throughout the entire third *Critique*, are also marginal to the human being's realm of dominion. Kant thinks of them apparently not in terms of fishing and eating – rather he imagines them as free creatures which occasionally lend themselves to man's aesthetic contemplation at the liminal margin between land and sea. Furthermore, shells enter into this contemplation as empty enclosures, as 'coverings' without 'contents' or as a frame without a center, and these empty frames in turn are used for decorative frameworks – a doubled arabesque structure. (I only recall here the famous *Muschel-Saal* in the *Neues Palais* in Potsdam.) The "shell-work" decried by Winckelmann thus undergoes a legitimation as a free beauty. But why Kant's amazing obsession with "foliage for framework" and other arabesque parerga? Schiller already had noted this obsession with as much concision as concern: "Kant [...] claims, rather strangely, [...] that an arabesque and similar things, considered as beauty, are purer than the most perfect beauty of man".[24]

For Kant "art always has a determinate intention to produce something".[25] And since in this way "art always presupposes a purpose in the cause (and its causality), a concept of what the thing is intended to be must first of all be laid at its basis";[26] otherwise "its product cannot be ascribed to any art at all".[27] Pure aesthetic judgments, however, are applicable only to what pleases without purpose, intention, concept and

---

[21] Ibid. P. 82. (B 55. §17).

[22] Cf. Jacques Derrida: Parergon. In: Derrida: *La Vérité en Peinture*. Paris 1978. Pp. 19-168.

[23] Kant: *Critique of Judgement*. P. 76 (B 49, §16). P. 221 (B 248, §58). P. 224 (B 252, §58).

[24] Friedrich Schiller: Kallias oder Über die Schönheit. In: F. Schiller. *Sämtliche Werke*. Ed. Gerhard Fricke und Herbert G. Göpfert. 5th ed. Vol. V. Munich 1975. Pp. 394-433, here p. 395.

[25] Ibid. P. 174 (B 180, §45).

[26] Ibid. P. 179 (B 188, §48). Translation modified.

[27] Ibid. P. 178 (B 186, §47).

interest. In drawing on examples taken from nature Kant avoids this dilemma, but vis-à-vis problematical art he confronts it with a double strategy. On the one hand "fine art" [*schöne Kunst*], in order to be beautiful, must produce the illusion that it is no art at all, but rather "nature". Its unavoidable finality [*Zweckmäßigkeit*] must "appear unintentional, although it is intentional".[28] At least in the mode of illusion, of an 'as if' – that is, as if it were not art – fine art can be rescued for a pure aesthetic judgment. To be sure, Kant only follows this route toward the final paragraphs of the "Analytic of Aesthetic Judgment". At the same time, with the emphasis of a "must", an imperative of illusion, he runs the danger of falling into contradiction with himself, namely with his likewise categorical assertion that poetic composition should not "deceive by means of a beautiful illusion" as rhetoric does, but rather that in it "everything proceeds honestly and sincerely".[29]

In the first paragraphs of the "Analytic of Aesthetic Judgment", on the other hand, Kant looks for a beauty of art [*das Kunstschöne*] that corresponds to the requirements of a pure aesthetic judgment *without* deception and illusion.[30] And since artworks in the genuine sense here are disqualified, Kant resorts to the adjunct or "minor works", the

---

[28] Ibid, P. 174 (B 180, §45). Translation modified.

[29] Ibid, P. 197 (B 216-217, §53). Translation modified.

[30] Both the "analytic" and the "deduction" offer though a second reflection upon the 'impurity' of aesthetic judgements regarding products of fine art: namely their recognition which attempts to understand the "impairing of beauty's purity" [*der Reinigkeit der Schönheit Abbruch thun*] not simply as a lack, but rather as a "gain" [*Gewinn*] for "the *entire faculty* of representation" [*das* gesamte Vermögen *der Vorstellungskraft*] (pp. 230-231 [B 50-52, §60], translation modified). "When we judge artistic beauty", i.e. a beauty, which according to Kant is necessarily linked to a purpose, we shall consequently "have to assess the thing's perfection as well" (p. 179 [B 188, §48]) – thus a quality of which pure beauty should be "wholly independent" (p. 73-75, [B 44-48, §15]). Yet such a connection between beauty and what is "actually" foreign to it (p. 78, [B 51, §16]) is also present in the "ideal" of beauty of nature ["das Naturschöne"] itself: namely in man (pp. 80-81, [B 55-56, §17]). Just as in man, the 'impurity' of beauty in art – its inextricable connection to "perfection", which demotes it to a "merely adherent beauty" (p. 76, [B 48-49, §16]) – is not simply a deficit, but rather a paradoxical mode of intensification as pollution. For Kant, when he legitimates the – mixed – beauty of art, also refers to the analogical impurity of the aesthetic judgement regarding man (p. 179, [B 188-189, §48]).

decorative "parerga".[31] These are beneficiaries of a negative-parasitic economy: they draw their freedom not positively from the 'genuine' works, but from the fact that the latter by their very definition include the moment of purpose and intention and thus remove the aesthetically 'impure' component of art from their ornamental supplements. The artwork incorporates and as it were 'handles' the problematical element, so that in the difference between the work and the arabesque addendum a possibility of a "pure" and "free beauty" opens up which otherwise would remain unattainable for art.[32] Consequently, parerga are para-sitic in a double sense: first, they are spatially situated next to an ergon; second, they profit functionally from this para-situatedness in that they draw from it their power and the particular surplus of their being. Only as a parergon, as an addition to itself, is it possible for art to be "purely" beautiful without having to deceive. The free play of all faculties becomes possible to the extent that beauty – its Kantian correlate – is banished from the work to its frame. The arabesque "foliage for frameworks" and its analogs thus not only are prime examples, but even represent the condition of possibility of purely aesthetic asignificance and of conceptless non-representationality. An echo of this revalorization of the "parerga" [Nebenwerke] also can be heard in Kant's theory of "supplementary representations" [Nebenvorstellungen] or aesthetic attributes:

> If forms do not constitute the exhibition of a given concept itself, but are only supplementary [Neben-]representations of the imagination, expressing the concept's implications and its kinship with other concepts, then they are called (aesthetic) attributes of an object. [...They present] something that prompts the imagination to spread over a multitude of kindred presentations that arouse more thought than can be expressed in a specific concept determined by words.[33]

Although itself a part of the aesthetic work, the para-representation produces a similar side-step, a spreading and straying along the borders

---

[31] Cf. also Kant: *Anthropologie in pragmatischer Hinsicht*. In: *Kants gesammelte Schriften*. Ed. Königlich Preußischen Akademie der Wissenschaften. Berlin 1917. Vol. 7. P. 243.

[32] Also in the discourse on the sublime, when the question of the "artistic presentation" of the sublime arises, Kant once again resorts to beautiful accessory works: "The sublime is indeed not an object for taste, but rather for the feeling of being moved [Rührung]; but the artistic presentation of the same in the description and attire (in accessory works, parerga) can and should be beautiful" (*Anthropologie in pragmatischer Hinsicht*. P. 243).

[33] Kant: *Critique of Judgement*. P. 183 (B 195, §52).

similar to what the parergon of beautiful frames does. Both evade the
center, because both evade the concept for the sake of the aesthetic.

To put it formally, the purely aesthetic beauty of art thus resides in
establishing and processing the difference between ergon and parergon.
Even if it was only established in order to be blurred, this difference
opens up within art a space, a field of self-reflection which the Romantics then held to be the prime feature of art. Both of these types of
beauty in art – that of the ergon and that of the parergon – are equally
dependent on the absence of a determinate concept. Yet in each respec-
tive case this conceptual indeterminateness generates a different and
even opposing effect: in the case of the 'authentic' artistic productions
of genius it reveals precisely the infinite meaningfulness of the aesthetic
idea; in the case of the parerga, however, Kant explicitly speaks of their
"meaning nothing" [*nichts bedeuten*]. Hence there results a series of
several correlative oppositions: parergon vs. ergon, aesthetically pure
vs. aesthetically impure, free vs. adherent beauty, 'meaning nothing' vs.
infinitely meaningful. To be sure, the *Critique of Judgment* does not
develop these correlative oppositions simultaneously. Rather, its focus
shifts successively from one side to the other: from the pure beauty of
ornamental parerga at the beginning, to the theory of infinitely meaningful erga which do not, however, allow for an "entirely pure" judgment
of taste, at the conclusion of the Analytic.

By virtue of his emphasis on the parerga, Kant radically reevaluates
the margins, frames and digressions as compared to the 'actual' artworks. He locates the inner and "pure" field of the beauty of art in
precisely those marginal figures of framing which constitute the crossing of inside and outside, or more precisely – which articulate the
inside/outside difference at the outermost margin of the work. Kant is
no longer concerned here with the frame's effects on what is enframed –
regardless whether it playfully defigures the enframed image, as in the
Rococo-arabesque, or whether it confirms and enhances it, as in Classicism. On the other hand, he also does not transform the ornament into a
self-sufficient abstract artwork, as would occur later on in modern art.
For Kant insists that the arabesque has its genuine place on or beside a
work and thus indeed is a parergon. But this "para" is little more than a
transcendental metonymy. It signifies nothing but parergonality itself as
the condition of the possibility of a pure aesthetic judgment and does
not imply any specific interaction between the particular content levels
of ergon and parergon. The assumptions traditionally underlying the
ornament – "that the ornament emphazises the value of the object it
decorates and must itself be appropriate to it, that it simultaneously

'interprets' what it decorates"[34] – are suspended in this now entirely abstract relationship. By virtue of this naked and transcendental metonymy, the ornament ends up in the rigorously sought-after position of aesthetic autonomy, exactly because it is the "only genre of art that cannot exist autonomously".[35] Even so, the ornament is not required to surrender its para-sitic dependence on some other ergon.

Kant's insight into the autonomy of the aesthetic is thus essentially an insight into the para-heteronomy of this central phantom of modern aesthetics. A consequence of this insight, however, is that Kant suspends the requirement of aesthetic purity for all non-parergonal and hence for almost all art, just as for the "ideal of the beautiful"; in fact, he superimposes on the tendency toward aesthetic purity a contrary tendency toward enhancing the aesthetic by contaminating it with practical und theoretical dimensions.[36] It is only with regard to this shift towards legitimating aesthetic impurity that one can account for the fact that when Kant finally addresses the beauty of artworks near the end of the "Analytic" he no longer mentions the parerga at all – though at the beginning they had served as a pivotal paradigm for the exposition of the very concept of beauty and of "entirely pure" judgments of taste. This displacement in the diachrony of the Kantian text reflects a fundamental tension about how to determine the autonomy of the aesthetic in terms of its pure self-reference. On the one hand the third *Critique* strives for a completely autochthonic principle of aesthetic judgment and excludes from it every theoretical concept as well as every purpose and every practical interest. On the other, the field of the aesthetic is construed precisely as a reconciliation between theory and praxis and hence as a function of a systemic architecture that is presupposed in its basic elements. The concept, as an "indefinite" one, is allowed to return in this field as well; indeed Kant demands – despite the polemically accentuated disinterestedness [*Interesselosigkeit*] – precisely that both artist and recipient take an "intellectual interest" in the beautiful, as a veritable seal of quality in aesthetic appreciation. The theory of the parergon thus marks the puristic self-referential pole of a fundamental ambivalence perceptible throughout the third *Critique*, while the theory of the ergon marks the integrating function of art. Only when seen together[37] do these conflicting elements point to a cardinal desideratum

---

[34] Hans Sedlmayr: *Die Revolution der modernen Kunst*. Hamburg 1955. Pp. 46-47.

[35] Ibid.

[36] Cf. footnote 31.

[37] Niklas Luhmann strictly separates this double movement, which on the one hand revalorizes and on the other hand devalues the ornament. Conforming to the interpretation of 20th-century non-representational art as absolute ornament

of Kantian as well as of subsequent Idealist aesthetics: how art can follow only its own "rules" and at the same time, by virtue of its formal structure, generate effects which bear on ethical and theoretical problems. Under two conditions this intervention does not compromise the autonomy of the aesthetic: first, its effects must be unattainable by anything other than the aesthetic; second, they must relate to problems not solvable at the levels proper to theoretical and practical philosophy (namely, to the problem of their unity). Moreover, rather than solving these problems of theoretical und practical philosophy, the aesthetic only sets them in motion, 'agitating' what cannot be solved at all in any coherent theoretical sense.

Kant's intervention in the discourse on the arabesque has been largely, often completely, ignored by literary historical research on the

---

(*Die Kunst der Gesellschaft*. Frankfurt a.M. 1995. P. 360), he understands the development of the modern system of art *entirely* as the development into a pure combinatorics of forms. Under pre-modern conditions the ornament was that upon which this combinatorics could be "as it were practiced", in order subsequently, in an evolutionary step, to progress from a "preadaptive advance" into the standard of art. Luhmann can therefore only condemn the "parallel" phenomenon of a "devaluation of the ornamental as mere decoration" for being a mere conceptual error in the "self-description" of the system of art, or being a lack of consistency that "sabotages the possibility of denoting the unity of art itself, for what could this unity be if beauty as perfection [of ornamental combinations of form – W.M.] still required a supplement?" (p. 353). Even though Luhmann otherwise likes to insist on distinctions in contexts where they aren't made – for example the distinction between code and program in the "self-description" of the system of art – in this case he does not want to grant validity to a distinction that has been maintained with a certain insistency, namely, "the distinction between artwork and ornament". Contrary to Luhmann and in agreement with the 'tradition' I find that precisely this processing and ambivalent transformation of the difference between ergon and parergon is something quite interesting. For already at the 'origin' of aesthetic autonomy it indicates an awareness of the precarious nature of art's self-grounding – an awareness that Luhmann allows for only in later phases of art's self-exhaustion, as wrought by an incessant and purely internal pressure of innovation. Moreover, I doubt that for the understanding of any artwork it suffices to define it as a purely ornamental combination of forms, if that combination means nothing other than that "differences accord with [previously made, W.M.] differences", and if the only rejoinder to the 'code value' of Beauty that this definition can offer is an extremely boiled-down version of the venerable doctrine of "harmony" (p. 286). Luhmann refrains from offering any formal criterion for such "harmony" (when does a difference "accord" or "fit" with another and when *not*?) while at the same time stripping it of every metaphysical or transcendental significance (in the sense of the ancient doctrine of cosmological harmony or the Kantian interplay of mental capacities).

theory of arabesque (for instance Karl Konrad Polheim's comprehensive treatment *Die Arabeske*[38]); the absence of the word[39] evidently occluded the argument as well. In research on Kant, the situation is widely similar.[40] To be sure, in a brilliant study Jacques Derrida analyzed Kant's

[38] Cf. Polheim's chapter: Das Wort Arabeske vor F. Schlegel. In: Karl Konrad Polheim: *Die Arabeske*. Pp. 17-21.

[39] The non-mention of the word 'arabesque' can be read, on the one hand, as pointing to the lack of a need to mention it explicitly: given the numerous treatises on the arabesque that preceded the appearance of Kant's third *Critique*, Kant could presume that his contemporaries were familiar with the locus of his intervention. On the other hand a strategy of conflict avoidance may also be involved here. For by forgoing the use of the word 'arabesque', Kant could avoid an open conflict with the enlightenment condemnation of the arabesque that was so eloquently formulated by Adolf Riem in 1788.

[40] An exception is Harries: *The Broken Frame*. Pp. 82-83. In a very interesting article, which appeared after completion of the present study, Harries addresses again, and this time more comprehensively, the problem of ornament in Kant's third *Critique* (Laubwerk auf Tapeten. In: *Idealismus mit Folgen. Die Epochenschwelle um 1800 in Kunst und Geisteswissenschaften. Festschrift zum 65. Geburtstag vom Otto Pöggeler*. Ed. Hans-Jürgen Gawoll and Christoph Jamme. Munich 1994. Pp. 87-96). Several of my elaborations coincide closely with Harries' article. Harries, however, seems to be unfamiliar with the arabesque debate in the 1780s and 1790s, the scholarly work done on this debate, as well as with Derrida's confrontation with Kant's parergon; at least he does not mention them at all. Rather, without referring to the classicist positions (like those of Moritz or Goethe), he relates Kant's examples directly and exclusively to the art of the rocaille. One consequence of this strategy is Harries' tendency to underemphasize the parergonal element in Kant's examples. Yet in contrast to the rocaille's undoing the difference between ergon and parergon, Kant maintains a clear and essential distinction between border and center, despite effacing the hermeneutical relationships between them. This is true not only for the "picture-frames, or garments on statues, or colonnades around magnificent buildings" (*Critique of Judgement*. P. 72 [B 43]. Translation modified); it is also true for Harries' titular example of the "foliage on wallpaper", which in the context of the contemporary debate should be seen more as a parergonal ornamentation of rooms rather than as an absolute decorative pattern. If one adds the construction of a parergonal ornaments in nature in Kant's animal examples as well (see above) – which is completely overlooked by Harries because of his exclusive concentration on the wallpaper pattern –, then Kant's examples attain a considerable, indeed almost uncanny rigor, and are surely not, as Harries surmises, "probably adduced without much reflection" (p. 96). Likewise Harries' observation, that "Kant uses as examples of pure beauty not paintings or sculptures, but something like foliage on wallpaper" (p. 94), seems to miss the logic underlying the series of Kant's examples. For the foliage, as a parergonal part of the art of adorning rooms, is an exact parallel to the "picture-frames, or garments on

orientation toward the parergon, but he related the over-determination of the frame above all to a theoretical problem of the third *Critique* itself: namely its taking, without any further justification, its own frame from the *Logic* and moreover tacitly from an implicit anthropology.[41] Following Derrida, the logic of the parergon has then been generalized into a universal subversion of occidental reason and its principle of identity.[42] But this standpoint overlooks the contemporary aesthetic locus of the third *Critique*'s apparently so eccentric series of examples. The entire argument of the text begins to speak differently, and far more specifically, only when the frame circumscribing the frame-obsession, namely the theory of arabesque, is itself brought into view.

For Friedrich Schlegel the arabesque was "the genuine mother, the embryo of all of modern painting"[43] – a determination that is most persuasive with reference to rocaille forms. But Schlegel went further than this. He declared the arabesque to be indeed "the oldest and original form of human fantasy".[44] Consequently it is the return of the "arabesque" that, according to Schlegel, accounts for "the entire advantage of the so-called novel of the age".[45] In Schlegel, the Kantian parergo-

---

statues". The primary distinction, therefore, is not being made between wallpapers as decorative patterns on the one hand and paintings or sculptures on the other, but between the parergonal series wallpaper, picture-frames, statues' drapery and the ergonal series room, painting, statue.

[41] Cf. Derrida: Parergon. Pp. 64-71 and 111-113.

[42] Cf. Ulrike Dünkelsbühler: *Kritik der Rahmen-Vernunft. Parergon – Versionen nach Kant und Derrida.* Munich 1991. Pp. 50-62. Dünkelsbühler often considerably overstrains the wording of the third *Critique* in her endeavor to see "the identity principle of Western provenance per se" undermined in the Kantian parergon. She attempts to complicate Kant's exclusion of the "golden frame" (*Critique of Judgement*, P. 72 [B 43, §14]) from the paradigm of "purely" beautiful "frameworks" [*Einfassungen*] with the comment that Kant after all concedes a "pure" beauty of "simple colours" and gold is just such a pure colour (p. 52). Yet the aesthetic "impurity" of the gold frame rests for Kant clearly on the "charm" [*Reiz*] and the interest entailed by the *costliness* of the *material* gold independently of its form and colour. Also the "*like*" [*wie*] in Kant's exemplificatory expression "like frameworks of paintings, or garments on statues", etc. should hardly be read as "*not completely like*" [*nicht ganz wie*] or, as Dünkelsbühler holds, as "a kind of translation or metaphorization". Not least of all because of these two forced and skewed distinctions does Dünkelsbühler lose sight of the aesthetic locus of the Kantian determinations.

[43] Friedrich Schlegel: *Literarische Notizen 1797-1801. Literary Notebooks.* Ed. Hans Eichner. Frankfurt a.M./Berlin/Vienna 1980. Number 313.

[44] *Kritische Friedrich-Schlegel-Ausgabe.* Vol. 2. P. 319.

[45] Schlegel: *Literarische Notizen.* Number 1743.

nality breaks through from the margins of the work into its center; indeed it becomes the very essence of the work itself as an unending reflection. The adjunct work ceases to be a mere addition; instead, it becomes incorporated into the ergon's own principle of form. The ornamental addendum is transformed into an ironic-reflexive supplement. To this extent, the difference between ergon and parergon is reintroduced into the ergon itself, and possibilities for endless re-entries of the Kantian difference in the interplay of different textual levels are being opened up. The arabesque no longer merely ornamentally demarcates the inner field of art against its exterior, and it no longer merely inversely displaces the purity of the aesthetic onto the – itself external – border dividing inside from outside. Rather, it turns the entire distinction towards the inside. This entropic movement does not sublate the central distinction of frame and enframed, but rather permits it to propagate itself all the more obstinately and diversely, in the mode of delirium. Schlegel speaks of an "artificially regulated confusion"[46] that is continually being produced by the parergonal disruption of a work from its own tendencies. Another name for this effect is the romantic cipher of "chaos".[47] Hence Schlegel parallels "chaotic form -- arabesque, *Märchen*".[48] This relationship between chaos and arabesque is also reflected in the *Discourse on Mythology* [*Rede über die Mythologie*][49] and in the sequence "Romantic Chaos", "*Naturarabeske*" and "Poem composed of nothing" in the self-advertisement of *Lucinde*.[50]

Embellishments of rooms, preeminently those done by Raphael in the Vatican, were for Moritz still the paradigm of the aesthetic of the arabesque – just as they were earlier in Heinse's *Ardinghello* (1787) and Goethe's article "Von Arabesken" (1789). This discourse, which primarily pertained to the fine arts until 1790, was then widely appropriated by philosophy, poetics and literature. The intersection of all these disciplines in the term "arabesque" marks the origin of a new thinking about art in general. Kant, in his search for a pure and free beauty, discovered parergonal structures in numerous natural and social phenomena. And between 1797 and 1801, Friedrich Schlegel applied the concept in a both original and persuasive way to literature. He had

[46] *Kritische Friedrich-Schlegel-Ausgabe*. Vol. 2. P. 318.
[47] Ibid. P. 319.
[48] Schlegel: *Literarische Notizen 1797-1801*. Number 1804.
[49] *Kritische Friedrich-Schlegel-Ausgabe*. Ed. Ernst Behler with Jean Jacques Anstett und Hans Eichner. Paderborn/Munich/Vienna/Zürich 1958ff. Vol. 2. P. 319.
[50] Ibid. Vol. 16. P. 247.

precursors in some remarks by Herder[51] and especially in the context of the poetics of the fairy tale [*Feenmärchen*]. In 1790 Friedrich Justin Bertuch compared Count Anton Hamilton's fairy tales with the "famous arabesques in the loges of the Vatican", and he named precisely the characteristics of the pre-Romantic traditions which were then developed in the earliest Romantic poetics: "the maddest and most hilarious imagination, playfulness, caprice, [...] the most colorful and most hilarious texture". Bertuch's introduction to the *Blaue Bibliothek aller Nationen* contains similar wording: "The Blue Library of all Nations will be a universal and ongoing collection of all wondrous tales [*Wundermärchen*], legends and adventure stories and novels, of all peoples, so to speak, the arabesques and grotesques of all known literatures".[52]

The affinity between arabesque ornament and fairy tales is based above all on two characteristics. Like the ornament, the fairy tale – at least as it was understood by most late 18th-century authors – suspends the practical ends and theoretical concepts of the (everyday) understanding and establishes its own proper arena of 'mischievous imagination'. Herder in his *Adrastea* (1801) still calls fairy tales "flower[s] of arabesque", precisely because they are "stories without understanding and purpose"; he requires, however, that the "caprices and whims" of this "extinct world" be given a new, "most unexpected turn".[53] The second common characteristic is the structure of interlacing in ornamental patterning and wondrous fairy tales. Meanders, snake-like lines, even the snake itself are preferred forms in arabesque decorations in architecture; narrative interlacings – and likewise often the snake as an old *Märchen* motif – characterize the Enlightenment fairy tale and its Romantic rewriting as linguistic *figurae serpentinatae*, as analogs of the famous line of beauty.[54] The "free", never entirely predictable curved line at the same time accounts for the interrelation of fairy tale and the romantic idea of chance [*Zufall*]; one of Schlegel's literary notes laconically explicates the "*Märchen*-like, arabesque" as "the infinitely capricious and contingent".[55] What Moritz had called the "play of chance" in his incrimination of the arabesque now becomes the central concept of a Romantic theory of the "chance" and "non-coherence" of *Märchen*.

[51] Cf. J.G. Herder: Briefe zur Beförderung der Humanität. In: J.G. Herder, *Sämtliche Werke*. Ed. Bernhard Suphan. Vol. 18. Berlin 1883. P. 43.
[52] Quoted in Oesterle: Arabeske und Roman. Pp. 238-239.
[53] J. G. Herder: Adrastea. In: J. G. Herder: *Sämtliche Werke*. Ed. Bernhard Suphan.Vol. 23. Leipzig 1883. Pp. 285-286.
[54] Cf. here Erwin Rotermund: Musikalische und dichterische 'Arabeske' bei E.T.A. Hoffmann. Pp. 51-54; and Oesterle: Arabeske, Schrift und Poesie in E.T.A. Hoffmanns Kunstmärchen "Der goldne Topf". Pp. 72-92.
[55] Schlegel: *Literarische Notizen 1797-1801*. Number 1065.

44

Winckelmann's "void" and Riem's condemnation of the "senseless-ness" [*das Sinnlose*] of the arabesque return as a poetics of what is "without any sense" [*ohne allen Sinn*] and of "nonsense" [*Unsinn*]. Schlegel's definition of the *Märchen* as an "arabesque composition for fantasy's pleasure"[56] unmistakably continues the pre-Romantic conception of the fairy tale. However, Schlegel never explicitly applied this definition to *Feenmärchen*, but exclusively to their radical Roman-tic modification. One of his earliest comments on the theory of *Märchen* refers to the "poetic arabesques, which [Tieck] formed out of several old *Märchen*".[57] In the following reflections I focus on one of these poetic arabesques which at the same time is one of the most delightful and yet least known texts of early German Romanticism: the narrative *The Seven Wives of Bluebeard*. This arabesque, explicitly subtitled so by Tieck, is much more than simply one of the many works upon which Schlegel practiced the permutations of his conceptual alchemy. For this tale's theoretical reflections directly anticipate many of Schlegel's thoughts and also exhibit elements that go beyond his ruminations.

In Tieck, the disputed 'meaninglessness' of the arabesque is no longer justified by the constraints of a philosophical system that requires art to be without concept and intention, but instead by a critique of the con-straints and ideological violence inherent in the imperative to be mean-ingful. It is also not, as in Schlegel, dialecticized into a prerequisite for infinite meaning, but on the contrary is functionalized into resisting the new hermeneutical paradigm. The sober realization, that "in the whole of human life there is no goal and no coherence to be found", that life quite literally "means nothing",[58] should for Tieck finally produce consequences in literature: on the one hand as an anti-idealistic 'real-ism', and on the other hand as the liberation of life from the expectation that it should be poetically meaningful. As an arabesque pattern, litera-ture should "shake" the hermeneutical postulates of meaning "loose like a saddle and reins".[59] Tieck thereby polemically exploits a possibility which the arabesque accrued only against the background of the new paradigm of sense. As a beauty free in the Kantian sense, that is, with-out concept, purpose or interest, the arabesque has its field beyond the difference between sense and nonsense: it is without sense, without, however, being nonsensical. Yet the arabesque can become the producer of nonsense-effects, where its indifference toward sense is itself placed and exploited within the field of sense.

[56] *Kritische Friedrich-Schlegel-Ausgabe*. Vol. 2. Pp. 357-358.
[57] Ibid. P. 245.
[58] Ludwig Tieck: *Die sieben Weiber des Blaubart*. In: Tieck: *Schriften*. 28 vols. Berlin 1828 (Reprint Berlin/New York 1974). Vol. 9. P. 193.
[59] Ibid. P. 220.

In Tieck's text, even Kant's arabesque parergonality finds a more literal counterpart than in Schlegel's theory. For the entire narrative presents one single parergon to the plot of the *Märchen* itself: it describes only its margins and avoids the center. Blaubart-*Märchen* preeminently, and often exclusively, narrate the story of the final wife who brings the murderous career of the fiend to an end. It is precisely this narrative core which Tieck leaves out. It becomes merely the subject of an allusion to Tieck's recently published *Blaubart* -drama: "I am therefore not obligated to add anything here, because I assume that each of my readers has read the *Blaubart*, and therefore it is very easy for me to write this last chapter, in which I do not need to present anything".[60] In the sense of Propp's morphology, Blaubart figures solely as the evil counterpart of the positive heroine who brings the serial murders to an end. Precisely because this main protagonist of the Blaubart-*Märchen* disappears from the circle of Tieck's arabesque 'presentation' [*'Darstellung'*], the *Märchen*'s distinctive focus on the hero[61] is inverted into figurations of the hero's literal exclusion: into the involutions and branchings of a plot that finally consists only of secondary figures and antagonists. The repeat offender, the serial killer Blaubart thus becomes the ideal subject of a form which is essentially defined through serial proliferation, through repetitions of a recurrent pattern. Even the bloody and central phantom in the plot of *Blaubart*, the shocking presence of the women's corpses in the forbidden chamber, gives way to a more than discrete arabesque. It is replaced by a leaden head, which is and means nothing to Blaubart's women, and which is not even perceived by them at all. This leaden head only marginally 'fills' an empty space, without removing the vacuum: Winckelmann's very definition of the arabesque "flourish" [*Schnirkel*]. Not only the head's spatial positioning on a chamber wall, but also its metamorphic ability reveal it to be a derivative of those much-discussed wall-decorations. When Blaubart smashes the head, a tiny snake slips out of it – that (fairy-tale) animal which occurs as both a pictorial figure and the formal principle of interlacing and serpentine lines in Raphael's Vatican arabesques. Similarly, the very attribute of the 'blue beard', taken literally as a peripheral adornment of the protagonist's face, figures primarily as an arabesque within Tieck's arabesque.

As a final note, I would like to single out the construction of the narrative's conclusion among the numerous examples of these arabesque figurations and disfigurations. After the "conclusion" [*Beschluß*]

---

[60] Ibid. P. 241.
[61] Cf. Eleasar Meletinsky/ S. Nekludov/ E. Novik/ D. Segal: Problems of the Structural Analysis of Fairytales. In: *Soviet Structural Folkloristics*. Ed. P. Maranda. Vol. 1. The Hague/Paris 1974. Pp. 73-139. Esp. p. 87.

of the "story" [*Geschichte*], in which Tieck while alluding to his Blau-bart drama simply announces that he will forgo depicting the announced conclusion, there follows a further, explicitly titled "final chapter". What comes on the heels of the *Beschluß* (the subtitle of the 32nd chapter) of the thereby concluded "story" as a "thirty-third, or final chapter" [p. 241] – as supplementary note, appendix, paralipomenon, etc. – can easily be called a parergon *sensu stricto*. By nonetheless integrating this parergon, this "final chapter" *after* the final chapter, into the ergon, Tieck once again lays bare the work's pervasive and literal parergonality, which like an arabesque snakes about the margins of a narrative center that is both omitted and yet presupposed. Elsewhere in his critical writings Tieck explicitly praises "those arabesques with their flourishes and embellishments that have come alive",[62] and he also uses the Kantian term *Nebenwerk* or parergon: "The parergon [*Nebenwerk*] is made into the main subject".[63] This arabesque inversion and inversion of arabesque[64] does not by chance haunt both Kant and early Romanti-cism. Rather, it responds in the mode of caprice and whimsical play to some of the basic problems inherent in the very formation of modern art and aesthetics.

[62] Ludwig Tieck, *Kritische Schriften*. 4 vols. Leipzig 1848. (Reprint Ber-lin/New York 1974.) Vol. 1. P. 162.
[63] Ibid. Vol. 1. P. 119.
[64] For a more comprehensive treatment of the Kantian and early Romantic poetics of ornament and of nonsense see my book *Lob des Unsinns. Über Kant, Tieck und Blaubart*. Frankfurt a.M. 1995. [Editor's note: This article is adapted from material appearing in *In Praise of Nonsense* by Winfried Men-ninghaus (Stanford University Press, 1999). It is published here with the permission of Stanford University Press and Suhrkamp Verlag.]

Helmut Mueller-Sievers

Tidings of the Earth:
Towards a History of Romantic *Erdkunde*[1]

Romantic Geography (Erdkunde) *strives to find natural coordinates for any location on earth. Enlightenment geography (and its auxiliary practices surveying, cartography, and navigation), conscious of the essential impossibility of applying geometrical measurements to the curved surface of the globe, had attempted to achieve orientation by means of approximative techniques. For Immanuel Kant, the impossibility of purely transitive (geometrical) orientation and the concomitant necessity of self-orientation became the organizing principle for the critique of human reason. Against his admission of constitutive fissures in the relation between knowledge and earth, romantic geography mobilizes all the sciences to argue for an organic development of the earth's surface, for the physiognomic individuality of each location and, ultimately, for the belonging of humans to their native location* (Heimat).

The goal of all Romantic sciences is the end of Enlightenment geography and the beginning of *Erdkunde*. They all contribute to the endeavor of rendering the description of the earth independent from unearthly, quantifying discourses (such as astronomy and geometry) and to furnish, in the form of magnetic, electrical, and chemical variables, immanent scientific coordinates by which any place on earth is identified as unique and unmistakable. This is not to say that the other sciences lose their identity, or that their subservience to *Erdkunde* is explicit and theoretically reflected. Yet the tidings of the earth (as *Erdkunde* might be translated), the self-expression of any earthly place in the strata of its temporal growth, is not just one project of Romantic science among many; it is its central concern. For if the earth tells us where we are, we can know who we are; then our place on earth ceases to be a contingent assignation and turns into an *Ursprung*, a *Heimat*. The development of *Erdkunde* is thus supported by a philosophy of subjectivity that conceives of itself as nostalgia, as driven by the question that haunts the epoch: "Where

---

[1] A first version of this essay was presented in June 1997 at the conference "Varieties of Scientific Experience" at the Max-Planck-Institut für Wissenschaftsgeschichte in Berlin. I owe much to the fellows of this extraordinary institution.

are we going?"
"Always towards home". Much in the interpretation of German Romanticism hinges on the understanding of how this answer, given in Novalis' *Heinrich von Ofterdingen*, relates to its question.[2] For it is by no means sure that the staccato of questions in the novel comes to an end in this famous answer. It is not clear, without strong interpretative presuppositions, whether each of the questions finds "its" answer, and whether the quest at the heart of the novel, and of so much romantic writing, can reach its destination. It might well be that the question persists against all answers, that the quest always exceeds and misses its goal, and that Romantic literature, philosophy, and science (if thus they can be separated) are marked by this missage.[3]

Philosophically inclined scholarship has traced the retreat of the answer in Romantic discourse to the persistence of a philosophical question – Fichte's "insight" into the ungrounded reflexivity of self-consciousness.[4] In this view, Romantic literature and science are charged with providing an answer – a ground – that philosophy alone cannot give. Philosophical hermeneutics, a product of early Romanticism, stakes its plausibility on the premise that in works of literature such answers are attempted and that a philosophically attuned art of understanding can indeed retrieve them. Many historians of science, eager to demonstrate their credentials as humanists, have espoused the hermeneutic paradigm of question and answer. To them, Romantic science – at first sight a deplorable step backward in the progressive history of scientific conquest – was spurred on to ever more expansive answers by the institutional and discursive indifference of science, philosophy, and literature. This is, on the whole, a productive view of Romantic science, more productive in any case than the wholesale condemnation that had reigned unchallenged in the scientific community since the meeting of the *Gesellschaft deutscher Naturforscher und Ärzte* in Berlin in 1828. Yet the hermeneutic sequence of question and answer is at best a heuristic model, for it implies a teleology of the answer, it imposes an order which remains outside its own argumentative control, it relies on a common space – the famous "hermeneutic horizon" – it can

---

[2] "Wo gehn wir denn hin?" "Immer nach Hause". Novalis: *Heinrich von Ofterdingen*. In: *Werke*. Ed. Gerhard Schulz. 3rd ed. Munich 1987. P. 267.
[3] This is a concept used by Hélène Cixous in a seminar on romantic literature (Northwestern University, Fall 1996).
[4] Most impressively in the work of Manfred Frank. See his: *Einführung in die frühromantische Ästhetik*. Frankfurt a.M. 1989.

only invoke.[5]

This essay challenges the dominance of the hermeneutic sequence in an oblique way. It is not so much concerned with the theoretical questions of grounding and the hermeneutic postulate of a horizon, but with the earth – ground as such – and the human circum-stance establishing a horizon. The history of geography, if viewed as a set of answers, shows that the question at its origin – where am I? – is, strictly speaking, unanswerable. From the facts and dilemmas of orientation – all related to the upright human stance or, as the Greeks said, to *ethos* – springs a history of practices (surveying, cartography, navigation) that, at the end of the Enlightenment, reaches a certain point of saturation. Kant's *Critique of Pure Reason*, permeated through and through by geographical terminology, is a transcendental geography because it too is concerned with the impossibility and the necessity of orientation. Critical thought realizes that the *regressus ad infinitum* that threatens geography and metaphysics – the impossibility of finding a last reliable point of orientation – can be suspended only if the original question is understood as positing itself.

Only against this backdrop does the Romantics' attempt to re-fashion geography become understandable in its full scope. It is fueled by the desire to overcome what Idealist philosophers and Romantic scientists alike perceived as the source of fatal disorientation in Kant's philosophy, its unnatural and overly mathematical view of reason. The new science of *Erdkunde* is part of a large-scale effort to naturalize reason and achieve its repatriation into an organic whole, into a world that would, at last, provide a home.

Orientation: Facts and History

Orientation, i.e. the unequivocal determination of one's location on the surface of the earth, is an impossible task. It is impossible because a roundish rotating body like the earth might have natural south and north poles, but no natural east and west to complete the

[5] "To question the question – But what is not a question? – is to condemn the hermeneutic order dominated by the schema of question and answer to vacuity to the degree that the supposed subject matter can no longer impose itself as a task, much less as a positive fact, but sinks into an unavoidable void from which it would be impossible to secure a place of possible fulfillment. Nothing would be spoken in the conversation from which we measure our existence, so it would be questionable whether 'we' – and all that we are – have ever existed in a past we can 'retrieve'". Peter Fenves: *"Chatter". Language and History in Kierkegaard.* Stanford 1993. P. 22.

coordinates of location. It is a task because the axis of the human body is a prolongation of the earth's radius; it is at the center of a celestial meridian – a circle with the center of the earth as its nadir, the human on the surface of the earth as its center, and the zenith equidistant above – which in turn allows the determination of a terrestrial meridian. A terrestrial meridian is a great circle, and location on spherical bodies is determined in relation to great circles. (It is for lack of this human circumstance that quadrupeds cannot, or need not, orient themselves.) With the equator as one great circle established – since the earth's north-south axis is stable this can be done by external, astronomical measurement – such determination is possible if this terrestrial meridian is de-individualized. If we can measure the distance of our individual meridian not only to the equator, but also to a previously fixed "prime" meridian, the coordinates necessary for orientation are complete. But in the absence of a natural orient, this necessary prime meridian can be established only by an "unnatural" convention.[6]

In a way, the establishment of a prime meridian flattens and stops the earth; it tries to bestow a border onto its curved surface and give it the properties of Euclidean flat space onto which geography and geometry can be inscribed. The impossibility of representing a spherical surface in graphically or metrically undistorted form on a flat surface is embedded in the impossibility of orientation. Euclidean geometry – the geometry of maps – holds only in two-dimensional, infinite space. The surface of the earth is curved and finite: meridians are parallels that intersect. As long as the surface of representation is characterized by Euclidean parameters, this difference cannot be overcome, not even by the "invention" of consistent geometries of curved surfaces. Not only orientation, but also geo-metry, in a very literal sense, is impossible.

Maps are supposed to show the relative distance of places. These distances are measured by surveyors triangulating the terrain: the distance between points is determined by measuring the angle they form with the two ends of an established baseline. The laws of trigonometry employed in this procedure are analytic in the sense in which Leibniz and Kant understood this term: they derive from the definitions of triangles alone. Large scale triangulations, as they are undertaken from the middle of the sixteenth century onward, presuppose a sound geometrical realism on the basis of which the *loci*

---

[6] For details see David Greenhood: *Mapping*. Chicago 1964; and Immanuel Kant: *Physische Geographie*. In: *Gesammelte Schriften. (Akademie-Ausgabe)*. Berlin 1908 -. Vol. IX. Pp. 151-180.

naturales of scholastic physics can be inscribed, without the loss of essential properties, onto the homogenous plane of representation, the map; this inscription both presupposes and fosters the possession of large expanses of land and its military and administrative domination.[7] The disturbances unvaryingly encountered, such as the difficulties in establishing an exact base line, the distortion produced by the angles of elevation, the changes in the gravitational field (and thus the impossibility of getting a true plumb line) are all deemed negligible, or at least manageable.[8]

Epistemologically, triangulation repeats the main features of Cartesian philosophy. As the very work of the surveyor shows, the exclusion of the surveying subject from the field of survey is constitutive for the success of the measurement. The *cogito* remains outside the world of extension, which nonetheless is supposed to conform to the axioms of plane geometry. This structure of constitutive exclusion reappears in the use of maps. The utterance of cartographic self-orientation – to indicate a point on a map and to say "I'm here" – is felicitous only if it is not true, just as the "utterance" of a stationary map – "you are here" – is true, strictly speaking, only for the map itself.[9] This paradoxical "bilocation", and the inaccuracies accumulated in triangulation, need not be prohibitive as long as maps serve either purely representative purposes, or else are on a sufficiently large scale to allow for visual reconnaissance. As soon as maps are used to install and maintain territorial power on larger expanses of land, the inherent distortions seriously compromise their usability.

Cartographic distortions increase as the scale of the map decreases. The dilemmatic structure characterizing the practices of orientation here takes the following form: maps are conformal, i.e. they preserve the shapes and outlines (of a continent, say), or they are equal-area, i.e. they preserve the relative extension (of land and water, of a state, etc.). In addition, they are never, except at their points of contact, consistently true to scale. Within the space of

---

[7] See W. Schäffner: Operationale Topographie. Representationsräume in den Niederlanden um 1600. In: *Räume des Wissens. Repräsentation, Codierung, Spur*. Ed. H.-J. Rheinberger, M. Hagner, B. Wahrig-Schmidt. Berlin 1997. Pp. 63-90. Equally important in this context is Svetlana Alpers: *The Art of Describing. Dutch Art in the Seventeenth Century*. Chicago 1983.

[8] The travails of some surveying expeditions and the material problems of establishing reliable baselines and good sight lines are recounted in *The Shape of the Earth*. Chicago/ New York/ San Francisco 1991. Pp. 110-169.

[9] See Chr. Jacob: *L'empire des cartes*. Paris 1992. Pp. 427-434; also Schäffner. P. 66.

Euclidean geometry – the space of the flat map – there is no solution to this dilemma. Points on a spherical surface have positive curvature; they are intrinsically different from points on flat or on cylindrical surfaces.[10] (This is why rotary presses work; it is also the reason why many map projections, including the famous Mercator projection, are cylindrical.) The dilemma between conformal or equal-area representation requires that at the origin of every map there be a practical choice: sometimes it is more important where a ship arrives than when it arrives (conformal projections); at other times statistical incidence (like population) has to be related to the extent of a geographical area (equal-area projections). The starkest distortions in either projection can be smoothed over, but no internal solution is possible.

The extrinsic reason why maps cannot solve the problem of orientation is that on the greater part of the globe there is nothing to map. The oceans invert the problem of territorial mapping – their surfaces are smooth (and could therefore be measured with much greater accuracy than the irregular surfaces of continents) – but the landmarks on which to take the sightings are submerged. On the oceans the problem of orientation thus takes on its simplest form: one does not know from any observation independent of the moving vessel how far east or west one has traveled. Navigational devices, such as the sextant, the compass, and lunar tables only insufficiently alleviate these dangerous uncertainties.

From the dilemma at the heart of orientation – its necessity and its impossibility – unfolds a history in which surveyors, cartographers, and navigators seek to negotiate the straits of their task. During the eighteenth century these problems were confronted with characteristic optimism. The largest and most representative surveying project of the era, Cassini's *Carte de France*, is based on a thorough and ever more detailed triangulation of the kingdom completed in 1744, anchored by a prime meridian going, of course, through the observatory in Paris. As its mode of financing shows – the 180 maps were available by subscription between 1756 and 1815 – the representation of the French lands was no longer conceived as an inventory of the King's possessions, nor was it yet a military or state secret. Like the contemporaneous *Encyclopédie*, the maps were supposed to function as a public display of information, and foster graphically the idea of national identity.[11] During the same

---

[10] See Lawrence Sklar: *Space, Time and Spacetime*. Berkeley 1974. P. 41.
[11] See B.-H. Vayssière: La 'Carte de France'. In: *Cartes et figures de la Terre*. Paris (Centre Georges Pompidou). Pp. 252-265.

time, the triangulation of a degree of longitude in the polar region and near the equator served as one of the most resounding confirmations of the predictive power of Newtonian physics. So pervasive and transgressive of political boundaries was the trust put in triangulation that in 1787 French and English surveyors met at the English Channel to complete the first transnational triangulation.

The dilemma between conformal and equal-area projection may admit of no "pure", i.e. strictly geometrical solution, but the success of Newton and Leibniz in mathematizing the trajectories of physical bodies – the calculus – carried here as well. The map projections in use until 1772 were arrived at by strictly geometrical means. They were understood as spatial arrangements between the sphere of the earth, a point of projection (often represented as a source of light), and a plane of projection. Gnomonic, stereographic, orthographic, cylindrical, and conical projections are all derived from the mutual displacement of these three elements.[12] The basic constellation – the globe in its spatial relation to the source of light and to the plane of projection – had never been questioned. The properties of maps, such as the conformality of stereographic and Mercator projections, was either not understood at all or regarded as a contingent attribute. Mercator himself seems to have configured the spacing of latitudes on his map by actually translating the distances of parallels from a globe onto the map; only later was a mathematical analysis of it properties undertaken.[13]

It was the great Enlightenment *savant* Jean-Henri Lambert who realized:

> The question has not been asked whether this property [conformality] occurs only in the two methods of representation mentioned or whether these two representations [Mercator and stereographic], so different in appearances, can be made to approach each other through intermediate stages. [...] If there are stages intermediate to these two representations, they must be sought by allowing the angle of intersection of the meridians to be arbitrarily larger or smaller than its value on the surface of the sphere. This is the way in which I shall now proceed.[14]

[12] A good overview of the geometrical properties of the various projections can be found in Norman J. W. Thrower: *Maps & Civilization*. Chicago 1996. P. 222.

[13] See John P. Snyder: Flattening the Earth. Two Thousand Years of Map Projections. Chicago 1993. P. 47.

[14] Jean-Henri Lambert: Notes and Comments on the Composition of Terrestrial and Celestial Maps. (Trans. and intr. W.R. Tobler). Department of Geography, University of Michigan 1972. P. 28. Original: Anmerkungen und Zusätze zur Entwerfung der Land- und Himmelscharten. In: Beyträge zum

In this question, conformality (and, by implication, equivalence) is no longer regarded as an accidental property that can only be copied or described, but as a quality to be actively constructed. The attention of the cartographer shifts from the constellation of projection, in which the plane of projection is regarded as given, to the construction of that plane itself.[15] The use of cylindrical and other conical surfaces already had pointed in this direction, but the properties of these surfaces – meridians and parallels intersecting at constant angles – were passively accepted. Lambert, the first to apply infinitesimal calculus to the problem of map projection, opens an active, algebraic way of transporting the angles of intersection from the globe to the plane of the map. While the position of the plane of projection remains the characteristic difference between the map projections, within each genus Lambert is able to minimize the stark difference between conformality and equivalence. The disjunction between a true representation of shape and a true representation of area (both under the limitation of distortions in scale) could now be "overcome" by selecting conformal projections (like the cylindrical) and bending the graticule in such a way as to approach an equal-area map, and vice versa. The geometrical problem of projection, in which a sphere and a plane are seen in immediate, and therefore immutable, relation is thus "solved" by an algebraic procedure that no longer makes any appeal to spatial intuition. The spacing of parallels and meridians can no longer be determined by geometrical means; they are graphs of differential equations.[16] Through these equations Lambert was able to construct the graticule of various maps *a priori*, rather than just describing them from existing or imagined projections. Lambert, who

---

Gebrauche der Mathematik und deren Anwendung durch J. H. Lambert. Dritter Theil. Berlin 1772. Repr. in: *Oswalds Klassiker der exakten Naturwissenschaften.* Vol. 54. Leipzig 1891. Pp. 24-25.

[15] The emphasis on "construction" here and in the following derives not only from Kant's, and later Schelling's, use of the term, but from the remarkable study by David Rapport Lachterman: *The Ethics of Geometry. A Genealogy of Modernity.* New York 1989. Lachterman sees the difference between the ancients and the moderns in the shift from theorem-proving to problem-solving, and in the modern concept, inaugurated by Descartes, of geometrical construction.

[16] See J.J. Levallois: L'Œuvre cartographique de Lambert. In: *Colloque International et Interdisciplinaire Jean-Henri Lambert.* Paris 1979. P. 302; and Snyder: *Flattening.* Pp. 76-94, who gives the equations for all of Lambert's projections.

incidentally came very close to developing a consistent geometry of curved surfaces, thus managed to control the difference separating curved and plane surfaces by making it infinitely small.[17] Like the surveyors' ignoring the difference between measurement and ground, active construction (rather than passive projection) is not, strictly speaking, a solution: both are strategies of approximation.

The same is true for the third problem of orientation – finding a means to establish longitude. In 1714, the British Parliament offered an award of 20,000 pounds sterling for a means to "ascertain longitude". This wording seems to suggest that longitude is a spatial relation which, like latitude, can be determined by geometrical (astronomical) means. In a coherent geometrical worldview, as it was held by the British astronomical establishment, longitude could indeed be "found" if spatial boundaries could be established within which the earth rotates. Exhaustive lunar tables were used as such a means of orienting an object on earth with relation to a point – the moon – in predictable and calculable motion. In this view, longitude was conceived as a straight line between two points on a plane with vast, but not indefinite, coordinates, while the curvature of the earth disappeared in the flatness of astronomical and geometrical space.

"Longitude" Harrison and the chronometric faction instead understood Parliament as simply asking for a means to come as close as possible to a solution. By staggering the prize money in proportion to the accuracy of the solution, Parliament had implicitly encouraged a method of approximation in which longitude is understood as a limit to be approached in ever smaller increments. In this view, longitude is not a straight line within a larger plane, but a moving point on a rotating curved surface, the location of which cannot be determined by strictly geometrical means. The time measured by Harrison and his predecessors to approach the limit of longitude was not the qualitative time of human experience or of terrestrial history (as the Romantics will understand it), but the mere repetition of as stable an interval as possible. It was "spatial" time in precisely the sense that it could be made visible – not only on the dials of Harrison's timepieces, but also to the august Board of Longitude when it demanded to see the interior of Harrison's chronometer. There was not, as is often stated, a secret to Harrison's chronometers; rather, they constituted a complex riddle which, once solved and demonstrated, could be, and was, reproduced infinitely. The key to Harrison's success was to secure the greatest independence of his

---

[17] J.-H. Lambert: Theorie der Parallellinien. In: *Magazin für reine und angewandte Mathematik.* Vol 2. Pp. 137-164. Vol. 3. Pp. 325-358.

system of measurement from all other spatial influences, to insulate the chronometer from its means of conveyance, from the dangers of the climate, from the changes in the gravitational field – insulation which an open chronometer like the pendulum clock had been unable to achieve.[18]

The similarity to Newton's methods of "fluxions" in the *Principia* is striking. The traveling timepiece *performs* the continuity of a function. True, the time it keeps is visible and structured by intervals, but it measures the distance between two points by measuring it continuously. The condition of its functioning as a device to provide spatial orientation is that it never stops counting off regular, measured intervals, and that, in its maximal contraction, it does not stop timing itself. The ticking timepiece thus traces the graph of a continuous function upon the coordinate system of the earth, relating physical discreteness and geometric continuity in a way Newton could only postulate.

Triangluation, cartography, and navigation thus make significant progress in the eighteenth century despite the acknowledged dilemmas in their discourse and the resulting inaccuracies of their measurements. Triangulation is incapable of accounting for the physiognomy of the terrain it measures, incapable, for example, of predicting how much physical exertion is necessary to get from point A to point B. And still it is undertaken for the first time on a national, even international, scale. Map projections proliferate because they are, strictly speaking, no longer projections but constructions. Longitude is not actually "found" but approached, experimentally verified by a time-keeping device the accuracy of which, in the absence of an absolute measure of time, could not be determined except by its success. The three practices of orientation overcome their internal contradictions on different levels of reflection: triangulation by *ignoring* the discrepancy between measurement and measured terrain; cartography by *constructing*, rather than describing, map projections; navigation by *performing* the integration of geometrical space and physical motion.

A Summons to Orientation: Kant

It is tempting to interpret the triad of ignoring, constructing, and

[18] See Silvio Bedini: *The Pulse of Time. Galilei Galileo, the Determination of Longitude, and the Pendulum Clock.* Florence 1991. Unfortunately, these, and many other points are missing from David Sobel's sensationalistic: *Longitude. The True Story of a Lone Genius Who Solved the Greatest Scientific Problem of his Time.* New York 1995.

performing as typical arrogations of the faculties of sensibility, understanding, and reason such as Kant diagnosed them in the *Critique of Pure Reason*. Beyond this architectonic resemblance, Kant inserted both elaborate allegories (like B 295) and very specific images (like B 790) into the text of the first *Critique* which link the questions of geographical orientation tightly to the task of transcendental critique.[19] As his *Reflexionen* show, Kant would repeatedly exemplify the limits of philosophical questioning by referring to a geographical situation: it is as misguided to expect an answer to certain questions from human reason as it is meaningless to ask where east and west are when one stands on the north pole.[20] On a biographical level, one should not forget that Kant was a great admirer of Jean-Henri Lambert; that he most certainly knew the *Anmerkungen und Zusätze*; and that he actually intended to dedicate the *Critique of Pure Reason* to Lambert.

The geographic concerns in Kant's critical thought go far beyond the textual and biographical level. The problems of geodesy, navigation, and cartography all converge on the question of the ontological status of geometrical objects, and this question is at the heart, at the origin even, of critical philosophy. The point of convergence can be located in what Freud would have called the 'antithetical meaning', the *Gegensinn* of "vermessen" – the opposition *and* identity of surveying (accomplished in the Transcendental Analytic) *and* presuming (critiqued in the Transcendental Dialectic).

Kant's geographical *exempla* seek to reinforce the argument that transcendental philosophy is an investigation for which no question can arise that it cannot also answer. In the *Reflexionen* Kant argues:

> There cannot be any question of transcendental philosophy to which the answer would be unknown to us. For if the predicate is not determined by the subject it means that the question in itself is nothing, because the predicate in this case has no meaning at all, being neither affirmative nor its contrary opposite. Just like when, being at the pole, I ask where to look for the east.[21]

---

[19] As is customary, the *Critique of Pure Reason* is quoted (in the text as CPR) using the page numbers of the first (A) or second (B) edition. The English translations are from *Immanuel Kant's Critique of Pure Reason*. Trans. Norman Kemp Smith. New York 1965.

[20] Immanuel Kant: *Reflexionen zur Metaphysik*. In: *Gesammelte Schriften* (*Akademie-Ausgabe*). Berlin 1908 -. Vol. XVIII. Reflexion 4944, 4945.

[21] Refl. 4945, p. 37: "Es kann keine quaestionen der transcendentalphilosophie geben, deren Beantwortung uns unbekannt wäre. Denn wenn das praedicat nicht durch das subiect determinirt ist, so bedeutet es, daß die Frage an sich selbst nichts sey, weil das praedicat in diesem Falle gar keine Bedeu-

The same argument, without the geographical simile, appears repeatedly in the *Critique of Pure Reason*:

> Now I maintain that transcendental philosophy is unique in the whole field
> of speculative knowledge, in that no question which concerns an object
> given to pure reason can be insoluble for this same human reason, and that
> no excuse of an unavoidable ignorance, or of the problem's unfathomable
> depth, can release us from the obligation to answer it thoroughly and com-
> pletely. (CPR B 505 / A 477).[22]

This cannot mean, of course, that reason is conceived as potentially
omniscient and limited only actually, in its human incarnation (as
Leibniz would have it). Rather, human reason has the ability to judge
what can be a question for it at all, and this judgment entails a potential answer. There are an infinite number of questions, one could
paraphrase Kafka, but not for us. The answer to the question which
question belongs to the set of "questions for us" cannot come from
outside this set, for then the legitimacy of that answer would itself
be in question, and so forth.[23] On the other hand, the set of possible
questions cannot be closed either, for then, technically speaking, all
truth would be analytic, and the possibility of experience (at stake in
the first *Critique*) would remain unproved. Kant articulated this
dilemma in the very first sentence of the first edition of the *Critique*
when he stated that human reason is "molested" by questions "which
it is not able to ignore, but which [...] it is also not able to answer"
(CPR A vii).

It is this need for answers and their simultaneous impossibility
that likens the first question of metaphysics to the quest for orientation. Just as it is the human posture (ek-sistence in the most literal
sense) that demands and denies orientation, so it is the problem of
positing questions that agitates transcendental philosophy. In order

---

tung hat, nicht beiahend noch ihr *oppositum contrarium* ist. so wie wenn ich
frage, wo ich doch, wenn ich unter dem Pole bin, Osten suchen soll".
[22] See also the 'Division of General Logic into Analytic and Dialectic' (B 82):
"To know what questions may responsibly be asked is already a great and
necessary proof of sagacity and insight". Indeed, the breakthrough to the
Critique in the famous letter to Marcus Herz (Feb. 21, 1772) appears as a
question Kant poses to himself: "I asked myself: on what grounds rests the
relation of that which we call representation to the object?" (*Akademie-
Ausgabe*. Vol. X. P. 124)
[23] For a version of this argument (which derives from Russell's critique of
Frege's *Grundgesetze*) see Walter Benjamin: *Ursprung des deutschen Trauerspiels*. Frankfurt a.M. 1978. P. 12.

not to curtail the spontaneity of reason, its questions cannot come merely from the outside, and yet, in order not to dissipate in arbitrariness, these questions cannot be generated entirely from within. This coincidence of opposites is entailed in the enlightened proposition "Die Vernunft muß sich Fragen stellen" – its *Gegensinn* demands that reason ask itself questions *and* that reason expose itself to questions. Reason is fraught with this dilemma insofar as it imposes itself, and yet liberated insofar as it can recognize it as its own. The coincidence of imposition and liberation Kant conceives, in the period just before the *Critique of Practical Reason* (1788), as a selfaddressed summons, as a *Geheiß*. What does it mean: to summon? Or, to give the question its characteristic transcendental doubling: "Was heißt heißen?" Here, a threefold *Gegensinn* disrupts the possibility of unilinear understanding. For "heißen" asks the question of naming, the question of summoning, and the question of meaning. It is precisely in their irrepressible co-presence and counter-position within the concept of "heißen" that the three critical questions posit *themselves*. Each is present and absent in the other, each is both within and without the domain that the other opens up and investigates.

Kant had articulated this trinity of questions in the title question of his essay: *Was heißt: sich im Denken orientiren?* of 1786.[24] Ostensibly engaged in settling the dispute between faith and knowledge, this philosophical intervention relies in the body of its text chiefly on the analogy between orientation on earth and orientation in thought; but in its title it puts to use the *Gegensinn* of *heißen*. True to the definition of transcendental philosophy given in the first *Critique*, the answer is entailed in the question; not, however, as its analytical implication but as the co-presence of antithetical meanings. The standard translations: *What is Orientation in Thinking?*[25], even the more faithful *What does it mean: to orient oneself in thought?* only transmit a fraction of the question. For it remains also in question what it is that is named: "to orient oneself in thought". And at the same time it asks what it is that summons (itself) to orient itself in thought.[26] It is this non-analytical co-

---

[24] *Akademie-Ausgabe.* Vol. VIII. Pp. 131-147.
[25] In: *The Philosophy of Immanuel Kant.* Ed. Lewis White Beck. New York 1976. Pp. 293-305.
[26] It is the self-posed colon that regulates the reading of the title. A more expansive interpretation of the nature of a self-issued summons would have to discuss the role of the colon in Kant's philosophy. The *Critique of Pure Reason*, in its second edition, is interspersed with more than 1209 colons. Furthermore, the first sentence (A vii, but even the first sentence of the motto),

presence (of meanings, of sense, of directions in reading) that vali-
dates the question *Was heißt: sich im Denken orientiren?* as a question of transcendental philosophy, as a question for us.

As we will see, the peculiar notion that a question imposes itself
and yet does not stifle the spontaneity of the quest distinguishes
Kant's philosophy from the Romantic search for a last source of
meaning. For Kant, the question of orientation on earth is equivalent to the question of orientation in thought – there is no answer
for either. The oscillation of practical and theoretical concerns in
the antithetical meaning – that one *must* orient oneself in thought,
that one must orient oneself *in thought* – points to the essential
deductive incompleteness of critical philosophy which Fichte,
Schelling, and Hegel so vehemently denounced.

Kant's philosophy is therefore not concerned with the identity of
origins or the longing for unique location. The finite nature of
reason – "Our reason is not like a plane indefinitely far extended
[...] but must rather be compared to a sphere, the radius of which
can be determined from the curvature of the arc of its surface"
(CPR, B 790) – calls for a cosmopolitan philosophy, one that
embraces human exposure and disorientation and, ideally, turns it
into wanderlust. Kant mused in one of his *Reflexionen*: "It [sc.
critical philosophy] is the opposite of the inclination that binds us
to our fatherland (nostalgia). A desire to lose ourselves outside our
circles and to move into other worlds".[27]

Speculative Reorientations

"Philosophy is really nostalgia – a desire to be at home everywhere".[28] The reorientation towards a *Heim* and center, announced
in Novalis' famous dictum, characterizes Romantic *Naturphilosophie* regardless of the difference between individual authors. The
irritation and dissatisfaction of Idealist philosophers with Kant's
theoretical and moral philosophy – with his insistence on the tran-

---

the highest sentence ("Das: Ich denke [...]", B 131) and the last sentence (B
884) are all interrupted by a colon. I propose such an interpretation of self-
interruption in a forthcoming book with W. Schäffner on mathematical points
and interpunction.

[27] Refl. 5073: "Sie [sc. die Critik der reinen Vernunft] ist das Gegentheil von
der Neigung, die uns an unser Vaterland fesselt (Heimweh). Eine Sehnsucht,
uns ausser unsern Kreise zu verlieren und andere Welten zu beziehen".

[28] "Die Philosophie ist eigentlich Heimweh – *Trieb überall zu Hause zu
sein*". Novalis: *Aus dem "Allgemeinen Brouillon"*. In Novalis: *Werke* . Ed. G.
Schulz. 3rd. ed. Munich 1987. P. 491.

scendental homelessness of human reason – as well as the systematic concerns of Romantic scientists found expression in their attempts to reconstitute a new science of the earth. No longer should the globe be treated as a dead, "unnatural" geometrical entity from which the human being sticks out in precarious fashion, but as a living organism, as the locus of nature herself. The help of all natural sciences was enlisted in this campaign.

In a first step, the difference between north and south needed to be naturalized. In pre-Kantian and Kantian geography, the North and South Poles, and, by extension, the northern and southern hemispheres, formed symmetrical opposites (*Gegenden*) in which each climate recurred and which, therefore, could be distinguished only extrinsically, in relation to the celestial sphere. In *Naturphilosophie*, the North and South Poles become the prime example of the underlying polarity in nature. Polarity – one of the master concepts of the epoch – means: north and south are not only the other of each other, they are, as concentrations and loci of different forces, intrinsically distinguishable.[29] Schelling realized that such a view translates the former mathematical distinction between the poles into a dynamical, physical one:

If the difference between directions in the world, e.g. between North and South, ceases to be simply a mathematical difference and the idea slowly emerges that a physical cause, active throughout the solar system, has instituted [*gestiftet*] this difference, why should gravitation not turn from a mathematical into a physical phenomenon?[30]

[29] See, e.g., F.W.J. Schelling: Von der Weltseele, eine Hypothese der höheren Physik zur Erklärung des allgemeinen Organismus (1798). Nebst einer Abhandlung über das Verhältnis des Realen und Idealen in der Natur. In: *Schellings Werke.* Ed. Manfred Schröter. Munich 1927. Vol. I. P. 527: "Es ist erstes Princip einer philosophischen Naturlehre, in der ganzen Natur auf Polarität und Dualismus auszugehen". This is, of course, but one of innumerable evocations of polarity in Schelling's work, and in that of his contemporaries. For an exhaustive overview see the index of F.W.J. Schelling: *Historisch-Kritische Ausgabe. Ergänzungsband zu Werke 5 bis 9.* Stuttgart 1994. For the conceptual history of polarity cf. Jean-Jacques Wunenburger: Antagonisme et Polarités de Kant à F. von Baader. In *Kantstudien* 79 (1988). Pp. 201-217; R. Chr. Zimmermann: Goethes Polaritätsdenken im geistigen Kontext des 18. Jahrhunderts. In: *Jahrbuch der deutschen Schillergesellschaft* 18 (1974). Pp. 304-347.
[30] F.W.J. Schelling: *Erster Entwurf eines Systems der Naturphilosophie* (1799). In: *Schellings Werke.* Ed. Schröter. Vol. II. P. 113: "Wenn selbst der Unterschied der Weltgegenden, z. B. von Süden und Norden, aufhört, ein bloß mathematischer Unterschied zu seyn, und man allmählich auf die Idee kommt,

With this turn the relation between the measuring instrument and the measured object – a constant source of distortion in the practice of surveying – is also inverted: the magnetic compass indicates north-south direction not because of an arbitrary convention, but because it is, in the parlance of the epoch, a symbol of the earth, naturally related to the large magnet from which it is taken. The fashion of magnetism in the last decade of the eighteenth and the first decades of the nineteenth century feeds off this relocation of the magnet. For the *Naturphilosophen* with ambitions to systematic closure it is important that magnetism, although seemingly a spatial and immediate phenomenon, can be conceived as a process, as an infinitely slow, but potentially temporal relation. It just so happens that the temporal indicators, because the north-south axis of the earth rotates around itself, show zero.

The east-west distinction, in contrast, because it partakes in the earth's diurnal motion, expresses temporality to the highest degree; therefore, the physical process to which it is related also has to be the fastest. In the hierarchy of Romantic sciences, this is electricity, with its almost instantaneous discharge between two separate bodies. Together, magnetic and electrical forces would provide a grid on which the slowest and the fastest physical process intersect. Henrich Steffens and Hegel, the prominent Romantic scientist and the systematic philosopher, both argue for this new, electro-magnetic graticule:

North-South polarity is designated by magnetic opposition, East-West polarity by electrical opposition [...] by virtue of the magnetic opposition every individual is subjected to the schema of the line, by virtue of the electrical opposition to the schema of area [...] the axis of the planet, in opposition to the equator, represents passivity, rest; the equator in opposition to the fixed axis represents activity, mobility [...]. Quadruplicity appears in space as compass bearings [*Weltgegenden*] where the North-South line and its determined direction takes precedence while the East-West line connects space with time.[31]

---

daß eine physische allgemein durch das ganze Sonnensystem wirkende Ursache diesen Unterschied zuerst gestiftet, warum sollte nicht endlich auch die Attraktion aus einem bloß mathematischen in ein physikalisches Phänomen übergehen?"

[31] Henrich Steffens: *Grundzüge der philosophischen Naturwissenschaft*. Berlin 1806. Pp. 41-43: "Die Nordsüd-Polarität wird durch den magnetischen Gegensatz, die Ostwest-Polarität durch den elektrischen bezeichnet [...]. Vermöge des magnetischen Gegensatzes ist alles Einzelne dem Schema der Linie unterworfen, vermöge des elektrischen Gegensatzes dem Schema der

The general revolution of the earth as such, i.e. its revolution around its axis, which is its East-West polarity, determines the North-South polarity, the direction of the axis at rest. Oerstedt discovered that electrical and magnetic activity, insofar as they are related to direction in space, are opposed to each other in such a way that they intersect. Electrical activity is directed from east to west, magnetic activity from north to south; but one can also reverse the direction.[32]

In this view, the geometrical problems arising from the Cartesian coordinates projected upon the globe in the form of parallel circles and meridians (and/or the projection of these curved coordinates onto a flat map) have become secondary: they are only the representation of a real, non-geometrical event, of the intersection of physical forces.

And yet, although magnetism and electricity make it possible to determine any location on the globe according to its magnetic polarization and its electrical charge, this would remain an abstract, literally superficial procedure ("one can also reverse the direction"), were it not for the third dimension provided by chemism. Among the Romantic sciences chemism could claim the highest rank because time, dormant in magnetism and evanescent in the electrical reaction, is visibly "at work" in the chemical process. Unlike the spatial indifference of magnetic simultaneity and the superficial spatiality of electrical time, chemical time is fully interiorized in the change of one body: it is the time of becoming, of growth. Chemical processes built up the content of the earth from its inner core outward and thus regulate the qualitative distribution of matter upon its surface. Chemism provides the dimension of depth that is inaccessible to any geography based on the geometry of surfaces. This is not

---

Fläche [...]. Die Axe des Planeten stellt im Gegensatz gegen den Aequator das Passive, Ruhende; der Aequator im Gegensatz gegen die fixirte Axe, das Aktive, Bewegliche dar [...]. Die Quadruplicität stellt sich im Raume durch die Weltgegenden dar, wo die Nordsüd-Linie und die bestimmte Richtung die hervortretende ist, die Ostwest-Linie aber, den Raum mit der Zeit verknüpft".

[32] G.W.F. Hegel: *Enzyklopädie der philosophischen Wissenschaften*. In: *Werke*. Vol. 9. Frankfurt a.M. 1986. P. 290: "Durch die allgemeine Revolution der Erde überhaupt, als ihre Umdrehung um ihre Achse, welche die Ost- und Westpolarität ist, wird die Süd-Nord-Polarität, die Richtung der ruhenden Achse, bestimmt. Oersted fand, daß die elektrische und die magnetische Tätigkeit, insofern sie als Richtungen auf den Raum bezogen sind, sich auch einander entgegengesetzt sind, indem sie einander kreuzen. Die elektrische Tätigkeit ist von Westen nach Osten gerichtet, während die magnetische von Norden nach Süden; man kann es aber auch umkehren".

only the third dimension of physical space but the dimension of manifest time, of geological history. The four directions of the compass (*Weltgegenden*) all have a prevalent chemical characteristic. North is the area with the highest concentration of carbon; the south abounds with nitrogen; east, "on the axis of becoming", is richer in oxygen; and the west in hydrogen.[33] If combined with the magnetic and electrical coordinates, every place on earth can be located by its unique physical composition.

Franz von Baader's essay *Über das phythagoräische Quadrat in der Natur und die vier Weltgegenden* of 1798 is an early, highly influential example of this qualitative mapping. Baader polemicized against the external, quantitative physics of the Newtonians and Kantians by insisting that the individuality of material bodies is expressed in their specific weight (*Schwere*). The Kantian forces of expansion and attraction alone (which Baader associated with the chemical elements of fire and water) are insufficient to account for the individuality (and location) of each body on the earth. With its specific weight each body participates, in various degrees of proximity, in the earth, its third element. These three dimensions (or, as Baader said, these three *Gegenden*) of fire, water, and earth (and their scientific notation as expansion, contraction, and weight) constitute the necessary determination for any material object. The sufficient reason granting it its individuality, however, is given by an element that is out of this world. Quite predictably, in Baader's revival of ancient cosmology this fourth element is air. Air is not

---

[33] See Henrich Steffens: *Grundzüge*. Pp. 45-48; see also his *Beyträge zu einer innern Naturgeschichte der Erde*. Freyberg 1801. Pp. 260-266. On the question of the naturalness of east and west Goethe drew the line between his own science and *Naturphilosophie*. As early as Jan. 26, 1801 Schelling writes a sprawling letter to Goethe about physical orientation which goes unanswered. But it is on the occasion of reading Steffens' *Grundzüge* in 1806 that Goethe distances himself (in a letter to Wilhelm von Humboldt): "North and south, east and west, oxygen and hydrogen thus become puppets and ghosts of such bizarre topics that one is terrified out of one's good will. I'll say again that I'm not hostile to the use of such a symbolism, that I often feel compelled to use it; but these gentlemen go far beyond my convictions, and it is unpleasant to have to leave those whom one had accompanied so willingly". In: *Goethe-Jahrbuch*. NF 26 (1965). P. 311. In a letter to Steffens himself (in: *Werke*. Herausgegeben im Auftrage der Großherzogin Sophie von Sachsen [WA]. Weimar: Böhlau, 1887-1919. Pt. IV. Vol. 30. P. 90) Goethe writes: "Let me confess openly! In the beginning it was painful to me to see the multiform nature of the earth, from the intuition of which I had just returned, fidget on the cross of the four directions of the world. But now this feeling has become much milder".

internal to the construction of matter, it intervenes – inspires – "from above", thus giving everything its first direction (*erste Weltgegend*), its orient (*Aufgang*).[34] Baader's sign for this relation was a triangle with an internal point (*Inpunkt*).

This triangle is no longer the externally applied geometrical form that always excludes the measuring subject and that only insufficiently approaches the physiognomy of the earth's surface, as the theory and practice of triangulation would have it. It is much rather the abstraction of a triangular intersection of physical forces in which the subject is included as a product. Baader's *Inpunkt* is a *locus naturalis* of subjectivity, a direct answer to the emptiness of the Cartesian triangle and an indirect answer to the homelessness of the Kantian subject. And yet, by locating the *origin* of the *Inpunkt* outside the interplay of terrestrial forces, Baader recognized that orientation, i.e. univocal location on the spheroid body of the earth, always has to come from, or relate to, the non-spherical outside. Enlightenment science had tried to "find" this outside either in the completeness and accuracy of its maps, in the vast space of the solar system, or within the insulated mechanism of the chronometer. Kant had insisted that the location of the orient is always the "unnatural" result of a decision, a concretization of the difficult *Geheiß* of orientation. With his Paulinian solution, Baader tried to turn the world towards its theological orient, towards its *Aufgang*, both in the sense of creation and of final dissolution.

The importance of Baader's essay for the development of Romantic *Naturphilosophie* can hardly be overestimated. His "quaternal" hypothesis had an immediate and lasting impact on the early Romantics, notably on Novalis, F. Schlegel, Steffens, J. Ritter, and Schelling, but also on Goethe and Hegel. The problem he tried to solve is common to all thinkers of natural orientation; it arises from the circumstance that, while dynamic processes might be able to account for the shape and content of the earth, the human subject on the earth is given to wandering, to exile, to ex-perience. To complete the project of a natural geography for the human being, the earth had to be related to its inhabitants in such a way that their location could be measured against a point of origin.

The philosophical task of forging this essential bond was articulated in the Idealist argument that the gaps, paradoxa, and disorienting doublings in Kant's philosophy arise from the unwarranted

---

[34] *Franz von Baader's Sämmtliche Werke.* Leipzig 1852. Vol. 1. P. 267. For a fuller account of Baader's philosophy of nature see Johann Sauter: *Baader und Kant.* Jena 1928. Pp. 261-340.

opposition between the geometrical (mathematical) and the physical (dynamical) categories of the understanding. Kant, such was the explicit or implicit claim of Fichte, Schelling, and Hegel, had been unable to see that the categories are genetically related to each other, that the mathematical categories are superseded by their dynamical continuations. The categories of relation in particular exhibit temporality well before their schematic application to the data of sensibility. From this organic interdependence of the categories it follows that Kant's radical distinction between the categories of the understanding and the "intuitions" of sensibility could also be abolished. Rather than being applied, the categories grow out of the sensory manifold, just as the understanding grows out of sensibility – not in the linear sense in which Locke and the empiricists had misunderstood it, but as organic generation and non-linear growth.[35] This means that physical processes, such as magnetism, electricity, and chemism are in fact archaic forms of subjectivity. "Electricity, like magnetism, is not the effect of a particular cause, but a general category of matter",[36] Schelling writes. The intersection of meridians and parallel circles, for example, is the earth's way of schematizing, of temporalizing sheer spatial discreteness.

Schelling's *System des transcendentalen Idealismus* of 1800, and even more so his magnificent *System der gesammten Philosophie und der Naturphilosophie insbesondere* of 1804, are devoted to the narration of this slow rise of subjectivity from the most basic configurations of matter to the heights of philosophy, politics, and art. The inherent difficulties of this philosophical narrative lie less in its global scope than in the need to argue for an ever more essential and "living" bond, or copula, between the earth and the wandering inhabitants who think (on) it. These difficulties lead Schelling to break out of the immanentism of his natural philosophy and to argue, in his *Über das Wesen der menschlichen Freiheit*, that the desire to wander is the essence of human freedom, and that it requires a decision on the part of the ethical subject to either stray from the created ground or to remain close and true to the origin.

Naturphilosophen with smaller philosophical ambitions, like H. Steffens or Lorenz Oken, argue for the bond between human beings and the earth mostly in the form of analogies. Steffens' "inner

---

[35] For a good reconstruction of this re-valuation and re-organization of Kantian elements in Hegel's thought see R.P. Horstmann: *Wahrheit aus dem Begriff.* Frankfurt a.M. 1990, esp. pp. 46-54.

[36] *System der gesammten Philosophie und der Naturphilosophie insbesondere.* F.W.J. Schelling: *Ausgewählte Schriften.* Ed. Manfred Frank. Frankfurt a.M. 1985. Vol. 3. P. 348.

history of the earth" sees the distribution of land on the planet in direct relation to the prevalent chemical activities in the four corners of the world. The human being is able to understand these processes because s/he is at their intersection.[37] In a bolder way, Oken in his *Über das Universum als Fortsetzung des Sinnensystems. Ein pythagoräisches Fragment*[38] of 1808 construes the solar system (like Hegel in his *Habilitationsschrift*[39]) as a single living organism in which the dynamical processes correspond to sensory perception and thus link the human being to the earth, and the earth to the universe. J.W. Ritter, although his vision is much more fragmented, also analogizes, even identifies the human being with the earth; for him the link between earth and human being is part of the overall process of birthing and cosmic copulation that characterizes physical phenomena.[40]

Although these authors set out to show where on earth human beings belong, they mostly exhaust themselves in showing that they belong on earth at all. It required the speculative energy of Hegel's philosophy to argue that the copula between the earth ("the universal individual"[41]) and the conscious subject is both logical and historical. Not only is the formation of the earth itself logically explicable, but also the presence and exact location on this earth of the spirit:

> [...] the land in general is split into two parts, i.e. the old world, which is shaped like a horseshoe, and the new world, the main extent of which is north-south. The existence of the new world became actual through the connection created when it was discovered, and so brought into the general system of peoples. This discovery was fortuitous however, and its recency is not the only factor in the newness of the continent, for everything within it is new. As civilization has developed there with neither horse nor iron, it has lacked the powerful instruments of positive difference. No continent of the old world has been coerced by another, while America is merely a part of Europe's booty. Its fauna is weaker than that of the old world, although

---

[37] H. Steffens: *Beyträge zu einer innern Naturgeschichte der Erde.* P. 265.

[38] Jena 1808. ("Pythagoräisch" is a clear reference to Baader's earlier essay.) See also his *Abriss der Naturphilosophie. Bestimmt zur Grundlage seiner Vorlesungen über Biologie.* Göttingen 1805.

[39] G.W.F. Hegel: *Dissertatio de Orbitis Planetarum. Philosophische Erörterung über die Planetenbahnen* Ed. W. Neuser. Weinheim 1986. P. 81.

[40] His geognostic speculations can be found in: *Fragmente aus dem Nachlaß eines jungen Physikers.* Leipzig 1984. Aphorismen No. 26, 48, 52, 67, 76, 173, 176, 368, 370, 419, 420(!), 444, 453, 525, 527, 634, and p. 303 (*Die Physik als Kunst*).

[41] *Enzyklopädie. Werke.* Vol. 9. P. 344; *Phänomenologie des Geistes.* Frankfurt a.M. 1977. P. 224.

it possesses an exuberant flora. The mountain ranges of the old world generally run from west to east, or from south-west to north-east, while in America, which is the butment [*Widerlage*] of the old world, they run from south to north. American rivers flow eastwards however, particularly in South America. In general, the new world exhibits an incomplete division like that of the magnet, separated as it is into a northern and a southern part. The old world exhibits a complete tripartite division however. Its primary part is Africa, which corresponds to compact metal or the lunar principle, and is stunned by the heat. Its humanity is sunk in torpor, it is the dull spirit which does not enter into consciousness. Its second part is Asia, which is the bacchantic eccentricity of the comet, the wild middle, which brings forth only from itself, engenders without form, and is unable to master its centre. Its third part is Europe, which constitutes the rational region of the earth, or consciousness, and forms an equilibrium of rivers, valleys, and mountains, the centre of which is Germany. Consequently, the continents are not contingent, for as divisions they are not a matter of convenience, but embody essential differences.[42]

These deductions of Germany were part of a general, if mostly less spectacular, reorientation of German culture in the nineteenth century. The compass bearings valid throughout the eighteenth century were turned ninety degrees: the climatic opposition between north and south that had dominated the debates ever since Winckelmann was replaced by a historical relation of origination and inheritance between east and west. This is the beginning of a peculiar (because mostly imaginary) brand of orientalism in which the study of Sanskrit (W.v. Humboldt, Fr. Bopp) and the "wisdom" of the Indians (Fr. Schlegel) challenge – and complete – the classical paradigm of cultural tradition. Dionysos appeared behind Apollo.

Erdkunde as Normal Science

It would be easy to dismiss this reorientation of philosophy and the sciences as speculative aberrations were it not for the very real practices by which they were accompanied. It is through the amalgamation of speculative geography and the technological developments accompanying the slow industrialization of the German countries that the idea of *Heimat*, of a hereditary and accustomed place on the earth for an individual or certain group of people took a firm hold.[43] The intense interest, both popular and scientific, in

---

[42] *Enzyklopädie*. P. 350-351. Translation from: *Hegel's Philosophy of Nature*. Ed. and transl. with an introduction and explanatory notes by Michael John Petry. London 1970. Vol. III. P. 24.

[43] This is, of course, not to say that the concepts of "Heimat" and nostalgia are

the study of geological formations (geognosy) and in the classification of minerals (oryctognosy) focused geographical investigations on the depth of the third dimension. The impossibility of geometrical orientation on the globe was due to its fixation on ahistorical, geometrical surface measurements; in particular, it had utilized the radius of the earth only to determine the celestial meridian. In the qualitative description of the earth, as the Romantic geographers proposed it, this radius must instead serve as the scale of terrestrial time, as the indicator of the earth's growth and history. Geognosy thus studied sedimented time, and its main debates revolved around the continuity (neptunism) or discontinuity (volcanism) of this sedimentation. Oryctognosy concentrated on the classification and location of minerals in much the same fashion as natural history had assigned specific marks and locations to the living beings on the globe. Not only did this combined vivification provide the earth with the central attribute of organic beings (temporal extension in space = growth), it also gave it a unique surface – a face – and called for its physiognomic description. The earth became, to repeat Hegel's word, "the general individual".

The investigation of Romantic institutions has shown how well the philosophical and scientific developments answered to the administrative and economic needs of early nineteenth century states.[44] Gottlieb Abraham Werner and the *Bergakademie* in Freiberg both had an extraordinary influence on the philosophical and literary imagination and provided the emerging forms of industrial production with access to much needed raw materials. This conjunction of practical applicability and esoteric speculation is embodied strikingly in Novalis' engagement to Julie Charpentier, the daughter of Werner's "practical" antipode at Freiberg, Johann Friedrich Wilhelm Charpentier, a specialist in industrial-scale mining and metallurgy.[45] "The mysterious inward way" (*der geheimnisvolle Weg nach Innen*) of which Novalis speaks, is both that into the sediments of one's own soul and into the pits which the students at Freiberg had to visit as part of their training. It is again a *Gegensinn*, that of deep and high (*altus*), that coincides in the image of the

---

unique to German Romanticism. It is the collaboration of the physical sciences, philosophy, literature and technology to justify and ontologize what otherwise would be regarded as a psychological phenomenon that characterizes the developments in the Germany.

[44] Theodore Ziolkowski: *German Romanticism and Its Institutions*. Princeton 1990. Pp. 18-63.

[45] For a first hand account of the atmosphere at Freiberg see H. Steffens: *Was ich erlebte*. Munich 1956. Pp. 127-172.

70

pit.[46]

Goethe's life-long interest in geology was awakened when he was put in charge of silver mining in Sachsen-Weimar. It was soon integrated into his own brand of *Naturphilosophie* which, however idiosyncratic, shares with his Romantic contemporaries the general dismissal and denigration of geometrical and mathematical methods in the sciences of nature.[47] Alexander von Humboldt, who embodied Goethe's ideal of a *Naturforscher*, had also been a student at the Freiberg academy. The literary-scientific results of his expeditions to South America, the *Ansichten der Natur*, the *Kosmos*-work (subtitle: *Attempt at a Physical Description of the Earth*), but also the *Ideen zu einer Physiognomik der Gewächse* are born from the opposition to the geometrical (or simply narrative) descriptions of the earth.[48] His brother Wilhelm's concomitant endeavors to locate languages and to map the diversity and individuality of languages onto the individually distinguished parts of the earth complement Alexander's physical description of the globe in such a way that the geological formations, fauna, and flora have their unmistakable place, as do the peoples that inhabit it and the languages they speak.[49]

The scientific works of Goethe and the brothers Humboldt are the most important conduits from the esoteric speculations of the Idealists and the early Romantic scientist into the mainstream of geographical teaching and research in German high-schools and universities. It is with Carl Ritter's massive and massively influential work, which began publication in 1817, that this transition of the new geography into a normal science is achieved. The title of his textbook is programmatic: *Die Erdkunde im Verhältnis zur Natur und zur Geschichte des Menschen, oder allgemeine, vergleichende Geographie als sichere Grundlage des Studiums und Unterrichts in physikalischen und historischen Wissenschaften* ("*Erdkunde* in relation to nature and to the history of man, or universal and com-

---

[46] See also N. Rupke: Caves, Fossils, and the History of Earth. In: *Romanticism and the Sciences*. Ed. Andrew Cunningham and Nicholas Jardine. Cambridge 1990. Pp. 241-259.

[47] See my: Skullduggery. Goethe and Oken, Natural Philosophy and Freedom of the Press. In: *Modern Language Quarterly* 59.2 (1998). Pp. 231-259.

[48] See Michael Hagner: Zur Physiognomik bei Alexander von Humboldt. In: *Geschichten der Physiognomik*. Ed. R. Campe, M. Schneider. Berlin 1996. Pp. 431-452.

[49] Kurt Mueller-Vollmer: *Wilhelm von Humboldts Sprachwissenschaft. Ein kommentiertes Verzeichnis des sprachwissenschaftlichen Nachlasses*. Paderborn 1993.

parative geography as secure foundation for the study and teaching in physical and historical sciences"). For in order to give tidings (*Kunde*) of itself, the earth has to be oriented, it has to be other than just a geometrical object. Although Ritter is more cautious than Steffens, Hegel, or Schelling, he, too, harbors the hope that there be a natural orient which would provide for the earth "a final resting point in space":

> We still do not know whether there is not in the physical world the beginning of something stable [sc. concerning east and west], invisible to us, the largest extent of which would be the division into the two continents on the hemispheres, and the dominant natural activity of which we would have to seek in the Asian orient from which the earliest and highest development of life on earth seems to have originated.[50]

In the absence of a spatial point of absolute orientation it is the physiognomic individuality of the land and the cultural history of the peoples that *express* the difference of location:

> Not only these countries and their sky, their vegetation and their animals speak of this [sc. their characteristic difference]: the voices of the peoples express it in the development of their cultural history, in their songs, religions, philosophies, languages.[51]

The "thick" descriptions of *Erdkunde* not only identify geographical location and geological features, but also demonstrate why a particular people lives in its *Heimat*. This multidimensional account therefore cannot rely on technical resources, such as cartography, for which the transition from three to two dimensions is unsolvable. Ritter reserves the few polemical remarks in his introduction for maps and for those geographers who exhibit "critical industriousness" in designing maps but do not know the country they attempt

---

[50] *Erdkunde*. Berlin 1817. Vol. 1. P. 9: "Noch sind wir nicht zu der Erkenntnis gelangt, ob diesem im Wechsel erscheinenden, dennoch nicht schon in der physichen Welt, obwohl uns unsichtbar, der Anfang eines Beharrlichen zum Grunde gelegt ist, dessen weitesten Umfang etwa die beiden großen Landvesten auf beiden Erdhalben bezeichnen möchten, und dessen vorherrschende Naturthätigkeit wir dann im Asiatischen Orient zu suchen haben würden, von dem die frühere und höhere Entwicklung des Erdenlebens ausgegangen zu seyn scheint".
[51] *Erdkunde*. P. 10: "Nicht nur diese Länder und ihr Himmel, ihre Gewächse und ihre Thiere sagen dieses; auch die Stimmen aller Völker drücken es im Gang ihrer Cultur=Geschichte, in ihren Gesängen, Religionen, Philosophien, Sprachen aus".

to represent from "proper intuition of nature". Instead of an image of nature, Ritter objects, maps produce a distortion "which physical *Erdkunde* should reject just as much as physiognomy disregards incorrect silhouettes. Even the best maps relate to the study of universal comparative *Erdkunde* like the collection of anatomical specimen to physiology".[52]

The personal intuition of nature, which C. Ritter opposes to the study of maps and travel reports and which he counts as the first and foremost source for *Erdkunde*, does away with the armchair Physical Geographies of the type in which Kant and his contemporaries delighted.[53] Its patron saint, invoked innumerable times in Ritter's text, is Alexander von Humboldt. The cosmopolitanism of Enlightenment narratives, in which not the accuracy and individuality of the description, but the curiosity for moral and political difference was the dominant feature, is replaced by the unequivocal, expressive coordination of place, history, and culture. It is no accident that this relation, in turn, is strengthened by the ideal forms of Romantic literature. The fairy tale, the folk song, the saga, the anecdote, the rediscovered medieval manuscript are all part of a literary aesthetics in which subjective originality is replaced by orientation in the geographical sense developed in *Erdkunde*: original is what belongs to this place, what is offered up by this region. The verb *künden* well expresses this mode of authorless literature.[54]

Erdkunde has had a secure place in the curricula of German universities and high schools throughout the nineteenth and twentieth centuries. There were times when the relation between peoples and

[52] *Erdkunde*. P. 30: "Kritischer Fleiß", "eigne Naturanschauung", "es tritt statt des Bildes der Natur ein Zerrbild hervor, welches die physikalische Erdkunde eben so als Quelle verwerfen sollte, wie die Physiognomik schon unrichtig gezeichnete Schattenrisse keiner Aufmerksamkeit würdig hält. Aber auch die besten Landkarten verhalten sich zum Studium der allgemeinen vergleichenden Erdkunde wie die Präparatensammlung zu Physiologie".

[53] Kant had attributed to Physical Geography primarily a social and conversational value (*Physische Geopgraphie*. In: *Akademie-Ausgabe*. Vol. IX. P. 165): "The use of these studies is quite extended. It serves the purposeful order of our knowledge, as well as our enjoyment, and it offers rich material for social entertainment". ("Der Nutzen dieses Studiums ist sehr ausgedehnt. Es dient zur zweckmäßigen Anordnung unserer Erkenntnisse, zu unserem eigenen Vergnügen und gewährt reichen Stoff zu gesellschaftlichen Unterhaltungen".)

[54] For Kant, *Erdkunde* was still an empirical and restricted form of wordly knowledge; see CPR B 787: "Aber das lehrt mich die Erfahrung: daß, wohin ich nur komme, ich immer einen Raum um mich sehe, dahin ich weiter fortgehen könnte; mithin erkenne ich Schranken meiner jedesmal wirklichen Erdkunde, aber nicht die Grenzen aller möglichen Erdbeschreibung".

their location were tightened to such a degree that scientific justifications for the recuperation of lost original territory became the paramount preoccupation of this science. To say nothing of the condemnation of a people that wandered the earth in diasporic homelessness. Recent attempts to resuscitate Germany as a "self-confident nation" have, predictably, invoked "Erde und Heimat" as the values that would restore the nation's mental health.[55]

There also has been a powerful current in twentieth-century philosophy to rethink and reformulate the romantic critique of Kant's philosophy of homelessness. The unacknowledged debt of Heidegger's *Geviert* to Baader's "quaternal" hypothesis in particular would provide a productive starting point for an investigation into the possibilities and dangers of *Naturphilosophie* at the end of the twentieth century. The history of geographical thought from the geometrical calculations of the Enlightenment to the organic determinations of Romanticism is an indispensable basis for such an investigation.

---

[55] See G. Bergfleth: Erde und Heimat. Über das Ende der Ära des Unheils. In: *Die selbstbewußte Nation.* Ed. H. Schwilk, U. Schacht. Frankfurt a.M. 1994. Pp. 101-123.

Jonathan M. Hess

Kant's Critique of Historical Judgment: Aesthetic Autonomy and the Displacement of Politics[1]

This essay explores the relationship between Kant's concept of historical judgment in his 1784 "Idee zu einer allgemeinen Geschichte in weltbürgerlicher Absicht" and his concept of aesthetic autonomy in his 1790 Kritik der Urtheilskraft. *The universal history essay does not merely present an initial elaboration of Kant's concept of reflective judgment; it also explicitly links its concept of judgment to a theory of political agency, thus articulating a perspective from which it becomes possible to evaluate the political function of aesthetic autonomy in the* Kritik der Urtheilskraft. *Positioned in this context, the Kantian concept of aesthetic autonomy does not seek to escape or withdraw from the political. On a formal level, rather, aesthetic autonomy engages directly with the political, embodying, realizing and ultimately subverting the political agency of historical judgment.*

In a move that paradoxically reproduces the logic of its perceived opponent, contemporary literary criticism has both celebrated a "return to history" and also continued to frame its interest in historical issues as an interest in something essentially external to the work of art as such. In a critical climate that often tends to regard the concept of aesthetic autonomy as a simple escape from the realm of the empirical, the interest in historical issues is typically seen as a concern with something radically "other" to the aesthetic; indeed, history has often come to figure as the "unconscious" of the aesthetic, as that which the particular work of art had to repress or displace in order to establish itself as such – and as that which the critic in turn must strive to restore to the allegedly autonomous aesthetic object.[2] In the wake of Jerome McGann's 1983 *The Romantic Ideology*, much historically oriented Romanticist criticism has worked in precisely this vein, routinely seeking to dismantle the

---

[1] The argument presented in this essay is elaborated at much greater length in chapters 6 and 7 of Jonathan M. Hess: *Reconstituting the Body Politic: Enlightenment, Public Culture and the Invention of Aesthetic Autonomy.* Detroit 1999.

[2] The most prominent example of this mode of reading, of course, is Fredric Jameson: *The Political Unconscious.* Ithaca 1981.

romantic "grand illusion that poetry can set one free of the ruins of history and culture" by unmasking the ways in which Romantic texts "occlude and disguise their own involvement in a certain nexus of historical relations".[3] Rather than actually rethinking the construction of their object, such modes of criticism have often continued to define their object by precisely that rigid opposition they seek to overcome, reinscribing a concept of history as the aesthetic's external other.

In terms of the basic categories within which it operates, this "return to history" has not been all that historically reflexive. For in their emergence in the eighteenth century, of course, the discursive fields of "history" and "aesthetics" were closely and intensely interrelated.[4] Far from being positioned antithetically toward each other, the philosophical disciplines of history and aesthetics construct themselves against the same conceptual backdrop, as responses to two very similar groups of problems. If the notion of autonomous art serves as some sort of negation or repression of history or the historical, the context in which it established itself as such would certainly merit closer examination. This paper seeks thus to illuminate the mutually constitutive relation between discourses of history and aesthetics by undertaking a case study, focusing on the text typically credited with the canonical formulation of the concept of aesthetic autonomy, Kant's 1790 *Kritik der Urtheilskraft*.[5] Reading Kant's concept of autonomous art in the third *Kritik* alongside his 1784 "Idee zu einer allgemeinen Geschichte in weltbürgerlicher Absicht", I would like to explore and critique what is typically obscured in the repression and displacement scenarios that

---

[3] Jerome McGann: *The Romantic Ideology: A Critical Investigation*. Chicago 1983. Pp. 82, 91-92. See the discussion and critique of McGann in: Jonathan M. Hess: Wordsworth's Aesthetic State: The Poetics of Liberty. In: *Studies in Romanticism* 33 (1994). Pp. 3-29. My frame of reference here, I should note, is Romanticist criticism in general rather than solely work on German Romanticism.

[4] See here, for instance, Rodolphe Gasché: Of Aesthetic and Historical Determination. In: *Post-Structuralism and the Question of History*. Ed. Derek Attridge, Geoff Bennington and Robert Young. Cambridge 1987. Pp. 139-161. Also Alfred Baeumler: *Das Irrationalitätsproblem in der Ästhetik und Logik des 18. Jahrhunderts bis zur Kritik der Urteilskraft*. Halle 1923.

[5] See, on the emergence of the concept of aesthetic autonomy, for instance, M.H. Abrams: Kant and the Theology of Art. In: *Notre Dame English Journal* 13 (1981). Pp. 75-105. Abrams: Art-as-Such: The Sociology of Modern Aesthetics. In: *Bulletin of the American Academy of Arts and Sciences* 38.6 (1985). Pp. 8-33. Martha Woodmansee: *The Author, Art, and the Market: Rereading the History of Aesthetics*. New York 1994.

dominate so much historically oriented Romanticist scholarship: namely, the extent to which, in its inception, the very concept of aesthetic autonomy is politically invested. The Kantian concept of aesthetic autonomy, I shall argue, is constructed not in an effort to withdraw from the realms of history and politics, but as an attempt to construct aesthetics itself as a mode of political agency.[6]

My reasons for taking the "Idee zu einer allgemeinen Geschichte in weltbürgerlicher Absicht" – and not, say, Kant's later historical writings, his writings on natural history, or the section of the *Kritik der Urtheilskraft* that is itself dedicated to the problem of history – as a point of entry are manifold. Published in the *Berlinische Monatsschrift* one month before Kant's famous "Beantwortung der Frage: Was ist Aufklärung?", the universal history essay is more squarely positioned within the realm of political discourse than many of Kant's other writings.[7] In discusing the "Idee zu einer allgemeinen Geschichte in weltbürgerlicher Absicht", accordingly, it will be necessary to stress its relation to the reflections on the limits of political agency vis-à-vis the absolutist body politic Kant offers in his enlightenment essay. For it is within this context that the universal history essay concerns itself with the question of the political agency of the historian, and it does so by constructing a concept of political history that is utterly distinct from the notion of history that emerges from Kant's ethics, that is, the understanding of history as a moral task, as an imperative to realize the "highest good".[8] Politics in the universal history essay is constitutively distinct from morality; indeed, if one reads this essay as a serious reflection on history and political agency, I argue, then history as the product of rational moral agency is by definition politically irrelevant. What counts here is solely the construction of history as a cognitive object. From the perspective of Kant's universal history essay, we shall see, the human being simply cannot be the direct "maker" of history, but only its judger – and yet it is precisely in this act of judgment that the exemplary political agency of the historian lies.

---

[6] For an elaboration of the historical and theoretical presuppositions of this argument, see Hess: *Reconstituting the Body Politic*. Particularly pp. 35-118.

[7] The "Idee zu einer allgemeinen Geschichte in weltbürgerlicher Absicht" was published in the *Berlinische Monatsschrift* in November 1783; the "Beantwortung der Frage: Was ist Aufklärung?" appeared in the December issue. For a discussion of the *Berlinische Monatsschrift* and enlightenment public culture, see Hess: *Reconstituting the Body Politic*. Particularly pp. 37-57.

[8] Compare here, on Kant's concept of history as a moral task, Yirmiyahu Yovel: *Kant and the Philosophy of History*. Princeton 1980.

Clearly, this conceptualization of the relationship between morality and politics does not sit well with the systematic framework Kant himself provides for his critical philosophy. Kant's explicit concern in the third *Kritik*, of course, is to envision the possible realization of moral freedom in the phenomenal realm, not to delineate the political agency of the historian. The *Kritik der Urtheilskraft* represents part of Kant's attempt to finish his "kritisches Geschäft" by forging a "Brücke" or "Mittelglied" to connect the phenomenal world of the *Kritik der reinen Vernunft* with the noumenal world of the *Kritik der praktischen Vernunft.*[9] As much as this bridge-making project might have political implications, its central thrust is obviously moral, not political; it would be difficult to argue that Kant's critical philosophy gestures toward a concept of the political in which rational moral agency would be irrelevant. In the "Idee zu einer allgemeinen Geschichte in weltbürgerlicher Absicht", however, precisely such a concept of politics is at work, and this model of politics is important, I shall argue, because it is in precisely this context that Kant first elaborates the critical problem of reflective judgment. The 1784 universal history essay offers, in other words, a critique of historical judgment, and it does so within a decidedly political context.

In what follows, accordingly, I approach Kant's concept of aesthetic autonomy from the perspective of this 1784 critique of historical judgment, a perspective that is obviously not in line with the explicit terms in which Kant introduces his third *Kritik*. My goal here, however, is not simply to establish chronological priority, nor is it to claim that all or even most of the problems of the third *Kritik* are prefigured in this essay. Indeed, the concept of history that Kant elaborates in §83 and following in the *Kritik der Urtheilskraft* is closely linked to his writings on morality in a way the universal history essay is not,[10] and it will not be possible in the context of this essay to put forth a reading of the *Kritik der Urtheilskraft* as a whole. I would like, rather, to explore the functional relationship between the concept of historical judgment in the universal history essay and Kant's concept of aesthetic autonomy in the third *Kritik*, a concept, I shall argue, that is similarly unsettling to the systematic project of Kant's critical enterprise. In this way, we shall see that the relationship between the realms of autonomous art and history is not one governed solely by notions like repression.

---

[9] Kant: *Akademie-Ausgabe.* Vol. V. Pp. 170, 175. All further references to Kant will be indicated parenthetically in the text by volume and page number referring to the *Akademie-Ausgabe.*

[10] See here Yovel: *Kant and the Philosophy of History.*

For when approached from the perspective of Kant's earlier formulation of the problem of reflective judgment, the *Kritik der Urtheilskraft* reveals that the concept of aesthetic autonomy is constructed very much *within* the discursive space of history. The problem with autonomous art in this context is not that it seeks to escape or repress the political. Quite on the contrary, the problem is that it *is* political, and that it succeeds in being political only too well.

From the Judgment of History to the Critique of Judgment

Before discussing the *Kritik der Urtheilskraft*, let us approach the universal history from a perhaps more familiar point of departure, positioning it in relation to Kant's reflections on the limits of enlightenment political agency in his "Beantwortung der Frage: Was ist Aufklärung?"[11] Enlightenment, as Kant conceives it, does not merely perform what he terms in the *Anthropologie* the most important "Revolution" within the human being, the "Ausgang desselben aus seiner selbstverschuldeten Unmündigkeit" (VII, 229). Enlightenment represents more than the emancipation of the reasoning subject to become "mündig" and make use of its reason "ohne Leitung eines andern" (VII, 35). Enlightenment also forges a collective realm of such individuals, a sphere of "öffentliche Gebrauch" of reason that has the task of disseminating "den Geist einer vernünftigen Schätzung des eigenen Werths und des Berufs jedes Menschen selbst zu denken" (VII, 36). As a collective realm that promotes individual enlightenment, moreover, this public space always exists in relation to another public realm, the realm of the absolutist state and its "öffentliche Zwecke" (VIII, 37). In his famous equation of the "Zeitalter der Aufklärung" with the "Jahrhundert *Friedrichs*" (VIII, 40), Kant clearly pays his respects to the absolutist monarch. He credits Frederick the Great with having the political wisdom first to provide a "wohldisciplinirtes zahlreiches Heer zum Bürgen der öffentlichen Ruhe" and *then* to say *"räsonnirt, so viel ihr wollt, und worüber ihr wollt; nur gehorcht!"* (VIII, 41). But Kant of course does much more than unilaterally subordinate enlightenment rationality to the absolutist state that guarantees freedom of thought and makes enlightenment discourse possible. For within this framework, he also endeavors to secure an active role for the enlightenment public in the state, to guarantee the possibility of *cooperation* be-

---

[11] I offer a much more substantial reading of the enlightenment essay, its context and its theoretical presuppositions in *Reconstituting the Body Politic*, particularly chapter 6, "Kant's Political Anthropology and the Prehistory of Judgment". Pp. 189-210.

tween these two potentially competing public realms. The enlightenment essay thus envisions a public forum where politically powerless political subjects would have the right to enter into critical debate about political matters, and to do so in such a way as to make the absolutist state accountable to its enlightened public. In this context, Kant issues the imperative that the legislative head of state heed the rational debate of the enlightened public, ultimately imposing only those laws on his subjects that they would actually legislate to themselves:

> Der Probirstein alles dessen, was über ein Volk als Gesetz beschlossen werden kann, liegt in der Frage: ob ein Volk sich selbst wohl ein solches Gesetz auferlegen könnte. [...] Was aber nicht einmal ein Volk über sich selbst beschließen darf, das darf noch weniger ein Monarch über das Volk beschließen; denn sein gesetzgebendes Ansehen beruht eben darauf, daß er den gesammten Volkswillen in dem seinigen vereinigt. (VII, 39-40)

In this schema, enlightenment does much more than encourage individuals to think for themselves. The process of enlightenment aspires to grant a public of politically powerless intellectuals influence in the process of government, to force absolutism to pay attention to the critical debates of enlightenment intellectuals so that it might be able in its legislation to simulate the process of representative self-government. In calling upon Frederick the Great in this way to govern the absolutist state as if it were a republic, Kant defines enlightenment as a movement that strives to politicize itself, a movement that issues imperatives to the head of state but does so without any political agency, a movement that attempts to transform its freedom of thought into legislative political action. Excluded from political power, enlightenment both aspires to political action and yet lacks any form of agency to perform such action. It is in this context that Kant both concedes and resolves a fundamental paradox:

> So zeigt sich hier ein befremdlicher, nicht erwarteter Gang menschlicher Dinge; so wie auch sonst, wenn man ihn im Großen betrachtet, darin fast alles paradox ist. Ein größerer Grad bürgerlicher Freiheit scheint der Freiheit des *Geistes* des Volks vortheilhaft und setzt ihr doch unübersteigliche Schranken; ein Grad weniger von jener verschafft hingegen diesem Raum, sich nach allem seinen Vermögen auszubreiten. Wenn denn die Natur unter dieser harten Hülle den Keim, für den sie am zärtlichsten sorgt, nämlich den Hang und Beruf zum freien *Denken*, ausgewickelt hat: so wirkt dieser allmählig zurück auf die Sinnesart des Volks (wodurch dieses der Freiheit zu handeln nach und nach fähiger wird) und endlich auch sogar auf die Grundsätze der Regierung, die es ihr selbst zuträglich findet, den Menschen,

der nur *mehr als Maschine* ist, seiner Würde gemäß zu behandeln. (VII, 41-42)

In the strange and unexpected course of human affairs, everything may appear to be paradoxical. This certainly seems to be the case with the given disparity between freedom of thought and freedom of action, between "Freiheit des Geistes" and true "bürgerliche Freiheit", between "freie[s] *Denken*" and the "Freiheit zu handeln". By introducing the teleology of natural development into this scenario, however, Kant is able to resolve the apparent paradox and envision a scenario in which freedom of action and freedom of thought will coincide, a scenario in which the absolutist body politic will no longer need to function as a "Maschine" or "Mechanism" that treats its subjects as "passive Glieder" in the state (VIII, 37). Viewing the absolutist state's necessary restrictions of "bürgerliche Freiheit" from the perspective of a utopian future, Kant argues that the lack of civil freedom in the present will dialectically overcome itself in the course of history, yielding an increased freedom of thought that will enable the enlightenment public to make the absolutist state grant its subjects freedom of action and thus become itself something "mehr als Maschine".[12]

It is "nature" that comes to the rescue here. The impasse of enlightenment – its lack of political agency vis-à-vis the absolutist body politic – can be overcome only by recourse to a concept of history as natural teleology. Enlightenment, in this conception, hinges on a concept of history that casts the human being not as a free agent, not as the "maker" of history, but only as its passive spectator. In this sense, Michel Foucault's location of Kant's enlightenment essay at a "crossroads of critical reflection and reflection on history" appears somewhat insufficient.[13] For Kant's concept of enlightenment does not merely mark a crossroads of critical reflection and reflection on history. It also illuminates why the teleology of historical progress is necessary for Kant, why the faith in historical progress is so crucial to the project of enlightenment. And a critical reflection on history, moreover, is precisely what the

[12] The implicit shift Kant delineates here from a concept of the state as "mechanism" toward a concept of the state as "organism" plays a central role in the *Kritik der Urtheilskraft* as well; see here, for instance, §59 and §65. On "mechanistic" and "organic" models of the body politic in the late eighteenth century and their roles in the formulation of the concept of aesthetic autonomy see Hess: *Reconstituting the Body Politic.*
[13] Michel Foucault: What is Enlightenment? In: *The Foucault Reader*. Ed. Paul Rabinow. New York 1984. Pp. 32-50, here p. 38.

enlightenment essay lacks. As much as Kant demonstrates the political conditions under which the concept of a natural teleology of historical development becomes necessary, nowhere in the enlightenment essay does he inquire into its conditions of possibility. This does not mean, however, that the readers of the *Berlinische Monatsschrift* would have taken this assumption of a natural teleology of historical progress simply as a question of faith. Indeed, the lead article of the *Berlinische Monatsschrift* just one month earlier had been Kant's "Idee zu einer allgemeinen Geschichte in weltbürgerlicher Absicht", an essay which explored the logical and epistemological conditions underlying precisely such an assumption of a natural teleology of historical progress in the political realm. The enlightenment essay establishes the limits of the political agency of enlightenment rationality and the extent to which these limits necessitate a recourse to a natural teleology of political progress. The essay on universal history defends this natural teleology of progress, defining progress in such a way as to envision a suprahuman, suprarational form of political agency able to promote the political goals enlightenment could not realize on its own.

If enlightenment aspires to a localized project of political emancipation it cannot complete, universal history takes the history of the entire human race as its object, attempting from this perspective to reflect on the possibilities of a "verborgenen Plan der Natur" (VIII, 27) according to which, unbeknownst to particular individuals, humanity as a whole is nevertheless progressing toward the republican and cosmopolitan future enlightenment could not realize on its own. Kant's concern in this essay, accordingly, is not primarily with what he calls "die Bearbeitung der eigentlichen bloß *empirisch* abgefaßten Historie"; he seeks, rather, to formulate the concept of a history – a *Geschichte* – that would be governed to a certain extent by a "Leitfaden *a priori*" (VIII, 30). Unlike the work of empirical *Historie*, the construction of universal history is grounded *a priori* in its "weltbürgerliche Absicht", in the *a priori* notion of a "verborgenen Plan der Natur" according to which humanity is progressing toward its republican and cosmopolitan future. The fundamental ambition of the essay, accordingly, is not to provide empirical proof of this cosmopolitan "Absicht", but to explore the conditions under which this *a priori* rule of universal history might be possible.

In the basic gesture of its argument, then, the essay on universal history clearly mimics the transcendental strategies of the critical philosophy, signaling here an important convergence of the transcendental method of critique with the political ambitions of enlightenment public culture.[14] To this basic similarity in form, however, there does not – or at least not yet – correspond a similarity in content. Indeed, the concept of history Kant elaborates in the universal history essay does not fall within the parameters of either the epistemology of the recently published *Kritik der reinen Vernunft* (1781) or the moral philosophy of his current critical projects in 1784, the *Grundlegung zur Metaphysik der Sitten* (1785) and the *Kritik der praktischen Vernunft* (1788). As the opening passage of the essay makes clear, history is governed by a form of *a priori* legislation that has not yet found its place within the critical philosophy:

Was man sich auch in metaphysischer Absicht für einen Begriff von der *Freiheit des Willens* machen mag: so sind doch die *Erscheinungen* desselben, die menschlichen Handlungen, eben so wohl als jede andere Naturbegebenheit, nach allgemeinen Naturgesetzen bestimmt. Die Geschichte, welche sich mit der Erzählung dieser Erscheinungen beschäftigt, so tief auch deren Ursachen verborgen sein mögen, läßt dennoch von sich hoffen: daß, wenn sie das Spiel der Freiheit des menschlichen Willens *im Großen* betrachtet, sie einen regelmäßigen Gang derselben entdecken könne; und daß auf die Art, was an einzelnen Subjekten verwickelt und regellos in die Augen fällt, an der ganzen Gattung doch als eine stetig fortgehende obgleich langsame Entwickelung der ursprünglichen Anlagen derselben werde

---

[14] My argument that the essential strategy of the essay on universal history is critical in form is intended to challenge those readings of this essay (and, more generally, of Kant's early philosophy of history) that insist that Kant seems here to "transgress the boundaries of critical reason and commit a 'dogmatic' fallacy"; see Yovel: *Kant and the Philosophy of History*. P. 127. This view, though common, is not universal. Willi Goetschel argues that this essay illuminates the *Critique*'s "moral-political core". Goetschel: *Constituting Critique: Kant's Writing as Critical Praxis*. Trans. Eric Schwab. Durham 1994. P. 145. Ernst Cassirer emphasizes that this essay "adopts the standpoint of the transcendental inquiry" and that it is thus "the essential method of this view of history, not its content, that has a primary claim on our interest". Cassirer: *Kant's Life and Thought*. Trans. James Haden. New Haven 1981. P. 226. Manfred Riedel, moreover, locates in this particular essay a "critical turn" in historiography. Riedel: Geschichte als Aufklärung: Kants Geschichtsphilosophie und die Grundlagenkrise der Historiographie. In: *Neue Rundschau* 84 (1973). Pp. 289-308. My narrow concern here with Kant's concept of political history in its relation to his definition of enlightenment and his concept of aesthetic autonomy forces me to bracket the relationship between this concept of history as natural teleology and Kant's writings on natural history; see here, for an alternative reading of the universal history essay, Peter D. Fenves: *A Peculiar Fate: Metaphysics and World-History in Kant*. Ithaca 1991.

erkannt werden können. (VIII, 17)

History deals neither with the noumenal domain of (inner) freedom and the legislation of the will, the realm of practical reason Kant will demarcate in the second *Kritik*, nor with the phenomenal domain of the understanding (*Verstand*) and its legislation, the realm of theoretical reason demarcated in the first *Kritik*. Concerned with the realm of human actions, the sphere of external freedom, history here marks a subcategory not of the realm of morality but of the phenomenal realm of nature, and yet not of that nature which formed the subject of the *Kritik der reinen Vernunft*. For the "allgemeine Naturgesetze" governing the "regelmäßigen Gang" of history in the phenomenal realm are not, like the categories, laws that the human understanding *prescribes* to nature in its construction of an object of experience. The philosophical historian views these "Naturgesetze", rather, as symptoms of a greater intentionality, symptoms of the "weltbürgerliche Absicht" one ascribes to nature itself. The *a priori* principle which Kant attributes to history marks neither the legislation of the understanding nor the legislation of practical reason but a third law-giving force conceived of as deriving from nature itself.

For Kant, of course, strictly empirical history must form the basis for any historical undertaking. What philosophical history does in this context is to attempt to discern in history the "Vollziehung eines verborgenen Plans der Natur" (VIII, 27); in this way, it is able "ein sonst planloses *Aggregat* menschlicher Handlungen wenigstens im Großen als ein *System* darzustellen" (VIII, 29). In this sense, Kant's concept of philosophical history relates directly to the enlightenment essay's approach to the "befremdlicher, nicht erwarteter Gang menschlicher Dinge; so wie auch sonst, wenn man ihn im Großen betrachtet, darin fast alles paradox ist". Indeed, Kant argues in the passage above that as a whole, the phenomenal realm of human actions is clearly a lawless affair, a *Spiel* – play or game – that obeys no plan or rules of its own. Using the assumption of a "verborgenen Plan der Natur" as an *a priori* guide, however, the philosophical historian is able to reconceptualize the random empirical particulars of *Historie* as the systematic presentation of a natural law. Universal history transforms the lawless realm of external freedom into a realm that conforms to its own form of legislation, a realm that lawfully progresses toward that complete synthesis of freedom and law that is for Kant the earmark of the republican state. In this way, the proposal of a legislation of nature becomes the perfect substitute for political action. In the context of Kant's philosophy of history, the legislation of the republican political order of the future is not a work of human artifice or the product of a social contract. The republican politics that emerges here is – quite conveniently for the politically powerless subjects of absolutist monarchy – a function of the legislation of nature.

The concept of history that Kant is developing here is clearly not the notion of history that emerges from his ethics, the understanding of history as a moral task, as an imperative to realize the "highest good".[15] The moral legislation of the will clearly assumes a privileged position in the critical philosophy as a whole. When it comes to the phenomenal realm of political history, however, Kant makes it clear that the noumenal legislation of practical reason is for all practical *political* purposes irrelevant. Indeed, if we take seriously the enlightenment essay's reflections on the limits of political agency in the face of absolutism, it becomes clear that morality has for Kant here no direct political import whatsoever; the legislative power of the will of political subjects has no sway in the phenomenal realm of politics. From the perspective of the enlightenment essay's demarcation of the limits of political agency, the human being simply cannot be the direct maker of history but only its passive spectator, and we shall see that is in precisely this act of judging history that the exemplary political agency of the philosophical historian lies.

By proposing the notion of a legislation of nature, the philosophy of history empowers the enlightenment public with recourse to precisely that "legislative" authority it otherwise lacks. In the universal history essay, the politically powerless enlightenment public does not simply issue the imperative that the legislative head of state only impose those laws on his people that he perceives they might impose on themselves. Devoid of any actual legislative authority of its own, the enlightenment public finds in the universal history essay's notion of an *a priori* legislation of nature governing the phenomenal realm of politics a perfect substitute for the process of political legislation, precisely that which the enlightenment essay

---

[15] My insistence upon Kant's strict demarcation of history from the legislation of the will here marks the point of departure for the major differences between my understanding of this essay and its relation to the project of enlightenment and that found in Goetschel and Cassirer, both of whom are eager to read this essay as an appendage to the critical philosophy. Cassirer links Kant's early philosophy of history primarily to his ethics. Cassirer: *Kant's Life and Thought*. Pp. 218-231. Goetschel stresses its "moral-political core" and does not integrate into his discussion the extent to which Kant explicitly makes morality marginal to the project of universal history.

aspired to but could not achieve. Unlike the critical debates of the enlightenment public, the construction of this legislation of nature is more than a helpful supplement to the legislative head of state who might be inclined to govern an absolutist state as if it were a self-governing republic. More than a vain attempt to introduce a simulation of representative government into the language of absolutist monarchy, the legislation of nature promises an objective realization of a republican political order.[16]

If enlightenment marks the emancipation of the reasoning subject, then universal history marks the reasoning subject's attempt to move beyond itself to claim the realm of the nonrational as its own legislative domain, as the agent of its own political ambitions. It is crucial in this context that unlike the nature constructed by the legislation of the understanding, the realm of nature that formed the subject of the first *Kritik*, the phenomenal realm to which history belongs is for Kant clearly and explicitly marked as a nonrational domain of nature, a "vernunftlosen Naturreich" (VIII, 30). It is the task of universal history, accordingly, to confront this nonrational domain of empirical *Historie* and attempt to regard it as if it were somehow governed by a rational, legislative force of its own, thus representing the "planloses *Aggregat* menschlicher Handlungen" as if it were a system. And this "as if" is crucial here. For regardless of how this might sound, the universal history essay does not mark a regression into the purely speculative, dogmatic metaphysics that Kant sought to put an end to with the *Kritik der reinen Vernunft*.[17] Kant insists toward the end of the essay that the work of the philosophical historian attempts in no way to usurp or repress (*verdrängen*) the work of empirical history (VIII, 30). The project of universal history is clearly not to transcend experience. Philosophical history never claims that the realm of human actions does in fact form a system in nature. Kant never goes so far as to propose a form of *a priori* legislation that would belong to nature itself. Universal history makes no objective claims about nature as such but attempts merely to develop an *a priori* rule for *judging* the apparently random play of human actions in the phenomenal realm. The *a priori* universality of universal history is primarily a subjective,

[16] On the central role of the metaphor of "legislation" in articulating the relationship between Kant's critical philosophy and his political writings, see Hess: *Reconstituting the Body Politic*. Pp. 211-222.
[17] Compare Yovel, *Kant and the Philosophy of History*, who reads the early essays on history as precisely such a regression. Yovel overcomes this problem by reintegrating them into the critical system, and not by reading them on their own terms.

not an objective phenomenon. The *a priori* rule of philosophical history merely opens us up to the possibility of *representing* the nonrational "*Aggregat* menschlicher Handlungen" as if it were a rationally organized diachronic system. As Kant emphasizes in the paragraph quoted above, the sole concern of universal history is to allow us to "hope", to explore the conditions under which progress might be possible.

Kant can secure a solid epistemological ground for universal history, then, only by marking it as a mode of judgment, only by grounding it in an *a priori* principle that is strictly subjective. Yet Kant's inquiry into the conditions of possibility for this legislation of nature ultimately amounts to more than an act of delimiting critique. Indeed, it is precisely this critical delimitation of history to a function of subjective judgment that constructs this domain as the most effective form of political agency open to the enlightenment public. As counterintuitive and paradoxical as this might sound, the judgment of history can be an effective political weapon precisely because it lacks all ontological authority:

Ein philosophischer Versuch, die allgemeine Weltgeschichte nach einem Plane der Natur, der auf die vollkommene bürgerliche Vereinigung in der Menschengattung abziele, zu bearbeiten, muß als möglich, und *selbst für diese Naturabsicht beförderlich* angesehen werden [my emphasis]. Es ist zwar ein befremdlicher und dem Anscheine nach ungereimter Anschlag, nach einer Idee, wie der Weltlauf gehen müßte, wenn er gewissen vernünfti-gen Zwecken angemessen sein sollte, eine *Geschichte* abfassen zu wollen; es scheint, in einer solchen Absicht könne nur ein *Roman* zu Stande kommen. Wenn man indessen annehmen darf: daß die Natur selbst im Spiele der menschlichen Freiheit nicht ohne Plan und Endabsicht verfahre, so könnte diese Idee doch wohl brauchbar werden. (VII, 29)

The legislation of the judgment of history may be a subjective operation, yet it nevertheless has definite objective manifestations. Universal history is not merely about progress. It is itself a sign of the progress that it posits, a means of enacting the end of which it speaks. By discerning the "verborgenen Plan der Natur" and con-structing a narrative of political progress, the philosophical histo-rian contributes directly to the realization of this progress. By constructing the possibility that the nonrational domain of human actions is organized by an overarching rational intention, universal history empowers itself as an agent of this alternative form of rational legislation, composing a "Roman" that turns out to be fact rather than fiction. In this way, the project of philosophical history enables the subjects of the absolutist state to move beyond the political limits of enlightenment and become more than passive spectators to the political world. Kant's universal history essay claims for the enlightenment public a form of judgment that marks the nonrational domain as its legislative domain, and that constructs this realm in such a way that it might serve to realize the political ambitions of enlightenment rationality. Through the judgment of history, the passive spectator becomes a political actor. Kant's philosophy of history proposes in this way a solution to the paradox of enlightenment, claiming a form of political agency for the enlightenment public that will make the absolutist state yield up an alternative political order and become thus more than a mere machine. The judgment of history thus salvages the possibility of a politicized enlightenment, granting the enlightenment public a form of political agency that secures the possibility of a republican politics.

In its solution to the paradoxes of enlightenment, the universal history essay does more than follow the transcendental method of the critical philosophy. There is more at stake here than simply a similarity in form. The delineation of the workings of the *a priori* principle at the root of historical judgment also links this particular mode of political practice directly and explicitly to that type of *a priori* legislation which Kant himself will mark six years later as the critical problem of judgment. Following Kant's own pronouncements – primarily his letter to Karl Leonhard Reinhold of 28 and 31 December, 1787 (X, 513-15) – Kant scholarship has traditionally situated the formulation of the concept of reflective judgment at a much later juncture in Kant's critical development.[18] The central pivot around which we have seen Kant construct his concept of a universal history, however, is precisely that crucial distinction between "determinant" and "reflective" judgment that figures so prominently in the conception of the third *Kritik*. Kant explains in the introduction to the *Kritik der Urtheilskraft*:

> Urtheilskraft überhaupt ist das Vermögen, das Besondere als enthalten unter dem Allgemeinen zu denken. Ist das Allgemeine (die Regel, das Princip, das Gesetz) gegeben, so ist die Urtheilskraft, welche das Besondere darunter subsumirt, (auch, wenn sie, als transcendentale Urtheilskraft, *a priori* die Bedingungen angiebt, welchen gemäß allein unter jenem Allgemeinen subsumirt werden kann) *bestimmend*. Ist aber nur das Besondere gegeben, wozu

---

[18] See here, for instance, John Zammito: *The Genesis of Kant's Critique of Judgment*. Chicago 1992. Pp. 167ff.

sie das Allgemeine finden soll, so ist die Urtheilskraft bloß *reflectierend.* (V, 179)

Determinant judgment – "bestimmende Urtheilskraft" – is the business of the understanding, whose universal laws are given *a priori* and subsequently prescribed unto nature. Determinant judgment does deal with the empirical particular in nature but only to the extent that it figures as a function of the universal laws of the understanding. Like universal history, on the other hand, reflective judgment takes as its point of departure the realm of empirical particulars not "determined" by the understanding in this way, a realm which, from the perspective of our understanding, can only be considered "zufällig" (V, 180). Reflective judgment does not attempt to subsume the particulars of this realm under an already existing universal law. It attempts, rather, to discern the organizing principle of this nonrational domain, or, as Kant explains in the first version of the introduction to the third *Kritik,* in words reminiscent of the essay on universal history, "das *Aggregat* besonderer Erfahrungen als *System* derselben zu betrachten".[19] Like the way in which the universal historian reads empirical *Historie* as the "Vollziehung eines verborgenen Plans der Natur", the process of reflective judgment attempts to conceive of the "undetermined" empirical particulars given in nature as the systematic presentation of their own form of legality.

Reflective judgment, like universal history, confronts that realm of nature not under the legislation of the understanding and takes on the task of regarding this nonrational realm as if it were governed by a rational intent. And again, the "as if" is crucial here. For the form of *a priori* legislation which the third *Kritik* calls reflective judgment makes no claims to objectivity. Like the universality of universal history, this legislation too is a strictly subjective operation:

Nun kann dieses Princip [der reflectierenden Urtheilskraft] kein anderes sein, als: daß, da allgemeine Naturgesetze ihren Grund in unserem Verstande haben, der sie der Natur (ob zwar nur nach dem allgemeinen Begriffe von ihr als Natur) vorschreibt, die besonderen empirischen Gesetze in Ansehung dessen, was in ihnen durch jene unbestimmt gelassen ist, nach einer solchen Einheit betrachtet werden müssen, als ob gleichfalls ein Verstand (wenn gleich nicht der unsrige) sie zum Behuf unserer Erkenntnisvermögen, um ein System der Erfahrung nach besonderen Naturgesetzen möglich zu machen, gegeben hätte. Nicht, als wenn auf diese Art wirklich ein solcher

---

[19] Kant: Erste Fassung der Einleitung in die Kritik der Urteilskraft. In: *Werkausgabe.* Ed. Wilhelm Weischedel. Frankfurt a.M. 1989. Vol. X. P. 16.

Verstand angenommen werden müßte (denn es ist nur die reflectierende
Urtheilskraft, der diese Idee zum Princip dient, zum Reflectieren, nicht zum
Bestimmen); sondern dieses Vermögen giebt sich dadurch selbst, und nicht
der Natur, ein Gesetz. (V, 180)

Unlike determinant judgment, reflective judgment has no actual
domain for its legislation. Reflective judgment may *deal* with the
realm of nature "undetermined" by the universal *a priori* laws of the
understanding. Like the universal historian, however, it can *legislate*
solely unto itself, giving itself the *a priori* law that the "undetermined" aggregates of empirical particulars in nature can indeed be
read as the systematic presentation of a law. This is the context in
which Kant introduces his famous concept of the "Zweckmäßigkeit"
or purposiveness of nature. Reflective judgment makes no metaphysical claims that the contingent realm of empirical particulars
was in fact ordered purposively by a suprahuman understanding, by a
"verborgenen Plan der Natur". The purposiveness reflective judgment ascribes to nature is merely a regulative principle used to guide
itself in coming to terms with the nonrational realm.

By tracing Kant's reflections on the possibilities of political
agency vis-à-vis the absolutist body politic, then, we have indeed
arrived at the central problem of the *Kritik der Urtheilskraft*. It is,
moreover, not just judgment in general but also aesthetic judgment
in particular that unfolds in a clear analogy to the judgment of
history. The judgment of history attempts to conceive of a nonrational domain of phenomenal nature, the world of human actions as
a whole, as if it were governed by a rational legislating force of its
own. Confronted with a nonrational domain of empirical particulars,
aesthetic judgment finds in beauty a similar "Plan der Natur", a
similar "Absicht" or, as Kant says here, a "Technik" that would
figure as the organizing ground of the nonrational domain of nature:

Die selbstständige Naturschönheit entdeckt uns eine Technik der Natur,
welche sie als ein System nach Gesetzen, deren Princip wir in unserm ganzen Verstandesvermögen nicht antreffen, vorstellig macht, nämlich dem
einer Zweckmäßigkeit respectiv auf den Gebrauch der Urtheilskraft in Ansehung der Erscheinungen, so daß diese nicht bloß als zur Natur in ihrem
zwecklosen Mechanism, sondern auch als zur Analogie mit der Kunst ge-
hörig beurtheilt werden müssen. Sie erweitert also wirklich zwar nicht unsere Erkenntniß der Naturobjecte, aber doch unsern Begriff von der Natur,
nämlich als bloßem Mechanism, zu dem Begriff von eben derselben als
Kunst: welches zu tiefen Untersuchungen über die Möglichkeit einer solchen Form einladet. (V, 246)

"Kunst", of course, refers at this point in the *Kritik der Urtheilskraft* not to "schöne Kunst" or fine art, to products of human artifice that are pronounced beautiful, but to the strictly subjective process of judgment that regards the nonrational domain of nature as if it were a purposive system governed by laws of its own, as if it were the product – the art – of a suprahuman understanding. The objective of the judgment of history was not to make definitive objective judgments about the collective realm of human actions but merely to secure hope, to explore the conditions under which a "verborgener Plan der Natur" might be possible. Similarly, the judgment of taste, Kant insists here, "erweitert [...] nicht unsere Erkenntniß der Naturobjecte". It only leads "zu tiefen Untersuchungen" into the *concept* of nature as belonging to something analogous to art. The pleasure one experiences contemplating beauty in nature serves as a sign of the formal purposiveness of nature in general, and thus, like the judgment of history, as a sign of the possibility of political progress as well.

The Genius and the Historian:
Aesthetic Autonomy and the Displacement of Politics

The mere fact of this basic parallel between historical and aesthetic judgment, however, only begins to address the question of the actual relationship between aesthetics and history in Kant, not to mention the issue what it might mean for this relationship that the *Kritik der Urtheilskraft* ultimately does much more than offer a transcendental deduction of the "art" of aesthetic judgment. In §43 and following, of course, the *Kritik der Urtheilskraft* also delineates a very particular concept of "fine art" or "free art" as distinguished from "mercenary art" (*Lohnkunst*). In this move, as countless commentators have noted, Kant offers one of the first elaborations of the concept of aesthetic autonomy, a high philosophical account of the normative distinction between instrumental works of artifice and noninstrumental works of art Karl Philipp Moritz had formulated in his 1785 *Berlinische Monatsschrift* essay, "Versuch einer Vereinigung aller schönen Künste und Wissenschaften unter dem Begriff des in sich selbst Vollendeten".[20] Unlike the tradition of normative poetics that

---

[20] Karl Philipp Moritz: Versuch einer Vereinigung aller schönen Künste und Wissenschaften unter dem Begriff des in sich selbst Vollendeten. In: *Berlinische Monatsschrift* 5 (1785). Pp. 225-236. On aesthetic autonomy, see note 5 above. On Moritz's role in the formulation of the concept of aesthetic autonomy, and on the question of the relationship between Kant and Moritz's

had judged what we call artworks in reference to their function, their utility, Kant insists that fine art has no instrumental purpose whatsoever. Unlike "mercenary art", "fine art" for Kant always involves a mode of production that is purposive in itself. Art for Kant has no use or exchange value; it is, rather, a playful "free doing" that produces an object that by definition can be seen to have no other purpose than simply providing the occasion for the disinterested judgment of taste.

The question I would like to explore in this section, accordingly, is the relationship between this notion of aesthetic autonomy and Kant's concept of the political agency of historical judgment. In focusing so much attention on Kant's concept of aesthetic autonomy, I am clearly not approaching the *Kritik der Urtheilskraft* from the perspective of its most explicit concerns. (In this sense, my approach to Kant in this section parallels my use of universal history essay as a point of entry into the third *Kritik*.) Indeed, it is crucial to recognize that Kant's primary concern in the section of the *Kritik der Urtheilskraft* devoted to aesthetics is with the aesthetic judgment of natural beauty, not with these works of fine art that might also provide the occasion for the judgment of taste. Hegel opens his *Vorlesungen über die Ästhetik* by excluding natural beauty from the realm of the aesthetic, redefining natural beauty as merely "ein Reflex des dem Geiste angehörigen Schönen".[21] Kant's third *Kritik*, however, explicitly privileges the beauty of nature over the type of beauty that might be achieved by a work of art. In its primary emphasis, Kant's aesthetics is an aesthetics of the judging subject in its relation to nature, not a philosophy of art or an elaboration of the concept of aesthetic autonomy. It is, indeed, crucial for the function aesthetic judgment assumes within the critical philosophy that it *not* be autonomous. Unlike the legislations of the understanding and practical reason, judgment lacks an objective domain, an independent realm in which its laws would be universally valid; in the vocabulary of the critical philosophy, the legislation of judgment is not "constitutive", like that of the understanding or practical reason, but merely "regulative", unable to prescribe laws to anything other than itself. For this reason, Kant insists, judgment has to be considered as a "heautonomous" rather than an "autono-

---

configurations of the relationship between aesthetics, politics and public culture, see Hess: *Reconstituting the Body Politic*. Pp. 119-188.
[21] Georg Wilhelm Friedrich Hegel: *Vorlesungen über die Ästhetik I*. Frankfurt a.M. 1970. P. 15.

mous" form of legislation.[22] The task Kant assigns aesthetic judgment in completing the critical philosophy – forging the necessary
"Brücke" over the "unübersehbare Kluft" (V, 175) separating the
phenomenal world of the *Kritik der reinen Vernunft* from the
noumenal world of the *Kritik der praktischen Vernunft* – requires, in
fact, that judgment not have an objective domain of its own in
which its own laws would be valid. It is the aesthetic's constitutive
lack of autonomy that marks its importance to Kant.

Elsewhere I have argued that the systematic function of aesthetic
judgment within the critical enterprise is inextricably linked to its
function vis-à-vis Kant's reflections on the limits of enlightenment
political agency. Aesthetic judgment, I have suggested, does not just
provide what Kant calls a "symbol" (§59), a sensible illustration, of
the noumenal ideas of morality. It also forges a bridge to the process
of republican political legislation as well, offering up a symbolic
articulation of precisely that political order Kant sought in the
universal history to effect through the agency of historical judgment.[23] Presupposing this discussion, I would like to trace here how
Kant's concept of fine art in §43 and following considerably *com-
plicates* the bridge-making project of the third *Kritik*, whether one
conceives of this as a bridge between the phenomenal domain of
nature and the noumenal domain of morality and freedom (the
explicit terms of the third *Kritik*) *or* as a bridge between the processes of aesthetic and historical judgment. Kant's concept of fine
art, we shall see, emerges from tensions within his concept of the
aesthetic judgment of nature, and it does so in such a way as to grant
the "heautonomy" of aesthetic judgment precisely that objective
domain – precisely that autonomy – it lacked and needed to lack to
perform its function. It is in this context that I would like to pose
the question of the ultimate relationship between historical judgment
and "aesthetic autonomy" in Kant and explore the role aesthetic
autonomy might play in the displacement of politics.

Let us begin by exploring those tensions out of which Kant's concept of aesthetic autonomy emerges. It is in the section "Vom
intellectuellen Interesse am Schönen" (§42) that Kant argues most
explicitly for the superiority of natural beauty to the type of beauty
achieved by a work of fine art. "[D]as Interesse am *Schönen der
Kunst*", Kant comments, furnishes "gar keinen Beweis einer dem

---

[22] See here, for instance, Vol. V. Pp. 185-86, also the first introduction, Kant:
Werkausgabe. Vol. X. P. 39.
[23] See Hess: *Reconstituting the Body Politic*. Particularly pp. 211-242.

Moralisch-Guten anhänglichen, oder auch nur dazu geneigten Denkungsart"; natural beauty, in contrast, arouses an immediate interest in those individuals who have an interest in the morally good (V, 298). As would seem appropriate in an aesthetics that culminates in constructing beauty as the "symbol" of morality (§59), Kant roots this "interest" in the process of reading and interpreting the language, the "Sprache, die die Natur zu uns führt" (V, 304):

> Da es aber die Vernunft auch interessirt, daß die Ideen (für die die im moralischen Gefühle ein unmittelbares Interesse bewirkt) auch objective Realität haben, d.i. daß die Natur wenigstens eine Spur zeige, oder einen Wink gebe, sie enthalte in sich irgend einen Grund, eine gesetzmäßige Übereinstimmung ihrer Producte zu unserm von allem Interesse unabhängigen Wohlgefallen (welches wir a priori für jedermann als Gesetz erkennen, ohne dieses auf Beweisen gründen zu können) anzunehmen: so muß die Vernunft an jeder Äußerung der Natur von einer dieser ähnlichen Übereinstimmung ein Interesse nehmen; folglich kann das Gemüth über die Schönheit der Natur nicht nachdenken, ohne sich dabei zugleich interessirt zu finden. Dieses Interesse aber ist der Verwandtschaft nach moralisch; und der, welcher es am Schönen der Natur nimmt, kann es nur sofern an demselben nehmen, als er vorher schon sein Interesse am Sittlich-Guten wohlgegründet hat. Wen also die Schönheit der Natur unmittelbar interessirt, bei dem hat man Ursache, wenigstens eine Anlage zu guter moralischen Gesinnung zu vermuthen. Man wird sagen: diese Deutung ästhetischer Urtheile auf Verwandtschaft mit dem moralischen Gefühl sehe gar zu studirt aus, um sie für die wahre Auslegung der Chiffreschrift zu halten, wodurch die Natur in ihren schönen Formen figürlich zu uns spricht. (V, 300-301)

As Kant describes it here, our intellectual interest in the beautiful is grounded in the interests of practical reason. Wanting to find its noumenal ideas represented in the phenomenal world, reason looks for a "Spur", a "Wink" or an "Äußerung" which it might read as the objective realization of practical reason. For those who have firmly established their interest in the morally good, beautiful forms in nature can become a form of figurative language, a "Chiffreschrift" that the judging subject can *interpret* as the objective presentation of moral ideas. What matters most about this interpretive activity, as Kant himself emphasizes, is not its result, not that which one gets after decoding the language of nature, but solely the process of interpretation: "Wenigstens so deuten wir die Natur aus, es mag der gleichen ihre Absicht sein oder nicht" (V, 302).[24]

---

[24] My primary interest in the concept of aesthetic autonomy forces me to bracket some of the other important issues that Kant raises here, among them

In interpreting nature's "language" as a symbolic medium that represents moral ideas, aesthetic judgment posits an *Absicht*, a design or intention, that may or may not be proper to nature itself. Rather than deciphering the *Chiffreschrift* of nature and definitively arriving at the "message" this encoded language is assumed to transmit, all aesthetic judgment can do is read this language as if it did in fact have intentionality, as if it were an encoded message. As a function of reflective judgment, the *Chiffreschrift* of nature is thus a writing with an indeterminate intentionality, a form of encoded, figurative language that both "einen höheren Sinn zu haben scheint" (V, 302) and is yet also potentially empty, devoid of any intrinsic link to that which it is taken to signify.[25] In this context, Kant's concession that his own "Auslegung der Chiffreschrift [...], wodurch die Natur in ihren schönen Formen figürlich zu uns spricht" might seem to be forced and didactic deserves to be read for the concession that it is, a concession that he has to make if he is not to fall back into the dogmatic metaphysics his critical philosophy seeks to overcome. All the aesthetically judging subject can do is to interpret nature as if it did in fact have meaning, as if it were purposive, as if it were symbolic. In the passage above, as in both the *Kritik der Urtheilskraft* as a whole and the universal history essay, it is clear that what motivates this interpretive process is not nature itself, but the interests of reason.

It is in the context of this tenuous bridge between the realm of nature and the realm of morality that Kant insists on the superiority of natural beauty to its counterpart in the work of art. In its attempt to envision the possible realization of moral ideas, practical reason wants its ideas to have objective reality in nature, not in the simulated world of the work of human artifice. However tenuous a form of language the *Chiffreschrift* of nature may be, Kant ranks beauty in nature far above beauty in art, which he describes here only in terms of its deceptive imitation of nature:

Aber dieses Interesse, welches wir hier an Schönheit nehmen, bedarf durchaus, daß es Schönheit der Natur sei; und es verschwindet ganz, sobald man bemerkt, man sei getäuscht, und es sei nur Kunst: so gar, daß auch der

---

the Kantian concept of the "beautiful soul" as it is elaborated in §42. See on this question Robert E. Norton: *The Beautiful Soul: Aesthetic Morality in the Eighteenth Century*. Ithaca 1995. Pp. 210-225.

[25] The etymology of the German *Chiffre*, borrowed from the French, manifests precisely this ambivalence. See "Chiffre" in: Jacob and Wilhelm Grimm: *Deutsches Wörterbuch*. Leipzig 1873.

Geschmack alsdann nichts Schönes, oder das Gesicht etwas Reizendes mehr daran finden kann. (V, 302)

Aesthetic pleasure is bound up with seeing natural beauty as a product of nature, as nature's art, and as Kant describes it here, beauty in human-produced artworks is by nature deceptive, an attempt to upstage natural beauty and surreptitiously supplant it. Beauty in art impedes the bridge-making project of the *Kritik der Urtheilskraft*, creating for the judging subject a deceptive world of seemingly natural artifice that prevents the objective realization of the ideas of morality in the realm of nature.

Kant's insistence on the superiority of natural beauty to the beautiful work of art thus both opens up the question of beauty in art and also attempts to position human artworks, fine art, in an altogether different domain from the products of nature's art. Kant initiates his comparison between the beautiful in nature and the beautiful in art, accordingly, by setting up a hierarchy between natural original and artistic imitation, a hierarchy designed to prevent art from upstaging nature:

An einem Producte der schönen Kunst muß man sich bewußt werden, daß es Kunst sei und nicht Natur; aber doch muß die Zweckmäßigkeit in der Form desselben von allem Zwange willkürlicher Regeln so frei scheinen, als ob es ein Product der bloßen Natur sei. [...] Die Natur war schön, wenn die zugleich als Kunst aussah; und die Kunst kann nur schön genannt werden, wenn wir uns bewußt sind, sie sei Kunst, und sie uns doch als Natur aussieht. [...] Also muß die Zweckmäßigkeit im Producte der schönen Kunst, ob sie zwar absichtlich ist, doch nicht absichtlich scheinen; d.i. schöne Kunst muß als Natur *anzusehen* sein, ob man sich ihrer zwar als Kunst bewußt ist. (V, 306-07)

The aesthetic pleasure afforded by natural beauty, we remember, was bound up with seeing nature in "Analogie mit der Kunst" (V, 246), as the product of a suprahuman art of nature. As Kant describes it here, the aesthetic pleasure occasioned by fine art derives from its essential similarity to this art of nature, not to nature itself. Fine art does not imitate the appearance of nature, the nature that is accessible to the understanding, but the purposiveness that reflective judgment posits at the base of nature, the "Technik der Natur". The similarity between beautiful art and beauty in nature lies not in art's content – not, say, in a particular natural object art might represent – but solely in art's formal semblance of natural purposiveness. In this way, Kant salvages fine art from its status as a deceptive imitation of natural beauty, redefining art as a formal imitation of the suprahuman *Absicht* that reflective judgment posits as belonging to nature. What art imitates is not the *Chiffreschrift* of nature's beautiful forms but the intentionality that the interpretive activity of aesthetic judgment posited (and could only posit) behind these beautiful forms. It is this point that marks the essential difference between beauty in art and natural beauty. For unlike the *Chiffreschrift* of nature, Kant points out here, art does have a design, an *Absicht*. In simulating natural purposiveness, accordingly, art must always suppress this design and seem not to have a purpose, simulating the undesigned contingency of nature so that the judging subject might then regard the work of art as analogous to the art of nature. The work of art, which as a product of human artifice is by definition purposive, must always feign unpurposiveness so as to make it possible for aesthetic judgment to regard it as if it were purposive.

By defining fine art as an imitation of nature's art, Kant reworks the inherited concept of *mimesis*, marking human art as a formal imitation of the process by which nature was created. There is more at stake here, however, than simply the common eighteenth-century shift from imitation to creation. For as an imitation of nature's art, fine art is itself also a *product* of nature, a creation of genius, which Kant defines as an "angeborne Gemüthsanlage (*ingenium*), *durch welche* die Natur der Kunst die Regel giebt"; as a "Talent" or "Naturgabe", genius itself *belongs to nature* ("selbst zur Natur gehört") (V, 307). The human being who imitates nature's art, then, does so as an *agent* of nature. Like the philosophical historian – and we will return to this parallel below – the genius too becomes an agent of a suprahuman natural purposiveness. The work of art can simulate natural purposiveness, that is, because it is itself an indirect product of nature, a secondary reflex of nature that embodies the natural purposiveness aesthetic judgment wanted to find in nature. Like Baumgarten, Lessing and Moritz, then, Kant here introduces art as a sort of displaced theology,[26] but he does so with a critical difference: that which art displaces in Kant is never perceived to be actually present in nature itself. The suprahuman art of nature which aesthetic judgment uses as a regulative principle is just that, a regulative principle for aesthetic judgment, and not a constitutive feature of nature itself. In this sense, the artifice of natural purposiveness which Kant marks as the constitutive feature of the work of art has to be seen as a process of *compensation*, a process of creating a simulation of that which was potentially *not* present in nature. The temporal scheme Kant outlines in the passage above

[26] See here Abrams: Kant and the Theology of Art (note 5).

thus deserves to be taken seriously, particularly because it goes against the grain of what Kant states explicitly about the superiority of natural beauty: "Die Natur war schön, wenn die zugleich als Kunst aussah; und die Kunst kann nur schön genannt werden, wenn wir uns bewußt sind, sie sei Kunst, und sie uns doch als Natur aussieht". At this point in the *Kritik der Urtheilskraft*, nature is apparently already no longer beautiful, and it becomes the task of nature's deputy, the genius, to bring to life precisely that internal purposiveness that aesthetic judgment posited and could only posit as the organizing ground of nature. In its simulation of natural purposiveness, art achieves precisely what nature could not.

As a secondary phenomenon, the simulated purposiveness of the work of art assumes primary significance, becoming the permanent representative of a natural purposiveness that may or may not have been proper to nature itself. For all his insistence on the superiority of natural beauty, Kant transforms the hypothetical principle by which one judged and interpreted the symbolic language of nature into the constitutive feature of a domain of human-produced art that ultimately comes to displace nature. Kant's reflections on the figurative language of the genius make the dynamic of this displacement explicit. Marked by an essential indeterminacy, the *Chiffre-schrift* of nature could be seen only as a possible sign of natural purposiveness, as a form of figurative language that both "einen höheren Sinn zu haben scheint" and yet was also potentially empty, devoid of any intrinsic link to that which it was taken to signify. As a secondary reflex of natural purposiveness, the genius overcomes this problem, producing a type of figurative language whose essential indeterminacy allows it to express the infinite:

Nun behaupte ich, dieses Princip sei nichts anders, als das Vermögen der Darstellung *ästhetischer Ideen*; unter einer ästhetischen Idee aber verstehe ich diejenige Vorstellung der Einbildungskraft, die viel zu denken veranlaßt, ohne daß ihr doch irgend ein bestimmter Gedanke, d.i. *Begriff*, adäquat sein kann, die folglich keine Sprache völlig erreicht und verständlich machen kann. – Man sieht leicht, daß sie das Gegenstück (Pendant) von einer *Vernunftidee* sei, welche umgekehrt ein Begriff ist, dem keine *Anschauung* (Vorstellung der Einbildungskraft) adäquat sein kann. Die Einbildungskraft (als produktives Erkenntnisvermögen) ist nämlich sehr mächtig in Schaffung einer andern Natur aus dem Stoffe, den ihr die wirkliche giebt. (V, 313-14)

Kant insists here that the language of art is essentially intransitive, a signifier to which no definitive concept can be adequate.[27] In its refusal to signify any particular concept, moreover, the aesthetic idea occasions a free play between the imagination and the understanding that seems to point toward precisely that which the understanding cannot grasp. In its indeterminacy, the "aesthetic idea" expresses precisely what language cannot. As intuitions which occasion much thought yet to which no concept can be adequate, aesthetic ideas strive "zu etwas über die Erfahrungsgränze hinaus Liegendem [...] und so einer Darstellung der Vernunftbegriffe (der intellectuellen Ideen) nahe zu kommen suchen, welches ihnen den Anschein einer objectiven Realität giebt" (V, 314). The aesthetic idea is indeed the perfect "Gegenstück" to the idea of reason, precisely that which reason needs in order to be represented in the sensible realm.

Clearly, Kant is doing more here than elaborating how the work of art can occasion a judgment of taste in a manner analogous to natural beauty. Through the medium of the genius, nature surpasses itself and creates "another nature", a second nature with a formal purposiveness that expresses what nature itself could not. In the production of an aesthetic idea, the imagination emulates the "Vernunft-Vorspiele in Erreichung eines Größten", going beyond the "Schranken der Erfahrung" to present ideas of reason to sense "in einer Vollständigkeit [...], für die sich in der Natur kein Beispiel findet" (V, 314). The figurative language of art clearly surpasses the *Chiffreschrift* of nature, producing through its indeterminacy what the indeterminacy of *Chiffreschrift* could not, the apparent reality of the ideas of reason. Whereas the *Chiffreschrift* of nature was always potentially empty and devoid of meaning, the aesthetic idea is marked by an excess of meaning that points toward what nature could not represent.

Once Kant delineates how art can surpass nature, moreover, he spells out the consequences:

Man kann überhaupt Schönheit (sie mag Natur- oder Kunstschönheit) den *Ausdruck* ästhetischer Ideen, nennen: nur daß in der schönen Kunst diese Idee durch einen Begriff vom Object veranlaßt werden muß, in der schönen Natur aber die bloße Reflexion über eine gegebene Anschauung ohne Begriff von dem, was der Gegenstand sein soll, zur Erweckung und Mittheilung der Idee, von welcher jenes Object als der *Ausdruck* betrachtet wird, hinreichend ist. (V, 320)

Once Kant defines genius as an agent of natural purposiveness en-

---

[27] On the concept of aesthetic intransitivity, see Tzvetan Todorov: *Theories of the Symbol*. Trans. Catherine Porter. Ithaca 1982. Pp. 147-221.

dowed with the faculty of producing aesthetic ideas that surpass nature, he remakes nature in the image of fine art, describing *all* beauty here – "Natur- oder Kunstschönheit" – as the expression of aesthetic ideas. The discourse that began by regarding nature as if it belonged to something analogous to suprahuman art ends up here by regarding fine art as the model for nature. The aesthetic ideas of the genius are not merely a secondary reflex of natural purposiveness analogous to the *Chiffreschrift* of nature. In this context, the language of fine art becomes the *model* for the language of nature, a model that nature itself will never be able to equal. The judgment of taste does not simply conceive of nature as if it were art in the most general sense of the term, as if it were something made by a suprahuman understanding. It is, rather, human works of fine art that provide the ultimate model for judging nature.

For all his emphasis on the superiority of natural beauty, then, Kant here anticipates the Hegelian argument that natural beauty is but a reflex of beauty in art. What ultimately matters here, however, is less to what extent Kant actually anticipates Hegel's argument than the dynamic and the function of this concession of the apparent superiority of fine art to nature within the *Kritik der Urtheilskraft* itself. For within the context of the critical philosophy, this slippage has serious consequences of its own. Kant's demarcation of an objective realm of human aesthetic production that reenacts the original purposiveness that judgment posited at the base of nature may indeed represent a secondary moment within the *Kritik der Urtheilskraft*, but it is a secondary moment that, once introduced, quickly gains primary significance. The introduction of art grants autonomy to the aesthetic, causing art to embody natural purposiveness to such a degree as to supplant nature, replacing the indeterminate, hypothetical purposiveness of nature with a formal artifice of purposiveness that in its indeterminacy can be counted on to give the ideas of reason the semblance of a phenomenal presentation. Rather than forging a bridge between the noumenal realm of reason and the phenomenal realm of nature, art infinitely defers this bridge, supplanting nature by casting itself as the ideal domain for aesthetic judgment. The mediating function of aesthetic judgment within the critical enterprise hinges on its ability to read symbolically, and it seems that it is ultimately the artwork – and not nature – that provides the perfect domain for this activity.

Art does not just unsettle the function of aesthetic judgment within the critical philosophy. The conception of an autonomous aesthetic domain also has serious consequences for the relationship between aesthetic and historical judgment. The political agency of the judgment of history, we remember, lay in its strict delimitation to the status of subjective judgment; it was by renouncing all claims to objectivity that this judgment was able to empower itself as an agent of natural purposiveness, as a means of contributing to the realization of precisely that political order enlightenment could not achieve on its own. Universal history was thus not merely about envisioning progress; it was itself a sign of the progress that it posited, a means to enacting the end of which it spoke. By discerning the "verborgenen Plan der Natur" and constructing a narrative of political progress, the philosophical historian contributed directly to the realization of this progress, casting itself as an agent of the natural purposiveness it could only posit in nature.

As long as we were talking solely about aesthetic judgment, we could indeed make the argument that aesthetics and history were compatible, perhaps even mutually complementary. The demarcation of an objective realm of human aesthetic production that reenacts the original purposiveness that judgment posited at the base of nature, however, has rather serious ramifications here. For in the case of the aesthetic judgment *of art*, judgment is not empowered as an agent of natural purposiveness but transported and confined to a newly autonomous realm that finds natural purposiveness *realized* in the work of art. In the *Kritik der Urtheilskraft*, it is the genius – and not the historian – who emerges as the ideal agent of natural purposiveness. The philosophical historian may indeed have contributed to the possibility of political progress conceived of as part of the purposiveness of nature. The genius, however, realizes the purposiveness of nature, and does so in a realm that is not that of history. The introduction of Kant's concept of fine art grants autonomy to the aesthetic, causing it to embody natural purposiveness to such a degree as to supplant the political ambitions of the judgment of history, displacing the model of political progress as diachronic purposiveness with a perfected synchronic model of purposiveness in the work of art. The work of art no longer allows judgment to become the agent of a "verborgenen Plan der Natur". Art makes this "verborgenen Plan" manifest – and does so in a realm that is no longer that of history.

Political interpretations of the *Kritik der Urtheilskraft* have become a burgeoning industry in recent years, often taking their lead from Hannah Arendt's posthumously published *Lectures on Kant's Political Philosophy*, Jean-François Lyotard's *The Differend* or numerous other works that argue that Kant's theory of aesthetic judgment or his analytic of the sublime represent models for poli-

tics.[28] By approaching the *Kritik der Urtheilskraft* from the perspective of Kant's formulation of the political agency of reflective
judgment in the universal history essay, I have been trying to stress
the extent to which Kant's model of the aesthetic is itself *already*
constructed from within a discursive space occupied by history and
politics. What matters here, accordingly, is not simply the question
how or whether one might seek to recuperate the *Kritik der
Urtheilskraft* as a model for politics. For in its inception, as we have
seen, the very construction of the Kantian aesthetic is *already* a
political act, and it is a political act that culminates, it seems, not in
the analytic of the beautiful or the sublime, but in the construction
of precisely that autonomous domain judgment needed to lack in
order to perform its proper function. In this context – to return to
my original point of departure – the problem with aesthetic autonomy is clearly not that it is not political, that it simply escapes or
seeks to repress the political. Quite on the contrary, the problem
with the Kantian concept of autonomous art is that it *is* political,
that it realizes the political ambitions of enlightenment rationality
to such an extent as to make any further politics superfluous. By
realizing the natural purposiveness of historical progress within the
simulated natural world of the work of human artifice, the work of
art certainly does not withdraw from politics. The concept of aesthetic autonomy, rather, embodies, realizes and *subverts* the form of
political agency Kant negotiated for the philosophical historian. If
contemporary criticism is indeed going to move beyond the con-
strictions of the concept of aesthetic autonomy – and given Kant's
formulation of the concept of autonomous art, this would appear a
desirable imperative – it would seem that such formal elements of
allegedly autonomous art would have to provide at least one of our
fundamental points of departure.

[28] Hannah Arendt: *Lectures on Kant's Political Philosophy*. Ed. Ronald
Beiner. Chicago 1982. Jean-François Lyotard: *The Differend. Phrases in
Dispute*. Trans. Georges Van Den Abbeele. Minneapolis 1988.

Marc Redfield

Lucinde's Obscenity

Friedrich Schlegel's Lucinde *has scandalized philosophers because its eroticism and double entendres enact the aesthetic and philosophical scandal that Schlegel calls "irony". A close reading of* Lucinde, *particularly of the section entitled "Eine Reflexion", reveals that in this text, gender identity is ironic because it undermines itself. The novel thus suggests the performativity of gender and the materiality of the body, where materiality is understood not as substance, but as the pressure of an uncertainty that enables and destabilizes gender difference.*

The subject for discussion here is Friedrich Schlegel's celebrated novel *Lucinde*, the gospel of Young Germany and the system for its *Rehabiliation des Fleisches*, which was an abomination to Hegel. But this discussion is not without its difficulties, because, inasmuch as *Lucinde* is a very obscene book, as is well known, by citing some parts of it for more detailed consideration I run the risk of making it impossible for even the purest reader to escape altogether unscathed. I shall, however, be as circumspect and careful as possible.[1]

It has been many years since anyone needed to apologize for reading or writing about *Lucinde*. Over the course of the twentieth century, Schlegel's odd, fragmentary novel has become, in Hans Eichner's words, the "meistgelesene Roman der Romantik", as well as an integral and incontestable part of the German Romantic canon.[2] It has become easy to dismiss comments such as those of Kierkegaard,

[1] Søren Kierkegaard: *The Concept of Irony, with Continual Reference to Socrates*. Ed. and trans. Howard V. Hong and Edna H. Hong. Princeton 1989. P. 286.

[2] Hans Eichner: *Lucinde*. In: Friedrich Schlegel: *Kritische Friedrich-Schlegel-Ausgabe*. Ed. Ernst Behler with Jean-Jacques Anstett and Hans Eichner. Paderborn 1958-. Vol. V. P. lv. References to Schlegel's texts are drawn from this edition: citation is by volume and page number. It should be noted that the canonization of *Lucinde* in our era has occurred thanks in great part to the extraordinary philological and critical work of Ernst Behler and Hans Eichner.

quoted above, as the distractions of an obsolete system of manners and proprieties. Yet the nature of *Lucinde*'s scandal resists easy explanation. It is one thing for a text taken as a salacious *roman à clef* to shock and titillate its immediate audience, as *Lucinde* did when it was first published in 1799. But the novel retained its power to scandalize when it was reissued in 1835, six years prior to Kierkegaard's *Concept of Irony*; and as late as 1870 Wilhelm Dilthey was calling it "ästhetisch betrachtet ein kleines Ungeheuer"[3] while Rudolph Haym, in *Die romantische Schule*, denounced it as not just an "ästhetischer Frevel" but "zugleich ein moralischer Frevel".[4] With the professionalization of German studies in the twentieth-century academy, *Lucinde* ceased to occasion axiological and ethical hyperbole; but the resulting gains in scholarly understanding may have been obtained by aestheticizing the text to the point that we have become blind to its unruliness. What "obscenity" did Kierkegaard, like his then-master Hegel before him, sense to be at work in the novel? No doubt *Lucinde*'s extramarital eroticism and *double entendres* had something to do with it, and no doubt the chapter in praise of laziness irritated more than one generation of the nineteenth-century *Bildungsbürgertum*. But the text's ability to disturb (or delight) its readers seems out of proportion to its actual offense against public *moeurs*. *Lucinde* is possibly the only novel in the world that owes some of its fame to the fact that it has been attacked and defended by philosophers (Hegel and Kierkegaard on one side, Fichte and Schleiermacher on the other); and as Dilthey's and Haym's comments make clear, the novel's scandal was always also an aesthetic, which is to say to some extent a "philosophical" scandal.[5] Indeed, *Lucinde* may even be argued to have become "obscene" in the first place because of its offense against form.

These questions haunt our contemporary efforts to interpret *Lucinde* insofar as they recall the sheer difficulty of *reading* this "meistgelesene Roman der Romantik". *Lucinde*'s allegories resist interpretation not because they are forbiddingly esoteric but because of their ironic and slightly absurdist flavor – no matter how one parses the "Allegorie von der Frechheit", for instance, one is likely to feel unsatisfied; it will never be entirely certain whether the allegorical figures of the "echten Romanen, vier an der Zahl" are telling us something about Schlegel's aesthetic, or whether they are

---

[3] Wilhelm Dilthey: *Leben Schleiermachers*. Berlin 1870. P. 492.
[4] Rudolf Haym: *Die romantische Schule. Ein Beitrag zur Geschichte des deutschen Geistes*. Second Edition. Berlin 1906. P. 501.
[5] For a helpful overview of *Lucinde*'s reception, see Eichner. Pp. xlvi-lv.

mainly out to pull our readerly leg (V, 16). Arguments for the novel's unity rarely seem to get far beyond the minimalist observation that the "Lehrjahre der Männlichkeit" comes in the middle of the text, flanked by six sections before and after (if, that is, one doesn't count the "Prolog"); though the text's narrator claims to have set out "den rohen Zufall zu bilden und ihn zum Zwecke gestalten" (9), it is never entirely clear that a higher purpose or *Zweck* will emerge out of the seemingly aleatory scene-changes. Most studies of *Lucinde* consequently focus on the "Lehrjahre" section, in order to understand the novel as a *Bildungsroman* and ignore as much as possible the text's slippery irony.[6] For in this novel, Schlegel's irony, besides being a "klares Bewußtsein der ewigen Agilität, des unendlich vollen Chaos" (II, 263), seems to function as a "permanente Parekbase" (XVIII, 85) that constantly disrupts its own illusions.[7] In order to interpret the text, one needs to take certain statements literally (or figuratively) and close off alternatives – but in this novel the alternatives nag. Thus every interpretation of

---

[6] At the cost of a further irony, since the genre of the Bildungsroman is itself an ironic mirage. For discussion see my *Phantom Formations: Aesthetic Ideology and the Bildungsroman*. Ithaca 1996. The "Lehrjahre" chapter is also arguably *Lucinde*'s flattest, most woodenly narrated episode: Schlegel has set a high price on comprehensibility.

[7] I refer here of course to two of Schlegel's more famous epigrammatic definitions of irony: "Ironie ist klares Bewußtsein der ewigen Agilität, des unendlich vollen Chaos" (II, 263); "Ironie ist eine permanente Parekbase" (XVIII, 85). I shall return briefly to the vast and much-discussed topic of Schlegel's notion of irony later in this essay, but for reasons of economy shall be forced to refer readers interested in this topic to the copious secondary literature. For a recent, strongly argued account of Schlegelian irony as dialectical synthesis, see Eric Miller: Masks of Negation: Greek eironeia and Schlegel's Ironie. In: *European Romantic Review* 8.4 (1997). Pp. 360-85. Other important accounts of Schlegel's irony that move in a similar direction include: Beda Allemann: *Ironie und Dichtung*. Pfullingen 1956; Rüdiger Bubner: Zur dialektischen Bedeutung romantischer Ironie. In: *Die Aktualität der Frühromantik*. Ed. Ernst Behler. Paderborn 1987. Pp. 85-95; Ingrid Strohschneider-Kohrs: *Die romantische Ironie in Theorie und Gestaltung*.Tübingen 1960. The present essay discovers at work in Schlegel's text an irony better described by Paul de Man: The Concept of Irony. In: Paul de Man: *Aesthetic Ideology*. Minneapolis 1996. Pp. 163-84. See also Georgia Albert: Understanding Irony: Three Essays on Friedrich Schlegel. In: *MLN* 108 (1993). Pp. 825-48; Kevin Newmark: *L'Absolu littéraire*: Friedrich Schlegel and the Myth of Irony. In: *MLN* 107 (1992). Pp. 905-30.

Lucinde inevitably becomes in its turn the "Bekenntnisse eines Ungeschickten".

In the pages that follow I propose to take up here the question of *Lucinde*'s irony in relation to what Kierkegaard called the novel's "obscenity", on the one hand, and to some of the questions that recent critics of the novel address as issues of gender, desire, and sexuality, on the other. My essential claim here will be that Schlegel's text enacts a literary reading of philosophical discourse, such that literature, irony, and obscenity become insistently over-lapping categories. The novel's eroticism and *double entendres*, in other words, enact the aesthetic and philosophical scandal that Schlegel calls "irony". In the process, the novel suggests what Judith Butler calls the "performativity" of gender: the constructedness, that is, of gender identity, with construction understood as "neither a subject nor its act, but a process of reiteration by which both 'subjects' and 'acts' come to appear".[8] *Lucinde* furthermore, I shall argue, suggests that we understand gender identity as "ironic" in the sense of being potentially illegible, and that we understand the mate-riality of the body as the pressure of an uncertainty that enables and destabilizes gender. These claims emerge out of a close reading of the section of *Lucinde* entitled "Eine Reflexion". Before attempting that reading, however, I propose to spend a few pages recalling a long essay by Philippe Lacoue-Labarthe, "The Unpresentable", which examines Hegel's allusions to Schlegel's novel, and can help situtate Kierkegaard's sense of *Lucinde*'s "obscenity" within a philosophical tradition.

I

Lacoue-Labarthe's "L'Imprésentable" belongs to a group of essays from the mid-1970's that worry the question of "a possible literary *filiation* of philosophy". This particular piece travels paths similar to those pursued in Lacoue-Labarthe and Jean-Luc Nancy's *L'absolu littéraire* (1978), and sets itself the ambitious task of aligning the question of literature-and-philosophy with that of romanticism, on the one hand, and that of the figure of "woman" within speculative philosophy, on the other.[9] Lacoue-Labarthe's "example" is

---

[8] Judith Butler: *Bodies that Matter: On the Discursive Limits of "Sex"*. New York 1993. P. 9.
[9] Philippe Lacoue-Labarthe: The Unpresentable. Trans. Claudette Sartiliot. In: Philippe Lacoue-Labarthe: *The Subject of Philosophy*. Ed. Thomas Trezise. Minneapolis 1993. Pp. 116-157, here p. 102. Lacoue-Labarthe chose not to

Lucinde, though he doesn't focus on Schlegel's text, refers to it only in passing, and, indeed, never once quotes from it: in this he is tacitly and carefully miming Hegel, whose rare, fleeting, and seemingly inconsequent references to *Lucinde* are what Lacoue-Labarthe sets out to analyze.[10] Focusing on a moment in the *Aesthetics* in which *Lucinde*'s moral depravity (*Liederlichkeit*) is denounced, and on a marginal note (consisting of one word: "*Lucinde*") handwritten in a copy of the *Philosophy of Right* that Hegel used as a teaching copy, Lacoue-Labarthe elicits links between romanticism, irony, literature, and the feminine that make of *Lucinde* a figure of the "scandal of the aesthetic" (156). I cannot, of course, do justice here to the care – a care not at all adverse to risk, even to a certain recklessness – with which Lacoue-Labarthe performs his argument; but our sense of *Lucinde*'s performance within the critical and philosophical tradition will be sharper if we follow out the main turns of his essay, and put some pressure on one or two of his claims.

Hegel's offhand denunciation of *Lucinde* in the *Aesthetics* occurs in a chapter titled "Die Auflösung der klassischen Kunstform", which is to say at a point in Hegel's historical narrative in which classical art yields to romantic art, and aesthetic religion to Christianity, or revealed religion. Its era over, art becomes a thing of the past: as romantic art, it survives as a form that, willingly or not, registers the fact that aesthetic representation no longer serves as the Spirit's essential manifestation. Hegel identifies good and bad varieties of aesthetic self-dissolution: the good kind tends to be exemplified by Schiller, and the bad or dissolute kind by Friedrich Schlegel. Hegel contrasts Schiller's *Götter Griechenlands*, which movingly portrays the disappearance of the anthropomorphic Greek pantheon, with Parny's satiric *La guerre des Dieux*, which makes fun of "christlichen Vorstellungen". There is worse than Parny, though: "Die Späße sollen aber nichts weiter als ausgelassene Leicht-

---

collect this essay in his *Le sujet de la philosophie*. Paris 1979. The essay originally appeared as: L'Imprésentable. In: *Poétique* 21 (1975). Pp. 53-95. Subsequent references to this essay over the next few pages are to the English-language version, and are given parenthetically in the text.

[10] Lacoue-Labarthe characterizes his essay as the "first part" of a longer work – "the first part, which can be considered as an introduction to the (a) 'reading of *Lucinde*'" (p. 183 note 4). To my knowledge a second part never appeared, though years later Lacoue-Labarthe published a short, relatively informal essay that discusses *Lucinde*: L'avortement de la littérature. In: *Du féminin*. Ed. Mireille Calle. Sainte-Foy (Quebec) 1993.

fertigkeit sein, und es soll nicht etwa die Liederlichkeit zur Heiligkeit und höchsten Vortrefflichkeit gemacht werden, wie zur Zeit von Friedrich Schlegels *Lucinde*".[11] In his next sentence Hegel turns back to Parny's poem, and we hear no more of *Lucinde*, the appearance of which in this context is in any case rather peculiar: as Lacoue-Labarthe notes, Schlegel's novel has nothing to do with the gods of Greece or their disappearance, and receives mention here purely as an example of the scandalous and frivolous per se.

What goes into the making of the opposition between Schiller and Schlegel? Putting pressure at once on Hegel's historical narrative and on the Hegelian relation between poetry and philosophy, Lacoue-Labarthe suggests that Schiller's "philosophical poetry" represents for Hegel the promise or guarantee of a necessary aesthetic moment within speculative dialectics:

> [...] Schiller did not merely take the aesthetic a decisive step forward *within* aesthetics; he was also able to relate to philosophy itself this premonitory conception of art, thus accomplishing – Hegel almost says so outright – what *had* to be accomplished in order for the speculative as such to be established, namely, the unity of sense and the sensuous without the presupposition of which, it is easy to understand, no phenomenology of the Spirit, no absolutizing of the phenomenon (and hence none of what Heidegger calls the *onto-theio-logical*) would have been conceivable. (124-25)

Art's function is thus to establish a "unity of sense and the sensuous" that speculative philosophy relies on and transcends. Such dependence on aesthetic or poetic practice carries its dangers, however. Romanticism represents the corrosion, the bad dissolution, of art, in which philosophy fails to recognize itself. This corrosive force bears many names: depravity, subjectivity, and above all and most formally, irony. Here we may simply recall that romantic irony, in Hegel's analysis, derives from an appropriation of Fichtean subjectivism, and that, as Lacoue-Labarthe summarizes, "subjectivism equals immoralism" because it occasions "the desubstantialization of the substantial" (128), or, more precisely, because it "does not attain to the truth of dissolution, that is, to the speculative, reconciling truth of *determined* negativity" (129). "Literature", Lacoue-Labarthe adds, emerges here as a concept closely related to

---

[11] G.W.F. Hegel: *Vorlesungen über die Ästhetik*. In: *Werke*. Ed. Eva Moldenhauer and Karl Markus Michel. Frankfurt a.M. 1970. Vol. XIV. P. 116. Subsequent references to Hegel's texts are to this edition of the collected works.

that of irony – that is, to "this nondialectical or predialectical, insufficiently speculative 'aesthetics' which the *Aesthetics* itself proposes to correct and to redress, be it on the basis of a firm and salutary 'return to Schiller'" (129). And *Lucinde* haunts this return as the figure of literature itself: dissolute, ironic, and out of step with the historical progress of Spirit.

At this point Lacoue-Labarthe turns to his second object of analysis: a marginal reference to *Lucinde* alongside the Remark to Paragraph 164 of the *Philosophie des Rechts*. The "substantiality" of marriage – which *Lucinde*, given its exemplary *Frechheit*, cannot grasp – consists in the sublation of natural sexual difference into a concrete unity in which the sensuous is negated and preserved.[12] This sublation of sexual difference performs "the speculative distribution itself" (133) in distributing masculine and feminine roles. Marriage, one could say, transforms sex into gender, and gender into specula-

---

[12] Lacoue-Labarthe's commentary refers itself to a single handwritten word, "Lucinde", written beside the final lines of the Remark to Paragraph 164 in one of Hegel's teaching copies of the *Philosophy of Right* – lines in which the inability to grasp the ethical dimension of marriage is called "impertinence [*die Frechheit*]". Oddly, Lacoue-Labarthe does not refer to the "oral addition" to Paragraph 164 that one finds in Eduard Gans's 1833 edition of the *Philosophy of Right*. Gans's "additions", drawn from student notes taken at Hegel's lectures, are controversial (for a succinct account of the editorial questions involved, see Moldenhauer and Michel's afterword to Vol. VII of the *Werke*, pp. 524-31); but it seems a bit odd that Lacoue-Labarthe would ignore them, given that his main object of analysis, the *Aesthetics*, is itself made up entirely of lecture transcripts. The "Zusatz" to Paragraph 164, in any case, mentions *Lucinde* explicitly and supports Lacoue-Labarthe's argument quite dramatically: "Daß die Zeremonie der Schließung der Ehe überflüssig und eine Formalität sei, die weggelassen werden könnte, weil die Liebe das Substantielle ist und sogar durch diese Feierlichkeit an Wert verliert, ist von *Friedrich von Schlegel* in der *Lucinde* und von einem Nachtreter desselben in den Briefen eines Ungenannten (Lübeck und Leipzig 1800) aufgestellt worden. Die sinnliche Hingebung wird dort vorgestellt als gefordert für den Beweis der Freiheit und Innigkeit der Liebe, eine Argumentation, die Verführern nicht fremd ist". Hegel goes on to reinforce the principles of gender difference that he enunciates in this section of the *Philosophy of Right*: "Es ist über das Verhältnis von Mann und Frau zu bemerken, daß das Mädchen in der sinnlichen Hingebung ihre Ehre aufgibt, was bei dem Manne, der noch ein anderes Feld seiner sittlichen Tätigkeit als die Familie hat, nicht so der Fall ist. Die Bestimmung des Mädchens besteht wesentlich nur im Verhältnis der Ehe [...]". G.W.F. Hegel: *Grundlinien der Philosophie des Rechts oder Naturrecht und Staatswissenschaft im Grundrisse. Mit Hegels eigenhändigen Notizen und den mündlichen Zusätzen*. In: *Werke*. Vol. VII. Pp. 317-18.

tive philosophical discourse, by transforming "natural" difference into the active, ethical, differential destiny of man, and the passive, subjective, undifferentiated identity of woman.[13] "One recognizes here", as Lacoue-Labarthe comments dryly, "the major tenets of 'phallogocentrism'" (134). Furthermore, this passage through a "sexual symbolic" grants to knowledge a figural register in which it can represent itself to itself:

[13] We may note briefly that the paragraph that elicited Hegel's marginal note "Lucinde" is richly suggestive in ways that Lacoue-Labarthe does not pursue. In the *Philosophy of Right*, Hegel argues that the stipulation of a contract involves the genuine transfer of the property in question – that, in other words, a contract is a performative (or, in Hegelian language, a contract is "das Dasein meines Willensbeschlusses" [Par. 79; III, p. 162]). Thus, in Paragraph 164, the marrying parties' declaration of consent to enter into marriage, and the recognition of this declaration by the community, constitutes the actuality [*Wirklichkeit*] of marriage: "[...] so daß diese Verbindung nur durch das *Vorangehen* dieser Zeremonie als der Vollbringung des *Substantiellen* durch das *Zeichen*, die Sprache, als das geistigste Dasein des Geistigen, als sittlich konstituiert ist" (VII, p. 315). Language makes marriage an ethical reality, because it is language's function to symbolize and thus grant determinate existence to ideas: "Jene zustande gekommene Übereinkunft ist, für sich im Unterschiede von der Leistung, ein Vorgestelltes, welchem daher nach der eigentümlichen Weise des *Daseins der Vorstellungen in Zeichen* [...] ein besonderes Dasein, in dem Ausdrucke der *Stipulation* durch Förmlichkeiten der *Gebärden* und anderer symbolischer Handlungen, insbesondere in bestimmter Erklärung durch die *Sprache*, dem der geistigen Vorstellung würdigsten Elemente, zu geben ist" (Par. 78, VII, p. 161). My ellipsis replaces Hegel's cross-reference to his challenging discussion of the sign in Paragraph 458 of the *Enzyclopädie der philosophischen Wissenschaften*, in which the sign is defined as "irgendeine unmittelbare Anschauung, die einen ganz anderen Inhalt vorstellt, als den sie für sich hat; – die *Pyramide*, in welche eine fremde Seele versetzt und aufbewahrt ist" (X, p. 270). It is at this point in the *Enzyclopädie* that Hegel distinguishes the sign from the symbol, characterizes the sign as the expression and product of the free power of intelligence, and links the sign to memory (*Gedächtnis*). The passage has elicited strong interpretations from Jacques Derrida: The Pit and the Pyramid: Introduction to Hegel's Semiology. In: Jacques Derrida: *Margins of Philosophy*. Trans. Alan Bass. Chicago 1982. Pp. 69-108; and Paul de Man: Sign and Symbol in Hegel's *Aesthetics*. In: Paul de Man: *Aesthetic Ideology*. Ed. Andrzej Warminski. Minneapolis 1996. Pp. 91-104. In Paragraph 164 of the *Philosophie des Rechts*, in other words, the complex question of the sign intersects with what Lacoue-Labarthe, in the passage quoted below, calls Hegel's "sexual symbolic". It is possible that Hegel's marginal note "Lucinde" was spurred by his disapproval not just of *Lucinde*'s supposed ethical levity, but of its specifically semiotic, which is to say *literary*, playfulness.

For what is at stake in this very differentiation is no less than the possibility of the philosophical as such. As we shall verify from other texts, nothing in the speculative is alien to what, for lack of a better word, we are compelled to call a "sexual" "symbolic" (in the most general sense) constitutive, in the mode of a kind of *anthropo-phenomeno-logic*, of the "figuratic" in which emerging knowledge must necessarily (re)present itself [...]. (134)

And if, with the aesthetic and ethical scandal of *Lucinde* in mind, we refer this sexual symbolism back to the question of the artwork, we find that "woman", within the differential system of marriage, plays a role analogous to that played by art and the aesthetic within speculative philosophy. Woman figures the union of the spiritual and the sensuous, and thus figures the aesthetic realm, "which her ethical (male) destination sublates [...]. Between woman and art, the 'symbolic' equivalence, or the analogy, is rigorous and strong" (136). Lacoue-Labarthe thus aligns the question of woman with the questions of aesthetics, literature, romanticism, and irony that Hegel summarizes and dismisses under the sign of *"Lucinde"*. Noting that Hegel defends nudity in classical sculpture by affirming the ancient Greeks' indifference to purely sensual desire, yet that, while he finds classical male nudity acceptable, Hegel requires the aesthetic female figure to be veiled, Lacoue-Labarthe concludes that "if woman alone needs to be veiled, it is because she alone expresses – and arouses? – *sensual* desire [...]. [T]here is, properly speaking, no *pudendum* other than female *pudendum*; or, what amounts to the same thing, male homosexual desire (we should write: *hommosexual* desire) is spiritual desire: the phallus is the "organ" of the Spirit" (141). It is precisely because woman expresses sensual desire that she becomes – when veiled – the figure of the beautiful. Since beauty is the unity of sensuousness and spirit, the male figure cannot represent the beautiful: being indifferent to the sensual, the male figure is always already moving beyond beauty, toward the unveiling of the spiritual. Or, as Lacoue-Labarthe puts it: the male figure is "figured only in being feminized". Woman, however, becomes the figure of beauty when her sensuousness hides itself in the doubling of body and clothes – the latter serving as "a sensuous veil thrown over the sensuous" (142). Hegel, Lacoue-Labarthe suggests, is wrestling here with the problem of the necessity of manifestation itself; and in the closing pages of his essay he names the threat represented by woman as that of aesthetics as "the theory of fiction", "the locus where fiction, the fictional in general, becomes worthy of theory" (151):

And it is in such a conflict, in such a struggle with philosophy, that woman is at stake. [...] Woman is at stake because she represents, not as Hegel through Schiller would have liked, the sensuous itself in opposition to the spiritual, or – which amounts to the same once it has been rigged with a veil – the "inner fusion of the sensuous and the spiritual", but the sensuous in *its* truth, which is the "truth" of figure and the fictional. (155)

Venus or Aphrodite, the one exception, according to Hegel, to the rule that the aesthetic woman must be veiled, is the "figure" of this figurality, which Lacoue-Labarthe names as the *"the scandal of the aesthetic* – which, like every scandal in the eyes of knowledge and the Spirit, consists in having revealed that *there is nothing to unveil*. Or at least that there might be nothing to unveil" (156).

A number of questions arise in the wake of Lacoue-Labarthe's ambitious reading. His final gesture has about it the aura of a well-planned gamble; and much depends on how, and in what context, one decides – or feels compelled – to play one's cards. Is this Aphrodite, this tutelary goddess of aesthetics, the *necessary* figure for the scandal of the aesthetic? Does this figure perhaps repeat or mime a little too programmatically the Hegelian, "phallogocentric" identification of woman with the sensuous, the fictional, the narcissistic – that is, the hypersubjective, which is to say, the scandalous? And what do we make of the fetishistic gesture toward anti-fetishism that closes off Lacoue-Labarthe's text? The staging, the bringing onto stage, of the naked body of a woman (indeed, of Venus herself); the zooming in toward a lack ("there is nothing to unveil") that perhaps *n'en est pas un* ("or at least there might be nothing to unveil")? Lacoue-Labarthe is well aware of these questions; he would probably accept them as the necessary fallout of any critical attempt to mime and displace Hegel's text. And they remain questions without easy answers. "[W]e cannot do without the feminine", Drucilla Cornell comments; and her sense of the feminine as "an aesthetic idea that breaks open the ground of fundamental metaphysical concepts", and is thus "always the door to a radical future", accords with Lacoue-Labarthe's emphasis on the "fictional".[14] Yet the feminine in this sense – as an utopian, ethical instance, radically

---

[14] Drucilla Cornell, in: The Future of Sexual Difference: An Interview with Judith Butler and Drucilla Cornell. Interviewers: Pheng Cheah and Elizabeth Grosz. In: *Diacritics* 28. 1 (1998). Pp. 24, 23. For an extended account of the ethical and cognitive necessity of the "feminine" in this poststructuralist sense, see Drucilla Cornell: *Beyond Accommodation: Ethical Feminism, Decon-struction, and the Law*. New York and London 1991.

other to the real – would also exceed and disrupt the dualisms of the symbolic order; and to the extent that Lacoue-Labarthe's figure of sexual difference tends, in "The Unpresentable", to remain a binary opposition, it risks simplifying the tensions and compromises at work in philosophy's gendered self-representations, and produces unwieldy heterosexist generalities. It is highly questionable, for instance, whether "male homosexual desire" has ever been success-fully quarantined within the parameters of "spiritual desire" in the Western tradition; it is equally uncertain, for that matter, whether one can justify the notion of a specifically "homosexual desire", particularly one that would span continuously, without fracture or detour, the entirety of Western philosophical discourse. What concerns us here, thankfully, is a more modest issue: the radically misleading character of such generalizations within the conceptual and rhetorical world of Schlegel's *Lucinde*. Lacoue-Labarthe's analy-sis of Hegel's allusions to this novel helps us situate within the history of philosophical aesthetics Hegel's famous identification of "woman" as "die ewige Ironie des Gemeinwesens"; but in order to grasp Schlegel's difference from Hegel – from the official, philoso-phical Hegel, in any case – it will not suffice simply to reverse Hegel's values while keeping intact the equation between woman and irony.[15] A close reading of *Lucinde* demonstrates the advantage of thinking gender in terms of irony rather than irony in terms of gender, and consequently, as we shall see, suggests that the "scandal of the aesthetic" is better characterized as a certain materiality of signification rather than as a "sensuous truth" incarnated in "woman".

---

[15] G.W.F. Hegel: *Phänomenologie des Geistes*. In: *Werke*. Vol. III. P. 352. It should be noted that complex and powerful acts of reading have resulted from a certain straightforward appropriation of Hegel's phrase. "No red-blooded woman, after all, can fail to enjoy the irony of wearing Hegel's slur as some-thing of a crown", Carol Jacobs writes ironically in her recent: Dusting Anti-gone. In: *MLN* 111 (1996). Pp. 889-917, here p. 889-90. For an exemplary appropriation of Hegel's phrase, see Luce Irigaray: *Speculum of the Other Woman*. Trans. Gillian C. Gill. Ithaca 1985; see especially pp. 214-26, and for discussion, see Jacobs. Important readings of Hegel that suggest the complex-ity and ambiguity of his texts' deployment of sex and gender difference in-clude: Jacques Derrida: *Glas*. Paris 1974; and Werner Hamacher: pleroma. In: G.W.F. Hegel: *Der Geist des Christentums: Schriften 1796-1800*. Ed. Werner Hamacher. Frankfurt a.M. 1978.

II

Feminist criticism has not been slow, however, to discern in *Lucinde* the pretenses and ruses of phallocentrism; and it would certainly be difficult to deny that Schlegel's novel frequently seems to be offering us a subtler and more playful version of the Hegelian sexual symbolic. The character and sometime narrator Julius's male narcissism and androcentric allegorizing are not derailed by the fact that Lucinde herself is on to his game, and only half willing to play:

> Nicht ich, mein Julius, bin die die Du so heilig malst; obschon ich klagen möchte wie die Nachtigall, und, wie ich innig fühle, nur der Nacht geweiht bin. Du bist's, es ist die Wunderblume Deiner Fantasie, die Du in mir, die ewig Dein ist, dann erblickst, wenn das Gewühl verhüllt ist und nichts Gemeines Deinen hohen Geist zerstreut. (V, 78-79)

No matter: Lucinde will remain the mirror of male desire, the lamp toward which Julius strives; she is the lunar *lux* to his *veritas*, the passivity into which he voyages to find himself. As numerous critics have shown, the novel's ideal of androgyny is heterosexist and masculinist in contour, and "serves in a regulatory manner to inscribe binaristic codes and to naturalize the proper unity between love and marriage".[16] The novel's highly traditional discrimination between friendship and love, for instance, excludes woman from the former: "Die Freundschaft ist für euch" – says Julius to Lucinde – "zu vielseiting und einseitig. Sie muß ganz geistig sein und durchaus bestimmte Grenzen haben" (34). The pure spirituality of friendship

---

[16] Catriona MacLeod: The "Third Sex" in an Age of Difference: Androgyny and Homosexuality in Winckelmann, Friedrich Schlegel, and Kleist. In: *Outing Goethe and his Age*. Ed. Alice A. Kuzniar. Stanford 1996. Pp. 194-214, here p. 214. See also Sara Friedrichsmeyer: *The Androgyne in Early German Romanticism: Friedrich Schlegel, Novalis, and the Metaphysics of Love*. New York 1983; and Kari Weil: *Androgyny and the Denial of Difference*. Charlottesville 1992. Feminist readings that interpret the novel as a fundamentally male fantasy include: Barbara Becker-Canterino: Schlegels Lucinde: Zur Frauenbild der Frühromantik. In: *Colloquia Germanica* 10 (1976-77). Pp. 128-39; Eva Domoradzki: *Und alle Fremdheit ist verschwunden. Status und Funktion des Weiblichen im Werk Friedrich Schlegels. Zur Geschlechtigkeit einer Denkform*. Innsbruck 1982; Sigrid Weigel: Wider die romantische Mode: Zur ästhetischen Funktion des Weiblichen in Friedrich Schlegels Lucinde. In: *Die verborgene Frau. Sechs Beiträge zu einer feministischen Literaturwissenschaft*. Ed. Inge Stephan and Sigrid Weigel. Berlin 1983. Pp. 67-82.

exceeds the grasp of woman, whose nature it is to represent the natural as the sensuous – and, as we have seen Lacoue-Labarthe extract from Hegel, to represent the beautiful as the synthesis of sensuousness and spirit. Friendship is spirit, and furthermore, *limited* spirit; its "Absonderung" is the province of male striving: "Diese Absonderung würde euer Wesen nur auf eine feinere Art eben so vollkommen zerstören wie bloße Sinnlichkeit ohne Liebe" (34). The doubleness of the homoerotic bond – loving, but purely spiritual, and thus defined through a limit: *not* sexual – opposes itself to the singleness of women, who "mitten im Schoß der menschlichen Gesellschaft Naturmenschen geblieben sind" (55).

Yet these phallocentric structures also repeatedly turn fuzzy and uncertain in *Lucinde*. In the first place, as Martha Helfer has recently argued, the text's autoerotic and homoerotic registers frequently turn intensely sensual, and become legible as "same-sex desire".[17] At the beginning of his "Lehrjahre" Julius pursues young men with a love that dares to speak its name rather passionately:

> Die Frauen kannte er eigentlich gar nicht, ungeachtet er schon früh gewohnt war, mit ihnen zu sein. Sie erschienen ihm wunderbar fremd, oft ganz unbegreiflich und kaum wie Wesen seiner Gattung. Junge Männer aber, die ihm einigermaßen glichen, umfaßte er mit heißer Liebe und mit einer wahren Wut von Freundschaft. (36)

And a little later in his mini-*Bildungsroman*, having had some painful heterosexual experiences, Julius goes through a phase when he decides to make of "männliche Freundschaft" the "eigentlichen Geschäft seines Lebens": "Jeden Mann, der ihm interessant erschien, suchte er, und ruhte nicht, bis er ihn gewonnen und die Zurückhaltung des andern durch seine jugendliche Zudringlichkeit und Zuversicht besiegt hatte" (45). (And the narrator adds: "Es läßt sich denken, daß er, der sich eigentlich alles erlaubt hielt und sich selbst über das Lächerliche wegsetzen konnte, eine andre Schicklichkeit im Sinne und vor Augen hatte als die, welche allgemein gilt".) In one of Julius's letters to Antonio which follow the "Lehrjahre" section, he tells off his friend with more than a touch of campy bitchiness: "Ich eile zu Eduard. Alles ist verabredet. Wir wollen nicht bloß zusammen leben, sondern im brüderlichen Bunde vereint wirken und handeln" (76). The text warns us on the same page that friendship is possibly "etwas Falsches und Verkehrtes" (76). We should also note that as

---

[17] Martha B. Helfer: "Confessions of an Improper Man": Friedrich Schlegel's *Lucinde*. In: *Outing Goethe and His Age*. Pp. 174-93, here p. 177.

part of *Lucinde*'s destabilization of Lacoue-Labarthe's "Hegelian" identification of the homoerotic and the spiritual, the novel renders shifty the difference between friendship and love.[18] At one point Lucinde is Julius's "volkommende Freundin" (10); at another point, love becomes a term capable of absorbing its spiritualized double: "Es ist alles in der Liebe: Freundschaft, schöner Umgang, Sinnlichkeit, und auch Leidenschaft" (35). The "Rhetorik der Liebe", we are told, should be directed at women – but "nächstdem," the text adds, in a democratic spirit, "freilich auch an die Jünglinge, und an die Männer die noch Jünglinge geblieben sind" (20-21). It is true, as Catriona MacLeod writes, that the novel tends to depict "male homosexuality as a seductive but perilous phase in the hero's erotic Bildung, a phase that is domesticated in favor of the relationship with a woman, and a woman who is also, and importantly, a mother".[19] But it is nonetheless also true that no process or state of "erotic Bildung" achieves real stability in *Lucinde*. Julius's letter to Antonio about Eduard, for instance, as noted a moment ago, comes *after* the "Lehrjahre" interlude; and *Lucinde*'s narrative organization is sufficiently underdetermined, or at least sufficiently opaque to analysis, that one could imagine a second part of *Lucinde* – the part Schlegel never completed – made up of any number of erotic permutations.

The phallocentric economy thus incorporates into its workings a good deal of ambiguity and slippage; and I suggest that there is reason to take the "etwas Falsches und Verkehrtes" that labors, at least potentially, at the heart of friendship, as a version of something Schlegel elsewhere calls irony. We may consider at this point a bit of dialogue from one of his fragmentary drafts for the second part of *Lucinde* entitled "Vom Wesen der Freundschaft", in which two men, Julius and Lorenzo, discuss irony as part of a discussion of joking, pain, and friendship. "Der Scherz darf mit allem scherzen, der Scherz ist frei und allgemein", Julius remarks. For this reason he is opposed to jokes: "Es giebt Stellen meines Daseyns und zwar des innigsten, wo also an gemeine Verletzung nicht zu denken ist, und an diesen Stellen kann ich den Scherz nicht ertragen". Thus, he continues, "die Ironie ist es, die mich in der Musik der Freundschaft oft

---

[18] Of the many studies that have recently advanced our understanding of the play of the "homoerotic" in various European cultures, perhaps the most indispensable are those of Eve Sedgwick. See Eve Kosofsky Sedgwick: *Between Men: English Literature and Male Homosocial Desire*. New York 1985; and *Epistemology of the Closet*. Berkeley 1990.
[19] MacLeod (note 16). Pp. 207-08.

durch einen hellen Mislaut gestört hat" (85). Lorenzo, however, suggests that irony and friendship are inextricable, if not always entirely compatible, and the discussion takes one of those dizzying turns we associate with Schlegel on irony:

> *Lorenzo*: Und wer weiß ob das nicht die Ironie der Ironie ist, daß man sie am Ende doch auch nicht mag.
> *Julius*: Die möcht' ich eher darin finden, daß es Dir unmöglich zu werden scheint, ohne Ironie über die Ironie zu reden.
> *Lorenzo*: Ich fürchte grade das Gegentheil. Wo sollte da die Ironie herkommen, wenn man in bitterm Ernst nicht weiß, woran man ist. Und je mehr ich denke, je unbegreiflicher wirds mir. (V, 85)

What is remarkable here is that Lorenzo goes on to specify that what is incomprehensible is that Julian should find irony incompatible with friendship: "Nun wenn die Ironie nicht das eigentliche Wesen der Freundschaft ist, so mögen es die Götter wissen, was sie eigentlich ist, oder sie mag es selbst wissen. Ich weiß es dann nicht" (86).

Note that Lorenzo is canny enough – ironic enough – to overstate and understate his claim in the same breath: irony may not be the essence of friendship, since Lorenzo may not know what irony is; on the other hand it seems that if irony has anything to do with friendship, the relation will be essential. Irony, it seems, has something fundamental – if also something fundamentally uncertain – to do with social life and libidinal relations. Love itself, it turns out, is always possibly another name for irony.[20] The irony of eros binds the social order: "das Feinste und das Beste" of good society is "der Scherz mit der Liebe und die Liebe zum Scherz" (V, 34). Yet this binding is also a wounding.[21] In the present context it is perhaps worth emphasizing not so much the incomprehensibility of irony as the aesthetic effectivity that characterizes this incomprehensibility.

[20] As Schlegel was in fact to write many years later, at the beginning of the third of his Dresden lectures of 1829: "Die wahre Ironie, da es doch auch eine falsche giebt – und diese eine Bemerkung habe ich nur noch zu dem Vorhergehenden anzufügen – ist die Ironie der Liebe" (X, 357).
[21] Furthermore, because love and friendship slide easily into each other in *Lucinde*, the pain of friendship reappears, linked to the wounding powers of language, as that of a woman submitted to (presumably heterosexual) intercourse: "Laß auch die Worte oder die Menschen ein Mißverständnis zwischen uns erregen! Der tiefe Schmerz würde flüchtig sein und sich bald in vollkommenere Harmonie auflösen. Ich würde ihn so wenig achten, wie die liebende Geliebte im Enthusiasmus der Wollust die kleine Verletzung achtet" (V, 12).

Irony disturbs friendship but threatens to be its essence, causing pain in the "innigsten" places of being. The freedom and universality of the joke makes its contact with the world unpredictable, but if anything more forceful for being incalculable. Irony's "absolute power to do anything", as Kierkegaard puts it, does not result in or derive from a flight from historical actuality: irony rather inscribes itself on the world precisely *because* it is incalculable.[22] Nor is this force simply negative in its effects: friendship and love themselves possibly derive from the pains (or pleasures) of irony.

How might gender difference and sexual identity be thought in relation to this performative power of irony? The question is not as strange as it might at first sound. If Schlegel is thinking of irony as a force capable of wounding, inspiring, and perhaps even constructing a desiring self, his notion of irony would resemble aspects of what Judith Butler calls the "psychic life of power". Far from being either the rhetorical strategem or the self-reflexive play of a self-conscious subject, irony would be a movement of "Unverständlichkeit" that enables (and destabilizes) the acts of meaning-production through which bodies and subjects come into being. Contemporary theory has various vocabularies in which to indicate these formative acts; Butler's exemplary texts draw on – and critique, and displace – speculations by Foucault and Althusser as well as Lacan and Freud (among many other texts, of course), in order to mount arguments for the radical constructedness of gender identity, sexual orientation, and the body. Building on Freud's resonant claim that "the ego is first and foremost a bodily ego",[23] Butler suggests that both the body and the ego are constructed through fantasmatic processes of projection, incorporation, and exclusion: that gender is "performed" as a reiteration of norms and conventions that constitutes the (gendered) subject in and as this very process of reiteration; that the (sexed) body is "material" in and as a somewhat analogous process of "materialization". "To claim that discourse is formative is not to claim that it originates, causes, or exhaustively composes that which it concedes", Butler writes; "rather, it is to claim that there is no reference to a pure body which is not at the same time a further

---

[22] Kierkegaard: op. cit., p. 275: Irony, in the wake of Schlegel and Tieck's misreading of Fichte, "functioned as that for which nothingness was an existent, as that which finished with everything, and also as that which had the absolute power to do everything".
[23] Sigmund Freud: *The Ego and the Id*. In: *The Standard Edition of the Complete Psychological Works of Sigmund Freud*. Ed. James Strachey. London 1953-74. Vol. XIX. P. 16.

formation of that body". Both in the case of the gendered subject or the sexed body, in other words, "the constative claim is always to some degree performative": the process of reiteration *generates* the illusion of an "essential" gender, a "material" body.[24] To name Schlegel's uncanny notion of irony as the transcendental precondition of such processes of subjection is in a sense to do no more than to insist on their radical ungroundedness. But one can also follow out in a Schlegelian vein Butler's recent speculations on the melancholy character of gender identity. The argument here is that the achievement of a gendered identity, above all a heterosexual one, not only requires the subject to renounce other (above all, same-sex) love objects, but also requires the subject to disavow this very renunciation: "what ensues is a culture of gender melancholy in which masculinity and femininity emerge as the traces of an ungrieved and ungrievable love".[25] Melancholy may not be the mood one tends to associate with *Lucinde*, but like Sterne's *Tristram Shandy*, Schlegel's novel skirts the edges of pain and disaster: *Musik* can become *Mislaut* (85); "blundering" can turn violent.[26] And what Schlegel calls "irony" would here name something like the inevitable risk of damage and loss: an immemorial risk that leaves in its wake irreducible possibilities of melancholy as well as of mirth.

Lucinde addresses the ironic instability of gender systematically in the chapter entitled "Eine Reflexion". Parodying Fichtean metaphysics, this chapter proleptically deconstructs Hegel's canonical definition of Romantic irony as a concept that has its "tieferen Grund [...] nach einer ihrer Seiten hin, in der *Fichteschen* Philosophie, insofern die Prinzipien dieser Philosophie auf die Kunst angewendet wurden".[27] *Pace* Hegel, "Eine Reflexion" tells a story about

---

[24] Judith Butler: *Bodies that Matter.* Pp. 10-11. See also Butler's earlier *Gender Trouble: Feminism and the Subversion of Identity.* New York and London 1990.

[25] See especially: Melancholy Gender/ Refused Identification. In: Judith Butler: *The Psychic Life of Power: Theories in Subjection.* Stanford 1997. Pp. 132-50, here p. 140.

[26] As in the novel's bizarre closing section, "Tändelein der Fantasie", for instance, where the first-person narrator fantasizes the premature death of his own (as yet, presumably, unborn) son, followed by an erotic approach to his brother's wife: "Gedankenvoll streue ich Blumen auf das Grab des zu früh entschlafnen Sohnes, die ich bald voll Freude und voll Hoffnung der Braut des geliebten Bruders darreiche [...]" (81).

[27] *Vorlesungen über die Ästhetik.* XIII. P. 93. This because, in the abstract space of the Fichtean ego, "[ist] jede Besonderheit, Bestimmtheit, jeder Inhalt in demselben negiert – denn alle Sache geht in diese abstrakte Freiheit und

the uncertain formation of identity, and does so via the sort of *double entendre* that the male voice of "Treue und Scherz" recommends: "Dazu sind die Zweideutigkeiten auch gut, nur sind sie so selten zweideutig, und wenn sie es nicht sind und nur einen Sinn zulassen, das ist eben nicht unsittlich, aber zudringlich und platt" (34). In the process, the text destabilizes gender difference and disarticulates identity, to the point that one is forced to conclude that if *Lucinde* is a *Bildungsroman*, as the secondary literature occasionally suggests, it is so only in the ironic sense in which Schlegel understood *Bildung*:

> *Bildung* ist antithetische Synthesis, und Vollendung bis zur Ironie. – Bei einem Menschen, der eine gewisse Höhe und Universalität d[er] Bildung erreicht hat, ist sein Innres eine fortgehende Kette der ungeheuersten Revoluzionen. (XVIII, 82-83)

III

Lucinde, as we have seen, constantly reflects upon sexual difference, but never more vibrantly or crazily than in "Eine Reflexion". It and the "Dithyrambische Fantasie über die schönste Situation" were the two sections of the novel that most scandalized the "gebildete Redner" of the era, who, Schlegel tells us, would prefer to name sexual matters "nur durch ihre Namenlosigkeit" – a prohibition that the Reflection both respects and violates through a running *double entendre*:

> Es ist meinem Gemüt nicht selten sonderbar aufgefallen, wie verständige und würdige Menschen mit nie ermüdender Industrie und mit so großem Ernst das kleine Spiel in ewigem Kreislauf immer von neuem wiederholen können, welches doch offenbar weder Nutzen bringt noch sich einem Ziele nähert, obgleich es das früheste aller Spiele sein mag. Dann fragte mein Geist, was wohl die Natur, die überall so viel denkt, die List im Großen treibt und statt witzig zu reden, gleich witzig handelt, bei jenen naiven Andeutung denken mag, welche gebildete Redner nur durch ihre Namenlosigkeit benennen.

Einheit unter [...]"; and the ego rejoices in an empty, yet corrosive potency: "Was ist, ist nur durch das Ich, und was durch mich ist, kann ich ebensosehr auch wieder vernichten [...]" (93). "[I]n keiner Sphäre der Sittlichkeit, Rechtlichkeit, des Menschlichen und Göttlichen, Profanen und Heiligen gibt es etwas, das nicht durch Ich erst zu setzen wäre und deshalb von Ich ebensosehr könnte zunichte gemacht werden. Dadurch ist alles Anundfürsichseiende nur ein *Schein* [...]" (94).

Und diese Namenlosigkeit selbst ist von zweideutiger Bedeutung. Je ver-
schämter und je moderner man ist, je mehr wird es Mode sie aufs Scham-
lose zu deuten. Für die alten Götter hingegen hat alles Leben eine gewisse
klassische Würde und so auch die unverschämte Heldenkunst lebendig zu
machen. Die Menge solcher Werke und die Größe der Erfindungskraft in ihr
bestimmt Rang und Adel im Reiche der Mythologie. (72)

Before it can even be said to be well underway, the Reflection has
gathered enough density to slow commentary to a crawl. And it has
done so in that inimitable Schlegelian tone – half sly, half enthusiastic – that for two centuries has infuriated certain readers of Schlegel:
the tone of an *ernsten Scherz* which renders ludicrous, or as Schlegel
would say, *ungeschickt*, the interpretive activity it provokes.[28] Nor
is there a graceful way out from such blundering: if one were to stride
through the difficulties of the Reflection with, for instance, the
insouciance of an aesthete, enjoying Schlegel's joke and paying no
mind to his text's difficulties, one would simply blunder more ludi-
crously. The entire scandal of *Lucinde* replays itself in miniature and
at triple speed in "Eine Reflexion": the text thematizes a sexual,
aesthetic, and hermeneutic "obscenity" that, because of the radically
unstable character of its irony, it also *performs*. But if we are con-
demned to blunder, this fate has its consolations: as the text gathers
density here, it reflects upon the language of gender that structures
Schlegel's novel. Blundering is a male prerogative in *Lucinde*; but
what is it to be male as we approach the force-field of the obscene?
Is blundering gendered at such points, or is gender itself the effect, or
act, of a certain blundering?

As a first step, or stumble, toward such issues we need to consider
the way in which the text speaks the unspokenness of "sex" – the
little game played, like that of interpretation, with such ludicrous
earnestness, over and over again. The game, a parodic double of
Schillerian *Spiel*, has no usefulness and no goal (*Ziel*); oddly enough,
it doesn't even seem to be motivated by what we ordinarily think of
as desire. Elsewhere in *Lucinde* Schlegel writes eloquently of the

---

[28] The phrase "diese sehr ernsten Scherze" is Goethe's description of *Faust* in
a letter to Humboldt that was the last letter he wrote before his death (17
March 1832); for commentary see Ehrhard Bahr: *Die Ironie im Spätwerk
Goethes*. Berlin 1972. Pp. 13-39. From this perspective one may understand
Schlegel's irony as an irony *of* irony: an ironization of the aesthetic irony that
Bahr discerns in Goethe, or of the philosophico-aesthetic irony that many
critics have sought to discern in Schlegel (see note 7, above). "Mit der Ironie
ist durchaus nicht zu scherzen", Schlegel warns us (jokingly and seriously, of
course) in "Über die Unverständlichkeit" (II, 369).

pleasures of the body, but here the game's players seem driven by a compulsion so absurd as to make any sort of pleasure, even aesthetic pleasure, irrelevant. In its sheer formalism the "little game" also has nothing to do with the reproductive sexuality celebrated by *Lucinde*'s narrator in the first of the "Zwei Briefe" that precede "Eine Reflexion". When the narrator asks himself what Nature was thinking of when she invented this game – asks, that is, after the meaning of the game – he pointedly avoids naturalistic or teleological language, and instead emphasizes "language" per se: "Dann fragte mein Geist, was wohl die Natur [...] bei jenen naiven Andeutung denken mag, welche gebildete Redner nur durch ihre Namenlosigkeit benennen". As an "Andeutung", the sexual game is a textual act, a referral of meaning elsewhere – which accords with the game's repetitive character. The sexual act refers for its meaning to other instances of its own repetition: to the sheer iterability through which the game retains its identity. Its meaning is its performance; and indeed, "Nature", in Schlegel's odd allegory, lends nothing natural to the game – neither affective content nor reproductive purpose – but rather seems to personify the performative force of language. Nature, who "statt witzig zu reden, gleich witzig handelt", emits "Andeutungen" that *occur* as the witticism of sex.

Sex, then, is akin to a speech-act: the game is a performance, and has no constative function. Yet the narrator, keen to know Nature's thoughts, asks after the game's meaning anyway; and indeed, the performative's iterative structure translates performance into meaning as tautology, as we have already seen. The meaning of fucking is fucking; the act "means" the formality of its own occurrence as repetition. At this point, however, Schlegel's text introduces a further complication. Confronted by the denaturalized linguistic performance of the *kleinen Spiel*, cultured people, the *gebildete Redner* – that is, anyone capable of reading, let alone writing, *Lucinde* – name it through and as its "Namenlosigkeit". This trope, Schlegel's narrator tells us, is a perversion particular to our modern era. The ancients troped the sexual act with dignity, in the figural language of myth; we moderns react against the shame with which we are burdened by shamelessly pretending that we can name namelessness. The trope "Namenlosigkeit" is the product and the denegation of shame. *Lucinde* offers us here a compressed version of Freud's insight that sexual repression makes culture and its *gebildeten Redner* possible, yet also suggests the pertinence of Foucault's sly twist: the repression exists in order to confirm, indeed, to generate, the existence of something called "sexuality" in the first place. The prohibition is enormously productive: of witticism and double-entendre; of respectability and scandal; in a Foucaultian vein one might extrapolate the production of scientific or medico-legal discourses that would pursue the nameless truth of reality as "sexual identity". In its abstract, single-minded negativity, the trope "Namenlosigkeit" pretends to be a name rather than a figure; and the more literally one thinks one is naming the thing in question, the more deluded one is – which, of course, makes us the real bunglers when we think we have named the referent of *Lucinde*'s parody ("the sexual act"), let alone when we uncork late-twentieth-century rhetorical timidities ("the meaning of fucking is fucking") as I did a moment ago. "Namenlosigkeit" totalizes the endless, mechanical iteration of a performative (Nature's performative, the "little game") into meaning as the absence of meaning. Like the phallus, the sign of lack that organizes the symbolic order, "Namenlosigkeit" symbolizes a sexual prohibition that would be coextensive with language itself. Naming the impossibility of naming, it is castration as pure signifier, signifying the endless displacement of meaning. Such is Schlegel's allegory of the phallus: the idealization of repetition as lack.

Yet though in a certain sense the phallus has already arrived on the scene, sex and gender differences have been hesitating in the wings. The "little game", contentless as it is, thus far could be played by anyone and is played by everyone, and thus presumably entails any and every possible ensemble of sexes, genders, and erotic dispensations. Sexual difference and heterosexual emplotment only emerge after the "Reflexion" has moved fully into its parody of Fichte:

> Diese Zahl und diese Kraft sind gut, aber sie sind nicht das Höchste. Wo schlummert also das ersehnte Ideal verborgen? Oder findet das strebende Herz in der höchsten aller darstellenden Künste ewig nur andere Manieren und nie einen vollendeten Styl?
> Das Denken hat die Eigenheit, daß es nächst sich selbst am liebsten über das denkt, worüber es ohne Ende denken kann. Darum ist das Leben des gebildeten und sinnigen Menschen ein stetes Bilden und Sinnen über das schöne Rätsel seiner Bestimmung. Er bestimmt sie immer neu, denn eben das ist seine ganze Bestimmung, bestimmt zu werden und zu bestimmen. Nur in seinem Suchen selbst findet der Geist der Menschen das Geheimnis welches er sucht.
> Was ist denn aber das Bestimmende oder das Bestimmte selbst? In der Männlichkeit ist es das Namenlose. Und was ist das Namenlose in der Weiblichkeit? – das Unbestimmte. (72)

Classical art, empowered by its healthy language of myth, achieved a good way of naming of the nameless; but the "darstellende Künste" of the era of the French Revolution, *Wilhelm Meister*, and Fichte's philosophy can perhaps aspire to an even more glorious mode of *Darstellung* – to a "vollendeten Styl" – because of the self-developing self-determination of Fichtean humanity. Schlegel's first extended *double entendre* had concerned the useless and direction-less "little game" that sensible and respectable people repeat end-lessly, "mit nie ermüdender Industrie und mit so großem Ernst"; now, he transposes that activity into a Fichtean key: "Darum ist das Leben des gebildeten und sinnigen Menschen ein stetes Bilden und Sinnen über das schöne Rätsel seiner Bestimmung". *Namenlosigkeit* becomes the *Rätsel* or *Geheimnis* fueling the human subject's endless self-reflexive self-development; and in Schlegel's hands the Fichtean process of *Bildung* becomes as absurdly mechanical and repetitive as the little game it plays: "Er bestimmt [seine Bestimmung] immer neu, denn eben das ist seine ganze Bestimmung, bestimmt zu werden und zu bestimmen". This magnificently tautological stutter repeats the repetitive insistence of the *kleinen Spiel*, but repeats it as the illusory activity of a subject. The *Bestimmung* is an illusion because it defines itself as self-defining, whereas in fact it repeats Nature's performance. Nature, which "überall so viel denkt", is echoed as subjective thought: "Das Denken hat die Eigenheit, daß es nächst sich selbst am liebsten über das denkt, worüber es ohne Ende denken kann" – the endless object of thought being, of course (thanks to the inevitable *double entendre*) the "little game". And since this little game *is* Nature's thought as sheer performance or act, the Fichtean language of *Selbstbestimmung* is doubly deluded: it is a repetition that pretends to be a self-sufficiency, and it is a translation of sheer performative repetition into a *Bildungsgeschichte*. A visibly illusory *Bildungsgeschichte*, to be sure, so long as the "Bestimmung des Menschen" remains a comic tautology.

It is at this point that the Reflection reflects on sex and gender difference, in a dense paragraph that provides a hinge upon which the episode turns: "Was ist denn aber das Bestimmende oder das Bestimmte selbst? In der Männlichkeit ist es das Namenlose. Und was ist das Namenlose in der Weiblichkeit? – das Unbestimmte". I shall return shortly to the difficult role played by the "Namenlose" in this passage; for the moment we may register the obvious fact that, thanks to the mediation of this *Namenlose*, the difference between "Männlichkeit" and "Weiblichkeit" becomes that between the *Bestimmende/Bestimmte*, on the one hand, and the *Unbestimmte* on the other. A difference, that is, becomes an *opposition*: a logical and ontological binary opposition capable of organizing a universe. And that is exactly what happens in the remaining paragraphs of

"Eine Reflexion" as modalities of determination and indetermination, gendered masculine and feminine, divide out existence itself:

Das Unbestimmte ist geheimnisreicher, aber das Bestimmte hat mehr Zauberkraft. Die reizende Verwirrung des Unbestimmten ist romantischer, aber die erhabene Bildung des Bestimmten ist genialischer [...]. Wer kann messen und wer kann vergleichen was eines wie das andre unendlichen Wert hat, wenn beides verbunden ist in der wirklichen Bestimmung, die bestimmt ist, alle Lücken zu ergänzen und Mittlerin zu sein zwischen dem männlichen und weiblichen Einzelnen und der unendlichen Menschheit? Das Bestimmte und das Unbestimmte und die ganze Fülle ihrer bestimmten und unbestimmten Beziehungen; das is das Eine und Ganze [...]. Das Universum selbst ist nur ein Spielwerk des Bestimmten und des Unbestimmten und das wirkliche Bestimmen des Bestimmbaren ist eine allegorische Miniatur auf das Leben und Weben der ewig strömenden Schöpfung. (72-73)

Schlegel's text retains its sly irony: the play of the determined and the undetermined is a "Spiel*werk*", a term that retains a hint of the mechanical repetition of the "kleinen Spiel" with which the Reflection began. And the contrasting qualities of the *Bestimmten* and *Unbestimmten* are pseudo-oppositions: their characteristics are paired contrastively ("the determined is X, but the undetermined is not-X"), but don't actually oppose each other ("geheimnisreicher"/"mehr Zauberkraft"; "romantischer"/"genialischer"; etc.). More than a hint of zaniness thus enlivens a phallocentric speculation that is submitting masculine determination and feminine indetermination to the priapic rule of a "wirklichen Bestimmung, die bestimmt ist, alle Lücken zu ergänzen". With the invocation of this truer, higher *Bestimmung*, the Reflection sums up, in terms that mix the sparkle of *double entendre* into the august colors of speculative philosophy, the novel's androcentric androgyny. The masculine is the whole and the part, and the feminine is the part and the lack. And the masculine is the male and the feminine is the female, since gender difference, infused with the powers of the Fichtean dialectic, absorbs sexual difference. And the masculine, as male, and the feminine, as female, pair with each other to redefine the "little game" as a heterosexual one. Thus the repetitive, emptily mechanical little game, infused with gender content and refigured as a heterosexual dialectic, becomes *Lucinde*'s version of the striving of Fichtean man, who forever creates himself in an asymptotic approach to the total freedom of self-determination.

The Reflection's playful tone, disjointed binary oppositions, and running *double entendre* do not incapacitate its phallocentrism; but such a degree of textual density does suggest the wisdom of reading the section with as much care as possible, particularly at the moment in which it represents the emergence of gender difference. It is never a good idea to imagine that one knows what's going on in *Lucinde*, particularly in the nameless reaches of sexuality, as becomes clear – as clear as anything becomes in this text, anyway – if we return to reexamine the peculiar role played by "das Namenlose" in the appearance of masculine and feminine:

> Was ist denn aber das Bestimmende oder das Bestimmte selbst? In der Männlichkeit ist es das Namenlose. Und was ist das Namenlose in der Weiblichkeit? – das Unbestimmte.

Given the paragraph's rhetorical structure we might have expected Schlegel to retain "determining or determined" as the mediating term which is being split into masculine and feminine (i.e.: "But what is the determining or determined itself? For the masculine it is X; for the feminine it is Y"). Instead the question of "das Bestimmende oder das Bestimmte selbst" is left dangling, attached only to the "masculine"; and a new term, the neuter abstraction "das Namenlose", enters to link, or suture, masculine to feminine, and determination to indetermination. One effect of this rhetorical zigzag is to grant the terms "Männlichkeit" and "Weiblichkeit" the dignity of primary terms, since they seize upon "das Namenlose" from the outside, as it were, to determine it in their various ways (as determination, as indetermination).[29] And at the same time, as we

---

[29] Apart from its generally Fichtean language of striving, self-determination, and so on, Schlegel's text may be parodying here one of Fichte's more peculiar propositions in the *Grundlage des Naturrechts* (1797), which is that sexual difference is ontologically prior to nature. Sexual difference, in fact, makes "Nature" possible, by making form possible: without sexual difference, Nature's "bildende Kraft" would have nowhere to pause, and there would be a constant transformation of forms, a process of becoming in which no being could come to presence. "So ist keine Natur möglich", Fichte comments. "Sollte sie möglich seyn, so mußte die Gattung noch eine andere organische Existenz haben, ausser der als Gattung; doch aber als Gattung da seyn, um sich fortpflanzen zu können. Dies war nur dadurch möglich, daß die Gattung bildende Kraft vertheilt, gleichsam in zwei absolut zusammen gehörende, und nur in ihrer Vereinigung ein sich fortpflanzendes Ganzes ausmachende Hälften zerrissen würde". J.G. Fichte: *Grundlage des Naturrechts nach Principien der Wissenschaftslehre*. In: *J.G. Fichte-Gesamtausgabe der Bayerischen Akademie*

have seen, phallocentrism installs itself as the logic of this binary opposition (for if, as we had been told in the previous paragraph, "der gebildete und sinnige Mensch" is that which determines itself, the masculine becomes the very essence and destiny of this self-determining power). But the term "Namenlose", slightly but significantly different from the term "Namenlosigkeit" that had earlier served as the privileged trope for *das kleine Spiel*, sutures the terms of the phallocentric, heterosexual conceptual universe at a cost. "Die Namenlosigkeit" is an abstract noun with an illusory but determined relation to its referent ("welche gebildete Redner nur durch ihre Namenlosigkeit benennen"); the little game, in other words, is taken to possess a quality, *Namenlosigkeit*, that educated people use as a synecdoche to describe the game itself. "Das Namenlose", however, though it inevitably triggers the *double entendre* and suggests the little game, also recedes from it. "Das Namenlose" is not a quality but an entity, at once specific and indeterminate: an entity named as the nameless and only as the nameless. The formal emptiness of the little game achieves here a certain radical purity. And in the process all tropes that would seek to substitute for, and thereby interpret or grant meaning to the *Namenlose*, including the mock-Schillerian trope of a "kleinen Spiel", become legibly arbitrary and uncertain. The *double entendre* may be inevitable, but here also becomes as uncertain – let us also say, as unsophisticated, as blundering – as any other meaning.

Though the terms "Männlichkeit" and "Weiblichkeit" assert themselves as fundamental terms, their contact with the "Namenlose" infects and destabilizes both them and the speculative dialectic they enable. The Reflection's parody of Fichte turns on the legibility of a difference between the nameless in the masculine and the nameless in the feminine: only thus can there be a certain difference between the determined and the undetermined – or, for that matter, a stable difference between masculine and feminine. This difference – the difference between one "Namenlose" and another – is inherently uncertain, precisely because the *Namenlose* is *namenlos*: uncertainly singular or dual or plural, uncertainly self-identical or self-different. Masculinity and femininity become a binary opposition thanks to a passage through a neutral space in which all determination is lost – as well as all "indetermination", to the extent that indetermination is opposed to determination, and thus determined

der Wissenschaften. Ed. Reihnard Lauth, Hans Jacobs, and Hans Gliwitsky. Stuttgart-Bad Cannstatt 1964-. Vol. I,4. P. 96. Subsequent references to Fichte are to this edition.

by and ultimately reducible to it. Masculinity and femininity become the violent, arbitrary *taking* of a difference. Gender imposes itself as a performance and a fiction: the fictional transformation of uncertainty into the determinations of identity.

Das Namenlose thus "names" an uncertainty at the heart of the abstract negativity of *Namenlosigkeit* and its dialectic of *Bildung*. The *Namenlose* provides for the emergence of the opposition between determination and indetermination, and, through the lens of gender, it "names" the essence of determination ("Was ist denn aber das Bestimmende oder das Bestimmte *selbst*? [...]"), but only through the non-essence of an indeterminate indeterminacy. At the turning point of the phallo-ontological system, one cannot tell the diference between determination or indetermination, masculinity or femininity; and this hinge-point is also by no means either sexless or "androgynous", for the absence or presence or copresence or synthesis of genders is just as uncertain as the genders themselves. The *Namenlose* is both inside and outside the phallo-ontological system; it is the neutral at work in the negative, the blank screen upon which the phallus, as image of lack, is projected. In the terms of the metaphor that Rodolphe Gasché has elaborated out of Derrida's work, the *Namenlose* is the "tain of the mirror": the dull, unreflecting support that enables the universe of mimesis, but remains unassimilable to it.[30] Schlegel's parody of Fichte is thus also a rigorous and radical critique of speculative philosophy. A Schlegelian reader of Fichte might, for instance, hear the neutral tones of the *Namenlose* in the third-person *Ich* of Fichte's *Wissenschaftslehre*: "Das Ich setzt ursprünglich schlechthin sein eignes Seyn", where the third person registers the trace of the neutral, the otherness that resists yet enables the self-positing of the I – the uncertainty which, as Werner Hamacher argues, must characterize any genuine act of positing, yet which must also instantly be forgotten.[31] In the gender allegory of

---

[30] Rodolphe Gasché: *The Tain of the Mirror: Derrida and the Philosophy of Reflection*. Cambridge, Mass. 1986.
[31] J.G. Fichte: *Grundlage der gesammten Wissenschaftslehre* (1794). In: J.G. Fichte: *Gesamtausgabe*. Vol. I, 2. P. 261. Werner Hamacher's analysis of the Fichtean proposition of the I discerns a tension that Hamacher describes as an incompatibility between constative and performative language: "Der unbedingte Grundsatz des Ich ist reines Setzen und als solches Vollzug und Ereignis, Handlung und Prozeß des Satzes; aber er ist zugleich das Gesetzte und als solches schon das Produkt, das Ergebnis, das Faktum des Satzes. Als reines Setzen ist er offen, irreferentiell, kontext- und bedeutungslos; als Gesetztes ist er abgeschlossen, eine Tatsache und ebensosehr das bestimmte – nicht

"Eine Reflexion", one could rephrase this unthinkable, random neutrality as the shadow of the German indefinite pronoun "man" within "Mann" (or "Mensch", or "Weib"). "Nun ist alles klar! Daher die Allgegenwart der *namenlosen* unbekannten Gottheit" (73), the narrator tells us near the end of "Eine Reflection", pretending to affirm a genial sort of pantheism, and actually registering the force of a neutrality that ruins all clarity and all presence. The little game's "ewigen Kreislauf" thus becomes the figure of the performative force of this neutrality: the active pressure of its unbearable passivity. And at this point, in a comic reverse parabasis, the Reflection forgets itself and disappears: "Sich vertiefend in diese Individualität nahm die Reflexion eine so individuelle Richtung, daß sie bald anfing aufzuhören und sich selbst zu vergessen".

To bring the present reflection on "Eine Reflection" to a less dramatic end, we may note that *Lucinde* confirms the performativity of gender, and teaches us furthermore that the "materiality" of the body is best understood as a name for the nameless uncertainty through which signification occurs, and through which bodies achieve shape and meaning. Such materiality may be thought of as "linguistic" insofar as the trope of language suggests an irreducible coimplication of materiality and difference. Sexuality in *Lucinde* can occur only as a disguised and displaced version of such radical uncertainty. The regime of heterosexuality is at once coercive and fragile, as *Lucinde* takes pleasure in showing us. Yet the text's flashily camp moments are no more and no less mobile and erratic, no more and no less represent the sexual "truth" of the novel, than do the seemingly heterosexual idylls of "Sehnsucht und Ruhe" and "Tändelein der Fantasie" with which this fragmentary novel "ends", or the polymorphous perversity of little Wilhelmine with which it more or less begins. This is not to suggest that sexuality escapes history, but rather that sex and gender are historical through and through, and this precisely because they are always figures, uncer-

---

mehr bloß bestimmende – Subjekt wie das mögliche Objekt von Aussagen". Thus "[d]er Doppelsatz, der dem Fichteschen Grundsatz eingeschrieben ist, reißt diesen Grundsatz also auseinander: schiere Performation, ist die Setzung *Ich* keiner Konstatierung fähig, ist sie absoluter Exzeß über jede mögliche Vergegenständlichung und jedes sich in einem Objekt also sich selbst reflektierende Subjekt". Werner Hamacher: *Entferntes Verstehen: Studien zu Philosophie und Literatur von Kant bis Celan.* Frankfurt a.M. 1998. Pp. 205, 208. See Hamacher's chapter, "Der ausgesetzte Satz: Friedrich Schlegels poetologische Umsetzung von Fichtes absolutem Grundsatz". In: *Entferntes Verstehen,* pp. 195-234.

tainly inscribed, constantly in need of reconfirmation and rein-
forcement. For the inscription of figure occurs via the uncertainty
of the *Namenlose*, which names the impossible condition of the
production of meaning. The meanings of the body are manifold and
mobile. The *materiality* of the body is the "Namenlose" as the
disruptive condition, which is to say the fundamental ob-scenity, of
all bodily figures and combinations. *Lucinde*'s truth of sex, in other
words, is a permanent ironic parabasis; and from this perspective
Kierkegaard was right: it may be that even the purest readers, blundering through this novel, will not escape unscathed. In this risk lies
the promise of the kind of textual event that, after Schlegel, we call
literature.

Michel Chaouli

Critical Mass, Fission, Fusion
Friedrich Schlegel's Volatile System

The essay attempts to understand the relationship of fragment and system in the early work of Friedrich Schlegel neither in dialectical nor organic terms, but rather as an inorganic system, modeled on Schlegel's notion of writing, that consists of the process of division and combination. Taken in homology with the social sphere, this dynamic system would seem to offer the promise of euphoric freedom from rigid structures, yet it does so at the cost of a sudden break-down in communication that yields not freedom but social psychosis.

> Viele Leute halten nur das für ein System, was einen großen Klumpen in der Mitte hat.
> – Friedrich Schlegel[1]

> Fragmentary writing is risk, it would seem: risk itself.
> – Maurice Blanchot[2]

Why would one try – as I will here – to chase down the elusive idea of *system* in the early work of Friedrich Schlegel? The effort seems doubly wrongheaded: either we take him at his word ("Da ich überall in Poesie und Philosophie zuerst und aus Instinkt auf das System gegangen bin, so bin ich wohl ein Universalsystematiker [...]" [KA 18, 38, No. 214]), in which case we have to address the question of why and in what ways yet another late eighteenth-century systematic thinker is of interest to us. Or we perversely emphasize the apparently scattered, disseminal, *anti*-systematic character of the work against Schlegel's own description of his philosophy as "ein System von Fragmenten" (KA 18, 100, No. 857), in which case we may end up putting so much pressure on the notion of system that it breaks. In this essay, I will end up doing some of each: reading

---

[1] *Kritische Friedrich-Schlegel-Ausgabe*. Ed. Ernst Behler et al. Munich, Paderborn, Vienna 1958ff. Cited as KA, followed by volume, page, and, where appropriate, fragment number; here KA 18, 63, No. 432.
[2] Maurice Blanchot: *The Writing of Disaster*. Trans. Ann Smok. Lincoln 1995. P. 59.

Schlegel against Schlegel while upholding a recognizable idea of system.

The question of Schlegel and system comes in three distinct though interrelated guises, and my argument, even when it is concerned with a local point, will attempt to keep all three in mind. They are:

1. The philosophical problem: At least since Horkheimer and Adorno's *Dialektik der Aufklärung* (itself programmatically subtitled *Philosophische Fragmente*) the idea of a system has been connected to a scientistically inspired, expansionist exercise of reason that, in attempting to give an account of the totality of the world, runs the danger of preparing the ground for totalitarianism. The discredit redounding to the idea of system through this unsavory association is easily countered, at least for our present purposes: regardless of the misfortunes that have befallen the idea of the system recently, there is little doubt it was among *the* crucial concepts in eighteenth-century Continental philosophy, and a historical study of its deployment in Schlegel's work would surely be uncontroversial. Uncontroversial, and quite uninteresting. Rather than focussing on its demise, I would begin by pointing to the continued vigor of the system even – *especially* – when it has been sliced and diced into fragments. For all the difference in context and argumentative force, when Horkheimer and Adorno (or for that matter Nietzsche or Blanchot) try their hands at fragmentary writing, they must – like Schlegel – concede, if only implicitly, that a fragment can only be a fragment of *something*, and though this something itself has become fragmentary (it lacks a morsel – the fragment – that has been broken off), it is at least notionally coherent, unbroken, whole – a system. As we shall see in Schlegel, the relationship of the two is not that of a static opposition (system entails fragment, fragment system). Rather, a peculiar oscillation (quite distinct from a dialectic, as we shall see) takes hold of the process, overwhelming the "volonté fragmentaire"[3] by rushing it toward the systematic pole (whether this is a dreaded or a euphoric place remains an open question), only to have it thrown back again. Though the critique of the homogenous, self-same system – be it a system of knowledge, a system of the self, or a system of society – has become as familiar to us as the air we breathe, we must for that very reason constantly contend with the appearance of the system; as Adorno has put it,

[3] Philippe Lacoue-Labarthe and Jean-Luc Nancy: Noli me frangere. In: *Revue des Sciences Humaines* 185 (1982). Pp. 83-92, here p. 87.

"Kritik liquidiert aber nicht einfach das System".[4] In few places is the dialectic of fragment and system to my knowledge more force-fully resisted and at the same time more eagerly sought than in the earliest instance of a will to fragments, which is to say in Schlegel's work.

2. The literary-historical problem: Much of the dizzying fluctuation in the ways Schlegel and early romanticism have been received hinges on the pedantic-seeming decision as to whether his writing should be put into the box labeled "Enlightenment" or in the one labeled "reactions to the Enlightenment"[5]; this decision in turn is crucially influenced by the more basic decision as to whether his work is systematic or not, since the idea of the system is closely identified with the Enlightenment. Emphasizing one or the other choice causes critics to drive Schlegel (and with him much of roman-ticism) either into Kant's arms or into the bosom of mystical irra-tionalism. That such a dichotomy is unsatisfactory, should at this point not concern us; the crucial thing is that it has been operative for almost two centuries. Ever since Hegel judged Schlegel to be unfit for philosophical argumentation,[6] the charge of irrationalism against the so-called romantic school has been a mainstay of critics, literary historians, and philosophers.[7] Right after 1945, it carried the maxi-mum political baggage when writers as ideologically at odds as Tho-mas Mann and Georg Lukács advanced the thesis of romanticism as the intellectual parent of Nazism,[8] a thesis that has shown few signs

---

[4] T.W. Adorno: *Negative Dialektik*. Frankfurt a.M. 1980. P. 35.
[5] I capitalize the term to refer specifically to a period of intellectual history in the eighteenth century, as distinct from the lower-case enlightenment of ration-alism and scientific verifiability, which in the Occidental tradition is as old as philosophy itself.
[6] G.W.F. Hegel: *Vorlesungen zur Ästhetik. Werke*. Ed. Eva Moldenhauer and Karl Markus Michel. Frankfurt a.M. 1968. Vol. 13. Pp. 92ff.
[7] See Karl Heinz Bohrer: *Die Kritik der Romantik*. Frankfurt a.M. 1989.
[8] Thomas Mann's most explicit critique of romanticism comes in a speech held at the Library of Congress in June 1945, and first published as *Deutsch-land und die Deutschen* (Stockholm 1947); the discussion of romanticism is on pages 31-37. He offers perhaps his most withering version of that critique in *Doktor Faustus* (1947) which dramatizes the trajectory from romanticism to Nazism. Lukács's argument about the intellectual complicity of romanticism – via irrationalism – with Nazism is first broached in *Fortschritt und Reaktion in der Deutschen Literatur* (also 1947) and later articulated at length in *Die Zerstörung der Vernunft*. 3rd ed. Darmstadt 1981. Pp. 84-172.

of exhaustion.[9] Opposing the thesis of the "annulment of Enlightenment"[10] and emphasizing the continuity of Schlegel's work, including his "will to fragment", with rationalism, would seem to put some distance between him and such bad company[11]; this has indeed been the case of the criticism of the last thirty years, especially in the exuberant reception that early romanticism received in Germany in the wake of the student protests of 1968. In this view, Schlegel and the Jena group are seen as continuing the process of enlightenment precisely by applying it to itself ("die Aufklärung über sich selbst aufzuklären und so zu retten", in the nigh-eschatological terms of the preface to a collection of criticism whose title – *Romantische Utopie – Utopische Romantik* – could well serve as the heading for a whole generation of romantic reception[12]). Far from huddling on the dark side of rationalism, romanticism now performs a "mimesis of Enlightenment",[13] due in part to the prominence given to the idea of the system. A detailed reception history of early romanticism would make clear what begins to emerge here, namely how high the historico-political stakes of the idea of the system are.

[9] Jürgen Habermas has lent renewed intellectual legitimacy to the idea of romantic irrationalism by characterizing it as a messianic, philosophically unfounded celebration of dionysian mythology. Jürgen Habermas: *Der philosophische Diskurs der Moderne*. Frankfurt a.M. 1985. Pp. 110-115. More recently the historian Gordon Craig has associated romanticism (in which he of course includes Schlegel) not only with the rise of Hitler but also with forms of violent extremism in postwar Germany, notably the terrorism of the Red Army Fraction. Gordon Craig: *The Germans*. New York 1991. Pp. 190-212.

[10] H.A. and E. Frenzel: *Daten deutscher Dichtung*. Munich 1987. Vol. 1. P. 300.

[11] Not always: Alfred Baeumler, in 1926, unequivocally connects Schlegel to the Enlightenment only to celebrate the fact that in his and Novalis' work it drew its last gasps and gave way to the *real* romanticism of an authentic connection to the earth, to nature, and to the *Volk*. See his Introduction to Johann Jakob Bachofen: *Der Mythus von Orient und Occident*. Ed. Manfred Schröter. Munich 1926. Pp. CLXIX-CLXX. Though it is not difficult to imagine that such an argumentation was to find an eager audience a few years later, it is still good to have it documented by Ralf Klausnitzer: Blaue Blume unterm Hakenkreuz. Zur literaturwissenschaftlichen Romantikrezeption im Dritten Reich. In: *Zeitschrift für Germanistik* 7.3 (1997). Pp. 521-542.

[12] *Romantische Utopie – Utopische Romantik*. Ed. Gisela Dischner and Richard Faber. Hildesheim 1979. P. 12.

[13] Helmut Schanze: *Romantik und Aufklärung*. 2nd. ed. Nürnberg 1976 (Erlanger Beiträge zur Sprach- und Kunstwissenschaft 27). P. 11.

3. The aesthetic problem: While in the hands of its severest critics romanticism is reduced to the status of an amorphous (and not disprovable) element of German mentality (Craig calls it the "*malaise allemand*"[14]), the celebrations of utopian romanticism describe its achievements primarily in the language of philosophy. What is largely missing from both appropriations is an adequate reading of the *artistic* innovations of the early (as well as the later) romantics. It is with this crucial omission in mind that we must understand Paul de Man's modest claim that "[i]t would hardly be hyperbolic to say [...] that the whole discipline of *Germanistik* has developed for the single reason of dodging Friedrich Schlegel".[15] We may expect such dodging in accounts largely hostile to early romantic texts, yet even laudatory critics tend to neglect the specific aesthetic achievements of those texts. Even such shrewd and sympathetic readers as Philippe Lacoue-Labarthe and Jean-Luc Nancy, who acclaim the *Frühromantik* "without any exaggeration [as] the first 'avant-garde' group in history",[16] maintain: "although it is not entirely or simply philosophical, romanticism is rigorously comprehensible (or even accessible) only on a philosophical basis [...]. If romanticism is approachable, in other words, it is approachable only by means of the 'philosophical path' [...]".[17] *Only* on a philosophical basis, *only* by means of a "philosophical path". As the quotation marks around "philosophical path" suggest, philosophy in Lacoue-Labarthe and Nancy's argument is by no means a homogeneous intellectual practice that may be assured of its own orientation; the burden of *The Literary Absolute* is to throw philosophy into a critical confrontation with literature, a confrontation that is not always productive or recuperable (that is, in short, risky).

Yet the critics who undertake this risky confrontation are standing on the ground of philosophy – even as their work is designed to be, literally speaking, groundbreaking – and using the currency of philosophy – even when they insist how worn-out it is. Lacoue-Labarthe and Nancy are of course not alone in this; some of the best recent work on the *Frühromantik* finds itself approaching the texts

---

[14] *The Germans*. P. 191.
[15] Paul de Man: *Aesthetic Ideology*. Ed. Andrzej Warminski. Minneapolis 1996. P. 168. What de Man says a bit further about *Lucinde* can surely be applied to the passage quoted here: "It is a joke, but we know that jokes are not innocent, and this is certainly not an innocent passage" (p. 169).
[16] Philippe Lacoue-Labarthe and Jean-Luc Nancy: *The Literary Absolute*. Trans. Philip Barnard and Cheryl Lester. Albany 1988. P. 8.
[17] Ibid. P. 29.

with philosophical questions.[18] It may well be that for the purposes of asking certain questions – including questions that this essay will attempt to raise – we have no choice but to stand on broken ground and use a worn-out currency; this may indeed be the predicament of criticism, or of critical thinking in general. But I suspect that what draws some of us to Schlegel is in fact that he tried to write his way into another situation, not one entirely free of the philosophical paradox I have been sketching (namely how to ask about the relationship of philosophy and literature without already being on the side of philosophy), but a predicament that is at least of his own making. That shift hinges on the notion of *Darstellung*,[19] the lexical, grammatical, and graphical presentation that is not the presentation *of* the system but rather *is* the system. The very concept of a Schlegelian aesthetic theory depends on the generic innovation with which the ideas are presented, on their irreducibly different *Darstellung* that both controls the content of such a theory and makes its coherent articulation finally impossible. A reading that poses the question of genre is not only well-equipped to see that the novelty in a romantic theory of artistic production and reception relies on, indeed is made possible by, the radical innovation in its form, but it will also concede that the materiality of the form always leaves a remainder. This remainder, not readily recuperable or digestible by philosophy, is the very aesthetic excess of *Darstellung* that forms a system according to rules not controlled by philosophy. The true challenge that Schlegel's work poses for philosophy ultimately resides not in an *opposition* to the idea of system (itself already a philosophical idea) but rather in a joyous and thoroughly sensuous (i.e., aesthetic) *embrace* of system. How we might understand such a system, and what it implies for philosophy and politics, is the subject of this essay.

"Es ist gleich tödlich für den Geist, ein System zu haben, und keins zu haben", a well-known *Athenäum* Fragment begins. "Er wird sich also wohl entschließen müssen, beides zu verbinden" (KA 2, 173, No. 53). What is usually overlooked about this clever fragment is that it proposes – no: prescribes – nothing less than the combination of two alternatives that are *deadly*. But why exactly are they deadly? And does the *Verbindung*, the binding or bonding, of two such lethal forces yield anything but more death (and what sense, if any, does a

---

[18] See for instance the superb essays in: *Die Aktualität der Frühromantik*. Ed. Ernst Behler and Jochen Hörisch. Paderborn 1987.

[19] See Martha B. Helfer: *The Retreat of Representation. The Concept of Darstellung in German Critical Discourse*. Albany 1996.

phrase like "more death" make)? Can two deaths make a life? Then there is the question of the position occupied by the spirit or mind that "will have to decide": while it is deciding to link the two alternatives, is it residing with the system or its opposite? The same question also goes for the voice of the fragment itself: is it, while enjoining us to join the fatal options, systematic or nonsystematic? Or can it be that despite the laws of logic there is a third term between system and nonsystem, that in Schlegel *tertium datur*?

The notion of two deaths, though suggestive and worth returning to, may be too melodramatic to express clearly the dilemma in which Schlegel and many of his contemporaries found themselves, namely the question of whether Enlightenment thinking, by canceling the transcendent claims of meaning-giving systems (chief among them religion), is left with a plethora of unconnected beings, or whether a totality cannot after all be fashioned from the manifold. For Schlegel the answer is, as we shall see, that if there is to be a totality, it must be a *poetic* one that takes stock of the thorough fragmentation of the world, which includes, crucially, a fragmentation of writing; indeed, Schlegel's trademark will be to seek totality – of what kind, remains to be seen – *in* written fragmentation. He understands the fragmentation of modern works of art not just figuratively (i.e., as a symbol for the alienation of the subject vis-à-vis the world) but quite literally, as the writing of inherently incomplete pieces. He counters Winckelmann's project of an *imitation* of Greek art (1755) with the *study* of Greek poetry ("Über das Studium der griechischen Poesie" [1795-96]) because the conditions under which an imitation of the ancients was still possible have, in his view, vanished.[20] A caesura now separates the moderns from the ancients.

Schlegel formulates the symptoms of this new situation specifically in relation to the idea of totality and fragment: "Viele Werke der Alten sind Fragmente geworden. Viele Werke der Neuern sind es gleich bei der Entstehung" (KA 2, 169, No. 24). Thus the romantic project – "die Poesie lebendig und gesellig, und das Leben und die Gesellschaft poetisch machen", as Schlegel would have it in *Athenäum* Fragment 116 (KA 2, 182) – is intertwined with the very generic properties of the fragments. In what for Schlegel is a moment of utopia, the genre of the fragment reverses the direction of the story of the fall from the state of grace: it does not begin with a self-posited Whole that disintegrates into a slew of atomized, decen-

---

[20] This is a point Peter Szondi makes in *Poetik und Geschichtsphilosophie I*. Ed. Senta Metz and Hans-Hagen Hildebrandt. Frankfurt a.M. 1974. P. 103.

tered, meaningless pieces, but posits instead the fragmentary in order to offer the promise of a future melding (or smelting, as we shall see[21]). The allure of the fragment as genre lies in the fact that the very characteristics that make the fragment fragmentary imply its opposite, the system. In this sense, Schlegel's utopia is above all a utopia of genre. A determinedly formal reading of the fragments will reveal a new and paradoxical conception of totality, one that does not so much rule its parts as consist of the differences between them. The post-Kantian totality that Schlegel seeks does not rely, I shall argue, on the smooth homogeneity of the system as an *organic* whole but advances the notion of an inorganic system in which the elements interact in fluid and unexpected ways.

To make clear how far-reaching such a move is, we should keep in mind how inseparably the notions of *organic* and of *system* have been treated by the philosophical tradition that concerns us here, and what consequences that inseparability has wrought. For Kant, a proper organization of knowledge is only imaginable if it takes the form of a system ("Unter der Regierung der Vernunft dürfen unsere Erkenntnisse überhaupt keine Rhapsodie, sondern sie müssen ein System ausmachen"[22]), for a system provides "die Einheit der mannigfaltigen Erkenntnisse unter einer Idee"[23] in order to form a totality (*das Ganze*). But to be a system, the totality must have, dixit Kant, a particular shape: "Das Ganze ist also gegliedert (*articulatio*) und nicht gehäuft (*coacervatio*); es kann zwar innerlich [...], aber nicht äußerlich [...] wachsen, wie ein tierischer Körper".[24] Transcendental philosophy is a system forming a unity (*Einheit*) "in welcher ein jedes Glied, wie in einem organisierten Körper, um aller anderen und alle um eines willen dasind".[25] The mechanical connotations of the Greek root of *system* (*synistanai: to combine, put together*) have been superseded by an organic model; for all the architectural metaphors that pervade Kant's critical philosophy, it is ultimately the articulated body that serves as the model for the system. Thus

---

[21] As Peter Kapitza has shown, chemistry around 1800, which Schlegel knew well, understood mixing (*Mischung*) not as a mechanical agglomeration of parts, but rather as a process yielding a new substance different from the ones one started with, much like the present-day concept of compound (*Verbindung*). Peter Kapitza: *Die frühromantische Theorie der Mischung*. Munich 1968. Pp. 12-13.

[22] Immanuel Kant: *Kritik der reinen Vernunft*. Ed. Wilhelm Weischedel. Frankfurt a.M. 1976. A 832, B 860.

[23] Ibid.

[24] Ibid. A 833, B 861.

[25] Ibid. B XXIII.

Krug's philosophical dictionary of 1829 has no trouble putting the scientific system into a metonymic chain with "Knochensystem, Sonnensystem, Staatensystem, u.s.w".,[26] for all these systems – knowledge, the universe, the state – are thought to draw their metaphorical force from the body. The connection of the two is so powerfully evident to Enlightenment and post-Enlightenment thinking that the very first meaning of system given by Grimm's *Deutsches Wörterbuch* is "ein sinnvoll gegliedertes Ganzes". The nexus between system and organicity is simply assumed whenever the idea of a totality is invoked, be it to celebrate it (Hegel: "Das Wahre ist das Ganze"[27]) or to denounce it (Adorno: "Das Ganze ist das Unwahre"[28]). The assumption seems to be that *any* representation of a totality cannot but be organic.

We may speculate that the seductive charge of the organic lies in offering a coherent and homogenous picture of the world at precisely the time – the late eighteenth century – when the mechanization of life was in full swing. And by "life" we can literally understand the body and its reproduction, for the notion of life as organic becomes entrenched exactly when human life itself becomes imaginable as mechanical; indeed, the more manipulable life processes become, the stronger the allure of the intactness of "nature". This wishful notion of nature is today perhaps stronger than ever: we clutch to the holistic "ecosystem" all the more forcefully, the more the control of nature spreads; and the "sacredness" of life stands in direct proportion to the successes of biological engineering. The idea of the natural order becomes ideology when other formations – the universe, the state, the subject, the collection of knowledge, the artwork – are taken to stand in a homologous relationship with it, for then a *given* order (given by God or a personified Nature) comes to occupy the place of a *made* order. In this sense, the argumentative deployment of "organic nature" assumes a "cancellation of analytic thinking".[29] The recourse to an organic explanation may well be the ideological move par excellence.

We must set the generic properties of Schlegelian fragments against the background of the steeply rising success of the notion of the organic system. Schlegel wrote the fragments *as* fragments, pub-

---

[26] Wilhelm Traugott Krug: *Allgemeines Wörterbuch der philosophischen Wissenschaft*. Vol. 4. Leipzig 1829. P. 103.
[27] G.W.F. Hegel: *Phänomenologie des Geistes*. Frankfurt a.M. 1977. P. 24.
[28] T.W. Adorno: *Minima Moralia*. Frankfurt a.M. 1951. P. 57.
[29] *Faszination des Organischen*. Ed. Hartmut Eggert et.al. Munich 1995. P. 10.

lished a few hundred of them in three batches, and left thousands more in his *Nachlaß*.[30] Publishing a series of pithy aphorisms is by no means a Schlegelian innovation; indeed Schlegel avows his indebtedness to Chamfort's *Pensées, maximes, anecdotes, dialogues* (published in 1795) in a letter to Novalis by calling his *Lyceum* collection a "kritische Chamfortiade" (KA 24, 21). Yet despite its historical pedigree, Schlegel explicitly conceives of the fragment as a new form. The *Athenäum* fragments, he promises his brother August Wilhelm, will be "eine ganz neue Gattung" (KA 24, 51); his fragments are "on top of the fashion", he says in somewhat hapless English (KA 24, 113); they constitute "die eigentliche Form der Universalphilosophie" (KA 2, 209, No. 259). Underlining their radical novelty, Novalis goes so far as to establish an equivalence between the Schlegelian fragments and the fliers posted by revolutionary forces in Paris: "Deine Fragmente sind durchaus *neu* – ächte, revolutionaire Affichen" (KA 24, 69).

Whether they are historically speaking revolutionary and, if so, in what sense, is a question to be determined in another context. But they were evidently *meant* as a break with the tradition of La Rochefoucauld, Chamfort, and Lichtenberg. It could not have escaped the attention of Schlegel, the classical philologist, that the etymology of *aphorism* goes back to *aphorizein, to define*, derived from *horizein, to bound* (whence our *horizon*), while *fragment* derives from *frangere, to break*.[31] And the first thing the fragment was intended to break was the continuity with the tradition of the aphorism. What at first seems to be a terminological quirk quickly reveals itself to carry important generic and philosophical implications, for while the aphorism always contains the promise of autonomous comprehensibility, offering itself as a shrink-wrapped version of thinking, the fragment explicitly calls attention to its own incompleteness. If the eighteenth-century aphorism attempts to bound the horizon of our understanding by offering a central point of focus, the very generic structure of the Schlegelian fragment aims at breaking it open. Put in terms of the logic of organicity: the fragments are not projects meant for complete articulation; their incompleteness does not (following our conventional understanding of fragment) result from the intrusion of death or loss, but includes them from the beginning. They are in their very making (*gleich bei der Entstehung*) marked by an irrecuperable loss.

---

[30] The former are reproduced in KA 2; the latter in KA 16-19.

[31] See Franz Mautner: Der Aphorismus als literarische Gattung. In: *Zeitschrift für Ästhetik und Allgemeine Kunstwissenschaft*. 27.2 (1933). Pp. 132-175, esp. pp. 145-153.

But is there not a lot of evidence that Schlegel, just like the philosophical discourse that was operative around him, promoted and
sought the organic unity of things? Does he not follow the traditional triad of *Vielheit, Allheit,* and *Einheit,* where the order by which
phenomena are subsumed under concepts becomes successively more
coherent and also more organic?[32] Certainly Schlegel's later work is
filled with references to an organic system, and there is plenty of
evidence for it even in the early period that concerns us here. "Je
organischer, je systematischer", declares a posthumously published
fragment (KA 16, 164, No. 940); "*Systeme* müssen wachsen; der
Keim in jedem System muß *organisch* sein", another maintains (KA
16, 165, No. 953). And *Athenäum* Fragment 22 offers somewhat
cryptically, "Ein Projekt ist der subjektive Keim eines werdenden
Objekts. Ein vollkommenes Projekt müßte zugleich ganz subjektiv,
und ganz objektiv, ein unteilbares und lebendiges Individuum sein"
(KA 2, 168).

Even critics who have attempted to push a reading of the fragments beyond a teleological narrative that invariably leads to the
system, critics who are generally suspicious of the organic, have
tended to see an organic continuum between fragment and system in
Schlegel. For Lacoue-Labarthe and Nancy the "genre of the fragment is the genre of generation" since the fragment itself is "no
more than germinating", and fragmentation a "dispersal that leads
to future dissemination and harvest".[33] Peter Szondi reads the just
quoted *Athenäum* Fragment 22 as a key to a utopian understanding
of the fragmentary project: "Das Fragment wird als Projekt aufgefaßt, als der 'subjektive Keim eines werdenden Objekts', als Vorbereitung der ersehnten Synthese. Im Fragment wird nicht mehr das
Nicht-Erreichte, das Bruchstück-Gebliebene gesehen, vielmehr die
Vorwegnahme, das Versprechen".[34] Thus the utopian force of the
fragments consists in the promise that the fragmentary germ will
grow into full-blown and harmonious systematicity, the longed-for
synthesis. Rodolphe Gasché collapses the temporal (and thus utopian) component in Szondi's reading into the isolated punctuality of
the fragments, bundling their entire philosophical force into their
presence, yet his argument still depends upon the organic intactness
of the fragments; he notes that "all fragments are systems *in nuce*",
and that these "singular organic totalities" achieve systematic status

[32] See Hans-Joachim Heiner: *Das Ganzheitsdenken Friedrich Schlegels.*
Stuttgart 1971, esp. pp. 21-33.
[33] *The Literary Absolute.* P. 49.
[34] Peter Szondi: Friedrich Schlegel und die romantische Ironie. In: *Satz und
Gegensatz.* Frankfurt a.M. 1964. P. 13.

not by pointing to another order nor by an internal logic that may reside in their ensemble but by their strict "ab-soluteness".[35]

One of the places to which most critics interested in providing a physiognomy of the fragments return is *Athenäum* Fragment 206, which appears to establish the equivalence between fragments, art works, and organic individuals in the most economic manner. In its entirety, it reads: "Ein Fragment muß gleich einem kleinen Kunstwerke von der umgebenden Welt ganz abgesondert und in sich selbst vollendet sein wie ein Igel" (KA 2, 197). It could hardly be stated more clearly: the autonomous work of art is nothing but the hedgehog-like self-enclosure of the fragment, a sensibly articulated whole ("sinnvoll gegliedertes Ganzes") if there ever was one. Moreover, in true Schlegelian fashion, this definition appears to double back and apply to the very fragment that offers it (fulfilling the promise of "zugleich Poesie und Poesie der Poesie" [KA 2, 204, No. 238]). Lacoue-Labarthe and Nancy take Fragment 206 to be evidence that the fragment's "existential obligation, if not its existence [...], is indeed formed by the integrity and the wholeness of the organic individual".[36] Lothar Pikulik finds confirmation for a reading of the fragment as autonomously self-enclosed in the hedgehog's spikes, which he reads as a defensive measure against heteronomous aesthetic standards.[37] And Gasché, citing 206, concludes that "[f]ragments are individuals, singular organic totalitites, that is, systems in miniature".[38]

But we can also see something quite different and more interesting happening here. Linked by two analogies to a small work of art and to a hedgehog ("[...] gleich einem Kunstwerk [...] wie ein Igel"), the fragment straddles the two realms – art and nature – that define the spectrum of discussion in late eighteenth-century aesthetics: if to our initial surprise the fragment is not identified as an artwork but merely compared to one (and a small one at that) it is because, as *Athenäum* Fragment 116 reminds us, the completion of romantic poetry is a project for the infinite future (indeed, strictly speaking, an infinite project, for "[d]ie romantische Dichtart ist noch im

[35] Rodolphe Gasché: Foreword. In: Friedrich Schlegel: *Philosophical Fragments*. Trans. Peter Firchow. Minneapolis 1991. P. xii.

[36] *The Literary Absolute*. P. 43

[37] Lothar Pikulik: *Frühromantik. Epoche – Werke – Wirkung.* Munich 1992. P. 126.

[38] *Philosophical Fragments*. P. xii. Among the critics that I have consulted, only Harald Fricke promotes an ironic reading of Fragment 206, one that remains sketchy, however, due to the constraints of his study. See his *Aphorismus*. Stuttgart 1984. P. 88.

Werden; ja das ist ihr eigentliches Wesen, daß sie ewig nur werden, nie vollendet sein kann" [KA 2, 183]). Thus the introduction of the analogical turn counteracts the very thesis that the fragment ostensibly proposes, for were the fragment an expression of completion, then it would *be* a work of art rather than merely *like* one. Indeed, if we read the fragment literally (and with Schlegel we had better, for "Der Buchstabe ist der wahre Zauberstab" [KA 18, 265, No. 846]), it never says that fragments *are* detached and complete, but, much more precisely, that they *must* be so, echoing the prospective vision of Fragment 116 and thereby admitting the essential incompletion of present fragments. Thus the fragment's very mode of argumentation – definition by analogy – pulls the rug from under it.

The real ironic-paradoxical twist comes with the last word of the fragment: even if up to this point we believed in the happy isolation of the self-satisfied, autonomous fragment, the hedgehog pops that bubble. For a hedgehog is, of course, neither detached from its environs nor complete in itself, thus giving the lie to the comparative *wie.* If Fragment 206 demonstrates anything (*demonstrate* not understood in the sense of *argue* but of *show, present, darstellen*) it is that fragments are prickly beasts; they not only betray our trust in analogies (in the space of some twenty words two likenesses prove treacherous), they also undermine what they say as they say it (again: "zugleich Poesie und Poesie der Poesie"). This then would be an exemplary case of romantic irony.

While Schlegel espouses the thesis of the organic system for most of his life – the older he gets, the more obstinately so – for a few years, between about 1795 and the end of the decade, he offers a notion of the system in which the senses of multiplicity, totality, and unity at first overlap and ultimately coincide. What may have begun as a conceptual imprecision ends up carrying far-reaching aesthetic and political implications, for what we witness here is the construction of a system that foregoes, indeed undermines, the organic qualities that classically define it; while Schlegel directs his considerable polemical powers against solidity, stringent architectonics, and above all purity – the very ingredients that are to make the system as triumphant in the early nineteenth century as it is untenable in the twentieth – he relies more and more on a concept of system that does not so much tolerate difference as consist of it.

What sort of a system might this be? The short answer is again almost painfully literal: the alternative to the organic system turns out to be the *in*organic or, as Schlegel prefers to call it, the *chemical* system. What romantic poetry is destined to do to poetry, philosophy, sociability, rhetoric, criticism (and the list in *Athenäum* Fragment 116 goes on), is to mix and fuse them ("bald mischen, bald verschmelzen" [KA 2, 182]), in other words to combine them in a manner modeled by chemistry.[39] "Wo [Poesie und Praxis] sich ganz durchdringen und in eins schmelzen, da entsteht Philosophie" (KA 2, 216, No. 304), Schlegel writes; this chemical reaction does not yield a philosophy that remains coherent and stable, but one that is nothing but the ceaseless process of analysis and synthesis, "die Wissenschaft aller sich ewig mischenden und wieder trennenden Wissenschaften, eine logische Chemie" (KA 2, 200, No. 220), which he also calls "eine Art von transzendentaler Chemie" (KA 18, 89, No. 716). In this context, the prescription of *Athenäum* Fragment 53 to combine the two deadly alternatives of system and non-system ("wird sich also wohl entschließen müssen, beides zu verbinden") begins to make sense, for the choice of *verbinden* signals to us that we are in the world of chemistry. This bond does not, through an act of creationist magic, add up to a vital whole; nor does the union of two fatal elements imply that the ensuing result will be dead or even deadly. Schlegel locates the process that is neither dead nor alive – we might imagine it as consisting of the activity of pure expenditure – in the endless and vigorous movement *between* life and death. In this sense, the inorganic, as that which is both not organic *anymore* and *not yet* organic, would be a precise term for such a fleeting entity.

What makes this process of impersonal bonding stranger still is that Schlegel does not extend it to the fragments' conceptual or lexical content alone, but rather to their very material form. This means an almost obsessive interest in the question of how their presentation on the printed page – without explanation or transition to guide the reader – would yield a unity on the level of the ensemble. He repeatedly argues against splitting up the collection of fragments into two issues of *Athenäum* (e.g., KA 24, 64), warning that it would result in "Zerstückelung *eines Ganzen*" (KA 24, 102). "Die Epideixis der Universalität", as he likes to call the performative *Darstellung* of the romantic ideal that the fragments aspire to, "würde durch die reale Abstrakzion und praktische Kritik des Ganzen in beyde Stücke eine formale Destrukzion erleiden" (KA 24, 105). He is driven by two impulses that only at first seem contradictory, but which we now recognize as two sides of the same coin: on the

---

[39] Mixing and fusing is to be found all over early (and also late) romanticism, for example in the promiscuous mixing of genres. See Judith Ryan: Hybrid Forms in German Romanticism. In: *Prosimetrum. Crosscultural Perspectives on Narrative in Prose and Verse*. Ed. Joseph Harris and Karl Reichl. Cambridge 1997. Pp. 165-181.

one hand, his interest lies in pure numbers, in the sheer quantity of the fragments – "Wie schön sind die einzelnen, und wie erst in Masse", he exclaims about a new batch of fragments that August Wilhelm has just sent him (KA 24, 91).[40] On the other hand, the result of this open-ended, entirely fluid process of mass production becomes, once bonded, a Whole. The fragments are "Mitglied[er] einer Masse, die sich nicht trennen läßt", he writes and adds in exasperation: "Ueberhaupt hängen die verdammten Dinge so zusammen" (KA 24, 97).

What emerges then is something akin to critical mass (a term Schlegel would have certainly savored had it been available to him): the sheer numerical plenitude of fragments, in a force field of reciprocal pressures and attractions, combines to become a whole. This idea of a unified totality relies as much on difference as on incoherence; it is indebted neither to a mystical immediacy, nor to the implacable teleology of a dialectic, nor to the seemingly natural developmental narrative of an organism. Its spatial and temporal structure is very different from any of these. Rather than a unity guaranteed either through the assurance of immediacy, at one extreme (where the temporal vector would be zero), or by the infinite progression of the idea or the maturation of a germ, at the other (where the temporal vector would always point in the same direction), the chemical system is the expression of a series of oscillations of "part" into "whole" and "whole" into "part". I put "part" and "whole" into inverted commas because logical chemistry is not a form of philosophical alchemy; Schlegel does not offer us a series of distinct entities whose essence might consist of "partness" (say, the fragments) and whose destiny (their *Bestimmung*, in the language of *Athenäum* Fragment 116) would lead them to an entity whose essence in turn might be called "wholeness". For if we can even use a metaphysical concept such as "wholeness", it would – as Schlegel's verbs (*werden, entstehen, verschmelzen, mischen, durchdringen*) suggest – consist of the *process* of metamorphosis, of becoming rather than being. And since the fragments offer no progression – either up or down – or change (things are constantly becoming each other), it lacks the two crucial mainstays of the metaphysically imagined system: motivating force and telic movement; in other words, it lacks center, ground, axiomatic beginning, seed, the lump in the middle.

---

[40] Or, in another letter to August Wilhelm: "Glaubt mir, je *mehr* Fragmente gegeben werden, je weniger Monotonie, und je mehr Popularität. Die Menge muß es machen" (KA 24, 88).

What I have argued thus far might lead us to imagine a young Schlegel who offers us, instead of Kant's dour rationalism, a gay science of anti-foundationalism, a Schlegel who, through his embrace of the system, refuses to abandon the utopian potential of the Enlightenment (neither for an irrationalist mysticism nor for a messianism) and yet has no wish to adopt its dialectical or organicist versions. It would be temptingly easy to draw political conclusions from this and celebrate a Schlegel who embraces difference against identity, dialogism against monologism. After all, Schlegel often imagines fragments as members of a *social* system: "Manche witzige Einfälle sind wie das überraschende Wiedersehen zwei befreundeter Gedanken nach einer langen Trennung" (KA 2, 171, No. 37). Even if fragments are little more than "ein bunter Haufen von Einfällen", they are bonded – *verbunden* – by "jenes freie und gleiche Beisammensein, worin sich auch die Bürger des vollkommnen Staats [...] dereinst befinden werden" (KA 2, 159, No. 103). It is not hard to guess that a society based on elective affinities is very different from the one Schlegel inhabited; in case his readers missed the utopian charge of this model, he reminds them, "Das Zeitalter ist gleichfalls ein chemisches Zeitalter. Revolutionen sind universelle nicht organische, sondern chemische Bewegungen" (KA 2, 248, No. 426).

Before embracing such a philosophical/ textual/ social model, we ought to look carefully at what precisely might be implied by such an idea of constant oscillation. For oscillation is – at least in Schlegel's practice – impossible to think without having to contend with the movement of irony. And here is where the fragments may turn out to be the "Wespennest" for which Goethe recognized them.[41] Take a fragment that appears to assert the endorsable equivalence of fragment, system, work, and individual,[42] but contains a stinger that undoes the whole equation: "Nur ein System ist eigentlich ein *Werk*. Jede andre Schrift kann nicht schließen, nur abschneiden, oder aufhören; sie endigt also immer nothwendig annihilirend oder ironirend" (KA 16, 162, No. 902). A less ironic writer may want to end up on the side of *Werk* (which is to say system), but it becomes quite clear that Schlegel's own "work" falls on the side of irony, annihilation, interruption – in short, of *Schrift*.

The abrupt cut (*abschneiden, aufhören*) is of course a defining mark of the fragments. It marks not merely the end of the fragment collections but also the end of each and every fragment; a collection

---

[41] Letter to Schiller of July 25, 1798. J.W. Goethe: *Briefwechesel mit Schiller*. In: *Gedenkausgabe der Werke, Briefe und Gespräche*. Ed. Ernst Beutler. Vol. 20. Zurich 1950. P. 605.
[42] Thus Gasché's reading: *Philosophical Fragments*. P. xi.

consists, in this sense, as much of the white spaces separating the fragments as of the fragments themselves, of the interruptions in reading and the disjointed *Darstellung* as of the texts. What is more crucial, the interruptions are not confined to the space *between* fragments, but are lodged at the very heart of every fragment. As Paul de Man has shown convincingly, permanent interruptions are nothing but the expression of Schlegelian irony, the very sort of irony that in his view has led *Germanistik* to dodge Schlegel; according to de Man, Schlegelian irony occurs in those moments when there has been an interruption in the narrative line, specifically an interruption of the kind that on stage is called an aside, technically speaking a parabasis.[43] It is not hard to see how this creates an ironic text, even according to the most banal understandings of irony, for with the parabasis the character, or the textual voice, creates a distance between two discourses with the result that doubt is cast on the reliability of both. But Schlegel goes further, defining irony as a *"permanente* Parekbase" (KA 18, 85, No. 668, emphasis added), as interruption of *all* points in the narrative, which, as de Man correctly points out, "is saying something violently paradoxical",[44] for an interruption can only happen against a continuous background. Parabasis undercuts the notion that the fragments, either individually or as an ensemble, might yield to an organic reading, since the very foundation of an organic entity depends on its harmonious, unruffled order. It is not much good for something to be *in nuce* if its design requires a constant state of abortion.

Thus according to the rules of Schlegelian "chemische Philosophie" (KA 16, 179, No. 1144) – every synthesis implies a prior analysis, every analysis a synthesis – creating a whole by means of a permanent parabasis means that the whole can last only in the space of two interruptions, indeed that the whole, in the manner of a chain of chain reactions, gets permanently combined and recombined as one reads and rereads the fragments. Only in this sense can we understand the system to be a work, more precisely a work-in-progress. The system then can be held only at the expense of its radical inconstancy; it can be produced but its half-life approaches zero. This is, perhaps, why another deeply cryptic fragment places parabasis where other writers would put a lump, namely at the very center of systems: "In jedem systematischen Werk muß ein *Prolog* sein, ein *Epilog* und ein *Centrolog* (oder eine *Parekbase*)" (KA 16, 164, No. 942). Thus if there is to be a fusion, a chemical *Ver-*

---

[43] Paul de Man: *Aesthetic Ideology*. Pp. 178-179.
[44] Ibid. P. 179.

bindung, of system and non-system, it can only come about with a violent fission that enables the combination as it undoes it. This is not a philosophy in which one can put one's feet up; it is uncomfortable *at all points*. And the social model that we were (encouraged by Schlegel) tempted to draw by analogy is, if such a thing is possible, more troubling still. If we are willing to accept that fragments and individuals in society are to be imagined analogously – the meeting of two friendly thoughts after a long separation – then we must admit that we have subscribed to a disturbing model of social interaction. For such a meeting, as Schlegel takes pains to point out, must always be interruptable: "Selbst ein freundschaftliches Gespräch, was nicht *in jedem Augenblick* frei abbrechen kann, aus unbedingter Willkür, hat etwas Illiberales" (KA 2, 151, No. 37, emphasis added). This is Lacan's short session *avant la lettre*, with two radicalizing features: first, it is not confined to the structured context of an analytic situation but comprises all social interactions; and second, it extends the privilege of arbitrary interruption reserved for the analyst to all members of a communicative situation. We should be more precise, for it is not the speakers but the conversation itself, the subject of the quoted sentence (*Gespräch*), that, lest it be constrained, must take the liberty of performing the interruption. Interruption, irony, parabasis is not the result of an agent intervening in a discourse but of the discourse, the speech act, intervening into itself. Given this context, the seemingly anodyne opening sentence of the "Gespräch über die Poesie" – "Alle Gemüter, die sie lieben, befreundet und bindet Poesie mit unauflöslichen Banden" (KA 2, 284) – gains a certain disquieting edge, for we now know what sort of bonding (*binden*, *Banden*) poetry performs. We must be careful what we wish for. If we regard the social model implied in the fragments to be utopian, then utopia implies the possibility of a *permanent* revolution, a ceaseless transformation of the very conditions of interaction, the chance that a relationship will go dead at *any* moment. This condition is not far from the most extreme form of social psychosis.

This is, as I hope to have made clear, not the same thing as counter-Enlightenment irrationalism. If anything, there is an excess at work here that Blanchot has identified as "an excess of thought".[45] This excess should remind us to take great care in using formulas such as "mimesis of Enlightenment" or "enlightenment of Enlightenment", for the moment of repetition, of distance, of

---

[45] Maurice Blanchot: *The Infinite Conversation*. Trans. Susan Hanson. Minneapolis 1995. P. 353.

doubling (always also an ironic moment) creates a space between the Schlegelian move and the Enlightenment that makes all the difference. The excess of thinking is the mark and the maker of this difference. The difference begins at the heart of an artistic project and propagates itself into the structure of philosophy, yielding a social model that promotes radical egalitarianism only if it can be suspended as soon as it is founded.

Azade Seyhan

Allegorie der Allegorie:
Romantische Allegorese als kulturelle Erinnerung

Dem Andenken meines Doktorvaters Ernst Behler

The visible return of allegory in the critical discourse of postmodernity after its devalorization with regard to the symbol in the nineteenth century calls for a reassessment of the history of this trope. The following essay undertakes an interpretative analysis of the concept of allegory in early German Romanticism, in order to synthesize the diverse applications and implications of this figure for modern literary theory. Drawing on the critical insights of Walter Benjamin, Angus Fletcher, and Paul de Man, the essay illustrates that in early Romantic and postmodern criticism, allegory and allegoresis are intimately linked to cultural memory.

In jeder Geschichte wird etwas vergessen, verdrängt oder ausgelassen, etwas, was die Grenzen des Aussprechlichen sprengt und der sprachlichen Darstellung entkommt. Trotz dieses Schweigens der Sprache verraten bestimmte rhetorische Traditionen die unaussprechlichen Bedürfnisse der Epochen, die an der Schwelle sozialer, sittlicher oder geistiger Krisen stehen. Was dem Bewußtsein verheimlicht wird, offenbart sich in den Falten und Spalten der Sprache selbst, und unsere Geschichten, Erinnerungen und Krisen werden durch bestimmte Tropen, rhetorische Formen und Narrationen weitergetragen. In dieser "radikalen Geschichtlichkeit der Sprache", so der Kritiker Iain Chambers, "treffen wir nicht nur auf die Grammatik des Seins, sondern auch auf die Tatsache, daß es spricht: auf die Rede eines bestimmten kulturellen Gewebes, Erbes und Netzwerks, in dem das Aufgeschriebene und das Vorgeschriebene umgeschrieben werden".[1]

Die figurativen Repräsentationsformen, die unseren vielfältigen kulturellen Erinnerungen, Mythen und Identitäten Zugang gewähren, werden zum Schauplatz der ständigen Auseinandersetzung von Macht und Ohnmacht in der Geschichte. Die aus der kritischen Wendung

---

[1] Iain Chambers: *Migration, Kultur, Identität*. Übersetzt von Gudrun Schmidt und Jürgen Freudl. Tübingen 1996. S. 161-162.

der modernen Literaturtheorie abzuleitende systematische Unter-
suchung der rhetorischen Ausdrucksformen geht, wie u. a. Hans-
Georg Gadamer, Tzvetan Todorov[2] und Paul de Man ausführen, über
die Grenzen des ästhetischen Bewußtseins hinaus und deutet auf den
Wandel der philosophischen Tendenzen hin. Gadamer und de Man
finden in der Geschichte des Gegensatzes zwischen Symbol und Allegorie den Schwerpunkt einer philosophischen Debatte über das
Schicksal der modernen Kunstkritik. Die sichtbare Rückkehr der
Allegorie in dem rhetorischen Diskurs der Postmoderne nach ihrer
Herabsetzung zugunsten des Symbols im 19. Jahrhundert erfordert
eine Neuinterpretation der Geschichte des allegorischen Denkens.

Die Konkurrenz zwischen Symbol und Allegorie findet ihren umrissenen Ausdruck bei Goethe. In *Wahrheit und Methode* sieht Gadamer in "Goethes kunsttheoretischen Bemühungen" eine starke Tendenz "das Symbolische zum positiven, das Allegorische zum negativ-
künstlerischen Begriff zu stempeln". Der von Goethe selbst aus-
geprägte Maßstab der "Erlebtheit" galt im 19. Jahrhundert als der
leitende Wertbegriff. "Was sich in Goethes Werk diesem Maßstab
nicht fügte, – so die Alterspoesie Goethes – wurde dem realistischen
Geiste des Jahrhunderts gemäß als allegorisch 'überladen' hintange-
setzt".[3] In seinem letzten Maxim über den Gegensatz von Allegorie
und Symbol aus dem Nachlaß bringt Goethe die Problematik auf den
Punkt:

Die Allegorie verwandelt die Erscheinung in einen Begriff, den Begriff in
ein Bild, doch so, daß der Begriff im Bilde immer noch begrenzt und vollständig zu halten und zu haben und andemselben auszusprechen sei.

Die Symbolik verwandelt die Erscheinung in Idee, die Idee in ein Bild, und
so, daß die Idee im Bild immer unendlich wirksam und unerreichbar bleibt
und, selbst in allen Sprachen ausgesprochen, doch unaussprechlich bliebe.[4]

Mit anderen Worten: Das Symbol schafft eine Kette von Signifikanten als Teil eines signifizierenden Systems. Hier behandelt Goethe
die Vielfalt des symbolischen Ausdrucks durch die kritische Einsicht,
daß das Symbol das Phänomen in eine Reihe von sich fortsetzenden
Ideen übersetzt. Diese kontinuierliche Fortsetzung/ Übersetzung
negiert sowohl Transparenz als auch abschliessende Erklärung. Im

---

[2] Siehe insbesondere Tzvetan Todorov: *Théories du Symbole*. Paris 1977.
[3] Hans-Georg Gadamer: *Wahrheit und Methode. Grundzüge einer
philosophischen Hermeneutik*. Tübingen 1960. S. 75.
[4] Johann Wolfgang von Goethe: Maximen und Reflexionen. In:
Gedenkausgabe. Hg. von Ernst Beutler. Zürich 1949. Bd. 9. S. 639.

Gegensatz zum Symbol übersetzt die Allegorie das Phänomen in ein Bild, in dem der Begriff immer durchschaubar und zugänglich bleibt. Kurz, Goethes Urteil beruht auf einer Dichotomie von Opazität und Transparenz, wobei das Symbol wegen seines schwer zu entziffernden Charakters immer neue Interpretationen erzeugt und daher der begrenzten Bildlichkeit der Allegorie überlegen ist. Aber ist diese Grenze zwischen den zwei Figuren eine absolute? Ist die Beziehung der beiden Tropen nicht eher ergänzend als widersprüchlich? Und ist diese Abwertung des Ausdrucksvermögens der allegorischen Darstellungsweise zugunsten des Symbols auch teilweise in der Mißdeutung Goethes Formulierungen begründet?

Hier soll daran erinnert werden, daß Goethe dem abstrakten Charakter der modernen Wissenschaftslehre und der Unzulänglichkeit deren Sprache, in der er den frühen Tod des Poetischen erblickte, kritisch gegenüberstand[5] und deswegen nicht dazu geneigt war, großen Wert auf den von ihm als verstandesmäßig und abstrakt rezipierten Begriff der Allegorie zu legen. Diese Skepsis dem Allegorischen gegenüber wiederholt sich in Goethes Diskussion über den allegorischen, symbolischen und mystischen Gebrauch der Farbe in der *Farbenlehre*. Im symbolischen Gebrauch der Farbe, laut Goethe, wird "die Farbe ihrer Wirkung gemäß angewendet". Im Gegensatz zu dem "wahre[n] Verhältnis" zwischen der Farbe und ihrer Bedeutung im symbolischen Gebrauch (z.B. Purpur bezeichnet die Majestät) wird die Bedeutung im allegorischen Gebrauch durch Konvention diktiert und setzt eine Vorkenntnis voraus (wie z.B. die grüne Farbe, die der Hoffnung zugeteilt wird).[6] Hier scheint die Auseinandersetzung selbst höchst willkürlich, denn in beiden Fällen ist die Bedeutung, die der Farbe zugeschrieben wird, keine immanente sondern eine konstruierte.

Letzten Endes muß selbst der Gebrauch dieser Termini relativiert werden, wenn wir ihre Bindung an historisch-ästhetische Grundbegriffe erkennen. Die Hochschätzung des Allegorischen von den Philosophen der Romantik, der das Verhältnis des Unsagbaren zum poetischem Ausdruck zugrunde liegt, wurde

von dem Bildungshumanismus des 19. Jahrhunderts nicht mehr festgehalten worden. Man berief sich auf die Weimarer Klassik, und in der Tat, die Abwertung der Allegorie war das beherrschende Anliegen der deutschen Klassik, das sich ganz notwendig aus der Befreiung der Kunst von den Fes-

---

[5] Siehe z.B. den Abschnitt, "Schlußbetrachtung über Sprache und Terminologie". In Goethes *Schriften zur Farbenlehre*. In: *Gedenkausgabe*. Bd. 16. S. 203-204.
[6] Johann Wolfgang von Goethe: *Farbenlehre*. S. 233-234.

seln des Rationalismus und der Auszeichnung des Geniebegriffs ergab. Die
Allegorie ist gewiß nicht allein Sache des Genies. Sie beruht auf festen Traditionen und hat stets eine bestimmte, angebbare Bedeutung, die sich gar
nicht dem verstandesmäßigen Erfassen durch den Begriff widersetzt [...].[7]

Aus der "Wortgeschichte von Symbol und Allegorie" zieht Gadamer
die Folgerung, daß dieser Begriffsgegensatz fragwürdig wird, wenn die
"Erlebnisästhetik" ihre Geltung nicht mehr behaupten kann. Nun
hinterfragt Gadamer den "unter dem Vorurteil der Erlebnisästhetik"
absolut scheinenden Gegensatz von Symbol und Allegorie und verweist auf die kontinuierliche Existenz des Allegorischen im Bereich
der symbolischen Tätigkeit:

> Die Grundlage der Ästhetik des 19. Jahrhunderts war die Freiheit der sym-
> bolisierenden Tätigkeit des Gemüts. Aber ist das eine tragende Basis? Ist
> diese symbolisierende Tätigkeit in Wahrheit nicht auch heute noch durch
> das Fortleben einer mythisch-allegorischen Tradition begrenzt?[8]

Diese Bemerkungen implizieren eine fortwährende Revision der
hermeneutischen Konsequenzen von ästhetischen Werten und
spitzen die Erklärung der Beziehung zwischen Kunst und historisch
bestimmten Wertbegriffen zu.

Die von Gadamer hier erwähnte "gewisse [...] Ehrenrettung der
Allegorie"[9] durch die Wiederentdeckung der Kunst des Barocks und
der barocken Poesie wurde in den letzten Jahrzehnten von zeitgenössischen Kritikern mit großem Erfolg durchgeführt. Benjamins Rehabilitierung der Allegorie folgend, hat Paul de Man den diese Trope
betreffenden Vorwurf der Dogmatik und Starrheit mit großer theoretischer Anstrengung zurückgewiesen, indem er die Ungewißheit des
Allegorischen zum entscheidenden Kennzeichen der Kunst erhebt
und die Allegorie als die Darstellung der Aporie des Wissens
bestimmt:

> Allegory is frequently dismissed as wooden, barren (*kahl*), ineffective, or
> ugly, yet the reasons for its ineffectiveness, far from being a shortcoming,
> are of such all-encompassing magnitude that they coincide with the furthest
> reaching achievements available to the mind and reveal boundaries that
> aesthetically more successful works of art, because of this very success, were
> unable to perceive [...]. Allegory is the purveyor of demanding truths, and
> thus its burden is to articulate an epistemological order of truth and deceit
> with a narrative or compositional order of persuasion [...]. Why is it that

---

[7] Hans-Georg Gadamer: *Wahrheit und Methode*. S. 75.
[8] Hans-Georg Gadamer: *Wahrheit und Methode*. S. 76.
[9] Hans-Georg Gadamer: *Wahrheit und Methode*. S. 76.

the furthest reaching truths about ourselves and the world have to be stated in such a lopsided, referentially indirect mode? Or, to be more specific, why is it that texts that attempt the articulation of epistemology with persuasion turn out to be inconclusive about their own intelligibility in the same manner and for the same reasons that produce allegory?[10]

Im Einklang mit de Mans Formulierungen stellt Joel Fineman in der Allegorie den Ort der Mehrdeutigkeit und das Paradigma der kritischen Hinterfragung fest und beschreibt diese Figur als

trope of tropes, representative of the figurality of all language, of the distance between signifier and signified, and, correlavitely, the response to allegory becomes representative of critical activity *per se* [...]. This tendency on the part of allegory to read itself, for its theme to dominate its narrative, or [...] to prescribe the direction of its commentary, suggests the formal or phenomenological affinities of the genre with criticism.[11]

Die Allegorie bezeichnet also kritische Tätigkeit *par excellence*, weil in ihr, im romantischen Sinne, Kunst und Kritik übereinstimmen, das heißt, sie repräsentiert zugleich sich selbst und ihre Reflexionsstruktur. In seiner umfangreichen Studie über die Geschichte und Theorie der Allegorie stellt Angus Fletcher die Ansicht, daß Allegorien an Starrheit leiden, in Frage und unterstreicht dagegen ihre symbolische Rolle als Fürsprecher der verschwiegenen Geschichten.[12] Diese zeitgenössischen Bewertungen der Allegorie sprechen eine Umkehr der im 19. Jahrhundert herrschenden Abwertung der Trope aus und belegen durch ausführliche Analysen ihr ästhetisches und verstandesmäßiges Potential. Aus diesen Debatten kann gefolgert werden, daß das Allegorische ein Zeichen komplizierter und bedeutungsschwerer Epochen ist[13] und, ihrer Struktur gemäß, ein ständiges Verlangen nach Interpretation repräsentiert.

---

[10] Paul de Man: Pascal's Allegory of Persuasion. In: *Allegory and Representation*. Hg. von Stephen J. Greenblatt. Baltimore und London 1981. S. 1-25, hier S. 1-2.
[11] Joel Fineman: The Structure of Allegorical Desire. In: *Allegory and Representation*. S. 26-60, hier S. 27-28.
[12] "Allegories are far less often the dull sytems that they are reputed to be than they are symbolic power struggles. If they are often rigid, muscle-bound structures, that follows from their involvement with authoritarian conflict". Angus Fletcher: *Allegory: The Theory of a Symbolic Mode*. Ithaca und London 1964. S. 23.
[13] In seinem bekannten Essay *"Figura"* schreibt Erich Auerbach der figurativen Interpretation, die er mit der Allegorie im engsten Zusammenhang behandelt, einen historischen Charakter zu, während er im Symbol eine direkte

Eine implizite Hochschätzung der Allegorie und die Anerkennung ihres Verhältnises zu dem ästhetischen Bewußtsein der Zeit sind in dem rhetorischen Diskurs der Frühromantik zu erkennen. Hier werden rhetorische Sprache und Analyse in ihrem Eigenrecht gegenüber politischer, historischer und philosophischer Methodologie anerkannt. Im Licht der Wiederentdeckung der frühromantischen Poesie durch poststrukturalistische Literaturtheorie, der Neudeutung der rhetorischen Tradition der Moderne und des zunehmenden Bewußtseins von der Rolle kultureller Erinnerung in Identitätsformation, muß die Funktion der Tropen in frühromantischer Kritik neu bewertet werden. Den modernen kritischen Einsichten von Sigmund Freud, Walter Benjamin, Angus Fletcher und Paul de Man folgend, wird im folgenden die Allegoriekonzeption der Frühromantik ausgelegt und zerlegt, um mit einer weiteren Wendung zusammengesetzt zu werden. Entscheidend für meine Benjamin und de Man verpflichtete Interpretation des frühromantischen Allegoriebegriffs bleibt die Auffassung der Allegorie als die Trope des Unaussprechlichen und zugleich des Vergessenen und des Unvergeßlichen.

Die gebrochenen politischen und metaphysischen Hoffnungen eines Zeitalters, das die Nachbeben der französischen Revolution am eigenen Leibe verspürt hat, kommen im frühromantischen Diskurs zur Sprache. Revolutionen, Kriege und Besatzungen verursachen Umwälzungen und Brüche, die oft zu einer Verarmung, sogar Erschöpfung des kulturellen Erbes der Völker und Nationen führen. Dieser Verlust bedarf einer öffentlichen und kollektiven Erinnerungsarbeit, um eine bedeutsame, ungetrübte und moralisch unbefleckte Vergangenheit wiederzufinden. Gedächtnis stattet Geschehnis mit einer formalen (Bild)ung aus und baut aus den Trümmern der Geschichte Gedenkstätte.

Die Frühromatiker reagierten auf die Krise der nachrevolutionären Zeit mit einem höchst intellektuellen Projekt, das den Anspruch erhob, die gescheiterte Geschichte der europäischen Kultur als eine Art "neue Mythologie" umzuschreiben. Dieses Umschreiben erforderte eine implizite Strategie der Entdeckung verlorener und verdunkelter Ausdrucksformen der Literatur- und Kulturgeschichte und deren Ausrüstung mit der sprachlichen Kraft der kritischen

---

Interpretation des Lebens und der Natur sieht. *Figura* und figurative Auslegung sind, laut Auerbach, durch eine bestimmte kulturelle Reife und historische Erfahrung gekennzeichnet und sind Produkte späterer Zeiten. Siehe Erich Auerbach: *Figura*. In: *Scenes from the Drama of European Literature*. Übersetzt von Ralph Manheim. New York 1959. S. 57.

Reflexion. Kritik übernimmt also die Verantwortung für das Bewahren und Weitergeben eines kulturellen Gedächtnisses, das die Vergangenheit nicht im Sinne einer realen Erfahrung versteht, sondern diese Vorzeit aus den fragmentarischen Bildern und Schriften der Geschichte zusammensetzt. Die bevorzugten Figuren der Romantik – Allegorie, Ironie und Fragment – verneinen alle Arten der Sytematisierung und stellen jede Form der Totalität und des Abschlusses in Frage durch eine Praxis des Schreibens, die die Welt der Erfahrung in ihrer sich widersprüchlichen Gesamtheit erfaßt. Hier widersetzen sich sowohl Phantasie und Poesie als auch empirische Wahrnehmung der abschließenden Erklärung. Ernst Behler betont, daß Friedrich Schlegel das Fragmentarische keineswegs als einen "vorübergehenden Zustand bezeichnet, der vom vollendeten Erkennen und Schreiben überwunden wird, sondern im Fragmentarischen vielmehr die angemessene Form menschlichen Verstehens und Mitteilens erblickt".[14]

In der Wiederentdeckung der Frühromantik durch die moderne Literaturtheorie zeichnen Allegorie und Ironie den Schwerpunkt der rhetorischen Analyse auf. In ihren politischen und ästhetischen Dimensionen wirkt Allegorie als ein fortwährender Prozeß der konstruktiven Interpretation. Es wäre aufschlußreich, den Terminus, wie dieser in der romantischen Literaturtheorie zu verstehen ist, zu definieren. Aber die Behandlung der Allegorie von den Frühromantikern findet nicht in einer fertigen Theorie Ausdruck, sondern spricht sich in mehreren Bruchstücken, fragmentarischen Feststellungen und generativen Signifikanten aus, die selbst durch formale allegorische Züge gekennzeichnet sind. Deswegen kann von einem fest umrissenen Platz der Allegorie in der rhetorischen Tradition der Romantik nicht die Rede sein. Außerdem kommt weder eine systematisch noch eine konsequent ausgedachte Differenzierung zwischen den Spielräumen von Symbol und Allegorie in den frühromantischen Schriften zum Ausdruck. Novalis beschreibt das Symbol als Teil eines Systems, das endgültigen Interpretationen widersteht und im Bereich der Sprache eine progressive Signifikation erzeugt. Daß das Symbol auf eine interpretatorische und kritische Weise rezipiert werden soll, suggeriert Novalis im folgenden Fragment:

Jedes Symbol kann durch sein Symbolisirtes wieder Symbolisirt werden [...]. Auf Verwechselung des *Symbols* mit dem Symbolisirten – auf ihre Identisirung – auf den Glauben an wahrhafte, vollständige Repraesentation – und Relation des Bildes und des Originals – der Erscheinung und der Sub-

[14] Ernst Behler: *Frühromantik*. Berlin und New York 1992. S. 254.

stanz – auf der Folgerung von äußerer Aehnlichkeit – auf durchgängige innre Übereinstimmung und Zusammenhang – kurz auf Verwechselungen von Subject und Object beruht der ganze Aberglaube und Irrthum aller Zeiten, und Völker und Individuen [...].
(Alles kann Symbol des Andern seyn – Symbolische Function.)[15]

Sowie in moderner Literaturtheorie als auch in frühromantischer Poesie wird Repräsentation häufig durch diesen Bruch von Signifikat und Signifikant gekennzeichnet. Obwohl in frühromantischen Artikulierungen der Symbol- und Allegoriebegriffe diese Termini oft austauschbar sind, insoweit sie schlechthin das Wirkungsfeld der figurativen Sprache bezeichnen, deutet das Allegorische immer etwas Undarstellbares an.

In dem rhetorischen Diskurs der Frühromantik erscheint die Allegorie häufig als der Tropus *par excellence* des Unaussprechlichen. "Das Höchste kann man eben weil es unaussprechlich ist, nur allegorisch sagen", heißt es in Friedrich Schlegels *Gespräch über die Poesie*.[16] Das Verständnis für Allegorie erfordert eine Anerkennung der Mechanismen der Sprache selbst als Repräsentation, d.h. die Erkenntnis, daß, was angedeutet, gesagt, ausgedrückt, zitiert wird, schon eine Repräsentation ist. In mehreren Fragmenten hebt Novalis den indirekt darstellenden Charakter des Allegorischen hervor: "Höchstens kann wahre Poësie einen *allegorischen* Sinn im Großen haben und eine indirecte Wirckung wie Musik etc. thun".[17] In einem Brief an seinen Bruder Karl schreibt Novalis, daß "die Nachahmung der Natur, der Wircklichkeit nur allegorisch"[18] ausgedrückt, ausgeführt werden kann. Und in einem philosophischen Fragment von Friedrich Schlegel heißt es: "Die Unmöglichkeit das *Höchste* durch Reflexion positiv zu erreichen führt zur Allegorie [...]".[19] An die Stelle der Ungewißheit, der Aporie des Wissens tritt die Allegorie, das Bild.[20] Allegorie wird also zum formalen Ausdruck der Unmöglichkeit das Absolute logisch zu erfassen. Diese Formulierungen teilen der allegorischen Figur eine privilegierte Sprachposition zu, indem sie ihre Reflexionsstruktur nachdrücklich vorführen.

---

[15] Novalis: *Das Allgemeine Brouillon*. In: *Schriften*. Hg. von Richard Samuel. Stuttgart 1960. Bd. 3. S. 397-398.
[16] Friedrich Schlegel: *Gespräch über die Poesie*. In: *Kritische Ausgabe*. Hg. von Ernst Behler. Paderborn 1958. Bd. 2. S. 324.
[17] Novalis: *Schriften*. Bd. 3. S. 572.
[18] Novalis: *Schriften*. Bd. 4. S. 327.
[19] Friedrich Schlegel: *Kritische Ausgabe*. Bd. 19. S. 25.
[20] Siehe Friedrich Schlegel: *Kritische Ausgabe*. Bd. 19. S. 5.

Die prinzipielle Rehabilitierung der Allegorie für die Moderne wurde hauptsächlich von Benjamin und de Man durch eine Neuinterpretation der Trope, die ihre Zeitlichkeit in Anspruch nimmt, ausgeführt. In seiner Übersicht der Geschichte des Allegoriebegriffs in der Romantik bespricht Benjamin das Werk der Kritiker Friedrich Creuzer und Joseph Görres und verweist auf die geistige Brisanz ihrer Einführung der Kategorie "Zeit" in das semiotische Feld des Verhältnisses von Symbol und Allegorie, was eine bahnbrechende Erkenntnis des geschichtlicen Status beider Tropen und eine neue Formulierung ihrer theoretischen Grenzlinien ermöglicht:

Unter der entscheidenden Kategorie der Zeit, welche in dieses Gebiet der Semiotik getragen zu haben die große romantische Einsicht dieser Denker war, läßt das Verhältnis von Symbol und Allegorie eindringlich und formelhaft sich festlegen. Während im Symbol mit der Verklärung des Unterganges das transfigurierte Antlitz der Natur im Lichte der Erlösung flüchtig sich offenbart, liegt in der Allegorie die facies hippocratica der Geschichte als erstarrte Urlandschaft dem Betrachter vor Augen [...]. Das ist der Kern der allegorischen Betrachtung, der barocken, weltlichen Exposition der Geschichte als Leidengeschichte der Welt; bedeutend ist sie nur in den Stationen ihres Verfalls. Soviel Bedeutung, soviel Todverfallenheit, weil am tiefsten der Tod die zackige Demarkationslinie zwischen Physis und Bedeutung eingräbt [...]. Mit einer sonderbaren Verschränkung von Natur und Geschichte tritt der allegorische Ausdruck selbst in die Welt.[21]

Hier stellt Benjamin fest, daß Allegorie und Symbol grundsätzlich Darstellungen der Zeit sind. Während das Symbol die Brüche der Zeit und Geschichte in eine Art transzendentes Bild umwandelt, bewahrt die Allegorie die bildliche Erinnerung der Geschichte im Moment ihres Bruches. Allegorie versucht das von der Zeit schwer gezeichnete Gesicht der menschlichen Geschichte durch interpretatorische Praxis zu retten. Die Bruchstücke der Erinnerung werden gesammelt, erneut erinnert, neu gelesen, umgeschrieben, und in diesem fortwährenden Kommentar wird die Geschichte aufgeweckt. Die Benjaminsche Deutung der Allegorie als Zeichen des Verlustes – als Verfallen und Tod – und demgemäß einer Abwesenheit, die sie repräsentiert, wird von Benjamin nachfolgenden zeitgenössischen Kritikern in ihren Kommentaren über die Dialektik von Verlust und Ersatz (als figurative Kompensation) in der Allegorie aufgenommen. Fineman liest die Allegorie als "the mode that makes up for the distance, or

---

[21] Walter Benjamin: *Ursprung des deutschen Trauerspiels*. In *Gesammelte Schriften*. Hg. von Rolf Tiedemann und Hermann Schweppenhäuser. Frankfurt a.M. 1972. Bd. 1.1. S. 342-344.

heals the gap, between the present and a disappearing past, which, without interpretation, would otherwise be irretrievable and foreclosed [...]".[22] Die Allegorie bewahrt also eine Vergangenheit, die "mit jeder Gegenwart zu verschwinden droht",[23] vor der Gefahr der Vergänglichkeit und hebt sie im Kommentar auf. "Die biographische Geschichtlichkeit"[24] des Menschen, so Benjamin, wird in der rätselhaften Figur der Allegorie als Streben nach Interpretation geschildert.

In einem pointierten Essay über die Vergänglichkeit behauptet Sigmund Freud, daß die Erfahrung des Verlustes von etwas, was von uns geschätzt und geliebt war, der Trauer zugrunde liegt. Obwohl wir diese Trauer als selbstverständlich erklären, ist sie für den Psychologen "ein großes Rätsel, eines jener Phänomene, die man selbst nicht klärt, auf die man aber anderes Dunkle zurückführt".[25] Wenn unsere Liebesfähigkeit (Libido) sich vom Ich abwendet und auf Objekte zielt, werden diese gewissermaßen in unser Ich hineingenommen. Wenn diese Objekte verloren oder zerstört sind, wird die Libido wieder frei und kehrt entweder zeitweise zum Ich zurück oder eignet Ersatzobjekte an. Was jedoch nicht zu verstehen ist, ist warum diese Ablösung der Libido von ihren Objekten solch ein schmerzhaftes Erlebnis hervorruft. Die Libido, laut Freud, klammert sich an ihre Objekte und kann ihren Verlust nicht leiden, auch "wenn der Ersatz bereit liegt. Das also ist die Trauer".[26] Diese kurze Exposition der Trauer in dem Essay "Vergänglichkeit" gibt Freud Anlaß, die Destruktion des Krieges und den daraus entstehenden Verlust der Kulturgüter und kultureller Erinnerungen auf die Tagesordnung zu setzen. Er hofft jedoch darauf, daß die Trauer, die die Erfahrung der "Gebrechlichkeit" unsrer Kulturgüter hervorgerufen hat, durch das Ersetzen des Verlorenen überwunden werden kann.[27] Aus dieser Perspektive gesehen funktioniert die Allegorie bei Benjamin als figuratives Ersatzobjekt: "Auf dem Passionswege des Melancholikers sind die Allegorien die Stationen".[28] Die Allegorie interpretiert den Verlust und die dadurch verursachte Trauer als die "Leidengeschichte der

---

[22] Joel Fineman: The Structure of Allegorical Desire (Anm. 11). S. 29.

[23] Walter Benjamin: Über den Begriff der Geschichte. In: *Gesammelte Schriften*. Bd. 1.2. S. 695.

[24] Walter Benjamin: *Ursprung des deutschen Trauerspiels*. S. 343.

[25] Sigmund Freud: Vergänglichkeit. In: *Gesammelte Werke*. Hg. von Anna Freud. London 1945. Bd. 10. S. 360.

[26] Sigmund Freud: Vergänglichkeit. S. 360.

[27] Sigmund Freud: Vergänglichkeit. S. 361.

[28] Walter Benjamin: Zentralpark. In: *Gesammelte Schriften*. Bd. 1.2. S. 663.

Welt"[29] und setzt zugleich das verlorene oder zerstückelte Kulturgut erinnernd zusammen, oder übersetzt es in Schrift: "Wo die Romantik in dem Namen der Unendlichkeit, der Form und der Idee das vollendete Gebilde kritisch potenziert, da verwandelt mit einem Schlage der allegorische Tiefblick Dinge und Werke in erregende Schrift".[30] Das reflektierte Pathos der allegorischen Sprache ist ein unverkennbares Zeichen der vielfältigen Geschichten und Erinnerungen.

Paul de Man hat seinerseits mit großer theoretischer Anstrengung das historisch umgestaltende Genie der Allegorie herausgearbeitet. Indem de Man, Benjamin folgend, Ironie und Allegorie als die regulierenden Tropen der Zeitlichkeit bestimmt und ihre interpretatorische Kapazität grundsätzlich belegt, mißt er insbesondere der Allegorie eine erhebliche Bedeutung bei. In seinem oft zitierten Essay "The Rhetoric of Temporality" bringt er die zeitliche Dimension und das Zeitbewußtsein der Allegorie überzeugend zur Geltung:

Whereas the symbol postulates the possibility of an identity or identification, allegory designates primarily a distance in relation to its own origin, and, renouncing the nostalgia and the desire to coincide, it establishes its language in the void of this temporal difference. In so doing, it prevents the self from an illusory identification with the non-self, which is now fully, though painfully, recognized as a non-self. It is this painful knowledge that we perceive at the moments when early romantic literature finds its true voice. It is ironically revealing that this voice is so rarely recognized for what it really is [...].
We are led, in conclusion, to a historical scheme that differs entirely from the customary picture. The dialectical relationship between subject and object is no longer the central statement of romantic thought, but this dialectic is now located entirely in the temporal relationships that exist within a system of allegorical signs. It becomes a conflict between a conception of the self seen in its authentically temporal predicament and a defensive strategy that tries to hide from this negative self-knowledge. On the level of language the asserted superiority of the symbol over allegory, so frequent during the nineteenth century, is one of the forms taken by this tenacious self-mystification.[31]

Die Allegorie entmystizifiert also die im Symbol herrschende Einheit von Bild und Essenz und Ursprung und Präsenz. Im Gegensatz zu dem von Zeitlichkeit unberührten Symbol, das das Bewußtsein des in der

---

[29] Walter Benjamin: *Ursprung des deutschen Trauerspiels.* S. 343.
[30] Walter Benjamin: *Ursprung des deutschen Trauerspiels.* S. 352.
[31] Paul de Man: The Rhetoric of Temporality. In: *Blindness and Insight: Essays in the Rhetoric of Contemporary Criticism.* Minneapolis 1983. S. 207-208.

Zeit gespaltenen Subjekts negiert, ist die Allegorie zu einer kom-
promißlosen Erkenntnis ihres zeitlichen Dilemmas verurteilt. Und in
diesem Dilemma steht sie der Ironie nahe:

> The act of irony, as we now understand it, reveals the existence of a tempo-
> rality that is definitely not organic, in that it relates to its source only in
> terms of distance and difference and allows for no end, for no totality [...].
> Allegory and irony are thus linked in their common discovery of a truly
> temporal predicament. They are also linked in their common demystifica-
> tion of an organic world postulated in a symbolic mode of analogical corre-
> spondences or in a mimetic mode of representation in which fiction and
> reality could coincide. [32]

Obwohl die Anwendbarkeit der Ironie für einen Neuansatz der
rhetorischen Tradition von den Romantikern ausführlich besprochen
wurde, blieb eine genauere Formulierung der Form und Funktion der
Allegorie selbst unaussprechlich und ist im romantischen Sinne nur in
der Struktur der Allegorie flüchtig zu erkennen. Die Form der Allegorie, wie die der Erinnerung, gibt uns zu wissen, daß das, was dargestellt
ist, in einer Geographie und Historie der verdunkelten Ursprünge und
verschobenen Endpunkte steht. Die Literaturtheorie der Romantik
basiert auf der kritischen Einsicht, daß alle Formen aus sich selbst
ihre eigene Theorie herausarbeiten. Folglich wird jede Aufführung,
jedes Spiel des Allegorischen im romantischem Diskurs, in Schlegels
berühmter Formulierung, "in einer endlosen Reihe von Spiegeln"[33]
vervielfacht. Die Allegorie erkennt sich im Spiegel der romantischen
Poesie als ihre eigene Theorie, als Allegorie der Allegorie, wieder.
Ein genuines Verständnis der Formen und Tropen negiert jede
systematische Analyse und kann nur poetisch dargestellt werden.
Trotzdem ist es Creuzer, Görres, Benjamin und Paul de Man gelungen, dieses kühne Unterfangen – das Poetische theoretisch
darzustellen – zu leisten. Indem sie Allegorie auf eine generative
Weise mit Zeitlichkeit, Geschichte und Erinnerung in Verbindung
brachten, konnten sie aus den fragmentarischen Formulierungen des
Allegoriebegriffs einen erkenntnistheoretischen Bau errichten.
    Sobald Reflexionen über die Natur der Zeitlichkeit und die In-
kommensurabilität der Zeit angestellt werden, erzeugt das Nachdenken eine Reihe von metaphysichen Fragen, wie z.B. die Gegenwart definiert oder das Vergehen der Zeit festgestellt werden kann,
also Fragen, die anscheinend leicht zu beantworten sind aber sich
hartnäckig allen Antworten widersetzen. Diese Probleme sind nicht

---

[32] Paul de Man: The Rhetoric of Temporality. S. 222.
[33] Friedrich Schlegel: *Kritische Ausgabe*. Bd. 2. S. 182-183.

bloße Konsequenzen einer Sprachblindheit und ergeben sich nicht aus der Unzulänglichkeit der Sprache, sondern sind in unserer Erfahrung der Zeit begründet. Zeit ist die Voraussetzung aller Repräsentation, ist aber selbst nicht repräsentierbar. Da die Allegorie selbst Tropus der Undarstellbarkeit ist, kann vielleicht ihre Beziehung zur Zeit mit der Einführung der Kategorie der Erinnerung ausgedrückt werden. "Wenn es die Phantasie ist, die der Erinnerung die Korrespondenzen darbringt, so ist es das Denken, das ihr die Allegorien widmet. Die Erinnerung führt beide zu einander",[34] schreibt Benjamin in "Zentralpark".

Die Psychoanalyse als "die letzte Erinnerungskunst unserer Kultur"[35] represäntiert, laut Fineman, eine Erweiterung und Ergänzung der allegorischen Tradition, der sie entstammt.[36] In diesem Zusammenhang kann der romantische Allegoriebegriff in einer engen formalen Verwandtschaft mit Traumbildern bzw. Erinnerung verstanden werden. Während die Allegorie auf das Problem der Repräsentation, auf die immer von einem Verlust überschattete Sprache hindeutet, erinnern die Formen der Erinnerung an die Undarstellbarkeit der Zeit. Was steht in Gefahr in dieser irreduziblen Undarstellbarkeit? Die Kulturgüter der Epochen? Die Bedeutung der Geschichte selbst? Oder die menschliche Existenz überhaupt? In seiner Jenaer Vorlesung über Transzendentalphilosophie überwindet Schlegel in ästhetischer (ja selbst allegorischer) Form die Gefahr der Vergänglichkeit, indem er den Ursprung der menschlichen Existenz und Erkenntnis mit der Wahrnehmung der Allegorie gleichsetzt:

Warum ist das Unendliche aus sich herausgegangen und hat sich endlich gemacht? – das heißt mit andren Worten: *Warum sind Individua?* Oder:*Warum läuft das Spiel der Natur nicht in einem Nu ab, so daß also gar nichts existirt?* Die Antwort auf diese Frage ist nur möglich, wenn wir einen Begriff einschieben. Wir haben nämlich die Begriffe *eine, unendliche Substanz* – und *Individua.* Wenn wir uns den Übergang von dem einen zu den andern erklären wollen, so können wir dies nicht anders, als daß wir zwischen beyden noch einen Begriff einschieben, nämlich den Begriff *des Bildes* oder *Darstellung, Allegorie.* Das Individium ist also *ein Bild* der *einen unendlichen Substanz.*

[34] Walter Benjamin: Zentralpark. S. 669.
[35] "Psychoanalysis is our culture's last Art of Memory". Richard Terdiman: *Present Past: Modernity and the Memory Crisis.* Ithaca und London 1993. S. 240.
[36] Joel Fineman: The Structure of Allegorical Desire. S. 27.

(Man könnte dies auch ausdrücken: Gott hat die Welt hervorgebracht, um sich selbst darzustellen).[37]

Die Allegorie markiert also den Übergang zwischen Chaos und Form. Sie zeichnet aber keinen geschichtlich oder wissenschaftlich feststellbaren Moment auf, sondern ein erinnertes, ja erfundenes Gleichnis, eine sich immer wiederholende Instanz der (Bild)ung. Ohne Allegorie als *aide de memoire* und Interpretationsinstrument würde die Vergangenheit die Gefahr laufen von der Gegenwart vergessen zu werden, und die großen Leistungen der menschlichen Kultur könnten im Chaos der undarstellbaren Zeit verloren gehen.

In der Welt der romantischen Kritik haben Poesie, Fabel, Mythos und Gesang die Herrschaft von Erklärung und Logik mit einer Poetik unterbrochen, die verschiedenartige Formen der Erkenntnis anerkennt. Die Dialektik von Konstruktion und Zerstörung, die die Ironie kennzeichnet, kann als eine Art der Geschichtsphilosophie gelten. Als eine häufig vorkommende Trope der Geschichtsschreibung[38] bricht Ironie die begrenzten Protokollen analytisch-wissenschaftlicher Geschichte auf und übersetzt die überlieferten Konzeptionen von Erfahrung, Geschehnis, Subjekt und Identität in die Sprache der ästhetischen Mehrdeutigkeit. Die von einer durchgehenden und durchglänzenden Ironie geprägten romantischen Erzählungen, wie Achim von Arnims *Isabella von Ägypten* oder Kleists *Der Zweikampf*, sind oft auf historische Fakte basiert, stellen aber durch vielfältige Repräsentationsformen – wie z.B. die Rahmengeschichte, verschiedene Erzählperspektiven und zweideutige Endungen – die Faktizität der Geschichte und die Grenzen der Wirklichkeit in Frage. So erhebt die Ironie verdrängte Ungewissheiten auf eine Ebene, wo eine effektive Auseinandersetzung mit dem oft nicht problematisierten Verständnis von Realität und Wahrheit möglich ist.

Die Allegorie ihrerseits verhüllt einen Zeitverlust, der einen Palimpsest von Erinnerungen, historischem Trauma und poetischen Träumen simuliert. Folglich kann die Allegorie nur fragmentarisch sein und erhebt keine Ansprüche auf die Offenbarung einer historischen Wahrheit. Sie erzählt ihre Geschichte in der poetischen Sprache der Erinnerung durch die Stimme der Ahnung. Diese allego-

---

[37] Friedrich Schlegel: *Kritische Ausgabe.* Bd. 12. S. 39.
[38] Siehe Hayden Whites umfassende Diskussion über die Poetik der Geschichtsschreibung in: *Metahistory: The Historical Imagination in Nineteenth-Century Europe.* Baltimore und London 1973; insb. Kapitel 1, 2 und 10.

risch erinnernde poetische Historiographie wird in Novalis' *Heinrich von Ofterdingen* folgendermaßen aufgezeichnet:

> Der eigentliche Sinn für die Geschichten der Menschen entwickelt sich erst spät, und mehr unter den stillen Einflüssen der Erinnerung, als unter den gewaltsameren Eindrücken der Gegenwart. Die nächsten Ereignisse scheinen nur locker verknüpft, aber sie sympathisieren desto wunderbarer mit den entfernteren; und nur dann, wenn man imstande ist, eine lange Reihe zu übersehn und weder alles buchstäblich zu nehmen, noch auch mit mutwilligen Träumen die eigentliche Ordnung zu verwirren, bemerkt man die geheime Verkettung des Ehemaligen und Künftigen, und lernt die Geschichte aus Hoffnung und Erinnerung zusammensetzen.[39]

Wie die Erinnerung, zieht die poetische Kraft des Allegorischen die faktische Geschichte in Zweifel und führt die Simultanität des Vergessens und des Nachdenkens aus. Die Allegorie verkörpert ein kulturelles Gedächtnis, das gleichzeitig diachronisch und synchronisch erinnert. Im Benjaminschen Sinne löst sie die Fragmente der Ereignisse und Erfahrungen aus ihren historischen Rahmen und fügt sie schöpferisch-erinnernd in die veränderlichen Bedeutungskonstellationen der Gegenwart ein. Die romantische Allegorie akzentuiert die Forderung, das Sprachliche und das Sinnliche in der Geschichte und dem Gedächtnis der Kultur zu finden und diese poetisch weiterzugeben. Sie überläßt sich jedoch keiner Nostalgie für eine in der Vorstellung verklärte Vergangenheit; denn sie will erinnern nicht als Sklavin des Vergangenen, sondern als dessen Interpretin, die ein scharfes Verständnis "vom Nutzen und Nachteil der Historie für das Leben" hat. Vielleicht nicht immer ausdrücklich, aber jedoch nachdrücklich, fungiert die Allegorie in der frühromantischen Poesie als die Trope der Erinnerung, während die Ironie, da sie die veränderliche Syntax der Zeiten gut versteht, mit den instabilen Bedeutungen der Kultur gerne spielt und eine vielschichtige Verlagerung ihrer Wahrheiten darstellt, sich als die Trope der Geschichte bekennt.

Entscheidend für eine kritische Schlußfolgerung ist die Anerkennung, daß das Verständnis für Allegorie durch die Einstellung einer Kultur zu den miteinander in Konkurrenz stehenden Diskursen eines Zeitalters diktiert wird. Northrop Frye erkennt in allen Formen der Kritik eine Art des Allegorisierens, denn Schreiben und Interpretieren sind schon Akte der Aneignung, des Umschreibens:

---

[39] Novalis: *Heinrich von Ofterdingen*. In: *Schriften*. Bd. 1. S. 257-258.

It is not often realized that all commentary is allegorical interpretation, an attaching of ideas to the structure of poetic imagery. The instant that any critic permits himself to make a genuine comment about a poem (e.g., "In *Hamlet* Shakespeare appears to be portraying the tragedy of irresolution") he has begun to allegorize. Commentary thus looks at literature as, in its formal phase, a potential allegory of events and ideas.[40]

Maureen Quilligan sieht einen erheblichen Unterschied zwischen Allegorie als Redefigur und Allegorese (*allegoresis*), die einen interpretatorischen Akt bezeichnet. Während die Allegorie als figurative Sprechweise durch formale Eigenschaften wie Personifizierung und progressive Signifikation gekennzeichnet ist, bekundet sich in der Allegorese eine bewußte Art des Kommentars und der Korrektur. Die moderne Rehabilitierung der Allegorie, so Quilligan, ist eigentlich als eine Wiederherstellung und Legitimierung der interpretatorischen Funktion der Allegorese zu verstehen.[41] In ihrer literarischen Praxis haben die Frühromantiker, Benjamin und de Man sowohl die eidetische, bildliche Fassungskraft der Allegorie als auch die kommentierende Sprache der Allegorese zur Geltung gebracht. Ähnlicherweise hat Benjamin Erinnerungen, die für die Gegenwart das (bild)ende Potential des Vergangenen liefern, als Umdeutungen der Geschichte bewertet. Diese erfinden neu in allegorisch-poetischer Gestalt die Erfahrungen und Kenntnisse der Geschichte. Die Erinnerung bedient sich der Allegorie, da diese nachdrücklich die Flüchtigkeit aller Repräsentation betont und die Stabilität des Weltbildes ablehnt, indem sie dessen Fragmentierung in der Zeit darstellt. Mit dem Vergehen der Zeit wird die Vergangenheit immer unzugänglicher, kann aber durch die eidetische Kapazität der Erinnerung restituiert werden: "Nur als Bild, das auf Nimmerwiedersehen im Augenblick seiner Erkennbarkeit eben aufblitzt, ist die Vergangenheit festzuhalten".[42] Die emanzipatorische Erinnerung nimmt die Form eines Bildes, einer Allegorie an. Die fragmentierten Bruchstücke der Geschichte formen keine "Abfolge von Begebenheiten [...] wie einen Rosenkranz",[43] aber wie das Erinnerungsvermögen oder das Allegorische (bild)en sie neue Konstellationen. Da diese einander durch kulturelle Erinnerungen reflektieren, verbinden sie unsere Zeit mit anderen Zeiten und machen eine unreflektierte Darstellung der Vergangenheit unhaltbar. In diesem Akt der Reflexion,

---

[40] Northrop Frye: *Anatomy of Criticism: Four Essays*. Princeton 1971. S. 89.
[41] Siehe Maureen Quilligan: *The Language of Allegory: Defining the Genre*. Ithaca und New York 1979.
[42] Walter Benjamin: *Über den Begriff der Geschichte*. S. 695.
[43] Walter Benjamin: *Über den Begriff der Geschichte*. S. 704.

wo die Allegorie über die bloß signifizierende Grenze hinausgeht, kommt nach Fletcher ihre erlösende soziale Dimension zum Vorschein.[44]

Als *figura* der Zersplitterung und Zusammenfügung der Lebenskontexte im Benjaminschen Sinne, hinterfragt Allegorie geschlossene Narrationen, fixierte Identitäten und offizielle Geschichten. "Das von der allegorischen Intention Betroffene wird aus den Zusammenhängen des Lebens ausgesondert: es wird zerschlagen und konserviert zugleich" heißt es in einem der vielen Fragmente über die Allegorie in Benjamins "Zentralpark".[45] Es ist diese allegorische Intention, die die Kritiker immer wieder dazu antreibt, um mit Ernst Behler zu sprechen, "aus dem Geflecht des frühromantischen Denk- und Dichtungszusammenhanges jeweils verschiedene Themen" hervorzuheben und diese "nicht als in sich abgeschlossene Gebilde [...], sondern als Stadien einer stets fortgehenden Reflexion, die ihrer Natur nach nicht zu einem Abschluß gelangt",[46] aufzufassen. Die allegorische Tendenz der kulturellen Erinnerung interpretiert die Geschichte immer neu, sprengt bestimmte Epochen "aus dem homogenen Verlauf der Geschichte"[47] heraus, um "das bruchstückhafte Erbe der Vergangenheit zusammen mit aktuelleren Anleihen und Anregungen in eine bedeutungsvolle Gegenwart umzuformen".[48] Wir schreiben an einem unendlichen Buch der Erinnerungen weiter.

---

[44] "Both this satirical criticism and the apocalyptical escape into an infinite space and time tend toward high human goals. In both cases allegory is serving major social and spiritual needs. When we add to these the functions of education (the didactic strain) and entertainment (the riddling or romantic strains), we have a modality of symbolism which we must respect". Angus Fletcher: *Allegory*. S. 23.

[45] Walter Benjamin: Zentralpark. S. 666.

[46] Ernst Behler: *Frühromantik*. S. 29.

[47] Walter Benjamin: Über den Begriff der Geschichte. S. 703.

[48] Iain Chambers: *Migration*. S. 124.

Karin Schutjer

A Ground of One's Own:
Hölderlin, *Eigentum* and *Eigentümlichkeit*

Poetry is a kind of property in Hölderlin's thinking, a ground of one's own in which individuality emerges. The metaphor of the poet's "ground", which is by now overdetermined by nationalist resonances, is multivalent in Hölderlin's usage, suggesting not only a proper cultural soil but also, in Hölderlin's philosophical specula-tions, an undifferentiated continuity that defies categories such as self and nation. Partially in reaction to the aesthetics of his mentor Schiller, Hölderlin develops a notion of poetry as a middle condition between individual rootedness and a deep, universal rootlessness.

In the tumultuous final years of the eighteenth century, Hölderlin developed a pressing preoccupation with the nature of individual property. According to the logic that one needs a proper space to cultivate one's moral individuality, *Eigentum* becomes linked in Hölderlin's thinking to particular character, to *Eigentümlichkeit*.[1] Hölderlin conceives of property as *eigener Grund*, a ground of one's own, without which the individual is threatened. In his poem 'Mein Eigentum' (1799) he describes the fate of the soul with no proper ground: it becomes like a rootless, wilted plant scorched in the heat of day: "Denn, wie die Pflanze, wurzelt auf eignem Grund/ sie nicht,/ verglüht die Seele des Sterblichen,/ Der mit dem Tageslichte nur, ein/ Armer, auf heiliger Erde wandelt".[2] The poet eventually proposes song as his proper sphere: the poem is to be his "asylum" and the "garden" where he might dwell (StA 1.1: 307). Yet, as we will see, private property is a precarious notion for Hölderlin, for it rests on deeper, undifferentiated ground. This essay will explore Hölderlin's

---

[1] In this point, as in so many others, Hölderlin anticipates Hegel's later writings. According to Hegel's *Philosophy of Right*, to become fully realized an individual needs an external sphere: "Die Person muß sich eine äußere *Sphäre ihrer Freiheit* geben, um als Idee zu seyn". Hegel thus equates "Eigen-tum" with "[das] Daseyn der Persönlichkeit". Georg Wilhelm Freidrich Hegel: *Sämtliche Werke*. 20 vols. Stuttgart-Bad Cannstatt 1964. Vol. 7. Pp. 94, 104.

[2] Friedrich Hölderlin: *Sämtliche Werke und Briefe*. Ed. Friedrich Beissner. 7 vols. Stuttgart 1943-77. Vol. 1. P. 306. Hereafter all references to this edition will appear parenthetically in the text under the abbreviation "StA". The poem is quoted in its entirety below.

vision for poetry as a sphere both personal and impersonal. Both in response to his own lack of a social and economic foothold, and in reaction to the "obstinate pride of the others, who already are something"[3] (and who thereby fail to understand their dependence on something outside of themselves), Hölderlin imagines a poetic sphere that could be at once individual and common property.

auf eignem Wege

One does not have to look far to find in Hölderlin's life a whole host of dilemmas stimulating this philosophical and metaphorical investigation of property. Much of Hölderlin's short career was spent simply trying to create the conditions under which he could work. While he imagined that a career as writer and philosopher could secure him some economic and social independence "auf eignem Wege" (StA 6.1: 292), an independent existence also appeared to be the precondition of writing. He thus looked for some provisional social space in which to write, seeking to avoid at all costs the fixed bourgeois roles of pastor, spouse and father, which he associated with suffocating constraint. In a letter to his mother he explains his resistance to this prescribed career and life path with reference to his *Eigentümlichkeit*. He considers it a duty to comprehend one's own peculiar character and seek conditions favorable to it.

> Liebe Mutter! es ist Pflicht, seinen *eigentümlichen* Charakter zu kennen, sei er nun gut oder schlimm, und so viel möglich, sich in Umständen zu erhalten, oder sich in solche zu versezen zu suchen, welche gerade diesem Charakter günstig sind. (StA 6.1: 122; italics mine)

In his attempt to avoid the clergy and nourish his own character through intellectual pursuits, Hölderlin thus began his career as a family tutor. His first position with the von Kalbs in Walthershausen in 1794 initially seemed to offer him both social exchange and intellectual privacy. He participated in the family culture of reading aloud, of playful and serious conversation, yet as he writes to his

---

[3] In this passage, Hölderlin reaffirms his commitment to his friend Neuffer, despite the fact that "ich noch nichts bin, und vieleicht, ich werde nie nichts werden". In the search for self-understanding, friendship is essential: "[...] des Freundes Zuruf [ist] unentbehrlich, um mit uns wieder eins zu werden, wenn unsre eigne Seele, unser bestes Leben uns entlaidet worden, durch die Albernheiten der gemeinen Menschen, und *den eigensinnigen Stolz der andern, die schon etwas sind*" (StA 6.1: 278-9; italics mine).

mother, he was also given space to work: "Wenn ich aber über einer eignen Arbeit etwas zerstreut bin und Gesichter schneide, so weis man schon, wie's gemeint ist, und ich brauche nicht unterhaltend zu sein, wenn ich nicht in der Laune bin" (StA 6.1: 115).

This balance between privacy and social exchange soon eroded, however, for a curious reason: his young ward, Fritz, turned out to be an inveterate nighttime masturbator, a habit thought sure to lead to moral and physical decay by the doctors and educators of his day. Hölderlin was himself certain that he could recognize the traces of this "vice" in the boy and that indeed he was witnessing his pupil's further deterioration with every passing day (StA 6.1: 147-8). In an attempt to protect the child from himself, Hölderlin kept nighttime vigils that eventually destroyed his own concentration and capacity to work. He writes to his mother, "Das ängstliche Wachen bei Nacht zerstörte meinen Kopf und machte mich für mein Tagwerk beinahe unfähig" (StA 6.1: 148). This "vice" associated with private places both disturbed and put pressure on Hölderlin's own private activity of writing and contemplation.[4] The dangers of solitary reverie reemerge in the novel *Hyperion* when Hyperion awakes from a dream of communion and discovers with dismay his own (onanistic) solipsism, "es ist als fühlt' ich ihn, den Geist der Welt, wie eines Freundes warme Hand, aber ich erwache und meine, ich habe meine eignen Finger gehalten" (StA 3: 12). For Hölderlin, then, total privacy can be associated with self-involved delusion and eventually even self-destruction.[5]

In November 1794, Hölderlin left the family von Kalb and moved to nearby Jena with a small financial bonus from the von Kalbs for his good efforts, and with the hope, at least for the time being, "mit eignen Arbeiten Leib und Seele zu nähren" (StA 6.1: 149). Seven months later, for reasons that remain unclear, Hölderlin abruptly

---

[4] La Planche sees a much more thorough threat to Hölderlin's entire psychic organization at this juncture, identifying in Hölderlin's harsh reaction to the boy an initial schizophrenic episode. According to La Planche's Lacanian reading, Fritz's uninhibited phallic play brings to the fore Hölderlin's own lack of a paternal law within which to integrate the phallus. Jean Laplanche: *Hölderlin und die Suche nach dem Vater.* Stuttgart-Bad Cannstatt 1975 (Problemata 38). Pp. 39-41.
[5] Of course Hölderlin's novel about "der Eremit in Griechenland" describes many different forms of solitude, which are viewed as more or less legitimate. Solitude does not amount to solipsism in every case.

abandoned Jena for home in Nürtingen.[6] By January 1796 he had assumed a second position as family tutor, this time with the Gontard family in Frankfurt. Not surprisingly, letters to friends and family preserved from this period reveal little about Hölderlin's romantic involvement with the children's mother, Susette Gontard, or about the details of his strained relationship with her husband. But in a letter to his mother he does describe in cryptic terms a struggle in the Gontard household between two parties, one for him, the other against him; one rendering him almost overconfident, the other making him depressed and bitter. He portrays the extremity of this situation as resulting from a lack of his own domestic space:

> Das beste wäre freilich gewesen, sich still und in Entfernung, und mit beeden Theilen die Beziehungen so allgemein, als möglich, zu erhalten. Aber diß geht wohl an, wenn einer sein eignes Haus und keine besondern Verhältnisse hat, wo man oft in häufige Beziehungen geraten *muß*. (StA 6.1: 256)

Hölderlin concludes that he must simply do his best to concentrate on himself in the midst of this domestic strife: "Es ist also für itz nichts anders zu thun, als alle Kunst und alle Vorsicht zu gebrauchen, um die Gesellschaft, worinn ich lebe, nicht sehr störend auf mich wirken zu lassen, und still. und vest auf meinem eignen Wesen zu beruhen" (StA 6.1: 257).

Eventually Hölderlin left the Gontard household and occupied an apartment of his own in nearby Bad Homburg, where he was in the proximity of friends and from which he secretly continued contact with Susette Gontard. In a letter to his sister he describes his apartment as a space that opens out onto the external world – it has pictures on the walls of the four corners of the world, a window looking out onto trees, and chairs for good friends:

> Ein paar hübsche kleine Zimmer, wovon ich mir das eine, wo ich wohne, mit den Karten der 4 Welttheile dekorirt habe, einen eigenen großen Tisch im Speissaal der auch zugleich das Schlafzimmer ist, und eine Kommode

---

[6] His letter to Schiller of July 23rd, 1795 suggests that he fled his mentor's overwhelming presence (StA 6.1: 175-6). Adolf Beck first discovered evidence that Hölderlin might have been fleeing responsibility for the pregnancy of Wilhelmine Marianne Kirms, Charlotte von Kalb's young friend. Adolf Beck: Die Gesellschafterin Charlottens von Kalb. In: *Hölderlin-Jahrbuch* 1957. Pp. 46-66. La Planche sees Hölderlin's flight from Schiller and his (possible) flight from the situation with Kirms as closely related psychologically. La Planche. P. 61.

daselbst, und hier im Kabinet einen Schreibtisch wo die Kasse verwahrt ist, und wieder einen Tisch, wo die Bücher und Papiere liegen, und noch ein kleines Tischchen am Fenster, an den Bäumen, wo ich eigentlich zu Hauße bin, und mein Wesen treibe, und Stühle hab' ich auch für ein paar gute Freunde [...]. (StA 6.1: 352)

That Hölderlin sought more than retreat and refuge in this domestic space is clear in a letter he wrote to Sinklair after returning from a visit with his friend to the Rastatt Congress, the negotiations with the French over the future of German territories. His hopes have been rejuvenated by the new friends he met there, who share his faith in humanity as well, implicity, as his revolutionary aspirations. His thoughts of these new, politically engaged friends provide relief from his four walls and from the (unspecified) evil demon that threatens to overwhelm him in his solitude:

Sag es ihnen nur, den Deinen und Meinen, daß ich manchmal an sie denke, wenn mirs sei, als gäb es außer mir und ein paar Einsamen, die ich im Herzen trage, nichts, als meine vier Wände, und daß sie mir seyen, wie eine Melodie, zu der man seine Zuflucht nimmt, wenn einen der böse Dämon überwältigen will. (StA 6.1:300)

Here again solitude appears haunting and ominous for Hölderlin. In a letter to Neuffer from around the same time he describes retreat as defeat at the hands of the world, "Ach! die Welt hat meinen Geist von früher Jugend an in sich zurükgescheucht, und daran leid' ich noch immer" (StA 6.1: 289). Hölderlin clearly conceived his space for writing as a space from which he could safely radiate outwards and transform an external world that seemed otherwise so inhospitable to him.

The apartment in Bad Homburg was only a short-term solution: Hölderlin had saved enough money from his time in Frankfurt to support himself for approximately a year. He had hoped that his work-in-progress *Empedokles* might at last secure his career. As his progress on the drama slowed, however, he turned to the development of a "humanistic" journal, for which he sought contributions from his old contacts in Jena and Weimar, including, to no avail, Schiller and Goethe. Soon his failure to secure commitments from other authors forced him to give up the project. He turned to Schiller one more time, from his mother's home in Nürtingen in 1801, with a proposal to return to Jena as a lecturer in Greek literature. This plan, too, derailed for apparent lack of support. By the end of that year, as he set out for Bordeaux to assume another position as family tutor, Hölderlin foresaw no easy homecoming.

Propertied Poets

Schiller and Goethe, to whom Hölderlin looked in vain for help with his journal, were of course the age's great success stories, the prime models of propertied poets born into the middle class. Goethe, with his acquired title of nobility, was then well situated in his elegant house *am Frauenplan* in Weimar; Schiller – who would receive a title of nobility in 1802 – struggled a great deal more than Goethe but by the late nineties was securely installed in his *Gartenhaus* in Jena. I contend that Hölderlin eventually develops his own notion of aesthetic property in opposition to the models presented by these men, particularly to the aesthetics of his former mentor Schiller. In his very first letter to Schiller, in 1794, Hölderlin characterizes himself as "poor" next to Schiller's spiritual wealth. We turn first to consider how Schiller comes to regard this "poverty" in Hölderlin and then to suggest how Hölderlin ultimately rejects Schiller's analysis.[7]

Schiller clearly understood well the social plight of young poets and felt for Hölderlin. In a letter to Goethe he refers to Hölderlin as his "Freund" and "Schutzbefohlene[r]" on whom he does not want to give up.[8] Yet the tone of his exchange with Goethe concerning his protegé is patronizing and self-congratulatory at best. For example, he refers to Hölderlin and his friend Siegfried Schmid as "Leutchen" (NA 29: 111), who will have to gather their courage to dare an audience with Goethe during his stay in Frankfurt. This condescension towards the younger, less successful Hölderlin has a clear psychological payoff for Schiller. In distancing himself from Hölderlin, he distances himself from an image of his earlier self as intensely subjective and philosophical:

> Aufrichtig, ich fand in diesen Gedichten [von Hölderlin] viel von meiner eigenen sonstigen Gestalt, und es ist nicht das erstemal, daß mich der Verfasser an mich mahnte. Er hat eine heftige Subjectivität und verbindet damit einen gewißen philosophischen Geist und Tiefsinn. Sein Zustand ist gefährlich, da solchen Naturen so gar schwer beyzukommen ist. (NA 29: 92-3)

---

[7] Hölderlin writes to Schiller: "Warum muß ich so arm sein, und so viel Interesse haben um den Reichtum eines Geistes?" StA 6.1: 113.

[8] Friedrich von Schiller: *Schillers Werke*. Ed. Julius Petersen et al. 42 vols. Weimar 1943-77. Vol. 29. P. 92. Hereafter all references to this edition will appear parenthetically in the text under the abbreviation "NA".

This critique of Hölderlin simultaneously reinforces Schiller's bonds of friendship to Goethe. By rejecting his own excessively philosophical inclinations, Schiller offers Goethe an apparent disavowal of his own former tendency towards abstraction in poetry before, through his friendship with Goethe, he had learned a greater appreciation for the sensory world. Goethe rewards Schiller with an assurance that while he finds something of Schiller in Hölderlin's poems, these poems "[...] haben weder die Fülle, noch die Stärke, noch die Tiefe Ihrer Arbeiten".[9]

The core of Schiller's critique of Hölderlin is that he fails to achieve proper aesthetic grasp of his object, that he is, in effect, aesthetically dispossessed. An aesthetic relation to an object would consist, according to Schiller's Kantian aesthetics, in a harmonious tension between the particular and the general. In clear contrast to his ideal of balanced aesthetic play, Schiller describes poets like Hölderlin, whom he groups with Schmid and Jean Paul Richter, as "einseitig" and "überspannt" (NA 29: 118). Schiller views Hölderlin as too philosophical, which is to say *too general*; and yet he simultaneously suggests that Hölderlin, because he is too out of touch with empirical reality, is too inward and idiosyncratic and in turn *not generalizable enough*. The outcome is the same either way: through too much generality or too much idiosyncracy, one fails to achieve the desired aesthetic reconciliation of a material world with generalizable forms of consciousness. Objects repel [*zurückstoßen*] rather than secure [*festhalten*] such poets. While they develop a certain "Ernst" and "Innigkeit", these poets lack "Ruhe", "Klarheit" and "Freiheit" (NA 29: 118).

Aesthetic propertylessness may indeed be the product of particular social conditions, according to Schiller. He concurs with an earlier comment by Goethe that this inwardness and lack of freedom is found in poets from a certain social class, who meet too much opposition from the empirical world (NA 29: 118). Schmid, the poet Schiller repeatedly pairs with Hölderlin, thus becomes a caricature in reverse of the vulgar world of Frankfurt: just as the Frankfurters have no time to look into themselves, Schmid and his sort (i.e. Hölderlin) are not able to emerge out of themselves. Whereas in Frankfurt one finds the naked, empty object without feeling, in Schmid one finds feeling but no object for it (NA 29: 118).

Schiller laments this predicament for poets: "[...] wenn gleich ein mächtiges und glückliches Naturell über alles siegt, so däucht mir

[9] Johann Wolfgang von Goethe: *Goethes Werke*. 127 vols. Weimar 1887-1919. Part IV. Vol. 12. P. 177.

doch, daß manches brave Talent auf diese Art verloren geht" (NA 29: 118). One can invert the emphasis of this sentence without changing its logic: even if some worthy talent gets lost in this way, a powerful and felicitous nature triumphs over everything. In this inversion, one detects more clearly Schiller's self-justification. Although in the earlier letter he has identified Hölderlin with his earlier self, Schiller, unlike Hölderlin, has implicitly overcome the threat posed by the environment.

Furthermore, the assertion that a powerful natural talent or disposition triumphs even over the most difficult social conditions serves as a crucial caveat if Schiller is to remain committed to his own aesthetic program. In his Aesthetic Letters Schiller indeed acknowledges a practical dilemma: for political conditions to change, individual character must change, yet for individual character to change, political influences must change (NA 20: 332). To break this vicious circle that degrades individual character and sustains bad political institutions, Schiller turns to beauty as a source and instrument that can ennoble individuals even under less than ideal conditions (NA 20: 333). In Schiller's vision every empirical individual has the possibility of becoming free through aesthetic play. The transformation of society thus begins with the aesthetic harmony of the individual and builds toward a true state reflecting the inner balance of its citizens. In this progression, beauty reconciles the conflict between individuals and society that Schiller finds so pronounced in Hölderlin. In Schiller's vision, *Eigentümlichkeit*, the character of aesthetically balanced individuals, can be carried into this aesthetic communal whole:

> Ist der innere Mensch mit sich einig, so wird er auch bey der höchsten Universalisierung seines Betragens seine *Eigentümlichkeit* retten, und der Staat wird bloß der Ausleger seines schönen Instinkts, die deutlichere Formel seiner innern Gesetzgebung sein. (NA 20: 318; italics mine)

Schiller and Goethe's advice to Hölderlin is thus to give up his excessive philosophizing and to focus on achieving aesthetic harmony. Schiller writes to him in 1796:

> Fliehen Sie wo möglich die philosophischen Stoffe, sie sind die undankbarsten, und in fruchtlosem Ringen mit denselben verzehrt sich oft die beßte Kraft, bleiben Sie der Sinnenwelt näher, so werden Sie weniger in Gefahr seyn, die Nüchternheit in der Begeisterung zu verlieren, oder in einen gekünstelten Ausdruck zu verirren. (NA 29: 13)

During their meeting in Frankfurt, Goethe also urges Hölderlin to restrict the range and subject of his poetry. He advises Hölderlin "kleine Gedichte zu machen und sich zu jedem einen menschlich interessanten Gegenstand zu wählen".[10] The more limited poetic domain that Goethe recommends to Hölderlin here begs comparison with a private, petit-bourgeois sphere. Schiller and Goethe both seem to be telling Hölderlin to give up his universalistic ambitions and to focus on a more domestic, aesthetic space. In this smaller sphere, Hölderlin should be able to overcome his strained relationship with a hostile, external world and develop inner harmony.

While Hölderlin's bearing towards Schiller (and Goethe) appears to have been in every instance deferential, it is clear that he meanwhile rejected the Schillerian model of the negotiation between private and public spheres. We can find the seeds of Hölderlin's critique of his mentor in a letter which seems simply a lament about his own vulnerabilities. Hölderlin views Schiller's insulation from the external world as a kind of *Eigentum* he lacks:[11]

ich glaube, daß diß das *Eigentum* der seltnen Menschen ist, daß sie geben können, ohne zu empfangen, daß sie sich auch "am Eise wärmen" können. Ich fühle nur zu oft, daß ich eben kein seltner Mensch bin. Ich friere und starre in dem Winter, der mich umgiebt. So eisern mein Himmel ist, so steinern bin ich. (StA 6.1: 181)

Hölderlin's apparent admiration for Schiller here will turn into a criticism of the sort of person who could be so indifferent to the external world that he could warm himself on ice. In a letter to his brother-in-law in 1797, he considers the kind of independence he has implicitly attributed to Schiller untenable:

Ich fühle immer mehr, wie unzertrennlich unser Wirken und Leben mit den Kräften zusammenhängt, die um uns her sich regen, und so ist natürlich, daß ich es lange nicht hinreichend halte, aus sich selber zu schöpfen, und seine Eigenthümlichkeit, wäre sie auch die allgemeingültigste, blindlings unter die Gegenstände hineinzuwerfen. (StA 6.1: 261)

---

[10] Goethe: *Goethes Werke*, Part IV. Vol. 12. P. 263.
[11] While in the following quotation, Hölderlin does not directly identify Schiller as "der seltne Mensch" who is oblivious to his environment, such is implied from the preceding lines in which Hölderlin notes how unaffected Schiller was by his conversation partner, how little distressed by the "cloudy and unpolished mirror" in which Hölderlin reflected Schiller's formulations back to him.

We can begin now to anticipate the divergence between Schiller and Hölderlin, to which we will return below. Schiller views the private aesthetic sphere as a secure, independent starting point, as the fundamental endowment of all human beings.[12] At the same time, however, he assumes a basic uniformity in the human constitution, so that individuals, once properly balanced and attuned, can join together unproblematically into a political state or social whole, without sacrificing what is proper to them, their *Eigentümlichkeit*. Individuality is thus well fortified, and social harmony a matter of proper alignment. By contrast, Hölderlin imagines his own individual foothold as, from the first, far more fragile and interdependent. Yet, as we will see, he simultaneously stresses a diversity of individual positions and character that make unification more complex and heterogenous.

Narrow and Open Ground

A pervasive metaphor through which Hölderlin understands the relationship between personal and public spheres appeared in our opening image from 'Mein Eigentum': the poet is like a plant that needs to take root in ground of its own so as not to be scorched by the sun. The image of a plant seeking proper soil comes up repeatedly, not only in Hölderlin's literary works, but in his letters as well. In a letter to his brother in the summer of 1796 he describes himself as an old flower stem that had fallen with its flowerpot and soil onto the street, that had lost its buds and suffered damage to its roots, and that, despite replanting, remained withered and deformed (StA 6.1: 211). To Schiller a year later, he describes himself as a plant that has just been set in soil and needs to be covered at midday (StA 6.1: 251). In February of 1798 he asserts to his brother, "Wir leben in dem Dichterklima nicht. Darum gedeiht auch unter zehn solcher Pflanzen kaum *eine*" (StA 6.1: 264).

This metaphor of human beings as plants needing to have strong roots is by now overdetermined by nationalist resonances. An obvious contemporary association would have been Herder's descriptions

---

[12] Martha Woodmansee has argued that Schiller's conception of autonomy in his classical aesthetics emerged in reaction against marketplace pressures on publishing. That Schiller had a noble patron beginning in 1791 allowed him the freedom to make a polemical assault against the marketplace and a *general* claim about the autonomy of art that in fact did not represent the reality of most artistic production. Martha Woodmansee: *The Author, Art and the Marketplace: Rereading the History of Aesthetics*. New York 1994. Pp. 57-86.

in his *Ideen* of human beings as plant-like in their relationship to their environment, a conception which underlies Herder's analysis of distinctions among particular peoples and cultures. It is unnecessary to rehearse the nineteenth-century history of the metaphor as it increasingly assumes a chauvinistic, antisemitic tenor: Richard Wagner's "Judentum in der Musik" can stand as a single example. Jews cannot be artists, according to Wagner, because they are ungrounded, belonging only to an uprooted stem: "Der Jude stand [...] einsam mit seinem Jehova in einem zersplitterten, bodenlosen Volksstamme [...]".[13] The nationalistic apotheosis of this ideal of art as organically bound to the soil is of course the Nazi promotion of "Blut und Boden" literature.

Yet in Hölderlin we need to read the organic metaphor as multivalent, as not only suggesting the possibility of individual or cultural soil in which one can take root, but also pointing to the existence of an underlying, unbordered continuity that defies such categories as self and nation. In a letter to his brother on January 1st, 1799, he ridicules the narrow domestic sphere that is the focus of the Germans. The Germans are literally or metaphorically "an ihre Erdscholle gefesselt", and have no sense of *common property*:

Jeder ist nur in dem zu Hauße, worinn er geboren ist, und kann und mag mit seinem Interesse und seinen Begriffen nur selten darüber hinaus. Daher jener Mangel an Elasticität, an Trieb, an mannigfaltiger Entwiklung der Kräfte, daher die finstere, wegwerfende Scheue oder auch die furchtsame unterwürfig blinde Andacht, womit sie alles aufnehmen, was außer ihrer ängstlich engen Sphäre liegt; daher auch diese Gefühllosigkeit für gemeinschaftliche Ehre und *gemeinschaftliches Eigentum*, die freilich bei den modernen Völkern sehr allgemein, aber meines Erachtens unter den Deutschen in eminentem Grade vorhanden ist. (StA 6.1: 303; italics mine)

He contrasts this narrow German attachment to house and soil with the experience of the open field, which he considers the precondition of any genuinely individual life:

Und wie nur der in seiner Stube sich gefällt, der auch im freien Felde lebt, so kann ohne Allgemeinsinn und offnen Blik in die Welt auch das individuelle, jedem eigene Leben nicht bestehen [...]. (StA 6.1: 303)

Indeed in this letter to his brother, Hölderlin proposes a radical therapy for the Germans: the new (Kantian) philosophy which

---

[13] Richard Wagner: *Sämtliche Schriften und Dichtungen*. Leipzig 1911. P. 71.

insists to an extreme extent upon universal interests (StA 6.1: 304). Hölderlin calls Kant the "Moses of our nation" who can lead the Germans out of their lethargy "into the free, solitary wilderness of speculation".[14]

Thus, far from renouncing philosophical speculation to focus on a smaller poetic sphere, Hölderlin asserts here that philosophy is precisely what the Germans need to free them from their narrow domestic spaces. The open field, even the free wilderness of speculation, counteract the German attachment to their individual clumps of earth. Philosophy surveys the deep, roaming ground without which, according to Hölderlin, there can be no genuine conception of individuality.

Philosophy versus Poetry

It makes sense that Hölderlin would view philosophy, too, as a sort of metaphorical ground, because the term "Grund" plays such an important role in the philosophical discourse of the era. At the end of the eighteenth century, the word was heavily employed in the debate over whether philosophy had to begin with a first principle or "erster Grundsatz". For example, Karl Leonhard Reinhold, a professor at Jena who eventually broke with "Grundsatzphilosophie", enumerates three kinds of grounds: empirical grounds which appear in experience; transcendental grounds which are the *a priori* conditions of experience which Kant investigates; and a transcendent, final ground which outstrips all conceptualization.[15] In a letter to his

---

[14] "Kant ist der Moses unserer Nation, der sie aus der ägyptischen Erschlaffung in die freie einsame Wüste seiner Speculation führt, und der das energische Gesez vom heiligen Berge bringt" (StA 6.1: 304). It is of course curious that Hölderlin holds Kant up as a leader in the wilderness of speculation here, since, as will be discussed below, Hölderlin had already gone beyond Kant's *Grundsatzphilosophie* in his own thinking. Hölderlin seems to hold Kant up as a model chiefly in letters to his younger brother, as part of an attempt to educate his brother in contemporary philosophy and particularly in ethics. It could strike a reader as a paradox in my analysis that Hölderlin suggests Kant as a remedy for the sort of domesticity which I have loosely associated with Schiller's aesthetic standpoint, since Schiller explicitly identified himself as a Kantian. Yet in Schiller's alliance with Goethe he was clearly disavowing his former, more philosophical tendencies in favor of Goethe's "realism".

[15] Karl Leonhard Reinhold: *Beyträge zur Berichtigung bisheriger Mißverständnisse der Philosophie* Vol. 2. Jena 1794. Pp. 6-9. The metaphorical shifting grounds in Hölderlin's poetic work thus overlap with shifting notions of ground in contemporary philosophical discourse. On Reinhold's contribu-

brother of June, 1796, Hölderlin similarly distinguishes different sorts of grounds or foundations as they operate for the understanding or reason. He too refers to a "höchste[r] Grund", upon which even rational principles are dependent (StA 6.1: 208).

Indeed, during his stay in Jena, Hölderlin actively contributed to the breakthrough that marked the beginning of Early Romantic philosophy: the move beyond a search for first principles to the recognition of a final ground outside of rational thought. In his philosophical sketch "Urtheil und Seyn" (1795) he outlined what Dieter Henrich has called the "Grund im Bewußtsein".[16] According to this two-page manuscript, the oppositions and relations that structure our conscious thought presuppose an absolute ground of unity, "Seyn schlechthin", which can however never be recovered in consciousness. Thus, underlying all of our empirical judgments, all of our categorizations, identifications and differentiations, is a non-propositional claim about Being as such. Judgment, *Urtheil*, according to Hölderlin's apocryphal etymology, thus involves an original division, an *Ur-theilung* of a ground once whole.

The outcome of Hölderlin's philosophical speculation is his insight into a seamless continuity of Being upon which our conscious life is dependent. And yet this absolute basis of human experience is not inhabitable ground. Indeed in the same letter to his brother in which Hölderlin proposes philosophy as a cure for the German attachment to narrow plots of ground, he adds that political-philosophical education is not enough – poetry is also needed. To make his point about the limits of philosophy, he employs the example of landscape painting: the measuring out of ground according to optical principles does not render a full picture:

> Der nach optischen Regeln gezeichnete Vor- und Mittel- und Hintergrund ist noch lange nicht die Landschaft, die sich neben das lebendige Werk der Natur allenfalls stellen möchte. (StA 6.1: 307)

Philosophy can sketch a theoretical framework for our experiences but cannot produce a livable landscape.

---

tion to the move in Jena beyond a philosophy of first principles (in which Hölderlin participated), see Manfred Frank: Philosophische Grundlagen der Frühromantik. In: *Athenäum. Jahrbuch für Romantik* 4 (1994). Pp. 37-130, here pp. 42-46.

[16] Dieter Henrich: *Der Grund im Bewußtsein. Untersuchungen zu Hölderlins Denken (1794-1795)*. Stuttgart 1992. Henrich's book is an invaluable resource on the entire intellectual context surrounding "Urtheil und Seyn".

In a letter to his mother in the same month he describes the difference between philosophy and poetry once again in terms of a relationship to land. Philosophy makes him passionate and gives him no repose. Like the work of a footloose soldier, the task of philosophy is unnatural to him. His affinity for poetry, on the other hand, is *eigentümlich* and like that of a shepherd for his valley and his flock:

> Ich wußte lange nicht, warum das Studium der Philosophie, das sonst den hartnäckigen Fleiß, den es erfordert, mit Ruhe belohnt, warum es mich, je uneingeschränkter ich mich ihm hingab, nur immer um so friedenloser und selbst leidenschaftlich machte; und ich erkläre es jetzt daraus, daß ich mich in höherm Grade, als es nötig war, von meiner *eigentümlichen* Neigung entfernte, und mein Herz seufzte bei der unnatürlichen Arbeit nach seinem lieben Geschäffte, wie die Schweizerhirten im Soldatenleben nach ihrem Thal und ihrer Heerde sich sehnen. (StA 6.1: 311; italics mine)

Poetry represents home to Hölderlin in a way that philosophy never does. To Neuffer in November 1798 he writes of poetry as the "süße[..] Heimath der Musen" from which he cannot bear to be separated and from which mere chance has driven him (StA 6.1: 289).

Thus, Hölderlin returns from philosophy to poetry in order to cultivate a ground of his own. Philosophy, while it fathoms the universal ground of all differentiation – the "Seyn schlechthin" – also reveals a kind of groundlessness to individual life, since this ultimate ground, pure Being, is incompatible with the structure of our thought and experience. For Hölderlin individual spheres emerge out of, and are dependent on, an uninhabitable wilderness. Or to use a metaphor of vertical layers, which also frequently emerges in Hölderlin's thinking: *eigener Grund* rests necessarily upon a deep, undifferentiated *Grund*, which, in its boundlessness, can become the equivalent of an *Abgrund*.[17] Poetry must tend to an individual sphere, while simultaneously providing, like philosophy, a vision of

---

[17] One finds this imagery, for example, in the poem 'Achill' (1799). Achilles, having lost his loved ones on earth, his interpersonal grounding, stands on rocky cliffs and is called by his heart into the holy abyss, *heilige[r] Abgrund*, of the sea where his mother Thetis resides (StA: 1.1: 271). These sacred depths clearly mean both the annihilation of the individual and the foundation (the mother) of individual life. The crater of the volcano in *Empedokles* has a similar function, representing both the source and the destruction of the protagonist's individuality.

limitless connection that could dislodge any certain claim to one's local plot of land.

The Wanderer's Song

We now return to the poem 'Mein Eigentum', with which we began. For the reader's convenience I quote this lesser-known ode in full:

In seiner Fülle ruhet der Herbstag nun,
Geläutert ist die Traub und der Hain ist roth
Vom Obst, wenn schon der holden Blüthen
Manche der Erde zum Danke fielen.

5 Und rings im Felde, wo ich den Pfad hinaus
Den stillen wandle, ist den Zufriedenen
Ihr Gut gereift und viel der frohen
Mühe gewähret der Reichtum ihnen.

Vom Himmel bliket zu den Geschäfftigen
10 Durch ihre Bäume milde das Licht herab,
Die Freude theilend, denn es wuchs durch
Hände der Menschen allein die Frucht nicht.

Und leuchtest du, o Goldnes, auch mir, und wehst
Auch du mir wieder, Lüftchen, als seegnetest
15 Du eine Freude mir, wie einst, und
Irrst, wie um Glükliche, mir am Busen?

Einst war ichs, doch wie Rosen, vergänglich war
Das fromme Leben, ach! und es mahnen noch,
Die blühend mir geblieben sind, die
20 Holden Gestirne zu oft mich dessen.

Beglükt, wer, ruhig liebend ein frommes Weib,
Am eignen Heerd in rühmlicher Heimath lebt,
Es leuchtet über vestem Boden
Schöner dem sicheren Mann sein Himmel.

25 Denn, wie die Pflanze, wurzelt auf eignem Grund
Sie nicht, verglüht die Seele des Sterblichen,
Der mit dem Tageslichte nur, ein
Armer, auf heiliger Erde wandelt.

Zu mächtig ach! ihr himmlischen Höhen zieht
30   Ihr mich empor, bei Stürmen, am heitern Tag
    Fühl ich verzehrend euch im Busen
    Wechseln, ihr wandelnden Götterkräfte.

Doch heute laß mich stille den trauten Pfad
    Zum Haine gehn, dem golden die Wipfel schmükt
35   Sein sterbend Laub, und kränzt auch mir die
    Stirne, ihr holden Erinnerungen!

Und daß mir auch zu retten mein sterblich Herz,
    Wie andern eine bleibende Stätte sei,
    Und heimathlos die Seele mir nicht
40   Über das Leben hinweg sich sehne,

Sei du, Gesang, mein freundlich Asyl! sei du
    Beglükender! mit sorgender Liebe mir
    Gepflegt, der Garten, wo ich, wandelnd
    Unter den Blüthen, den immerjungen,

45 In sichrer Einfalt wohne, wenn draußen mir
    Mit ihren Wellen allen die mächtige Zeit
    Die Wandelbare fern rauscht und die
    Stillere Sonne mein Wirken fördert.

Ihr seegnet gütig über den Sterblichen
50   Ihr Himmelskräfte! jedem sein Eigentum,
    O seegnet meines auch und daß zu
    Frühe die Parze den Traum nicht ende. (StA 1.1: 306-7)

The poet's account of his autumnal walk and reflections divides into three parts. In stanzas one through three, the poet surveys the harvest scene. In the second segment, beginning with the first word of stanza four, "Einst", he reflects upon his current condition of alienation and remembers a time in the past when this was not so. In the third part, introduced by "Doch heute" in stanza nine and continuing through to the end, he formulates a wish or hope for refuge through his own song.[18]

---

[18] Compare Pál Kiséry: Hölderlin: Mein Eigentum. Eine Interpretation. In: *Német filológiai tanulmányok /Arbeiten zur Deutschen Philologie* 5 (1970). Pp. 57-64, here p. 58. Kiséry views the third stage of the poem as beginning in stanza eight rather than nine. This seems to me counter-intuitive since a

Thematically the poem is organized throughout by a contrast between restless motion and fixed position. The term "wandeln", which describes the poet's stroll in the second stanza, shows up as a stem five times in the poem. We have seen the word already in the passage quoted in the opening: the soul of the mortal is in danger of being burned which is not rooted in its own ground but: "[...] mit dem Tageslichte nur, ein/ Armer auf heiliger Erde *wandelt*" (l. 26-7; italics mine). Yet this term describing both the poet's stroll and the threatened condition of a rootless soul, also describes the transforming character of time: "die mächtge Zeit, / Die Wandelbare" (l. 46-7), and the gods: "ihr wandelnden Götterkräfte" (l. 32), who consume the poet by pulling him too forcefully aloft. The wandering of the poet is thus both dangerous and sacred. We might associate it with the images of a speculative wandering we have seen in Hölderlin's letters, of Moses in the wilderness or of the soldier-philosopher remote from his own valley. The wanderer may gain a necessary breadth of insight, but his condition is also intolerable.

Hölderlin seems to present an idyllic alternative to this wandering in the image of the harvest in the first few stanzas. From the first line of the poem we have an image of repose to contrast the poet's wandering: "In seiner Fülle ruhet der Herbsttag nun" (l. 1). The activity of the harvesters is itself a form of satisfaction rather than restlessness: for the "Geschäfftigen" (l. 9) here are also described as the "Zufriedenen" (l. 6). Unlike the pure daylight which may scorch the soul of the rootless wandering mortal, the light of heaven looks down mildly through the trees to these busy ones, dividing and sharing the joy (l. 9-11). Later in the poem, in the sixth stanza, Hölderlin provides an extremeley idealized, even clichéed vision of this stable life on solid ground: the man is blessed who lives in an honorable homeland, calmly loving a pious wife by his own hearth (l. 21-2). In this image, the man implicitly possesses his own source of heat and light in his wife and hearth and is spared the scorching impact of the direct sun. Thus the sky radiates more beautifully for him: "Es leuchtet über vestem Boden/ Schöner dem sichern Mann sein Himmel" (l. 23-4).

Is this vision of happy labor and peaceful rewards thus the ultimate ideal of the poem? Without ever revoking its validity, Hölderlin calls the stability of this existence into question.[19] For example,

---

contrastive "Doch" in the beginning of stanza nine marks the beginning of a series of wishes or hopes that continue until the end of the poem.

[19] An advantage of an analysis of this poem based on Hölderlin's theory of tonal modulation, as undertaken by both Lawrence Ryan and Meta Corssen, is

in the second stanza, Hölderlin describes the farmers' satisfaction as they greet what is theirs – the ripe produce: "Und rings im Felde, [...] ist den Zufriedenen/ Ihr Gut gereift" (l. 5-7). And yet in the statement that follows, Hölderlin undermines the notion that this produce is essentially theirs at all. A prominent account associated with John Locke holds that one's right to private property stems from the labor involved in its appropriation.[20] Hölderlin turns that

---

that it identifies the oppositional subtones at work in each stanza. For example, both Ryan and Corssen see the opening stanzas as naive in tone, even as a heroic, passionate subtone sounds through the voice of the alienated poet. Lawrence Ryan: *Hölderlins Wechsel der Töne*. Stuttgart 1960. Pp. 110-1; Meta Corssen: Der Wechsel der Töne in Hölderlins Lyrik. In: *Hölderlin - Jahrbuch* (1951). Pp. 19-49, here p. 26.

[20] In his *Second Treatise of Civil Government* John Locke explains that since a person's labor is unquestionably his own, he can appropriate other things through the addition of his labor: "Whatsoever, then, he removes out of the state that nature hath provided and left it in, he hath mixed his labour with, and joined to it something that is his own, and thereby makes it his property". John Locke: *The Second Treatise of Civil Government and A Letter Concerning Toleration*. Oxford 1946. P. 15. While I have no direct proof of Hölderlin's exposure to Locke's Treatise, it seems not improbable that he would have been familiar with its contents, for the following reasons: a) the Second Treatise had been translated into German as early as 1718 (Dorothee Tidow: Zur Übersetzung. In John Locke: *Über die Regierung*. Ed. Peter Cornelious Meyer-Tasch. Reinbek 1966. Pp. 193-4, here p. 193); b) although primarily due to his epistemology, Locke was a central figure in popular Enlightenment thought in Germany for some years (see Frederick C. Beiser: *The Fate of Reason: German Philosophy from Kant to Fichte*. Cambridge 1987. Pp. 165-192); c) because Hölderlin was so clearly interested in both law and politics, it is hard to imagine that he would not have known a work so central to the revolutionary politics of the age.
I asserted in note 1 that Hölderlin's view of property has affinity with Hegel's later formulations. In a book on rights-based arguments for private property, Jeremy Waldron contrasts the Lockean account (also associated with Robert Nozick) with the Hegelian line of argument: "On the Hegelian approach, this is a basic human interest which everyone has: owning property contributes immensely to the ethical development of the individual person. On the Lockean approach, the interest which commands respect is one which people have only on account of what they happen to have done or what has happened to them. A man who has mixed his labour with a piece of land, or acquired it legitimately from someone else, has an interest in ownership which the government must respect; but a man who has done neither of these things, but would simply *rather like* to own something, has no such constraining interest. The Lockean right to property, in other words, is a special right, whereas the

logic around, drawing our attention to his reversal by inverting normal word order: "und viel der frohen/ Mühe gewähret der Reichtum ihnen" (l. 7-8). Here it is not the happy effort that grants the people riches, but the riches that grant the people happy effort. That human labor does not by itself secure one's right to property is even more explicit in the third stanza: "denn es wuchs durch/ Hände der Menschen allein die Frucht nicht" (l. 11-12). The last line of the first stanza reminds us that it is the earth to whom the gratitude is due: the many blossoms that preceded the fruit have fallen to the earth in thanks. A boundless earth and sky, rather than individual merit, are the foundation of all wealth.

Furthermore, the vision in stanza six of the happy, secure man who rests on solid ground with his own wife and hearth comes from the part of the poem in which the poet is recollecting his own lost happiness. While it is never explicit that the poet is describing his own past in stanza six, the previous stanza, in which he laments his own losses, seems to contain traces of the description to follow. Stanza six idealizes the love for a "*frommes* Weib" (l. 21); stanza five declares "Vergänglich war/ Das *fromme* Leben" (l. 17-18). In stanza six heaven radiates more beautifully for the man on solid ground; in stanza five only the stars above still blossom to remind him of his previous life. Thus the solid ground of the secure man seems to have already emerged within the narrative present as transitory and uncertain.

If a state of peaceful security is unattainable, what condition can the poet imagine for himself in lieu of wilting like a rootless, scorched plant? In the final third of the poem the poet articulates his hope that his *song* might be a kind of refuge or garden in which the blossoms remain ever young. How does this reflective reality of poetry, constructed of memory and imagination, differ from the solid ground of the secure man? Its stability is only relative, as suggested by Hölderlin's use of comparatives: its simplicity is *more* secure (l. 45), the sun supporting his work is *more* still (l. 48). The roar of changing time, "Die Wandelbare", is now distant – but presumably not inaudible (l. 46-7). Indeed in the last line the poet acknowledges that this refuge is but a dream, which, he prays, the fates will not end too soon. If song amounts to a kind of property, it remains but temporary and fragile.

Perhaps most significant within the economy of the poem is that the poet continues to wander within his garden: "der Garten, wo ich,

Hegelian one is a general right". Jeremy Waldron: *The Right to Private Property*. Oxford 1988. Pp. 3-4.

wandelnd/ Unter den Blüthen [...] wohne" (l. 43-4). That is, poetry remains in motion, as a middle condition between rootedness and rootlessness, between a propertied state and and a state of dispossession. Pierre Bertaux maintains that Hölderlin, "ein rüstiger Wanderer", with a genuine need to roam outdoors, worked out many of his poetic compositions while underway to the rhythm of his own stride.[21] Whether or not walking was tied to Hölderlin's compositional practice in this manner, it is clear that internal motion or roaming is fundamental to Hölderlin's conception of the proper sphere of poetry.

Internal Differentiation

I argued above that Schiller's aesthetics does not provide, for Hölderlin's purposes, a robust enough account of individual difference *or* interdependence. In a fragment that was indeed probably intended as a reply to Schiller's Aesthetic Letters, Hölderlin formulates his own theory of how poetry can function simultaneously as a distinctly individual sphere and as a mode of intersubjective engagement.[22] (While religion is the apparent concern of the fragment, which Beissner calls "Über Religion", Hölderlin equates religion here with myth and sees it as "ihrem Wesen nach *poetisch*" [StA 4.1: 281; italics mine].) In what appears then to be his "Neue Briefe über die ästhetische Erziehung des Menschen", Hölderlin emphasizes the irreducible character of individual experience, its resistance to any abstract formulation. And yet he supposes that everyone can discover in the individual web of his or her life, a surplus, a richness of relation outstripping the necessary conjunctions of logic and mechanics. Hölderlin asserts that insofar as each person has his or her

---

[21] Bertaux constructs an impressive list of cross-country journeys Hölderlin undertook by foot and concludes that Hölderlin could easily and with pleasure traverse 50 kilometers a day. Furthermore, according to Bertaux, his fast stride is reflected in his poetry: for example his hexameter is read aloud most effectively at a quick tempo. Pierre Bertaux: *Friedrich Hölderlin.* Frankfurt a.M. 1978. Pp. 250-267.

[22] In a letter written in February, 1796 Hölderlin had promised Niethammer an essay for his *Philosophisches Journal* entitled "Neue Briefe über die ästhetische Erziehung". His précis in the letter to Niethammer resembles in important ways the extant fragment. Sattler dates the fragment in the second half of 1796 or the beginning of 1797. Friedrich Hölderlin: *Sämtliche Werke: Kritische Textausgabe* . Ed. D.E. Sattler. 20 vols. Darmstadt und Neuwied 1984-. Vol. 14. P. 21.

own sphere in which he or she operates and experiences, each develops through memory and gratitude an intimately individual conception of a higher life or divinity. Thus the recognition of a surplus of relationship within one's individual sphere simultaneously engenders a respect or empathy towards others:

> Es muß aber hiebei nicht vergessen werden, daß der Mensch sich wohl auch in die Lage des andern versezen, daß er die Sphäre des andern zu seiner eigenen Sphäre machen kann, daß es also dem einen natürlicher weise, nicht so schwer fallen kann, die Empfindungsweise und Vorstellung zu billigen von Göttlichem, die sich aus den besondern Beziehungen bildet, in denen er mit der Welt steht [...]. (StA 4.1: 278-9)

Because these spheres are organized, each in its own way, around an insight into something more than individual, a communal god or religion can emerge naturally out of the association of these individual visions of a higher life or deeper ground. Thus the drive for unification arises out of an honest comprehension of one's own individuality.[23]

Hölderlin again describes the intersubjective structure of poetry in opposition to Schillerian aesthetics in his letter to his brother on New Year's 1799. Without mentioning Schiller by name, Hölderlin rejects Schiller's description of social unification through aesthetic "play", asserting that it fails to preserve *Eigentümlichkeit*:

> [die Kunst, besonders die Poësie] nähert die Menschen, und bringt sie zusammen, nicht wie das *Spiel*, wo sie nur dadurch vereiniget sind, daß jeder sich vergißt und die lebendige *Eigenthümlichkeit* von keinem zum Vorschein kommt. (StA. 6.1: 305; italics mine)

Hölderlin views poetry in contrast to play as the medium of a more heterogeneous unification:

> Nicht wie das Spiel, vereinige die Poesie die Menschen sagt' ich; sie vereinigt sie nemlich, wenn sie ächt ist und ächt wirkt, mit all dem mannigfaltigen Laid und Glük und Streben und Hoffen und Fürchten, mit all ihren Meinungen und Fehlern, all ihren Tugenden und Ideen, mit allem Großen

---

[23] I have argued elsewhere that there are clear traces within the essay of a crisis in the intersubjective economy Hölderlin sketches here, a crisis which leads Hölderlin to experiment with the more extreme gesture of tragic negation in his *Empedokles* drama: The Semiotics of Individuality and the Problem of Reception in Hölderlin's Tragic Drama. In: *Colloquia Germanica* 3 (1997). Pp. 227-250, here pp. 227-230.

und Kleinen, das unter ihnen ist, immer mehr, zu einem lebendigen
tausendfach gegliederten innigen Ganzen, denn eben diß soll die Pöesie selber seyn, und wie die Ursache, so die Wirkung. (StA. 6.1: 305)

Poetry must unify, then, but without dissolving, as aesthetic play
does, the oppositions, such as pain and happiness, virtue and error,
that distinguish individual lives. This passage provides no overt
description of the authentic poetry that is to produce such a social
unification. The only clue is a direct correlation Hölderlin makes
between poetry and the diverse community which is its effect, "eben
diß soll die Pöesie selber seyn" and "wie die Ursache, so die
Wirkung". If poetry must reflect the social whole it aims to create,
it must presumably fit the description of that whole as "ein[..]
lebendige[s] tausendfach gegliederte[s] innige[s] Ganze[..]".[24] The
individual poetic work must itself be internally differentiated in order
to anticipate the internally differentiated social totality it is supposed to cultivate.

Internal motion and engagement with difference is indeed the goal
of Hölderlin's poetic experimentation around the turn of the century. The legitimacy and meaningfulness of poetry increasingly
depends for Hölderlin on a movement away from one's own narrow
ground in order to show one's relationship to a deeper ground.
Hölderlin's essay "Grund zum Empedokles" theorizes the importance of leaving one's "eigentümliche[..] Sphäre" in order to achieve
a freer, more secure, "gründlicher" return through the experience
and knowledge of heterogeneity. Hölderlin explains that meaning,
"the right truth", depends on this poetic projection of oneself into
something foreign:

> Es ist nicht mehr der Dichter und seine eigene Erfahrung, was erscheint,
> wenn schon jedes Gedicht, so auch das tragische aus poetischem Leben und
> Wirklichkeit, aus des Dichters eigener Welt und Seele hervorgegangen seyn
> muß, weil sonst überall die rechte Wahrheit fehlt, und überhaupt nichts
> verstanden und belebt werden kann, wenn wir nicht das eigene Gemüth und
> die eigene Erfahrung in einen fremden analogischen Stoff übertragen können.
> (StA 4.1: 150)

According to Hölderlin's theory of a poetic variation of tones, what
Hölderlin calls a "Grundton" or "Grundstimmung" must modulate
into other, oppositional tones in order to produce "Bedeutung", a

---

[24] Compare Stephan Wackwitz: *Friedrich Hölderlin*. Stuttgart 1985
(Sammlung Metzler. Realien zur Literatur 215). P. 79.

middle, unifying condition, which Hölderlin also identifies as a kind of "Grund" (StA 4.1: 266, 244).[25]

We see then that one's proper ground is in Hölderlin's view not a stable entitlement but a fragile encampment upon an existential foundation that resists appropriation as such. True individuality entails an insight into the uncertain character of one's own foothold, just as intersubjectivity depends not on human uniformity but on the common recognition of this *Grund* or *Abgrund* underlying all individual spheres. It is the role of poetry to plumb the deep ground of all individuality and unification without dissolving self and other. Poetry walks a middle path between the naked, dispossessing universality of philosophy, and the grasping domesticity Hölderlin criticizes in the Germans. Property thus emerges only as a poetic, creative relation – of oneself to other selves, and of selfhood as category to an undifferentiated ground of reality.

In 1801, after failing to secure a position for himself as a lecturer in Jena, Hölderlin set off for France by foot, both in sorrow and with a conviction that this self-imposed exile was his only appropriate choice. In a farewell letter to his brother on December 4th, he offers the paradox that while he has never felt so connected to his home, he must nevertheless journey abroad:

> So viel darf ich gestehen, daß ich in meinem Leben nie so vest gewurzelt war ans Vaterland [...]. Aber ich fühl' es, mir ist besser, draußen zu seyn, und Du, mein Theurer! fühlst es selber, daß zum einen, wie zum andern, zum Bleiben, wie zum Wandern, Gottes Schuz gehört, wenn wir bestehen sollen. (StA 6.1: 424)

Hölderlin's famous letter to Böhlendorff, written the same day, reveals the logic of this leave-taking in a discussion of the German relationship to Greece: "Aber das eigene muß so gut gelernt seyn, wie das Fremde. Deßwegen sind uns die Griechen unentbehrlich" (StA 6.1: 426). The Germans, like the Greeks, become more proficient through the course of their education at what is not natively theirs,

---

[25] I am drawing these terms from both *Über den Unterschied der Dichtarten* and *Über die Verfahrungsweise des poetischen Geistes*. Hölderlin's various uses of the terms *Grund* and *Begründung* are particularly complex in the latter essay. See Lawrence Ryan's exposition, pp. 37-42. Ryan points out the paradox, "daß dieser 'Grund' nicht ausschließlich als Ursprungsbereich zu betrachten ist, sondern unter einem anderen Gesichtspunkt auch den 'mittleren' Charakter bildet, in dem die beiden Pole – Geist und Stoff – sich vereinigen" (42).

for education involves taking on what is foreign. Therefore, to discover at last what is one's own, one must learn it, not at home, but through a reciprocal encounter with the other, who presumably has assumed what is native to oneself as something foreign. The Greeks are indispensible, precisely because one can receive from them "das eigene". Peter Szondi shows how this letter was historically misread as a document of Hölderlin's "vaterländische Umkehr", of his turn away from classical models towards his homeland.[26] Quite to the contrary, the letter to Böhlendorff evinces again the always displaced, paradoxical character of homeland and the structural impossibility of a complete return. A ground of one's own must be endlessly appropriated through a tireless journey of relationship.

[26] "[...] keine Heimkehr ins Eigene wird erstrebt, wie es die These von der 'vaterländischen Umkehr' wahrhaben möchte, sondern beide Elemente, das Eigene und das Fremde, die *Präzision* und die *Wärme*, sollen der dichterischen Sprache integriert werden". Peter Szondi: *Hölderlin Studien. Mit einem Traktat über philologische Erkenntnis.* Frankfurt a.M. 1967. P. 110. Szondi too connects the content of the letter to Hölderlin's theory of tonal modulation. Jochen Schmidt denies that the term "vaterländische Umkehr" as it actually turns up in Hölderlin's *Anmerkungen zur Antigonä* has Germany as a referent at all: "Und das 'Vaterland' ist nun eine Chiffre für das Allumfassende, Totale des Geschehens". Jochen Schmidt: Deutschland und Frankreich als Gegenmodelle in Hölderlins Geschichtsdenken: Evolution statt Revolution. In: *Dichter und ihre Nation.* Ed. Helmut Scheuer. Frankfurt a.M. 1993. Pp. 176-199, here p. 195.

Angela Esterhammer

Hölderlin and the Inter/Subjective Speech Act

In Hyperion *and* Der Tod des Empedokles, *intersubjective speech acts that operate in terms of sociopolitical authority, convention, and uptake are subordinated to utterances that place the speaker subjectively in the world and establish I-you relationships. Hölderlin's attempt to discover a form of utterance that combines subjective with intersubjective validity reflects the concerns of linguistic philosophy during the early Romantic period, which regarded the speech act as a simultaneously cognitive and communicative phenomenon.*

> Jezt aber tagts! Ich harrt und sah es kommen,
> Und was ich sah, das Heilige sei mein Wort.[1]

In Hölderlin's poetry, as in the critical corpus, these lines from the beginning of the third stanza of "Wie wenn am Feiertage..." constitute a nexus for his concept of how self, word, and world act on one another. They form the focus of Heidegger's reading of the poem, for he regards the poet's decisive act of naming "the holy" as the act by which the holy, or nature, comes into being:

> Weil es aber genannt wird, ja sogar selbst die Nennung fordert, kommt das Erwachen 'der Natur' in den Klang des dichtenden Wortes. Im Wort enthüllt sich das Wesen des Genannten. Denn das Wort scheidet, indem es das Wesenhafte nennt, das Wesen vom Unwesen.[2]

The deictic "now" with which Hölderlin's line begins is, for Heidegger, a conclusive indication that the advent of the holy happens in the utterance itself: "Das 'Jezt' nennt ja doch eindeutig den Zeitpunkt, in dem Hölderlin selbst sagt: 'Jezt aber tagts!'"[3] But Paul de Man, in an early review of Heidegger's exegeses of Hölderlin, challenges the philoso-

---

[1] *StA* 2.118. All quotations from Hölderlin's work are drawn from Friedrich Hölderlin: *Sämtliche Werke* (Große Stuttgarter Ausgabe = *StA*). Ed. Friedrich Beissner. 8 vols. Stuttgart 1946-1985. Quotations from *Der Tod des Empedokles* are identified by line number, all others by volume and page number.

[2] Martin Heidegger: *Erläuterungen zu Hölderlins Dichtung.* 4th rev. ed. Frankfurt a.M. 1971. P. 58.

[3] *Erläuterungen zu Hölderlins Dichtung.* P. 75.

pher's enthusiastic reading of these lines, arguing instead that they call into question the entire possibility of naming Being:

> [Hölderlin] does not say: das Heilige *ist* mein Wort. The subjunctive is here really an optative; it indicates prayer, it marks desire, and these lines state the eternal poetic intention, but immediately state also that it can be no more than intention[4]

For de Man, the event that occurs in these lines is not the coming-into-being of the holy, but the split between immediate Being and a mediating language, or the articulation of the difference between absolute Being and the "non-simple form" of being that is the only one available to human language.

Further perspectives on the function of the word in these lines are opened up by both Romantic and modern philosophies of language as action. The same year that saw the publication of de Man's critique of Heideggerian ontology, 1955, has come to represent the birth of speech-act theory – the most influential branch of modern linguistic pragmatics, or the discipline that studies verbal utterances in terms of the relationships among the speaker, the hearer, language, and the world. According to J.L. Austin's and John R. Searle's theory of performative language, Hölderlin's phrase "das Heilige sei mein Wort" is a *declaration*, an utterance that fits words to the world at the same time that it transforms reality so as to fit the world to the words.[5] Yet questions would arise, within the bounds of this theory, about the source of the speaker's authority and the conditions necessary to the success of his declaration. According to the rules of language, where Searle in particular seeks his criteria for the definition of illocutionary acts, the utterance institutes a new state of affairs for the speaking subject (in which "das Heilige" = "mein Wort"). But in intersubjective terms, or in terms of the social conventions that Austin stresses and Searle also brings to bear when defining declarations, speech-act theory exposes the fallibility of Hölderlin's lines: the poet simply lacks any apparent authority to issue such a declaration, and any indication of "uptake" or acknowledgement by a hearer or audience is conspicuously absent.

The work of Emile Benveniste provides an answer of sorts to the

[4] Paul de Man: Heidegger's Exegeses of Hölderlin. In: *Blindness and Insight: Essays in the Rhetoric of Contemporary Criticism.* Minneapolis 1983. Pp. 246-66, here p. 258.

[5] John R. Searle: *Expression and Meaning: Studies in the Theory of Speech Acts.* Cambridge 1979. Pp. 16-20.

question of authority, inasmuch as it calls attention to the way these lines themselves create the speaker's subjectivity and ground his discourse in his ability to articulate himself – for the first time in the poem – as "I". In attempting to make Austin's definition of the performative more rigorous, Benveniste considers the relationship between authority and action that obtains in performative utterances. Authority often includes sociopolitical power, but it also depends on the speaker's unique right to make his or her own commitments, pledges, or promises: "acts of authority are first and always utterances made by those to whom the right to utter them belongs".[6] This self-reflexive notion of authority as ultimate responsibility for one's own acts, which is interwoven with Benveniste's belief that subjectivity itself depends on the ability to place oneself within language as "I",[7] *might* validate Hölderlin's translation of "was *ich* sah" into "*mein* Wort". Since the speaker is responsible for defining the position of the self by articulating it in language, he is also responsible for declarations that orient themselves by the position of the I and involve its perceptions and commitments.

But "das Heilige sei mein Wort" is also a rather exact demonstration of the type of speech act discussed by linguistic philosophers of the early nineteenth century. German Romantic philosophy of language, which has yet to be properly acknowledged as an important background for the use of language in literary texts, manifests a pragmatic perspective of its own. Beginning in the 1790s, a new understanding of grammar and discourse arose that focused on individual acts of utterance, or what Saussure later called *parole*; on the *verb* as the active centre of language, and thus the most important part of speech; on *pronouns* as the parts of speech that establish the positions of speaker and hearer, and the relationship between them; on the indispensable role of language in *cognition*, or the formation of both self and world; and on the intrinsically *dialogic* nature of language.[8] Exponents of this new Ro-

---

[6] Emile Benveniste: *Problems in General Linguistics*. Trans. Mary Elizabeth Meek. Coral Gables 1971. P. 236.

[7] *Problems in General Linguistics*. P. 224.

[8] For an overview of these trends, which historians of linguistics have begun to focus on during the past decade, see Brigitte Nerlich and David D. Clarke: *Language, Action, and Context: The Early History of Pragmatics in Europe and America, 1780-1930*. Amsterdam 1996; Werner Neumann: Sprachhandlungsauffassungen an der Wende vom 18. zum 19. Jahrhundert. In: *Sprachtheorie. Der Sprachbegriff in Wissenschaft und Alltag*. Ed. Rainer Wimmer. Düsseldorf 1987. Pp. 121-42; Brigitte Schlieben-Lange: Elemente einer pragmatischen Sprachtheorie in den Grammaires générales um 1800. In:

mantic linguistics are J.G. Hamann, J.G. Herder, and A.F. Bernhardi, all of whom responded to Kantian and idealist epistemology by developing a philosophical grammar that affirms the essential role of language in forming judgements and in representing, or even conceptualizing, Being. Yet even the language that brings individual minds into a subject-object relationship with the world is intrinsically intersubjective, as Herder insists in his *Abhandlung über den Ursprung der Sprache*:

> Ich kann nicht den ersten menschlichen Gedanken denken, nicht das erste besonnene Urteil reihen, ohne daß ich in meiner Seele dialogisiere oder zu dialogisieren strebe; der erste menschliche Gedanke bereitet also seinem Wesen nach, mit Andern dialogisieren zu können![9]

The Jena Romantics reach the same conclusion about the simultaneously dialogic and cognitive function of language. For Friedrich Schlegel, Novalis, and Schleiermacher, in particular, an I-you relationship is the paradigm for the mind's interaction with the external world, and language inevitably plays a central role in establishing and developing this relationship. "Außendinge", Schlegel claims in his Cologne lectures of 1804, "sind nicht Nicht-Ich außer dem Ich; nicht bloß ein toter, matter, leerer, sinnlicher Widerschein des Ichs [...] sondern, wie gesagt, ein lebendiges, kräftiges *Gegen-Ich*, ein *Du*". This *du* reveals itself by speaking to us and being understood by us: "das *Du* spricht in dem Augenblicke, wo das Wesen *in seinem Ganzen vom Ich verstanden* wird, spricht es an und *offenbart ihm das Wesen seines Daseins*".[10]

But the foremost example of a linguistic thinker who interweaves the cognitive and communicative function of language is Wilhelm von Humboldt, who, in a long series of manuscripts, publications, and public lectures, beginning with fragments of the 1790s and proceeding to the full-fledged theory of language published after his death in 1834 as *Über die Verschiedenheit des menschlichen Sprachbaues und ihren Einfluss auf die geistige Entwicklung des Menschengeschlechts*, insists that the use of language determines our subjective as much as our

---

Zeitschrift für Literaturwissenschaft und Linguistik (LiLi) 19 (1988). Pp. 76-93.

[9] Johann Gottfried Herder: *Sprachphilosophische Schriften*. 2nd ed. Ed. Erich Heintel. Hamburg 1975. P. 30.

[10] Friedrich Schlegel: *Kritische Friedrich-Schlegel-Ausgabe*. Ed. Ernst Behler with Jean-Jacques Anstett and Hans Eichner. Munich 1958-. Vol. 12. Pp. 337, 350.

intersubjective mode of being in the world. Like most of his contemporaries, Humboldt believes that language is essential to thought, and regards dialogue as the central principle of linguistic structure, even in solitary or private speech. His speaker always stands in a dialogic relationship with a real or imagined human addressee, as well as with whatever element of the world he or she designates, through utterance, as an object, and finally also with *the word itself*, conceived of as a semi-material Other that enters into dialogue with the speaker's mind. The crucial operation of language, which Humboldt came to call "den Act des selbstthätigen Setzens durch Zusammenfassung", is an interaction by which the verbal object, which the mind forms out of impressions of the world, reacts back on the mind itself: "Der Geist schafft, stellt sich aber das Geschaffene durch denselben Act gegenüber und lässt es, als Objekt, auf sich zurückwirken".[11]

For an illustration of Humboldt's idea of the relationship between mind, word, and world, we may return to Hölderlin's "Jezt aber tagts! Ich harrt und sah es kommen, / Und was ich sah, das Heilige sei mein Wort". The indeterminate "es" that approaches from some place external to the speaker is objectified by his utterance as "das Heilige". It is brought into relation with the speaking subject *by* his word – that is, because language itself bestows on "das Heilige" the status of an object – and also *as* his word. The act of making "das Heilige" into a word, an act that the utterance both names and performs, alters, in turn, the poet's position in the world. Among other things, it allows him to identify himself with the community of holy poets who have thus far only been named in the third person, but for whom he henceforth speaks in the first person plural.

Like the speech act as Humboldt describes it, Hölderlin's line captures an ambiguity in the relationship between the speaker and language. On one hand, the poet's claim is grounded in human consciousness, sensory perception, and past experience. In this sense, it might be (clumsily) paraphrased, "I saw the holy, and I shall henceforth represent what I saw by my word" – a paraphrase that assigns language a basically referential or constative role. But it is also possible that experience is being subordinated to the performative power of language, as if to say, "(I posit that) my word, which I hereby bring into existence, shall be the holy and shall substitute for what (I say) I saw". Is the holy (or at least an objectified version of it) *embodied in* the poet's word, or

---

[11] Wilhelm von Humboldt: *Gesammelte Schriften*. Ed. Albert Leitzmann. 17 vols. 1903-36. Rpt. Berlin 1968. Vol. 7. P. 213.

does the word itself, in the form of Hölderlin's poem and of this specific performative utterance, *generate* the holy? The speech act engages a reciprocal relationship between speaking subject and articulated object, between I and other, and between language and reality, in which it is impossible to assign priority to one term over the other. On the contrary, the ambiguity between representational and performative aspects of the word in Hölderlin's line tends to confirm Humboldt's paradoxical assertion that language is an independent agent precisely *because* it is also dependent on human intentionality and intuitions: "Die Sprache ist gerade insofern Object und selbstständig, als sie Subject und abhängig ist".[12]

In their openness to both Romantic and contemporary formulations of performative utterance, the lines from "Wie wenn am Feiertage..." stand as an emblem for the aspect of Hölderlin's language that is to be examined in this essay. At issue here is the paradoxical way utterance is generated by subjectivity, at the same time that subjectivity is generated by utterance – so that the identity of the speaker and the effect of speech somehow depend on one another. But this aspect of speech is complemented, and further complicated, by the question of what words do in an intersubjective sphere, or how they establish and alter relationships between speakers. In early Romantic philosophy of language, as I have already suggested, subjective and intersubjective dimensions tend to be superimposed. An utterance establishes the speaker's relationship to the objective world at the same time, and in an analogous (if not identical) manner, as it establishes relationships between speaker and addressee; language forms and alters the speaker's conception of the world at the same time that it forms and alters his or her identity in relation to other human agents. In modern linguistic philosophy, on the other hand, the subjective and intersubjective dimensions of utterance are more likely to be in tension, or even conflict, with one another. Thus Jürgen Habermas (from whom, primarily, I draw the distinction between "subjective", "intersubjective", and "objective" spheres) gladly acknowledges the influence of Humboldt's view of language as intersubjective discourse or *Gespräch*. He credits Humboldt with opening up space for a theory of culture and society by envisioning a discursive relationship between an "Ego" and an "Alter Ego" that is recognized as being Other, yet as having a common origin with the I. For Humboldt, as for Habermas, society is constituted by the speech acts that link individuals to one another:

[12] *Gesammelte Schriften*. Vol. 6. P. 181.

Schon Humboldt versteht die Sprechakte als Koppelungen für Interak-
tionen; er begreift Verständigung als den erzeugenden Mechanismus der
Vergesellschaftung – zunächst als Mechanismus der Handlungs-
koordinierung und der gesellschaftlichen Integration, dann aber auch als
Medium der Fortsetzung kultureller Überlieferungen und der Sozialisa-
tion.[13]

In Habermas' view, however, Humboldt is held back from a modern
understanding of social discourse by his residual Romantic commitment to a view of language as individual expression. It is typical of
Humboldt's disparate, often paradoxical legacy that a hermeneutic
critic like Paul Ricoeur values exactly this subjective, "Romantic"
aspect of Humboldt as a model for his own notion of verbal performance. Ricoeur identifies with Humboldt's profoundly dynamic concept
of language as "the generation [...] of the work of speech in each and
every case",[14] and credits Humboldt with being one of the first to regard
language as a process rather than a system. To understand language in
terms of actual discursive events, rather than as a system that exists
only *in potentia*, is, according to Ricoeur, the task of phenomenology:

> Phenomenology's task becomes more precise: this positing of the subject,
> which the entire tradition of the *cogito* invokes, must henceforth be per-
> formed in language and not alongside it [...]. This positing must be made to
> appear in the occurrence of discourse, that is, in the act by which the poten-
> tial system of language becomes the actual event of speech.[15]

What Ricoeur here describes as the enterprise of phenomenology is
exactly Humboldt's enterprise: to analyze how the positing of the
subject and the development of the subject's representations of the
world occur in language as a discursive act. What allows Ricoeur to
enlist Humboldt into the project of phenomenology, while Habermas
enlists him for his own theory of communicative action, is that Hum-

---

[13] Jürgen Habermas: Entgegnung. In: *Kommunikatives Handeln. Beiträge zu
Jürgen Habermas' 'Theorie des kommunikativen Handelns'*. Ed. Axel Hon-
neth and Hans Joas. Frankfurt a.M. 1986. Pp. 327-405, here p. 332.
[14] Paul Ricoeur: Structure, Word, Event. Trans. Robert Sweeney. In: *The
Conflict of Interpretations: Essays in Hermeneutics*. Ed. Don Ihde. Evanston
1974. Pp. 79-96, here p. 84.
[15] Paul Ricoeur: The Question of the Subject: The Challenge of Semiology.
Trans. Kathleen McLaughlin. In: *The Conflict of Interpretations*. Pp. 236-66,
here p. 256.

boldt's work – which is in this sense representative of the work of contemporaries from Herder and Bernhardi to Friedrich Schlegel and Schleiermacher – encompasses a wide-ranging exploration of the way language performs identity within the interrelated realms of subjectivity, objective reality, and social or intersubjective experience.

In the remainder of this essay, I propose to examine the effect of speech on the subjective and intersubjective world in the two long texts that Hölderlin produced in the late 1790s, arguably the time at which speculation on language as discourse, dialogue, and representation was most intense among his contemporaries.[16] Speech-act principles can, to begin with, generate a reading of Hölderlin's novel *Hyperion, oder der Eremit in Griechenland* as the tragedy of a protagonist caught between ineffective words on the one hand and overly rigid social speech acts on the other, who therefore fails to fulfil his own potential for productive, performative utterance. *Der Tod des Empedokles* – which, as a drama, intrinsically foregrounds verbal action – illustrates still more clearly how subjective and intersubjective dimensions of utterance overlap and conflict in the confrontation between the philosopher Empedokles and the community of Agrigent. At one extreme, Hölderlin examines the way institutional utterances, such as the vow to a secret brotherhood or excommunication from a society, impose control on interpersonal relationships; but, typically for a Romantic thinker, his sense of the effects of words in social contexts is rooted in a phenomenological understanding of the way language creates relationships between self and other in the first place. Modern speech-act theory, and the terminology associated with it (performative, constative, illocution, perlocution, uptake, and so forth) opens up a perspective on utterance as a function of authority and social convention that, I hope to show, is also taken account of in Hölderlin's texts. But Hölderlin generally critiques these forms of utterance, putting in their place a speech act that, if it is to have an effect in the discursive community, must do so by grounding intersubjective relationships in a subjective or phenomenological placing of the self in the world. *Hyperion* and *Der Tod des Empedokles* reflect the crucial role(s) that speech acts begin to play among linguistic

---

[16] Cf. Brigitte Nerlich's claim that German pragmatic thinking about language, and particularly the prehistory of speech-act theory, "all started in 1795" (The Notion of 'Speech Act' in German Linguistics, Philosophy and Psychology between 1830 and 1970. In: *Speech Acts and Linguistic Research: Proceedings of the Workshop, July 15 - 17, 1994*. Ed. Elisabetta Fava. Padova 1995. Pp. 1-20, here p. 1).

philosophers of the post-Kantian generation, who attempt to analyze the function of language in light of two spectacular paradigm shifts: the Kantian system with its redefinition of the phenomenal world, and the French Revolution with its redefinition of the role and force of public utterances.[17] Hölderlin's texts – including his poetry, which almost always sets up a dialogic speech situation – therefore benefit from being read against the background of Romantic and modern philosophy of language.

Hyperion appears at first to deny the performativity of language entirely; the majority of references to speech in the novel are sceptical ones.[18] Its narrator repeatedly laments the failure of his words to have an effect, and the futility of language in general; these failures of the word are embedded in the other failures he experiences, as he loses, in turn, his mentor, his father, his beloved, and his best friend. "Ich

[17] On the influence of the French Revolution on pragmatic theories of language, see Brigitte Schlieben-Lange: Die Französische Revolution und die Sprache. In: *Zeitschrift für Literaturwissenschaft und Linguistik (LiLi)* 11 (1981). Pp. 90-123; Jacques Guilhaumou: *Sprache und Politik in der Französischen Revolution. Vom Ereignis zur Sprache des Volkes (1789 bis 1794)*. Trans. Kathrina Menke. Frankfurt a.M. 1989.

[18] Important secondary texts for the following discussion are Brigitte Haberer's studies of speech and discourse in Hölderlin, particularly *Sprechen, Schweigen, Schauen. Rede und Blick in Hölderlins "Der Tod des Empedokles" und "Hyperion"*. Bonn 1991. Haberer demonstrates that *Hyperion* does not simply condemn "Sprechen" in favour of "Schweigen", as is sometimes assumed; rather, the narrator alternates between "eine geradezu kindliche Gläubigkeit an die Macht des Wortes", and a rejection of it as an effective medium (p. 255). Other characters, too, have both positive and negative experiences of speech: Diotima begins as the silent one [die Schweigende] but becomes an enthusiastic speaker as she approaches her death, while Alabanda develops in the opposite direction. Haberer's book is valuable not only for the new interpretations it proposes of Hölderlin's two longest works, but also because of her comprehensive review of Hölderlin scholarship as it concerns the topics of language and discourse. In contrast to existing studies, Haberer aims to place new emphasis on the social context of discourse in Hölderlin's drama and his novel. Her frame of reference includes theories of dramatic monologue and dialogue and a Foucauldian concept of the gaze, but she relies primarily on traditions of myth, ritual, and superstition to define verbal acts, and consequently focuses on the magical power of the word [Sprachmagie] rather than the illocutionary force that words acquire within specific discursive contexts. My reading agrees with Haberer's in many respects, but differs in setting *Hyperion* and *Der Tod des Empedokles* explicitly in the context of speech-act theory and Romantic philosophy of language.

möchte sprechen können", he laments (*StA* 3.50), but "Worte sind, wie
Schneeflocken, unnüz, und machen die Luft nur trüber" (*StA* 3.95); "die
Sprache ist ein großer Überfluß" (*StA* 3.118).[19] But the first-person
narrative form allows, and indeed requires, us to contextualize the
deprecations of language that appear in Hyperion's letters by relating
them to his experience and development. Hyperion may be regarded as
a protagonist who senses that it lies within his reach to employ the
performative power of language, but whose tragedy is precisely that he
fails to take up the role of one whose words are effective in changing
his world. He might have become, we learn, a teacher or a poet; this is
the role that Diotima represents to him in the central scene of the novel,
when they discuss their future and the future of Greece during a visit to
the pre-eminent site of Greece's past, the Acropolis. At that moment
Hyperion declares, using explicit performatives, his readiness to take
up the role of a speaker. But this mission requires a form of language
that combines the power of individual creativity with the validating
response of a community; and, although the novel seems to offer examples of such a hybrid, "inter/subjective" speech act, Hyperion fails to
place his faith in it. The second volume records his attempts to channel
his energy toward violent physical action rather than verbal action, and
chronicles the losses that result. However, the unexpected mitigation of
Hyperion's crisis in the last letter represents a semi-recovery of the
performative, as his final utterance points to the way language might
restore dialogic relationships between self and other.

The type of language to which Hyperion does accord world-altering
power is the magical word, conceived of either as a magic formula or as
a mystical act of naming. Under certain circumstances Hyperion is able
to participate in epiphanic scenes of naming, or else to discover a soul-
changing experience in expressive, creative, individual utterance. The
possibility of such a word first arises in the context of Hyperion's
conversations with Adamas, to whom Hyperion is alluding when he
describes the regenerative and educative power of a "brave man's"
word:

Ein freundlich Wort aus eines tapfern Mannes Herzen, ein Lächeln, worinn
die verzehrende Herrlichkeit des Geistes sich verbirgt, ist wenig und viel,
wie ein zauberisch Loosungswort, das Tod und Leben in seiner einfältigen

---

[19] Haberer calls attention to the important distinctions between these negative
allusions to speech, distinguishing between unwillingness to speak, inability to
speak, and prohibitions against speaking (*Sprechen, Schweigen, Schauen*. Pp.
196-203 and 265-70).

Sylbe verbirgt, ist, wie ein geistig Wasser, das aus der Tiefe der Berge quillt, und die geheime Kraft der Erde uns mittheilt in seinem krystallenen Tropfen. (*StA* 3.12)

But this early characterization of the word as restorative water is undercut by later passages that figure the word negatively in terms of other natural elements: as snowflakes that trouble the air (*StA* 3.95), as fire that flares up and is gone (*StA* 3.159), or as a thing that only the winds hear (*StA* 3.151). The problem with the magical word, and with the spiritual language that Adamas' teaching seems to represent, is that there is no guarantee for its effectiveness. As soon as Hyperion leaves his study of nature and ancient culture with Adamas, and enters instead into a context of political action with his friend Alabanda, the magical word has to be rejected, as if it required an uptake that it will not find among a hostile public. With Alabanda Hyperion discusses grandiose plans for the future, but not, he assures Bellarmin, as if they think to bring them about through magical formulas:

nicht, als hätten wir, unmännlich, unsre Welt, wie durch ein Zauberwort, geschaffen, und kindisch unerfahren keinen Widerstand berechnet, dazu war Alabanda zu verständig und zu tapfer. (*StA* 3.27)

The rejection of the magical performative is quite precise. Characterized in the context of Adamas' instruction as the word spoken by a "tapfern Mann[..]", it is now abandoned as unmanly and childish, and Alabanda is too "tapfer" to use it. Later, Hyperion berates himself for relying on words that are unable to achieve what Alabanda achieves through pure action: "und mit Worten möchtest du ausreichen, und mit Zauberformeln beschwörst du die Welt?" (*StA* 3.95). Hyperion's rejection of magical words, and of the spiritual language of his philosophical mentor, is a first indication of his inability to conceive of an effective role for speech acts in the sociopolitical world.

An alternative model for the performative, which has a more intrinsic social dimension, is the act of naming as a recognition of the other and the establishment of a relationship with him or her. Brigitte Haberer shows how Hyperion's relationship with Diotima comes about in and as a few crucial acts of naming, of which the most important is the climactic scene where they declare their love for one another.[20] This declaration apparently consists solely of uttering one another's names,

---

[20] *Sprechen, Schweigen, Schauen.* Pp. 203-11.

since no other conversation is possible:

> Ach! mein Hyperion! rief jezt mir eine Stimme entgegen; ich stürzt' hinzu;
> »meine Diotima! o meine Diotima!« weiter hatt' ich kein Wort und keinen
> Othem, kein Bewußtseyn [...]
> Es ist hier eine Lüke in meinem Daseyn. Ich starb, und wie ich erwachte,
> lag ich am Herzen des himmlischen Mädchens. (*StA* 3.72)

Naming and utterance are implicated here in existence [*Daseyn*] itself.
Recognizing the existence of the other by uttering his or her name
causes a figurative death, yet this is followed by restoration to a fuller
life. In key scenes of the novel, as Haberer notes, alterity and existence
are brought together by an emphatic utterance of the phrase *du bist*.
Diotima recalls this same moment of mutual naming in her letter to
Hyperion as a scene of discourse in which both partners desperately
seek affirmation of the existence of a *du*: "bist dus? bist du es wirklich?" (*StA* 3.110). Exactly the same formula marks the reunion of
Hyperion with Alabanda, as the latter, unable to distinguish Hyperion
in the dusk but recognizing his voice, calls out, "bist du's?" (*StA*
3.106). Both Hyperion and Diotima, finally, echo these utterances in
relation to elements of nature, calling them by name and addressing
them as *du*. During the happy days of their betrothal, Diotima uses her
intimate relationship with nature to give new and better names to the
flowers in her garden (*StA* 3.56), while she and Hyperion use the metaphorical language of poets to re-name earth and heaven for themselves:
"Wir nannten die Erde eine der Blumen des Himmels, und den Himmel
nannten wir den unendlichen Garten des Lebens" (*StA* 3.54).

But the act of creative naming still provides no reliable basis for a
performative that will function in a social context beyond one-to-one
dialogue. Instead, as a sharp contrast to the inwardness and intense
dialogism of these forms of language, Hyperion experiences the alienation brought about by conventionalized, social speech acts that relate
human beings to one another in rigid, unfeeling ways. Alabanda's oath
to the *Bund der Nemesis* can be characterized as the paradigm of a
destructive institutional speech act; he relates how he made over his
"blood and soul" to the *Bund* in a "solemn" or "ceremonial" [*feierlich*]
procedure (*StA* 3.139). The oath is, in its essence, a convention-bound
performative, in which the oath-swearer commits him- or herself with
respect to future behaviour by the utterance of a set form of words; the
oath to a secret brotherhood, which adds on top of the conventions for
oath-swearing ritual elements specific to that society, is even more so.

In *Hyperion*, the rigid conventionality of this speech act is specifically opposed to feeling, passionate friendship, and the freedom to choose with whom one will enter into dialogue. "Um meines Lieblings willen brach ich meinen Eid", Alabanda relates, narrating how his love for Hyperion left him no choice but to break with his society brothers (*StA* 3.139). If the words of Adamas, and Diotima's acts of naming, are motivated by love and spiritual autonomy – but apparently have no basis for effectiveness in a larger social context – Alabanda's oath is caught in the opposite bind. It is *overly* effective in shaping the social order, to the extent that its power cannot be suspended. Alabanda departs from Hyperion to return to the *Bund* in the expectation of being killed for his treachery; his oath disallows behaviour based on sentiment and freedom.

Two events in Hyperion's story do, however, provide a model for utterance that combines individual creativity with convention, and brings subjective identity into harmony with intersubjective relations. The climax of Hyperion's experience with Adamas occurs when the two climb Mount Cynthus on Delos, the site of an ancient festival in honour of the sun-god, and Adamas symbolically dedicates his pupil to the rising sun:

> Jezt kam er herauf in seiner ewigen Jugend, der alte Sonnengott, zufrieden und mühelos, wie immer, flog der unsterbliche Titan mit seinen tausend eignen Freuden herauf, und lächelt' herab auf sein verödet Land, auf seine Tempel, seine Säulen, die das Schiksaal vor ihn hingeworfen hatte, wie die dürren Rosenblätter, die im Verübergehen ein Kind gedankenlos vom Strauche riß, und auf die Erde säete.
> Sei, wie dieser! rief mir Adamas zu, ergriff mich bei der Hand und hielt sie dem Gott entgegen, und mir war, als trügen uns die Morgenwinde mit sich fort, und brächten uns in's Geleite des heiligen Wesens, das nun hinaufstieg auf den Gipfel des Himmels, freundlich und groß, und wunderbar mit seiner Kraft und seinem Geist die Welt und uns erfüllte. (*StA* 3.15-16)

Since the unnamed sun-god is, in fact, the god Hyperion, Adamas' exhortation to his pupil to "Be like him!", accompanied by a ceremonial raising of Hyperion's hand toward the sun, constitutes a kind of baptism.[21] As such, it combines semi-conventional and completely private elements. "Conventional" are the authority Adamas exercises as

---

[21] I am grateful to Cyrus Hamlin for drawing my attention to the performative implications of this scene and its parallel to the betrothal scene in the second volume.

Hyperion's elder and mentor, the setting of the episode in a ritually significant location (i.e., on a mountaintop, and at the site of a traditional festival), and the use of an explicit performative, "Be like him" – which could, in this context, be either a command or an identity-altering declaration. Yet the words spoken by Adamas do not correspond to any prescribed formula, nor does he hold any official position that would authorize him to perform such a ritual. Rather, his motivation for teaching Hyperion and for performing the symbolic baptism is love and spontaneous choice.

The immediate effect of Adamas' utterance is spectacular: Hyperion experiences an ecstatic exhilaration, as if he were in fact being drawn through the heavens with the god whose name he bears. Even in retrospect, he can be inspired by Adamas' words to reflect on the god-like potential of the human soul. Yet as he recounts the experience to Bellarmin, Hyperion also places it in a context of grief and loss. The next words of Adamas that he recalls are "Du wirst einsam seyn", for at this moment Adamas announces his intended departure (StA 3.16). Even the possibility of recollecting the enthusiastic experience is threatened by the burdensome present, that counters the memory of Adamas' performative act with an unspecified curse: "Ach! es kann ja nicht einmal ein schöner Traum gedeihen unter dem Fluche, der über uns lastet" (StA 3.15).

Hyperion's quasi-baptism at the beginning of the first volume has a counterpart at the beginning of the second volume: the formal betrothal or quasi-marriage that he and Diotima celebrate on the evening before Hyperion's departure for battle. This is the other relationship the novel refers to as a "Bund" (StA 3.100), which suggests that it also needs to be seen as a redemptive counterpart to the Bund der Nemesis and Alabanda's oath. Hyperion asks Diotima's mother to bless and sanctify their union, with their assembled friends as witnesses, in anticipation of their official marriage when he returns. The couple proceeds to kneel before her mother and each of them utters a kind of marriage vow – addressed neither to the other nor to God, but to nature:

> Längst, rief ich, o Natur! ist unser Leben Eines mit dir und himmlisch-jugendlich, wie du und deine Götter all', ist unsre eigne Welt durch Liebe. In deinen Hainen wandelten wir, fuhr Diotima fort, und waren, wie du, an deinen Quellen saßen wir und waren, wie du, dort über die Berge giengen wir, mit deinen Kindern, den Sternen, wie du. (StA 3.101)

Following these testimonials, which are formulaic in rhetorical structure yet original in sentiment, Diotima's mother and the assembled companions are called on to witness that their love is "holy and eternal" like nature itself:

> Ich zeug es, sprach die Mutter.
> Wir zeugen es, riefen die andern.

The scene – which imitates a marriage ceremony, but uses non-conventional formulas and relies on an authority that is not derived from any state or religious institution – matches quite exactly one of the possible "misfires" Austin describes for the speech act of marrying. A "misapplication" of the performative occurs when it is a non-ordained mother, and not a priest, who is conducting the ceremony.[22] Clearly it is not the invalidity of these utterances that is being highlighted in *Hyperion*, though, but rather the meaningfulness they acquire precisely from the fact that conventions are being deformed. Diotima's mother is invested with the power to bless the couple's union, and the friends to witness it, by the love and trust that subsist among them. Here the freedom that is missing from Alabanda's overly institutionalized vow extends to a freedom to choose and re-make speech-act conventions. The ceremony that results from this process of altering the conventions is a hybrid of public, institutional forms (the vow, the act of witnessing) and the I-you dialogue with nature that the novel values, but otherwise locates outside of a societal context. The quasi-marriage of Hyperion and Diotima also represents a marriage of the two types of performative: the social and the subjective speech act.

But the marriage scene has a tragic coda, in which one further utterance affirms the link between speaking and being, and demonstrates that the performative can at least figuratively kill:

> Nun war kein Wort mehr für uns übrig. Ich fühlte mein höchstes Herz; ich fühlte mich reif zum Abschied. Jetzt will ich fort, ihr Lieben! sagt' ich, und das Leben schwand von allen Gesichtern. Diotima stand, wie ein Marmorbild und ihre Hand starb fühlbar in meiner. Alles hatt' ich um mich her getödtet, ich war einsam und mir schwindelte vor der grenzenlosen Stille, wo mein überwallend Leben keinen Halt mehr fand. (*StA* 3.101)

A moment after Diotima's mother has pronounced their love eternal, Hyperion's utterance "Jetzt will ich fort" re-introduces temporality with

---

[22] J.L. Austin: *How to Do Things with Words*. Ed. J.O. Urmson and Marina Sbisà. 2nd ed. Cambridge 1975. Pp. 15-16.

the deictic "now", re-introduces the autonomy of the I after I has supposedly been dissolved within the I-you-we relationship of the lovers and nature – and it kills all around it. In contrast to the active uptake that the lovers' vows found among their assembled friends, Hyperion's word meets with silence. His utterance is clearly effective, but the effect is mortal: if the marriage scene is, to complicate Austin, a *felicitous misfire*, then Hyperion's utterance finds its mark. His re-assertion of an independent subjectivity already counts as a kind of departure from the union, and the utterance figuratively kills Diotima just as his actual departure will lead to her actual death. It is, according to Hölderlin's use of the term in the annotations to his translation of *Antigone*, a *tödtlichfaktisches Wort* – a fatally factual word (*StA* 5.269-70).

The baptism scene and, even more, the marriage scene, suggest models for speech acts that place the self in the world, relating it to others and to nature in an act of spontaneous choice,[23] yet also take account of mechanisms of interaction within a community. The potential of this type of performative is called into question at the midpoint of the novel, in the scene that is critical for Hyperion's development. At the end of the first volume, he, Diotima, and some of their companions visit the Acropolis, where Hyperion is moved to make a long speech on the Greek past, on art, philosophy, reason, love, and the ideal of *hen diapheron eauto* ('the one differentiated within itself') as the basis for spiritual and social order. Joining the intellectual debate, Diotima raises it to a meta-level by making Hyperion's discourse itself the subject of her arguments. She urges him to give his people what he has to give – his intellect, his words – and predicts that he will become "Erzieher unsers Volks" and "ein großer Mensch". Hyperion is inspired by his own rhetoric and hers to proclaim the inauguration of a new world-order:

> Es werde von Grund aus anders! Aus der Wurzel der Menschheit sprosse die neue Welt! Eine neue Gottheit walte über ihnen, eine neue Zukunft kläre vor ihnen sich auf.
> In der Werkstatt, in den Häusern, in den Versammlungen, in den Tempeln, überall werd' es anders! (*StA* 3.89)

---

[23] "Spontaneous choice" is used here in Humboldt's sense, when he refers to the "Spontaneität der Wahl" exercised by a speaker in choosing a "you" with which to enter into dialogue (*Gesammelte Schriften*. Vol. 6. P. 26), or describes the pronouns *ich* and *du* as follows: "Sie werden wirklich innerlich empfunden, das *Ich* im Selbstgefühl, das *Du* in der eigenen Wahl" (Vol. 6. Pp. 165 and 309).

This explicit performative represents the climactic moment of the novel; it is the pivotal point for the forces that determine Hyperion's own fate and that of his people. If his declaration is to be effective, it must secure the uptake not only of Diotima and his other friends (who have, ironically and ominously, left the couple alone, preferring to converse with two British antiquarians), but also of the Greek people in general. But the people must first be brought to the point where they can assent to a new world-order in harmony with nature and culture, which can only happen through the instruction that Hyperion, as educator, will provide. If the people assent to his proclamation of a new order, he will be their educator and a great man; if he educates them successfully, they will assent to his proclamation of a new order. This is the paradox of the performative, always particularly acute in the language of Romanticism, where speech acts do not operate according to pre-established rules so much as they themselves establish the interpersonal relationships within which they will operate. The inability to accept the challenge posed by this paradox is Hyperion's tragedy. No sooner has he uttered his declaration than he begins to doubt its effectiveness. When Diotima tells him he will have to spend three to four years travelling and studying before he can take up his vocation, he is no less eager, yet he already begins to read this delay in the fulfilment of his declaration as a fatal dehiscence of word from deed and decision from action: "Giebt's denn Zufriedenheit zwischen dem Entschluß und der That?" Diotima must reassure him that he is the kind of speaker whose words *are* acts: "Es ist die Ruhe des Helden, sagte Diotima, es gibt Entschlüsse, die, wie Götterworte, Gebot und Erfüllung zugleich sind, und so ist der deine" (*StA* 3.89).

But Hyperion, doubting, chooses to subordinate language to immediate, physical, and violent action, by rejoining Alabanda and leaguing himself with the Russians in their battle against the Turks. He attempts to transpose his declaration of a new world-order into the context of armed rebellion, insisting to Alabanda, "es muß sich alles verjüngen, es muß von Grund aus anders sein" (*StA* 3.111). But the altered form of this utterance is revealing: no longer a declaration ("Es werde von Grund aus anders!"), it is now a statement ("Es muß von Grund aus anders seyn") used in a frenzied exhortation to action, but perhaps already with an anticipation of despair. The context Hyperion has chosen, in which words are used to command and to rouse to rebellion, is not on par with his declaration of a new world to an enlightened community, his baptism by Adamas, or his vows to Diotima and nature – profounder and more complex performatives that invoke the very spirit of speaker and addressee and alter their mode of being in the world. Abandoning the mission to which he had committed himself while with Diotima, he figures his earlier utterances as a now broken promise: "Ach! ich habe dir ein Griechenland versprochen und du bekommst ein Klaglied nun dafür" (StA 3.118).

Two redemptive moments remain. The first lies in the form of the novel itself, and the implications, analyzed by Lawrence Ryan and Friedbert Aspetsberger, of Hyperion's recollecting his experience and repeating it in language from a standpoint at the end of the process of development that he is describing. In the first paragraphs of the novel Hölderlin laments his original decision in favour of physical action: "O hätt' ich doch nie gehandelt! um wie manche Hoffnung wär' ich reicher!" (StA 3.8). But in writing the letters to Bellarmin he finally does exchange physical action for verbal action as a way of affecting the world and shaping his own identity. "Die Sprache ist seine Verbindung zu Bellarmin und zur Veränderung der Welt in eine bessere Zukunft", Aspetsberger writes, stressing the reflective and communicative function of language in Hyperion's letters – although he adds that the letters thereby also expose the inability of language to express immediate experience.[24] Haberer summarizes the significance of the novel's epistolary and recollective form for a discourse-centred reading: "*Als* Sprache erst gewinnen die Erlebnisse der Vergangenheit, die ja zugleich zu jener im Briefschreiben deutlich werdenden Sprachfähigkeit geführt haben, ihre identitätsbildende Bedeutung".[25]

The second redemptive moment occurs in the enigmatic ending of the novel. Hyperion ends his letters still denouncing the "empty words" of society in general: "Ach! viel der leeren Worte haben die Wunderlichen gemacht" (StA 3.159). But in this same context he ironically reaffirms the role of language in performing identity and bringing at least private dialogic relationships into being. Hyperion relates how, surrounded by the charms of nature on a spring day, he finds his way back to a dialogic recognition of the Other. Echoing the forms of speech that, in this novel, characterize intimate conversation, Hyperion

---

[24] Friedbert Aspetsberger: *Welteinheit und epische Gestaltung. Studien zur Ichform von Hölderlins Roman "Hyperion"*. Munich 1971. Pp. 158-60. See also Lawrence Ryan, who analyzes the reflective, "epic" character imposed on events by the narrative perspective (*Hölderlins "Hyperion": Exzentrische Bahn und Dichterberuf*. Stuttgart 1965).

[25] Brigitte Haberer: Zwischen Sprachmagie und Schweigen. Metamorphosen des Sprechens in Hölderlins *Hyperion oder Der Eremit in Griechenland*. In: *Hölderlin-Jahrbuch* 26 (1988-9). Pp. 117-33, here p. 133.

once again addresses the sun and the breezes as *du* and calls them his brothers, then gives voice to his intense desire for Diotima: "Diotima, rief ich, wo bist du, o wo bist du?" (*StA* 3.158). Against all expectation, his question is answered; he seems to hear Diotima's voice in the natural surroundings, a "dear word from a sacred mouth" (*StA* 3.159).

Hyperion's response to this experience, the passage of lyrical prose with which the novel ends, confirms the impression that his utterance itself is here re-establishing relationships and even calling Diotima back into existence:

Auch wir, auch wir sind nicht geschieden, Diotima, und die Thränen um dich verstehen es nicht. Lebendige Töne sind wir, stimmen zusammen in deinem Wohllaut, Natur! wer reißt den? wer mag die Liebenden scheiden?– O Seele! Seele! Schönheit der Welt! du unzerstörbare! du entzükende! mit deiner ewigen Jugend! *du bist*; was ist denn der Tod und alles Wehe der Menschen? (*StA* 3.159; my italics)

These dramatic apostrophes reaffirm the illocutionary effect of the vows that Hyperion and Diotima exchanged with each other and with nature; despite the death of Diotima and his own grief, Hyperion testifies that the union of lover, beloved, and nature is undissolved. But besides alluding to this unity, Hyperion performs it. Describing the united entities as voices in harmony with one another, Hyperion loses his voice in theirs, so that the referential structure of his language begins to dissolve. Who or what is the referent of "du unzerstörbare" and "du entzükende"? "Seele" and "Schönheit der Welt" are both possible antecedents, but the ultimate referent could equally well be "Natur" or "Diotima". Suddenly all these terms become grammatically as well as spiritually indistinguishable. To this no-longer-differentiated addressee Hyperion addresses the words that resonate with his previous, intimate exchanges with Diotima, Alabanda, and elements of nature: *du bist*. More than a recognition of the other, this is a recognition that the self is merged with the other; and the ability to utter *du bist* in this absolute way[26] marks the recovery of some sense of self beyond loss and disillusion. If Hyperion fails to discover a socially or politically effective form of expression, he at least ends by reaffirming, more

---

[26] Cf. Cyrus Hamlin's comment on this utterance, in the course of a detailed reading of the final pages of *Hyperion*: "Where else does Hölderlin use such an absolute sense of the verb 'to be'? It appears to affirm an existential condition beyond all human limits, beyond all mortal time" (*Hermeneutics of Form: Romantic Poetics in Theory and Practice*. New Haven 1998. P. 155).

strongly than before, the role of language in placing the self phenomenologically and dialogically in the world.

Only through creative utterance arising from individual will, one might conclude from a reading of Hölderlin's novel, can private feeling and intellect modify the otherwise rigid and even tyrannical forms of social life; but individual utterance always runs the risk of misfiring. Even the privileged performatives in the novel – the symbolic baptism, the exchange of vows, and the declaration at the Acropolis – are immediately followed by departure and loss, as if to indicate their ultimate failure to establish a stable discursive community. Innovative speech acts require the uptake of addressees, but must themselves establish the conditions under which that uptake can be given, or the conditions within which they count as meaningful social actions. Hyperion's tragedy is that he cannot risk, trust, negotiate, or perhaps even understand his own potential for performative utterance, and is caught in or discouraged by its paradoxes. Such a reading ascribes to Hyperion himself most of the responsibility for his own misfortune – mitigated, perhaps, by the fact that the paradoxes that baffle him are real and persistent properties of expressive utterance in a political world.

In contrast to *Hyperion*, a number of obvious and general reasons could be offered for regarding Hölderlin's uncompleted drama *Der Tod des Empedokles* as a speech-act text. The word "word" appears in it with obsessive frequency, often because characters are explicitly pondering the effects of language on others or on themselves. The drama contains remarkably little action, and the main "events" that do occur are either verbal utterances or responses to utterances. One crucial speech act takes place before the play begins: the philosopher Empedokles has apparently committed an act of blasphemy in declaring himself equal to the gods. This causes Hermokrates, priest of the town of Agrigent, to curse Empedokles by banning him from communication with any of the townspeople. The curse brings about the only real movement in the drama, Empedokles' wandering from Agrigent to Mount Etna, but it also generates other responses in the form of further speech acts. Empedokles' young disciple Pausanias immediately pronounces a blessing on his master in an attempt to mitigate the priest's curse, while Empedokles himself angrily pronounces a counter-curse on the townspeople. At the end of the drama, once a delegation of citizens has come to ask forgiveness of Empedokles and bring him back to the town, the curses of both Hermokrates and Empedokles are annulled by Empedokles' blessing on the people, just before he departs from them again to seek reconciliation with nature and the gods by a suicidal leap into the volcano of Etna.

Not only does *Der Tod des Empedokles* operate primarily through verbal action, but it actually thematizes the issue of when and how speech acts become effective. The characters need to address these questions because the drama presents a situation in which subjective and intersubjective contexts for performative utterance collide. *Der Tod des Empedokles* shows how speech acts operate within a system of societal conventions and structures of authority, but also how expressions of individual will and creativity can cut across and deform those structures. By setting extremely individualistic, expressive, or phenomenological utterances against extremely conventional, institutional, or socially authoritative ones, the drama challenges us to consider the role of discourse in generating both subjective identity and the intersubjective sphere.

These two frames of reference, the subjective and the public, coalesce around Empedokles' initial, self-deifying pronouncement. Although it resonates throughout the play, the audience never hears this utterance directly. Rather, it is alluded to at length in a dialogue between Hermokrates and Kritias, and it is recalled (although carefully not repeated) in Empedokles' own monologues and his dialogues with Pausanias. Hermokrates claims twice that Empedokles called himself a god, and stresses that this utterance occurred in a public context:

> Denn es haben
> Die Götter seine Kraft von ihm genommen,
> Seit jenem Tage, da der trunkne Mann
> Vor allem Volk sich einen Gott genannt. (185-8)[27]

> Verruchter! wähntest du,
> Sie müsstens nachfrohlokken, da du jüngst
> Vor ihnen einen Gott dich selbst genannt? (614-16)

Hermokrates, whose own power as a priest depends on sociopolitical institutions and their discursive conventions, necessarily associates the transgressive aspect of Empedokles' words with their function as a

---

[27] Unless otherwise identified, quotations from *Der Tod des Empedokles* are drawn from the first of the three versions of the drama as printed in *StA*, the most complete and continuous available text. Variants in the second draft that have a significant bearing on the points being made are taken account of in footnotes.

public utterance.[28] Indeed, he cannot interpret Empedokles' speech act
otherwise than as an attempted play for political power:

> Dann hättest du geherrscht in Agrigent,
> Ein einziger allmächtiger Tyrann
> Und dein gewesen wäre, dein allein
> Das gute Volk und dieses schöne Land. (617-20)

But in performing his self-deifying declaration, according to Hermokrates, Empedokles misread the conventions. His proclamation of himself as god or tyrant does not win uptake from the people: they maintain
only a shocked silence ("Sie schwiegen nur; erschroken standen sie"
[621]). As the priest sees it, Empedokles' attempt to overturn the existing power structure is doomed because he underestimates the tenac-
ity of the rules about permitted and forbidden speech. Empedokles'
shocking declaration does not leave a dent in the discursive conventions, even if, as both Hermokrates and Kritias admit elsewhere, he has
succeeded in overturning other legal and social conventions in Agrigent:

> Krit: Das Volk ist trunken, wie er selber ist.
> Sie hören kein Gesez, und keine Noth
> Und keinen Richter; die Gebräuche sind
> Von unverständlichem Gebrause gleich
> Den friedlichen Gestaden überschwemmt. (189-93)

> Herm: Gesez und Kunst und Sitt und heilge Sage
> Und was vor ihm in guter Zeit gereift
> Das stört er auf und Lust und Frieden kann
> Er nimmer dulden bei den Lebenden. (231-4)

Empedokles himself confirms that he once claimed to be a god, or
mightier than the gods: "ich allein / War Gott, und sprachs im frechen
Stolz heraus" (482-3). But he places the utterance in a subjective context. As far as he is concerned, the transgression was not sociopolitical
but spiritual, since through his utterance he shattered the unity between
himself and a deified nature. But the accounts of Empedokles and

---

[28] In the second draft of the play, which Haberer analyzes in detail, Hermokrates accuses Empedokles of a different transgression, for which the public
context is still more of a determining factor: he intimates that Empedokles has
betrayed holy secrets to the lay people (*Sprechen, Schweigen, Schauen*. Pp. 73-
81).

Hermokrates agree on one point: that semantically, and in all likelihood grammatically, Empedokles' transgressive words were an "I am" utterance: "I am a god", he presumably said, or "I am equal to the gods". This formulation resonates not only with the "I am" utterances of Yahweh in the Hebrew and Jesus in the Christian Scriptures, but also with Hölderlin's philosophical context and Romantic philosophy of language. Empedokles sets himself up as something like a Fichtean Absolute I, or as the expanded individual ego as which the Romantics often understood the Fichtean I.[29] His utterance symbolically places him in the position of a first principle to which all other entities are related as objects, their existence dependent on his act of self-positing – which may be a way of interpreting Hermokrates' statement that Empedokles claimed the gods came into existence through his word (225).

Representing this act of self-positing as a specific utterance by which Empedokles has repositioned himself in the world, the drama illustrates how subject-positions are established in acts of speech. Pronouns, as Humboldt claims, take abstract "points of agency" and identify specific individuals with them: "Der wesentliche Begriff aller drei Pronomina ist immer der durch die Natur der Sprache selbst gegebene, dass sie die ursprünglichen und nothwendigen Beziehungspunkte des Wirkens durch Sprache, als solche, bezeichnen, und dieselben in Individuen verwandeln". But he goes on to specify that the central subject-position established by utterance is that of the "I" in relation to a "you": "*Ich* ist nicht das mit diesen Eigenschaften versehene, in diesen räumlichen Verhältnissen befindliche Individuum, sondern der sich in diesem Augenblick einem Andren im Bewusstseyn, als ein Subject, Gegenüberstellende".[30] The I-you relationship is exactly what Empedokles gave up in calling himself a god, whereby, as he recalls in his opening monologue, he "thought [only] of himself" ("dachtst du / An dich" [339-40]). By positing himself as an independent I, Empedokles relinquishes his former state of unity with nature and the gods, a state of *Erkenntnis* characterized by his ability to address natural objects, such as the light of heaven, as *du*: "Da kannt' ich dich, da rief ich es: du lebst!" (384). The primary self-assertion of the I that Fichtean philosophy sees as the birth of existence and knowledge here represents the

[29] For a detailed account of Hölderlin's response to Fichte, especially in relation to the proposition "I am I", see Dieter Henrich: *Der Grund im Bewußtsein. Untersuchungen zu Hölderlins Denken (1794-1795)*. Stuttgart 1992. Pp. 485-515.
[30] *Gesammelte Schriften*. Vol. 6. P. 306.

death of Empedokles' *Erkenntnis* and oneness with nature. Pausanias, overhearing Empedokles' self-recriminations without distinguishing the words, remarks on the "unfamiliar deathly tone" ("der fremde Todeston" [365]) that now colours his speech. In terms of the sequence of speech acts in the play, whereby Empedokles' self-deification calls forth Hermokrates' curse and instigates the chain of responses that culminates in Empedokles' resolution to commit suicide, the original self-deifying utterance is another "fatally factual" word: it not only represents the death of Empedokles' spiritual unity, but triggers his actual death.

Empedokles' "I am" utterance, then, has the illocutionary effect of altering his position in relation to nature, and the perlocutionary effect of making him feel spiritually alienated from his gods. And, even if the point of the self-deifying utterance was to set Empedokles apart from the intersubjective sphere in which ordinary humans interact with one another, it has further ramifications in precisely that sphere. In the context of the conventions for public discourse, Empedokles' illocution counts as an act of blasphemy. As such, it incurs the perlocutionary effect of angering Hermokrates and the citizens of Agrigent. Because the effect of the utterance is to bifurcate Empedokles' spiritual and social identity, and because it sets him in a new, distanced relation to nature as a world of objects, one might say that Empedokles' speech act *opens up the division between subjective, intersubjective, and objective spheres*. It is, in this sense, a truly originary utterance that is appropriately never voiced in the drama itself, but is present only in the responses, paraphrases, and allusions it elicits.

Positing that Empedokles' utterance had this form and this effect makes the question of identity, and how it is shaped by language, central to the drama. Empedokles' subjective identity and his social identity are altered by the act of declaring publicly "I am [a god]", and the question of who he is – or, rather, who he was and who he has now become – is repeatedly posed by Empedokles himself and by his interlocutors. "Ich wars!" he recalls in his first dialogue with Pausanias (410), but immediately questions, "Bin ich es noch?" (416), and then laments, "ich bin / Es nimmer" (428-9), even as Pausanias tries in vain to reassure him, "Du bist es noch, so wahr du es gewesen" (430). Hermokrates, preparing to pronounce his curse on Empedokles, challenges him to repeat his self-deifying claim before the people once more, by urging them to ask him who he is: "Ihr möget nur / Ihn selber fragen, wer er sei?" (546-7).

Once Empedokles' attempted self-deification opens up a gap be-

tween the way he sees himself (as an alienated sensibility) and the way
the public sees him (as a blasphemer), his subjective and intersubjective
identities develop separately over the course of the drama. Hermokrates, the champion of sociopolitical roles and institutional speech acts,
tries to impose on Empedokles a purely intersubjective identity by
altering the way others see him. He appears to succeed in doing so, as
Empedokles, driven out of the city, is identified even by a peasant in
the mountainous wilderness as the one marked by a priestly curse: "Ich
kenn euch. Wehe! das ist der Verfluchte / Von Agrigent" (1136-7). The
ability of utterances to alter public identity is a function of the response
or uptake they elicit in an audience – and uptake, or the question of
how utterances acquire validity in an interpersonal context, is one of the
central issues in *Der Tod des Empedokles*. A key phrase in the drama is
der Sinn des Volk – the mind of the people, or, perhaps, the collective
will. It is the object *on* which public speech acts work, but also the
means *by* which they work, and the play contains a number of discussions about how the mind of the people will determine the effectiveness
of speech.

Since Hermokrates' sociopolitical authority can, as the drama vividly
demonstrates, be revoked if the public refuses its consent, he shows the
liveliest concern for the *Sinn des Volk*. His first dialogue with Kritias
reveals their shared interest in the question of whose words, Hermokrates' or Empedokles', will win uptake from the public. Kritias poses,
almost formulaically, three questions to test the possibility that the
curse Hermokrates plans to pronounce on Empedokles will misfire:

Krit: Doch wenn des schwachen Volks
       Der Kühne sich bemeistert, fürchtest du
       Für mich und dich und deine Götter nicht?
Herm: Das Wort des Priesters bricht den kühnen Sinn.
Krit: Und werden sie den Langgeliebten dann
       Wenn Schmählich er vom heilgen Fluche leidet,
       Aus seinen Gärten, wo er gerne lebt,
       Und aus der heimatlichen Stadt vertreiben?
Herm: Wer darf den Sterblichen im Lande dulden,
       Den so der wohlverdiente Fluch gezeichnet?
Krit: Doch wenn du wie ein Lästerer erscheinst
       Vor denen, die als einen Gott ihn achten?
Herm: Der Taumel wird sich ändern, wenn sie erst
       Mit Augen wieder sehen den sie jezt schon
       Entschwunden in die Götterhöhe wähnen! (252-63)

Despite Hermokrates' apparent confidence in the power of priestly authority to overcome the "bold sense" that Empedokles' words have instilled in the people, his behaviour betrays uneasiness. He reveals, in fact, that he has already pre-tested the effectiveness of his public pronouncements, by promising the citizens a day earlier that he would bring them to Empedokles, and ordering them to stay at home until then:

Herm: Drauf sagt' ich ihnen, daß ich heute sie
Zu ihm geleiten wollt'; indessen soll
In seinem Hauße jeder ruhig weilen.
Und darum bat ich dich, mit mir heraus
Zu kommen, daß wir sähen, ob sie mir
Gehorcht. Du findest keinen hier. Nun komm. (271-6)

The townspeople stayed indoors at Hermokrates' command; the test has worked. But the scene in which Hermokrates curses Empedokles still dramatizes a struggle over the *Sinn des Volk* and thereby exposes the operation of intersubjective speech acts. The townspeople react to the first utterances of both Hermokrates and Empedokles with incomprehension and indecision:

Ein Agrigentiner: Was hat er da gesagt? (513)
Erster Agrigentiner: Was ist es denn, Hermokrates, warum
                     Der Mann die wunderlichen Worte spricht? (558-9)

But the second of these questions, wherein one of the citizens specifically asks *Hermokrates* for an interpretation of *Empedokles'* words, already indicates in whom the questioners will place their confidence. Their consent is forthcoming after Hermokrates' next utterance, in the form of an unusually explicit statement of uptake: "Wir glauben dir es wohl" (565). Hermokrates tests the will of the people yet once more before proceeding, by insinuating that Empedokles and Pausanias might in fact be allowed to get away with ignoring the conventions of public discourse, if they have won over the townspeople: "Wer sich das Volk gewonnen, redet, was/ Er will" (585-6). But the response is an even clearer declaration of solidarity from three of the citizens:

Dritter Agrigentiner: Ihr Bürger! ich mag nichts mit diesen Zween
                       Ins künftige zu schaffen haben.
Erster Agrigentiner: Sagt,
                       Wie kam es denn, daß dieser uns bethört?

Zweiter Agrigentiner: Sie müssen fort, der Jünger und der Meister. (592-5)

Having found the opportune moment – "So ist es Zeit!" (596) – Hermokrates now proceeds with his formal denunciation and excommunication of Empedokles. But he has been anticipated by the townspeople, who, in the lines cited above, assent to the banishment of Empedokles and Pausanias *before* Hermokrates has actually pronounced the curse. Moreover, in his remorse for the sin of blaspheming the gods, Empedokles testifies that he is already abandoned and alone, "wie ein Ausgestoßener" (424); he even offers to pronounce a curse over himself. When the priest's curse comes, it is, in at least two senses, a *citation*. As an institutional speech act, it cites a recognized formula for excommunication; beyond this, his words have been anticipated by his audience, including both the townspeople and Empedokles himself. The formal act of banishing takes effect because it has somehow already taken effect. By presenting this, the most explicit public speech act in the drama, as an echo of earlier speech acts, Hölderlin assigns sociopolitical performatives a secondary or belated status, implying that they merely confirm what subjective utterances have already achieved.

The citational quality of Hermokrates' curse also points to something inherently self-referential in the act of banishing. In forbidding all forms of communication between Empedokles and the citizens of Agrigent, the curse cuts Empedokles off from the conventions that would give his own utterances intersubjective validity. Hermokrates explicitly forbids the people to give assent to even one of Empedokles' words, or to perform even the most basic speech act of greeting:

Und wehe dem, von nun an, wer ein Wort
Von dir in seine Seele freundlich nimmt,
Wer dich begrüßt, und seine Hand dir beut [...] (644-6)

But Empedokles has already forfeited the uptake of the citizens – as they show by explicitly giving their assent to Hermokrates' words instead. Hermokrates can successfully shut Empedokles out from social discourse because his own discourse *does* have social validity; or, conversely, Empedokles is vulnerable to being shut out from discursive conventions because he is *already* shut out from discursive conventions, and therefore cannot appeal, as the priest can, to the *Sinn des Volk*. The speech act of excommunication, at least in the form in which Hermokrates performs it, has a special relevance for the issue of whether and how a speaker's utterances achieve intersubjective validity, since excommunication is itself the condition of being unable to "speak" within a discursive community. Perhaps this explains why it is the most explicit and detailed performative utterance in *Der Tod des Empedokles*, and forms a kind of counterpart to the central performative in *Hyperion* – Hyperion's declaration of a new world, that seeks to bring this world into existence, yet will only find uptake if the new world already exists.

Hermokrates' speech act, then, effectively gives a public name to the condition in which Empedokles finds himself throughout the first part of the drama. The priest's performative utterance is thereby relegated to the sociopolitical level – and the counter-example of Empedokles' utterances suggests that words perform their most profound acts elsewhere than in a political context. Although he does not have authority to challenge Hermokrates' curse on its own level, Empedokles responds with a counter-curse that invokes an entirely different use of language. Whereas Hermokrates annulled the *social* identity of Empedokles, Empedokles' curse annuls even the *ontological* existence of its addressees:

Emp: ha geht
Nun immerhin zu Grund, ihr Nahmenlosen!
Sterbt langsamen Tods, und euch geleite
Der Priesters Rabengesang! und weil sich Wölfe
Versammeln da, wo Leichname sind, so finde sich
Dann einer auch für euch; der sättige
Von eurem Blute sich, der reinige
Sicilien von euch; es stehe dürr
Das Land, wo sonst die Purpurtraube gern
Dem bessern Volke wuchs und goldne Frucht
Im dunkeln Hain, und edles Korn, und fragen
Wird einst der Fremde, wenn er auf den Schutt
Von euern Tempeln tritt, ob da die Stadt
Gestanden? (748-61)

As curse counters curse, Empedokles' preoccupation with subjective identity counters Hermokrates' preoccupation with intersubjective identity. Setting the citizens of Agrigent over against himself as *ihr*, he causes this *ihr* to disappear over the course of his speech until only an anonymous *er* ("der Fremde") is left. His curse, with its echoes of Hebrew prophecy, demonstrates that the performatives he utters rely not on sociopolitical conventions, but on the force of individual will.

Throughout the drama, characters testify to the identity-altering and even reality-altering effect of Empedokles' words. Kritias' daughter Panthea recalls "der /Geist in seinem Wort" (66-7), and Empedokles refers to himself as one "durch wen der Geist geredet" (1748). Pausanias recalls how a word from Empedokles, spoken in a sacred moment, changed his entire life (445-9).[31] Especially in one-to-one dialogue, Empedokles shows an extraordinary ability to persuade his interlocutors. Even after the excommunication has been pronounced, Kritias listens and agrees to Empedokles' request that he take Panthea away; Kritias and the townspeople later agree to leave him on Mount Etna, even though they desire to bring him back to Agrigent. Pausanias explicitly describes the way Empedokles' words persuade him, in despite of his own will, to obey:

> Mich meistert wunderbar dein Wort, ich muß
> Dir weichen, muß gehorchen, wills und will
> Es nicht. (1908-10)

As he describes this situation once more to Panthea and her friend Delia, Pausanias emphasizes that the words of Empedokles work differently from the normal process of persuasion. Although they overpower, they evoke liberty rather than submission in the listener:

> Er greift in meine Seele, wenn er mir
> Antwortet, was sein Will' ist....
>   Es ist
> Nicht eitel Überrredung, glaub es mir,
> Wenn er des Lebens sich bemächtiget....
>   doch wenn das Wort
> Entscheidend ihm von seinen Lippen kam;
> Dann wars, als tönt' ein Freudenhimmel wieder
> In ihm und mir und ohne Widerred'
> Ergriff es mich, doch fühlt ich nur mich freier. (2006-23)

Empedokles' words of power work by changing the addressee com-

---

[31] Intensifying these allusions, the second draft of the drama ends with Panthea's report that the citizens who sought out Empedokles on Mount Etna, and experienced his final exhortation and blessing, descended from the encounter with their faces glowing from the effect of his words, just as Moses' face shone when he descended the mountain after receiving the Ten Commandments from God: "Und ihnen glänzt' im Laide das Angesicht/ Vom Worte, das er gesprochen" (711-12).

pletely. According to Pausanias' account, they apparently acknowledge the subjectivity and freedom of the listener, yet alter the listener's mind and soul by bringing these into harmony with a superior will. By contrast, the priest persuades by attempting to negotiate the conventions of intersubjective discourse. *Der Tod des Empedokles* exposes the dangers of Hermokrates' approach, inasmuch as the uptake that was granted him can be – and here, is – rescinded again. In the final scenes of the play, Hermokrates and the townspeople seek out Empedokles and Pausanias on Mount Etna in order to retract the curse and beg them to return to the city. At this point, Hermokrates' utterances abruptly begin to fail of their expected uptake; his attempt to mollify Empedokles by reporting that the citizens have forgiven him elicits abuse rather than thanks. "So dankst du uns?" Hermokrates asks, incredulously, seeing his illocution fail (1327). The uptake he had counted on from the citizens also vanishes, as they assent instead to Pausanias' threat to take revenge on Hermokrates for the curse. One of the townspeople explicitly describes how Hermokrates, before and during the banishment scene, manipulated the public's *Sinn*:

> Zweiter:　　　　Regst du noch die Zunge? du,
> Du hast uns schlecht gemacht; hast allen Sinn
> Uns weggeschwatzt; hast uns des Halbgotts Liebe
> Gestohlen, du! er ists nicht mehr. (1397-1400)

Hermokrates' use of language, this passage suggests, is rooted in sociopolitical authority, and indeed prefigures the account of the performative given by the sociologist Pierre Bourdieu. *Contra* Austin, Bourdieu argues that the principle of performativity is not to be found within linguistic structure itself, but "comes to language from outside", from the societal power structure that endows certain speakers with authority.[32] But this authority, as Hermokrates' situation now illustrates, depends on the "complicity" of listeners, or even a failure of awareness on their part, that allows them to be duped into according the speaker performative power. "Misrecognition", Bourdieu suggests, "is the basis of all authority";[33] the citizens of Agrigent now seem to come to the same realization, and regret their complicity in responding to Hermokrates' utterance.

When this happens, Hermokrates himself, despite his careful analysis

---

[32] Pierre Bourdieu: *Language and Symbolic Power*. Ed. John B. Thompson. Trans. Gino Raymond and Matthew Adamson. Oxford 1991. P. 109.
[33] *Language and Symbolic Power*. P. 113.

of the *Sinn des Volk*, cannot control and does not fully understand the effect of his words. "Weißt du, was du gethan?" Empedokles asks him (1333), as does one of the citizens (1423); the only response Hermokrates is able to offer is "Den Rasenden begreif ich freilich nicht" (1358). Having successfully, if temporarily, altered the relation of Empedokles to the people, Hermokrates has simultaneously altered his own relation to them. Uttering the curse marks him in the eyes of the citizens as the public and verbal antagonist of Empedokles, and they now accuse him of calling up Empedokles' counter-curse (1407-9). Moreover, in terms of the logical sequence of speech acts in the drama, Hermokrates' act of banishment is the catalyst that motivates Empedokles to issue his parting speech to the townspeople on Mount Etna – a speech in which he changes his curse into a blessing, but also urges a full reformation of the social and political order. Once Empedokles has been shut out of the discursive conventions that constitute society, he can reflect on them and decree their transformation. Just as Empedokles' original act of self-deification had the opposite effect of what was intended, so Hermokrates' curse, in trying to uphold and confirm the conventions of sociopolitical discourse, ultimately generates the potential to overturn them.

The drama brings its participants to the point of a revolution in the relationship between utterance and identity. After reconciling with Empedokles, but before experiencing his call for a new world-order, the citizens try to implicate him in the existing sociopolitical conventions by offering to make him king. His response, "Diß ist die Zeit der Könige nicht mehr" (1449), meets with complete incomprehension on their part. Neither accepting nor declining their offer, Empedokles voids the offer itself by declaring that "king" is no longer a valid term in the sociopolitical order. Unable to situate themselves and him in terms of the conventions of discourse familiar to them, the townspeople respond by questioning Empedokles' identity on the most basic level: "Wer bist du, Mann?" (1450). The same question reappears shortly after in the context of one-to-one dialogue between Empedokles and Pausanias:

Emp: Wofür
        Erkennst du mich?
Paus: O Sohn Uraniens!
        Wie kannst du fragen? (1846-8)

In this instance, the dialogue eludes discursive conventions in a different way and on a different level, for the reader perceives an echo of the dialogue between Jesus and his disciples in the gospels, in which Peter confesses that he believes Jesus to be "the Christ, the Son of the living God" (Matthew 16:15-16). The allusion, unavailable to the speakers themselves, ironically implies some kind of fulfilment of Empedokles' claim to be a god, albeit on a level he can neither intend nor experience.

Instead, the restitution that Empedokles does experience in respect of his transgressive speech act occurs in his final speech. Addressed to "Jupiter the Liberator", this ecstatic monologue anticipates the reunion with the divine that Empedokles now expects to find only in death. The contemplation of non-being inspires him to a remarkable declaration of being:

> staunen muß ich noch, als fieng
> Ich erst zu leben an, denn all ists anders,
> Und *jezt erst bin ich, bin* – (1919-21; my italics)

These words constitute the *Aufhebung* of Empedokles' original transgressive speech act. While his first "I am" utterance is only paraphrased in the drama, this one is presented (its presentness intensified by the deictic "jezt erst"); while the former represented the death of unity, the latter announces reunion and rebirth; while the former claimed for Empedokles the status of an immortal, the latter rejoices in mortality. But the utterances are parallel in their focus on subjectivity and on the effort of articulating being in language – achieved here by the formulation "bin ich, bin" that literally contains the I within being.

The crucial difference between the assertions "I am a god" and "only now am I, am" is that the second is spoken in a context in which Empedokles is not thinking of himself, but intensely aware of the presence of the other – of "you". In this final speech, Empedokles declares "I am" in a context where "everything is otherwise". He addresses Jupiter, nature, his own heart, his eye, and even his own self as an immediately present *du*, and ends with an apostrophe to the rainbow: "*wie du bist*, so ist meine Freude" (1942; my italics). The last words spoken by Empedokles echo Hyperion's last words ("du unzerstörbare! du entzükende! mit deiner ewigen Jugend! du bist" [*StA* 3.159]), and embody the spirit of Hölderlin's philosophical writings when they suggest that a true act of self-identification involves recognizing oneself in the other. "Wie ist aber Selbstbewußtseyn möglich?" he asks in the fragment "Urtheil und Seyn": "Dadurch daß ich mich mir selbst entgegenseze, mich von mir selbst trenne, aber ungeachtet dieser Trennung mich im entgegenge-

sezten als dasselbe erkenne" (*StA* 4.217). At the same time, the restoring of an I-you relationship in this speech engages Romantic ideas
about language as the medium that establishes a connection between
the *Ich* and the *Gegen-Ich* of the natural world (Friedrich Schlegel), and
about the *ich*, placed opposite to a *du* in consciousness, as the element
on which a whole linguistic structure hinges (Humboldt). According to
the radically dialogical concept of identity that runs through the work
of the early Romantics, acknowledging the existence of the "you"
represents a more open and receptive, yet a truer and more stable way
of saying "I am" – and thereby also forms one of the touchstones of a
pragmatically conceived linguistics.

If Empedokles' original act of self-deification set him apart from
others and distanced him from the natural world, his final speech act
represents the achievement of another concept of identity, that understands the self as existing only within otherness. *Der Tod des Empedokles* achieves a certain fulfilment on this level of verbal action –
always subject, however, to the dark irony that Empedokles is about to
kill himself. Nevertheless, the drama implies that its protagonist's
expressive, phenomenological speech acts work even within the sociopolitical sphere, deforming its conventions and promising to transform
it even after his death. The speech acts of Hermokrates, on the other
hand, are represented as manipulative, for they exploit discursive
conventions so as to impose on the consciousness and identity of others; derivative, because they cite conventional formulas and perhaps
only enact on a sociopolitical level what is already the case on a deeper,
spiritual level; and temporary in their effect, because they can always
be superseded by later, more effective speech acts. Although the drama
hinges on the fatal consequences of Empedokles' utterance, it is ultimately his language that continues to be valorized as a performative
discourse that relies on individual will, on being itself rather than social
identity, and on an intimate relationship between two consciousnesses.

To the extent that both Hyperion and Empedokles count as analogues
for the poet, this reading of *Hyperion* and *Der Tod des Empedokles*
would find its logical continuation in interpretations of Hölderlin's
poetry that stress its powerful dialogic aspects. The situation of a
speaker who uses poetic language to posit relationships with specific
addressees is common to virtually all of his poems, although only
specific aspects of Hölderlin's dialogism have received critical attention.[34] Hyperion and Empedokles represent the poet-philosopher as a

---

[34] Gerhard Kurz calls attention to rhetorical, oratorical, and pragmatic

speaking subject in a social context, but one whose speech acts never quite bring subjective and intersubjective worlds into alignment. Their qualified failure indicates the situation of Hölderlin himself, for whom the relation to a discursive community is a vital aspect of the poet's vocation, but who never succeeds in winning intersubjective validity for the language with which he places himself subjectively in the world. Modern definitions of the performative, especially by philosophers like Austin and Bourdieu who define it according to sociopolitical conventions and relationships, can help bring out the intersubjective context of Hölderlin's poetry, and to delineate the issues of social convention and political authority in *Hyperion* and *Der Tod des Empedokles*. Yet speech acts that derive from sociopolitical authority or rigid convention are subordinated in these texts to speech acts that express individual will and creative force, and that instantiate relationships between self and world as a relationship between *ich* and *du*. In this sense, Hölderlin's notion of the pragmatic dimension of language reflects that of his early Romantic contemporaries, who described language as a simultaneously cognitive and communicative act, and called attention to the realignment of relationships that happens in and through each individual act of utterance.

---

dimensions of Hölderlin's poetry (Hölderlins poetische Sprache. In: *Hölderlin-Jahrbuch* 23 [1982-3]. Pp. 34-53). With reference to the historical and literary-historical context, William Scott McLean argues that in his mature work Hölderlin tried to develop a poetics of the intersubjective sphere, where value lies not in isolated individual identity, but in the individual's implication in a field of relationships to others and to the natural world (Private Song and the Public Sphere: Some Remarks on the Development of Hölderlin's Later Poetry. In: *Goethezeit. Studien zur Erkenntnis und Rezeption Goethes und seiner Zeitgenossen*. Ed. Gerhart Hoffmeister. Bern 1981. Pp. 265-80). Rolf Zuberbühler, finally, concentrates on Hölderlin's dedicatory poetry and provides a psychological interpretation of the drive to address a *du* that shapes all of his writing (*Die Sprache des Herzens. Hölderlins Widmungsdichtung*. Göttingen 1982).

Fritz Breithaupt

The Ego-Effect of Money

This essay asks how economics could emerge as a leading paradigm of our culture and it explains the omnipresence of economics by considering two conceptions of money: money as individuation and money as a medium. Both of these concepts develop out of the Romantic connection between money and individuality. According to Friedrich Schlegel and Tieck, money functions as a model of and competitor with human beings since it performs the very act by which individuality is established: self-extension. The later Romantics (Fouqué, Chamisso, and Müller), who try to rescue an individuality untouched by money, present a different concept of money as a neutral medium of exchange and community. The modern meaning and success of money can be described as an overlapping of these two concepts of money.

Our Western culture is a culture of money.[1] This not only means that actual business transactions occupy a prominent place in our society, but also that we rationalize non-monetary relationships in terms of money and economics. Today, economic explanations of even non-economic matters have the air of being "realistic". Why is that? What is the attraction or "reality" of money that explains its predominance?

The following article presents a partial answer to the question of how at the beginning of the nineteenth century the science of monetary circulation was able to become a general principle of other disciplines, rather than just remaining a "science of business administration". While it is often and rightfully assumed that the success story of modern economics has its roots in Adam Smith, I will argue that the economic model gained a specific attraction for non-business areas during its revision in German Romanticism, a revision that ties money to a certain notion of individuality (and the Romantic task of becoming). While popular discourse has opposed money and true individuality (money as abstract, individuality as concrete, etc.), I will argue that both money

[1] I thank Elizabeth Starr for her patient and thoughtful editing of this text, Karl-Heinz Maurer, Derek Hillard, and F. Corey Roberts for their many comments, and Martha B. Helfer for her indispensable suggestions which are too numerous to individually acknowledge.

and modern individuality possess the same structure. In fact, I will draw the perhaps extreme, perhaps very familiar conclusion that what came to be the *Ich* is generated by the very dynamic that characterizes capital. This is the reason why the attraction of money is not simply psychological: the *Ich* does not precede money. Rather, money itself produces the *Ich* that is attracted to money, so that the attraction to money is, in a certain sense, pre-psychological.

To map the dimensions of the wide sense of economy beyond mere economics means to present most major trends of thought of the last two centuries that have shaped the Western world. The wide sense of economy includes not only Marx's explanation of politics and society in terms of economy, but also Nietzsche's claim that all morals are based on the structure of creditor and debtor and Freud's use of economy for explaining the "household" of the psyche (Freud invents the apparatus of the psyche as an economic enterprise that organizes its actions in order to increase its "libido", the legal tender of the soul; see, for example, his *Zur Einführung des Narzißmus*). To be sure, the economic paradigm has not been reduced to "theory" but found its way in many "practices" that are manifested in social institutions organizing our behavior (institutions of education, work, and family, insurance companies, institutionalizations of the division of the private and the public and of the division of worktime and *Freizeit,* etc.). To avoid the naive opposition of theory and praxis, one could say that economy today occupies the place of "theory" that organizes our "praxis" from within. Indeed, talking about economy today immediately raises the question as to what, if anything, resists economy (this is Derrida's question in *Giving Time: Counterfeit Money*). Economics seem to offer a model for the explanation of the world that subsumes other models, and is has been claimed that other discourses like politics, morality, religion, aesthetics, culture, and philosophy are in the process of disappearing, only to reappear in the guise of economic interests.

The question, then, is what came to be economy. Jean-Joseph Goux has given us many insights into the structural similarity between economy and other areas such as language and the Freudian psyche.[2] But while Goux's project has been to show how any operation of substitution and any entity operating with substitutions can be seen as an economy, he makes it difficult to explain the rise of a universal concept of economy. In fact, following Goux's concepts, one would have to con-

---

[2] Jean-Joseph Goux: *Symbolic Economies: After Marx and Freud.* Ithaca 1990.

clude that economy was already structurally organizing social life long before modern capitalism emerged in the nineteenth century (indeed, Goux refers to the much older history of signification). It is here that I will take a slightly different turn by examining historical notions of economy. I will argue that a certain notion of economy that emerged in German Romanticism (departing from Adam Smith's economy of balance) made it attractive as a paradigm for manifold social interpretations by its linkage to a certain notion of individuality. Specifically, my hypothesis is that the Romantic concept of individuality is not only influenced by money, but based on an economic dynamic in such a way that this concept of individuality will inescapably produce the idea of money as its double. In turn, money becomes the model of individuality and the *Ich* an economic enterprise. One of the modern paradoxes deriving from this seems to be that one can only inscribe one's individuality into a work, put oneself fully into it, by economizing this work, which means rationalizing it in terms of an investment that will pay off for the individual by generating the very *Ich* as its benefactor. Thus, even though we ought to have reservations about the economization of the modern world, we cannot base our rejection of money on an idealist notion of individuality. And in turn it is difficult to critique economics in the age of individualism.

Talking about individuality requires talking about money. When individuality was reinvented by the early Romantics in Germany in a way that shares little with any previous thought about the matter, money entered the process of individuation. The early Romantics defined individuality as an act of self-extension *(Selbst-Bildung)*.[3] I t follows consequently that individuality cannot simply be assumed as a given, but as something that has to be brought about. This bringing about takes the form of a reflection of the subject on the subject. The

---

[3] Here and in the following, I translate the Romantic *Bildung* by the English word "extension" instead of the more common "formation" to emphasize the dynamic nature of *Bildung*. For the early Romantics and Goethe, *Bildung* was less a finished product and not even a shaping, but rather a process of a *Horizonterweiterung*. This extension does not result in any describable entity, gestalt, or form; in fact, this very indescribability belongs to the notion of *Bildung*. The word "formation", on the other hand, is used by Friedrich Schlegel only to mark the product, not the process; see the quotation in footnote 18. For the implications of the German notion of *Bildung*, see Marc Redfield: *Phantom Formation: Aesthetic Ideology and the "Bildungsroman"*. Ithaca and London 1996. Pp. 38-62.

result of this peculiar reflection is not to become oneself or to understand oneself as one is, but rather to extend oneself. The reflected being is extended by the very ability to reflect on itself, meaning by the reflecting faculty. In such a reflection on oneself, one is always more than the mere reflected being since the reflection generates the reflecting *Ich* as a surplus to the reflected being. Thus, individuality is the ability to be more than oneself.

In short, this surplus-individuality is structured like that which Schlegel describes as the dynamics of money and Marx later defined as capital: money that reflects on money, thereby growing or "extending itself" (*sich bilden*) by means of interest. This is what Marx's famous formula of the generation of capital states; money is exchanged for a commodity and the commodity is exchanged for a higher amount of money (M'): M-C-M'. The paradoxical nature of this formula is underlined when one emphasizes that each exchange is an equal exchange. The result, then, is that money is equal to more money (M = M'). It is exactly this "moreness" of capital that connects individuality and money. Thus, money (capital) could become not only an example of this new individuality, but in fact its prime proof due to the clear measurability of its growth. Money does not simply imitate human individuality, but appears to be the model of human individuality since it displays the very process of individuation uncontaminated by any content. This process of self-extension I will call the *ego-effect* of money. The interest in money produces interest, produces me as interest or surplus. Once this insight became available for the Romantics, the uncanny closeness of money and human individuality haunted their thought.

I will distinguish two basic approaches to the relationship of individuality and money within Romanticism and will define them as two models – money as individuation and money as a medium of society. The first approach is the one of the early Romantics (I will present Friedrich Schlegel and Tieck), who discover the problematic structural similarity of money's and individuality's extension. Money functions as the ideal of this individuality and, in fact, pure individuality. In this sense, the Romantic addiction to individuality is an addiction to money.

The later Romantics take a reactionary position that tries to rescue an individuality untouched by money. They apparently find it possible to neglect the importance of money for the practice of individuality and instead externalize money as the opposite of the pure individual. This move, however, leads them to idealize individuality without being able to define its essence. This second position within Romanticism is prepared by the novellas of authors such as Fouqué and Chamisso and culminates in Müller's economic concepts. Müller describes money not as a model of individual expansion but as a medium of integration that brings communities together in a harmonious way.

At the end of the paper, I will speculate about the predominance of the economic model beyond Romanticism and I will suggest that we need to consider the "overlap" of the two diametrically opposed Romantic paradigms. This overlap establishes a complex network that makes the economic model both attractive, since it promises a strengthening of ego-positions, *and* allows a cover-up of egotistic interests by presenting the use of money as a universally accepted form of behavior beyond suspicion.

For this generation of the *Ich*, the *ego-effect*, there is theoretically no difference whether its economy is played out on an economic, psychic, social, or political stage. What is money in the economic, is libido in the psychic, and power in the political realm. However, libido and power tend to remain more abstract without a "fetish" representation like that of money. The main advantage of the economic over other areas is that it gives the illusion that money as personal property can be withdrawn from universal circulation and can be stored as one's own at any time.

I

Prior to the early Romantics, Adam Smith's idea of a self-regulated household came to be a model for understanding not only business administration, but cultural institutions in general. In 1795 Goethe described the difference of nature and culture in terms of economy: "die Natur [kann] sich niemals verschulden, oder wohl gar bankrutt werden".[4] While nature can only treat and use everything that is there at a given time, culture apparently has the ability to use what is not (yet) there by going into debt. This distinction, however, highlights that for both nature and culture the guiding principle is that of a household with a balanced budget. The accounting of positive and negative values evokes the concept of an equilibrium, a balancing out of two debts. Thus, even by going into debt, culture expands the idea of a balance by including negative numbers which record the failed balance and submit it to memory, thereby indicating that even debts correspond to a bal-

---

[4] Johann Wolfgang von Goethe: *Werke* (Hamburger Ausgabe). Ed. Erich Trunz. Munich 1981. Vol. 13. P. 176.

anced budget as long as they are maintained as a negative value (or likewise as a profit). The positive or negative balances are manifested by money. Thus, money exists as a delay of a conclusion of an exchange that saddles the business partners with longstanding obligations. Money functions as a trope of equalization since it stores disproportion, thus hinting at a balanced budget. Money is there only to disappear, be sublated, and become zero.[5]

Bankruptcy, then, must be a catastrophe for a system seeking an equilibrium, since debts will remain unpaid and even the present elements of an economic unit will be eaten up by the mere negativity of debt. Culture as a whole is marked by its ability to go into debt, thereby risking bankruptcy and exposing itself to less than nothingness. Thus, the *Hand* in Goethe's *Das Märchen* becomes black and seems to disappear once a *Handel* involving debt is made. Perhaps Goethe would go so far as to say that a culture exists only by virtue of this very possibility and danger.

While Adam Smith's paradigm of a balanced household budget led to the establishment of the academic discipline of economics in England and Germany, the early Romantics introduced a completely different idea of economics that is based on expansion and extension, rather than on balance. To engage with this turn within the philosophy of economics – and the Romantics' turn to money – we need to consider the central place that expansion and extension came to occupy within their thought.

II

In the following, I will first present Schlegel's thinking from the time of the *Athenaeum*, which focuses on individuality and in which money played only a negative role. Then, we will consider how Schlegel, only a few years after the *Athenaeum*, suddenly changes his understanding of money in a way that aligns money and individuality. The uncanny closeness of (human) individuality and (inhuman) money leads the later Schlegel to distance himself from his early celebration of individuality

---

[5] Marc Shell analyzes Kant's rare use of metaphors of money and observes how Kant derives the concept of zero from a balancing out of two debts. Thus, Shell argues, money and its production of the concept of "zero" lead Kant to his concept of truth as an adequation or "Aufhebung". Marc Shell: *Money, Language, and Thought*. Baltimore 1982. Pp. 133-37.

and to embrace Catholicism instead.

For the Friedrich Schlegel of the time of the *Athenaeum* and thereafter, extension (*Bildung*) is always the extension of an individual.[6] Individuality is not simply a person's set of given unique features that makes him or her more or less different from others, but rather rests on an act of self-generation. Schlegel calls this act a *Reflexion, Potenzierung, Charakterisieren*, or, in some contexts, a *Kritik*. The result of this reflection on oneself is not to become oneself or to understand oneself as one is, but rather to extend oneself. By reflecting about itself, the *Ich* splits off from its identity and rises above "itself", thereby producing a surplus; this means it produces its reflecting *Ich* as a surplus that is not included in the reflected self.[7] Thus, the individual or *Ich* is not a given, but a "project".[8] The *Ich* is that which cannot be defined but is produced in an act of definition as a defining entity. Likewise, the reflection is a limitation of the reflected object that extends the limited object by the limiting force or *Ich*. If one were to define this surplus *Ich*, the *Ich* as a surplus, the act of this definition would inevitably escape its own reflection and produce another surplus *Ich*, an "Ich über Ich". *Ad infinitum.*[9]

When Schlegel states that only an individual can reflect, exponentialize itself (*potenzieren*), and be characterized, this means in turn that

[6] It was not until 1797 that Schlegel employed individuality as a positive term. Until then, his thought on individuality was connected with the manneristic, which he took as a defective or subjectively degenerated form, borrowing from Goethe's – misunderstood – category of "Manier" in *Über Einfache Nachahmung, Manier und Stil.* As we will see, Schlegel does not give up the notion of individuality in his later writings after the *Athenaeum*, but instead focuses on the forces of limitation that can control individuality's expansion.

[7] This is also the reason why the reflection does not, properly speaking, constitute a self-reflection, since the self that is reflected about and the reflecting agent are not the same.

[8] Philippe Lacoue-Labarthe and Jean-Luc Nancy have developed the characteristics of this individual as a "project", a "work in progress", or a "projection" of its own completion that is never achieved but always coming. Philippe Lacoue-Labarthe and Jean-Luc Nancy: *The Literary Absolute: The Theory of Literature in German Romanticism.* Albany 1988. Pp. 39-58.

[9] For the structure of this individuality and its aporias see the insightful text by Werner Hamacher: Der Satz der Gattung: Friedrich Schlegels poetische Umsetzung von Fichtes unbedingtem Grundsatz. In: *MLN* 95 (1980). Pp. 1155-80.

everything that can reflect and be characterized is an individual. As we will see later, this turn is quite crucial: "Alles was kritisirt werden soll, muß ein *Individuum* sein".[10] "Nur Individuen kann man charakteris- ieren".[11] "Die Potenzirung ist eine moderne Figur; Combinazion des Individuum mit sich selbst".[12] Thus, individuality is not reserved for human beings but also pertains to all cultural institutions that come about through 'reflections'.

Schlegel's concept of individuality does not exclude community but is, in fact, the condition of its possibility (although the early Schlegel will not arrive at a notion of a harmonious or complete synthesis with- out radical discongruency). The individual does not seclude itself from others, but exists by extending itself and extending itself to others, thereby displaying a genuine openness for what it is not. Thus, indi- viduality is the precondition of any community, since only by the act of becoming an individual can one reach beyond oneself. Accordingly, Schlegel does not see the individual and the universal as excluding each other, but as two sides of a coin.[13] Schlegel develops this in the famous opening page of the *Gespräch über die Poesie* (1800) in which he stresses radical individuality while at the same time asserting that this individuality will unite everybody:

Die Vernunft ist nur eine und in allen dieselbe: wie aber jeder Mensch seine *eigne* Natur hat und seine *eigne* Liebe, so trägt auch jeder seine *eigne* Poe- sie in sich. Die muß ihm bleiben und soll ihm bleiben, so gewiß er der ist, der er ist, so gewiß nur irgend etwas *Ursprüngliches in ihm* war; und keine Kritik kann und darf ihm sein *eigenstes* Wesen, seine *innerste* Kraft rauben,

[10] Friedrich Schlegel: *Kritische Friedrich-Schlegel Ausgabe* (= KA). Ed. Ernst Behler with assistance of Jean-Jacques Anstett and Hans Eichner. Munich, Paderborn, Vienna, Zürich 1958-. Vol. XVI. P. 138. No. 138. Compare also: "Kann man etwas anderes charakterisiren als Individuen?" KA II. P. 205. (*Athenaeum* fragment 242). This fragment also indicates that individuality is not limited to human beings: "Sind nicht alle Systeme Individuen, wie alle Individuen auch wenigstens im Keime und der Tendenz nach Systeme?"
[11] KA XVI. P. 142. No. 677. The interchangeableness of "charakterisiren", "kritisiren", and "potenziren" is clear from the context and stated explicitly in: KA XVIII. P. 48. No. 298.
[12] KA XVI. P. 163. No. 919. The following fragment reads: "Jedes In- div.[iduum] constituirt eine Masse".
[13] For the simultaneity of individuality and universality, compare KA XVIII. P. 229. No. 418 and Pp. 258-59. No. 782.

um ihn zu einem allgemeinen Bilde ohne Geist und ohne Sinn zu läutern und zu reinigen wie die Toren sich bemühen, die nicht wissen was sie wollen. *Aber* lehren soll ihn die hohe Wissenschaft echter Kritik, *wie er sich bilden muß in sich selbst*, und vor allem soll sie ihn lehren, auch jede *andre* selbständige Gestalt der Poesie in ihrer klassischen Kraft und Fülle zu fassen, daß die Blüte und der Kern *fremder* Geister Nahrung und Same werde für seine *eigne* Fantasie.[14]

While the significance of the *Eigne* is stated emphatically, Schlegel does not elucidate its content. No descriptive or constative statement accompanies the existence of the individual but only the performative "so gewiß er der ist, der er ist", which affirms only the unquestionability of its positedness without naming who or what carries out the act of its positing. Instead, the only "essence" of the *Eigne* is its self-grounding by an act of "bilden in sich selbst". The self thereby establishes itself only by extending itself beyond "itself". And it is this movement beyond itself that explains the essential openness of the individual in the process of becoming for other beings. Thus, Schlegel can assert that one can embrace "auch jede andre selbständige Gestalt" precisely because the individual consists of a genuine openness for what it is not. The contact between the individual in the process of becoming and other beings or forms does not take the form of a mediation which somehow establishes a link between two incommensurably different beings (a somewhat naive concept), but is a contact only because the *Eigne* in its essence provides its possibility and *is* this possibility.

Schlegel briefly touches on what he considers a wrong method for achieving a state of universality by stripping the individual of its individuality and making it a mere "allgemeine[s] Bild". A page or so later, Schlegel again emphasizes that the true task is to develop individuality and not "tötende Verallgemeinerung". At this point, Schlegel seems to feel confident enough only to mark this *Verallgemeinerung* as something to be avoided. In fact, he asserts that no criticism "kann und darf" take away the individual being ("eigne Wesen"), thus emphasizing the clear possibility of keeping the "allgemeine Bild" at bay. In numerous fragments from the time of the *Athenaeum*, this constellation of individuality returns along with the to-be-excluded abstraction or objectivity. And on several occasions, this negative generality or abstraction is

---

[14] KA II. P. 284, emphasis mine.

identified as money.[15] Thus, August Wilhelm Schlegel regrets the "ökonomische Geist" of his "Zeitalter": "Die [...] Zurückführung von allem Möglichen auf das sogenannte Nützliche, welches doch ohne Hinweisung auf das an sich Gute gar keine Realität hat, der ökonomische Geist mit einem Worte, ist eine der hervorstechendsten Eigenheiten des Zeitalters".[16] For both of the Schlegels, money seems to be very far from individuality.

III

Only a few years later, this abstraction and its danger to individuality returns. Yet now this abstraction is not something that can be avoided, but rather an essential aspect of individuation. Book 10 of Schlegel's 1804/05 Cologne lecture *Die Entwicklung der Philosophie in zwölf Büchern* is devoted to *Natur- und Staatsrecht* and Schlegel deduces the necessity of statehood from three social institutions: marriage, property, and punishment.[17] It is in the central discussion of property (*Eigentum*) that Schlegel engages with the question of individuality. In line with his earlier conception, he understands individuality not as a given entity but as the process of a certain self-extension or *Bildung*. This process of individuation relies on the process of acquiring *Eigentum*. "Ohne Eigentum würde der Mensch weder sich selbst und seine Kräfte, noch

---

[15] In *Über die Unverständlichkeit*, Friedrich Schlegel writes: "Schon oft hatte ich die Objektivität des Goldes im stillen bewundert, ja darf wohl sagen angebetet. [...] Kurz überall wo es nur einige Bildung und Aufklärung gibt, ist das Silber, das Gold verständlich und durch das Gold alles übrige". While this seems to suggest that gold provides the neutral and abstract "Medium" of communication that Schlegel pretends to search for, he suddenly turns around by pointing out that gold only covers up the essential unununderstandability: "Wenn nun erst jeder Künstler diese Materien [gold and silver] in hinreichender Quantität besitzt, so darf er ja nur seine Werke in Basrelief schreiben, mit goldnen Lettern auf silbernen Tafeln. Wer würde eine so schön gedruckte Schrift, mit der groben Äußerung, sie sei unverständlich, zurückweisen wollen?" KA II. P. 365. Gold is simply abstract and cannot provide meaning and, thus, is not suited for individuality and *Bildung*.

[16] August Wilhelm Schlegel: *Kritische Schriften und Briefe*. Ed. Edgar Lohner. Stuttgart 1964. Vol. III. P. 60.

[17] KA XIII. Pp. 104-41. In the following, I will quote from this text by giving the page number in the main text.

irgend eine Kunst ausbilden können" (115).[18] Schlegel now considers, as will Hegel later on, the affinity between *Eigentum* (property) and *Eigentümlichkeit* (individuality), an affinity that was already present in the "Eigene" of *Gespräch über die Poesie* as both individual and possession.[19]

Once there is *Eigentum* (which is, to repeat, the condition of possibility for *Eigentümlichkeit*), there will be trade and exchange. But "Handel ist ein gefährliches Prinzip", as Schlegel warns repeatedly.

[18] Also: "Bildung aber ist ohne Eigentum nicht möglich; sie ist der einzige sittliche Grund, der uns zum Besitze der äußern Dinge berechtigt" (128).

[19] This is a very interesting point, but since it is not essential for the course of my argument, I will limit myself to a few remarks on this correlation. Schlegel's question is what happens between owner and owned. While the object does not change physically when it is owned, the owner affects its way of being an object. The force of making *Eigentum* manifests itself on the material not as a physical entity, but as a limitation and shaping of the material's extension. Schlegel calls this limitation of the extension a "Formation": "Alles worauf ich meine Kraft angewandt habe, wird eben dadurch mein Eigentum – vor allem die *Formation*; habe ich den Stoff kultiviert, so ist er mein eigen; aber auch bei der Okkupation findet eine Kraftanwendung statt, und mithin ein Eigentumsrecht" (114). Schlegel can immediately move on to include the occupation of space as a similar use of force because he defines ownership as a limitation: by occupying a place, one first of all limits it, cuts it off from the unlimited space, by circumscribing its extension. In this act of defining, forming, or limiting of the material or space, the owner becomes the owner: s/he is the limit of her or his property. The limit is more than the mere object or space; it is the defining force, the surplus or *Ich* of the property.

Hegel is very close to Schlegel's concept of *Eigentum* when he compares acts of ownership, formation, and definition. In §54 of *Grundlinien der Philosophie des Rechts*, he stipulates: "Die Besitznahme ist teils die unmittelbare *körperliche Ergreifung*, teils die *Formierung*, teils die bloße *Bezeichnung*". Similar to Schlegel, Hegel will problematize the notion of contract as the "Entäußerung" of property that arises from property (see esp. §72).

Thus, appropriation of *Eigentum* is an act of *Eigentümlichkeit* (individuality). The empowerment and extension of the owner by means of ownership is in line with the *Selbst-Potenzierung* of the earlier text in which the *Ich* extends itself and opens itself up beyond the defined and limited *Ich* of its reflection. The *Eigentümer* who limits and thereby defines the *Eigentum* escapes his own definition, thus producing a surplus, an *Ich*, that supersedes its own act. The *Ich* in its *Eigentümlichkeit* is that which cannot be defined but is produced in an act of definition, limitation, and appropriation (*Eigentum*).

This danger culminates in money. The abstraction (money) that the earlier text from 1800 still believed to be able to control and to distinguish from true individuality now moves into the heart of individuality. Money is, first of all, nothing but a means of comparison, "ein allgemeiner objektiver Maßstab des Werts aller dem Handel und Wechsel unterworfenen Dinge" (119). Money promotes exchange, makes it go smoothly. But money starts a process that escapes the individual's control:

> Durch das Geld entsteht ein Handel in der zweiten Potenz, mit dem Gelde selbst, da derjenige, der viel Geld hat, sich viele Waren und durch diese wieder viel Geld verschafft. Dieses verzinst sich wieder, und so kann dieses immer weiter fortgehen. Es entsteht nun billig die Frage: darf der Staat solche Benutzung des Geldes erlauben, darf er Zinsen garantieren und sanktionieren? (119)

> Der Handel ist ein gefährliches Prinzip. Dies gilt vorzüglich vom auswärtigen Handel. Beim Handel geht, da das Geld sich immer in sich selbst vermehrt, das Steigen des Reichtums ins unermeßliche. (120)

The danger of money is not simply that of an abstraction (as the *Kulturpessimisten* had it a century later), but that of an individualization. By reflection on itself ("zweite Potenz") and by entertaining a relationship with itself ("sich immer in sich selbst vermehrt"), money performs the very act by which the individual becomes an individual: extension of itself. By reflecting upon itself, a human being produces an *Ich* as a surplus which escapes its own observations. In the limitation or definition of his property, the owner goes beyond his/her property, thereby extending himself/herself. Similarly, by investing money for money ("zweite Potenz"), money does not remain self-identical, but splits off from itself and grows out of its own dynamic. As Schlegel had asserted before, this non-identity achieved by reflection (*Potenzierung)* is the *sine qua non* of individuality. Thus, money not only executes the same act as the individual, it also *becomes* an individual by the same act. The *skandalon* money presents is that money individualizes itself and becomes an *Ich* by means of a reflection, since its essence consists of an extension of "itself" to what is not part of itself. *Es verselbständigt sich.* In this self-generation, money both mocks and performs the process of individualization, thereby compromising all human individuality. Thus, Hans Christian Anderson can write a fairy tale (*The Silver Shilling*) in which a coin tells its life story: "*I* [...]".

Money brings about the *Ich-Effekt*. This *ego-effect* of money poses a challenge to Schlegel's concept of individuality. Money consequently derives from the ex-tension of *Eigentümlichkeit*, but money ends the very extension of human individuality and threatens human *Eigentüm-lichkeit* because it has the ability to operate independently from human beings and to limit the space of their action. As long as individuality takes place in the form of money, human beings cannot escape the dilemma of producing a money that operates on its own and escapes human control. Thereby, human individuation potentially turns into a dehumanization of individuality and, perhaps, a de-individuation.

Money does not merely copy the movement of individuation executed by human beings, but rather performs the act in its purest form and is the incorporation of precisely this act. While all other possible candidates for individuality are "contaminated" by differentiations of some kind (like biological factors, nationality, gender, and memory), the money of investment (capital) is nothing but a self-extension, meaning its self is only "its" extension. Money is the only existing item that can fit the demands of the philosophical *Ich* as posited by Fichte, namely the demand of its essential emptiness and its independence from any prior ground. Thus, money not only is an external competitor for individuality that could be separated from the true and human individual, but also displays the mechanism of individuation as such. When Schlegel defines individuality as that which is always only becoming,[20] a "project", and "work-in-progress", he later on finds the essence of this becoming in money. Money structurally becomes the ideal of individuation, an ideal which human individuality can never achieve.

The essence of the *Ich* is its openness for the *Nicht-Ich*, meaning its ability to extend itself to what it is not. It is this non-identity and ex-tendibility that makes money the incorporation of the *Ich*, since money can embrace the whole world as a world of possible *Eigentum*. Money comes about as the incarnation of the process that should complete the human individual but which actually undermines its possibility. It both gives and withdraws the basis for the *Ich* in one double gesture: it

---

[20] As the famous 116 *Athenaeum* Fragment has it: "Die romantische Dichtart ist noch im Werden; ja das ist ihr eigentliches Wesen, daß sie ewig nur werden, nie vollendet sein kann". This fragment also describes the fascination of the "romantische Dichtart" with individuality: "Sie [romantische Poesie] kann sich so in das Dargestellte verlieren, daß man glauben möchte, poetische Individuen jeder Art zu charakterisieren, sei ihr Eins und Alles". KA II. P. 186.

establishes the *Ich*, since it functions as a model of a *Selbst-Potenzierung* that leads to an extension; and it withdraws the basis of the *Ich* since it detaches the *Selbst-Potenzierung* from the control of the human individual, thereby making individuality a non-human issue. Money neither simply becomes the abstract Other of individuality nor gains sufficient ground to be a proper individual, but is the self-abstraction of individuality, meaning the production of a self by means of an abstraction. Money individualizes abstraction and is an individuo-abstraction. Money exposes the individual to its *own* abstraction. Thus, money enters discourses of individuality, self-fulfillment, and authenticity to mock and undermine their validity while, at the same time, radicalizing and expanding them.

For the early Romantics, money is not a measurement of comparison, not a simple means of exchange, and not a medium of society (for the notion of medium, see below). Rather, money is a measurement of comparison only to itself, since it only counts its own growth. It is a means of exchange only insofar as it turns all objects (acts) into commodities (services) that exist within the world of exchange. And it is a medium of society only insofar as its extension erases all differences and reduces all social *com*munication to a mere monologue of money. Money is that faculty that already entails its producing a surplus and, therefore, is more than it is. Marx explains the concept of "Mehrwert" (which he takes as a translation of the English "surplus value") when he discusses the conversion of money to capital. While money is used simply as a means of exchanging two goods, capital is "Geld, das gleich mehr Geld, Wert, der größer als er selbst ist". Capital is generated when money is exchanged for a commodity only with the intent of being exchanged for money again, money of a higher amount. Capital is already more than it is; it is pure extendibility and *Ich*-ability.[21]

[21] In short, for Marx capital is that which Schlegel calls an individual, a self-extending, non- identical faculty: "Der Wert der Waren [...] verwandelt sich so in ein automatisches Subjekt. [...] In der Tat aber wird der Wert hier das Subjekt eines Prozesses, worin er unter dem beständigen Wechsel der Formen von Geld und Ware seine Größe selbst verändert, sich als Mehrwert von sich selbst als ursprünglichem Wert abstößt, sich selbst verwertet. Denn die Bewegung, worin er Mehrwert zusetzt, ist seine eigne Bewegung, seine Verwertung also Selbstverwertung". This subject is a self-creating subject since it could not exist unless it creates itself. There is no evidence for "value" in the natural world, so it can only exist by *its own* movement of self-creation. It is this highest degree of uncertainty, this necessity of positing itself, and of

IV

Thus, we have seen the genesis of Schlegel's thought and, in fact, even Schlegel's famous conversion to Catholicism and his turn away from the radical philosophy of the *Athenaeum* can be seen as a response to the danger that money poses for that very concept. This turn will bring the later Schlegel close to the position of Müller and other later Romantics.

The danger money and its individuation pose is not a mere philosophical danger, but threatens the ability of human beings to become individuals themselves. "Überhaupt führt das Eigentum notwendig zu einem großen Unterschied zwischen Armen und Reichen. Diese aber sind ein Übel, da sie praktisch untätig werden, und dem Staate zur Last fallen" (120). It has been observed that the deictic pointing of the "diese" remains unclear.[22] I suggest that it can be read both ways. For the poor, the accumulation of money in the hands of a few means that they only have reduced space left for the extension of their individuality. For the rich, their wealth means that they do not have to work and perform the act of individuation themselves. Thus, money potentially takes individuality away from the rich as well as the poor.

In order to limit the accumulation of money and the brutality of the free capitalism he was envisioning, Schlegel apparently found it necessary to establish a higher force or institution that could limit the extension of money. This meant to limit human individuality, as well. For Schlegel, the higher institution can only be another individual, an individual that performs the act of individuality (owning, defining, limiting), thereby extending itself. This institution, which exists by defining the individuals as citizens, is the state. Thus, the state is the *Ich*

---

performing a *verwerten* which brings about a *Wert* that the "fetish" of money shares with individuality. Karl Marx: *Das Kapital: Kritik der politischen Ökonomie*. In: Karl Marx und Friedrich Engels. *Werke*. Ed. Institut für Marxismus-Leninismus beim ZK der SED. Berlin 1989. 33rd. Edition. Vol. 23. Pp. 168-69.

[22] Ernst Behler felt that the context of this passage was clear enough that he suggested replacing the "diese" by "jene", since he thought that only the poor ones would be a burden for the state. However, would it not be possible that Schlegel might have meant to say that the rich ones become a burden for the state once their money does the work for them? Wealthy people might stop working and becoming, since their money replaces them in this task, leaving them behind as non-individuals. KA XIII. P. 455. Endnote 27.

distinct from what it defines, limits, and appropriates. Consequently, Schlegel calls the state both an "Individuum" and the "Obereigentümer".[23] Thus, Schlegel does not abandon his concept of individuality, but reduces the variety of individuals in the process of becoming to only one: the absolutist, Catholic state. Apparently this call for a strong state made it possible for Schlegel to engage with the ultra-conservative politics of Metternich, in whose service he found employment.

Schlegel maintains that the state does not simply exist, but only exists insofar as the independent human beings subject themselves to the state (which, in turn, unites them in one larger body). The self-limitation of human beings qualifies them as citizens. For Schlegel, this self-limitation is a belief: "Der Staat beruht auf dem Glauben" (122):

> Nun ist aber der Glaube ein sittliches Anhalten des Geistes, ein willkürlich sich selbst anhaltendes, beschränkendes, beharrendes Denken, nicht aus Armut und Trägheit des Geistes, sondern aus Überfluß von geistiger Kraft und Tätigkeit. Der Glaube ist also ein wahrhaft göttliches Denken. [...] Nimmt man allen Glauben weg, so geht das Denken nach allen Richtungen ins unendliche, welches notwendig endlich einen skeptischen Zustand herbeiführen muß. (123)

The religious citizen exercises his or her individuality only by taking it away. If, as said before, individuality arises by limiting (and thereby extending oneself), then believing is the limitation of the act of limit-

---

[23] Just as trade enabled by money is a danger to human individuals, so international trade is a danger for states. Thus, Schlegel, who envisions that international trade will get out of the hands of the state, demands that international trade be restricted. "Der Handel ist ein gefährliches Prinzip. Dies gilt vorzüglich vom auswärtigen Handel" (120). This is also Fichte's conclusion in *Der geschlossene Handelsstaat. Ein philosophischer Entwurf als Probe einer künftig zu liefernden Politik* (1804), in which he goes so far as to demand: "Aller Verkehr mit dem Ausländer muß dem Untertanen verboten seyn und unmöglich gemacht werden". Johann Gottlieb Fichte: *Sämmtliche Werke*. Ed. J.H. Fichte. Berlin 1845. Vol. 1. Part II. P. 419 (chapter 2). Like Schlegel, Fichte seems to turn away from his progressive thought once he deals with questions of statehood and economy in the years after 1800. But as in the case of Schlegel, it also could be shown that Fichte's politics of a strong state consequently derive from his radical theory of individuality, from the "unbedingte Grundsatz", and is not merely a reaction to the events in France, as has been argued.

ing. The act of believing is a self-limitation, a limitation of the very ability to perform the act of limiting. Thus, the act of believing is split in two. It is both the continuation and the end of individuality, a continuation and end because it can only end the act of individuality by another limitation. This is the moment in Schlegel's thought that comes close to Hegel's later notion of *Aufhebung* as destruction, elevation, and preservation at the same time: in self-limitation, individuals are *aufgehoben*. And perhaps, but this I can only bring up as a side thought, Hegel's *Phänomenologie des Geistes,* with its praxis of passing into and through nothingness, is ultimately a religious manifesto.

His radical concept of individuation leads Schlegel to the necessity of religion (a belief), a religion that is both the climax and the end of individuality. It is here where individuality and money are divorced. Money cannot perform the religious act of limiting its extension.

V

From this point on, money appears wherever individuals and individuality should be. From the Romantic age onward, money accompanies discourses of individuality and authenticity to invade, undermine, and perhaps twist them against their original intention. One can date the emergence of this individuality of/from money fairly precisely in the works of Schlegel, Novalis, Brentano, and Tieck around or after the year 1797.[24] In the works of Tieck, to limit ourselves to one other writer of this era, the turn to money takes place between *Der blonde Eckbert* (1797) and *Der Runenberg* (1804). *Der blonde Eckbert* is hardly a conventional story. In a detailed reading, one would have to examine the strange pattern of repetition that the protagonists experience and the elimination of all uniqueness and individuality within this repetition.[25]

[24] As is well known, 1797 is a decisive year for both English and French fiscal politics in reaction to the failed French experiment in paper money. However, the Romantic turn to money seems only indirectly promoted by these events. The reception of paper money is certainly not reduced to a mere semiotics that suddenly realizes the nature of arbitrary "signs" (paper money) that are not what they mean. Lessing and the writers of the Enlightenment already knew about this.

[25] A reading of the story would have to consider the four repetitions of the same structure: A person in the circle of a family somewhat irresponsibly runs away from this family (perhaps kills the members) and, after some time wandering through forests, finds a new family. In this second family, however,

However, the story's use of money is a quite unproblematic one of mere possession that can raise jealousy, and thus lead to murder.

However, Tieck's *Der Runenberg,* written seven years later, reveals a different approach to the correlation of individuality and money. The story has many structural similarities with *Der blonde Eckbert* in repeating a similar *rite de passage* of someone leaving a family harbor to enter some undefined space, finding a new family, and ultimately being haunted again by memories or appearances of the suppressed first family. Yet while *Der blonde Eckbert* uses this pattern to erase and pathologize individuality, *Der Runenberg* individualizes the pathological, meaning the story establishes the pathological struggles of the protagonist as the very essence of individuality. In the struggle of the protagonist of *Der Runenberg,* money plays a central role; it is linked to Christian's self-alienation. A strange desire is awakened in him by money that is not satisfied by the possession of money. Rather, the very

---

the suppressed first family returns in the form of names, ghosts or similarities (*Wiederkehr des Verdrängten*). Each time, money and possession appear as the stimulus for running away by causing jealousy and suspicion. In this pattern of repetition, this *Wiederholungszwang*, the different characters of the text are condensed into only two: the "bert"-character who leaves his or her family (Eck*bert* and *Bert*a) and the "alter"-character who is abandoned or murdered (Berta's *Elter*n, W*alter,* and the *Alte*). The repetition of these two characters under different disguises, as well as the four circles of this pattern, make a new beginning for the "bert"-character impossible and pathologize the possibility of any kind of self-determined individuality. Thus, Ernst Bloch suggests that the shocking return of the supressed, the déjà vu, figures as a return to the uncompleted: "Der Chok wäre dann stellvertretend für alle plötzliche Rückkehr zu einem Selbst, das nicht oder nicht überall so geriet, wie es sich meinte". Ernst Bloch: Bilder des déjà vu. In: *Gesamtausgabe*. Frankfurt a.M. 1959. Vol. 9. P. 238.

Also, a reading would have to consider the 'ununderstandability' of the text. The riddle *Der blonde Eckbert* poses to its readers can be seen in light of the way in which the text itself deals with riddles. Several times one of the characters unveils a secret of his or her life, and each time the result is a betrayal or loss. Bertha dies after telling Walther her story, and Eckbert loses his new friend Hugo after telling him of his secret. Thus, the story avoids its characters' mistakes by not giving away its secret. See: Wolfgang Rath: *Ludwig Tieck: Das vergessene Genie.* Paderborn 1996; and Bernhard Greiner: Pathologie des Erzählens: Tiecks Entwurf der Dichtung im *Blonden Eckbert*. In: *Deutschunterricht* 39.1 (1987). Pp. 111-23.

possession provokes an unexplained search that drives him from his house and household, the Goethean place of stability and balance. He is lured into this search by the shining of money, glittering stones, sparks, and a strange gold symbol, as he explains to his father who caught him staring at some coins at night:

> Ich verstehe mich selbst nicht mehr, weder bei Tage noch in der Nacht läßt es mir Ruhe; seht, wie es mich jetzt wieder anblickt, daß mir der rote Glanz tief in mein Herz hineingeht! Horcht, wie es klingt, dies güldene Blut! Das ruft mich, wenn ich schlafe, ich höre es, wenn Musik tönt, wenn der Wind bläst, wenn Leute auf der Gasse sprechen; scheint die Sonne, so sehe ich nur diese gelben Augen, wie es mir zublinzelt, und mir heimlich ein Liebeswort ins Ohr sagen will: so muß ich mich wohl nächtlicherweise aufmachen, um nur seinem Liebesdrang genugzutun, und dann fühle ich es innerlich jauchzen und frohlocken, wenn ich es mit meinen Fingern berühre, es wird vor Freuden immer röter und herrlicher; schaut nur die Glut der Entzückung an![26]

He eroticizes money and is eroticized by money, but this auto-eroticization finds no fulfillment and no proper object.[27] His search does not lead him to find a secure place, or to find himself, but seduces him to go underground into the mines and leads him astray. When, at the end, he appears again after years of wandering, he proudly presents his findings: nothing but a couple of ordinary flintstones that spark when struck together. While the stones do not interest him, the sparks (which are analogous to the glittering of money, as the text emphasizes through similar connotations) fascinate Christian, tempt him to go beyond himself and to expose himself to other beings. What Christian is looking for is not an essence that exists in a stable and fixed form within a body, but rather a sparking that occurs between two bodies. Thus, the sparks are the figure of an in-between that shows the contact between beings as an unregulated and uncontrolled occurrence of an *Außer-sich-gehen*.[28] The individual thus happens in the sparks between beings –

---

[26] Ludwig Tieck: *Werke in vier Bänden*. Ed. Marianne Thalmann. Munich 1964. Vol. 2. Pp. 74-75.

[27] For this eroticization, see Klaus F. Gille: Der Berg und die Seele: Überlegungen zu Tiecks *Runenberg*. In: *Neophilologus* 77.4 (1993). Pp. 611-623.

[28] The sparking and the constellation of *Blitz-Witz* are key concepts for the early Romantics. "Die Einbildungskraft muß [...] durch die Friktion freier Geselligkeit so [...] elektrisieren, daß der Reiz der leisesten freundlichen und

which also means that individuals are not beings. The sparks do not "mediate" between bodies (stones), do not harmonize their crashes, but play out their bizarre singularity. Similar to Schlegel, Tieck does not posit isolated individual beings, but rather an individuality that occurs between different beings in their collusion without ever becoming one. Thus, a stable marriage is impossible for Christian.

VI

Tieck's and Schlegel's concept of an individuality of/from money leads to a strong counteraction by the later Romantics (including the late Schlegel, as I argued above). The later Romantics try to tame the implications of this concept of money and to rescue an individuality that could be reserved exclusively for human beings. Instead of facing the addiction to money, an addiction that is at the same time an addiction to individuality, these later writers aimed to detach money from the human individual by rationalizing money as the most unindividual entity there is. In this attempt, they sacrificed the dynamics of individuality that Schlegel develops for an unexplained, mythical idea of the individual. This does not mean that individuality ceases to govern modern thought – quite the opposite, since the notion of individuality is brought out of reach for reinvestigation, thereby multiplying its strength. While for Schlegel, individuality was justified only as the condition of possibility of extending the singular to the universal and promoting dialogue, individuality merely functioned to glorify or dramatize human beings for the later Romantics. Their ideology is an ideology of mystification that is comfortable with celebrating a *je ne sais quoi* as the essence of humanity without further questioning.[29]

In the following, I will present the steps the detachment of money

---

feindlichen Berührung ihr blitzende Funken und leuchtende Strahlen [...] entlocken kann". KA II. P. 150 (*Lyceum* Fragment 34). "Witz ist die Erscheinung, der äußre Blitz der Fantasie. Daher seine Göttlichkeit, und das Witzähnliche der Mystik". KA II. P. 258 (*Ideen* 26). Novalis adds: "Echt geselliger Witz ist ohne Knall. Es gibt eine Art desselben, die nur magisches Farbenspiel in höhern Sphären ist". KA II. P. 214 (*Athenaeum* Fragment 289).

[29] One could also speculate that this obsession with an unexplainable essence of individuality promoted the interest of the later Romantics in the phenomena of man-like machines and vampires, since these showed man without his miraculous individuality.

from individuality took and how the very manner of this detaching allowed the observation of a different concept of money, namely money as a medium of society. While the earlier Romantics came to view money in the context of individuality, the later Romantics rationalized money as a force that could unite people despite their differences. In stories by Fouqué and Chamisso, money is presented as a danger for the individual from the outside, not from within as for Schlegel and Tieck. While these stories present money as an agent of the individual's annihilation, it is precisely this "non-individuality" of money that qualifies it as a bridge between distinct individuals. Adam Müller will draw this conclusion by celebrating money's ability to unite a community. Within a few years, Schlegel's individuality of money led to its extreme opposite in Müller's societability of money.

VII

Fouqué's *Das Galgenmännchen* (1809) is based on an implicit pun. In this story, Reichard purchases a "Galgenmännchen", a little devil-like being in a bottle that magically will give as much money to its owner as he or she wants.[30] However, if the owner dies before selling the *Galgenmännchen*, his or her soul will go to Hell. The problem is that the bottle has to be sold for less than what it was bought for. Ultimately, someone will be stuck with the bottle who cannot sell it for less. The "prisoner's dilemma" of this construct consists in deciding who cannot sell the bottle any longer, since his/her potential buyers might think that they themselves could not sell it to anyone else because their hypothetical buyers might be afraid to remain stuck with it. Thus, while the first motivation seems to be getting the money-devil, the real problem arises once one wants to rid oneself of it. While Reichard first buys the money-devil for a fairly high amount, after a series of exchanges, the bottle returns to him for the price of the smallest coin. Now he, the individual, is stuck, since the money cannot be divided further. For years, Reichard engages in a maddening search for a "Halbheller" (half-penny), meaning a coin smaller than the smallest coin, which would make it possible to sell the money-devil again. While he wants to rid himself of the money-devil, he, ironically, comes to be known as the "Halbheller", a nickname that only stresses his inseparableness

---

[30] For the sources of this text, see Winfried Freund: *Literarische Phantastik*. Stuttgart, Berlin, Cologne 1990. Pp. 35-44.

from money.

However, Fouqué's story introduces a pun as a solution to Reichard's dilemma. Reichard finds an aristocrat who coins "Drittelpfennige" for him and he also learns that one "Pfennig" in one currency is as much as three coins of a different currency, so that he could sell the bottle to someone with these coins of lower value (and indeed someone who already sold his soul to the devil volunteers to buy the bottle). The pun consists of the very word "individuality" – money is not an individual since it can always be further divided. Money only seems to be "in-dividable", but in fact is a "dividual". By playing around this implicit pun, the story makes its case that the human individual can always be separated from money since in their essence, they are different.

This solution, the dividability of money, rejects Schlegel's and Tieck's view of the structure of individuality, but it fails to offer a satisfying alternative as to what human individuality could be. The end presents a Reichard whose soul is saved and freed from the dangers of the false use of money as already anticipated in his name, Reich-hard (*Reich Herz*), which promises the possibility of a conflictless unity of wealth and life. Thereby, the story can only water down the significance of money but fails to explain the attraction to money that the very story exploits to motivate its course of events.

VIII

No other text has shaped the position of the later Romantics toward money as much as one novella that reached popularity throughout Europe: *Peter Schlemihl* (1813) by Chamisso, a story that tells how the title figure trades away his shadow to the devil for a magic bag that produces infinite amounts of money. The novella not only presents a strange deal, but in the creation of money as one of the commodities of a deal it presents the creation of the very possibility of a deal.

Schlemihl, a poor fellow who has been ignored by a group of wealthy people, is leaving their party when he suddenly is approached by a strange man who had shown abnormal powers in pulling the most astonishing and huge gifts out of his small pocket:

> "Möge der Herr meine Zudringlichkeit entschuldigen, wenn ich es wage, ihn so unbekannterweise aufzusuchen, ich habe eine Bitte an ihn. Vergönnen Sie gnädigst –" – "Aber um Gottes willen, mein Herr!" brach ich in meiner Angst aus, "was kann ich für einen Mann tun, der –" wir stutzten beide und wurden, wie mir deucht, rot.

Er nahm nach einem Augenblick des Schweigens wieder das Wort: "Während der kurzen Zeit, wo ich das Glück genoß, mich in Ihrer Nähe zu befinden, hab ich, mein Herr, einigemal – erlauben Sie, daß ich es Ihnen sage – wirklich mit unaussprechlicher Bewunderung den schönen, schönen Schatten betrachten können, den Sie in der Sonne und gleichsam mit einer gewissen edlen Verachtung, ohne selbst darauf zu merken, von sich werfen, den herrlichen Schatten da zu Ihren Füßen. Verzeihen Sie mir die freilich kühne Zumutung. Sollten Sie sich wohl nicht abgeneigt finden, mir diesen Ihren Schatten zu überlassen?" Er schwieg, und mir ging's wie ein Mühlrad im Kopfe herum. Was sollt' ich aus dem seltsamen Antrag machen, mir meinen Schatten abzukaufen? Er muß verrückt sein, dacht' ich, und mit verändertem Tone, der zu der Demut des seinigen besser paßte, erwiderte ich also: "Ei, ei! guter Freund, habt Ihr denn nicht an Eurem eignen Schatten genug? das heiß ich mir einen Handel von einer ganz absonderlichen Sorte". Er fiel sogleich wieder ein: "Ich hab in meiner Tasche manches, was dem Herrn nicht ganz unwert scheinen möchte; für diesen unschätzbaren Schatten halt ich den höchsten Preis zu gering". Nun überfiel es mich wieder kalt, da ich an die Tasche erinnert ward, und ich wußte nicht, wie ich ihn hatte guter Freund nennen können. Ich nahm wieder das Wort und suchte es, wo möglich, mit unendlicher Höflichkeit wiedergutzumachen. "Aber, mein Herr, verzeihen Sie Ihrem untertänigsten Knecht. Ich verstehe wohl Ihre Meinung nicht ganz gut, wie könnt' ich nur meinen Schatten – " Er unterbrach mich [...].[31]

Here, the stranger interrupts, repeats his offer, and, when Schlemihl indicates that he does not think this deal to be possible, rejects Schlemihl's hesitation by saying that this would only be his, the stranger's, problem. The stranger then starts to list the objects he would be willing to trade for the shadow, all magical devices including Fouqué's *Galgenmännchen*. Schlemihl is so intrigued by the mention of Fortuna's bag of luck that he overcomes his anxiety and agrees to the trade. They test the bag by pulling out ten gold ducats, then another ten, and another ten. Finally, Schlemihl watches how the stranger peels his shadow off the ground with "bewundernswürdiger Geschicklichkeit". Schlemihl, who is now rich, will very soon regret this deal with the stranger, since everyone – with the exception of one servant – gets an uncanny feeling standing next to someone without a shadow.

[31] Albert von Chamisso: *Peter Schlemihls wundersame Geschichte*. Stuttgart 1965. Pp. 16-17.

While most interpretations of this novella focus on what the allegorical meaning of this traded-away shadow could be – Schlemihl's soul, his morals, consciousness, national identity, or human qualities – the text suggests that this shadow does not have an allegorical meaning and does not even function as a shifter that can be filled with different meanings.[32] Rather, the shadow does not stand *for* something but stands *by* someone. It is something – if a shadow is something – unique and personal that resists exchange. However, the impossible exchange takes place. The catastrophe of the text is that the un-detach-able and un-abstract-able is detached and abstracted. So, how is this exchange made possible despite its impossibility?

The dialogue opens with two people who behave as if they were subordinate to each other. The stranger uses polite phrases that are embarrassing to young Schlemihl; Schlemihl, for his part, is afraid of a man who possesses powers that he himself does not have. Only once does Schlemihl transgress his subordinate behavior, but only to come back to it and "make up" for his transgression with "infinite politeness". Both use superlatives to express that they see the other and his belongings as infinitely superior to themselves. And it is these very superlatives that they exchange verbally. The stranger calls the shadow "unpriceable" and speaks of his "unspeakable admiration", while Schlemihl calls himself the stranger's "most subordinate servant". It seems that their trade can only happen once both acknowledge the absolute superiority of the other and his belongings.

It is a trade, then, of superlatives. What is negotiated are the two most impossible items of exchange. On the one hand, a money-making bag is by definition more valuable than any fixed price since it can

---

[32] See for the discussion of the meaning of the shadow Jochen Hörisch's rich study on money in literature: *Kopf oder Zahl: Die Poesie des Geldes*. Frankfurt a.M. 1996. Pp. 276-78. See also Rolf Günter Renner, who argues that the novella presents a shift from an imaginary to a symbolic order. However, his study does not problematize the notion of exchange and treats the shadow, money and the soul as equal objects of exchange: Schrift der Natur und Zeichen des Selbsts: Peter Schlemihls wundersame Geschichte im Zusammenhang von Chamissos Texten. In: *Deutsche Vierteljahrsschrift* 65 (1991). Pp 653-73. Alice A. Kuzniar was the first to move the discussion of Chamisso's novella away from simply filling the meaning of the shadow by suggesting that the shadow is indeed an empty shifter: "Spurlos...verschwunden": *Peter Schlemihl* und sein Schatten als der verlorene Signifikant. In: *Aurora* 45 (1985). Pp. 189-204.

immediately produce a higher amount of money. On the other hand, a shadow is the least tradeable item since it cannot be detached, remains unique, and is not even an entity but the mere absence of light. What Schlemihl gives up when he makes his deal seems to be nothing. So why should he hesitate?

The novella gives a clear signal. He should hesitate because what he would give up is exactly that which is nothing only from the perspective of money and exchange: by making this deal, he agrees that a deal like this can be made and that what he is giving up does not count (or does only "count"). He agrees that that which cannot be exchanged does not need to be considered and does not add to his wealth. By making this deal, Schlemihl agrees that there is no difference between a shadow and no shadow, meaning he stops acknowledging items that are not exchangeable. Thus, he agrees not only to this deal but to exchangeability as such. This deal is not only one of many deals, but a deal that brings about the very possibility of making a deal. Consequently, what Schlemihl gets in return is not simply some money, but the very source of money, Fortuna's bag, which is the condition of possibility for exchange. They negotiate (and exchange) the possibility of making an exchange. Indeed, Schlemihl's money allows him to buy everything (except a wife), but the condition for entering this order of exchange is to give up his individuality. As a medium of exchange, money consists of the detachment of the un-detach-able. By means of this detachment (money) the un-exchange-able and singular enters into an order of exchange. It is, indeed, "a deal of the strange kind".

Thus, Chamisso's novella displays the paradox surrounding the creation of money. When something is exchanged, it is not replaced by something equal – which is impossible: "for this unpriceable shadow, I consider the highest price too low" – but rather it is replaced by something that functions *as if* it were a replacement. Money, then, in one double gesture displays a gap and fills it with an as-if equality. It exposes all goods to a self-alienation, an alienation that Marx (who explicitly refers to Peter Schlemihl) described in "Fetischcharakter der Ware und sein Geheimnis".

While the shadow seemed to be nothing when Schlemihl owned it, it suddenly gains an enormous importance as that which he should not have been able to detach. What he loses when he trades the shadow is his own un-detach-ability (*Unveräußerlichkeit*). The un-detach-ability he trades away is something undefinable, a shadow, which does not have a positive value since it is in fact that which denies all value and exchange orientation. But, as Schlemihl has to learn, his individuality rests on this un-detach-ability.

As it is for Schlegel, trade is dangerous for individuality. But in contrast to Schlegel, the essence of Schlemihl's individuality is not at all related to trade or money; money and individuality are simply antagonists in Chamisso's novella. While Schlegel rationalizes that money performs an act corresponding to the very act by which the individual becomes an individual, an act of extension, Chamisso presents an individuality that is unproblematically given. Schlemihl's loss of individuality by means of money does not derive from the structure of individuality as it does for Schlegel. Instead, the essence of individuality appears to be the direct negation of money and exchange: un-exchange-ability. However, Chamisso never develops in positive terms precisely what individuality *is*, which explains the many interpretations of what it actually "stands for". By means of this mystification of individuality as a *je-ne-sais-quoi*, the individual is detached from money and trade. This is how Chamisso's novella can claim that there is a state of individuality free of money without ever presenting it, since it is only seen from the perspective of a paradise lost or "une ombre perdue".[33]

While the early Romantics like Schlegel and Tieck face and acknowledge a certain dilemma in their attempt to base individuality on an openness toward others, Chamisso and the later Romantics try to mask this problem within the structure of individuality by separating the individual from those compromising effects of individuality. Thus, the exchange comes to the "individual" Schlemihl from the outside, does not correspond to any of his own acts, and is diabolized, since it is initiated from the grey stranger or "Teufel".

In short, Chamisso's stigmatization of money functions as a rejection of Schlegel's insights without changing the underlying aporia of individuality. Only a naive person such as Schlemihl would even engage in such a contract or exchange by which the individual gives up what is his or her very essence. Indeed, we have to assume that that which Chamisso's novella presents as individuality is utterly naive. Chamisso's novella cannot explain the fascination money has for the individual by simply stigmatizing it as an evil principle conflicting with true individuality. It is an individuality that can only be mourned once

---

[33] For the peculiar status of the shadow in *Peter Schlemihl* as not nothing, see Wladimir Troubetzkoy: *L'Ombre et la Différence: Le Double en Europe*. Paris 1996. Pp. 109-36, here p. 111.

it is lost, just as the shadow attracts attention only when it is gone and not seen any longer.

A clue that Chamisso feels unsatisfied with his solution is that he cannot give Schlemihl's individuality – his what? – back to him. Instead, at the end of the story Schlemihl engages in practices of the age before individualism. Like the melancholic travelers of the seventeenth and earlier eighteenth centuries, he wanders around the globe with his seven-mile shoes to collect encyclopedic data that do not require any personality. Happiness and individuality have disappeared from his life.

IX

Once money is sufficiently distinguished from individuality, a more positive reevaluation of money is possible. While *Peter Schlemihl* portrays the dangers of money for individuality, other writers recognize in this non-individuality a "super-individuality" or "inter-individuality" that serves to mediate between individuals precisely because it cannot be claimed by the individual or subject alone. Ironically, Chamisso's novella, which openly displays its reservation toward all aspects of economics, helps to bring about a more positive concept of money.

Adam Müller, the so-called economist of the Romantics, rationalizes money as the very essence of community since money functions as a form of communication understood and accepted by everyone. Müller compares this ability of money to function as a medium that unites a people only with the mediating force of poetry.[34] While Schlegel had been critical of Smith's economy of balance and focused on the individual instead, Müller understands his work as an interpretation of Smith and elaborates on notions of balance and unity.

In his discussion of money, Müller distinguishes two kinds of *Eigentum*, the mere egotistic claim of "Allod" (private property) and the community-mediating "Feod" (from which "feudalism" derives). Feod in its essence is "Geld, welches nur circulirend, von einem zum anderen übergehend, und zwischen zwey Personen vermittelnd zu denken ist,

---

[34] "Die Macht der Waare, die um des Beyeinanderseyns Willen mit Allen von Allen gesucht wird, die Macht des Wortes oder des Glaubens, worin sich viele oder alle Mitglieder der bürgerlichen Gesellschaft vereinigen: beyde Mächte sind nur Offenbarungen des Bedürfnisses aller bey einander zu seyn". Adam Heinrich Müller: *Versuche einer neuen Theorie des Geldes*. Jena 1922. P. 31. Written in 1810/11, first published in 1816.

niemahls ein Gegenstand des unbedingten Privateigenthums seyn kann" (29). Müller's emphasis is on the mediating *Feod*. "Die Macht des Geldes liegt darin, daß es [...] zwischen Sachen und Personen [...] zu vermitteln im Stande ist" (33), and he calls money (*Feod*) the "persönliche Band" between workers and commodity. Money (*Feod*) is only money in the very moment of its transition from one to the other ("nur im Moment des Umsatzes oder der Cirkulation sind die Substanzen des Geldes wirklich Geld" [31]). Money exists only as a force of mediation and exists only in so far as it connects. From the perspective of this mediation, the connected beings only count in so far as they are united, mediated, and without difference. Elaborating on this notion of *Band* and connection, Müller describes marriage as the nucleus of feudalism ("[Die] Ehe [ist] eine Hauptquelle des Feudalismus" [34]). Marriage and money (*Feod*) have in common that they both produce offspring that are again capable of reproduction. "Es kommt nähmlich darauf an, daß das Produkt auch selbst wieder eine dauerhafte und fruchtbare Verbindung (eine Ehe) schließen könne; kurz es kömmt darauf an, etwas Produktives zu produciren" (36). What money produces is not simply profit, but itself as the force that will produce money. Private property (*Allod*), on the other hand, is rejected since it is not fruitful, and Müller misses few opportunities to discredit individual possession (that means the *notion* of private property, not actual possession; Müller only condemns the actual ownership of land).

Thus, Müller, who was a close friend of the later Schlegel, explicitly takes up the notions that marked Schlegel's early conception of an economy of individual expansion, accumulation, and surplus (*Erweiterung*, *Bereicherung*, and *Überschuß*) in order to reevaluate it in terms of his economy of mediation. Müller argues that there is no real or absolute surplus in a production since value has no essence to itself. Instead of being a surplus, profit only enables one to invest more, which will not lead to an increase in property but instead an increase in the "credit" given one by the society. This credit will only result in a strengthening of the mediation between the individual and the society, be a "Band an die bürgerliche Gesellschaft" (76).[35] The individual for Müller only exists in the credit it receives from the majority, and this

[35] "Es ergibt sich also für den Eigenthümer nie und an keiner Stelle ein absoluter Überschuß, welcher Gegenstand des ausschließenden Privateigenthums für ihn werden könnte: es ergibt sich für ihn nichts, als ein unsichtbares aber immer festeres zuverläßigeres Band an die bürgerliche Gesellschaft" (75-76).

credit consists solely in its connectibility.

In the tradition of this thought we can also see contemporary work, such as Niklas Luhmann's theory of economy. Luhmann defines money as a medium of communication, with medium meaning "die Einheit einer Differenz".[36] This perspective enables Luhmann to gain several interesting insights into the nature of social formations by means of money. By comparing economic communication to other forms of communication, Luhmann is able to describe the specificity of money communication.[37] While I will not give a full account of his at times brilliant work, it is remarkable that his "Einheit einer Differenz" still suffers from a problem that we see in Chamisso's novella, Müller's economic theses, and the late Schlegel's theory of statehood. The "Einheit einer Differenz" harmonizes the structure of money and individuality, since it can only presuppose individuality ("Differenz") without being able to question or define its status. Difference/individuality escapes observations that take place in the name of "media" and unification (the "difference" Luhmann considers instead is the difference between observer and observed). Just as the shadow is important only as a shadow lost, individuality exists for Luhmann's system only as an individuality lost. Thereby, Luhmann's formulation reduces money to its function of producing a unity, a unity that covers up what Marx described as the paradoxical nature of money not to bring about a real equality but only to function as an as-if equality (or fetish equality), taking the place of a "real" equality.

My objection does not aim to discredit the idea of money as a medium by simply pointing to a dilemma that might well arise from the very nature of individuality (and singularity), since individuality (sin-

[36] Niklas Luhmann: *Die Wirtschaft der Gesellschaft*. Frankfurt a.M. 1986. P. 232.
[37] Money allows "communication", but at the same time this communication does not result in a simple sharing of information and "richness of shared possibilities" (246) like the communication of other media. Rather, money forces both sides to give up the control over some entity. Once one has traded away one's belongings or faculties like a farmer trading away his or her land for food, one is limited in one's future ability to trade. While other forms of communication simply include those who participate and exclude those who do not, communication through money remains more complex, since the way one participates decides whether one will be included or excluded in future transactions/communications. The inclusion in economic communication constantly tends toward the exclusion of its participants.

gularity) by definition is that which escapes accurate observation and description. My point is rather that the attraction of the economic model cannot be explained without consideration of the promises money has for the individual (and more precisely: for creating individuality). Thus, a mere theory of money as a medium, a *Band*, marriage, or an abstract danger for one's individuality fails to explain the success of the economic model over other models. To understand this success, I believe we have to consider the combination of the concepts that were produced during the Romantic age – money as individuation and money as a medium.

X

Both models or "discourses" that I have presented – money as individuation and money as a medium – have influenced social interactions through their impact on the definition, organization, and perpetuation of social institutions that continue to inform our behavior today. Both have managed to coexist (and in their coexistence caused effects and conflicts), even though they logically seem to exclude each other, since they each have shaped different institutions or spheres (the ones we have started to discuss in this paper are the *Ich* and the capitalist community). This coexistence takes a very peculiar form. The overlap of the two models allows for mistaking an act of personal accumulation of property for an act of community building. And this confusion or "abuse" might explain the predominance of economy today. By "economizing" social interaction, personal interest can be inscribed in the social sphere. If my hypothesis is right, economy was able to become a leading paradigm of social interaction because its connector, money, functions as a universal and seemingly neutral medium of communication while at the same time allowing personal interests to be generated, to infiltrate money circulation secretly or openly, and to be withdrawn and stored as individual possession. Certainly, the condition of money's attraction is that it functions as a universal medium and shared concept. However, the attraction money produces is the attraction of gaining the connection or connectibility money promises *for oneself* (which means to withdraw it from others), thereby gaining oneself as the connecting force, the *Ich* that can extend itself to others by means of money.

When the later Romantics present money as a mere abstract medium, a medium of community or communication, this reconceptualization of money does not take away one's personal interest in money, but provides a hiding place for it in a universally accepted practice.[38] The two competing models of money that the Romantic age produced, Schlegel's concept of money as individuation and Müller's medium of community or communication, thus form a very successful conglomerate. The overlap masks the one as the other, thus making the success of economics a "joint enterprise" that is hard to analyze and critique since it conflates the expansion of individuality with social balance. Similarly, the idea of a "libertarian" or "free" economy is so successful because it masks the brutal competition of unequals as "freedom".

What I have called an overlap of two models of money might just as well be described in terms of forgetting: The modern *Ich* needs to forget that its essence is not its own since the *Ich* only exists as an empty self-extension modeled after the economics of interest. The *ego-effect* is rooted in economics but needs to forget this dependence to claim its autonomy. One invests in money, but hopes to liquidate this investment in the form of a pure *Ich*, free of money and its effects. Only through the use of money is the *Ich* able to believe in its independence from money.

---

[38] Luhmann offers a beautiful examination of a related overlap or slip of the meanings of money. When he discusses the effects money has on the administration of scarce resources, he asks why people tolerate (and perceive as normal) that a few people own a lot while many own very little. While there certainly is no justice to the unfair distribution of scarce properties, money offers an explanation as to why this unfairness is tolerated. Money allows us to say when someone is allowed to own a lot: "wenn er zahlt" (252). Luhmann, posing this answer to why people accept an unfair distribution of goods, does not go on to address why this answer, despite the dissatisfaction that we should have with it, still is widely accepted. Luhmann's explanation "wenn er zahlt" cannot, as he well knows, be a real explanation, but it functions *as if* it were the explanation, meaning it usually stops people from further questioning.
The persuasive quality of money consists of its ability to also function as a causal connector. So, the exchange 'A for B' and 'A equals B' can also be described, deceivingly, as: B because A was given for it. Money, then, is not simply a medium within exchange, but it is able to slip into other forms of connections like causality. Precisely because of this persuasive force, money subverts and avoids questions of justice and politics.

Anke Gilleir

"Als ob der Gegenstand der Gegenstand wäre"
Die Kunstbetrachtungen Wackenroders,
Friedrich Schlegels und Ludwig Tiecks

Whereas romantic aesthetics in general reject the idea of a rationally based, formal art as it was represented by Goethe's and Heinrich Meyer's classicism, the iconographical writings of Heinrich Wilhelm Wackenroder, Friedrich Schlegel and Ludwig Tieck reveal that their theologically inspired hermeneutics are heavily rooted in this cognitive and formal perception of art. Thus, the transcendental Revelation of the romantics takes place in the frame of a rational aesthetic representation (which explains why their writings do not include modern romantic art such as Füßli or Friedrich).

Wie ein Gemälde herkömmlicherweise in einen Rahmen eingefaßt ist, um als Kunstwerk (an)erkannt zu werden, so ist Kants Betrachtung über das Schöne eingeschrieben in die Transzendentalphilosophie, die als Leiste für die Auseindersetzung über das allgemeinmenschliche Erkennen von Schönheit fungiert. Diese Analogie ist in groben Zügen Derridas Lektüre von Kants Analytik des Schönen zu entnehmen, wo er die Rolle des "Parergons" für Kants auf "gewalttätige" Weise eingerahmte Auslegung von Schönheit erfaßt: "La violence de l'encadrement se multiplie. Elle enferme d'abord la théorie de l'esthétique dans une théorie du beau, celle-ci dans une théorie du goût et la théorie du goût dans une théorie du jugement".[1] Die Feststellung, daß es ohne Rahmen kein Kunstgebilde gibt, daß der Kontrast zwischen Innen (Werk) und Außen (Rahmen) die wesentliche Voraussetzung für das Anschauen und Erkennen der künstlerischen Darstellung ist und indes beide Aspekte des ästhetischen Artefaktes

---

[1] Jacques Derrida: *La vérité en peinture*. Paris 1978. S. 85. "La *Critique* se donne comme une oeuvre (ergon) à plusieurs côtés, elle devrait comme telle se laisser centrer et cadrer, délimiter son fond en le découpant, d'un cadre, sur un fond général. Or le cadre est problématique. Je ne sais pas ce qui est essentiel et accessoire dans une oeuvre. Et surtout je ne sais pas ce qu'est cette chose, ni essentielle ni accessoire, ni propre, ni impropre, que Kant appelle parergon, par exemple le cadre. Où le cadre a-t-il lieu. A-t-il lieu. Où commence-t-il. Où finit-il? [...]" (S. 73).

schwer auseinanderzuhalten sind, bildet den Ausgangspunkt für unsere Lektüre der romantischen Kunstbetrachtungen.[2] Obwohl Kant die Ästhetik zum Gegenstand der Philosophie gemacht hat und dabei das Individuelle mit dem Allgemeinen zu verknüpfen versuchte, hat er sich selber nicht mit konkreter Kunst oder Kunstgeschichte befaßt.[3] Während er sich, wie Zeeb andeutet, eher vorsichtig über die in der Kunst hergestellte Verbindung zwischen dem "individuell" Wahrgenommenen und der Sphäre der Vernunftideen äußert, hat mancher nachher diesen von ihm angedeuteten Weg entschieden eingeschlagen. Nicht nur in der Klassik, sondern ebenfalls bei den Romantikern setzen Schriftsteller sich mit bildender Kunst auseinander und überbrücken irgendwie jeweils die Kluft zwischen der ästhetischen Darstellung und dem Allgemeinen. Wo Schiller das allgemeingültige Fundament der klassizistischen Kunstpraxis schafft, indem er die Differenz zwischen vernünftig vermittelter Transzendenz und Kunstgebilde rückgängig macht,[4] so setzen Wilhelm Wackenroder, Friedrich Schlegel und Ludwig Tieck, die als namhafte Autoren gewissermaßen die Romantik verkörpern, sich mittels Kunstbeschreibungen mit der bildenden Kunst auseinander und bewirken damit eine Transformation des Ikonischen ins Sprachliche. Diese Verwandlung von Ikone in Rhetorik charakterisiert, Derrida zufolge, die Kunstgeschichte grundsätzlich, denn ihre (tau-

[2] Siehe auch: Ekkehard Zeeb: Kleist, Kant und Paul de Man – vor dem Rahmen der Kunst. In: *Heinrich von Kleist: Kriegfall – Rechtsfall – Sündenfall*. Hg. von Gerhard Neumann. Freiburg im Breisgau 1994. S. 299-336, hier S. 302.
[3] So bemerkt Arthur Schopenhauer, wie fremd es eigentlich ist, daß jemand wie Kant, der immerhin mit seiner *Kritik der Urteilskraft* der Kunstphilosophie ein dauerhaftes Fundament schuf, selber keine Ahnung von der Kunst seiner Zeit hatte. Siehe: Immanuel Kant: *Over schoonheid*. Hg. von Jean Pierre Rondas und Jacques de Visscher. Meppel 1978. S. 12. Tatsächlich streift Kant in jener *Kritik* die Kunst nur sehr vorsichtig und fordert den Leser sogar in einer Fußnote auf, seinen Entwurf zu einer möglichen Einteilung der schönen Künste nicht als beabsichtigte Theorie zu beurteilen. In seiner Darlegung betont Kant übrigens die Analogie der "Kunst mit der Art des Ausdrucks, dessen die Menschen sich im Sprechen bedienen [...]", allerdings mit der Einschränkung, "die bildenden Künste, oder, die des Ausdrucks der Ideen in der Sinnesanschauung (nicht durch Vorstellungen der bloßen Einbildungskraft, die durch Worte aufgeregt werden), sind entweder der Sinnenwahrheit oder des Sinnenscheins". Siehe: Immanuel Kant: Von der Einteilung der schönen Künste. In: *Kritik der Urteilskraft*. Frankfurt a.M. 1957. S. 257-264, hier S. 259.
[4] Ekkehard Zeeb: Kleist, Kant und Paul de Man. A.a.O. S. 305.

tologische) Anerkennung von "Kunst" hat die Form einer besonders strikten Auslegung, die das ästhetische Artefakt sprachlich einrahmt und vereinnahmt: "On se demande ainsi ce que veut dire une oeuvre plastique ou musicale en soumetant toutes les productions à l'autorité de la parole et des arts 'discursifs'".[5]

Das Vorhaben, die romantische Ästhetik über die künstlerische Repräsentation statt über die erkenntnistheoretische Grundlage zu erforschen, bringt uns also nur auf den ersten Blick aus dem Fachbereich der Literaturwissenschaft. Ikonographie gehört zwar in erster Linie der Kunstgeschichte an, die mittels genauer Bildbetrachtungen die Entwicklung von Figuren und Darstellungen festzustellen versucht, aber wie das Wort Ikonologie (*eikon* Bild + *logos* Wort) selber besagt, überschreitet diese Disziplin im Grunde die Grenze zwischen Bild und Sprache.[6] Daß die diskursive Auseinandersetzung mit Gemälden durchaus Teil der romantischen Ästhetik ist, belegt Friedrich Schlegel explizit in seinen Gemäldebeschreibungen:

> Für diejenigen, welche zu philosophieren lieben, erinnere ich nur noch, daß es zwar gar nicht schwer sein würde, was über Malerei als allein gut und richtig erkannt worden, mit noch allgemeineren Wahrheiten in Verbindung zu setzen, [...] aber eben, weil es nicht schwer ist, kann es auch füglich unterbleiben, da es überdem leicht zu einem ungeheuren Mißverständnisse führen, und sehr gegen die Würde der Kunst verstoßen könnte. Es ist nämlich die göttliche Kunst der Malerei etwas mehr als eine bloß notwendige Entwicklung der menschlichen Natur, wie sie es zu sein in einer Deduktion der Art scheinen müßte.[7]

Schlegel reißt sich mit dieser ausdrücklichen Abweisung von Schillers logischer, d.h. vernünftig-anthropologisch begründeten Definition von "Kunst" los. Entgegen jener ästhetischen Lehre der Klassik, die auf Grund vernünftiger Kriterien allgemeingültig wirkt, verbindet Schlegel die ikonische Darstellung mit göttlicher Transzendentalität. Will man Sinnvolles über Malerei, oder allgemeiner, über Kunst, aussagen, so muß man sich direkt mit den Artefakten selber auseinandersetzen, die zugleich aber mit der Andeutung "göttlich" als inkommensurabel erscheinen.

Insofern ist die Überschrift "Gemäldebeschreibungen" hervorzuheben, da sie impliziert, daß an erster Stelle empirisch-sinnliche Erfah-

[5] Jacques Derrida: *La vérité en peinture.* S. 26.
[6] *Wahrig. Deutsches Wörterbuch.* Gütersloh 1994. S. 827
[7] Friedrich Schlegel: Ansichten und Ideen von der christlichen Kunst. In: *Kritische Friedrich-Schlegel-Ausgabe* Bd. IV. Hg. von Hans Eichner. München-Paderborn-Wien 1957. S. 70.

rungen ausgedrückt werden, die dem Leser das ikonisch Dargebotene vermitteln wollen. Schlegels Schriften schließen sich so einer existierenden diskursiven Gattung an, die in unserer Epoche uneingeschränkter Bildreproduktion völlig aus dem Blick geraten ist, aber in einer Zeit, wo die Reproduktion durch Lithographie erst zögernd anfing, als wichtige Aussagemöglichkeit empfunden wurde, Kunstgebilde den Lesern aufzuschließen.[8] Zugleich aber wird das Problematische jener rhetorischen Kunstdarstellungen klar: wo die Lithographie oder die spätere Photographie von Kunstwerken dem Zuschauer selber die Beurteilung bzw. die sinnlichen Eindrücke überläßt, vermittelt die textuelle Darstellung eher das Verhältnis des schreibenden Subjekts in Bezug auf das Kunstobjekt, als das Kunstobjekt an sich. Im Fall der Romantik fällt überdies der Widerspruch des Konzepts "Gemäldebeschreibung" auf, denn deren "Ungenügen an der Normalität" (Lothar Pikulik) ist ja die Anregung zur Aufhebung der sprachlichen Unmittelbarkeit zugunsten einer reflexiven Dichtung.[9] So entsteht Peter Szondi zufolge eine Dichtung, die sich selber zum Gegenstand hat, zur "Poesie der Poesie wird".[10] Transponiert man das von Szondi analysierte Subjekt-Objekt-Verhältnis auf die diskursive Gat-

[8] Bernhard Ridderbos: Van Waagen tot Friedländer: het kunsthistorisch onderzoek naar de Oudnederlandse schilderkunst gedurende de negentiende en het begin van de twintigste eeuw. In: *De Vlaamse Primitieven – herontdekking, waardering en onderzoek*. Hg. von Bernhard Ridderbos und Henk van Veen. Nijmegen 1995. S. 189-235, hier S. 193.
[9] Wir beschränken uns auf diese grundsätzliche Feststellung, die schon eingehend von mehreren Seiten erforscht und erfaßt wurde. Hingewiesen sei auf Walter Benjamins Analyse der frühromantischen Kunstkritik: "Den Romantikern bekundet das reine Wesen der Reflexion sich an der rein formalen Erscheinung des Kunstwerks. Die Form ist also der gegenständliche Ausdruck der dem Werke eigenen Reflexion, welche sein Wesen bildet. Sie ist die Möglichkeit der Reflexion in dem Werke, sie liegt ihm also a priori als ein Daseinsprinzip zugrunde; durch seine Form ist das Kunstwerk ein lebendiges Zentrum der Reflexion". Walter Benjamin: *Der Begriff der Kunstkritik in der deutschen Romantik*. In: *Gesammelte Schriften* Bd. I.1. Hg. von Rolf Tiedemann und Hermann Schweppenhäuser. Frankfurt a.M. 1974. S. 9-122, hier S. 73. Auch Peter Szondis aufschlußreiche Lektüre über die romantische Ironie besagt das komplexe Verhältnis der romantischen Sprache zur Wirklichkeit: "Schlegel fordert eine Dichtung, die mit dem Objekt auch sich selber dichtet, die auch sich selbst zum Gegenstand hat und in dieser inneren Spaltung in Subjekt und Objekt sich potenziert, Poesie der Poesie wird". Peter Szondi: Friedrich Schlegel und die romantische Ironie. In: *Schriften*. Bd. II. Frankfurt a.M. 1978. S. 11-31, hier S. 17.
[10] Peter Szondi: Friedrich Schlegel. A.a.O. S. 19.

tung der Kunstbeschreibungen, so lassen sich hier möglicherweise die Grundsätze der romantischen Ästhetik herausdestillieren. Vorweggenommen ist damit Derridas Bemerkung, daß ohne Rahmen keine Kunst existiert, oder in diesem Fall, daß das Wortwerden der bildenden Kunst die einfache Vermittlung von ikonischen Elementen insofern übersteigt, als die romantische Ikonographie sich als Fremdbestäubung zwischen Betrachtung und Ästhetik erweist. Die Kunstbetrachtung, d.h. der Kunstgegenstand als Beschreibung der Darstellung, wirft ein Licht auf den Rahmen, d.h. auf das romantische Subjekt und die seinen "Beschreibungen" zugrundeliegende Lehre von Schönheit und göttlicher Transzendenz.

Wie oben erwähnt, erscheint es im Rahmen unserer Argumentation wichtig, die sich antagonistisch abhebende Lage der Romantik im "Feld der Ästhetik" zu erfassen.[11] Holt man sie aus ihrer "isolierten" Position heraus und erforscht man ihre Kontroverse mit der Klassik, so zeigt sich umso deutlicher, in welchen Rahmen die romantischen Kunstbetrachtungen eingefaßt sind und inwiefern sie Leiste und Artefakt amalgamieren. Daß die Romantik herkömmlicherweise als Aufbruch in die Moderne betrachtet wird, hängt nicht zuletzt damit zusammen, daß sie, auf Grund ihres Gefühls des existenziellen Verlustes, im Bereich der Kunst eine pluralistische Ästhetik befürwortet. Das besagen Friedrich Schlegels *Athenäumsfragmente*, insbesondere das vielzitierte 139. :

> Aus dem romantischen Gesichtspunkt haben auch die Abarten der Poesie, selbst die ekzentrischen und monströsen, ihren Wert, als Materialien und Vorübungen der Universalität, wenn nur irgendetwas drin ist, wenn sie nur original sind.[12]

---

[11] Mit dem Begriff "Feld der Kultur" verweisen wir auf die Kultursoziologie Pierre Bourdieus, dessen Betrachtung über die Konfiguration von Positionen im französischen Kulturleben Mitte des 19. Jahrhunderts durchaus auf die Topographie der "anspruchsvollen" deutschen Kulturproduktion um 1800 angewendet werden kann, zumal die Voraussetzung über ein Feld der Kultur sprechen zu können, die explizite Abwendung der Kulturprotagonisten von der Öffentlichkeit bzw. vom Treiben des "großen Haufens" (Kant) sich sowohl bei den "Klassikern" wie bei den "Romantikern" nachweisen läßt. Siehe: Pierre Bourdieu: *Les règles de l'art. Génèse et structure du champ littéraire*. Paris 1992.

[12] Friedrich Schlegel: Charakteristiken und Kritiken (1796-1808). In: *Kritische Friedrich-Schlegel-Ausgabe* Bd.II. Hg. von Hans Eichner. München-Paderborn-Wien 1967. S. 187.

Die Prägnanz dieser programmatischen Aussage gewinnt erst volle
Bedeutung, sobald man sie innerhalb der existierenden Ästhetik an-
siedelt und bemerkt, wie hier die Kluft mit der ästhetischen Norm-
strenge des Klassizismus sich auftut. Die Kontroverse mit jener "anderen" Ästhetik zieht sich immerhin wie ein roter Faden – um einen
Ausdruck Goethes zu verwenden – durch die romantischen Kunstbetrachtungen. Als um die Jahrhundertwende und in den ersten Jahrzehnten des 19. Jahrhunderts die Kontroverse zwischen Klassik und
Romantik hoch aufflackert, ist der gemeinsame Einsatz dieses Strei-
tes das Monopol auf die moderne Kultur;[13] sowohl bei Schlegel wie
bei Goethe erweist sich der gemeinsame Auslöser der polemischen
Energie als die abgründige Unzufriedenheit mit den zeitgenössischen
Kunstentwicklungen.[14] Obgleich Schlegels Grundsatz, daß die Theorie
der Kunst nicht von der Anschauung getrennt werden kann, sowohl
für Klassiker wie für Romantiker Gültigkeit beansprucht, und beide
das Allgemeine mit dem Besonderen in Zusammenhang bringen,
prallen die jeweiligen "Betrachtungen" aneinander ab. Schlegel bringt

[13] Das Grundmuster für diese Rekonstruktion des ästhetischen "ordre du
discours" ist erneut Bourdieus Kultursoziologie entnommen, dessen prägnante
Feststellung über die oppositionelle Struktur um den gemeinsamen Kampf für
das "Monopol" über die "wahre" Ästhetik in der Moderne auf fruchtbare
Weise den engen Rahmen des Literarischen sprengt. Über den Maler Edouard
Manet, der ästhetische Autonomie in bezug auf die *Académie* erringt, heißt es,
er habe die monopolische akademische Kontrolle zugunsten eines internen
Konkurrenzverhältnisses verlassen und damit die modernen Kulturverhältnisse
eingeleitet. Da es in Deutschland keine ähnliche autoritäre Kulturinstanz
gegeben hat, ist ab dem Anfang der bürgerlichen Epoche das Feld frei für
widersprüchliche Kulturauffassungen. Vgl. Pierre Bourdieu: *Les règles de
l'art.* S. 191. Da Bourdieu aber auf keinerlei Weise eine eingehende Lektüre in
seine Analyse einschiebt, greifen wir als Ergänzung auf Foucaults Text *L'ordre
du discours* zurück, der das Schwergewicht einer Epochenuntersuchung auf die
diskursive Materialisierung verlagert. Vgl. Michel Foucault: *L'ordre du
discours. Leçon inaugurale au Collège de France le 2 décembre 1970.* Paris
1971.
[14] Schlegels Stoßseufzer über die Gründe, weshalb es keine guten Künstler
mehr gibt, hören sich wie ein Echo von Schillers Zeitdiagnose in den *Briefen
über die ästhetische Erziehung* an: "Die universelle Bildung und intellektuelle
Vielseitigkeit, als charakteristische Eigenschaft und allgemeiner Hang unsres
Zeitalters, führt leicht zur Zersplitterung der geistigen Kraft und verträgt sich
schwer mit einer konzentrierten Wirkung in fortschreitender Steigerung, und
mit einer Fülle vollendeter Hervorbringungen in einer bestimmten positiven
Art". Friedrich Schlegel: Ansichten und Ideen von der christlichen Kunst.
A.a.O. S. 148. Hiernach verwenden wir die Abkürzung FS.

Poesie und Malerei auf den gleichen Nenner und transformiert die Kunstanschauung zum literarisch-poetischen Verfahren:

> [...] ist nicht jede richtige in das Innre ganz eindringende und auch alles Einzelne aufmerksam ergreifende Anschauung eines organischen Ganzen durchaus Poesie? Selbst der äußeren Form nach, wenn die Anschauung des Ganzen anders nicht in uns verborgen bleiben, sondern auch in äußeren Worten deutlich ausgesprochen werden soll? (FS 33)

Poesie und Malerei in eins zu setzen, bedeutet eine Absage an den scharfen Schnitt, den die Klassik zwischen den unterschiedlichen Kunstgattungen vornimmt. Überdies ersetzt die Verknüpfung von "Anschauung" und "in das Innere eindringend" die objektive Beschreibung durch eine ästhetische Hermeneutik, die den Schwerpunkt auf das beschauende Subjekt und seine ganze Innenwelt verlagert.

In Winckelmanns Kielwasser haben Protagonisten des deutschen Klassizismus, wie Goethe, Heinrich Meyer oder Carl Ludwig Fernow, sich zeitlebens als Begründung und Manifestation ihrer Ästhetik mit der historischen Kunst auseinandergesetzt.[15] In Weimar ist es vor allem Heinrich Meyer, der ab ovo in den Horen und Propyläen bis in Kunst und Altertum neben Goethe die konkreten Kunstforderungen der Klassik anhand von Kunstbeschreibungen aufzeigt. So artikuliert er 1798 in den Propyläen das Axiom des klassischen Schönheitsideals: der Künstler hat bei der "Wahl des Gegenstandes besonders vorsichtig zu seyn", denn ein "schlechter oder widerstrebender Gegenstand [...] ermüdet und schlägt nieder".[16] Damit wird klar ersichtlich, daß im dialektischen Verhältnis zwischen Objekt und Subjekt hier das Kunstwerk zentral steht. Indem, genauer noch, die klassische Ästhetik das Schlaglicht auf das Kunstobjekt richtet, wird die hermeneutische Tätigkeit des Zuschauers minimalisiert, so daß, im Gegensatz zu

---

[15] Der Schweizer Maler Heinrich Meyer ist in der Goethe- und Klassikforschung zugunsten des Verhältnisses zwischen Goethe und Schiller aus dem Blickfeld geraten. Dennoch war er, der Goethe während seiner Italienreise in Rom begegnete, als klassizistischer Maler und Kunstkenner Goethe in der Entwicklung der klassischen Ästhetik unentbehrlich. Als Direktor der Weimarer Kunstakademie lebte er zeitlebens in dessen Nähe und starb nach einer fünfzigjährigen Freundschaft im gleichen Jahr wie der Autor. Schiller, der sich zum Theoretiker des neuen Klassizismus entwickelte, hatte in Bezug auf die bildende Kunst genauso wenig praktische Kenntnisse wie Kant. Vgl. Heinrich Meyer: *Kleine Schriften zur Kunst*. Hg. von Paul Weizsäcker. 2. Ausgabe. Nendeln/Liechtenstein 1968.

[16] Heinrich Meyer: Über die Gegenstände der bildenden Kunst. In: *Kleine Schriften zur Kunst*. A.a.O. S. 21-45, hier S. 21.

Schlegels Interiorisierungsprozeß, die Kunstbetrachtung daraus besteht, die sinnliche Materialisierung des Schönen zu erkennen. Die
Grundlage des klassischen Artefaktes bilden immerhin universell an-
erkannte und wissenschaftlich erforschte Schönheitskriterien.[17] Ver-
ankert diese "objektive" Begründung von Schönheit das klassische
Kunstideal im Bereich der menschlichen Größenverhältnisse, so impliziert das nicht nur, daß das Kunstobjekt in erster Linie menschliche Schönheit darstellen soll, sondern überdies, daß Schönheit sich
sinnlich-logisch messen und ausdrücken läßt.[18] Die Selbstsuffizienz
der artistischen Darstellung erhebt die Plastik zur höchsten Kunstgattung schlechthin: sie repräsentiert das Ideal der menschlichen
Schönheit am meisten und verkleinert insofern umgekehrt propor-
tional die Anteilnahme des Zuschauers. Die Statue Laokoon verkörpert die Kunstwahrheit und fungiert unter diesem Gesichtspunkt als
Symbol der klassischen Kunstidee schlechthin. Strebt die klassizisti-
sche Malerei die kunstvoll abgemessene Darstellung von Gruppen im
Räumlichen an, so widerhallen diese verständlichen Proportionen in
der Kunstbeschreibung des Zuschauers: Begriffe wie Symmetrie, Selbständigkeit, Geschlossenheit, Anmut, Kolorit und Gruppierung sind
Kernworte, die den akademischen Geist der Kunst erfassen.[19] Weil
Kunstobjekt und Zuschauer in der Klassik auf den gleichen Nenner
gebracht werden, geschehen die Kunstbeschreibungen im Rahmen

[17] Goethe: Der Sammler und die Seinigen. In: *Werke*. Bd. 19. Berlin 1973. S.
207-272, hier S. 246.
[18] "Alle hohen Kunstwerke stellen die menschliche Natur dar, die bildenden
Künste beschäftigen sich besonders mit dem menschlichen Körper; wir reden
gegenwärtig nur von diesen. [...] Die höchsten Kunstwerke die wir kennen,
zeigen uns: Lebendige, hochorganisierte Naturen". Goethe: Über Laokoon. In:
Werke. Bd. 19. A.a.O., S. 40-48, hier S. 42. Der apodiktische Ton dieser
"Feststellungen" enthüllt jedenfalls den programmatischen Charakter von
Goethes Kunstbetrachtungen in bezug auf das derzeitige Kulturleben. In
Anbetracht der Feststellung, daß die Schönheit des Menschen zum
Zentralthema der Kunst erhoben wird, leuchtet es ein, daß der Romanheld
Wilhelm Meister nach einer mißlungenen Theaterlaufbahn schließlich
Wundarzt wird. Insofern krönt er mit diesem Beruf seine ästhetische
Erziehung, als nun sein Ziel daraus besteht, die natürliche Harmonie des
grundsätzlich gesunden, aber verwundeten menschlichen Körpers (denn er wird
nicht einfach *Arzt* sondern *Wundarzt*) wiederherzustellen. So überschneidet
sich seine Arbeit mit dem Künstlerischen. Siehe: Goethe: *Wilhelm Meisters
Wanderjahre*. In: *Werke*. Bd.8. Hg. von Erich Trunz. München 1988. S. 322-
334.
[19] Vgl. Herbert von Einem: *Deutsche Malerei des Klassizismus und der
Romantik 1760 bis 1840*. München 1978. S. 42-53.

eines ästhetischen Passepartouts, dessen normative Proportionen die Qualität des Gemäldes fixieren.[20]

In Anbetracht dieser strengen Kunstbetrachtung stellt sich nun die Frage nach dem Rahmen der romantischen Ikonologie. Der Ausgangspunkt jener "anderen" Lehre bildet allerdings nicht Friedrich Schlegel, sondern Wackenroders Kunstroman *Herzensergießungen eines kunstliebenden Klosterbruders* (1795). Den christlichen Glauben als Rahmen der Kunst zu fixieren, die "Frömmigkeit als alleiniges Fundament derselben" festzusetzen nach dem von Goethe ironisch erfaßten Motto, "einige Mönche waren Künstler, deshalb sollen alle Künstler Mönche sein", wurde von Wackenroder eingeführt und in den folgenden Jahrzehnten von den Romantikern weiter verfolgt.[21] Indem er aber Kunst mit Religion verknüpft und das Kunstobjekt als Offenbarungsinstanz des Göttlichen interpretiert, weicht Wackenroder entschieden von der Selbstbezogenheit des klassizistischen Ästhetizismus ab. Mit dieser Verschiebung geht sowohl eine Veränderung der Hermeneutik wie der Ästhetik einher, denn statt einfach das Maß des Gebildes zu bestimmen, muß der Beschauer hier dessen seelische Botschaft erfassen.

Insofern weigert der Romantiker sich, Schönheit in der "Sprache des Wortes" auszudrücken und als objektive Begebenheit darzustellen. So wie die Überschriften "Herzensergießungen" und "Phantasien über die Kunst" schon eine Verlagerung vom Objektiven zum Subjektiven andeuteten, hebt Ludwig Tieck in der Einführung zu den Schriften seines frühverstorbenen Freundes nochmals die zentrale Position des Rezipienten hervor: er betont nämlich die "Originalität" von Wackenroders Kunsterlebnissen und verbindet dieses Unorthodoxe unmittelbar mit dem Begriff "Wahrheit".[22] Dirk Kemper hebt in seiner eingehenden Analyse hervor, daß Wackenroder nicht die Sprache an sich ablehnt, sondern gegen das aufklärerische Rationalitätskriterium plädiert, das den Menschen dazu veranlaßt, mittels der Sprache die Welt aufzuschließen und zu demystifizieren.[23] Die objektive Sprache, die "Sprache des Wortes" also, erweist sich aber als

---

[20] Auch die nicht-klassische Kunst wird mit dem antikisch begründeten Maß gemessen. Vgl. Goethe: Ältere Gemälde. Neuere Restaurationen in Venedig, betrachtet 1790. In: *Werke*. Bd. 19. Berlin 1973. S. 100.

[21] Goethe: Tag- und Jahreshefte. In: *Werke*. Bd. 16. Berlin 1973. S. 101.

[22] Ludwig Tieck: Vorrede. In: Wilhelm Heinrich Wackenroder: *Werke und Briefe in einem Band*. Heidelberg 1968. (Hiernach im Text als WR zitiert.) S. 270.

[23] Dirk Kemper: *Die Sprache der Dichtung. Wilhelm Heinrich Wackenroder im Kontext der Spätaufklärung*. Stuttgart 1993. S. 22 f.

unzulänglich für das Unsichtbare, das Göttliche und vor allem für das in der Kunst vermittelte Gefühl der Religiosität, das zum Fundament der romantischen Existenz schlechthin wird:

> Durch Worte herrschen wir über den ganzen Erdkreis; durch Worte erhandeln wir uns mit leichter Mühe alle Schätze der Erde. Nur das Unsichtbare, das über uns schwebt, ziehen Worte nicht in unser Gemüt herab. Die irdischen Dinge haben wir in unsrer Hand, wenn wir ihre Namen aussprechen; – aber wenn wir die Allgüte Gottes oder die Tugend der Heiligen nennen hören, welches doch Gegenstände sind, die unser ganzes Wesen ergreifen sollten, so wird allein unser Ohr mit leeren Schallen gefüllt und unseren Geist nicht, wie es sollte, erhoben.[24]

Jenseits der "Wortsprache" existiert eine Welt von "dunklen" Gefühlen, die durch sprachliche Benennung nicht vereinnahmt werden kann, sondern nur durch gefühlvolles Erleben erfahrbar ist. Indes bedarf Wackenroder trotz Abweisung eines objektiven Mitteilungsmediums und trotz ahnungsvollem Erleben des Transzendentalen dennoch einer Kommunikationsmöglichkeit, will er nicht mit seiner Begeisterung über die Kunst isoliert im Wortlosen enden.[25] In dieser Hinsicht ist es signifikant, daß er der Sprachmetaphorik sowie dem archetypisch aufklärerischen Konzept "Wahrheit" insoweit verhaftet bleibt, als er sich um die Vorführung einer "anderen", romantischen Sprache bemüht.[26] Statt der rationalen Sprache des Systemdenkens betont Wackenroder die Sprachen der Natur und der Kunst, die beide jeweils auf verschiedene, dennoch auf ähnliche Weise

---

[24] Wilhelm Heinrich Wackenroder: *Herzensergießungen eines kunstliebenden Klosterbruders.* In: *Werke und Briefe in einem Band.* A.a.O. S. 7-131, hier S. 67.

[25] Bedeutungsvoll erscheint es bezüglich der Aporie, das sprachlich Unfaßbare der Kunsterfahrung mitteilen zu wollen, daß Tieck in der Einführung zur Neuveröffentlichung der *Phantasien über die Kunst* im Jahr 1814 bemerkt, Wackenroder wäre "ohne alle Absicht im Schreiben" verfallen, "seine Worte einem von der Welt abgeschiedenen Geistlichen in den Mund zu legen, denn er dachte bei diesen Ergießungen seines Gemüts anfangs nicht daran, sie durch den Druck auch andern, als seinen vertrautesten Freunden mitzuteilen". Ludwig Tieck: Vorrede. A.a.O. S. 269.

[26] Er stellt das göttlich offenbarende *"Erklärungsbuch* der Natur" der objektiven Sprache gegenüber: "Das Säuseln in den Wipfeln des Waldes, und das Rollen des Donners, haben mir geheimnisvolle Dinge von ihm *erzählt*, die ich in Worten nicht aufsetzen kann. [...] es ist große Gnade von Gott, daß er uns *diese echten Zeugen der Wahrheit* herabsendet". Wilhelm Heinrich Wackenroder: *Herzensergießungen.* A.a.O. S. 68-69. (Hervorhebung AG)

"durch dunkle und geheime Wege, eine wunderbare Kraft" im Herzen des Menschen erregen:[27]

> Sie redet durch Bilder der Menschen und bedienet sich also einer Hieroglyphenschrift, deren Zeichen wir dem Äußern nach kennen und verstehen. Aber sie schmelzt das Geistige und Unsinnliche, auf eine so rührende und bewunderswürdige Weise, in die sichtbaren Gestalten hinein, daß wiederum unser ganzes Wesen und alles, was an uns ist, von Grund auf bewegt und erschüttert wird. [...] Die Kunst aber, die durch sinnreiche Zusammensetzungen von gefärbter Erde und etwas Feuchtigkeit, die menschliche Gestalt in einem engen, begrenzten Raume, nach innerer Vollendung strebend, nachahmt (eine Art von Schöpfung, wie sie sterblichen Wesen hervorzubringen vergönnt ward) – sie schließt uns die Schätze der menschlichen Brust auf, richtet unsern Blick in unser Inneres und zeigt uns das Unsichtbare [...]. (WR 69-70)

Auf den Zeichencharakter des Bildes verweist eben der Begriff "Hieroglyphe", dessen mimetisch-sinnliche Außenseite als Vorlage des Numinosen erscheint. Die Kunstbetrachtung wird zu einer hermeneutischen Tätigkeit, die mittels poetischer Sprache das grundsätzlich Unsagbare des endlosen Gefühls zu fassen versucht.[28]

Im Kontext unserer Fragestellung ruft diese neue Definition der Kunsterfahrung die Frage nach der romantischen Ästhetik auf. Es erscheint sinnvoll, sich zu fragen, welche Art von Kunst als Vermittlung der religiösen Erfahrung fungiert, denn immerhin bildet die gemalte Darstellung, wenngleich nicht mehr als eine Zusammensetzung von "gefärbter Erde und etwas Feuchtigkeit", als sinnlicher Aspekt den Sockel der göttlichen Offenbarung. Wie bereits in Bezug auf Schlegels ästhetischen Pluralismus erwähnt, erscheint die Romantik, allerdings auf den ersten Blick, als total unterschieden von der Klassik und ihren rigiden Schönheitsregeln. Wackenroder plädiert für "Toleranz und Menschenliebe in der Kunst" und widerspricht der geläufigen klassisch-aufklärerischen Ansicht, "das Mittelalter" solle verdammt werden, weil "es nicht solche Tempel wie in Griechenland baute" (WR 53). Die Kunst kann nach keinem "System" beurteilt werden:

---

[27] Wilhelm Heinrich Wackenroder: *Herzensergießungen*. A.a.O. S. 69.

[28] Bei der "Beschreibung" der Kunst wird die Schönheit des Kunstgebildes in das Medium der poetischen Sprache verwandelt, das auf "andere Art" die ihr übergeordnete Idee vermittelt. Vgl. Dirk Kemper: *Die Sprache der Dichtung*. S. 251-254.

Es erblickt in jeglichem Werke der Kunst, unter allen Zonen der Erde, die
Spur von dem himmlischen Funken, der, von ihm ausgegangen, durch die
Brust des Menschen hindurch, in dessen kleine Schöpfungen überging [...].
Ihm ist der gotische Tempel so wohlgefällig als der Tempel des Griechen.
(WR 52)

Die Feststellung, daß jede Kunst im Grunde Beachtung verdient, kann
indes nicht verhindern, daß Wackenroder selber implizit eine Ästhetik fixiert, die ihn zum exklusiven Zuschauer macht. So heißt es in
Anbetracht von Dürers Werk: "wenigen muß es gegeben sein, die
Seele in deinen Bildern so zu verstehen, und das Eigne und Besondre
darin mit solcher Innigkeit zu genießen, als der Himmel es mir [...]
vergönnt zu haben scheint" (WR 58). Andeutungen wie "Eignes" und
"Besonderes" widersprechen der Idee einer verständlich
entwickelten, allgemeingültigen Schönheit und lenken stattdessen
den Blick auf die Individualität der bildlichen Darstellung. Dürer wird
als charakteristisches Produkt seiner Zeit und seiner Landschaft betrachtet und als solches bewundert; es habe keinen Sinn, zu bedauern,
daß er nicht eine "Zeitlang in Rom gehauset hätte [...] und die echte
Schönheit und das Idealische von Raffael abgelernt" (WR 63). Hier
zeigt sich aber gleich der Widerspruch in Wackenroders Kunstdiskurs. Obwohl er besagt, daß es keine universale Schönheitshierarchie
gibt, will er Dürer nicht mit Malern wie Raffael oder Michelangelo
vergleichen, weil deren Werk eben die "wahre" Schönheit verkörpert. Die implizit hypostasierte Überzeugung, daß eine solche Gegenüberstellung negativ für Dürer ausfallen würde, zeigt, daß Wackenroders angekündigter ästhetischer Pluralismus nur teilweise als Passe-
partout der Kunstanschauungen fungiert. Stattdessen entsteht die
Vermutung, daß die "akademischen" Schönheitsprinzipien eher als
ikonische Vermittlung fungieren. Wie Hans Eichner in der Einführung zu Schlegels Gemäldebeschreibungen hervorhebt, hat die über
vierzig Jahre alte Forschung Robson-Scotts schon klar nachgewiesen,
daß Wackenroder nicht wirklich für die mittelalterliche Kunst eine
Lanze bricht,[29] denn die romanische oder sogar die gotische Kunst ist
ihm vollkommen fremd. Im Gegensatz zum Gemeinplatz über die
romantische Liebe für das Mittelalter stellt es sich heraus, daß jeden-

---

[29] "For the fact of the matter is that the Middle Ages play an utterly
insignificant role in the *Herzensergießungen*. Medieval art proper – the
paintings of the Italian Pre-raffaelites and the German Primitives, Gothic or
romanesque sculpture or architecture is barely mentioned in their pages". W.D.
Robson-Scott: Wackenroder and the Middle Ages. In: *The Modern Language
Review* 50.2 (1955). S. 156-167, hier S. 159.

falls Wackenroders Kunstbetrachtung zwischen objektiven Schön-
heitsvorstellungen nach klassischem Muster und seelischer Einfüh-
lung oszilliert. Zwar nimmt die Religion, die nach romantischer Ansicht das Kunstgebilde umfaßt, sich als flexibler Rahmen aus, der zu
vielen Ikonen paßt, aber hinter dieser Konstruktion dämmern indes
die klassizistischen Schönheitskriterien der vernünftig verwurzelten
Größenverhältnisse, die das Transzendentale wiederum einrahmen.

Ähnliches ergibt sich, wenn man liest, wie Michelangelo, der
"große Buonarroti", auf dessen Kunst der "göttliche Geist Christi
ruht", bewundert wird um seine herrlichen Vorstellungen von
menschlichen Körpern, die wiederum auf anatomischen Kenntnissen
basieren: "Er ergründete das innerliche Triebwerk der Menschenma-
schine bis in die verborgensten Wirkungen [...] um die üppige Fülle
seiner Geisteskraft auch in den körperlichen Teilen der Kunst auszu-
lassen und zu befriedigen" (WR 86). Die formale Darstellung der
"körperlichen Teile" mündet in die Konstruktion einer ästhetischen
Skala, worauf Watteau das eine Ende und der übermäßig bewunderte
Raffael das andere bildet. Gelingt es Raffael, musterhaft in der Darstellung von Kinderfiguren, die wahre Sphäre des erhabenen religiösen Gefühls zu erfassen, so müssen Watteaus Gemälde gleichfalls
wegen ihres sinnlichen Reizes anerkannt werden. Watteau, dessen
allegorische Gebilde zwar keine "Begeisterung, kein Streben nach
dem Himmel" aussprechen, fungiert als Beispiel der meisterhaften
profanen Kunst, die unter dem Gesichtspunkt der "objektiven" Ästhetik mit Raffael verglichen werden kann. Sinnliche Schönheit pur
sang braucht es im Reich der Kunst, denn der Mensch bleibt immerhin teilweise der sichtbaren Welt verhaftet: "aus größern Ursachen
ist es auch wohl gut, wenn wir das Hohe der Kunst innigst fühlen [...]
zuweilen wieder durch lustige Geister in die nähere Umgebung zurück-
gerufen zu sein".[30] Weil Watteaus Bilder keine eschatologische Ver-
weisfunktion haben, vermitteln sie desto deutlicher die der religiösen
Erfahrung zugrundeliegenden ästhetischen Kriterien, die sich im
Grunde mit den klassischen überschneiden: zentral steht die Verklärung der Menschengestalt, die bei den Malern der Renaissance und
des Barock eben auf Grund ihrer formalen Orientierung den Höhe-
punkt erreicht.

---

[30] Wilhelm Heinrich Wackenroder: Phantasien über die Kunst. In: *Werke und
Briefe in einem Band*. A.a.O. S. 133-266, hier S. 177. Ein analoges
Verhältnis zwischen dem Sinnlichen und dem Himmlischen läßt sich bei
Wackenroders Unterschied zwischen Tanzmusik und Kirchenmusik
nachweisen, wobei die profane Gattung nicht abgewiesen wird, sondern als
reizendes Gleichgewicht zum Erhabenen des Religiösen fungiert (S. 211).

In der Betrachtung über die Sankt Petruskirche in Rom oszilliert Wackenroder erneut zwischen Schönheitsbeschreibung und Offenbarungserlebnis, zwischen objektiver Ästhetik und dem Gefühl des Numinosen, und stellt es sich auf ähnliche Weise heraus, daß er der barocken Kunst näher steht als der pietätvollen mittelalterlichen. Der Unterschied zwischen Watteaus Malerei und jenem Barockgebäude liegt nur in der Erhabenheit jenes Gebäudes, das aus göttlicher Begeisterung errichtet wurde und eben als religiöse Kunst das Menschliche selber übersteigt:

> Menschen erschufen dich, und du bist höherer Natur als das Geschlecht deiner Schöpfer [...]. Wohl dem vergänglichen Menschen, daß er Unvergänglichkeit zu schaffen vermag! [...] Unter dem Himmel der frommen Kunst treibt die sterbliche Zeugungskraft eine goldene Frucht, edler als Stamm und Wurzel, hervor; wie Wurzel mag vergehen, die goldene Frucht verschließt göttliche Kräfte.[31]

Wackenroder versucht die Distanz zwischen Subjekt und Objekt zu überwinden, indem er mittels direkter Anrede an das Gebäude ("Du erweckst mit deiner stummen Unendlichkeit Gedanken auf Gedanken") den archimedischen Standpunkt der objektiven Rationalität verläßt und sich auf die gleiche Ebene des Kunstgebildes stellt. Eine Kunstbeschreibung in dem Sinn, daß man sich als Leser nachher die Kirche vorstellen könnte, liegt also nicht wirklich vor. Indes erweist Wackenroder sich dennoch der Tatsache wiederum bewußt, daß die Voraussetzung seines romantisch-religiösen Erlebnisses mit der sinnlichen Schönheit des Kirchengebäudes zusammenhängt, und daß in dieser Hinsicht die architektonischen Verhältnisse als Scharnier fungieren. Wortwörtlich betont er die "Angeltugenden" der edlen Kunst, die als "sinnliches Bild der schönen Regelmäßigkeit, der Festigkeit und Zweckmäßigkeit" fixiert werden (WR 172). Daß die Anregung zum seelischen Kunstgenuß der sinnliche Aspekt der Kunst ist, und daß dieser sinnliche Reiz besonders klassisch anmutet mit Andeutungen wie "regelmäßig" und "fest", bestätigt unsere oben dargelegte Einrahmung.

Betrachten wir nun kurz die Gedichte in den *Herzensergießungen,* die Wackenroder mit dem Titel "Gemäldeschilderungen" versieht, nämlich "Die heilige Jungfrau mit dem Christuskinde und der kleine Johannes" und "Die Anbetung der drei Weisen aus dem Morgenlande", so tritt die Aporie der romantischen Ikonographie erneut ans Licht:

---

[31] Wilhelm Heinrich Wackenroder: Phantasien über die Kunst. A.a.O. S. 172.

Ein schönes Bild oder Gemälde ist, meinem Sinne nach, eigentlich gar nicht zu beschreiben; denn in dem Augenblicke, da man mehr als ein einziges Wort darüber sagt, fliegt die Einbildung von der Tafel weg, und gaukelt für sich allein in den Lüften. (WR 47)

Die sinnliche bzw. formale Schönheit der gemalten Darstellung, die zunächst die Aufmerksamkeit des Kunstbetrachters lenkt, um ihn das Göttliche berühren zu lassen, kann nicht nach dem Maßstab der objektiven Ästhetik ausgedrückt werden, so daß die informative Frage, was für Wackenroder ein "schönes Bild oder Gemälde" ist, hier in der Schwebe bleibt. Fehlt im herkömmlichen kunsthistorischen Sinn das ikonographische Scharnier, so will Wackenroder andererseits den Geist des Gemäldes, die "Einbildung auf der Tafel", von der allerdings anzunehmen ist, daß sie durch das Schöne vermittelt wird, auf angewandt poetische Weise erfassen. Die "Wahrheit" jener Kunstsprache erscheint als ätherisches Gut, welches nur durch unmittelbares Einfühlen erfaßbar wird: darum bietet der Zuschauer/ Erzähler dem Leser zwei sprachliche "Proben", die ihm "von selbst in den Sinn gekommen sind, um der eigenen Art willen". Vertuscht Wackenroder einerseits die objektiven Konturen zugunsten der romantischen Aussagekraft, so nimmt die sprachliche Erfassung, obwohl es sich um "Proben" handelt, andererseits wiederum die Form eines formalen Sprachgebildes an, womit die Tatsache, daß der seelischen Erfahrung eine entschiedene Schönheitsnorm zugrundeliegt, symptomatisch ersichtlich wird. In den Gedichten kommen die unterschiedlichen gemalten Figuren zu Wort und tritt die Stimme des Dichters/ Sprechers, der nur in kurzen Überschriften andeutet, wer jeweils spricht, in den Hintergrund. Damit wird, genau wie bei der Betrachtung der Sankt Petruskirche, die Distanz zwischen Subjekt und Objekt verwischt: obwohl die formale Struktur der Sprache schon auf die dichtende Instanz hinweist, kommen jeweils die gemalten Objekte zu Wort, wodurch eine Synthese von Beobachter und Artefakt entsteht. In vierzig Zeilen, der symbolischen Zahl von Tagen, die zur Auferstehung Christi führen, sprechen im ersten Gedicht Maria, das Jesuskind und "der kleine Johannes" nacheinander und bekunden aus eingeschränkter Sicht ihre Existenz als Kunstobjekt und Vermittler des Göttlichen. Marias "Aussage":

Nur mit Lächeln und mit tiefer Wehmut
kann ich auf dem Götterkinde ruhen,
Und mein Blick vermag es nicht, zum Himmel,
Und zum güt'gen Vater aufzusteigen.
Nimmer werden meine Augen müde

Dieses Kind, das mir im Schoße spielet,
Anzusehen mit tiefer Herzensfreude. (WR 49)

vermittelt einiges über Figurenkonstellation und Gesichtsausdruck:
das Kind auf dem Schoß, den Blick nach unten, melancholisches Lächeln, während andererseits die Idee des Unsagbaren diese Figuren
mit dem Beobachter in eins setzt. Die Selbstaussage des "Jesuskind-
leins" in Bezug auf die "drei Weisen aus dem Morgenlande" im zweiten Gedicht belegt das Schwanken zwischen Beschreibung und Erlebnis:

Denn wie herrlich sind die Männer!
Aber wie so alt und prächtig?
Ach! das ist die tiefe Weisheit,
Daß sie goldne Königsmäntel,
Silberweise Häupter haben [...].
Und ich weiß mir nicht zu sagen,
Wie ich sie recht nennen soll. (WR 50)

Das existenzielle Staunen bekundet paradoxerweise ikonographische
Information über Farbe und Ausdruck, während die letzten Zeilen das
ewige Problem der "Schilderung" darstellen: wie soll die göttliche
Herrlichkeit, oder, allgemeiner, die verführerische Ahnung des Transzendentalen, die von den Gemälden herabspricht, in Sprache erfaßt
werden. Greift man in Anbetracht dieses Verstummens vor dem
künstlerischen Artefakt auf die im Text zerstreuten Indizien der Ästhetik zurück, so wird der sinnliche Ansatz zu Wackenroders "inne-
rem" Erleben und damit der ästhetische, vernünftige Rahmen seiner
Offenbarung sichtbar.

Friedrich Schlegel verfolgt in seinen ikonographischen Schriften
Wackenroders Spur und rahmt seine Kunstbetrachtungen in den ka-
tholischen Glauben ein. Während aber ersterer in seiner Anschauung
von Watteaus Malerei die "klassischen" Fundamente der Offenba-
rungsästhetik erkennen läßt, lehnt Schlegel die "neueste französische
Schule" entschieden ab, die sowohl das "falsche Ideal antikischer
Nachahmerei", wie "den grellen Effekt" anstrebt. (FS 135) Dieser
Unterschied ist symptomatisch für den logischen Aufbau von Schlegels Ästhetik, die er in seinen Gemäldebeschreibungen, einer Reihe
von Aufsätzen in der Zeitschrift "Europa" zwischen 1802 und 1804,
entfaltet.[32] Schlegel verläßt sich nicht auf eine unklare Ästhetik, die

---

[32] Wir konzentrieren uns auf Schlegels "Gemäldebeschreibungen aus Paris und
den Niederlanden" und lassen seine Beurteilung der zeitgenössischen

sich bei näherem Zusehen mit dem klassischen Geschmack überschneidet. Die formale Lage seiner Gemäldebeschreibungen, so wird
am Anfang des Textes bald deutlich, weicht erheblich von den eher
lässigen *Herzensergießungen* ab. Angesiedelt in einer neu gegründe-
ten Zeitschrift, deren programmatischer Charakter auffällt, deutet
Schlegel jeweils den Ort an, wo sich die Gemälde befinden, verfährt
mit katalogischer Aufzählung mit Nummern und siedelt die Kunstgebilde schließlich in der Kunstgeschichte an. Daß er damit die akademische Form der klassischen Historiographie übernimmt und das
"Poetische" der wackenroderschen Romantik ausklammert, hängt
mit der polemischen Schärfe zusammen, welche die Kunstansichten
kennzeichnet.[33]

Programmatisch hebt er in Anbetracht eines Gemäldes von Cor-
reggio hervor, daß "schöne Stellen nicht zufällig da sind", daß es sich
nicht um die "sinnliche Schönheit" an sich handelt, "sondern um den
Gedanken oder das tiefe individuelle Gefühl des Ganzen", das die
göttliche Botschaft offenbart (FS 25). Die Betonung des "Individuellen" eines jeweiligen Gemäldes rückt, wie bei Wackenroder, das
beobachtende Subjekt ins Blickfeld. Statt wie im Klassizismus dem
Kunstwerk objektive Kriterien abzugewinnen, muß das künstlerische
Verstehen den eschatologischen Sinn der ästhetischen Komposition
herauskristallisieren.[34] Die Frage ist aber wiederum, ob Schlegels Ikonographie, die sich entschieden in Richtung des Poetischen bewegt,
tatsächlich den ästhetischen Pluralismus seiner Athenäumsfragmente
materialisiert und so die Verbindung des individuell Sinnlichen einer

---

nazarenischen Kunst zwanzig Jahre nach den "Beschreibungen" außer Betracht.
Daß aber die Kontroverse mit der Klassik bis dann hartnäckig verharrt, belegt
Goethes Schadenfreude über den Mißerfolg einer romantisch-christlichen
Kunstausstellung im Palazzo Caffarelli in Rom 1819: "Ich gönnt' ihnen gerne
Lob und Ehre/ Könnens aber nicht von *außen* haben. /Sie sehen endlich doch
ihre Lehre/ In *Caffarelli* begraben". Zitiert in: Friedrich Schlegel: Ansichten
und Ideen von der christlichen Kunst. A.a.O. S. XLIII.
[33] Eine Andeutung wie jene am Anfang der Europa-Aufsätze, es gebe sogar
"Dichter von Genie", die trotz einer lebenslänglichen Beschäftigung mit
Kunst, nie das Gefühl fürs Schöne erringen, spricht in dieser Hinsicht Bände.
[34] Auch Hegel distanziert sich bekanntlich von der romantischen Kunsttheorie
und deren "Obstination, mit der sie in dem Teufelskreis der permanenten
Selbstinszenierung und Selbstanzeige [...] verharrt". Emanuel Hirsch: Die
Beisetzung der Romantiker in Hegels Phänomenologie. Ein Kommentar zu
dem Abschnitte über die Moralität. In: *Materialien zu Hegels Phänomenologie
des Geistes*. Hg. von Hans Friedrich Fulda und Dieter Henrich. Frankfurt a.M.
1973. S. 245-275, zitiert in: Bart Philipsen: *Die List der Einfalt. Eine
NachLese zu Hölderlins spätester Dichtung*. Tübingen 1995. S. 105.

Darstellung mit der teleologischen Immanenz herstellt. Insofern würde der Rahmen der romantischen Kunst sich als universell herausstellen.

Aus der Sicht Walter Benjamins verliert Friedrich Schlegel als Erkenntnistheoretiker seine methodische Kraft, wenn dieser nach 1800 die Religion an Stelle des Absoluten des Kunstwerkes setzt: "Er verlangt in ihm die eigentümlichen Züge seines religiösen Kosmos wiederzufinden, während zugleich, zum Zeichen jener Unklarheit, seine Idee der Form um nichts gewinnt".[35] Hans Eichner, der Herausgeber von Schlegels Oeuvre, zeigt sich sogar einigermaßen geniert über die Kunstbetrachtungen, die der ältere Romantiker (anläßlich einer Italienreise) erörtert:

> man erschrickt fast über die Einseitigkeit, zu der die schlimme Gewohnheit, alles und jedes, auch das Unpassendste, an seiner religiösen Bedeutung zu messen, diesen in seinen jüngeren Jahren so umfassenden Geist verleitete; aber freilich, wenn man bedenkt, daß er schon 1808 die Skulptur der Alten als eine "falsche" Kunst verdammen und mit der Bemerkung Papst Adrians V. "sunt idola paganorum" abtun konnte, wird man es kaum von ihm erwarten, diesem Aspekt Italiens noch viel Aufmerksamkeit zu schenken.[36]

Religion transformiert Schlegel als Ästhetiker indes nicht unmittelbar in einen Dogmatiker: die Tatsache, daß Malerei als Kunstgattung das Göttliche zu offenbaren hat, schafft sogar umgekehrt dem Individuellen und Phantasiereichen Raum, denn es wird nicht a priori fixiert, wie sich das Göttliche malerisch übersetzten läßt. Die strikte Schönheitsnorm der Klassik, die "heidnischen" Ansichten über die "Vollkommenheit der organischen Gestalt", stehen laut Schlegels Ansichten erst am "Verschlossenen Eingang des ewigen Schönen" (S. 150), weil sie das Transzendentale rückgängig gemacht haben, indem es auf Verstandeseigenschaften reduziert wurde. Die Quelle der malerischen Schönheit liegt stattdessen im Gefühl. Die Auswirkung dieser Verfassung ist, daß es dem Künstler "Ernst" sein muß mit "dem tiefen religiösen Gefühl" (S. 149), das er über seine Malerei erscheinen läßt. Das Artefakt wird so zur Hieroglyphe, zum göttlichen Sinnbild,

---

[35] Walter Benjamin: *Der Begriff der Kunstkritik in der deutschen Romantik.* A.a.O. S. 74. Daß Schlegel mit diesen Kunstansichten seiner ehemaligen Idee über die Autonomie des Kunstwerkes widerspricht, betont auch Elisabeth Decultot: Friedrich Schlegel et l'art divin de la peinture. In: *Etudes Germaniques* 52.4 (1997). S. 629-648, hier S. 641.

[36] Hans Eichner in: Friedrich Schlegel: Ansichten und Ideen von der Christlichen Kunst. A.a.O. S. XL.

das vom Zuschauer empfunden werden soll. Daß Schlegel abermals das Kunstgebiet der Klassiker aus romantischer Perspektive vereinnahmt, wird deutlich, wenn er über Raffael spricht. Während bei Wackenroder die Anschauung von Raffael symptomatisch die einverleibte normative Ästhetik erkennen läßt, polemisiert Schlegel ausdrücklich, man habe bislang den Maler aus falschen Gründen bewundert: der universale Wert von Raffaels Werk liege keineswegs in der sogenannten "idealischen Schönheit", sondern in der Tatsache, daß dieser während seiner Jugendjahre als Maler an die "alte Schule" anknüpfte (FS 55). Den klassizistisch beeinflussten älteren Maler kann man kaum noch bewundern.

Damit ist aber die Frage, welche artistisch-sinnliche Darstellung als Eckstein des Numinosen fungiert, noch nicht beantwortet. Schlegel liefert einen beträchtlichen hermeneutischen Aufwand, um die Kunstprinzipien der Romantik zu fixieren. Während es den Klassikern nicht um die Originalität eines Künstlers geht, sondern um die Vollkommenheit der Schönheit, betont er die Phantasie, die Künstler anwenden, um ihr Ziel zu erreichen, und räumt dem Häßlichen, Sentimentalischen und der Trauer einen Platz in seiner Ästhetik ein. So führt er eine Interpretation von Corregios "Nacht" vor, wo nicht nur das herkömmlich Anmutige, sondern auch das Häßliche in der Gesamtbedeutung eine Rolle spielt:

> Was war in dieser Ansicht der Sache notwendiger als nicht bloß die Freude über den Glanz der göttlichen Erscheinung aus dem Reiz und dem Lächeln einiger schöner Gesichter und Gestalten zurückleuchten zu lassen, sondern auch die Häßlichkeit der dunklen Welt [...] in Erinnerung zu bringen? [...] Aber schwerlich werden diejenigen, welche in die Ansicht der Religion da sie ihrem Herzen fremd geworden ist, sich auch nicht einmal mit der Phantasie hinein versetzen können, jemals dahin gelangen, die alten Maler zu verstehen. (FS 24)

Phantasie und Häßlichkeit sind der klassischen Kunstlehre vollkommen fremd, während ihnen im religiös umrahmten romantischen Kunstdiskurs eine bedeutende Funktion zugeschrieben wird. So heißt es ebenfalls über Corregios allegorische Darstellung, die den Sieg der Tugend darstellt, und wo eine aus verschiedenen Tieren zusammengesetzte Mißgestalt vorgestellt wird: "ich halte es aber für diesen Künstler gar nicht für zu spitzfindig anzunehmen, daß er dieses Verworrene absichtlich gesucht habe, um dadurch die Natur des bösen Prinzips mit auszudrücken" (FS 29). Das Morbide und das Häßliche werden aber unter spezifischer Voraussetzung als neue Elemente in die Ästhetik eingeschlossen: der Sinn des Unschönen liegt nur im Kontrast zum Schönen, das auf diese Weise umso stärker zum Ausdruck kommt. Das Universelle jener Ästhetik stellt sich so als beschränkt heraus, indem es in der Kontrastfunktion dem Symmetriedenken der Klassik gleichkommt. In Bellinis "Heilige Familie" wird die Bedeutung jener widersprüchlichen Schönheitsauffasung offenbar, wo eine Heilige "von der vollendetesten Anmut und Schönheit" einen Kontrast bildet zur Heiligen Mutter, die "eher etwas leidendes oder kränkliches" hat:

> Der Gegensatz und das Absichtliche, die höhere Schönheit der Nebenfigur zu geben, ist auffallend. Es ist, als hätte der Maler sagen wollen, sie ist mehr als schön; und auf diesem Wege versucht das undarstellbare Göttliche, deutlich zu machen. [...] denn die Vereinigung des scheinbar widerstreitenden, die dennoch indirekt erreichte Darstellung des an sich Undarstellbaren ist ja gerade das einzige was auf diesen Namen wenigstens in der Malerei mit Recht Anspruch machen kann. (FS 69)

Schlegel zufolge ist der Gegenstand im Gemälde nie nur der Gegenstand an sich, sondern er erlangt Bedeutung im Ganzen des Gemäldes, dessen Immanenz aber wiederum im Rahmen des Transzendentalen verstanden werden muß. Die spezifische Toleranz dem Grotesken oder Karikaturalen gegenüber nimmt ein Ende, wenn beide Modi zur Darstellung an sich werden. Von Michelangelos "Parzenbild" wendet der Romantiker sich entschieden ab, denn es handelt sich um "das Extrem neuerer Kunstausbildung oder Entartung", "wo alle Kraft aufgeboten ist um die abscheulichste Häßlichkeit recht anschaulich zu machen" (FS 109). Das Charakteristische einer gemalten Darstellung darf also das Unschöne aufzeigen, indem es sinnvoll mit dem Ganzen verknüpft wird. So bekommt auch Dürer einen Ehrenplatz:

> Noch mehr aber war mir die Farbenwirkung an einem großen Ecce homo von Dürer merkwürdig; wie es entworfen sei, kann man sich leicht denken, da er diesen und die damit verwandten Gegenstände in Ölgemälden und Zeichnungen so vorzüglich oft variiert hat; der heilige Dulder von der höchsten sittlichen Schönheit, die höhnenden Krieger Karikaturen der Schlechtigkeit und Rohheit, Karikaturen von einer unergründlichen Bedeutsamkeit. (FS 105)

Zwei Schwerpunkte von Schlegels Ästhetik werden in Anbetracht von Dürer hypostasiert: die Wirkung des Häßlichen im Kontrast zur formalen Schönheit, die gemeinsam fixiert wird (und mit der Opposition von Gut und Böse verknüpft ist). Zweitens zeigt es sich, daß das wahre Thema der Kunst die christlichen Gegenstände sind. Unter diesem Gesichtspunkt erklärt sich ebenfalls die Begutachtung von Märtyrerszenen, die immerhin als Kunstobjekt in der altchristlichen

Malerei legion sind. Wiederum zollt Schlegel der klassischen Idee über diese Art von Vorstellungen Anerkennung, "wie kann aber, hör ich unsre Leser fragen, ein so grausamer Gegenstand der Stoff eines schönen Gemäldes sein?" (FS 87), aber widerlegt sie dennoch in seiner methodischen Darlegung der Schönheitsprinzipien. Darin zeigt es sich wiederum, daß auch in der Romantik die Darstellung menschlicher Grausamkeit zu bändigen ist, weil sie der Idee der formal-menschlichen Schönheit widerspricht. Auf dem von Schlegel bewunderten Gemälde, das "Märtyrertum der heiligen Agatha" von Sebastian del Piombo, befindet sich "kein Blut, kein krampfhafter Schmerz, keine Verwundung, denn noch haben die drohenden Marterwerkzeuge den Leib der Heiligen nicht wirklich berührt" (FS 88). Das von den Zuschauern als peinlich Empfundene liegt insofern mehr in der Art zu schauen als im Gemälde selber:

Der Künstler hat den Augenblick unmittelbar vor der Ausführung gewählt; schon nähern die glühenden Eisen sich den Brüsten und dem herrlichen entblößten Leibe des hohen Weibes, und die dadurch so heftige erregte Erwartung kann allerdings etwas Peinliches haben, aber doch könnte es wohl nur derjenige allzu peinlich finden, der in dieser Pein eben nichts sieht, nichts fühlt als die Pein, der gar nichts ahndet von der höhern göttlichen Bedeutung, und keine Freude hat an der herrlichen Form. (FS 88)

Die formale Schönheit wird zum Kern der ästhetischen Repräsentanz: alles Häßliche, sogar der "peinliche Eindruck gewaltsamer Fesselung" wurde ganz vermieden (FS 88), und stattdessen kreierte der Maler ein Musterbild irdischer Schönheit. Die junge Heilige besteht nicht aus "Lilien und Rosen", sondern hat einen Körper, an dem die "Farbe der ungeschwächten Gesundheit im hellsten Licht durchglüht", und die dunkeln Augen bekunden die "Glut des gefühlvollsten Weibes". Vollkommene Schönheit und Anmut repräsentieren das Göttliche und kombinieren so herkömmliche Schönheitsideale mit göttlicher Offenbarung. Schleicht sich an jenen Stellen in die theologische Interpretation der Gemälde die kognitiv-vernünftige Ästhetik ein, so heißt es andererseits über ein Gemälde von Raffael, der göttliche Gedanke sei darin "nicht zu vertilgen", obwohl es stark "restaurirt und retouchirt" wurde. Obgleich also von Raffaels Meisterhand wenig übrigbleibt und die formale Schönheit teilweise verloren gegangen ist, erregt sie beim Betrachter das Gefühl transzendentaler Offenbarung (FS 109).

Dieser Gegensatz kennzeichnet die Komplexität von Schlegels Ästhetik. Bleibt Schönheit die "Angeltugend" der numinosen Kunstauffassung, so ist dennoch nicht eindeutig, was visuell damit gemeint ist. Immerhin: einfache Nachahmung und das "Streben nach täuschender Natürlichkeit" führt Schlegel zufolge, den Klassikern ähnlich, zu "Plattheit des Sinns" (FS 124). Obwohl aber auch klassische Argumentation über objektive Schönheit ostentativ abgelehnt wird, ist sie dennoch zerstreut aber konstant in jenem romantischen Diskurs anwesend. Vergleicht Schlegel Tizian und Holbein, so schließt er, daß die Frauenfiguren des Italieners "bei gleicher Objektivität den Vorzug behaupten", während anderseits die Männergestalten von Holbein "wegen der größeren Tiefe und ausgeführten Gründlichkeit der Charakteristik" von größerer Bedeutung sind (FS 201). Oszillierend zwischen Gefühl und formaler Schönheit, zwischen "Auge" und "Nachdenken", münden Schlegels Beschreibungen schließlich in eine Definition:

> Die malerische Schönheit insonderheit, welche die körperliche Form nur im Umriß erraten lassen kann, dafür aber das Eigenste und wahrhaft Geistige im Sinnlichen zu ergreifen und in ihrem Farbenspiel magisch zu fixieren vermag, muß durchaus eine individuelle sein im Idealischen, aber freilich individuell in größerer Dimension, objektiv individuell, wie dies bei dem wahrhaft Lokalen und Nationalen der Fall ist. (FS 123, Hervorhebung AG)

Das Paradox der Verbindung von Individualität und Idealität verrät wiederum die Konfrontation mit dem klassischen Kunstmuster und dabei die Tatsache, daß letztendlich für Schlegel Schönheit und Ästhetik sich größtenteils überschneiden. Will er einerseits nicht in die homogene Flachheit der klassizistischen Muster verfallen, so lehnt er anderseits das Hässliche oder Groteske als Grundthema der Kunst ab. Sogar die erbauenden Malereien über christliches Leiden müssen körperliche Schönheit aufzeigen und dürfen nicht zu grauenerregenden Szenen "entarten".[37]

Die altdeutsche und altflämische Malerei, die gemäß der romantischen Ästhetik als Apotheose der Kunst schlechthin betrachtet wird, verkörpert die Lösung. Diese "alte Schule" verknüpft immerhin auf prägnante Weise das Individuelle mit dem Göttlich-Allgemeinen, das tiefe Gefühl des Glaubens mit schönen, individuellen Bildern. So gibt

---

[37] Günter Oesterles Ansicht, daß Schlegels Inkorporation des Häßlichen in die romantische Ästhetik als Grundsatz für die Autonomisierung der Kunst hinsichtlich gesellschaftlicher Vorurteile fungiert, trifft für den älteren Schlegel nicht zu. Aus klassizistischer Perspektive wirft man Schlegel ja vor, mit der Verknüpfung von Kunst und göttlicher Transzendenz die abgründige Selbstsuffizienz der Ästhetik verraten zu haben. Vgl. Günter Oesterle: Entwurf einer Theorie des ästhetisch Häßlichen. In: *Friedrich Schlegel und die Kunsttheorie seiner Zeit.* Hg. von Helmut Schanze. Darmstadt 1985. S. 397-451, hier S. 408.

Schlegel ihr den Titel der "originellen Kunst", aber immer noch vor dem Hintergrund des Ideellen, d.h. des formal Ästhetischen. Daß, wie gesagt, indes doch ein objektives Schönheitsmuster beibehalten bleibt, das als archimedischer Punkt der religiös-romantischen Empfindung fungiert, verrät Schlegels Kommentar zu einem "altdeutschen" Bild in Köln, in dem die "ganze Kunst beschlossen liegt" (FS 141). Dieses namenlose Triptychon mit der Darstellung der drei Könige, der heiligen Ursula und des Sankt Geryon inspiriert ihn schließlich zu einem Gedicht, mit dem er die poetische "Wahrheit" der künstlerischen Darstellung in wackenroderschen Sinn erfaßt. Auffallend ist allerdings, daß es um eine Darstellung von objektiver Schönheit geht, denn der namenlose Meister hat "das Auge der Schönheit gesehen und von ihrem Hauch sind alle seine Bildungen übergossen" (FS 140). Die "Schönheit", die ihn zu jenem romantischen Ausgangspunkt zurückführt, den die *Herzensergießungen* bekundeten, bleibt kognitiv-formal begründet: "die Farbenpracht ist fast in allen bewunderswürdig; das Blau durchaus ultramarin und auch andre Farben, nach Verhältnis die köstlichsten und glänzendsten" (FS 138).

Werfen wir schließlich im Rahmen unserer Argumentation einen Blick auf Ludwig Tiecks Kunstbetrachtungen, so zeigt sich auch hier die formale Ästhetik, die sich in Wackenroders und Schlegels Ikonographie nachweisen läßt. Allerdings hat Tieck sich weniger systematisch mit der sprachlichen Bewältigung der bildenden Kunst und insofern mit vernünftig begründeten Kriterien ästhetischer Darstellungen befaßt als Schlegel.[38] Er fungiert an erster Stelle als Vermittler. So tritt er als Herausgeber von Wackenroders nachgelassenen Schriften auf und führt den Faden von dessen vager kunsthistorischer Evokation weiter in dem Künstlerroman *Franz Sternbalds Wanderungen* (1799). Tieck hat ebenfalls Friedrich Schlegels Ansichten über Malerei weitgehend beeinflußt und nennt sogar in einem Gespräch mit Boisserée die Hälfte der Europa-Aufsätze sein geistiges Eigentum.[39] Daß Tieck die religiöse Hermeneutik der anderen Romantiker teilt, belegt die Feststellung, daß seine Kunstauffassungen den Maler Otto

---

[38] Diese Aussage gilt allerdings nur auf Grund von Tiecks veröffentlichten Schriften, denn in der Wiener Nationalbibliothek befindet sich das bislang unveröffentlichte Manuskript seiner "Geschichte und Theorie der bildenden Künste". Vgl. Roger Paulin: *Ludwig Tieck*. Stuttgart 1985. S. 112.

[39] Friedrich Schlegel: Ansichten und Ideen von der Christlichen Kunst. A.a.O. S. XIX. Allerdings verweist Schlegels Widmung "dem Freund in Dresden" auf Tieck.

Runge dazu anregten, Kunst mit Offenbarungsglauben zu verknüpfen.[40]

In Bezug auf die bildende Kunst erscheint Tieck insofern weiterhin interessant, als er das zumindest fremdartige Verhältnis der "literarischen" Romantiker zu der zeitgenössischen romantischen Kunst anschaulich macht. Immerhin fällt es auf, daß jene moderne Malerei, die ihrerseits das tiefe Gefühl menschlicher Verfremdung und Religiosität ikonisch auszudrücken versucht, weder in Wackenroders noch in Schlegels Schriften anwesend ist. Caspar David Friedrich (1774-1840) einerseits und der ältere Johann Heinrich Füßli (1741-1825) andererseits, zwei Maler, die man mit dem Etikett "romantisch" bezeichnen kann, bleiben im romantischen Kunstdiskurs größtenteils außer Betracht. Friedrichs unheimliche Landschaften, die (oft versehen mit einer winzigen Menschengestalt, die dem Zuschauer den Rücken zeigt) das Gefühl der Unendlichkeit verkörpern, werden negiert.[41] Füßli stellt pure Gefühle dar und, Edvard Munch vorwegnehmend, hebt die Distanz zum Zuschauer auf, indem er auf die formalen Orientierungstechniken verzichtet.[42] Dieser frühromantische Schweizer, der dasjenige bildlich zu erfassen versucht, was Schlegel und Wackenroder wenigstens anzudeuten scheinen, nämlich das Poetische, Häßliche und Verzerrte, ist ihnen zutiefst fremd.

Das belegt jedenfalls eine Rezension Tiecks über Zeichnungen zu Shakespeares Dramen. Zwar handelt es sich um eine frühe Kritik aus dem Jahr 1793, aber in der Einführung zur späteren Neuauflage widerruft Tieck allerdings keineswegs seine Meinung, so daß man

---

[40] Herbert von Einem: *Deutsche Malerei des Klassizismus und der Romantik.* S. 76. Über das Verhältnis zwischen Tieck und Otto Runge, in dem Tieck abermals als "Vermittler" auftritt, heißt es bei Paulin: "As with Novalis and so many others Tieck provides the important creative spark, without necessarily appreciating the full implications of his actions". Roger Paulin: *Ludwig Tieck. A Literary Biography.* Oxford 1986. S. 151.

[41] Allerdings aber nicht von einigen anderen Dichtern, wie Brentano oder Kleist, die anhand von Friedrichs "Mönch am Meer" dessen Zugehörigkeit zur Romantik erkannten.Vgl. Herbert von Einem: *Deutsche Malerei des Klassizismus und der Romantik.* S. 90-91. Ob Friedrich und Tieck sich jemals begegnet sind, bleibt fraglich. Nur ein – falsch buchstabierter – Verweis auf "Fridrich" deutet an, daß Tieck die Gemälde des Romantikers kannte. Allerdings nimmt seine Bewertung sich eher negativ aus, wenn er sich fragt, ob nicht die "overaccentuation of a personal manner or idiosyncrasy endanger the whole, the "Erscheinung"? Roger Paulin: *Ludwig Tieck. A Literary Biography.* S. 150.

[42] Herbert von Einem: *Deutsche Malerei des Klassizismus und der Romantik.* S. 91.

annehmen kann, daß sich hinsichtlich seiner Kunstansichten wenig geändert hat. Manche dieser Illustrationen stammen von Füßli. Obwohl sie aber buchstäblich das Poetische mit dem Malerischen verknüpfen, verstoßen sie, Tieck zufolge, fast alle gegen die Regeln des guten Geschmacks.[43] Man will eine "Höhe des Affectes" vorstellen, die "der Maler schwerlich ausdrücken kann, ohne widrig zu werden, viele Darstellungen wirken "unnatürlich" oder verfallen in "gräßliche Caricaturen".[44] Prägnanterweise schließt der Verfasser, der in Füßlis Werk nur "Übertriebenes" auffindet: "Unter allen Nachahmern des großen Michel Angelo gehört Füeßli vielleicht zu den schlechtesten".[45] Damit wird klar, daß Tiecks Anschauung durchaus von der Werteskala der formalen Ästhetik bestimmt ist. Daß jener Maler vielleicht absichtlich das neuzeitlich-klassische Muster verzerrt als Symptom der Tatsache, daß jenes stringente Beispiel das tiefe individuelle Einfühlen fesselt und paralysiert, wird nicht beachtet.[46] Die formale Schönheit muß auch hier das tiefe Einfühlen bändigen, so daß der Zuschauer nicht überwältigt wird. Dieses Oszillieren zwischen dem akademischen Stil der formalen Verklärung und dem Gefühlswert drückt Tieck implizit mittels eines Vergleichs zwischen dem Maler Murillo und dem Dichter Lenz aus:

Wenn wir in Galerien die schmuzigen Gassenjungen von Murillo gern anschauen und bewundern, weil sie vortrefflich gemalt sind, und also die Virtuosität den geringen Gegenstand adeln darf, so habe ich es nie begriffen, warum Lenz, nach einer kurzen Periode von Glorie, unbeachtet bleiben und vergessen werden sollte.[47]

Daß ein Kunstwerk dem Betrachter die Seele aufschließt, damit dieser die Unendlichkeit berührt, hat also als Voraussetzung, daß der künstlerische Urheber gewissen logisch-kognitiven Schönheitsforderungen folgt. Mit andern Worten: das Subjekt und seine Erfahrung der Transzendentalität, die in dem dialektischen Verhältnis zwischen Zuschauer und Artefakt zustandekommt, ist wiederum in eine rational

---

[43] Ludwig Tieck: Die Kupferstiche nach der Shakespeare-Gallerie in London. Briefe an einen Freund. In: *Kritische Schriften*. 2. Ausgabe. Bd. I. Berlin-New York 1974. S. 1-34.
[44] Ludwig Tieck: Shakespeare-Gallerie. A.a.O. S. 27.
[45] Ludwig Tieck: Shakespeare-Gallerie. A.a.O. S. 34.
[46] Diese Interpretation wird bestätigt durch Füßlis Rötelzeichnung "Der Künstler, verzweifelnd vor der Größe der antiken Trümmer", die einen Mann darstellt, der neben einem riesigen steinern Fuß sitzt. Während er eine Hand auf die enorme Plastik legt, hält er die andere verzweifelt vor das Gesicht.
[47] Ludwig Tieck: Vorrede. In: *Kritische Schriften*. Bd I. A.a.O. S. XV.

begründete Ästhetik eingefaßt. Die Komplexität jener Kunstanschauung, die insofern Symmetrie und pluralistischen Stil verknüpft, als sie zugleich dem Häßlichen neben dem Idealischen Platz einräumt und die "Höllenbrut" neben dem "Himmelsengel" bewundert, bekundet Tiecks Dresdner Novelle *Die Gemälde*.[48] Alle derzeitig herrschenden Meinungen über die Malerei werden allegorisch von unterschiedlichen Protagonisten verkörpert, aber Eulenböck, ein alter Trunkenbold, der die Zeit damit verbringt, alte Werke zu fälschen, um sie nachher als Originalkunst teuer zu verkaufen, nähert sich dem Ideal der Kunsterfahrung am besten. Zwar fixiert er mit Hilfe eines Vergleichs zwischen Weinsorten und Gemälden die hierarchische Anordnung des Geschmacks und spricht von einer "Himmelsleiter", die der Zuschauer/ Zecher erklettert, "um in das Paradies zu schauen".[49] Als Kopist alter Bilder tritt er aber wortwörtlich in die Spuren der alten Maler und erfaßt das Problem der Dialektik von Kunstwerk/Darstellung und Zuschauer/ Leser: "ein Kunstwerk ganz verstehen, heißt, es gewissermaßen erschaffen".[50] Durch diese "Paraphrase" des Objekts gelingt es dem Subjekt, die Bedeutung und die Schönheit des grundsätzlich autonomen Kunstwerks zu erfassen. Ob dieses Aufgehen in die Kunst, die Überwindung der Distanz zwischen Artefakt und Zuschauer, als "allgemeingültige Lösung" aufgefaßt werden sollte, bleibt fraglich. Immerhin spricht ein Maler, so daß eher der Eindruck entsteht, daß die Erfassung des Kunstobjekts nur im Kunstobjekt selber liegt. Sonst gilt ja das von Tieck formulierte Verhältnis, als sein Protagonist Eduard zum erstenmal die Gemäldesammlung des Vaters sieht: "[...] Rahmen drängte sich an Rahmen, einer kostbarer als der andere, und in ihnen alle jene verloren gewähnten Gemälde [...]".[51]

---

[48] Ludwig Tieck: *Die Gemälde*. In: *Werke in vier Bänden* Bd. III. München 1965. S. 7-73.
[49] Ludwig Tieck: *Die Gemälde*. A.a.O. S. 70.
[50] Ludwig Tieck: *Die Gemälde*. A.a.O. S. 54.
[51] Ludwig Tieck: *Die Gemälde*. A.a.O. S. 72. (Hervorhebung AG)

Helmut J. Schneider

Wahllandschaften:
Mobilisierung der Natur und das Darstellungsproblem
der Moderne in Goethes *Wahlverwandtschaften*

This article considers the prominent motif of the landscape park in Goethe's novel of 1809. The thesis is that Goethe uses this motif for the representation and problematization of modernity as mobility. Seen within the context of the history of gardening, Goethe sharply discerns the essential characteristic of the "English" park, which is the mobilization of nature for the sake of her reification as an illusionist, even virtual reality. Thus, he criticizes an important cultural phenomenon to which he himself had once contributed with the Weimar Ilmpark. Beyond this, the aesthetic transformation of "nature" into a series of images becomes the avatar of that dynamic process which Marx some thirty years later will call the "liquidization" [Verflüssigung] of all human conditions". Finally, it may also be seen as the symbol of an aesthetic re-rooting answering to historical uprooting. In this manner, the "landscape of choice", i.e. the self-made aesthetic nature inserts itself into the important self-referential dimension of Goethe's text.

I

Der englische Landschaftspark ist eines der großen kulturellen Phänomene der europäischen Aufklärung und Romantik, dem in den letzten beiden Jahrzehnten zurecht die intensive Aufmerksamkeit einer interdisziplinär ausgerichteten Forschung zuteil wurde.[1] Es handelte sich bei diesem neuen Typ der ästhetischen Naturgestaltung, der sich insbesondere von dem in der ersten Hälfte des 18. Jahrhunderts dominierenden französischen Park absetzte, um ein komplexes Gesamtkunstwerk, dem die Absicht einer totalen Illusionierung des Betrachters und – vor allem – Begehers zugrundelag. Für die neuere Landschaftsästhetik und überhaupt den neuzeitlichen Prozeß, den wir die "Entdeckung der Natur"

---

[1] Aus der Fülle der Literatur sei hier nur einer herausgegriffen: Norbert Miller: Die beseelte Natur. Der literarische Garten und die Theorie der Landschaft nach 1800. In: *Kunstliteratur als Italienerfahrung*. Hg. von Helmut Pfotenhauer. Tübingen 1991. S. 112-191.

nennen, kann seine Bedeutung kaum überschätzt werden; im englischen Park schulte sich unsere Landschaftswahrnehmung, unser landschaftliches Auge. Zentral hierfür war das Prinzip der Beweglichkeit, das er einführte und gegen die statische Überblicksperspektive des französischen Parks stellte. Der englische Landschaftsgarten war ausgelegt auf die Abwechslung der Blickpunkte und Durchsichten, der überraschenden Ansichten und Prospekte, der Szenen und Auftritte, die sich dem Spaziergänger in einer dem Anschein nach unendlichen Fülle darbieten sollten. So inszenierte er den Überraschungscharakter einer offenen – das heißt geöffneten, nachkopernikanischen – Welt; sie fiel hier in symbolischer Weise einem Subjekt zu, das das Gefühl einer unbegrenzten Bescherung mit dem anderen einer ebenso unbegrenzten Eroberungsfähigkeit verband. Wie es Joseph Addison in seinen programmatischen Essays über die "Vergnügungen der Einbildungskraft" zu Beginn des Jahrhunderts formulierte: Ein solcher Betrachter sieht sich der überwältigenden Mannigfaltigkeit der Welt genußreich ausgesetzt und eignet sie sich in ästhetischer Wahrnehmung an. Die entferntesten Gegenstände liegen gewissermaßen nur einen Lidschlag entfernt: "It is but opening the Eye, and the Scene enters".[2]

In der Welt von Goethes Roman *Die Wahlverwandtschaften* von 1809 nimmt der Landschaftsgarten bekanntlich einen bedeutenden Raum ein. Dabei wird er jedoch in ein eminent kritisches Licht gerückt; ein Licht, das (wie es für kritische Demontagen typisch ist) wesentliche Züge des Phänomens scharf heraushebt.[3] Kritik war schon vorher, auch von Goethe selbst, an der stilisierten oder affektierten Natürlichkeit des Landschaftsparks geübt worden. Der Roman führt aber den tiefsten Stoß gegen ihn – und damit, so läßt sich ohne Übertreibung sagen, den Stoß ins Herz der empfindsamen Landschaftsästhetik überhaupt. Er tut das insofern, als er ihn als zentrales Symbol gerade für die moderne

---

[2] Joseph Addison, Richard Steele and Others: *The Spectator*. Hg. von G. Smith. Bd. 3. London und New York 1963. S. 276-309 (= Nr. 411-4219); hier S. 277.

[3] Diesen Aspekt hat schon früh herausgearbeitet Siegmar Gerndt: *Idealisierte Natur. Die literarische Kontroverse um den Landschaftsgarten des 18. und frühen 19. Jahrhunderts in Deutschland*. Stuttgart 1981. S. 145ff. – Unter ikonographischer Perspektive (insbesondere in bezug auf die arkadische Tradition) analysiert den Park Bernhard Buschendorf: *Goethes mythische Denkform. Zur Ikonograpie der "Wahlverwandtschaften"*. Frankfurt a.M. 1986. – Die jüngste ausführliche Monographie ist Michael Niedermeier: *Das Ende der Idylle. Symbolik, Zeitbezug, 'Gartenrevolution' in Goethes Roman "Wahlverwandtschaften"*. Berlin u.a. 1992.

Natur*entfremdung* begreift.

Entfremdung heißt hier, daß der Mensch aus den naturwüchsigen Verhältnissen seiner Herkunft und angestammten Lebenswelt herausgerissen und in die sekundären Welten und Weiten der Bilder entführt wird. Für diesen epochalen Vorgang der Moderne, der den globalen Hintergrund des Romans bildet,[4] steht die ästhetische Vergegenständlichung der unmittelbaren Naturumgebung, die das von Charlotte initiierte und von den anderen Figuren in leidenschaftlichem Eifer aufgenommene Projekt der Umgestaltung des alten Schloßgartens ausmacht. Was die Ehethematik auf der sozial- und kulturgeschichtlichen Ebene bedeutet, nämlich die Auflösung der altständisch-vormodernen Ehe und ihre Transformation in die romantische Liebesbeziehung, das spiegelt sich auch in Natur und Landschaft; den Wahl*verwandt*schaften entsprechen die Wahl*land*schaften.

In der Umschaffung der 'natürlichen Natur' zu einer künstlichen Natürlichkeit wird das Problem einer "Wahl" von Natur, das der Titel für den familiären Bereich formuliert, unmittelbar anschaulich. Es ist das Problem der Moderne überhaupt, dem sich das aufklärerische Denken immer wieder ausgesetzt sah. Wie kann das, was von Natur, naturwüchsig ist, mit menschlicher Freiheit vereinbart werden? Der Natur durfte ja nicht der Stempel menschlicher Willkür aufgedrückt werden, wie es dem französischen Park als Ausdruck absolutistischen Herrschaftswillen vorgeworfen wurde. Vielmehr sollte sie *als* Natur *durch* den Menschen und sein Werk zur umso eindrucksvolleren Erscheinung kommen. Das Parkprojekt des "reichen Baron" und seiner Ehefrau, das die Handlung des Romans von Beginn an begleitet und zu einem signifikanten Teil bestimmt, mobilisiert das Hergebrachte und Naturwüchsige. Der über Jahrzehnte und Jahrhunderte gewachsene Landsitz wird in ein ästhetisches Bild überführt, das schließlich zu einer unbewohnten Totenlandschaft und zur Grabstätte seiner Bewohner wird. In Goethes früher Farce aus den siebziger Jahren, *Der Triumph der Empfindsamkeit*, trat im Gefolge eines gefühlvollen umherreisenden Prinzen ein Gärtner auf, der einen Koffer mit Naturrequisiten – den Requisiten des englischen Gartens – mit sich führte. Diese paro-

---

[4] Als Artikulation des Umbruchs des symbolischen Kultursystems um 1800 deutet den Goetheschen Roman die umfassende Analyse von David Wellbery: *Die Wahlverwandtschaften (1809)*. In: *Goethes Erzählwerk. Interpretationen.* Hg. von Paul Michael Lützeler. Stuttgart 1985. S. 291-318. Wellbery arbeitet eindringlich das Moment der Entgrenzung und "Entortung" in Imaginäre heraus.

distische "Reisenatur" nimmt der Roman jetzt in seine dargestellte Welt hinüber. Seine Handlung versetzt die altadlige Welt in den ästhetischen Schein und verleiht ihr ansatzweise einen virtuellen Charakter. Die Mobilisierung einer nun nicht mehr als fester und unverrückbarer "Grund und Boden" verstandenen Natur ist das wirksame Instrument wie auch das signifikante Bild für die Auflösung der traditionalen Bindungen.

Es ist keine Frage, daß Goethe der von ihm dargestellten Entwicklung kritisch gegenüberstand, deren Unvermeidlichkeit er gleichwohl sah und darstellte und die er vor allem im ästhetischen Darstellungsprinzip seines Romans reflektierte. Die *Wahlverwandtschaften* stellen die Auflösung von Ehe und patriarchalischer Ordnung durch eine entbundene Einbildungskraft nicht nur dar; sondern der Roman *vollzieht* diese Losbindung der Phantasie zugleich in seiner Form (die Form des von ihm inaugurierten modernen Eheromans). "Niemand glaubt sich in einem Garten behaglich", sagt Charlotte (die parkbegeisterte und zugleich doch eheerhaltende!), "der nicht einem freien Lande ähnlich sieht; an Kunst, an Zwang soll nichts erinnern, wir wollen völlig frei und unbedingt Atem schöpfen. Haben Sie wohl einen Begriff, mein Freund [sie redet zum Gehilfen, dem Erzieher von Ottilie], daß man aus diesem in einen andern, in den vorigen Zustand zurückkehren könne?" (II, 8; S. 454)[5] Ähnlich wie hier wird an anderen Stellen die Unmöglichkeit angesprochen, das einmal Befreite wieder einfangen zu können. Moderne ist irreversibel.

Das gilt natürlich vor allem von der entfesselten erotischen Leidenschaft, die im selben Maße eine "Richtung gegen das Unermeßliche" nimmt, wie die Freunde, "nicht mehr in ihrer Wohnung befangen", die neuen Anlagen dazu nutzen, ihre Spaziergänge immer weiter auszudehnen. (I, 7; S. 321) "Anlagen" ist ein bezeichnendes Wort, insofern es Raum und Psychologie, Äußeres und Inneres, und vor allem – mit Bezug auf beides – die gegensätzlichen Momente von Gestaltung und Naturgegebenheit verbindet. Zwischen der inneren und äußeren Entgrenzung herrscht eine symmetrische Wechselbeziehung. So dringt Eduard beispielsweise auf einem überwachsenen Fußpfad zur abgele-

---

[5] Johann Wolfgang Goethe: *Die Wahlverwandtschaften*. In: ders.: *Sämtliche Werke. Briefe, Tagebücher und Gespräche*. Vierzig Bände. Hg. von Friedmar Apel u.a. I. Abteilung. Bd. 8. In Zusammenarbeit mit Christoph Brecht hg. von Waltraut Wiethölter. Frankfurt a.M. 1994. – Alle Zitate aus dem Roman im folgenden nach dieser Ausgabe, wobei zuerst Teil und Kapitel (römische und arabische Ziffer), dann die Seitenzahl angegeben wird.

genen Mühle vor, wo sich das erste Liebesgeständnis zwischen ihm und Ottilie vollzieht, bevor dieser Entdeckungsgang ins Unbetretene (die innere Natur) als Spazierweg angelegt wird. Überschreitung der 'Hausnatur', wie wir ihre alte Form nennen könnten, zur Landschaftsnatur und Entfesselung der seelischen Leidenschaft sind miteinander verschränkt, ohne daß das eine als Ursache des anderen ausgemacht werden kann. Wohl aber gibt es das beständige Bemühen, das unbekannte Innen in der "neuen" Natur wiederzuerkennen und zu artikulieren. So wird die zum Landschaftspark umgeschaffene Natur aus einem *Lebens-* zu einem *Ausdrucks*raum, in dem sich das Individuum "völlig frei und unbedingt", wie Charlotte sagt, verwirklicht, wodurch es sich aber zugleich potentiell den festen Gegenhalt der Realität entzieht. Hierfür ist die mit der Parkanlage verknüpfte Wassersymbolik nur das einprägsamste Beispiel.

"Von der Natur", so sagt der Gehilfe, der damit auf deutliche Weise den vormodernen Standpunkt vertritt, "sollten wir nichts kennen, als was uns unmittelbar lebendig umgibt. Mit den Bäumen, die um uns blühen, grünen, Frucht tragen, mit jeder Staude an der wir vorübergehen, mit jedem Grashalm über den wir hinwandeln, haben wir ein wahres Verhältnis, sie sind unsre echten Kompatrioten". (II, 7; S. 451f.) Der Gehilfe wird zum exponiertesten Kritiker des neuen Parks, der die sichernde Einschränkung "ins Freie und Weite" durchbrochen habe. Früher habe man in einer Periode gelebt, "wo man Lust hatte sich manches zuzueignen, dieses Eigentum zu sichern, zu beschränken, einzuengen und in der Absonderung von der Welt seinen Genuß zu befestigen" (II, 8; S. 454). Diese Sicht wird bestätigt durch seinen modernen Gegenspieler, den reisenden Engländer, der im zweiten Teil des Romans auftritt. Er hat sein angestammtes Gut verlassen, um andere, immer neue Gegenden zu bereisen und dabei fremde Landsitze zu ästhetischen Panoramen umzuschaffen. Wir seien, so sagt dieser ewig Umherreisende in halb trauernder, halb faszinierter Selbstkritik – eben ein wahrer Moderner – "immer nur halb und halb zu Hause", wir führten eine Hotelexistenz, eine Existenz auf Abruf und Abbruch, wir wechselten die Orte wie Dekorationen einer Oper – oder aber, so können und so müssen wir im Kontext dieses Gesprächs und des gesamten Romans ergänzen, wie englische Parks: eben Wahllandschaften.

Die Hauptbeschäftigung des touristischen Aristokraten aus England – dem Land nicht nur des Landschaftsgartens, sondern auch der beginnenden industriellen Moderne – besteht darin, "die malerischen Aussichten des Parks in einer tragbaren dunklen Kammer aufzufangen und zu zeichnen" und so für sich und andere verfügbar zu machen. (II, 10;

S. 466) Die visuelle Aneignung der Welt lag im Ursprung des modernen Landschaftsparks und der mit ihm verbundenen Naturerfahrung,
wie es der eingangs zitierte Addison ebenfalls bereits formuliert hatte:
Die Natur bietet ihrem Liebhaber "a kind of property in everything he
sees, and makes the most remote parts of nature administer to his pleasures".[6] Der appropriative Blick ist freilich charakteristisch nicht nur
für die Landschaft, sondern die moderne Welterfahrung schlechthin.
Bei Goethe freuen sich die Zuschauer über die ihnen vom weitgereisten
Besucher dargebotenen Schätze, die es ihnen ermöglichen, "hier in
ihrer Einsamkeit die Welt so bequem zu durchreisen, Ufer und Häfen,
Berge, Seen und Flüsse, Städte, Kastelle und manches andre Lokal, das
in der Geschichte einen Namen hat, vor sich vorbeiziehen zu sehen".
(II, 10; S. 466f.) Die in Bilder eingefangene Welt kann jederzeit und
allenorts und jedermann zugänglich gemacht werden.

Aber ihre Verfügbarkeit rächt sich an dem, der selbst in ihrer Virtualität aufgeht. Auf die Frage, wo er denn, hätte er die Wahl, am liebsten
zuhause wäre, antwortet der Engländer zunächst mit der "Bequemlich-
keit" seiner Wanderexistenz, in der "andre für mich bauen, pflanzen
und sich häuslich bemühen". Dann aber beklagt er – in Worten, die
dem Gehilfen indirekt recht geben – das Desinteresse seines Sohns an
dem angestammten Besitztum, das der Vater doch nur für ihn "eigentlich [...] eingerichtet, dem ich es zu übergeben, mit dem ich es noch zu
genießen hoffte", der aber nun nach Indien ausgewandert sei:

> Gewiß wir machen viel zu viel vorarbeitenden Aufwand aufs Leben. Anstatt
> daß wir gleich anfingen uns in einem mäßigen Zustand behaglich zu finden,
> so gehen wir immer mehr ins Breite, um es uns immer unbequemer zu ma-
> chen. Wer genießt jetzt meine Gebäude, meinen Park, meine Gärten? Nicht
> ich, nicht einmal die Meinigen; fremde Gäste, Neugierige, unruhige Rei-
> sende. (II, 10; S. 467)

Also Leute wie er selbst, so müssen wir ergänzen. Unstets Reisen,
kolonialer Exotismus und englischer Park verbinden sich zur wurzel-
losen Mobilität der modernen Existenz, die, wieder in den selbstkriti-
schen Worten des Barons, "vielem entsagt, um vieles zu genießen". (II,
10; S. 468) Ottilie charakterisiert ihn als "heimatlos und freundlos", (II,
10; S. 469) wobei sie an ihren Geliebten Eduard denkt, der zur selben
Zeit (im zweiten Teil des Romans) seinen zum englischen Park umge-
schaffenen Stammsitz verlassen hat und unbehaust umherstreift.

Erinnern wir uns hier, daß es auch in Eduards und Charlottes Schloß

---

[6] Addison A.a.O. S. 278.

einen Erben gibt, der sein Erbe nie antreten wird, der gewissermaßen eine innere exotische Kolonie repräsentiert, in der er als Bild – als Phantasma eines zügellosen Begehrens – gezeugt wurde. Seine imaginäre Mutter Ottilie, selbst eltern- und herkunftslos, wird ihn im Park jenes Anwesens herumtragen, in das sie vor einem Jahr selbst "als Fremdling" eingetreten war und in dem sie nun, zusammen mit den neugepflanzten Blumen und Sträuchern, Wurzel geschlagen zu haben scheint: "Wenn sie um sich her sah, so verbarg sie sich nicht, zu welchem großen reichen Zustande das Kind geboren sei: denn fast alles wohin das Auge blickte, sollte dereinst ihm gehören". (II, 9; S. 461) Wir wissen, daß es anders kommt: Der Erbe wird in dem neu angelegten See ertrinken, und Ottilie wird sich zu dem Bild verzehren, in das Bild entrückt werden, das sie für den Roman und seine (männlichen) Figuren von Anfang an repräsentierte. Hierauf werde ich zurückkommen.

II

Bildwerdung bedeutet in Goethes Roman sowohl Verarmung wie Bereicherung. Dem Dahinschwinden gelebter Substanz entspricht die Weite der medial herangeholten Räume (wie der Zeiten, vgl. die historistische Renovierung der "altdeutschen" Kapelle), aber zugleich auch die Tiefe der so eröffneten Innerlichkeit. Wie beides zusammenhängt, wie Erweiterung und Entleerung ineinander greifen, kann mit Bezug auf unseren Gegenstand an dem Beginn des Romans aufgezeigt werden.

Vom Begründer der englischen Parkbewegung, William Kent, hieß es in einem vielzitierten Satz, er habe den Zaun – das heißt die Einzäunung des formalen, französischen Gartentyps – übersprungen und die freie Natur als Garten entdeckt.[7] Diesen symbolischen Einschnitt der Gartengeschichte inszeniert Goethe hundert Jahre später als einen sehr ambivalenten Befreiungsakt.[8] Die ersten Sätzen und Abschnitte

---

[7] Horace Walpole: Über die neuere Gartenkunst. In: *Historische, litterarische und unterhaltende Schriften übersetzt von A.W. Schlegel.* Leipzig 1800, S. 384-443 (zuerst als "Essay on Gardening", 1770). Hier zitiert nach Hans-Joachim Possin: *Natur und Landschaft bei Addison.* Tübingen 1965. S. 54 ("He leaped the fence and saw that all Nature was a Garden").
[8] Überhaupt kann man in der Darstellung des englischen Parks bei Goethe eine kritische Rücknahme des befreienden Gestus sehen, der im Ursprung der modernen Naturerfahrung erkennbar ist; der "Gestus des Hinaustretens", von

des Textes markieren den Bruch zwischen dem Alten und dem Neuen
so unauffällig wie unmißverständlich. Eduard, der "reiche Baron im
besten Mannesalter", war soeben in seiner Baumschule gärtnerisch
tätig, als er das Werkzeug zusammenlegt und nach "drüben in den
neuen Anlagen", auf der anderen Seite des Baches hinstrebt, wo seine
Frau eine Aussichtshütte fertiggestellt hat. "Man hat einen vortreffli-
chen Anblick", lobt der hinzugekommene Gärtner: "unten das Dorf, ein
wenig rechter Hand die Kirche, über deren Turmspitze man fast hin-
wegsieht; gegenüber das Schloß und die Gärten". (I, 1; S. 271)
    Von jetzt an, so läßt sich sagen, nimmt das Unheil seinen Lauf. Der
Sündenfall besteht darin, daß der praktische Umgang mit der Natur
durch ihren ästhetischen Anblick ersetzt wird.[9] Eduard wird aus seinem
Mittelpunkt heraus ins Grenzenlose gezogen, das sich schon bald aus
der Energie erotischer Passion speist. Er lebt nicht mehr *in* Schloß,
Garten, Dorf und Kirche, sondern steht ihnen exzentrisch *gegenüber*;

---

dem Adorno in diesem Zusammenhang spricht (*Ästhetische Theorie*. Frankfurt
a.M. 1970. S. 100f.), wird in den *Wahlverwandtschaften* zu einem Gestus des
"Übertretens", der gefährlichen Entgrenzung und Entfesselung. Dagegen hatte
insbesondere die frühe europäische Aufklärung sich im Gang "ins Freie",
hinaus vor die Tore der Stadt und in die offene Natur eins ihrer bedeutsamen
Symbole gegeben.
[9] Daß dies mit der bekannten Deutung der modernen Landschaft durch
Joachim Ritter übereinstimmt, sei wenigstens erwähnt. Für Ritter ist die – erst
durch die moderne Naturbeherrschung möglich gewordene – ästhetisch
distanzierte Vergegenständlichung der Natur im Bild konstitutiv; hierfür sind
übrigens Aufstieg sowie Rundblick 'von oben' wesentliche Momente, die er
als eine Kompensation für die verlorene antik-mittelalterliche Kosmosschau –
theoría thu kosmou – deutet. Wenn die Mooshütte aus ihren vier Fenstern
einen (symbolisch) gottgleichen Ausblick bietet, so entspricht dies freilich
einem (hier nur angedeuteten) hybriden neuzeitlichen Anspruch, wie er in der
Philemon und Baucis-Episode des *Faust. Zweiter Teil* mit katastrophalem
Ergebnis (Fausts Erblindung und Tod) ausgetragen wird (hierzu vgl. Verf.:
Utopie und Landschaft im 18. Jahrhundert. In: *Utopieforschung.*
Interdisziplinäre Studien zur neuzeitlichen Utopie. Hg. von Wilhelm
Voßkamp. Frankfurt a.M. 1985. Bd. 3. S. 172-190, hier S. 182f.) Ein weiterer
Paralleltext ist die *Novelle* von 1827, wo ebenfalls der Perspektivwechsel
zwischen altem und neuem Schloß (die Ästhetisierung der "alten Stammburg"
zum Bild) als Indikator eines sozialgeschichtlichen Umbruchs fungiert. –
Joachim Ritter: Landschaft. Zur Funktion des Ästhetischen in der modernen
Gesellschaft. In: *Subjektivität. Sechs Aufsätze*. Frankfurt a.M. 1974. S. 141-
163.

folgerichtig wird er sie einmal ganz verlassen und erst im Tod wieder in sie als ästhetisch irrealisierten Raum eingehen. Ebenso lösen sich die "neuen Anlagen" von ihrer Ausrichtung auf die alte Umgebung, die sie auf der anderen Seite des Hügels im Tal zwischen Teichen und Felsen aus dem Blick verlieren. Sie folgen der Blicklinie, die Charlottes Hütte geöffnet hat. "Dann", so hatte der Gärtner den geschilderten Nahblick in die Weite hinein fortgesetzt, "öffnet sich rechts das Tal und man sieht über die reichen Baumwiesen in eine heitere Ferne". (Ebd.) Der entgrenzten Landschaft entspricht das entbundene Begehren; und beides entspricht, um es zu wiederholen, einer dynamisierten, in grenzenlose Bewegung versetzten Welt.

Auffällig ist, was man die 'Mittelbarkeitsstruktur' dieser Eingangsszene nennen könnte. Dem zufrieden zurücktretenden Blick auf die getane Arbeit – bezeichnenderweise handelt es sich um das Anbringen "frisch erhaltener Pfropfreiser auf junge Stämme"[10] – folgt die Schilderung des Gärtners, die Eduard in eine vorgestellte Perspektive versetzt, bevor er dem vorausgeschickten Boten selbst auf dem angezeigten Weg zur Hütte folgt und die beschriebene Aussicht mit eigenen Augen genießt. Dort findet sodann die Unterredung über die Einladung des "Dritten" – des Hauptmanns – statt, dem eine Vierte – Ottilie – zur Seite gesetzt wird; wobei erstmals Schrift und Briefe ins Spiel kommen, die im Laufe des Romans eine so bedeutsame Rolle entfalten werden. Diese gewünschte – und gefürchtete – Ergänzung der Hausgemeinschaft, die einen empfundenen Mangel zugleich anzeigt und schafft, wird ihrerseits ergänzt durch den Wunsch nach Übersicht der gegenwärtigen und vergangenenen Lebensverhältnisse. Charlotte macht den Anfang, indem sie den weiblichen Drang, wie sie sagt, auf das "Zusammenhängende" auf ihre Spätehe anwendet und den Wunsch äußert, ihrer beider getrennte Vergangenheiten aus Tagebüchern und

---

[10] Die Interpreten haben diesem kleinen Umstand häufiger ihre Beachtung geschenkt. Neben dem symbolischen Bezug auf Eduards Spätehe mit der Jugendgeliebten Charlotte und der Vorausdeutung auf seine Beziehung zur jungen Ottilie ist in unserem Zusammenhang wichtig die kunstvolle Bearbeitung der Natur, die hier genau als ein "Aufpfropfen", gewissermaßen eine Adoption erscheint; zu beachten ist auch, daß die Reiser "frisch erhalten", also von außen kommen, d.h. zu der hier hervorgehobenen Mittelbarkeit passen. – Schließlich ist die symbolische Analogie zur Namensgebung hervorzuheben: "Eduard – so nennen wir [...]" – der Erzähler setzt ein mit dem willkürlichen (pfropfenden) Akt der Namensgebung, die bekanntlich in ein weitverzweigtes Netz von Verweisungen führt.

anderen "Papieren" jetzt gemeinsam in "ordentlicher Folge" als ein "erfreuliches Ganze zusammenzustellen", um derart "die Welt, die wir zusammen nicht sehen sollten, in der Erinnerung zu durchreisen". (I, 1; S. 275) Ist hiermit nicht bereits die Entwicklung eingeleitet, an deren Ende Ottilie der "häusliche Zirkel" nur noch "als ein Scheinbild des vorigen Lebens" erscheinen will? (II, 17; S. 517) Demselben Wunsch nach imaginärer Ganzheitsherstellung folgt Eduard, indem er seinen Besitz in gemeinsamen Begehungen mit dem Freund neu erobert und sich nun erst richtig, wie er meint, zueigen macht.

Das beginnt damit, daß der Hauptmann über den Aussichtspunkt von Charlottes Mooshütte hinausgeführt wird, "damit er", wie Eduard sagt, "nicht glaube, dieses beschränkte Tal nur sei unser Erbgut und Aufenthalt; der Blick wird oben freier und die Brust erweitert sich". (I, 3; S. 289) Der ästhetische Weitblick wird sogleich überführt in die systematische Landvermessung des "Erbguts", das Eduard nun "auf das deutlichste, aus dem Papier, wie eine neue Schöpfung, hervorgewachsen" erscheint und das er "jetzt erst recht kennen zu lernen", das ihm "jetzt erst recht zu gehören" glaubt. (I, 3; S. 290) Ästhetische und kartographische Objektivation der Natur gehen Hand in Hand, wie das auch kulturhistorisch für den englischen Landschaftspark nachweisbar ist. Nicht lange darauf – Ottilie ist mittlerweile angekommen, deren Anblick sogleich mit der schönen Ganzheit des Parkprojekts verbunden wird;[11] und die Reformierung des Dorfs wird in Angriff genommen, die nun auch die soziale Realität in die Bildschöpfung einbezieht – unterhält man sich damit, die geodetische Bestandsaufnahme neben "die englischen Parkbeschreibungen mit Kupfern" zu legen. "Man muß es erst problematisch und nur wie zum Scherz behandeln; der Ernst wird sich schon finden", so sagt Eduard, (I, 6; S. 318) der damit den Romanverlauf vorwegnimmt: nämlich das Spiel mit dem ererbten Grund und Boden, der bald in den tödlichen Ernst des Verlusts umschlägt.

Von jeher hat die berühmte Gleichnisrede des vierten Kapitels die Interpreten beschäftigt, in der man (zurecht) das verrätselte Konstruktionsprinzip des Romans angesprochen sah. Die andere

---

[11] Wie sehr der Park ein Bild der Ganzheit bieten soll, geht aus vielen Stellen hervor, beispielsweise der folgenden, die sich auf das neue Lusthaus und seine Umgebung bezieht (II, 10. S. 464): "Alles störend Kleinliche war rings umher entfernt; alles Gute der Landschaft, was die Natur, was die Zeit daran getan hatte, trat reinlich hervor und fiel ins Auge, und schon grünten die jungen Pflanzungen, die bestimmt waren, einige Lücken auszufüllen und die abgesonderten Teile angenehm zu verbinden".

"Abendunterhaltung" mit den Parkbüchern, die zwei Kapitel später stattfindet, hat den Vorteil, daß sie offensichtlicher, buchstäblich oberflächlich ist. Das setzt ihre symbolische Relevanz für die Romanhandlung nicht herab. Man schlägt die Parkbücher auf,

> worin man jedesmal den Grundriß der Gegend und ihre landschaftliche Ansicht in ihrem ersten rohen Naturzustande gezeichnet sah, sodann auf andern Blättern die Veränderung vorgestellt fand, welche die Kunst daran vorgenommen, um alles das bestehende Gute zu nutzen und zu steigern. Hievon war der Übergang zur eigenen Besitzung, zur eignen Umgebung, und zu dem was man daran ausbilden könnte, sehr leicht. (I, 6; S. 318)

Es entsprach einem gartenplanerischen Verfahren, die Karte einer bestehenden Lage mit transparenten Umgestaltungsentwürfen zu überdecken, bzw. auf die Pläne fremder Parkanlagen zum Vergleich die eigenen zu legen.[12] Nichts könnte die 'Mobilisierung' des (eben nur scheinbar) Festen, des Grunds und Bodens, deutlicher manifestieren. Das Wiedererstehen des "Erbguts" als eine "aus dem Papier" "hervorgewachsene" "neue Schöpfung" wird in Goethes Werk darüberhinaus zur selbstreflexiven Spiegelung der eigenen Romanfiktion, die die experimentelle Versuchsanordnung der Gleichnisrede auf der landschaftlichen Symbolebene aufgreift. Der Raum wird verschoben, er wird aufgelöst in virtuellen Szenerien.

In den derart beweglich gemachten Landschaftsraum, den die Figuren der *Wahlverwandtschaften* sich er-spazieren, zeichnen sie ihre Wünsche ein. So wird das Spiel mit der Karte zum Ernst der Leidenschaft. Der Wendepunkt ist dabei die Entscheidung, das neue "Lusthaus" nicht in Sichtweite des Schlosses und ihm gegenüber, sondern auf dem jenseitigen Abhang des Hügels zu errichten. Der Hauptmann wollte es dagegen in ein Ensemble mit dem bestehenden Schloßgebäude einbinden: es "sollte einen Bezug aufs Schloß haben, aus den Schloßfenstern sollte man es übersehen, von dorther Schloß und Gärten wieder bestreichen können". (I, 6; S.318) Das entspricht seiner ursprünglichen Absicht mit der gesamten Parkanlage, die er als erweiterten geselligen Raum konzipiert und "auf ein ruhig freundliches Zusammenleben berechnet" hatte. (I, 13) Ottilie ist es, die das Lusthaus ausdrücklich *außer* "Bezug" zum Herrschaftsgebäude setzen will; sie faßt die Idee, als die Gesellschaft den erwähnten Mühlenspaziergang in einem anmutig-geselligen Schlängelpfad zu verewigen gedenkt. Damit ist die wohlmeinende Absicht des Parkarchitekten bereits grundsätzlich

---

[12] Vgl. S. Gerndt a.a.O. S. 195, Anm. 22.

durchkreuzt:

> Ich würde, sagte Ottilie, indem sie den Finger auf die höchste Fläche der Anhöhe setzte, das Haus hieher bauen. Man sähe zwar das Schloß nicht: denn es wird von dem Wäldchen bedeckt; aber man befände sich auch dafür wie in einer andern und neuen Welt, indem zugleich das Dorf und alle Wohnungen verborgen wären. Die Aussicht auf die Teiche, nach der Mühle, auf die Höhen, in die Gebirge, nach dem Lande zu, ist außerordentlich schön [...]. (I, 7; S. 325f.)

Die damit von Ottilie ins Leben gerufene neue und andere Welt führt doch nur konsequent fort, was Charlottes Mooshütte begonnen hatte. Es handelt sich um eine Welt der gesellschaftsabgewandten Leidenschaft, die sich einem gewaltsamen initiierenden Akt voluntaristischer Setzung verdankt; Eduard, heißt es, "nahm einen Bleistift und strich ein längliches Viereck recht stark und derb auf die Höhe". Der Hauptmann verbirgt den Unmut über diese Verunstaltung seines "sorgfältigen, reinlich gezeichneten Plans" hinter diplomatischer Zustimmung, die typisch ist für den Gesellschaftston des Romans, unter dem sich das Unheil vorbereitet: "Wir verlangen Abwechselung und fremde Gegenstände", konzediert er dem Vorschlag, und rationalisiert weiter: "Das Schloß haben die Alten mit Vernunft hieher gebaut: denn es liegt geschützt vor den Winden, und nah an allen täglichen Bedürfnissen" usw. (I, 7; S. 326) – aber das alles, so ist zu ergänzen, genügt nun nicht mehr, man will das Andere und Ferne, den ästhetischen Exotismus, den Übertritt aus der gewohnten in eine fremde imaginäre Welt – eine Welt, die zugleich die Welt des Goetheschen Romans selbst ist.

III

Der Landschaftspark der *Wahlverwandtschaften* ist das herausragende Beispiel für die von vielen neueren Analysen hervorgehobene selbstreferentielle Schicht des Romans, die er andererseits eng mit der dargestellten Welt verknüpft. Er manifestiert das, was man "Goethes bemerkenswerte Gabe" genannt hat, "allegorisches Emblem und Treue gegenüber dem stilistischen Dekorum des Realismus zu vereinbaren".[13] Das soll zum Abschluß an einem Tagebucheintrag Ottiliens gezeigt

---

[13] J. Hillis Miller: Interlude as Anastomosis in *Die Wahlverwandtschaften*. In: *Goethe-Yearbook* 6 (1992). S. 115-122, hier S. 117 ("Goethe's extraordinary gift for reconciling allegorical emblem and obedience to the stylistic decorums of realism").

werden, der für die bisher skizzierte Thematik relevant erscheint. Gemeint ist der Eintrag mit dem berühmt gewordenen Diktum "Es wandelt niemand ungestraft unter Palmen".[14] Er befindet sich zwischen zwei Kapiteln, in denen pädagogische Probleme der Moderne erörtert werden: Wie sind Kinder auf eine offene Welt vorzubereiten, ohne sie "ins Grenzenlose" zu treiben; wie ist die Kontinuität der Generationen (und besonders zwischen Vater und Sohn) angesichts einer beschleunigten historischen Entwicklung zu wahren, wie ist Treue zur Herkunft mit der Freiheit des Individuums zu vereinbaren? Diese theoretischen Fragen bereiten die Geburt des Erben Ottos vor. (II, 7 und 8)

Ottilies Eintrag entzündet sich an ihrem Abscheu gegen Abbildungen von Affen und allgemeiner gegen "Karikaturen und Zerrbilder". (II, 7; S. 451) Sie fühlt sich hierin bestärkt durch die (bereits zitierte) Meinung des "guten Gehülfen", daß den Menschen nur seine unmittelbar lebendige Naturumgebung interessieren sollte. Wenig später (II, 9) wird, wiederum im Zusammenhang mit der Kindererziehung und Otto, eine ähnliche Stellungnahme des Gärtners gegen die modische exotische Bepflanzung angeführt, wie sie für den englischen Park typisch war und ihm von seiner Herrschaft jetzt aufgezwungen wird: "er [der Gärtner] hatte vor dem unendlichen Felde [!] der Botanik [...] und den darin herumsummenden Namen, eine Art von Scheu, die ihn verdrießlich machte". (II, 9; S. 460) Für Ottilie sind offensichtlich alle exotischen Lebewesen Karikaturen – bloße Zeichen ohne lebensweltliche Bedeutung. Mit dem Gehilfen fragt sie sich, "ob nicht ein jedes fremde, aus seiner Umgebung gerissene Geschöpf einen gewissen ängstlichen Eindruck auf uns macht, der nur durch Gewohnheit abgestumpft wird. Es gehört schon ein buntes geräuschvolles Leben dazu [hier ist an die lärmende Affenliebhaberin Luciane gedacht], um Affen, Papageien und Mohren um sich zu ertragen". (II, 7; S. 452) Aber Ottilie ist selbst ein fremdes, aus seiner Umgebung gerissenes Geschöpf; oder vielmehr, sie ist das "Geschöpf" ohne angestammte Umgebung, die ihre Wahlheimat in der Liebe findet, der jeder feste lebensweltliche 'Boden' fehlt und – das ist entscheidend – nach ihrem eigenen Willen auch fehlen soll. Als sie den Säugling durch sein künftiges Erbe trägt, verschmilzt ihr die Vision des fremden Eigentums und der fremden Genealogie mit dem

[14] Kulturhistorischen Hintergrund und Nachleben dieses Zitats und seines Kontextes leuchtet ausführlich aus: Gerhard Schulz: "Es wandelt niemand ungestraft unter Palmen". Über Goethe, Alexander von Humboldt und einen Satz aus den *Wahlverwandtschaften*. In: ders.: *Exotik der Gefühle. Goethe und seine Deutschen*. München 1998. S. 48-74.

Gefühl ihres eigenen Dahinschwindens; es ist, als ob sie ihr Blut an das
Leben des vorgestellten Bildes abgäbe:

> Ottilie fühlte dies alles so rein, daß sie sich's als entschieden wirklich
> dachte und sich selbst dabei gar nicht empfand. Unter diesem klaren Him-
> mel, bei diesem hellen Sonnenschein, ward es ihr auf einmal klar, daß ihre
> Liebe, um sich zu vollenden, völlig uneigennützig werden müsse [...]. (II, 9;
> S. 461)

Ottilie, die Waise und Fremde, ist zugleich der exzentrische Mittelpunkt einer eigenen, "zusammenhängenden" Welt. Sie verkörpert in
ihrem *Sein* und von Anfang an, was die anderen Figuren, vor allem das
grundherrliche Paar, erst *werden*, indem sie ihre überkommene Welt
überschreiten und zerstören. Dies macht ihre Bedeutung aus für die
Romanfiktion, begreift man diese im emphatischen Sinne der selbstreflexiven Konstruktion. Ottilie ist das reine Bild, in dem die Realität
zugunsten eines neuen Eigenlebens ausgelöscht ist.

In diesem Sinne scheint mir die Fortsetzung des fraglichen Eintrags
deutbar, die den Abscheu vor dem Exotischen relativiert und schließlich sogar zurücknimmt. Zunächst beruft die Schreibende den "Reisenden [...], der solche [exotischen] Wunder mit andern Wundern in lebendiger alltäglicher Verbindung sieht", der also, um in unserer Terminologie zu bleiben, das Exotische in seinen ursprünglichen Kontext zu-
rückversetzt. Freilich – und hier kommt das Zitat –: "Aber auch er wird
ein anderer Mensch. Es wandelt niemand ungestraft unter Palmen, und
die Gesinnungen ändern sich gewiß in einem Lande wo Elephanten und
Tiger zu Hause sind". (II, 7; S. 452) Nur um den Preis der *eigenen*
Selbstentfremdung, indem er sich an das Andere und Fremde anpaßt
und so selbst ein Anderer wird, kann der Reisende die exotischen Phänomene integrieren. Aber Ottilie bleibt hier nicht stehen. Es folgt der
Gedanke einer darstellerischen Rekontextualisierung, gewissermaßen
einer sekundären Einwurzelung des lebensweltlich fernen, von der
lebendigen Erfahrung isolierten, unzusammenhängenden Wissensstoffs,
wofür ihr (und hinter ihr dem Autor Goethe) das Beispiel des Naturfor-
schers und Reisenden Alexander von Humboldt steht, "der uns das
Fremdeste, Seltsamste, mit seiner Lokalität, mit aller Nachbarschaft,
jedesmal in dem eigensten Elemente zu schildern und darzustellen
weiß".

Vergessen wir nicht, daß Ottilie eifrige Leserin von exotischen
Reisebeschreibungen ist; mit einem solchen Buch in der Hand, wird sie
in dem Kahn verunglücken und den Tod des Kindes, das sie im selben

Arm trägt und daher nicht festhalten kann, verursachen. Ottilie, der heilende Smaragd und "wahre Augentrost", der den Menschen (Mann) "mit sich selbst und mit der Welt in Übereinstimmung" bringt (I, 6; S. 313), die alles zusammenfügt, so wie sie selbst nichts Unzusammenhängendes aufnehmen kann, Ottilie, die zum Schluß als Heilige und heiliges Bild verehrt wird: sie ist der Spiegel, in dem sich die moderne Fiktion als die grenzenlose Produktion des Imaginären erkennt, die das Reale als bloßes Stückwerk aufzehrt.

Als verkörpertes *Prinzip* des Parks gehört sie daher auch nur am Rande – exzentrisch – dessen *Raum* an, an dessen Planung sie am wenigsten beteiligt ist (bis auf die allerdings bedeutsame Bestimmung der Lage des Lusthauses, dem Haus der imaginären Zeugung und Geburt des Romanerben). Am liebsten hält sie sich im Innern des Hauses auf. Ebensowenig nimmt sie Anteil an der Kirchhof-Umgestaltung, nicht einmal an der Kapellenrenovierung, die vielmehr die Romanhandlung für sie schafft. Charlotte ist es, die den ersten Anstoß zur Parkgestaltung gegeben und damit den Ersatz der feudalen Welt durch deren ästhetischen Anblick eingeleitet hatte, die auch den zweiten Teil einleitet mit der Planierung der Grabstätten und sakralen Grabdenkmäler, die ins bloße Medium des Bildes und Gedächtnisses verflüchtigt werden: "Das reine Gefühl einer endlichen allgemeinen Gleichheit, wenigstens nach dem Tode, scheint mir beruhigender als dieses eigensinnige starre Fortsetzen unserer Persönlichkeiten, Anhänglichkeiten und Lebensverhältnisse". (II, 1; S. 397) Auch die Toten werden – entkörperlicht – in den Landschaftspark versetzt; völlig konsequent, wo dieser das scheinhafte Bild realer "Lebensverhältnisse" stellt; aber auch konsequent, daß die bildhafte Ottilie schließlich in seiner reinen Medialität aufgeht.

In der Figur der Ottilie wird evident, daß der Roman, der die imaginäre Entgrenzung der Moderne zum Thema hat, zugleich selbst an ihr teilhat. Man mag das auch als ein Stück Selbstgericht, zumindest eine kritische Selbstspiegelung des Autors Goethe sehen. Die Aufzehrung des gegebenen Realen durch eine verselbständigte Einbildungskraft hatte sich bereits in der Epoche der europäischen Empfindsamkeit und deren radikaler Version im deutschen Sturm und Drang artikuliert; Goethes Jugendroman *Werther* war ein maßgebliches Zeugnis hierfür. Freilich hatte sich dort die entbundene Phantasie des Subjekts noch als schöpferische Entbindung einer ontologisch verstandenen 'Natur' verstehen wollen. Nun verweist die autonome Einbildungskraft nicht mehr auf eine intensivere, vollere, wahrere Wirklichkeit hinter der scheinhaften Fassade der approbierten Realität, sondern sie setzt sich an deren Stelle. Die Natur verschwindet im Park, der sie nur noch darstellt; das Reale im Imaginären. Die Realität der Moderne erkennt sich im Spiegel der Virtualität, an der die Literatur partizipiert.

Susan Kassouf

Textuality and Manliness: Heinrich von Kleist's *Michael Kohlhaas* (1810) and the Journal *Phöbus**

Michael Kohlhaas *(1810) is usually read as the story of a man who demands his rights, and finally – albeit strangely – receives them. In contrast, the following reading emphasizes the emergence and disappearance of texts in the piece as they relate to masculinity. Placing* Kohlhaas *in its original context, namely the journal* Phöbus, *we can see a continuum that ranges from manly ideals in the journal to the ambivalences informing this ideal in the literary text.*

The transition to a textual age and the relative proliferation of written material during the late 18th and early 19th centuries gave rise to numerous discussions on and within the newly emergent literary sphere. Literary culture continually reflected on the textual medium as its dominant means of representation and communication; the materiality of the text became a sometimes explicit and sometimes tacit focal point for those participating in the production, reception and circulation of (literary) texts. The more the writers' world revolved around less controllable concerns of profit, career and production, the more their discourse emphasized arguably immaterial and stable values of freedom, honor and patriotism. [1] This denial of the material can be observed on an explicitly aesthetic level as well: the means of communication became the "silenced underground of writing"[2] around 1800, functioning as a measure of ex- or inclusion in the literary sphere. Whereas the material-

---

* I would like to thank Christine Havelock and Brian Lukacher for their helpful guidance in art history, and Jeffrey Schneider and Silke von der Emde for their encouragement, critique and suggestions.
[1] Ute Frevert: *Ehrenmänner. Das Duell in der bürgerlichen Gesellschaft.* Munich 1991. P. 153. See also Heinrich Bosse: *Autorschaft ist Werkherrschaft. Über die Entstehung des Urheberrechts aus dem Geist der Goethezeit.* Paderborn 1981; Friedrich Kittler: *Aufschreibesysteme 1800/1900.* Munich 1987; and Dorothea von Mücke: *Virtue and the Veil of Illusion. Generic Innovation and the Pedagogical Project in Eighteenth-Century Literature.* Stanford 1991.
[2] Barbara Hahn: 'Weiber verstehen alles à la lettre'. Briefkultur im beginnenden 19. Jahrhundert. In: *Deutsche Literatur von Frauen.* Ed. Gisela Brinker-Gabler. Munich 1988. Vol. 2. P. 23.

ity of writing often was projected onto women, in this essay I explore the meaning of immateriality for discourses of manliness.

The assertion that discourses on gender difference and textuality are inextricably linked around 1800 informs my reading of the journal *Phöbus* and Kleist's narrative *Michael Kohlhaas*. Constructions of gender among the bourgeoisie are simultaneously literary phenomena, just as constructions of literary culture are irrevocably gendered.[3] During the late 18th and early 19th centuries discourses on masculinity competed with each other, only to become more codified in the course of the 19th century.[4] So prevalent during the late Enlightenment and the Napoleonic Wars, as opposed to the possibly less stringent conceptions of Romanticism or *Empfindsamkeit*, "manliness" describes what developed into bourgeois normative ideals of male behavior. "Manly men" were seen as physically and mentally more powerful than women; their attributes included a readiness for battle, controlled aggression and a unity of spirit with a hard body.[5] Coupled with the discursive denial of the textual aspects of the writer's profession, these gendered characteristics served to construct the literary sphere as one composed of manly, spiritual or immaterial [*geistig*] men, a construction that allowed for a functioning, if illusory, stability.

Ferdinand Hartmann's image *Phöbus über Dresden* evokes this illusory stability by recalling the philhellenic tradition, a tradition made popular by the aesthetic writings of J.J. Winckelmann.[6] Origi-

---

[3] This assertion is explored (and explained) more fully in my dissertation, *Writing Masculinities Around 1800*. Diss. Cornell U, 1996. Ann Arbor 1997.

[4] As Britta Herrmann eloquently shows, Kleist struggled with all of these definitions: late Enlightenment conceptions, however, appear most relevant to the present discussion. To my knowledge, the importance of manliness for the Romantic era has yet to be explored in depth. See Britta Herrmann: Auf der Suche nach dem sicheren Geschlecht: die Briefe Heinrich von Kleists und Männlichkeit um 1800. In: *Wann ist der Mann ein Mann? Zur Geschichte der Männlichkeit*. Ed. Walter Erhart and Britta Herrmann. Stuttgart 1997. Pp. 212-234.

[5] See George Mosse: *The Image of Man. The Creation of Modern Masculinity*. New York 1996.

[6] See Alex Potts: *Flesh and the Ideal: Winckelmann and the Origins of Art History*. London 1994 and Suzanne Marchand: *Down from Olympus. Archaeology and Philhellenism in Germany, 1750-1970*. Princeton 1996. [Editor's note: A reproduction of *Phöbus über Dresden* is contained in *Phöbus. Ein Journal für die Kunst* (note 8); unfortunately, we were unable to obtain copyright permission to print the photograph here.] Marchand underlines the importance of philhellenism for Germany at this time by deeming it a "cultural obsession". While clearly more is at stake in Hartmann's allegorical

nally planned as a theater curtain design, *Phöbus über Dresden* graced the first five covers of the almost eponymous journal *Phöbus*, founded by Heinrich von Kleist and Adam Müller in 1808. The sixth edition, which contained the original version of *Michael Kohlhaas*, appeared without this cover, as if a textual horse dealer, namely Kohlhaas himself, had replaced the image of Phöbus, the illustrated horse driver.[7] Driving his four horses toward the viewer, Hartmann's Phöbus occupies, without dominating, the center. His placement in front of the sun visually underlines what Kleist described as his "rather boldly chosen" Grecian name, meaning light.[8] The calm, disinterested stance, underlined by the uneven distribution of weight in his hips, belies the control needed to reign in his rearing steeds. Relaxed, outstretched arms speak to this fantastical lack of tension and strain in his body; indeed, his cloak proves much more mobile than he himself. His posture evokes the pose of the Apollo Belvedere (Figure 1), a figure considered the quintessence of ideal masculinity during this Graecophilic era.[9] True to the oft-cited Winckelmannian ideal of "noble simplicity" and "serene grandeur", this athletic and self-sufficient hero rests in a state of tranquillity, undisturbed by passion or conflict; he seems the most still of all the figures in Hartmann's picture. Unlike that of "manly men" later in the nineteenth century, his strength expresses an indirect potential, even a softer power. We see beauty, grace and effeminate youth, as opposed to any brute strength or virile manliness.

---

illustration, in this reading my focus remains on the figure Phöbus and its philhellenic connotations.

[7] Helmut Sembdner: Anmerkungen. In: *Sämtliche Werke und Briefe* by Heinrich von Kleist. Vol. 2. Munich 1984. P. 962. Future references to Kleist's collected works will be indicated by volume and page number.

[8] "Ein wenig dreist gewählt" is how Kleist describes the title in a letter to Goethe of January 24, 1807. Heinrich von Kleist and Adam Müller: *Phöbus. Ein Journal für die Kunst*. Ed. Helmut Sembdner. Darmstadt 1961. P. 614. All translations are my own.

[9] Winckelmann's description of the Apollo Belevedere seems to capture Hartmann's Phöbus as well: "His build is sublimely superhuman, and his stance bears witness to the fullness of his grandeur. An eternal springtime, as if in blissful Elysium, clothes the charming manliness of maturity with graceful youthfulness and plays with soft tenderness on the proud build of his limbs". Quoted in Potts. P. 118.

Kleist christens his first edition of *Phöbus* with a prologue and epilogue that refer unmistakably to the cover picture.[10] Equally unmistakably, Kleist's reading differs radically from the philhellenic tradition to which the image speaks. In order to indicate the journal's explosive arrival, Kleist greets in verse the elemental strength and the colossal onward-and-upward movements of Phöbus with cries of "storm in" [*wettre hinein*] and "thunder along" [*donner einher*]. Despite the tranquillity of Hartmann's figure, he asserts that Phöbus' activity, here horse driving, stands in opposition to a more passive, aestheticized pose. Celebrating Phöbus' violent physical power, Kleist recontextualizes the "noble simplicity" and "simple grandeur" that the resting philhellenesque figure evokes. The fantasy of the free-standing, elevated self which Phöbus' figure promises seems to allow for these connotations of virile masculinity, indicating that philhellenic and manly masculinity may simply be differences of degree. This shift in emphasis bears witness to the historical changes at the turn of the 19th century. Under the pressure and patriotic fervor of the Napoleonic Wars, German philhellenism underwent a transformation. A more tranquil, even effeminate masculinity gave way to a more obviously virile one, one that theoretically could help Germany liberate itself from French domination.[11] To some extent, the newly prevalent nationalistic sentiments enabled Kleist's creative "reading" of Hartmann's image. Both he and Müller[12] employed the contemporary ideals of a virile and nationalistic masculinity to solicit subscribers for the journal and to establish what they believed to be a new, aesthetic community.

In the journal's initial prospectus, Kleist's descriptions of the journal *Phöbus* denigrate the tranquillity of the more classical era

---

[10] Collaboration between the visual arts and the written word was one of the founding motives of the journal. Helmut Sembdner: Zur Geschichte der Zeitschrift. In: *Phöbus* P. 604.

[11] In terms of Kleist's own biography, and his well-known struggle to find stable, (socially and personally) acceptable ways of being both a gendered and sexual being, the muted homoerotics to which a Winckelmannian figure such as Phöbus speaks might have given the author pause. Whereas Kleist was willing to express "Grecian" feelings in his loving letter to Ernst von Pfuel (January 7, 1805), the more public context of the journal might seem too threatening a venue in which to speak about desire.

[12] To what degree Müller or Kleist contributed to which announcement remains unclear up until today. For example, regarding the authorship of the first *Phöbus* prospectus, one critic asserts that it was written mainly by Adam Müller. Yet Kleist sends this same document in a letter to Cotta (December 22 1807), willing not only to sign his name to it, but to circulate it further. See Helmut Sembdner: Anmerkungen. Vol. 2. P. 961.

back to which the visual image hearkens. Kleist and Müller want to introduce an explicitly Germanic striving to replace what they perceive of as the harmful classical quietude surrounding them (2:446). [13] In a letter to Gentz on the differences between *Phöbus* and *Die Horen*, Müller distinguishes their journal from Schiller's, refusing any comparison whatsoever. [14] Accusing *Die Horen* of willingly degenerating into a stroller's paradise, fit only for leisurely Sundays, Müller rejects that "flaccid" [*schlaff*] view of life which can neither separate so-called art from life nor unify them completely (2:961). Preferring to ignite a sublime battle [*erhabenen Streit*] over and above a more quiet, passive beauty, Kleist and Müller endeavor to sell their journal as an energetic alternative to a cultural (and indolent) decline:

We do not represent the god, whose picture and name protects our exhibitions, as he appears resting, encircled by muses on Mount Parnassus, but rather as he guides his sun-horses in confident clarity [...]. The fine arts will intervene with rigor and seriousness, and without consideration for the playful and shallow spirit of the age. (2:446-7) [15]

Kleist and Müller distinguish themselves here by criticizing Anton Raphael Mengs' rendering of Apollo in *Parnassus*, a painting considered the pinnacle of German classicism. [16]

Though seeking a community, Kleist and Müller reject the notion of a guild as neither artistic nor noble enough. Hoping to create and cultivate an elite, intellectually and culturally active circle of men,

[13] "Die Kunst, in dem Bestreben recht vieler Gleichgesinnter, wenn auch noch so verschieden gestalteter Deutschen darzustellen, ist dem Charakter unsrer Nation angemessener, als wenn wir die Künstler und Kunstkritiker unsrer Zeit in einförmiger Symmetrie und im ruhigen Besitz um irgend einen Gipfel noch so herrlicher Schönheit versammeln möchten".

[14] However, in the original prospectus, Müller and Kleist framed *Phöbus* as a "modified" version of *Die Horen* (2:446). We might understand this bow to the older, more established journal as part of a less antagonistic marketing strategy that drew on readers' predilections.

[15] "Wir stellen den Gott, dessen Bild und Name unsre Ausstellungen beschirmt, nicht dar, wie er in Ruhe im Kreise der Musen auf Parnaß erscheint, sondern vielmehr, wie er in sichrer Klarheit die Sonnenpferde lenkt [...]. Die bildende Kunst wird ohne Rücksicht auf den spielenden und flachen Zeitgeist, mit Strenge und Ernst, [...] eingreifen".

[16] Hubert Schrade: *German Romantic Painting*. Trans. Maria Pelikan. New York 1977. Pp. 9-11. [Editor's note: A reproduction of Mengs' painting is contained in Schrade. Unfortunately, we were unable to obtain copyright permission to print the photograph here.]

they instead promote a unified coalition in which the individual artist and reader bond as a group: "in every way one will see how the unification of art which we have in mind is more valuable to us than the singular works, despite the good and great intentions with which they were written" (2:449). [17] In this typical description, a material culture of texts is downplayed, sacrificed to a more ideal concept of art: Kleist and Müller subordinate the smaller project of singular *written* works for a larger vision of unified *art*.

The other metaphors Kleist and Müller draw on to describe their envisioned artistic community emphasize activity, authenticity and competition: ideals not necessarily supported by Hartmann's image, but ideals essential for manly men of the nascent bourgeoisie and pertinent for a people enmeshed in the Wars of Liberation. [18] Mobilizing a virile, bellicose masculinity, Kleist and Müller want to win not "spoiled, effeminate souls", [*verwöhnte, weichliche Seelen*] but rather "active comrades" [*tätige Genossen*] (2:448). They encourage the submission of very varied works and opinions that lead to good healthy fights and discussions. To uniform symmetry and exquisite beauty, they prefer a level and nationalistic playing field with "artworks of the most opposite forms that need not share anything but strength, clarity and depth, the old established qualities of the Germans" (2:446). [19] Disregarding the lack of discord in Hartmann's image, their magazine encourages conflict: "But as we our-

[17] "Allenthalben wird man sehen, wie die Kunstvereinigung, welche wir im Sinne haben, uns mehr wert sei, als die eignen Arbeiten, in wie guter und großer Absicht sie auch geschrieben wären".

[18] For more on the emergence of sharply defined gender roles based on incommensurable differences during the late 18th and early 19th centuries, see Thomas Laqueur: *Making Sex. Body and Gender from the Greeks to Freud.* Cambridge 1990. For a specifically German context, see: Sylvia Bovenschen: *Die imaginierte Weiblichkeit. Exemplarische Untersuchungen zu kulturgeschichtlichen und literarischen Präsentationsformen des Weiblichen.* Frankfurt a.M. 1979; Barbara Duden: Das schöne Eigentum. Zur Herausbildung des bürgerlichen Frauenbildes an der Wende vom 18. zum 19. Jahrhundert. In: *Kursbuch 47* (1977). Pp. 125-140; Ute Frevert: *Ehrenmänner. Das Duell in der bürgerlichen Gesellschaft.* Munich 1991; Karin Hausen: Die Polarisierung der 'Geschlechtscharaktere' – Eine Spiegelung der Dissoziation von Erwerbs- und Familienleben. In: *Sozialgeschichte der Familie in der Neuzeit Europas.* Ed. Werner Conze. Stuttgart 1976. Pp. 363-393; and Claudia Honegger: *Die Ordnung der Geschlechter. Die Wissenschaften vom Menschen und das Weib 1750-1850.* New York 1991.

[19] "Kunstwerke, von den entgegengesetztesten Formen, welchen nichts gemeinschaftlich zu sein braucht, als Kraft, Klarheit und Tiefe, die alten anerkannten Vorzüge der Deutschen [...]".

selves are armed, so too will we not suffer next to us those unarmed
or only slightly armed on our battlefield which we hereby inaugurate". With militaristic metaphors, they invite only those heavily
armed warriors to compete on their battlefield.[20] The violence which
quietly underlies the Greek figures of Winckelmann's aesthetic is
foregrounded in Kleist and Müller's description.[21]

Admittedly, the journal eventually floundered. Because of insufficient financial backing, lack of support by big aesthetic guns such as
Goethe, and partly because of another philhellenic competitor, the
Viennese journal *Prometheus*, the journal folded soon after it began.[22] Striving for enlightenment and the persecution of all mystical
and tyrannical art authorities, Phöbus lost the fight.[23] Or, as one
contemporary maliciously observed, Phöbus had to shed his horses
and follow on foot the common path of literary progress.[24]

We might understand Kleist's dystopic construction of manliness
and texts in *Michael Kohlhaas* as implicitly related to the journal's
failure, a disappointed response to his unsuccessful attempt to construct a manly cultural community. *Kohlhaas'* appearance coincides
with the shift from the private publication of the journal to the
support of the Waltherschen Hofbuchhandlung in Dresden, a shift
understood by Kleist and Müller, as well as by onlookers, to indicate
the journal's financial failure.[25] Whereas *Phöbus über Dresden* and
Phöbus rely on traditions of philhellenism and manliness, respectively, *Michael Kohlhaas* reveals the ambivalences of these ideals in
a textual context; in *Kohlhaas*, texts come to disrupt conceptions of
a virile masculinity, and the immediacy and activity which they

[20] "Aber wie wir selbst bewaffnetsind, werden wir keinen andern Unbewaff-
neten oder auch nur leicht Bewaffnetenauf dem Kampfplatz, den wir hierdurch
eröffnen, neben uns leiden" (2:447). Ironically, the one known fight inspired by
the journal was a duel between Müller and Kleist. On the quarrels endemic to
their friendship, see Joachim Maass: *Kleist. A Biography.* Trans. Ralph
Manheim. New York 1983. Pp. 181-183.
[21] Both Potts (note 6) and Richter explore the underlying violence and pain of
the Greek figures. Simon Richter: *Laokoon's Body and the Aesthetics of Pain.*
Detroit 1992.
[22] *Phöbus.* Pp. 605-6.
[23] These are Müller's sentiments. *Phöbus.* P. 611.
[24] The words of their somewhat nefarious contemporary Karl August Böttiger
on the journal's first financial fiasco. *Phöbus.* P. 634.
[25] Kreutzer touches upon the relation between the financial failure and the final
version of *Kohlhaas*, but does not note any specific narrative significance.
Helmut Kreutzer: Michael Kohlhaas. In: *Die dichterische Entwicklung Hein-
richs von Kleist. Untersuchungen zu seinen Briefen und zu Chronologie und
Aufbau seiner Werke.* Berlin 1968. P. 251.

promise. The fantasy of gender to which the visual image gestures, and the journal itself speaks, does not emerge as unproblematically within Kleist's *Erzählung* itself. By examining the relation between manliness and texts, I want to "reread" *Michael Kohlhaas*, the other horse driver in question, in a gendered and textual context, as well as suggest a fundamental connection between the aesthetic set up in the image *Phöbus über Dresden* and in the journal *Phöbus*.

Heinrich von Kleist's *Michael Kohlhaas* is usually read as the story of a man who demands his rights, and finally receives them, if in a twisted sort of way. Traveling with two horses, the horse dealer is illegally stopped by a certain Junker named von Tronka. While von Tronka forces Kohlhaas to get hold of a permit for passage, his two horses must remain with the Junker as collateral. After discovering this permit requirement to be a farce, Kohlhaas returns, only to find that his horses have been worked almost to death. Kohlhaas takes legal action against the Junker; yet after a year of hesitation on the part of the government, he learns that von Tronka has shot down the suit through various connections. Lisbeth, Kohlhaas' wife, tries to help by attempting to bring his case directly before the sovereign. The attempt proves deadly for her when an overzealous guard hits her with his lance shaft. Overcome with grief and fury, the widowed Kohlhaas now attacks Tronkenburg and its occupants, ravaging the countryside with a murderous band of men. News of his terrible reign spreads; even Martin Luther will scold Kohlhaas, first in a letter and then in person. Luther negotiates an amnesty for Kohlhaas, whose conditions the government does not keep. Kohlhaas not only experiences trouble with those in positions of religious or political authority; he must also contend with unscrupulous bandits such as Nagelschmidt, who, with no interest in justice, attempt to proclaim their allegiance to Kohlhaas in order to better their own robberly reputations. Finally, the horse dealer is sentenced to death. Yet the Saxon Elector who broke the amnesty remains interested in Kohlhaas' fate, or rather in the fate of his neck and what hangs around it. Kohlhaas wears a capsule on a chain, given to him by a gypsy woman, that apparently contains a written prophecy about the future of this Elector's power. On the scaffold awaiting his execution, Kohlhaas opens the amulet, reads the message, swallows it and is beheaded by the sword. His horses restored to health and his claim against the Junker satisfied, he dies a simultaneously tragic and triumphant death.

In contrast to dominant interpretations of *Michael Kohlhaas*, which often take the story's publishing history as their structural cue,[26] I suggest a reading that emphasizes the emergence and disappearance of texts in the piece, specifically the importance of written materials in establishing and disturbing connections between men. In the narrative, texts (and one's relation to them) prove to be the dividing line between manly men and others. From the contorted, lengthy sentences to the more than ninety references to written material circulating within the piece itself, the textuality of Kleist's *Erzählung* is constantly on display. However, critics have yet to discuss the relation between gender and textuality in any detail: that the texts – except for the pivotal text of the gypsy – are written by and for men has remained a moot point. [27] As I intend to show in the following, when we take texts and gender, particularly manliness, into account, *Kohlhaas* reads as the ill-fated struggle of a *manly* individual against *his* textualized society.

The story begins with a death. It is the dying of an old and worthy man – although he is not Kohlhaas' biological father – that radically alters the horse dealer's life. Kohlhaas' troubles commence when he reaches a turnpike toll [*Schlagbaum*] that prevents his passage and threatens his livelihood. After inquiring, Kohlhaas learns there has been a changing of the male guard:

Als er an die Elbe kam, und [...] einen *Schlagbaum* traf, den er sonst auf diesem Wege nicht gefunden hatte [...fragte er...] Ist der alte Herr tot? – Am *Schlagfluß* gestorben, erwiderte der Zöllner, indem er den *Baum* in die

[26] The original version, published in *Phöbus*, ends shortly after Lisbeth's death and long before the appearance of the gypsy. For a short summary of the various structural interpretations of the story, see Bogdal: *Heinrich von Kleist*. Pp. 13-14, 48.

[27] Anthony Stephens does examine the status of different forms of expression (and he offers a brief but clear overview of the secondary literature concerned with this issue), but his argument does not necessarily rely on a distinction between texts and other forms of expression. See Anthony Stephens: "Eine Träne auf den Brief". Zum Status der Ausdrucksformen in Kleists Erzählungen. In: *Jahrbuch der deutschen Schillergesellschaft* (1984). Pp. 315-348. Timothy Mehigan's study: *Text as Contract. The Nature and Function of Narrative Discourse in the Erzählungen of Heinrich von Kleist*. New York 1988, examines the status of texts, but without attention to gender. For a specific discussion of (the dearth of) feminist criticism on Kleist, see Marjorie Gelus: Birth as Metaphor in Kleist's *Das Erdbeben in Chili*: A Comparison of Critical Methodologies. In: *Women in German Yearbook* 9 (1993). Pp.1-20. Gelus herself is apparently working on a book to correct this imbalance. See also Herrmann's excellent discussion of Kleist's search for a stable gender. Hers is probably the most recent and comprehensive analysis to date of Kleist's relation to manliness (Herrmann: "Auf der Suche" [note 4]).

Höhe ließ. – Hm! Schade! versetzte Kohlhaas. Ein würdiger alter Herr, der seine Freude am Verkehr der Menschen hatte, Handel und Wandel, wo er nur vermochte, forthalf, und einen Steindamm einst bauen ließ, weil mir eine Stute, draußen, wo der Weg ins Dorf geht, das Bein gebrochen. Er war aber noch kaum unter den *Schlagbaum* gekommen, als eine neue Stimme schon: halt dort, der Roßkamm! hinter ihm vom Turm erscholl [...] (2:9-10).[28]

The violence of this transition to a new order can be seen in the repeated use of the word *Schlag*. What was once a tree [*Baum*] becomes a barrier [*Schlagbaum*], while a stroke or *Schlagfluß* puts an end to the movement [*Fluß*] that the old man encouraged. The blow [*Schlag*] that kills both the old man and the tree signals the passing of the irretrievable old world and the introduction of the new.[29] This always already lost world is marked by its leader who took joy in the bonds between people, "Handel und Wandel", and in paperless passage.[30] As Kohlhaas nostalgically notes, the now deceased old man helped the horse dealer from Kohlhaasen*brück* build his own road, rather than hinder his movement. In contrast to the mobility etymologically present in the name of Kohlhaas' hometown, the more ominous title of von Tronka's home, namely Tronken*burg*, announces a new non-mobility or stasis. The manly world of movement, of the Phöbean horse driver that Kleist and Müller propound in their journal, exists only as a memory in the *Kohlhaas* narrative. The longing for an already vanished world, a

---

[28] "As he came to the Elbe, and [...] encountered a *tollgate*, that he otherwise had never found on this road [...he asked...] Is the old master dead? – Died of a *stroke*, replied the toll collector, while he let the *tree* in the air. – Hm! A shame! answered Kohlhaas. A worthy old master who took joy in the traffic of people, helped along trade and commerce wherever he could, and once had some cobblestones put down, because a mare of mine, outside, where the road leads into the village, had broken a leg. He had barely come under the *tollgate* when a new voice rang out from the tower behind him: stay there, the horse dealer!" (emphasis mine).

[29] Kohlhaas' awareness that his world has changed can be seen in his repeated question, "Was gibts hier Neues?" (2:9-10). The importance of the *Schlag* for this new world is repeated when the Saxon Elector learns about Kohlhaas' amulet: "er gebe alle Zeichen von sich, als ob ihn der Schlag gerührt!" (2:83). As it does Kohlhaas at the beginning, this *Schlag* initiates the Elector into the cycle of violence and textual pursuit.

[30] As if to underline the connections between the old man and Kohlhaas, the narrative later characterizes the horse dealer himself as one who participated vigorously in the trade (*Handel*) of horses (2:21).

world of the father(-figure), however, will come to permeate the
story and to determine Kohlhaas' actions.

Significantly, the sudden shift from the stable patriarchal realm to
the uncertain new one manifests itself not only in the death of the
father, but botanically in the shape of a felled tree.[31] As critics have
often noted, Kleist's writings generally favor the use of arboreal
metaphors.[32] In *Kohlhaas*, however, the story begins with the tree
already fallen and a number of blows already suffered. No longer
anthropomorphised, a tree serves as a regrettable human obstacle:

> "Ja, Alter", setzte er [Kohlhaas] noch hinzu, da dieser [Zollwärter]: hurtig!
> hurtig! murmelte, und über die Witterung fluchte: "wenn der Baum im
> Walde stehen geblieben wäre, wärs besser gewesen, für mich und Euch"
> (2:10).[33]

The change from an idealized world that required no texts to one
whose arbitrariness will demand them emerges in this tree imagery.
We might understand the now felled phallic tree as a sign of the
effeminate, castrated world that emerges, or we might view it much
more "literally". The dead tree, enabling the production of paper,
forms the boundary between Kohlhaas' lost realm and his entry into
this changed one. Suddenly he can go no further without a document:

> Kohlhaas fragte: der Paß*schein*? Er sagte, ein wenig betreten, daß er, soviel
> er wisse, keinen habe; daß man ihm aber nur beschreiben möchte, was dies
> für ein Ding des Herrn sei: so werde er vielleciht zufälligerweise damit
> versehen sein. Der Schloßvolgt, indem er ihn von der Seite ansah, ver-
> setzte, daß ohne einen landesherrlichen Erlaubnisschein, kein Roßkamm
> mit Pferden über die Grenze gelassesn würde. Der Roßkamm versicherte,
> daß er siebzehn Mal in seinem Leben, ohne einen solchen *Schein*, über die
> Grenze gezogen sei, [...] doch der Vogt erwiderte, daß er das achtzehnte
> Mal nicht durchschlüpfen würde, daß die Verordnung deshalb erst neuerlich

---

[31] Mehigan also discusses the relation between The Edenic Fall, trees and
language in his Chapter 2, "The Fall as 'Sprachversehen'". For more on the
Fall generally as central to Kleist's *oeuvre* see Ilse Graham: *Heinrich von
Kleist. Word into Flesh: A Poet's Quest for the Symbol*. New York 1977.

[32] One thinks of his fascination with the strong, sturdy yet simultaneously
imperiled oaks of *Penthesilea*, of *Familie Schroffenstein*, and of his letters. See
1:885 and 2:84, 594.

[33] "'Yes, old man,'" he [Kohlhaas] still added, as this one [toll collector]
mumbled 'quick! quick!' and cursed about the weather: 'if the tree would have
stayed in the forest, it would have been better, for me and for you'".

erschienen wäre, und daß er entweder den Paß*schein* noch hier lösen, oder zurückkehren müsse, wo er hergekommen sei (2:10).[34]

Like *Phöbus'* fatal decision to dismount, as Böttiger so vividly put it, Kohlhaas responds, not by turning back, but by stepping down from his horse and following the path expected of him. A new order, masquerading as an old one, grinds into gear at Kohlhaas' eighteenth border crossing, where relations between men are now governed through paper and legal regulations, not through the patriarchal interventions of an old and worthy man. Kohlhaas barely emerges from under the turnpike [*Schlagbaum*] (2:10) and his journey begins. The fall of the executioner's sword announces his journey's end.

Rather quickly, the Junker's textual demand reveals itself to be a farce, contained in the semantic tension of *Schein*, a word on whose connotations of paper, appearance and illusion the narrative repeatedly relies.[35] Whereas the irretrievable loss of the old world corresponds with the old man's death, entry into the new world begins with the Junker's trick, which reveals that the literal need for a *Schein* (paper) is pure *Schein* (illusion). Here Kleist departs significantly from the original chronicle of Hans Kohlhase. In the 1731 narrative, from which Kleist borrows freely, Kohlhase is required to get a piece of paper that proves he has not stolen the horses, but rather bought them honestly. Hans Kohlhase returns with textual proof that the horses belong to him, only to find the horses much worse for wear and the nobleman unwilling to buy them. Kleist's modifications emphasize the hindrance to mobility that the nobleman represents (Michael Kohlhaas cannot pass through his terri-

---

[34] "Kohlhaas asked: the pass *paper*? He said, a bit disconcerted, that he, as far as he knew, had none; that if they would just like to describe for him what sort of a thing of the master's this was: perhaps he accidentally might be equipped with it. The castellan, giving him a side-long glance, replied, that without a sovereign *document* of permission, no horse dealer with horses would be allowed over the border. The horseman affirmed that he had crossed the border seventeen times in his life without such a *paper* [...], but the castellan replied that he would not sneak through the eighteenth time, that the decree for that reason had just recently appeared, and that he either had to redeem the pass *paper* here, or turn back to whence he came" (emphasis mine).

[35] According to *Duden*, the West Germanic noun *Schein* originally indicated light and expanded to include "deceptive appearance" in the 15th century. Late Middle High German came to describe written proof of something as a *Schein*, in this case, that which was visible. *Duden. Etymologie. Herkunftswörterbuch der deutschen Sprache.* Ed. Günther Drodowski et al. Vol. 7. Mannheim 1963. P. 598.

tory) and underline the arbitrary nature of the nobleman's textual request.[36]

In Michael Kohlhaas' new world, meanings become unstable, even deceptive, and the name or appearance of things need not always correspond to the thing itself.[37] Kohlhaas' discussion with the nobles about his horses highlights the instability between the word and the object it describes, that is, between the signifier and the signified. The horses' arrival at the Tronkenburg already indicates a threat to their equine "essence": the horses are referred to as "deer", and they are put, like pigs, in a "pigsty", out of which they peek like "geese" (2:11, 19). The unstable relation between signs and their objects that permeates the nobles' world comes to assume gendered connotations as well. After time spent at the Tronkenburg, what were originally masculine *Rappen* metamorphose into the feminized *Mähre* (2:13).[38] The Junker's world threatens to make the horses not only less "horse-like" but also less male; thus, their transformation and deterioration are feminized. The nobles also disrupt the horses' apparently secure relation to their worth and to their rider. At first, Kohlhaas is willing to sell the nobles the horses for a price that reflects their value. He attempts to establish a correspondence between the sovereign rider and his horse, asserting that a visual illusion will not work:

[...] alle musterten die Tiere. Der eine lobte den Schweißfuchs mit der Blesse, dem andern gefiel der Kastanienbraune, der dritte streichelte den Schecken mit schwarzgelben Flecken [...] Kohlhaas erwiderte munter, daß die Pferde nicht besser wären, als die Ritter, die sie reiten sollten (2:11).[39]

---

[36] Klaus-Michael Bogdal reprints the original document – "Nachricht von Hans Kohlhasen" – in his study: *Heinrich von Kleist: Michael Kohlhaas*. Munich 1981. P. 76.

[37] Although she does not examine texts specifically, Graham also notes the "disastrous discrepancy between the material signs [...] and their spiritual significance" in *Michael Kohlhaas* and in Kleist's work generally. She makes the connection between Kohlhaas' desire to restore the horses' value and Frau Marthe's insistence on restoring the broken jug to its original state in *Der zerbrochene Krug*. Graham: *Heinrich von Kleist*. Pp. 213-16.

[38] *Mähre* originally described female horses who performed less well than their male counterparts; it eventually became a derogatory word for a bad horse. *Duden. Etymologie. Herkunftswörterbuch der deutschen Sprache*. Pp. 416-7.

[39] "[...]All scrutinized the animals. The one praised the sorrel with the blaze, the chestnut brown one pleased the other, the third stroked the piebald with the black-yellow spots [...]. Kohlhaas replied cheerfully that the horses would be no better than the knights who should ride them".

Despite the nobles' visual fixation on appearance and, implicitly, illusion – *Schein* – Kohlhaas asserts that the horses ultimately reflect the quality of their rider; and of course, Kohlhaas' back-handed flattery indicates that these particular riders cannot be helped by any horses, regardless of their quality.[40] After returning to the Tronkenburg and seeing the horses' deteriorated condition, Kohlhaas insists that they be restored to their original value: "'das *sind* nicht meine Pferde, gestrenger Herr! Das sind die *Pferde* nicht, die dreißig Goldgülden wert waren! Ich will meine wohlgenährten und gesunden Pferde wieder haben!'" (2:15).[41] Whereas the Hans Kohlhase of the original chronicle wanted money for his horses rather than any restoration of them, Kleist's transformation stresses the importance of the original object for Kohlhaas.[42] Part of Kohlhaas' triumph comes at the end of the narrative when the horses are restored to their original condition; shortly before being executed, Kohlhaas receives two *Rappen* who are miraculously restored to their original worth, their health and their gender.[43] The deceptive nature of the nobles' regime and the rampant familial nepotism which delay Kohlhaas' requests interminably serve as a foil to Kohlhaas' striving for authenticity and movement, attributes necessary for the manly man and for the man of commerce. At the pinnacle of the government's chicanery, Kohlhaas reacts strongly to their unfulfilled promise of amnesty:

> Denn nichts mißgönnte er der Regierung, mit der er zu tun hatte, mehr, als den *Schein der Gerechtigkeit*, während sie *in der Tat* die Amnestie, die sie ihm angelobt hatte, an ihm brach (2:71).[44]

The appearance and/or paper of justice [*Schein*] becomes the contextual opposite of fact and action [*in der Tat*] here, reinforcing the (gendered) continuum ranging from an unstable, paper world of

---

[40] Ironically, Kohlhaas' prophecy that the horses are no better than their riders appears to be true; parodying the Junker himself, the horses become "skinny" (*dürr*) and "careworn" (*abgehärmt*) after time at the Tronkenburg. Here, the name of the thing and the object it describes come together (2:8).

[41] "Those *are* not my horses, severe sir! Those are not the *horses* that were worth thirty gold guilders. I want my well-fed and healthy horses back!"

[42] See: "Nachricht von Hans Kohlhasen". Bogdal: *Heinrich von Kleist*. P. 76.

[43] Shortly before his execution Kohlhaas receives his horses: "von Wohlsein glänzenden, die Erde mit ihren Hufen stampfenden Rappen" (2:101).

[44] "Then he begrudged the government with which he dealt nothing more than the *appearance of justice* while it *in deed* broke the amnesty that it had promised him" (emphasis mine).

feminized, aristocratic inaction to an actual world of facts, reality and manly energy.[45]

Perhaps naively, when Kohlhaas deals with the authorities, he operates on the principle that a central point of male power exists to which one only needs access. Recalling the activity and force of Kleist's Phöbus, Kohlhaas prefers to act directly rather than negotiate the numerous channels necessary:

> Der Herr selbst, weiß ich, ist gerecht; und wenn es mir nur gelingt, durch die, die ihn umringen, bis an seine Person zu kommen, so zweifle ich nicht, ich verschaffe mir Recht [...]. (2:27)[46]

Kohlhaas typically will try to break through the various webs and barriers preventing access to authority with an elemental speed that evokes Kleist's descriptions of Phöbus (2:40, 55). Indeed, the idea that he will be guarded, that he will be surrounded by men who effectively watch and impede his movement, causes him considerable distress, which can be read in the visual stutter of the two dashes:

> Inzwischen, sagte der Prinz [...], du wirst auf die ersten Tage eine Wache annehmen müssen, die dich, in deinem Hause sowohl, als wenn du ausgehst, schütze! – – Kohlhaas sah betroffen vor sich nieder und schwieg [...]. Kohlhaas, der sich besonnen hatte, sprach: Gnädigster Herr! tut, was Ihr wollt! Gebt mir Euer Wort, die Wache, sobald ich es wünsche, wieder aufzuheben: so habe ich gegen diese Maßregel nichts einzuwenden! (2:58)[47]

Kohlhaas is willing to accept such humiliating conditions only with the Prince's manly word of honor,[48] an unwritten contract between

---

[45] For more examples on the symbiotic and necessary relation between manliness and action, see Friedrich Ehrenberg: *Der Charakter und die Bestimmung des Mannes*. Leipzig 1808. Pp. 20 and 32.

[46] "The sovereign himself, I know, is just; and if only I can succeed to reach his person through those that surround him, then I do not doubt that I will obtain justice for myself".

[47] "In the meantime, said the Prince [...], for the first days you will have to accept a guard who protects you in your house as well as when you go out! – – Kohlhaas looked down before himself dismayed and was silent [...]. Kohlhaas, who had recollected himself, spoke: Kind sir! do, what you wish! Give me your word that the guard, as soon as I wish, will be withdrawn; then I have nothing in this precaution to object to".

[48] Kleist discusses the importance of being true to one's word in his letters (2:489). For more on the relation between manliness and keeping one's word during this time, see Ehrenberg on *Wortbrüchigkeit*: "Auf sein Wort ist gerechnet, darum muß es wahr werden. An dieser Maxime hängt alles Ver-

men, that he be given power over this decision and over the restrictions on his autonomy. Upon learning that he must submit to this watch unconditionally and that his freedom of movement will be curtailed, Kohlhaas realizes the sham of the amnesty (2:80).

The very complex role that paper plays in this relation between "what is" and "what appears (not) to be", between truth and (im)probability, becomes particularly decisive in *Michael Kohlhaas*. The unstable connection between illusion and object and their textual connotations emerges in the Kleistian wordplay between *Wahrheit* and *Wahr*schein*lichkeit*, where *Schein* literally interrupts truth and turns it into (im)probability. [49] In answer to Nagelschmidt's campaign of posted mandates, in which the insidious bandit claims to be the horse dealer's viceroy, Kohlhaas convinces the prince that any such claims are based on improbability [*Unwahrscheinlichkeit*]: as so often in Kleist's work, here as elsewhere the improbable is correct (2:67). Nagelschmidt then takes it upon himself to write to Kohlhaas directly, offering to free him from his confinement so that they may form an alliance. This letter to Kohlhaas forces the Saxon Elector to reflect on the possible relation between the two. Basing his decision on probability [*Wahrscheinlichkeit*], the Elector initially refuses to take any action:

Der Kurfürst weigerte sich standhaft, auf den Grund bloß dieses Briefes, dem Kohlhaas das freie Geleit [...] zu brechen; er war vielmehr der Meinung, daß eine Art von *Wahrscheinlichkeit* aus dem Briefe des Nagelschmidt hervor-

---

trauen der Welt [...]. Wort halten ist die Ehre des Mannes". Ehrenberg: *Der Charakter*. Pp. 287-8. Rousseau also notes: "To be something, to be oneself and always one, a man must act as he speaks". Quoted in Joan Landes: *Women and the Public Sphere in the Age of the French Revolution*. Ithaca 1988. P. 74. The inability to keep one's word was attributed to those outsiders of the dominant, emergent manliness: for example, Jews, noblemen, the French and women were all seen to varying degrees as deceptive in their speech.

[49] See also Kleist's anecdote "Unwahrscheinliche Wahrhaftigkeiten": "Denn die Leute fordern, als erste Bedingung, von der Wahrheit, daß sie wahrscheinlich sei; und doch ist die Wahrscheinlichkeit, wie die Erfahrung lehrt, nicht immer auf Seiten der Wahrheit" (2:277-8). As Hubert Rast has pointed out to me, *Wahrlichkeit*, not *Wahrscheinlichkeit* would be the accurate result. However, Kleist's own reliance on *Wahrheit* as the second term in the quote above indicates he saw the tension to be between *Wahrheit* and *Wahrscheinlichkeit*. Similarly, in the *Kohlhaas* narrative, to describe the coincidental discovery of the original gypsy woman Kleist writes: "und wie denn die Wahrscheinlichkeit nicht immer auf Seiten der Wahrheit ist [...]" (2:96).

gehe, daß keine frühere Verbindung zwischen ihnen stattgefunden habe [...]. (2:75)[50]

Kohlhaas does respond to Nagelschmidt's entreaty, but in a letter written entirely in the subjunctive case, as if parodying the precarious probability on which his fate depends. The nobility, in particular Graf Kallheim, pounce on Kohlhaas' letter as proof of a relation to Nagelschmidt, despite its grammatical tendency to the contrary, thus contributing to the fatal decision to draw and quarter the horse dealer. Once Kohlhaas responds on paper [*Schein*] to Nagelschmidt, the connection between the two is assumed, although the suspected bond did not in fact exist. In this textual world, bonds between men become tested through paper, and the appearance of text leads to understanding it as true – a false assumption in which *Schein* becomes reality and *Wahrscheinlichkeit*, *Wahrheit*. In contrast to the world Phöbus occupies, where textual mediation between men is denied for the greater good of a unified community, harmful relations between men are sustained by duplicitous texts in *Michael Kohlhaas*.

As opposed to the lost world of the old man,[51] the gendered integrity of the men who comprise this realm of slippery textual illusion comes under constant scrutiny. First, we are encouraged to read the non-heroic stature of the nobles' bodies during an era in which bodies and souls came to be seen as mutually reflective of one another. "Der Burgvogt, indem er sich noch eine Weste über seinen weitläufigen Leib zuknüpfte, kam, und fragte, schief gegen die Wit-

---

[50] "The Elector refused resolutely just because of this letter to break Kohlhaas' safe-conduct [...]; he was much more of the opinion that a sort of *probability* followed from Nagelschmidt's letter that no earlier connection between the two had existed [...]" (emphasis mine).

[51] As Bogdal (*Heinrich von Kleist.*) notes, and we have already seen, not all of the men are criticized in the narrative. Those who try to help Kohlhaas, and who knew him previously, receive the description of "the most important (*bedeutendsten*) men of the land" (2:21). For example, the more sympathetic Prince of Meissen refuses to accept a chair from the rest of the nobles at their gathering in which they discuss Kohlhaas' fate, a gesture which not only separates him from the lower nobility, but which also shows his unwillingness to accept a sedentary, or passive, position. However, those men who initiate and contribute to Kohlhaas' downfall are sharply critiqued, often within the tradition of the Enlightened discourse on the (lower) nobility. The gendered connotations of this tradition become important for understanding the relation between manliness and these particular men.

318

terung gestellt, nach dem Paßschein" (2:10). [52] While the lopsided castellan is too fat, the Junker, who holds his coat to his freezing body, is too thin: "Nun! sprach der Junker, da eben das Wetter wieder zu stürmen anfing, und seine dürren Glieder durchsauste" (2:12). [53] The Junker speaks with "pale, quivering lips" and a "weak, shaky voice" (2:59, 56). [54] According to Friedrich Ehrenberg, the well-known Protestant German clergyman and author of *Der Charakter und die Bestimmung des Mannes* (1808), manly men remain physically and mentally unaffected by unpleasant influences, such as weather: "only the woman may tremble" he pronounces. [55] Feminized in their weakness, these nobles' bodies are further described as diseased and powerless. The Treasurer gets sick, the Junker succumbs to a rash, and the Saxon Elector suffers regularly from fainting spells [*Ohnmacht*]. At the scaffold, after an eerily noncorporeal Kohlhaas ingests the note, the Saxon Elector collapses into painful cramps (2:103). While few can boast a heroic build, the Junker is even incapable of dressing himself or keeping his clothes on: "Als man dem Junker ein Wams anlegt, und einen Helm aufgesetzt hatte, [...] er [verlor] mehreremal, ohne ihn zu vermissen, den Helm [...], den ihm ein Ritter von hinten wieder aufsetzte [...]" (2:39). [56] Just as he cannot stay in control of his appearance, showing a body that shivers and shakes, he cannot exercise control over his costume of power.

The Junker's less than manly physical build corresponds with his actions. Upon first meeting Kohlhaas at his newly established turnpike, the Junker proves too cowardly to confront Kohlhaas directly about the toll. When the Junker finally demands the *Paßschein* of Kohlhaas, he does so with an embarrassed face and his back to him (2:12). Moreover, the Junker and his kin are unable to show any manly, courageous solidarity of the sort we observe between Kohlhaas and his group of men. Kohlhaas wins his battles because his

---

[52] "The castellan, while he still buttoned closed a vest over his ample body, came, and asked, leaning slanted against the wind, for the pass paper".
[53] "Now! spoke the Junker, since the wind had just begun to storm and whistled through his skinny limbs".
[54] "Mit bleichen bebenden Lippen" and "schwacher zitternder Stimme".
[55] "Kein körperliches Mißbehagen stört ihn; keine Empfindung mischt sich verstimmend in sein Thun". Ehrenberg: *Der Charakter*. P. 28, see also p. 15. "Nur das Weib darf zittern". P. 21. For more in general on "the manly man" see George Mosse: *The Image of Man*.
[56] "As they put a jacket on the Junker and set a helmet on him [...] he [lost] the helmet several times, without even noticing [...] a rider from behind set on him again".

strategy requires men to stay together, as opposed to his enemies, who are incapable of precisely this kind of bonding. For example, when the provincial governor, Otto von Gorgas, orders Captain Gerstenberg to capture the raving horse dealer who has just set Wittenberg in flames, the Captain fails because of his faulty military strategy:

> denn da dieser Kriegsmann [Gerstenberg] sich in mehrere Abteilungen auflösete, um ihn [Kohlhaas], wie er meinte, zu umzingeln und zu erdrücken, ward er von Kohlhaas, der seinen Haufen zusammenhielt, auf vereinzelten Punkten angegriffen und geschlagen. (2:37)[57]

When Kohlhaas breaks into the nobles' gathering during the storming of the Tronkenburg, the Junker unwittingly parodies brotherly bonding. Crying "brothers, save yourselves!" he disappears immediately (2:32).[58] The Junker flees from Kohlhaas to a pointedly feminine sphere, namely to his aunt and her nunnery. Any true "brother", however, would stay and fight, as Kohlhaas demonstrates in his final words to his band before departing for Wittenberg: "Follow me, my brothers", he calls, upon which the group decimates the city (2:36).[59] While both the Junker and Kohlhaas use familial metaphors, the Junker's cries speak of noble, effeminate nepotism, whereas Kohlhaas' call indicates the "true" fraternity of a *Männerbund*.[60]

The nobles possess bodies that, to use Lee Edelman's words, "could, and must be, read".[61] In his article "Homographesis", Edel-

---

[57] "Since the warrior [Gerstenberg] broke up the squads into many divisions, in order to, as he believed, surround and to crush him [Kohlhaas], he was attacked and beaten at singular points by Kohlhaas, who kept his gang together".

[58] "Brüder, rettet euch!"

[59] "Folgt mir meine Brüder".

[60] For a similar, yet problematic understanding of gender relations in *Michael Kohlhaas* we find one contemporary critic who puts the Saxon Elector's decisiveness and heterosexual potency up for discussion: "The Elector is a weakling in all that he does, bowing to pressures rather than making decisions, and his relationship with Heloise is evidently much less than passionate". The critique goes on to denigrate the perceived feminine qualities of the Elector and von Tronka: namely, their lack of action, lack of courage and lack of self-control. Such an interpretation may foreclose any critical attention to gender, since it indiscriminately adopts rather than analyzes the *Erzählung*'s continuum of masculinity. See John Ellis: *Heinrich von Kleist. Studies in the Character and Meaning of his Writings*. Chapel Hill 1976. Pp. 80 and 84.

[61] Lee Edelman: Homographesis. In: *Homographesis. Essays in Gay Literary and Cultural Theory*. New York 1994. P. 6.

man explores the legibility of (male) homosexuality and the illegibility of (male) heterosexuality. Using Derrida as a springboard, Edelman posits a strong connection between constructions of sexuality and written culture. To this end, he coins the term "homographesis" to indicate the formation of a category of the homosexual whose "very condition of possibility is his relation to writing or textuality". [62] While more research needs to be done on the similarities between bourgeois representations of homosexuality, effeminacy and the (lower) nobility, particularly in the German context, Edelman's discussion of representation may already help elucidate the relations between men in *Michael Kohlhaas*. In contrast to the nobles, whose bodies offer a threatening excess of signs, Kohlhaas' exterior is rarely described. As far as is discernible, it does not seem Kohlhaas possesses a feminized body: in fact, he seems to possess no body at all. Neither weather nor illness affects him. He never actively "cries", but rather he "lets fall a tear on the letter", "a tear rolls over the cheek" or he will simply "dry his eyes" (2:22, 47, 48). [63] Unlike the other men who are physically readable, Kohlhaas is not: he offers no expression, no indication of the workings of his soul (2:60). [64] His person and his masculinity define themselves through self-restraint, following the popular notion that he who does not have himself under control will remain under foreign power. [65] If we modify Edelman's discussion of sexuality to apply it to gender, we see the way in which Kohlhaas' "manliness" is reinforced as "natural", that is, as unmarked, authentic and non-representational. [66] Similar to a gay sexuality that provides a site at which the unrepresentable finds representation, so too do the nobles remain central to Kohlhaas' construction as a manly, non-legible man. The horse dealer can be seen in the relief of his fellow characters, exhibiting a manliness that defines and stabilizes itself *ex negativo* by setting itself against portrayals of their noble, very material, legible bodies. Michael Kohlhaas represents what may be understood

---

[62] Edelman: "Homographesis". P. 9.

[63] "[...] daß Kohlhaas eine Träne auf den Brief [...] fallen ließ", "[...] indem ihm eine Träne über die Wangen rollte [...]", "[...] indem er sich die Augen trocknete [...]" (2:22, 47, 48). These tears would qualify as the sentimental disruptions that Herrmann finds throughout Kleist's attempts to adhere to late Enlightenment ideals of manliness and femininity. Herrmann: "Auf der Suche". P. 219.

[64] "[...] der mit keiner Miene, was in seiner Seele vorging, zu erkennen gab [...]".

[65] Ehrenberg: *Der Charakter*. P. 27.

[66] Edelman: Homographesis. P. 4.

as a legitimate or idealized masculinity that recalls the wishful thinking of Kleist and Müller in their *Phöbus* prospectus. Proper manly identity appears to avoid readability or *Schein*, here, appearance, illusion and textuality. Rather than suggesting that manly identity is about the unity of appearance and essence, the portrayal of Kohlhaas goes further, indicating that the manly man offers no appearance to interpret. Kohlhaas' manliness defines itself not as one inimical to texts, but as one that attempts to avoid interpretation completely. As the ending of the story reveals, this position of stable non-legibility is radically uninhabitable; as Michael Kohlhaas' raving trajectory shows, the project of manliness will ultimately fail.

While the tension between manly and unmanly men underlies the entire narrative, women generally do not play an important role in *Michael Kohlhaas* and disappear from the scene rather quickly. Yet, in the same breath that women in the plural are written out, or sent to Schwerin like Kohlhaas' family, Woman in the singular, in all her mythical, shape-shifting ability, takes center stage, here in her outsider position as a gypsy. The presence of this Ur-woman at the expense of women is both a function and creation of this male-dominated world, where women quickly deteriorate into a projection of Woman. The gypsy's character is so overdetermined that she is not only indistinguishable from Lisbeth, her mother and her Grandmother, but also interchangeable with herself, as when the Treasurer seeks a gypsy look-alike and finds the original instead. Shortly after his wife Lisbeth's death, Kohlhaas is present by chance at a marketplace meeting between this fantastical woman and the Electors of Brandenburg and Saxon. While she prophesies good fortune for the skeptical Brandenburg sovereign, she refuses to even tell the Saxon Elector about his fate. Instead, when the Saxon Elector asks from which side danger threatens his house, she takes coal [*Kohle*] and paper, preferring instead to write it down. She then seals the paper in an amulet, walks across the marketplace and gives the prophecy to an uncomprehending Kohlhaas. Only she appears capable of investing paper with meaning again, a specifically patriarchal meaning: she holds the key to the Saxon Elector's future. As a "truth teller" [*Wahrsagerin*],[67] she is described as representing a world of *Unwahr*schein*lichkeit*, a word whose "double" negations lead us somewhere back in the vicinity of truth. Significantly, the gypsy's paper is not described as the semantically oscillating *Schein*, but as a *Blatt*,[68] recalling the leaf of the original tree and a possible

---

[67] In the narrative, she is described as a gypsy who "wahrsagte" (2:82).
[68] It is even referred to as a "Wunderblatt" (2:98).

return to the Garden before the Fall,[69] to a tree that is not yet felled, and to a world where signifier and signified had not yet been sundered.

When Kohlhaas finally comes to understand the significance of this gift, he exults in the new power the written note gives him (2:97), a note worth more to the Elector than his very existence (2:86). In contrast to the original, illusory permit for passage required of Kohlhaas, the horse dealer now possesses a paper that bears great significance. Having refused the gypsy's advice to use the amulet to save his own life, Kohlhaas chooses to read and then ingest the note on the scaffold.[70] The second and final fall, here of the executioner's blade, appears to mark the end of his textual odyssey. This moment attempts to stand outside the textual world of the narrative,[71] the final reference to text occurring in the penultimate sentence, in reference to the Elector:

> Der Kurfürst von Sachsen kam bald darauf, zerrissen an Leib und Seele, nach Dresden zurück, *wo man das Weitere in der Geschichte nachlesen muß* (2:103).[72]

The story indicates that the Elector, his body, soul and story, remain trapped in text, recorded in books. Kohlhaas, on the other hand, becomes one with the text, experiencing a death that he has wished for himself: yet, his final (ingestive) assertion of agency is fatal, indicating the impossibility both of the manly man's survival within the new textual world and of the existence of a truly meaningful text. Significantly, one of the most simple sentences of the *Erzählung* emerges at this moment: "Hier endigt die Geschichte

[69] Her offering of an apple to Kohlhaas' child reinforces the biblical connotations (2:97).

[70] The ingestion can also be seen as a sort of Holy Communion with the text. For Kohlhaas, Communion or *Abendmahl*, a word which denotes eating, is a sacred ritual to whose (revealing) power he gives credence. In response to Herse's story about the Junker's abuse he offers to take Holy Communion to prove he believes it. While Luther denies Kohlhaas' request to receive the sacrament, Kohlhaas' final "communion" becomes his last sacrament in a world that has become textualized (2:20, 48).

[71] Rainer Nägele's observes in his study of *Götz von Berlichingen* that all attempts to find a non-mediated or atextual space within literary texts become exercises in irony. Rainer Nägele: Götz von Berlichingen. In: *Goethes Dramen: Neue Interpretationen*. Ed. Walter Hinderer. Stuttgart 1980.

[72] "The Elector of Sachsen came back to Dresden shortly thereafter, destroyed in body and soul, about the rest of which one must read up on in the history books" (emphasis mine).

vom Kohlhaas" (2:103).[73] The text stops, as if no longer wanting to
call attention to its willful syntactic complexity, its numerous relative and dependent clauses.

Kohlhaas' dramatic exit shows the negotiations required by the
historically changing relations between men and the rise of a textual
world. An (imagined) leave-taking of the textual realm of production and circulation, enabled by the fantastical Other figure of the
gypsy, informs the ending. The Saxon Elector's unanswered questions (when will he die, who will replace him, when will his family's
name disappear) are diffused and transferred, since the readers learn
the answers for Kohlhaas and not for the Elector: Kohlhaas dies
now, his sons will attend a *Pagenschule* and his family name is
carried on as "von Kohlhaas". In the final sentence we learn that
even in the past century happy and hardy descendants survive
(2:103). Kohlhaas, the narrative appears to tell us, can leave the
textual world only in death – there is no textually describable existence outside of it – but the Elector is plagued by remaining in a
textual world with no access to this final meaningful paper; his
history and his narrative, his *Geschichte*, must be read and re-
searched. Kohlhaas' death puts an end to his nostalgic longing for
immediacy, while the Elector remains trapped within a textual world
of mediation.

Whereas *Phöbus*, perhaps bowing to market pressures, can canter
about in a self-made forum for virile aesthetics, Kohlhaas, driving
his horses on the same continuum, stumbles upon many more road-
blocks. One can, and many critics do, take Kleist's first sentence as
their clue, examining "Kohlhaas" as one of the "upright" and "terrible" *people* of his time. In this interpretation, however, I have tried
to be more substantive, taking off from the second sentence's description of this extraordinary *man* (2:9).[74] In the novella-like story
of *Kohlhaas* the complexities of a transition from an (always)
already lost world of certainty and immediacy to a world of uncertain mediation are both gendered and textual. Kohlhaas stands alone,
a manly individual, surrounded by incompetent, conniving half-men
and disturbing papers. A world of meaningful texts, or of potentially
stable relations between signifier and signified (enabled by the improbable gypsy), may finally realize itself, but only in Kohlhaas'
death. Kohlhaas' dilemma speaks to a broader concern found among
male writers and their literary works during the early 19th century.
The conflict between their visions of manliness and their everyday

[73] "Here ends the story of Kohlhaas".
[74] "[...] einer der rechtschaffensten zugleich und entsetzlichsten Menschen
seiner Zeit. – Dieser außerordentliche Mann [...]".

authorial lives can be read in their literary as well as extra-literary writings. As Gottfried August Bürger's poem reflects:

> Der ist ein Mann, und der ist groß!
> Doch ringt sich aus der Menschheit Schooß
> Jahrhundert lang kaum Einer los.[75]

Our legacy of modern bourgeois masculinity must be located specifically within an intellectual class of men whose ideals of manliness often stand in bizarre refraction of what their lives require of them. Placing Kleist's story within the context of the journal *Phöbus* points to the structural relation between the male writer and his ideals of manliness in the early 19th century. Specifically, this relation illuminates the ways in which newly professional *Berufschriftsteller* attempt to "masculinize" their nascent profession both inside and outside their literary works. With varying degrees of success, as *Phöbus* and *Michael Kohlhaas* show, (male) writers understand and attempt to secure their aesthetic and gendered positions using concepts of an immaterial and illegible manliness. After removing the curtain which is Phöbus, we find a proliferation of literary and cultural discourses on manliness accompanied by the sneaking, self-reflexive suspicion that the position of the literary "manly" man is impossible to occupy.

---

[75] "He is a man, and he is great!/ Yet out of humanity's womb emerges/ for centuries long rarely any such one". Gottfried August Bürger: *Sämtliche Werke.* original 1779. Göttingen 1844. P. 257. Numerous poems by Bürger both celebrate the manly man and bemoan his scarcity.

Figure 1. Apollo Belvedere. Alex Potts: *Flesh and the Ideal: Winckelmann and the Origins of Art History*. London 1994. Photograph reproduced with the permission of the Istituto Centrale per il Catalogo e la Documentazione, Roma.

Claudia Brodsky Lacour

From the Pyramids to Romantic Poetry: Housing the Spirit in Hegel

In the Introduction to the Lectures on Aesthetics, *Hegel describes his "science of art" as "building" upon the "foundation" of Kant's* Critique, *claiming that, by "representing" "freedom", the "point of unification" of all opposition between spirit and nature, the* Critique *constitutes both a "turning point" within the history of philosophy and an "absolute point of departure" from which philosophy cannot turn back (Hegel, XIII: 83-84). While the* Critique *describes neither representation, nor its opposite, freedom, as a symbolic union of opposites, maintaining instead a strict separation of mental faculties and sensations across its tripartite organization, its own self-enclosing, architectonic structure is transformed into a representational moment by Hegel, the new beginning of a dialectical narrative representing all representation as historical and the rationale of history as the overcoming, by spirit, of representation itself. Parallel to this historicization of "Kantian philosophy" is Hegel's description of "pre-art" (XIII: 84, 393). These monumental "housings of the dead" constitute at once the dialectical beginning of and preparation for aesthetic representation because they prohibit representation: purposefully "indecipherable riddles", they contain a visually and mentally inaccessible content, bodies preserved for the first time "as dead" rather than as a subject of metamorphosis (XIII: 464-65, XIV: 291) In so severing any meaningful link between the two, the pyramids first represent materially the possibility of the complete "freedom" of spirit from matter (XIII: 459). They thus inaugurate aesthetic history by making art, first, semiotic; negating the intellectual union between bodily form and meaning, they compel their own perception as "sign" (XIV: 273). Yet what makes this first architectonic sign aesthetic – and thereby constitutes the aesthetic in Hegel – is its narrated relationship to the other, equally nonrepresentational "sign" of the* Aesthetics, *the formless "sounding as such" of romantic poetry (XIV: 140). Already figured by the Egyptian colossus whose stone was reported to "sound" in the light of dawn, the riddle-like relationship between the symbolic pyramids and romantic poetry renders semiotics historical and aesthetic by locating the meaning of each of these "meaningless sign[s]" in the temporally and formally removed perception of the other (XIII: 462, XV: 235).*

I. Architectonics and the Dialectic: How Hegel's *Aesthetics* "Builds" on Kant

It would be difficult to name a philosophical project with the announced aim of achieving the coherence of "science"[1] that is less architectonic in the Kantian sense than Hegel's historical theory of spirit. Yet, for Hegel, as for Kant, the specific kind of articulation embodied in the art of architecture performs an essential speculative function. Hegel's positioning of architecture at the origin of art, "the symbolic proper" (or "properly symbolic" [*die eigentliche Symbolik*][2]) – so-called because it gives first aesthetic form to a recognized division between

---

[1] It should be recalled that Hegel named his historical dialectic of spirit the only true "science", a conception of science radically at odds with the notion of a schematic investigation of natural phenomena with which we, since Kant, associate the word. Cf. G.W.F. Hegel: *Vorlesungen über die Ästhetik* (in vols. XIII-XV of Hegel: *Theorie Werkausgabe*. Ed. E. Moldenhauer and K.M. Michel, XX vols. Frankfurt a.M. 1977. Here Vol XII. P. 26), in which Hegel not only states his definition of philosphy as science but, most unusually, uses the first person singular ("ich") to do so, thereby indicating the particular, concrete source of this historical turn: "Die Kunst lädt uns zur denkenden Betrachtung ein, und zwar nicht zu dem Zwecke, Kunst wieder hervorzurufen, sondern, was die Kunst sei, wissentschaftlich zu erkennen. Wollen wir nun aber dieser Einladung Folge leisten, so begegnet uns die schon berührte Bedenklichkeit, dass die Kunst etwa wohl überhaupt für philosophische reflektierende, jedoch nicht eigentlich für systematisch wissenschaftliche Betrachtungen einen angemessenen Gegenstand abgebe. Hierin jedoch liegt zunächst die falsche Vorstellung, als ob eine philosophische Betrachtung auch unwissenschaftlich sein könne. Es ist über diesen Punkt hier nur in der Kürze zu sagen, dass, welche Vorstellungen man sonst von Philosophie und vom Philosophieren haben möge, *ich* das Philosophieren durchaus als von Wissenschaftlichkeit untrennbar erachte" [Art invites us to thoughtful consideration, not, however, in the aim of calling forth further art, but rather that of recognizing scientifically what art is. If, however, we want to follow up on this invitation, we run into doubts, already touched on above, as to whether art, while offering an appropriate object for considerations of a philosophically reflective kind, also properly offers itself as an object for considerations of a systematic scientific nature. But herein lies a false conception, as if philosophical consideration could ever be unscientific. On this point it should be stated in brief that, whatever conception of philosophy and philosophizing one may have, *I* consider philosophizing inseparable from the scientific] (emphasis added; all further quotations from Hegel will be from this edition; all translations are my own).
[2] Hegel: Vol XIII. Pp. 413-14.

form and content, initiating the dialectic of matter and intellect that is the subject of all art for Hegel – has recently been the object of renewed critical commentary,[3] and the pseudo-empirical primacy theoretically attributed to Egyptian architecture in the *Lectures on Aesthetics* will be considered in the following discussion. But the significance of Hegel's identification of architecture with the dialectical origin of art, like his identification of Kant's *Critique* with the origin of dialectical aesthetics, is foundational only in an oppositional, negative sense. As counterintuitive as this might seem, building in the *Aesthetics* is a transitory phenomenon – perhaps the most transitory of all art forms whose appearance Hegel narrates and describes – precisely because it is the most enduring, and comprehensive, in intention. This paradox, which serves ultimately to link architecture to the end of all art for Hegel, romantic poetry, is directly related in the *Aesthetics* to earlier conceptions of the aesthetic Hegel sets out to refute.

The object Hegel's "*science* of art"[4] immediately excludes from the purview of aesthetic theory is "nature",[5] and the name Hegel gives to

[3] See Denis Hollier: *La Prise de la Concorde*. Paris 1974; and Daniel Payot: *Le Philosophe et l'Aarchitecte*. Paris 1982. Concerned with the significance of architectural form for philosophy, both Hollier and Payot view architecture as a kind of metaphor for philosophy operative within philosophical discourse. In describing and analyzing the parallel between Hegel's readings of Kant's *Critique* and of the pyramids, I am not arguing that architecture serves Hegel as a general metaphor for philosophy.

[4] Hegel: Vol. XIII. P. 25 (emphasis in text).

[5] See Hegel: Vol. XIII. P. 13 (emphasis in text): "Der eigentliche Ausdruck jedoch für unsere Wissenschaft ist '*Philosophie der Kunst*' und bestimmter '*Philosophie der schönen Kunst*'[...]. Durch diesen Ausdruck nun schliessen wir sogleich das *Naturschöne* aus". [The proper expression for our science is '*philosophy of art*' and, more precisely, '*philosophy of beautiful art*.' (...) Now, through this expression we immediately exclude the *beauty of nature*]. Stated at the opening of the *Aesthetics*, this exclusion of natural beauty effects a turning point in the history of aesthetic theory, a break not only with Kant but with the entire empirical-skeptical tradition of conceiving sensory experience. In redefining the aesthetic as pertaining to "art" alone, i.e., sensory matter already reformed and "raised" by spirit, Hegel replaces the critical equation of aesthetic experience and sense perception, dominant in philosophy since Descartes, with an absolute idealism or aestheticization of the aesthetic. Although, or perhaps because, it has set the pattern for postromantic – modern and contemporary – conceptions of the aesthetic, Hegel's turn away from nature and toward the idealization of art has been little examined. See also Vol. XIII. Pp. 15, 48-49, and 220-21, on "nature" as "an undefined, empty

the inclusion of that object in speculative aesthetics is Kant. Implicitly and explicitly, Hegel takes Kant as his predecessor (and adversary) in theory of the aesthetic: "*Die Kantische Philosophie*" is the only philosophy to appear in the *Lectures on Aesthetics* as such, as what we might call, recalling the status accorded the pyramids, *die eigentliche Philosophie*, "philosophy proper". In the section entitled "Historical Deduction of the True Concept of Art",[6] "Kantian philosophy" provides the point of departure for the intellectual transition to philosophy as "science", Hegel's theory of the "truth" of contradictions resolved in and by way of the spirit that fostered them.[7]

Hegel's summary of the *Third Critique*, at this and other moments in the *Aesthetics*,[8] is both accurate and provocatively off the mark, a systematic theoretical deformation that bears close and extended inspection. But its immediate effect is unmistakable: in describing the formal content of "Kantian philosophy" Hegel historicizes Kant's philosophy. Directly preceding the opening of the "Historical Deduction" Hegel states of his own aesthetic project: "Hiergegen steht zu behaupten, dass die Kunst die *Wahrheit* in Form der sinnlichen Kunstgestaltung zu enthüllen, jenen versöhnten Gegensatz darzustellen berufen sei und somit ihren Endzweck in sich, in dieser Darstellung und Enthüllung selber habe"[9] [The claim posed here is that the aim of art is to reveal the *truth* in the form of sensory art forms, to represent that reconciled contradiction; and that art thus has its own final purpose in itself, in this representation and revelation]. The explanatory introduction to the "Historical Deduction" continues by describing and situating Hegel's philosophy as follows:

So ist dieser Standpunkt wie die Wiedererweckung der Philosophie im all-

---

word" whose meaning for the spirit is "already idealized".

[6] See Hegel: Vol. XIII. Pp. 83-89, for the part of this section explicitly devoted to Kant.

[7] See esp. Hegel: Vol. XIII. P. 82: "Die Philosophie gibt nur die denkende Einsicht in das Wesen des Gegensatzes, insofern sie zeigt, wie das, was Wahrheit ist, nur die Auflösung desselben ist" [Philosophie provides thinking insight into the essence of opposition insofar as it shows that that which is truth is only the dissolution of opposition].

[8] The *Lectures* in fact begin with an attack on Kant's (architectonic) positioning of aesthetic judgment as intermediary between reason and moral action (see Vol. XIII. Pp. 16-17), an objection grounded on Hegel's redefinition of the aesthetic as relating to the historical domain of artworks alone.

[9] Hegel: Vol. XIII. P. 82 (emphasis in text).

gemeinen so auch die Wiedererweckung der Wissenschaft der Kunst, ja dieser Wiedererweckung verdankt eigentlich die Ästhetik als Wissenschaft erst ihre wahrhafte Entstehung und die Kunst ihre höhere Würdigung. Ich will deshalb das Geschichtliche von diesem Übergange, das ich im Sinne habe, kurz berühren, teils um des Geschichtlichen willen, teils weil damit die Standpunkte näher bezeichnet sind, auf welche es ankommt und auf deren Grundlage wir fortbauen wollen. Diese Grundlage ihrer allgemeinsten Bestimmung nach besteht darin, dass das Kunstschöne als eine der Mitteln erkannt worden ist, welche jenen Gegensatz und Widerspruch des in sich abstrakt beruhenden Geistes und der Natur – sowohl der äusserlich ercheinenden als auch der innerlichen des subjektiven Gefühls und Gemüts – auflösen und zur Einheit zurückführen.
I. *Die Kantische Philosophie*
Es ist schon die *Kantische* Philosophie, welche diesen Vereinigungspunkt nicht nur seinem Bedürfnisse nach gefühlt, sondern denselben auch bestimmt erkannt und vor die Vorstellung gebracht hat.[10]

This standpoint is thus as much the reawakening of philosophy in general as it is the reawakening of the science of art, indeed, the aesthetic as science properly owes its true arisal, and art, its higher appreciation, to this reawakening.
I will thus briefly touch upon the historical dimension of the transition that I have in mind, partly for the sake of the historical, partly in order thereby to better point out those standpoints which are significant and upon whose foundation we want to build further. Generally defined, what constitutes this foundation is that artistic beauty has been recognized as one of the means which dissolve the opposition and contradiction between the spirit, resting abstractly in itself, and nature; and returns them to unity.
I. *Kantian Philosophy*
Already *Kantian* philosophy felt not only the need for this point of unification, but specifically recognized it and gave it conceptual [or imaginable] form.

Like the historical understanding of the "internal necessity" of art[11] that now succeeds them, there have been, in the past history of philosophy, certain fixed points or positions which constitute a kind of progressive "foundation" for Hegel's "science of art". "Kantian philosophy", ac-

---

[10] Hegel: Vol. XIII. Pp. 83-84.
[11] Ibid.: "Von diesem Standpunkte aus, in welchen sich die Reflexionsbetrachtung auflöst, ist es nun, dass wir den Begriff der Kunst seiner inneren Notwendigkeit nach erfassen müssen" [It is now from this standpoint, into which reflective consideration dissolves, that we must grasp the concept of art according to its inner necessity].

cording to Hegel, represents the first point in intellectual history at which "artistic beauty" was recognized for its scientific significance, that of serving to unite the spirit with its (temporary) negation, sensuous matter. But a philosophical "standpoint", dialectically defined, must include a recognition of the necessity of another point at which philosophy, like artistic beauty, will be insignificant, the "point of unification" signifying (if that verb still applies) the end of history, of all signification. "Kantian philosophy", in other words, constitutes a *Standpunkt* for Hegel because it recognized the need for an ultimate *Standpunkt*; it became a fixed and fixing point in history, a "founda - tion" on which Hegel's "science of art" and spirit itself could "build", at the moment it envisioned[12] the point within which all discrete points in history, all foundations for building, indeed, all properly symbolic, external articulations of spirit would vanish and be contained.

Kant foresaw such a "point of unification", according to Hegel, in his conception of "freedom". That conception is in turn described by Hegel as the "foundation" of the *Critique*: "[ü]berhaupt machte Kant, für die Intelligenz wie für den Willen, die sich auf sich beziehende Vernünftigkeit, die Freiheit [...] zur Grundlage [...]".[13] [on the whole Kant made freedom, reason related only to itself, (...) into the foundation of the intellect as well as the will]. The creation of a foundation for reason in freedom remains historically effective even when "Kantian philosophy" is not: "[...] und diese Erkenntnis der Absolutheit der Vernunft in sich selbst, welche den Wendepunkt der Philosophie in der neueren Zeit herbeigeführt hat, dieser absolute Ausgangspunkt, mag man auch die Kantische Philosophie für ungenügend erklären, ist anzuerkennen und an ihr nicht zu widerlegen"[14] [(...)and this recognition of the absolute nature of reason in itself, which brought about the turning point in modern philosophy, this absolute point of departure is to be appreciated and, even if one views Kantian philosophy as insufficient, it is not to be refuted in that philosophy]. Thus Kant's conception of "freedom" –

---

[12] The meaning of the term *Vorstellung* (in "vor die Vorstellung gebracht hat") ranges from that of an abstract "idea" or "conception" to "imagining" or (imagined) "representation". It is contrasted in the *Aesthetics*, as it is in Kant's *Critique*, with the more concrete term *Darstellung*, "imaging" or (mimetic) "representation". Hegel identifies *Vorstellung* as the medium of the highest and final stage of art, romantic poetry, "Poesie der Vorstellung" (Vol. XIII. P. 123). But, already at the opening of the *Aesthetics*, it is "Kantian philosophy" which Hegel describes as appealing to such an unlimited imaginative power.
[13] Hegel. Vol. XIII. P. 84.
[14] Ibid.

according to Hegel – as "point of unification" represents at once a "turning point in modern philosophy" and an "absolute point of departure" from which philosophy cannot turn back. What cannot be "refuted" in "Kantian philosophy" is that in so imagining "freedom" Kant moved philosophy forward toward the very *Vereinigungspunkt* in which it, too, will be dissolved, and it is Hegel's interest in presenting philosophy as a progressive movement akin to the movement of imagined or aesthetic forms that accounts for the number and variety of "points" "Kantian philosophy" is said to occupy – or make imaginable (bring to *Vorstellung*) – all at the same time.

Standpunkt, Wendepunkt, absoluter Ausgangspunkt: these three points mark, perfectly punctually or succinctly, the history of the spirit as it will be narrated by way of artistic *Vorstellungen* throughout the *Aesthetics*. All three will serve to describe individual, concrete man ifestations of *das Kunstschöne* which, while formally and temporally discrete, are also viewed dialectically to traverse time: to be a standpoint, a turning point, an absolute point of departure; to incorporate all those points by being the body which allows them to be linked in one conceptual movement. What cannot be refuted in "Kantian philosophy" is that it presents Hegel's science with a conceptual *point de repère* which is also a narrative structure. Hegel historicizes Kant by redefining his *Standpunkt* as performing three different, inherently distinct temporal functions. His description of the Kantian *Standpunkt* gives it the multivalent aspect of a continuous figure even as it remains a single point in historical time. Turning a discrete "point" into a consequential extension by identifying it as a foundation, Hegel spatializes and historicizes an entire conceptual system, and it is just such a dynamic notion of a "point", whether it be a concrete manifestation of art or Kant's critical system, that renders Hegel's own philosophy not "the Hegelian philosophy" but the revelation of the truth and the end of philosophy, "science".

What Hegel *does* refute in Kant is the kind of conceptual or imaginable form the progressively functional "point", "freedom", takes in the *Critique*. That form, Hegel states critically, is exclusively "subjective", lacking in a "demonstrable" and "adequate reality:" "Und so hat denn Kant den versöhnten Widerspruch wohl in die Vorstellung gebracht, doch dessen wahrhaftes Wesen weder wissenschaftlich entwickeln noch als das wahrhaft und allein Wirkliche dartun können"[15] [And so while Kant did make the reconciliation of contradiction conceivable (or

[15] Ibid.

imaginable), he could neither develop its true essence scientifically nor represent it as the true and solely real]. The practical reality of "freedom" for Kant lies in its nonrepresentable, nonphenomenal form, whose purpose he identified with two nonimitative, or nonrepresentational art forms: the "useful" art of architecture and the imaginative art of poetry. In criticizing the subjectivism of Kant's "freedom" Hegel reserves for "spirit" what Kant, according to Hegel, attributed to the mind alone. Yet the reconciliation of opposites which Hegel ascribes to spirit is one Kant never envisaged. Indeed, the refutation of the notion, presupposed by idealism and empirical skepticism alike, that such syntheses are the necesary ground of philosophy, is the defining task of Kant's own "critical" project.[16] As "freedom" is not an imaginable reconciliation of spirit and nature but the necessary condition of those human activities – such as aesthetic judgments and ethical actions – that are performed in independence from the *a priori* causal chain of phenomenal cognitions, so the beautiful and the sublime in the *Third Critique* offer not an objective yoking of sensuous form and spiritual content but an object of contemplation never identifiable with the speculative purposes of the mind. In using Kant as a "foundation" on which "to build further", Hegel must appear to complete Kant's already architectonic system. In order to read Kant's "subjective" "freedom" as a "point" in the prelude to the freedom of the spirit, he must also reread the (subjective) experience Kant ascribes to the aesthetic *and* the (objective) domain he submits to aesthetic judgment.

Hegel's recasting of Kant's analysis of aesthetic experience centers on his key notion of "purposiveness" [*Zweckmässigkeit*]. In a thinly veiled reference to the *Third Critique* at the opening of the *Aesthetics*, Hegel criticizes theories of art which raise art to too high a purpose; his focus is the mediating role first ascribed to art by Kant. Rehearsing the traditional objections that art attenuates the spirit, or that its ornamental nature, when not indeed morally injurious, is "in any case [...] unnecessary" [*(a)uf allen Fall (...) ein Überfluss*] and so hardly "worthy of scientific treatment" [*ob (...).einer wissenschaftlichen Behandlung würdig*], Hegel turns to the contrary thesis, that art could be of "practical necessity" and serve "serious purposes":

Es hat in dieser Rücksicht vielfach nötig geschienen,
die schönen Künste, von denen zugegeben wird, dass sie ein Luxus seien, in

---

[16] Immanuel Kant: *Prologemena*. (A 71). In: *Werkausgabe*. Frankfurt a.M. 1968. Vol. VI. Pp. 157-58.

betreff auf ihr Verhältnis zur *praktischen* Notwendigkeit überhaupt, und näher zur Moralität und Frömmigkeit, in Schutz zu nehmen und, da ihre Unschädlichkeit nicht zu erweisen ist, es wenigstens glaublich zu machen, dass dieser Luxus des Geistes etwa eine grössere Summe von *Vorteilen* gewähre als von *Nachteilen*. In dieser Hinsicht hat man der Kunst selbst ernste Zwecke zugeschrieben und sie vielfach als eine Vermittlerin zwischen Vernunft und Sinnlichkeit, zwischen Neigung und Pflicht, als eine Versöhnerin dieser in so hartem Kampf und Widerstreben aneinanderkommenden Elemente empfohlen. Aber man kann dafür halten, dass bei solchen zwar ernsteren Zwecken der Kunst Vernunft und Pflicht dennoch nichts durch jenen Versuch des Vermittelns gewönnen, weil sie eben ihrer Natur nach als unvermischbar sich solcher Transaktion nicht hergäben und dieselbe Reinheit forderten, welche sie in sich selbst haben. Und ausserdem sei die Kunst auch hierdurch der wissenschaftlichen Erörterung nicht würdiger geworden, indem sie doch immer nach zwei Seiten hin diene und neben höheren Zwecken ebensosehr auch Müssigkeit und Frivolität befördere, ja überhaupt in diesem Dienste, statt für sich selber Zweck zu sein, nur als Mittel erscheinen könne.[17]

In this regard it has appeared necessary in many ways to defend the beautiful arts that are granted to be a luxury with respect to their relationship to *practical* necessity generally and to morality and piety more specifically; and, since their harmlessness cannot be proven, to make at least credible that this luxury of the spirit guarantees a greater number of *advantages* than *disadvantages*. In this respect serious purposes have been ascribed to art itself and art has been recommended variously as a mediator between reason and sensousness, between inclination and duty: as a reconciliator of the hard struggle and opposition between elements that come together. But we can assume that, regarding such serious purposes of art, reason and duty can have gained nothing by this attempt at mediation because, being by their very nature unmixable, they would not give themselves to such a transaction and would demand the same purity that they have in themselves. Furthermore, art itself would not have been made worthier by this scientific explanation in that it must always serve two sides and, alongside higher purposes, must just as much further superfluity and frivolity; indeed art in this service can only appear as a means, rather than its own purpose.

Kant's ascription to the aesthetic of a higher purpose within a tripartite architectonic system – that of a bridge between "reason and sensuousness" [*Vernunft und Sinnlichkeit*], the realms of the Second and the First Critiques respectively – is criticized by Hegel on the grounds of the individual and discrete "purposes" [*Zwecke*] of reason and sensu-

---

[17] Hegel: Vol. XIII. Pp. 16-17.

ousness – which Hegel, in a thoroughly non-Kantian revision, calls neither intellectual faculties, nor powers of experience, but "elements" [*Elemente*]. Here, in the Introduction to the *Aesthetics*, as in the section devoted to "die Kantische Philosophie", Hegel truncates and virtually reverses Kant's critical conception of the basis of the beautiful: our perception in beautiful objects of a "purposiveness *without* a purpose" [*Zweckmässigkeit ohne Zweck*].[18] That negative definition posits no cultural norms, whether of content or style, and suggests no *a priori* positive preferences: "the form *of the normative idea* of a beautiful man is *based* in the country *where* this comparative notion is employed; [...] under these empirical conditions [every people] must have a different normative idea of the beauty of the form".[19] Nor does it prescribe a calculus for purely formal success: "[t]he *normative idea* is not deduced from proportions taken from experience as *definite rules*; rather rules for judging first become possible according to it [...]. It is, as one named Polykleitos' Doryphorus, the *rule* (Myron's Cow could also just as well have been used in its species)".[20] Representing "no purpose at all, whether objective or subjective", and "no object" other than itself, the formal dynamic Kant describes engages its perceiver in the particular pleasure of contemplation without relation to a conceptual determination and "without any interest" ("ohne alles Interesse"), an experience involving none of the partiality – and resulting in none of the intended gratification – which must attach itself to pleasure taken in a known "purpose".[21] For, "every purpose", Kant cautions, "when viewed as the basis of pleasure, carries with it an interest as the determining basis of one's judgment of the object of pleasure" ("[a]ller Zweck, wenn er als Grund des Wohlgefallens angesehen wird, führt immer ein Interesse, als Bestimmungsgrund des Urteils über den

---

[18] Immanuel Kant: *KU*, "Analytik des Schönen", §11, 12 (B 34-35). In: *Werkausgabe*. Frankfurt a.M. 1968. Vol. X. Pp. 135-36.

[19] "[...] so *liegt* diese Gestalt *der Normalidee* des schönen Mannes, in dem Lande, *wo* diese Vergleichung angestellt wird, *zum Grund*; daher ein Neger notwendig *unter diesen empirischen Bedingungen eine andere Normalidee* der Schönheit der Gestalt haben muss, als ein Weisser, der Chinese *ein andere*, als der Europäer" (*KU* B 58. Vol X. P. 153).

[20] "Diese *Normalidee* ist nicht aus von der Erfahrung hergenommenen Proportionen, als *bestimmten Regeln*, abgeleitet; sondern nach ihr werden allerest Regeln der Beurteilung möglich [...]. Sie ist, wie man Polyklets brühmten Doryphorus nannte, die *Regel* (eben dazu konnte auch Myrons Kuh in ihrer Gattung gebraucht werden" (*KU* B 58-59. Vol. X. P. 153).

[21] Kant: *KU*, §5 (B 17). Vol. X. P. 124.

Gegenstand der Lust, bei sich"[22]), when judgment should instead have
no basis other than "the state of mind in the free play of imagination
and understanding" ("der Gemutszustand in dem freien Spiel der Einbildungskraft und des Verstandes"[23]). What determines judgment of the
beautiful is a mutually unsettling play between our representational and
conceptual faculties; purpose casts the experience of the beautiful into
the opposite of play, an instrumental means to an end.

Supplanting Kantian "purposiveness without a purpose" with the
higher purposes of reason and duty (to which the beautiful must be
subordinate) and, ultimately, with the highest (historical) purpose, the
Aufhebung of purpose itself, Hegel denies, as he miscontrues, the
dynamic function of beauty acting "only as a means, rather than its own
purpose".[24] Having redefined "das Schöne" in Kant as "purposive in
itself" ("zweckmässig in sich selbst"), Hegel observes: "Was wir nun in
allen diesen Kantischen Sätzen finden, ist eine Ungetrenntheit dessen,
was sont in unserem Bewusstsein als geschieden vorausgesetzt ist.
Diese Trennung findet sich im Schönen aufgehoben, indem sich Allgemeines und Besonderes, Zweck und Mittel, Begriff und Gegenstand
vollkommen durchdringen"[25] [What we find then in all these Kantian
principles is the undividedness of that which otherwise is presupposed
as separate in our consciousness. This separation finds itself sublated in
the beautiful, in that general and particular, purpose and means, concept
and object fully penetrate one another].

A reader possessing even an elemental knowledge of the *Third
Critique* must find this summary description ridiculous: Kantian "free
play" is not an interpenetration of such Hegelian opposites as the universal and the particular, nor does the mediating role of the beautiful
threaten either to contaminate, by mixing, the faculties mediated, or to
weaken itself, understood (falsely) as its own purpose. The references
to the universal and the particular in Kant that Hegel goes on to cite
come from the Introduction to the *Third Critique*.[26] But rather than join
these terms in an overriding dialectic, Kant uses them to define *two
distinct kinds of judgment*: "bestimmend" (determining) and "reflek-
tierend" (reflective). A judgment that "subsumes" the particular to a
universal "rule, principle, or law" is "determining"; one that finds the

---

[22] Kant: *KU* §11 (B 35). Vol. X. P. 136.
[23] Kant: *KU* §9 (B 29). Vol. X. P. 132.
[24] See note 18.
[25] Hegel: Vol. XIII. P. 88.
[26] Kant: *KU* (BXXV-XXVI). Vol. X. P. 87.

general on the basis of a given particular is "reflective". The single general law that is generated by reflective judgment is, as Hegel goes on to state, "Zweckmässigkeit" (purposiveness).[27] But Kant specifically limits the scope of that general law to the *teleological*, rather than aesthetic, conception of nature, i.e., to nature viewed from the vantage of divine understanding, at a categorical remove from the free play of understanding and imagination: "D.i. die Natur wird durch diesen Begriff so vorgestellt, als ob ein Verstand den Grund der Einheit des Mannigfaltigen ihrer empirischen Gesetze enthalte"[28] [That is, nature is conceived according to this concept as if an understanding contained the reason for the unity of the manifold of her empirical laws]. Pertaining specifically to the "Critique of Teleological Judgment" that composes the second part of the *Critique of Judgment*, this conception of nature is expressly distinguished by Kant from the experience of beauty in nature *and* art described in the preceding "Critique of Aesthetic Judgment", according to which no "general law", reflecting a higher understanding, appears to account for phenomena at all. For precisely no presupposition of divine plan or purpose can underlie the play in the beautiful, and violent conflict in the sublime, that characterize the relationship between necessarily human understanding and imagination in *aesthetic* experience.

Furthermore, like Descartes before him, Kant openly criticized dialectical reason in his own explication of method. Having "degenerated" from a "use of pure understanding, abstracted from all sensory perception", into a form of "sophistry" which, freed from the limits imposed by such perceptions, argued any proposition on the basis of mere verbal "subtleties", dialectic, Kant argued, continues to abuse reason by using it to create only the "semblance of truth".[29] Indicating no preconception of Hegel's *historical* dialectic, Kant also flatly denied that there could be a "universal material criterion of truth", i.e., one that did not "abstract completely" from the very "differences" that constitute specific material objects.[30] Nor did he propose any point of unification between the "*universal formal* criteria of truth", those composing human logic (the "logical characteristics of the agreement of knowledge with itself"), and "objective truth", the truth of distinct material

---

[27] Hegel: Vol. XIII. P. 85.
[28] Kant: *KU* (BXXVIII). Vol. X. P. 89.
[29] Kant: *Logik* (A 32). Vol. VI. P. 452; (A 28). Vol. VI. P. 449.
[30] Kant: *Logik* (A 71). Vol. VI. P. 477.

objects.[31] The dialectial resolution of difference remained instead for Kant inimical to philosophy itself, a falsifying production of so-called universal truth "whereby nothing is actually said": "womit eigentlich gar nichts gesagt wäre".[32]

Like the rewriting of the dynamic "purposiveness without a purpose" that structures the objects of aesthetic experience internally, the (mis)reading in the *Aesthetics* of the dynamic function of that experience within the overall articulation of cognition and action Kant describes is formulated in terms so clearly originating in Hegel, rather than Kant, that one may wonder why Hegel adopted Kant's *Critique* as his *Ausgangspunkt* to begin with: a "point of departure" whose own axiomatic origins he effectively buries. That appeal to and misrepresentation of Kant makes the *Critique*, understood on its own terms, an inaccessible thing of the past – a past defined by Hegel and a thing one would have to dig through Hegel to recuperate – while at the same time transposing the past of philosophy into the future. Hegel renders Kantian aesthetics idealist and dialectical just as he historicizes Kantian philosophy, for although Kant introduced the concept of "freedom" into philosophy and aesthetics, he failed to foresee the eventual overcoming of both of these, the true "science" of a spirit freed from all phenomenal, discursive or sensuous, forms.

On that superhistorical, Hegelian view, art first, and religion and philosophy second and third, are merely different, sequential "forms" for bringing "absolute spirit to consciousness": "drei Reiche des absoluten Geistes nur duch die *Formen* unterschieden, in welchen sie ihr Objekt, das Absolute, zum Bewusstsein bringen".[33] Neither nature nor Kantian aesthetic theory *non*historicized can have a place in Hegel's *Aesthetics* precisely because they neither require nor indicate their further transformation, a transition through and beyond them. Like the phenomena of nature it includes, Kant's critical aesthetics – characterized by Hegel as merely "subjective" – is not subject to spirit, and for this reason Hegel must exclude the one (*das Naturschöne*) and recast the other (*die kantische Philosophie*). Any product of spirit for Hegel must surpass any product of nature, just as even the most "accidental" of "ideas" must surpass the evident "necessity" of the "sun":

Denn die Kunstschönheit ist die *aus dem Geiste geborene und wiederge-*

---

[31] Kant: *Logik* (A 72). Vol. VI. Pp. 477-78.
[32] Kant: *Logik* (A 17). Vol. VI. P. 477.
[33] Hegel: Vol. XIII. P. 139 (emphasis in text).

borene Schönheit, und um soviel der Geist und seine Produktionen höher steht als die Natur und ihre Erscheinungen, um soviel auch ist das Kunstschöne höher als die Schönheit der Natur. Ja *formell* betrachtet, ist selbst ein schlechter Einfall, wie er dem Menschen wohl durch den Kopf geht, *höher* als irgendein Naturprodukt, denn in solchem Einfalle ist immer die Geistigkeit und Freiheit präsent [...]; aber für sich genommen ist solche Naturexistenz wie die Sonne indifferent [...].[34]

For artistic beauty is beauty *born and reborn of spirit* and as much as spirit and its productions stand higher than nature and its appearances, so much higher than natural beauty stands artistic beauty. Considered *formally*, even a bad idea, in the way it goes through a person's head, is *higher* than any product of nature, for in such ideas or notions spirit and freedom are present [...]; but taken in itself such a natural existence as the sun is indifferent [...].

"*Formally*" means for Hegel, unlike Kant, temporally and dialectically, which is to say, anything but the formal, phenomenal occasion for a nonprogressive experience of faculties in "free play". In order to "build upon the foundation" of Kant's "standpoint" Hegel not only interprets it as containing a dialectical series of points leading to the unique point of total "unification", but he also transforms Kant's basic "principles". The ground for such extravagant appropriation lies in the necessary "historical" connection determined by Hegel between the formulation of aesthetics and the rebirth of philosophy itself, between "the science of art" and philosophy as "science".[35] *Following* Kant *and* retrospectively misconstruing his *Critique* – the limits upon reason posed by its epistemology as well as the necessary experience of aesthetic play and violence that this termination of the dream of pure reason entails – Hegel "builds upon" the "standpoint" of "Kantian philosophy" from which, on his "historical" account, the "transition" to the dissolution of the opposition between spirit and nature is already visible. After Kant, according to Hegel, aesthetics is "as much the reawakening of philosophy in general as it is the reawakening of the science of art"[36] – two notions that, *within* the terms of Kant's *Critique*, are not only not united but incompatible.

The architectonic formulation of Kant's *Critique*, like the formal basis

---

[34] Hegel: Vol. XIII. P. 14 (emphasis in text).
[35] Cf. Note 10.
[36] Ibid.

of his concept of *non* scientific aesthetic judgment, make "Kantian philosophy" an unlikely foundation upon which such a transformative history of spirit can "build". The entirely artificial, architectonic structure of the *Critique*, built to uphold its own "hypothesis" or "wager" [37] logically rather than provide temporary, representational housing for the phenomena of history – such a structure is not given to its own ruination. And precisely in this it resembles the point of departure of Hegel's *Aesthetics*: just as the pyramids, those enduring, self-determining structures and first representations of "immortality", take on the aspect of passing phenomena in a history of spirit surpassing all phenomenal manifestation, so the first true "turning point" in the history of philosophy takes on the deceiving quality of an aesthetic object, a *Kunstprodukt*, within Hegel's philosophy. Kant's notion of the "architectonic" is of a logically synchronic system of *a priori* mental forms and concepts whose synthetic mediation of sensory experience (as representation) constitutes (impure) theoretical knowledge. The suspension of that mediation in disinterested sensory experiences that cause pleasure (or pain), while remaining unrelated to cognitive representation, is aesthetic judgment. The suspension of all sensory experience and unmediated realization of reason hypothesized within the system is the unrepresentable form of moral action, "freedom". The encompassing, self-defining form of architectonics thus makes knowledge possible and impossible – representation inevitable and unavailable – depending on "where" one is "in" the total structure: on the kind of experience to which the subject is submitted, and, as a consequence, the faculties and sensations, and relationships or exclusions of relationships, that are called into play. At absolutely no moment in Kant does the system itself achieve synthesis: its many operations, faculties, and forms never take on a single shape or face. Instead, the active *negation* of each part of the system by the others (i.e., of free, moral action and aesthetic judgment by representational cognition, and, likewise, of cognition by action and aesthetic judgment, and of such judgment by cognition and action), both ensures the limits and integrity of each part and bars, at every moment, their symbolic unification.

With Hegel, this critical notion of nontransformable building is itself transformed into *a moment of representation*, an historical artifact with a narrative meaning. Like the impervious construction of the secretive pyramids, Kant's building of a rational system constructed to preserve a profoundly nonrational core – the "pure" practical reason of unrepre-

---

[37] Kant: *KrV* (BXXII-XXIII). Vol. II. P. 28.

sentable "freedom" – is enrolled by a "science" whose "reason" is instead the representational rationale of historicization itself. The very necessity of freedom to these two architectonic activities allows Hegel to "build" upon their "foundations" or "standpoints" equally (and equally improperly) so as to "further build" *his own beginning*. Monumental constructions, the pyramids and "Kantian philosophy" are historicized by Hegel to represent transitional representations of spirit progressing historically past both art and philosophy.

II. Mute Pyramids and the Riddle of the Symbol

The "timelessness", the pure, monumental spatiality of the pyramids make them an unlikely foundation for a "science of art" whose "formal" aspect is a temporal dialectics of change. Hegel's description of symbolic architecture, the first true *Kunstprodukt* according to the dialectic, reveals the parallel between the "beginning"[38] of art and the *Ausgangspunkt* Hegel finds in "Kantian philosophy":

> die Ägypter [sind] unter den bisherigen Völkern das eigentliche Volk der *Kunst* [...], ein bauendes Volk, das nach allen Seiten hin den Boden umgewühlt [...] und im Instinkte der Kunst nicht allein an das Tageslicht die ungeheuersten Konstruktion herausgestellt, sondern die gleich unermesslichen Bauwerke auch in den grössten Dimensionen in die Erde gewaltsam hineingearbeitet hat [...].
> *I. Ägyptische Anschauung und Darstellung des Toten; Pyramiden*
> Was nun die ägyptische Kunstanschauung ihren besonderen Seiten nach angeht, so finden wir hier zum erstenmal das Innere, der Unmittelbarkeit des Daseins gegenüber, für sich festgehalten. [...] Weiter aber bleiben die Ägypter nicht bei dieser unmittelbaren und selbst noch natürlichen Dauer den Toten stehen. Das natürlich Bewahrte wird auch in der *Vorstellung* als dauernd aufgefasst. Herodot sagt von den Ägyptern, sie seien die ersten gewesen, welche lehrten, dass die Seele des Menschen unsterblich sei. Bei ihnen zuerst also kommt auch in dieser höheren Weise die Lösung des Natürlichen und des Geistigen zum Vorschein, indem das nicht nur Natürliche für sich eine Selbstständigkeit erhält. Die Unsterblichkeit der Seele liegt der Freiheit des Geistes ganz nahe, indem das Ich sich erfasst als der Natür-

---

[38] Hegel: Die Eigentliche Symbolik. In: Vol. XIII. P. 452 (emphasis in text): "so *beginnt* doch das wahrhaft Innere sich erst aus dem Natürlichen herauszuringen [...]". [thus true interiority *begins* to wrest itself from the natural (...).] See also Vol. XIII. P. 453: "Das Innere überhaupt beginnt hier zur Selbständigkeit zu gedeihen [...]". [The internal in general begins here to progress toward independence (...).]

lichkeit des Daseins entnommen und auf sich beruhend; dies Sichwissen aber ist das Prinzip der Freiheit.[39]

of all the other people so far presented, the Egyptians are the proper people of *art* [...], a people that builds, that bores into the ground in all directions [...] and, with the instinct of art, produced enormous constructions not only under the light of day but also worked immeasurable buildings in the largest dimensions into the earth [...].

I.The Egyptian View and Representation of the Dead; Pyramids
As to the special aspects of the Egyptian perspective on art, we find that the internal, in its relation to the immediacy of being, is here held fast for the first time. [...] But, in addition, the Egyptians don't stop at the immediate and natural duration of the dead. That which is preserved naturally is also grasped as enduring in *representation*. Herodotus says of the Egyptians that they were the first who taught that the soul of men is immortal. The dissolution of the natural and the intellectual in this higher way first comes to appearance with them, as the not-only-natural receives independence for itself. The immortality of the soul lies very close to the freedom of the spirit, in that the I grasps itself as resting upon itself and removed from the naturalness of being; but this self-knowing is the principle of freedom.

Egyptian art marks the proper beginning of the history of art – that of the appearance of the "idea" of spirit – for Hegel because the pyramids represent the same turning point he distinguishes in "Kantian philosophy", the concept Kant called the "keystone" [*der Schlussstein*] of his architectonic *Critique*, "freedom".[40] The act of *representing* death in symbolic form signals "the principle of freedom" in that it turns from the preservation of nature toward independent intellectual activity, just as Kant's representational epistemology, whose only stipulated "positive" "use" is to ensure the freedom of pure, *practical* reason, posits hypothetically the existence of independent, or *a priori*, mental forms.[41]

---

[39] Hegel: Vol. XIII. Pp. 457-59 (emphasis in text).
[40] Kant: *KrV* (A 4). Vol. VII. Pp. 107-108. Cf. Claudia Brodsky: 'Freedom' in the Second Critique. In: *The Imposition of Form: Studies in Narrative Representation and Knowledge*. Princeton 1987. Pp. 68-87.
[41] See Kant: *KrV* (BXXV). Vol. XXX. P. 30 (Preface to the second edition of the *First Critique*; emphasis in text): "Daher ist eine Kritik, welche die erstere [die spekulative Vernunft] einschränkt, so fern zwar *negativ*, aber, indem sie dadurch zugleich ein Hindernis, welches den letztern Gebrauch einschränkt, oder gar zu vernichten droht, aufhebt, in der Tat *positivem* und sehr wichtigem Nutzen, so bald man überzeugt wird, dass es einen schlechterdings notwendigen praktischen Gebrauch der reinen Vernunft (den moralischen) gebe [...]".
[Thus a Critique, which limits (speculative reason), is to that extent, *negative*,

Both formal structures embody architectonically, i.e., in the least free form of artificial composition, the recognition that freedom resides in the most rigorous acts of building. "Buildings" [*Bauwerke*] not merely posed *upon*, but built "into the earth", "first" bring to appearance the "freedom of spirit" from "natural" grounding and "duration"; Kant's "building" [*Gebäude*] of an intellectual system of representational faculties creates a new basis for "freedom" by first hypothesizing the critical independence from nature of thought.[42] The name Hegel gives to such groundbreaking independence in the aesthetic realm is the symbol:

Das Symbol in der Bedeutung, in welcher wir das Wort hier gebrauchen, macht dem Begriffe wie der historischen Erscheinung nach den Anfang der Kunst und ist deshalb gleichsam nur als Vorkunst zu betrachten, welche hauptsächlich dem Morgenlande angehört und uns erst nach vielfachen Übergängen, Verwandlungen und Vermittlungen zu der echten Wirklichkeit des Ideals als der klassischen Kunstform hinüberführt.[43]

The symbol, in the meaning of the word that we use here, constitutes the beginning of art both conceptually and as an historical appearance. For this reason it is to be considered only, as it were, as pre-art, which belongs mainly to the Orient and first leads us, after various passages, transformations, and mediations, to the true reality of the ideal, as the classical form of art.

According to the temporally double "meaning" which Hegel's historicization of art must define, the symbol is both the "beginning of art" and has not yet begun to be art. As "pre-art" ("Vorkunst") the symbolic will lead to art defined as classical art, that is, art in which the "full unity of inner meaning and external form" "appears".[44] In classical

---

but in that it eliminates an obstacle which threatens to limit, or even to destroy, the use (of speculative reason), it is in fact of *positive* and very important use, as soon as one is persuaded that there is an absolutely necessary practical use of pure reason (the moral use) (...)].

[42] Ibid.

[43] Hegel: Vol. XIII. P. 393.

[44] "Die Eigentümlichkeit des Inhalts besteht [...] im Klassischen darin, dass er selbst konkrete Idee ist und als solche das konkret Geistige [...]. Diese Gestalt, welche die Idee als geistige – und zwar die individuell bestimmte Geistigkeit – an sich selbst hat, wenn sie sich in zeitliche Erscheinung herausmachen soll, ist die *menschliche Gestalt*" [The particularity of content in classical art is that it itself is a concrete idea and, as such, the concretely intellectual (...). The form

sculpture representing "the human form" "the idea of the beautiful" first attains necessary symmetry with "the beauty [of] the idea".[45] The famous dictum Hegel lays down at the opening of the *Aesthetics*, and repeats in related formulations later, that "art in its highest determination is and remains for us a thing of the past" ("die Kunst [ist und bleibt] nach der Seite ihrer höchsten Bestimmung für uns ein Vergangenes"),[46] seems to pronounce the postmortem of all art for all time.

---

which carries with itself the idea as the intellectual, and, moreover, as individually determined intelligence – that form, when it is to come to temporal appearance, is the *human form*] (Hegel: Vol. XIII. Pp. 109-110); "[i]n dieser Weise *sucht* die symbolische Kunst jene vollendete Einheit der inneren Bedeutung und äusseren Gestalt, welche die klassische in der Darstellung der substantiellen Individualität für die sinnliche Anschauung *findet* [...]". [in this way symbolic art *seeks* that full unity of internal meaning and external form which classical art *finds* in the representation for sensory vision of substantial individuality] (Hegel: Vol. XIII. P. 392).

[45] For Hegel's definition of the idea as beautiful and, reciprocally, of the beautiful as the idea, see the chapter "Begriff des Schönen überhaupt" [The Concept of the Beautiful in General] (Vol. XIII. Pp. 145-57; and Vol. XIII. P. 151), especially: "Indem [...] der Begriff unmittelbar in Einheit bleibt mit seiner äusseren Erscheinung, ist die Idee nicht nur wahr, sondern *schön*. Das *Schöne* bestimmt sich dadurch als das sinnliche *Scheinen* der Idee" [In that (...) the concept remains immediately united with its external appearance, the idea is not only true, but *beautiful*. The *beautiful* is thereby determined as the sensory *appearing* of the idea].

[46] Hegel: Vol. XIII. P. 25. In the opening of Part One, "Die Idee des Kunstschönen oder das Ideal" [The Idea of Artistic Beauty or the Ideal], Hegel defines the "point" at which "philosophy of art must begin" as the moment when infinite spirit "makes itself finite so as to transcend finitude", thereby replacing the function of art: "[d]adurch macht er sich in seinem höchsten Gebiete für sich selbst zum Gegenstande seines Wissens und Wollens" (Vol. XIII. P. 130; on "the highest, true dignity" of art, see also Vol. XIII. P. 131) [in this way [spirit] makes itself in its highest realm into the object for itself of its knowledge and will]. This "freedom", which art first makes manifest, is for Hegel "the highest determination of spirit" ("höchste Bestimmung des Geistes" [Vol. XIII. P. 134]). In his closing comments on the "first" of the three historical "forms" of spirit (art, religion, philosophy), Hegel relates both the general pastness of the "highest" function of art and the specific event of its rejection by the Reformation to the spirit's overcoming of its own objectification. If the art of "our time" no longer fulfills the "highest need of spirit", that is not because it is not the right art but because spirit – which alone creates the sequential "forms of artistic beauty" (the symbolic, classical, and romantic) and their individual species (architecture, sculpture, painting, music, and

Read, however, as it is written, from "our" ("for us") position in time, i.e., at the end of the dialectical history culminating in philosophy that Hegel considers "science", this pronouncement advances no transhistorical truth but rather refers to a specific historical moment, the era of the beautiful incorporation of the idea in classical art that, on the Hegelian view, has already transpired.

The "highest determination" of art is not and could not be a *purely aesthetic* highpoint for Hegel, a moment of beauty purified of the "concrete content" of the idea.[47] The very notion of such an appearance would be dialectically inconceivable. The "highest determination" of art is instead a *hermeneutic* one, in the specific sense propounded in the early nineteenth century: art made and understood in the service of *religious* meaning, the first (and, for Hegel, ultimately insufficiently abstract) realm of the idea. In a dialectical sequel to Baumgarten's transcendental aesthetics of perfected sensory cognitions (*aesthetices fines est perfectio cognitionis sensitivae* [*Aesthetica* §15]) and Schleiermacher's historical hermeneutics of sacred and literary texts, Hegel interprets art not as a perfect, and consequently, meaningless,

---

poetry) – no longer has need of art in general: "als aber der Trieb des Wissens und Forschens und das Bedürfnis innerer Geistigkeit die Reformation hervortrieben, ward auch die religiöse Vorstellung von dem sinnlichen Elemente abgerufen und auf die Innerlichkeit des Gemüts und Denkens zurückgeführt [...]. Ist aber der vollkommene Inhalt vollkommen in Kunstgestalten hervorgetreten, so wendet sich der weiterblickende Geist von dieser Objektivität in sein Inneres zurück und stösst sie von sich fort. Solch eine Zeit ist die unsrige. Man kann wohl hoffen, dass die Kunst immer mehr steigen und sich vollenden werde, *aber ihre Form hat aufgehört, das höchste Bedürfnis des Geistes zu sein.* Mögen wir die griechischen Götterbilder noch so vortrefflich finden und Gottvater, Christus, Maria noch so würdig und vollendet dargestellt sehen – es hilft nichts, unser Knie beugen wir doch nicht mehr" (Vol. XIII. P. 142 [my emphasis]) [but as the drive for knowledge and research and the need for inner spirituality drove the Reformation forward, religious conception was recalled from the sensory element and led back to the interiority of the mind and thought (...). Perfected content having come perfectly to the fore in artistic forms, however, so spirit, which looks onward, turns back inside itself from this objectivity and casts it aside. Such a time is ours. One can of course hope that art will always rise higher and continue to perfect itself, *but its form has stopped being the highest need of spirit.* We may still find the Greek images of gods just as splendid and we may still see God the Father, Christ, and Maria represented in as worthy and perfected a way – but this is to no avail, we no longer bend our knee].

[47] See note 43.

sensory experience but as the historical text for a transcendent hermeneutics. Indeed, in Hegel's intersecting, three-phase histories of the
progressive forms of the intellect (art, religion, and philosophy) and of
art (symbolic architecture, classical sculpture, and romantic painting,
music, and poetry), the arisal of art so nearly dovetails with the origin
of religious organization and representation that his brief description of
the phase, "Religion", situated between "Art" and the "third form of the
absolute spirit, Philosophy", largely recapitulates the longer exposition
of art as "the determined representation of the actions, life, and influence of the godly" ("die bestimmte Vorstellung vom Tun, Leben,
Wirken des Göttlichen") that precedes it.[48]

Architecture is the *first* art form or, as in the analysis of the pyramids, the "pre-art" form, because it "first clears the path for the adequate reality of God [...] out of the tangled growth of finitude and the
deformity of accident", "leveling a place for God, forming his external
environment and building him his temple, the space of the internal
congregation".[49] Architecture clears the way and prepares the place for
religious meaning, but "God himself enters the temple", and, with God,
the idea of religion, only "*secondly*", when "spirit itself" is represented
in sculpture, the artform that produces in inarticulate matter a perfect
interpenetration of "spiritual content" with "corporeal form".[50]

From the wilderness and accident of unmediated nature, architecture
determines a space which can and will be filled with (Christian) representations: to the empty, circumscribed place of God is added the body

---

[48] Hegel: Vol. XIII. P. 141. On the three phases of human intellectual history,
see Vol. XIII. Pp. 140-44; on the three phases of art forms, see Vol. XIII. Pp.
116-124.
[49] Hegel: Vol. XIII. P. 117: "Denn die Architektur bahnt der adäquaten Wirklichkeit des Gottes erst den Weg und müht sich in seinem Dienst mit der
objektiven Natur ab, um sie aus dem Gestrüppe der Endlichkeit und der
Missgestalt des Zufalls herauszuarbeiten. Dadurch ebnet sie den Platz für den
Gott, formt seine äussere Umgebung und baut ihm seinen Tempel als den
Raum für die innere Sammlung [...]".
[50] Hegel: Vol. XIII. Pp. 117-18 (emphasis in text): "in diesen Tempel *zweitens*
tritt sodann der Gott selber ein, indem der Blitz der Individualität in die träge
Masse schlägt, sie durchdringt und die unendliche, nicht mehr bloss symmetrische Form des Geistes selber die Leiblichkeit konzentriert und gestaltet.
Dies ist die Aufgabe der *Skulptur*" [*Secondly* the God himself enters this
temple, as the lightening of individuality strikes into inert mass, penetrates it,
and forms and concentrates the corporality of the infinite, no longer merely
symmetrical form of spirit itself. This is the task of *sculpture*].

and face of God. The progress of art Hegel defines is the addition, by representation, of a content to a container. To the exclusion of the eastern strains of Judaism and Islam that prohibit just such representations of the divine, the necessary content of art that is no longer pre-art but proper art – the beautiful unity of expressive form and internal meaning – is already religious by Hegel's account, just as "the determined content of religion" ("de[r] bestimmte[r] Inhalt der Religion") is first made available in art: "this would be the original, true position of art as the closest, unmediable self-satisfaction of the absolute spirit" ("dies wäre die ursprüngliche, wahre Stellung der Kunst als nächste unmittelbare Selbstbefriedigung des absoluten Geistes").[51]

"*Third*" and finally, with the entering of the congregation, "the unity of God represented in sculpture is broken into the multiplicity of individuated interiority", and "the wide realm of human feeling, desire, and shortcomings becomes itself the object of artistic representation".[52] The "sensory element" or "material" for representing particular internal experiences must "also be particularized" accordingly; in its medium as in its subject matter, spirit no longer manifests itself in unity but in differentiation.[53] Echoing the structure of Hegel's presentation of aesthetic theory – the establishment of the "idea" of the beautiful in Part One; the theoretical history of artistic "forms", defined as entire periods, in Part Two; and the description of "the system of the *individual arts*" that traverse those forms in Part Three[54] – Hegel's narration of the origin of art in religion progresses from an establishing act of abstraction (the symbolic clearing of a space by architecture), to a "totalizing" individual form (the filling of a space by classical, sculptural representation), to the forms of multiple individuation (color, music, and finally linguistic sound) that make up the differential, romantic systems of "painting, music, and poetry".[55]

The complication in this neat sequence of events becomes apparent

---

[51] Hegel: Vol. XIII. P. 141. On the "art of the sublime" [*Kunst der Erhabenheit*] in Hebrew poetry as the dissolution of the "one" of the symbolic into two, "the abstract being-for-itself of God, and the concrete being of the world", see Vol. XIII. Pp. 480-85.

[52] Hegel: Vol. XIII. P. 119: "Die gediegene Einheit in sich des Gottes in der Skulptur zerschlägt sich in die Vielheit vereinzelter Innerlichkeit, [...] und [...] so wird jetzt [...] das weite Bereich menschlichen Empfindens, Wollens und Unterlassens für sich selber Gegenstand der künstlerischen Darstellung".

[53] Ibid.

[54] Hegel: Vol. XIV. P. 246.

[55] Hegel: Vol. XIII. Pp. 118-20.

by its own lights. If the first art also preceded art, was both art and "pre-art", then the time of classical art which is now past – the time when art fulfilled, in objective representation, "the highest need of the spirit" – must likewise appear temporally indistinguishable from its passing.[56] Just as there is a "*Before*" of art, Hegel states emphatically, there is an "*After*", in which art "passes over into higher forms of consciousness".[57] But just as "pre-art" is the origin of art, this passage from art arises *with* "its highest determination", making "our time" appear – upon reflection – like any time in which beautiful, representational art is viewed at all:

> Die Kunst in ihren Anfängen lässt noch Mysteriöses, ein geheimnisvolles Ahnen und eine Sehnsucht übrig, weil ihre Gebilde noch ihren vollen Gehalt nicht vollendet für die bildliche Anschauung herausgestellt haben. *Ist aber der vollkommene Inhalt vollkommen in Kunstgestalten hervorgetreten, so wendet sich* der weiterblickende Geist von dieser Objektivität in sein Inneres zurück und stösst sie von sich fort.[58]

> In its beginnings art still leaves behind mysteriousness, a secretive sense of something and a yearning, because its images have not yet perfectly displayed their full content for sensory intuition. Perfected content *having come* perfectly to the fore in artistic forms, however, *so spirit*, which looks onward, *turns back inside itself* from this objectivity and casts it aside.

Against the activity of beginning, related in the time of the present ("lässt"), Hegel juxtaposes a completed action, expressed in the perfect tense: "ist [...] hervorgetreten" ("came [...]" or "having come to the fore"). Here the meaning of the form of a verb additionally mirrors the lexical and contextual meaning it is being used to express, the achievement by artistic form of "perfected" (or "fully finished": "vollendet") content. Yet precisely at that moment in the history of the making and experience of art whose narration requires the perfect tense, a nonnar-

---

[56] Hegel: Vol. XIII. P. 142.

[57] Hegel: Vol. XIII. P. 141: "Wie nun aber die Kunst in der Natur und den endlichen Gebieten des Lebens ihr *Vor* hat, ebenso hat sie auch ein *Nach* [...]. Denn die Kunst hat noch in sich selbst eine Schranke und geht deshalb in höhere Formen des Bewusstseins über" [Yet just as art has its *Before* in nature and the finite realms of life, so it also has an *After* (...). For art still contains a limitation within itself and for this reason passes over into higher forms of consciousness].

[58] Hegel: Vol. XIII. P. 142 (my emphasis). For the continuation of this citation, see note 39.

rative present tense enters Hegel's account again. In this instance, too, form reproduces content: Hegel's morphological turn from the perfect reflects the semantics of his text, the turn of the intellect, in and to present time, from the completed forms of the past: "so wendet sich der [...] Geist [...]", "so spirit turns [...]" . Coordinating the two clauses of this sentence by bare syntactic apposition, without explicit causal or temporal subordination, Hegel effectively renders past and present cotemporaneous: the perfection or completion of an act – itself represented in the content of that act, the completion of an object – is accompanied, syntactically and temporally, by a new, uncompleted activity, the rejection by spirit of all such acts of objectification.

Taken as a whole, the *verbal* time employed in this two-sentence summary of all aesthetic history makes the activity of the distant beginnings of art, formulated in the present tense, appear closer to the dialectical movement of spirit beyond art than the (immediate) past of art's perfection. Like the present-tense arisal of art, the turn from art occurs with the force of an axiom available at any moment. Hegel historicizes neither event in itself: only the reported appearance of a completed object divides them. The appearance of completion in a perfect tense that serves to distinguish present tenses first makes the telling of time possible, forming change from continuity. It also – for Hegel, necessarily – makes such narrated time significant by positioning intellectual activity (spirit) within it. The completed art object spirit produces serves in turn to articulate the intellect in time.

Yet this union of spirit with temporal differentiation has the second, inevitable consequence of making all such differentiation appear a mere grammatical trick. One can enunciate the past achievement of a perfected *form* in the *form* of the perfect tense; however, since Hegel's aesthetics is not a chronology of forms, but a history of the invention and surpassing of forms by mental activity called spirit, what spirit *does* cannot be identified with the objects that spirit *has made*. An art history – a history of the objective forms of art – does not tell the story of intellectual "yearning" and "leaving behind", of contemplating objects and turning away from them, that is the true, and temporally nearly inarticulable subject of Hegel's *Aesthetics*: the infinite activity of spirit becoming different from itself, so as to become itself. In this nonlinear narrative of productive anticipation and either failed or temporary realization, "perfected" art, like the "past" in general, is a purely artificial form of objectification: the morpheme of a verbal category (the perfect) or the blunt visual aid of a form of punctuation, the comma separating perfect and present in Hegel's text.

In this sense, in its highest determination, art *at any time* is and remains for us a thing of the past, precisely because it is not the activity of spirit but what remains of that activity to be seen, a product we can perceive. "The sensory *appearing* of the idea" is not a neoplatonic apparition but a technical and historical *Kunstprodukt*, the "making of spirit into an object in *sensory* form", "whereby content becomes visible and imaginable".[59] For the same reason, the time of art in its highest determination can have no independent duration, for any such duration would achieve a formal objectification of spirit at odds with the oppositional "content" of spirit itself, producing a synthesis of intellectual activity and matter which must be anti-intellectual in effect. In that it removes spirit from the concrete world spirit opposes, art in its highest determination relegates the vital task of abstraction to the appearance of eternal rest.

The pyramids, by contrast, give rest to the dead. Only at first glance is this function tautological. Contrary to a hypothetical present of art in its highest determination, and the complementary historicization of art as the means away from art to greater abstraction, these perfect constructions "contain" ("einschliessen") not the life but the death of the mind – "a spirit departed" or defunct ("einen abgeschiedenen Geist") – in a permanent present.[60] They give the *viewer* pause by refusing to represent any image of the intellect, erecting, with their very appearance, a total barrier between form and intellectual content: a wall that, truly perfected, closes everywhere upon itself.[61] Unlike a partition symbol-

---

[59] Hegel: Vol. XIII. P. 151 (cf. Note 38); Vol. XIII. Pp. 111, 102 (emphasis in text): "die Kunst überhaupt [macht...] den Geist, in *sinnlich* konkreter Form zum Gegenstande [...]"; "wodurch der Inhalt anschaubar und vorstellbar wird".

[60] Hegel: Vol. XIV. P. 294.

[61] On the planned impenetrability of the pyramids, see Hegel: Vol. II. P. 293: "Die Eingänge in die Pyramiden waren aufs festeste mit Quadersteinen verschlossen, und es scheint, die Ägypter suchten es beim Bau schon so einzurichten, dass der Eingang, wenn er auch bekannt war, doch nur mit grosser Schwierigkeit konnte wieder aufgefunden und eröffnet werden. Dies beweist, dass die Pyrmaiden verschlossen bleiben und nicht wieder gebraucht werden sollten" [The entrances to the pyramids were closed tight with squared stones, and it seems that the Egyptians tried to set up construction in such a way that the entrance, if previously known, could only be rediscovered and opened with great difficulty. This proves that the pyramids were supposed to remain sealed and not be used again].

izing a potential passage from one of its sides to the other, making the death it stands for seem something transient, the self-enclosing pyramids short-circuit all perspective for their traversal, destroying *de facto* Hegel's history of a "before" and "after" of art. And unlike the nonsymbolic death rites of religions (such as Hindu Brahmanism) which view nature as the incarnation of gods and dead bodies as reintegrable parts of nature – extensions, in death as in life, of the divine – Egyptian entombments block ahistorical transformation.[62] Without nostalgia they objectify negation. The first form to give life to art, their objective content is separated doubly from the living: hidden from view, the bodies they house remain "individual", inassimilable to a general concept; preserved, they are no longer organic, but "fixed" forever by embalming.[63]

Only with the Egyptians, Hegel writes, do we arrive at a "fixed distinction of the living from the dead as dead" ("dieser festen Unterscheidung der Lebendigen von den Toten als Toten"), with the result that, for the first time, "the opposition between the living and the dead comes forcefully to the fore" ("der Gegensatz des Lebendigen und Toten [tritt] mit Macht hervor").[64] Yet the "opposition" embodied by the pyramids defies their dialectical conversion into monuments to abstraction. For within these "housings for the dead" ("Behausungen für Tote") *are* and remain the dead, their reason for being: not a fleeting moment of life held still, or an idea given "temporal appearance",[65] by the illusory means of representation, but dead that remain what they are ("Toten als Toten") by permanently filling, and excluding the living from, a concrete place of their own.[66] As isolated from our senses as

---

[62] Hegel: Vol. XIV. Pp. 290-91.
[63] Hegel: Vol. XIII. P. 458: "Was nun die ägyptische Kunstanschauung ihren besonderen Seiten nach angeht, so finden wir hier zum erstenmal das Innere, der Unmittelbarkeit des Daseins gegenüber, für sich festgehalten, und zwar des Innere als das Negative der Lebendigkeit, als das Tote; nicht als die abstrakte Negation des Bösen, Verderblichen, wie Ahriman im Gegensatze des Ormuzd, sondern in selbst konkreter Gestalt" [With regard to the special aspects of the Egyptian view of art, for the first time we find here the internal fixed for itself in relation to the immediacy of being: the internal as the negative of life, as the dead; not as the abstract negation of evil, or the deadly, in the manner of Ahriman in opposition to Ormuzd, but the negative itself in concrete form]. (Ahriman and Ormuzd are the Zorastrian gods of evil and good respectively.)
[64] Hegel: Vol. XIV. P. 291.
[65] See note 43.
[66] Hegel: Vol. XIV. P. 291.

they themselves are powerless, these bodies "are" in a manner pertinent neither to objects of perception, subjects of action, nor ideas of religious representation. The pyramids give rest to the dead by relieving them of exactly those dialectical modes of being.

As little Hegelian in conception as Kantian architectonics, the pyramids nonethless provide the vantage point for the kind of historicization they are built to withstand. These housings also clear a permanent path to the dialectic. Viewed by Hegel as "pre-art" and "properly symbolic" art because, unlike classical art, they conceal their individual content, the pyramids can also be classified the first art because, by containing and preserving "the dead as dead" – by separating them from the transformations of intellectual no less than natural life – they *artificially* create a new point of departure, the existence of specific content: "[t]he dead are kept as individual and thus secured and preserved against the imagining of an overflowing into the natural, into the general drifting, indistinction, and dissolution" ("[d]ie Toten werden daher als ein Individuelles festgehalten und damit gegen die Vorstellung des Hinüberfliessens in das Natürliche, in die allgemeine Verschwebung, Verschwemmung und Auflösung befestigt und aufbewahrt").[67]

The first indication Hegel identifies of "the freedom of the spirit" from nature necessarily requires the extraordinarily unfree being of an embalmed corpse, a fabricated *rigor mortis* additionally preserved from the further animation of intellectual internaliztion by being permanently housed within a faceless, otherwise uninhabitable form.[68] This strange being, the hidden being of the inassimilably dead – those neither departed nor available in body – becomes in Hegel the basis of art, the strictly invisible basis for the construction of visible form. When Hegel names the pyramids "monstrous crystals" ("ungeheure Kristalle"), we may thus assume he has more than their size and shape in mind.[69] Enormity and inorganicism are indeed the aspects of pyramids that first strike the eye. Yet what makes *these* enormous, inorganic buildings the first art form is what they *withhold* from vision, the monstrousness of an immutable negation known only to the mind: death removed, by artful means, from both physical decay and philosophical historicization.

---

[67] Hegel: Vol. XIV. P. 291; cf. Vol. XIII. P. 458.
[68] Pyramids, in other words, are anything but museums, whose display of tombs *and* their preserved contents make them, in Hegel's sense, anything but preservers of art.
[69] Hegel: Vol. XIII. P. 459.

Kept from these twin ravages, the unnatural, terribly concrete content created by "the symbolic proper" remains the essential basis of art even as it thwarts art's progress. Architecture alone does both these things and does them in an equally Hegelian sense. In order to be the first art, the pyramids must also be the last art: art beginning as aesthetic impasse. Before the sphinx and before Oedipus, before the human embodiment and ventriloquism of art by which art bears a face and poses a question that we alone may answer – before art becomes itself (sculptural, classical) and we become ourselves (identified, destined) in the intellectual completion of its form – art is and remains the riddle of a nonrepresentational architectonic form:

Solche Bedeutung, in deren Entzifferung man freilich heutigentags oft zu weit geht, weil fast alle Gestalten sich in der Tat unmittelbar als Symbole geben, könnte nun – in derselben Art, wie wir sie uns zu erklären suchen – auch für die ägyptische Anschauung selbst als Bedeutung klar und verständlich gewesen sein. Aber die ägyptischen Symbole enthalten, wie wir gleich anfangs sahen, implizit viel, explizit nicht. Es sind Arbeiten, mit dem Versuche unternommen, sich selber klarzuwerden, doch sie bleiben bei dem Ringen nach dem an und für sich Deutlichen stehen. In diesem Sinne sehen wir es den ägyptischen Kunstwerken an, dass sie Rätsel enthalten, für welche zum Teil nicht nur uns, sondern am meisten denen, die sie sich selber aufgaben, die rechte entzifferung nicht gelingt.[70]

The kind of meaning in whose deciphering we clearly go too far today, since almost all forms present themselves immediately as symbols, could have been for the Egyptian perception – in the same way in which we try to explain it for ourselves – clear and understandable as meaning. But Egyptian symbols, as we just saw to begin with, contain much implicitly, not explicitly. These are works undertaken in the attempt to become clear about oneself, but during this struggle for meaning in and of itself, they remain, nonetheless, at a standstill. In this sense we perceive in Egyptian artworks that they contain riddles whose correct solution not only we, in part, cannot reach, but which, for the most part, cannot be reached by those themselves who posed them for themselves.

A riddle which cannot be solved – not then, not now – is the standstill the first art contains within it, like the dead which cannot be transformed. Architecture comes first because it compels thought *and* impedes it, and what it does not show the viewer, having never been lost, will not later be found. Hegel's solution to the riddle of symbolic

[70] Hegel: Vol. XIII. Pp. 464-65.

architecture – to the impasse constructed by his own theory of the origin and progress of art – is to replace one form of necessary invisibility with another. His discussion of Egyptian architecture must make what is hidden sing. Unlike the problem of finding a single identity that remains constant within a changing narrative context (who is it, who at morning, noon, and night...) – the Aristotelian problem of representation posed by riddles typically which, by separating subject and context, or vehicle and tenor, provide for and receive a single unifying answer ("man") – Hegel's riddle of the symbol requires a change in signifying medium if its solution is to leave the symbol, the impasse of art, behind. Architecture, in short, must become poetry. It does so, in Hegel, in the shortest scope, before the classical representational arts are formed.

III. Singing Colossuses and Romantic Poetry

Unlike those of classical and romantic architecture, the buildings of symbolic architecture cannot be classified according to a fixed correlation of content with external form. Hegel explains:

Fragen wir [...] nach einer näheren *Gliederung* dieses Kapitels [der selbständigen, symbolischen Architektur] und der Hauptgebilde, welche hierher gehören, so kann bei dieser Architektur nicht wie bei der klassischen und romantischen von bestimmten Formen, von der des Hauses z.B., ausgegangen werden; denn es lässt sich hier kein für sich fester Inhalt und damit auch keine feste Gestaltungsweise als Prinzip angeben, das sich dann in seiner Fortentwicklung auf den Kreis der verschiedenen Werke bezöge. Die Bedeutungen nämlich, welche zum Inhalt genommen werden, bleiben, wie im Symbolischen überhaupt, gleichsam unförmliche allgemeine Vorstellungen, elementarische, vielfach gesonderte und durcheinander-geworfene Abstraktionen des Naturlebens, mit Gedanken der geistigen Wirklichkeit gemischt, ohne als Momente *eines* Subjekts ideell zusammengefasst zu sein. Diese Losgebundenheit macht sie höchst mannigfaltig und wechselnd, und der Zweck der Architektur besteht nur darin, bald diese, bald jene Seite für die Anschauung sichtbar herauszusetzen, sie zu symbolisieren und durch Menschenarbeit vorstellig werden zu lassen. Bei dieser Vielfachheit des Inhalts kann deshalb hier weder erschöpfend noch systematisch davon zu sprechen die Meinung sein, und ich muss mich deshalb darauf beschränken, nur das Wichstigste, soweit es möglich ist, in den Zusammenhang einer vernünftigen Gliederung zu bringen.[71]

[71] Hegel: Vol. XIV. Pp. 274-75.

Should we inquire as to the *particular categories* of this chapter [on independent, symbolic architecture] and the principle objects which belong in it, we cannot take specific forms, such as that of the house, as our point of departure, as we would do in the cases of classical and romantic architecture. For no content, fixed in itself, and thus no fixed mode of formation can be given here as the principle to whose further development the different works in this group could be related. The meanings accomodated by content remain, in the symbolic, unformed, general imaginings: elementary, distinct abstractions of the life of nature, thrown together and mixed with thoughts of intellectual reality, without being ideally synthesized as moments of *a* subject. Their loose association makes these abstract imaginings highly varied and changing, and the aim of the architecture consists in making their various sides visible, to symbolize and render them conceivable through human work. Given this multiplicity of content, one cannot intend to speak of it exhaustively or systematically, and I must thus limit myself, insofar as possible, to bringing only the most important [aspect] within the framework of reasoned categorization.

Before turning to Hegel's description of its "most important [aspect]", we would do well to consider what is being said here of symbolic architecture in general. As massive "abstractions", these permanent forms without corresponding content are multiply suggestive, conceptually "changing". Fixed in their material being, they are unfixed in significance, the medium of varied, fleeting imaginings. The palpable disparity described here between form and content signals more than a lack of harmony; what makes the meaning of the pyramids ephemeral from a specifically Hegelian perspective is their very suggestion of timeless significance. The pyramids bring meaning and sensory appearance into a relation of contradiction, but that incompatability of perception and thought could only arise in the context of Hegel's *a priori* historicization of art. Architecture that seems to defy the passage of time appears paradoxically transient in meaning because its forms are not identifiable with the underlying and ongoing progress of intellectual history: their persistence effectively divorces them from "the moments of *a* [thinking] subject", those intellectual changes in the very possibility of meaning that Hegelian philosophy considers definitive. As no development of thought, no subject coming to knowledge, grounds them in time, the permanent forms of symbolic architecture exist apart from aesthetic forms of properly historical significance, the true appearances of meaning ("das sinnliche Scheinen der Idee"[72]) which only

---

[72] See note 44.

a unified subject of reflection can produce, recognize, and move beyond.

Buildings which cannot be "ideally" subordinated to a coherent subjectivity appear inexplicable by any specific "principle"; the same stability they embody instead invites disorderly variety on the semantic plane. Such artforms convey meanings by offering the material occasion for acts of imagining and conceptualization, but those meanings must themselves fail to convey "moments" in the history of spirit, to be meaningful for "a subject" – for once, and for all – in the irreversible and unequivocal, Hegelian sense. Determined for all time, they are unavailable to dialectical conceptualization, the single, overarching principle of determination in Hegel's historical system. What makes them available to speculation whatsoever is instead conceptualization of a different kind.

Forms which endure unchanged seem fleeting and ahistorical because they appear exclusively as forms, nonrepresentational, immutably abstract. Hegel defines this kind of form, the symbol, as a sign:

Das Symbol ist nun zunächst ein *Zeichen*. Bei der blossen Bezeichnung aber ist der Zusammenhang, den die Bedeutung und deren Ausdruck miteinander haben, nur eine ganz willkürliche Verknüpfung. Dieser Ausdruck, dies sinnliche Ding oder Bild stellt dann so wenig sich selber vor, dass es vielmehr einen ihm fremden Inhalt, mit dem es in gar keiner eigentümlichen Gemeinschaft zu stehen braucht, vor die Vorstellung bringt. So sind in den Sprachen z.B. die Töne Zeichen von irgendeiner Vorstellung, Empfindung usw. Der überwiegende Teil der Töne einer Sprache ist aber mit den Vorstellungen, die dadurch ausgedrückt werden, auf eine dem Gehalte zufällige Weise verknüpft, [...] und die Verschiedenheit der Sprachen besteht vornehmlich darin, dass dieselbe Vorstellung durch ein verschiedenes Tönen ausgedrückt ist.[73]

Now the symbol is first of all a *sign*. The connection between meaning and its expression in a mere designation is, however, an entirely arbitrary one. This expression, this sensory thing or image, so little represents itself that it rather brings to conception a content foreign to it, with which it needs share no common property. Thus in languages, for example, sounds are signs of

---

[73] Hegel: Vol. XIII. P. 394; see also Vol. XV. Pp. 144-45: "Durch diese Gleichgültigkeit der Sprachlaute als sinnlicher gegen den geistigen Inhalt der Vorstellungen usf., zu deren Mitteilung sie gebraucht werden, erhält der Ton hier wieder Selbständigkeit" [In the indifference of linguistic phonemes, as sensory content, with regard to the intellectual content of the conceptions they are used to communcate, sound again obtains independence].

any conception, feeling, etc. However, with regard to content, the overwhelming portion of the sounds of a language is joined with the conceptions expressed by way of them in an accidental manner, [...] and the difference among languages consists mainly in the fact that the same conception is expressed through a different sounding.

Although Hegel compares "independent, symbolic architecture" to a "soundless language" ("lautlose Sprache"), the independence of that "language" lies, *like* the arbitrary relationship of sound to content in spoken language, precisely in its separation from specific meaning.[74] No less than the sounds of spoken language, the symbols of this silent "language" define it as a language of signs. Both sounds and symbols "designate" – they do not represent – what they signify.

The *Aesthetics*, however, is not, or not only, a semiotics. In the inescapable course of the historicization of sensory appearances Hegel describes, sign serves hermeneusis: the *formal* identity of sounding and silent languages as sign systems also makes itself *perceptually* known in time. The sensory form of the symbolic which follows the pyramids in Hegel's theoretical history is the semi-sculptural building of the colossus and sphinx. Still architectonic, these silent forms strike the senses at a specific moment in the manner of sounding signs. Ordered "in countless quantities, lined up in rows by the hundreds",[75] they appear to the eye like characters written upon the landscape, mute symbols strung together forever into text. Yet they are also perceived discretely by the ear like individual phonemes, signs made to sound not by human vocalization but by the light of dawn:

Besonders merkwürdig sind jene kolossalen *Memnonen*, welche, in sich beruhend, bewegungslos, die Arme steif und unlebendig, der Sonne entgegengestellt sind, um von ihr den Strahl zu erwarten, der sie berühre, beseele und tönen mache. Herodot wenigstens erzählt, dass die Memnonen beim Sonnenaufgang einen Klang von sich gäben. Die höhere Kritik hat dies zwar bezweifelt, das Faktum jedoch des Tönens ist neuerdings wieder von Franzosen und Engländern bestätigt worden, und [...] so lässt er sich erklären, dass, wie es Mineralien gibt, welche im Wasser knistern, der Ton jener Steinbilder von dem Tau und der Morgenkühle und den sodann darauffallenden Sonnenstrahlen herkommt, insofern dadurch kleine Risse ent-

---

[74] Hegel: Vol. XIV. P. 273.
[75] Hegel: Vol. XIII. P. 465: "In zahlloser Menge, zu Hunderten in Reihen aufgestellt, finden sich Sphinxgestalten in Ägypten vor [...]". Cf. Vol. II. P. 284.

stehen, die wieder verschwinden.[76]

Especially noteworthy are those colossal [figures of] Memnon which –
resting in themselves, motionless, arms closed upon the body, feet close to
one another, rigid, stiff and lifeless – are positioned before the sun in order
to await the ray from it which touches them, animates them, and makes
them sound. Herodotus, at least, recounts, that the Memnon [figures] gave
out a sound at dawn. Professional criticism has cast doubt on this, but the
fact of this sounding has been reconfirmed recently by Frenchmen and
Englishmen [...] and can be explained in that, as there are minerals which
crackle in water, so the sound of those stone figures comes from the dew
and cool morning air, followed by the rays of the sun which then fall upon
them, insofar as small cracks thus arise, which later disappear once again.

Now, Hegel specifies that these colossal figures are *not* sculptures but
buildings: they compose the "second" of his three categories of "independent, symbolic architecture".[77] While the "third" category entails the
"transition" to "classical" architecture, a "housing for other meanings
no longer expressed in an immediately architectonic manner" ("einem
Gehäuse für andere, nicht unmittelbar selber architektonisch ausge-
drückte Bedeutungen"), the second group – *which sounds* – remains
fundamentally architectonic: "[o]n the other hand architecture presses
[...] to pass on to *sculpture*, to take on the organic forms of animal
shapes and human figures, to extend them massively, however, into the
colossal, to line them up next to each other, to add partitions, walls,
gates, and passages to them, and thereby to treat what is sculptural in
them in a purely architectonic manner" ("[a]uf der anderen Seite drängt
sich die Baukunst [...] zur *Skulptur* überzugehen, organische Formen
von Tiergestalten, menschlichen Figuren anzunehmen, sie jedoch ins
Kolossale hin massenhaft auszudehnen, aneinanderzureihen, Wände,
Mauern, Tore, Gänge hinzuzufügen und dadurch das Skulpturartige an
ihnen schlechthin architektonisch zu behandeln").[78]

Along with "the Egyptian sphinxes and great temple buildings", the
sounding Memnon figures "belong" to those "architectural works

---

[76] Hegel: Vol. XIII. P. 462. Cf. Vol. XIV. P. 282: "Die Ägypter und Äthipier
verehrten den Memnon, den Sohn der Morgenröte, und opferten ihm, wenn die
Sonne ihre ersten Strahlen sendet, wodurch das Bildnis mit seiner Stimme die
Anbetenden begrüsste" [The Egyptians and Ethiopians venerated the Memnon, the
son of dawn, and sacrificed to him at the first rays of the sun, whereby the
figure greeted the worshippers with his voice].
[77] Hegel: Vol. XIV. P. 275.
[78] Hegel: Vol. XIV. Pp. 276, 275 (emphasis in text).

ranging between architecture and sculpture" in which "architecture remains the pervasive [element]" ("die Baukunst [bleibt] das Durchgreifende").[79] Thus, before the symbolic becomes classical, before the sculptural ceases to be architectonic – a sign –, symbolic building emits pure, or meaningless, sound. It does this at daybreak and at the beginning of art, and in so doing it already foretells the twilight and end of art, "the meaningless sign" ("bedeutungslose[s] Zeichen") of romantic poetry.[80] The architectural origin of art contains both immutable bodies and the eventual history of art, the dead of the past and the future arisal and demise of individual subjectivity. The effect of such an architectonic *and* historicizing model upon our conception of poetry can perhaps be made clearest by way of reference to a recent critical debate.

The subject of the debate is Baudelaire, whose poems often link architecture with poetry.[81] The particular poem in question is his "Spleen II", in which the speaker is compared in closing to a sphinx singing at the characteristic Baudelairean moment, *crépuscule* . The critics, Hans Robert Jauss and Paul de Man, disagree as to whether the sphinx can be considered a figure for the poet, and his song, a figure for the poem, a representation of a subjectivity able to communicate itself which the poem had previously figured as lost.

Denying the identity between the sphinx and a poetic self refound in a monumental substitute for its absence, de Man refers directly to the architectonic nature of the sphinx, as described by Hegel:

> The transformation [in the poem] occurs as one moves from mind (as recollection) to pyramid and to sphinx. It occurs, in other words, by an itinerary that travels by way of Egypt. Egypt, in Hegel's *Aesthetics,* is the birthplace of truly symbolic art, which is monumental and architectural, not literary [...]. "[P]yramid", which connotes, of course Egypt, monument and

[79] Hegel: Vol. XIV. Pp. 275, 279. On the sphinxes as primarily architectonic, see Vol. XIV. P. 283: "Dies immense Gebilde nähert sich zwar mehr der eigentlichen Skulptur in deren kolosallstem Massstabe; ebensosehr jedoch wurden die Sphinxe auch zu Gängen reihenweise nebeneinandergestellt, wodurch sie sogleich einen vollständig architektonschen Charakter erhalten" [This immense work approaches actual sculpture in its most colossal scale; just the same, however, the sphinxes were also set next to each other in rows forming passages, whereby they immediately maintain a fully architectonic character].
[80] Hegel: Vol. XV. P. 235.
[81] Cf. my 'Terrible Novelty': Baudelaire's Vision of Building. In: *Nineteenth-Century French Studies in Literature*. Ed. Keith Busby. Amsterdam 1992. Pp. 43-57.

crypt, [...] also connotes, to a reader of Hegel, the emblem of the sign as opposed to the symbol [...] the deliberate forgetting of substantial, aesthetic, and pictorial symbols. Baudelaire, who in all likelihood never heard of Hegel, happens to hit on the same emblematic sequence [...]. [T]he crypt of recollection [...] is replaced by the sphinx, who, since he has a head and a face, can be apostrophized in the poetic speech of rhetorical figuration. But the sphinx is not an emblem of recollection, but, like Hegel's sign, an emblem of forgetting.[82]

As if in imitation of the Hegelian symbol itself, de Man here both indicates and buries the definition of symbol *as unmotivated sign* which Hegel purposefully constructs, and which makes his historical *Aesthetics*, beginning with the pyramids, possible. For Hegel's first or, in de Man's terms, "truly" symbolic art is, as de Man states, "monumental and architectural, not literary": the pyramid. Yet that symbol is anything but "pictorial": it is a crypt which, functioning as a sign, forever impedes "forgetting" even as it makes the content of memory absolutely inaccessible. Similarly, the more pictorial (or, in de Man's terms, symbolic) sphinx is indeed, in both de Man's and Hegel's terms, like a sign; stranger still, it is a singing sign, and the hour of its song is twilight, the time of poetry in Hegel. In the space of a few verse lines Baudelaire has effectively conflated the two outer limits of Hegel's millenial art history, its architectural origin *and* poetic end as sign. In equating mute symbols with singing signs as Hegel does, Baudelaire does *not* imply that the song of the sphinx is not poetry; he does imply, however, that it is not poetry in the sense of a recuperative, self-allegorizing consciousness claimed by Jauss, "the rising of beauty into song, which overcomes anxiety and atones for the loss of the 'I' [...] through the final form of its subject, which now becomes retrospectively recognizable in the first form (for who may say with greater right than the sphinx, 'j'ai plus de souvenirs que si j'avais mille ans'?).[83] In other words, while it is incorrect to say Baudelaire's image of the sphinx is not, in Hegel's terms, pervasively architectonic, it is also incorrect to state that it is not – again in Hegel's terms – an image of

---

[82] Paul de Man: Reading and History. In: *The Resistance to Theory*. Minneapolis. Pp. 69-70 (orig. pub.: "Introduction" to Jauss: *Toward an Aesthetic of Reception* [Minneapolis 1982]. P. xxv.).
[83] Hans Robert Jauss: The Poetic Text within the Change of Horizons of Reading: The Example of Baudelaire's 'Spleen II'. In: *Toward an Aesthetic of Reception*. Trans. Timothy Bahti. Introduction by Paul de Man. Minneapolis 1982. P. 169.

poetry, specifically romantic poetry, the ultimate art. Hegel's historical system includes poetry within the architectonic, but it is a poetry of sound without internal moorings. His description of the sound resulting from the external influence of the sun upon the stone colossuses continues:

> Als *Symbol* aber ist diesen Kolossen die Bedeutung zu geben, dass sie die geistige Seele nicht frei in sich selber haben und zur Belebung daher, statt sie aus dem Innern entnehmen zu können, welches Mass und Schönheit in sich trägt, von aussen des Lichts bedürfen, das erst den Ton der Seele aus ihnen herauslockt. Die menschliche Stimme dagegen tönt aus der eigenen Empfindung und dem eigenen Geiste ohne äussere Anstoss, wie die Höhe der Kunst überhaupt darin besteht, das Innere sich aus sich selber gestalten zu lassen. Das Innere aber der menschlichen Gestalt ist in Ägypten noch stumm und in seiner Beseelung nur das natürliche Moment berücksichtigt.[84]

> As *symbol*, however, the colossuses can be ascribed this meaning, that they do not have free within themselves an intellectual soul, and for their animation require external light, which first charms the sound of the soul out of them, rather than being able to produce such animation from the interior which carries measure and beauty in itself. The human voice, by contrast, sounds from its own feeling and own spirit without external impetus, just as the summit of art in general consists in allowing the interior to form itself from itself. The interior of the human form is, however, still mute in Egypt and in its animation only takes the natural moment into account.

The opposition Hegel draws here is as fundamental to the dialectic as the difference between external matter and internal spirit, sunlight and inner light, mute stone and sounding voice. It implies that the realms of architectonic and poetic art are indeed as far apart as "an intellectual soul" and "the natural moment", and thus themselves enact the grounds for refuting Kant's aesthetic theory, cited above: the incomparability of "beauty born and reborn of spirit" and "such a natural existence as the sun".[85] Yet the medium for these unmediatably opposed forms of production – and only for them – is one. The introduction to poetry, the last individual artform and chapter in the last phase of art and part of the *Aesthetics*, "Die romantische Künste", directly compares "Dichtkunst" with "Baukunst:"

> Wie vollständig deshalb auch die Poesie die ganze Totalität des Schönen

---

[84] Hegel: Vol. XIII. P. 462 (emphasis in text).
[85] See note 35 above.

noch einmal in geistigster Weise produziert, so macht dennoch die Geistigkeit gerade zugleich den Mangel dieses letzten Kunstgebiets aus. Wir können innerhalb des Systems der Künste die Dichtkunst in dieser Rücksicht der Architektur direkt entgegenstellen. Die Baukunst nämlich vermag das objektive Material dem geistigen Gehalt noch nicht so zu unterwerfen, dass die dasselbe zur adäquaten Gestalt des Geistes zu formieren imstande wäre; die Poesie umgekehrt geht in der negativen Behandlung ihres sinnlichen Elementes so weit, dass sie das Entgegengesetzte der schweren räumlichen Materie, den Ton, statt ihn, wie es die Baukunst mit ihrem Material tut, zu einem andeutenden Symbol zu gestalten, vielmehr zu einem bedeutungslosen Zeichen herabbringt.[86]

Thus, however completely poetry still produces the totality of the beautiful in an intellectual manner, it is precisely in such intellectualism that the lack of this last realm of art consists. In this respect we can directly oppose the art of poetry to architecture within the system of the arts. For the art of building cannot yet subordinate objective material to intellectual content in such a way as to form an adequate shape of the intellect; poetry, on the other hand, goes so far in its negative treatment of the sensory element that it debases sound, the opposite term to heavy spatial material, to a meaning-less sign, instead of forming it into a meaning-bearing symbol, as the art of building does with its material.

In attempting to describe the end of art, Hegel has recourse to the original art: ("romantic") poetry reflects ("symbolic) architecture, i.e., it inverts it. Poetry, Hegel states immediately preceding this paragraph, is "the individual art through which, at the same time, art itself begins to dissolve" [diejenige besondere Kunst, an welcher zugleich die Kunst selbst sich aufzulösen beginnt[87]], because its intellectual excess yields, in aesthetic terms, "a lack:" an absence of sensorily structured meaning. In order to be grasped within the realm of the aesthetic at all, the "negative treatment" of the "sensory element" within poetry which separates the matter of "sound" from meaning must be *compared aesthetically* with something that provides too much of what it is miss-ing, those buildings in whose excessively positive treatment of matter the imbalance between matter and meaning first took shape.

Yet, at the same time, it is through the very act of comparison that the specificity of these forms dissolves. In the context of its comparison with romantic poetry, "mute" architecture, so-called because in it "spirit [...] does not yet know how to speak the clear language of

---

[86] Hegel: Vol. XV. P. 235.
[87] Hegel: Vol. XV. P. 234.

spirit" and the "interiority" symbolized is instead itself "the negative", the intransmutably "dead",[88] is redefined as the "meaning-bearing symbol", while poetry, which, in the "symbolic" form of the Old Testament narrative and Hebrew Psalms, first effected the "expression" of the single "clear meaning" of an unrepresentable God,[89] becomes at the end of Hegel's dialectical history of art "a meaningless sign". Architecture and poetry have in effect exchanged places within that history: the Egyptian distinction and preservation of "den Toten als Toten" ("the dead as dead") which caused symbolic (pre-)art to come about is replaced in romantic poetry with its sensory dissolution *and* equivalent, "ein Tönen als solches, ohne Gegenständlichkeit und Gestalt" ("a sounding as such, without objectification and form").[90] *[Die] Toten* and *ein Tönen*: conceptually and materially opposed as death to life, and heavy matter to all that is light, these embodiments of "departed spirit" ("einen abgeschiedenen Geist") and arriving Spirit take on each other's characteristics. In part because they *do in fact sound similarly,* death as death (*Toten*) and sounding as such (*Tönen*) are very much the same: their dialectical differentiation depends upon solely on the temporal "standpoint" one takes in analyzing them. Verbal forms which sound like each other truly profer the death of the intellectual, because such sameness owes to the similarity of their sensory matter alone.

Yet Hegel's dead as such and sounding as such do not only "sound" alike, they are alike, that is, they are the stuff of "sign". And only from a temporal distance does sign appear not as "meaningless sign" but as "meaning-bearing symbol" – only as a vehicle of comparison does the "indecipherable" appear to speak "the clear language" which present signs "lack". As art dissolves with poetry into a formless sounding as such – "ein Schweben über den Wassern, ein Klingen über einer Welt, [...]". [a floating over the waters, a ringing over a world (...)] –, it becomes external to the world of appearances as such – "[...] welche in ihren und an ihren heterogenen Erscheinungen nur einen Gegenschein dieses Insichseins der Seele aufnehmen und widerspiegeln kann" [(...) which in and through heterogenous appearances can only take up and reflect a counter-appearance of this self-integral being (or "being-within-itself") of the soul].[91] Distinct from the metamorphoses of the

[88] Hegel: Vol. XIII. Pp. 457-58.
[89] Hegel: Vol. XIII. P. 480.
[90] Hegel: Vol. XIV. P. 140 (from the conclusion of the Introduction to Part III, "The Romantic Artform").
[91] Hegel: Vol. XIV. P. 141.

world, including artforms themselves, the sounding of poetry as "meaningless sign" echoes the fixed distinction between the dead and the living first made by the Egyptians. For with "the people who build" art arose and distinguished itself from the practices of those peoples who viewed life and death in metamorphic continuity. If Egyptian architecture, apparently the least verbal of the arts, led Hegel to state that "the symbol is, in the first place, a sign", then romantic poetry, apparently the most verbal art, leads him to conclude that the symbol is a sign in the last place, at the end of art. If Kant's *Critique*, while stating the fact of freedom from form, made no (dialectical) distinction between the aesthetic experience of the things of nature and the made or semiotic things of art, and thus is itself read by Hegel in the manner of the symbol, as a temporal pivot for the dialectic of the beautiful he narrates, then Hegel's sign, first and finally the representation of freedom from meaningful form, must take two distinct, symbolic forms of indecipherability, architecture and poetry, if it is to "mean" anything at all.

In an historic, hermeneutic view of the beautiful, the (inevitably "meaningless") sign must be deciphered by the symbol it is and is not: in contrast with romantic poetry, symbolic architecture must provide that meaning which, as riddle-like sign, it kept locked within itself. The dead housed permanently by the pyramids must be legible as their opposite, spirit, *Toten* must be unearthed as *Tönen*, even and especially in the absence of the natural light of the sun, if sign is to succeed sign – if meaninglessness is to succeed meaninglessness – in a meaningful way. In order for past and present indecipherability to yield an interpretive history, signs which are meaningless in themselves have to be exchanged. The fact that the sign, "this expression, this sensory thing or image represents it own self so little" [(d)ieser Ausdruck, dies sinnliche Ding oder Bild stellt dann so wenig sich selber vor], and that intellectual "meaning" and sensory "expression" are "arbitrarily" linked in the sign, can be discerned, Hegel observes, from languages themselves: "the difference among languages consists mostly in the fact that the same conception is expressed through a different sounding" [die Verschiedenheit der Sprachen besteht vornehmlich darin, dass dieselbe Vorstellung durch ein verschiedenes Tönen ausgedrückt ist].[92]

A nonarbitrary narrative *linking* the artificial expressions of spirit must, by contrast, move toward a sounding which is incomparably

---

[92] Hegel: Vol. XIII. P. 394; this explanation is the continuation of the passage defining the symbol as sign, cited above (see note 74).

"different": unsubordinated to meaning and thus "in itself" the meaning of art. Romantic poetry is, properly speaking, the *missing* solution of the riddle of the sign introduced by the pyramids, because this solution is the very dissolution of art into spirit which those "monstrous crystals" stand permanently, nondialectically against; and the pyramids house the missing body that the sounding of romantic poetry "lacks", because "in its highest determination", i.e., as spirit, this body is truly, properly dead. Together architecture and poetry do what the aesthetic is supposed to do and what the dialectic of all forms made by spirit must always do: house, so as to "reveal", the spirit *over time*. And together they demonstrate that they can never be together, that meaning will always reside with one of them at another – at the other's – time. The pyramids, signs built on and "into the ground" to traverse time, house a body that, dialectically speaking, requires no housing, while romantic poetry, "a sounding" like "a floating over the waters", lacks the body which would ground it as a structure in which meaning could temporarily reside. The pyramids and romantic poetry demonstrate why and how Hegel "builds" upon Kant: why, rejecting Kant's theory that the formal sensory experience of any object may be available at any moment to aesthetic judgment, Hegel's dialectical art history must first translate specific artforms into sign. "The truth" "reveal[ed]" in the necessary relation between these "sensory artforms" is that artforms must be viewed as "meaningless signs" in order to be compared meaningfully. For, as embodiments of the sign requiring not only each other but each other's reversal to be interpreted, the pyramids and romantic poetry prove that the sign that houses spirit can never reveal it, can never in itself constitute an aesthetic moment, if there *is to be* meaning to art. Art requires semiosis in Hegel because history requires art: only in the aestheticization of the "meaningless sign" can a theory of the beautiful produce meaningful time.

Carsten Strathausen

Eichendorff's *Das Marmorbild*
and the Demise of Romanticism

This reading of Eichendorff's Marmorbild *examines the relationship between word and image in the novella within the context of Romantic theory and media history. The author argues that the Marmorbild is situated at the faultline between Romantic aesthetic paradigms and the nascent discourse of modernity. Whereas the former relies on the creative power of poetic imagination to engage and produce art, the latter questions the authority of human imagination in light of specular forms of entertainment such as the phantasmagoria and other proto-cinematic devices.*

There are few examples in literary history where a text and its interpretation appear to converge as seamlessly as in Eichendorff's *Das Marmorbild*, for the essence of 20th-century critical reaction to the novella seems itself cast in stone and thus eager to emulate its subject of reference. Given Eichendorff's explicit endorsement of Catholicism, critics have generally focused their attention on the alleged binary structure of the *Marmorbild*, its "black and white"[1] representation of the religious conflict between damnable heathendom and redeeming Christianity. These readings highlight what is often referred to as the aesthetic rigidity and "statue-likeness" of the text itself, a "loss of inner tension" that separates it from other "more interesting" Romantic works.[2]

Most recent studies, however, regard this stasis to be grounded in the reification of traditional academic discourse rather than in

---

[1] Michael Sauter: Marmorbilder und Masochismus. Die Venusfiguren in Eichendorffs *Das Marmorbild* und in Sacher-Masochs *Venus im Pelz*. In: *Neophilologus* 75 (1991). P. 119.

[2] Hannelore Schlaffer: Mutterbilder, Marmorbilder. In: *Germanisch-Romanische Monatsschrift* 36 (1986). Pp. 304-19. Similarly Winfried Woesler: Frau Venus und das schöne Mädchen mit dem Blumenkranze. Zu Eichendorffs *Marmorbild*. In: *Aurora* 45 (1985). Pp. 33-48. For a comprehensive overview of similar criticism, see Waltraud Wietölter: Die Schule der Venus. Ein diskursanalytischer Versuch zu Eichendorffs *Das Marmorbild*. In: Michael Kessler and Helmut Koopmann (eds). *Eichendorffs Modernität*. Stuttgart 1989. Pp. 171-221.

Eichendorff's text. One critic argues that the fictional characters usually associated with either the Christian or the pagan realm are much more ambiguous and exhibit traces of both, while the plenitude of sexual imagery displayed in the text subverts at least tendentiously its moralistic ending.[3] These later readings indeed resonate with the very first reactions voiced by Eichendorff's contemporaries, who criticized the novella for being too "fantastic" and rich in images. Instead of denouncing it as being trivial and rigid, these critics on the contrary lamented what they perceived as a fragmented story full of "Gespensterspuk" and "Romantic hallucinations" ("romantische Blendbilder") which leave the reader completely bewildered and confused.[4]

It appears that the history of critical reception of Eichendorff's novella is caught up in the same oscillatory process of reification and movement ("Versteinerung und Bewegung"), contemplation and distraction ("Versenkung und Zerstreuung") which, as I will argue in this paper, marks the central motif in the *Marmorbild* and which lends itself to contradictory interpretations, depending on which perspective is emphasized. This essay refrains from endorsing either and instead accepts this ambiguity as characteristic of Eichendorff's text. To do so requires the reader to pursue various Romantic aesthetic theories and cultural practices as a means of examining the novella within the interdisciplinary context of the word-image relationship. The first part of my reading will thus repeat the oscillatory movement one follows through the text during the process of its interpretation. The second part of this essay advances a double thesis. I maintain that the story's peculiar suspension between simplicity and obscurity is anti-dialectical in nature and gives rise to a kind of "moving standstill" whose momentum fails to transcend the boundaries of the literary text. This literary confinement, I argue, derives from Eichendorff's rejection of the poetic power of human imagination to harmoniously unite the private and the public, self and world. I will also contend that this skepticism towards the mediating power of artistic creation was facilitated not only by late Romantic aesthetic discourse, but also by popular forms of specular entertainment such as the phantasmagoria projected by the magic lantern. As a consequence, Eichendorff's text is less con-

---

[3] Cf. Wietölter. Pp. 171-80. Similarly Simon Jan-Richter: Under the Sign of Venus: Eichendorff's *Marmorbild* and the Erotics of Allegory. In: *South Atlantic Review* 56.2 (1991). Pp. 59-71.

[4] See the Reclam edition of *Erläuterungen und Dokumente* entitled *Joseph von Eichendorff. Das Marmorbild*. Ed. Hanna H. Marks. Stuttgart 1989.

cerned with the self-conscious exploration of literary forms of representation than with working through the perceptual crisis caused by the rise of proto-cinematic devices and other cultural phenomena at the beginning of the 19th century.

I

The *Marmorbild* is a text about images. Throughout the novella, Florio is literally surrounded by a plethora of ubiquitous "Bilder" of all kinds and shapes, including paintings, landscapes, statues, memories, and dreams. When Florio perceives the Venus statue for the first time, he seems to recognize her image as one he had already known in his youth; in the Venus palace, he admires a series of paintings which seem to portray his own recent experiences, although he clearly remembers having seen similar pictures when he was a child. These are fairly typical examples for Romanticism's interest in the art of representation: alluding to a story within the story, the fictional hero is confronted with what appears to be yet another fictionalized version of his own history. This interlacing of various levels of representation initiates a series of displacements which exposes both the literary text and the pictures described therein as mere artifice, thus signifying the essence or meaning of art as an absolute ideal located beyond manifest forms of representation. In short, the frequent evocation of images in Eichendorff's text might function as a kind of "Romantic irony", a self-conscious reference to and exploration of various modes of artistic representation within the literary text meant to highlight the fragmentary and referential nature of art.

However, the *Marmorbild* not only describes various images in great detail, it portrays Florio's travels and even life itself as a continuous series of "ever-changing pictures" ("ewig wechselnden Bildern"),[5] an expression echoed repeatedly in the text as it recalls the "pictures of the day" ("Bilder[..] des Tages" [15]) or describes a social gathering as a "circle of merry pictures" ("den Kranz heiterer Bilder" [8]) in which Florio appears as yet another "lovely picture among other beautifully moving pictures" ("[...] wie ein anmutiges Bild, zwischen den schönen schweifenden Bildern" [27]). The text thus highlights its own visual quality with the help of an aestheti-

[5] Joseph von Eichendorff: *Das Marmorbild. Das Schloß Dürande.* Stuttgart 1993. Pp. 5-48, here pp. 7 and 38. All further citations refer to this edition and are given in the body of the text.

cizing gaze that transforms the fictional reality it presents into a series of representational pictures.[6]

Given the predominance of literary pictures in Eichendorff's text, it seems reasonable to situate the novella within the ekphrastic tradition, defined most broadly as literature's attempt to *describe*, or, using a more narrow definition, actually to *imitate* visual imagery, be it a person, an object or a place.[7] Ekphrasis in the second sense certainly proves interesting in our context, as it might help ascertain the specificity of Eichendorff's use of literary images. The general history of ekphrasis can be traced back to two canonical authors with contradictory views on the kinship and reciprocity between literature and the visual arts: Horace and Lessing. While the former issued his famous dictum "Ut pictura poesis" ("as in painting, so in poetry") in the belief that literature should consciously seek to imitate the visual arts, Lessing insists on the incommensurability of the two media. In his aesthetic treatise *Laokoon*, he locates the differences between text and image within the separate realms of time and space they inhabit. The visual arts such as painting and sculpture are characterized by simultaneity and spatial stasis, i.e., they extend in space and present themselves in their entirety to the first glance of the beholder. Literary texts, by contrast, do not possess any physical corporeality, Lessing argues.[8] They unfold in

[6] Grimm's *Wörterbuch* underlines the particular meaning of "Bild" as an artificially created image that may refer to both two- or three-dimensional forms of representation, but which always remains secondary behind the "Urbild" and thus of a derivative, aestheticized nature.

[7] A more precise definition of the term "ekphrasis" proves difficult since scholars disagree about its traditional scope and meaning. The broader definition used above is explicitly rejected by James A.W. Heffernan and W.J.T. Mitchell, both of whom argue that ekphrasis specifically refers to the verbal representation of graphic representation in order to distinguish it from iconicity and pictorialism encountered in almost every literary text. "What ekphrasis represents in words", Heffernan argues, "must itself be representational" (300), i.e., it must itself be another referential work of art. James A.W. Heffernan Ekphrasis and Representation. In: *New Literary History* 22 (1991). P. 299. Other scholars such as Mieke Bal avoid the term ekphrasis altogether, favoring the idea of a "visual poetics" as an attempt to examine the interdisciplinary relationship between word and image. See Mieke Bal: Introduction. Visual Poetics. In: *Style* 22. 2 (Summer 1988). Pp. 177-82.

[8] Lessing's apodictic claims have been modified in the history of art criticism, for example by Norman Bryson, who rightly asserts that we never perceive an image in its ideal state of totality. Images also do change over time, both materially and spiritually, i.e., with regard to their meaning. Nonetheless,

the course of time during the act of reading and thus cannot be perceived or "taken in" all at once. Art is static,; literature is agile. The two should therefore remain separate and distinct forms of art. Viewed from Lessing's perspective, Eichendorff's *Marmorbild* might be called a transgressive text as it focuses on the literary exploration of visual imagery. Yet the question remains as to exactly how texts such as the *Marmorbild* endeavor to overcome the considerable differences between literature and the arts. One possibility consists in defining the "ekphrastic principle" as the deliberate attempt of literature to "freeze" its own temporality so it can achieve corporal existence and "take on the still elements of plastic form", as Murray Krieger has argued.[9] Stylistic features such as redundancy, repetitiveness or circular patterns thus emerge as artistic means at the disposal of a "visual poetics". With regard to Eichendorff's *Marmorbild*, one might thus regard the often lamented "statue-likeness" of Eichendorff's text as a deliberate aesthetic device, a kind of physical assimilation meant to inscribe the differences of the spatial arts within the chronology of literary discourse.[10]

I do not, however, believe this to be an apt reading of the *Marmorbild*, a text too concerned with the narration of Florio's psychological development for it to escape the temporal constraints of language. Moreover, many of the images depicted in the story are characterized by their inner motion, giving rise to a series of "moving pictures" nicely illustrated at the very beginning of the text, as Florio strolls in the park of Luccia (note the abundance of present participles indicating movement):

Versteckte Musikchöre erschallten da von allen Seiten aus den blühenden Gebüschen, unter den hohen Bäumen wandelten sittige Frauen auf und nieder und ließen die schönen Augen musternd ergehen über die glänzende Wiese, lachend und plaudernd und mit den bunten Federn nickend im lauen Abendgolde wie ein Blumenbeet, das sich im Winde wiegt. Weiterhin auf einem heitergrünen Plan vergnügten sich mehrere Mädchen mit Ballspielen.

Bryson does seem to agree with Lessing regarding the immateriality of linguistic signifiers. He argues that texts "absolutely disobey the description of Aristotelian 'substance'. Texts are like this because they possess no embodiment. They are sheer information". Norman Bryson: Intertextuality and Visual Poetics. In: *Style* 22.2 (Summer 1988). P. 192.

[9] Murray Krieger: *The Play and Place of Criticism*. Baltimore 1967. P. 107.

[10] See W.J.T. Mitchell: *Iconology. Image, Text, Ideology*. Chicago 1986, and Grant F. Scott: The Rhetoric of Dilation: Ekphrasis and Ideology. In: *Word and Image* 7.4 (Oct.-Dec. 1991). Pp. 301-10.

Die buntgefiederten Bälle flatterten wie Schmetterlinge, glänzende Bogen
hin und her beschreibend, durch die blaue Luft, während die unten im
Grünen auf und nieder schwebenden Mädchenbilder den lieblichsten Anblick gewährten. (6-7)

This sense of perpetual movement does not stay confined to the
diegetic level of the story, but resonates in the structural composition of the entire text as well. Eichendorff's novella not only exhibits strong intertextual ties to tales by Novalis, Brentano, and
E.T.A. Hoffmann, but also tries to relocate the history of Romantic
discourse and imagery into the childhood of its fictional hero.[11]
Florio's Romantic fundus includes among others the ancient tales of
the wandering "Spielmann" (6), the "Wunderblume" (18) that
recalls Novalis' "blue flower", examples of old paintings as well as
Fortunato's ancient songs, all of which remind Florio of his own
youth that "he had almost forgotten due to the ever-changing
images encountered during his travels" ("[...] das er in seiner Kind-
heit oft gehört und seitdem über den wechselnden Bildern der Reise
fast vergessen hatte" [38]).

The novella's structural openness and mobility caused by the
abundance of intertextual references repeatedly intersects with the
depiction of moving pictures in the text. The perpetual sense of
movement thus emerges as one central characteristic of Eichendorff's text both on the descriptive and the thematic levels, emphasizing a similiarity in content and structure that culminates in the
animation of the Marmorbild as Florio perceives it for the first
time:

Der Mond, der eben über die Wipfel trat, beleuchtete scharf ein marmornes
Venusbild, das dort dicht am Ufer auf einem Steine stand, als wäre die Göt-
tin so eben erst aus den Wellen aufgetaucht und betrachte nun, selber ver-
zaubert, das Bild der eigenen Schönheit, das der trunkene Wasserspiegel
zwischen den leise aus dem Grund aufblühenden Sternen widerstrahlte.
Einige Schwäne beschrieben still ihre einförmigen Kreise um das Bild, ein
leises Rauschen ging durch die Bäume ringsumher. Florio stand wie
eingewurzelt im Schauen, denn ihm kam jenes Bild wie eine lang gesuchte,
nun plötzlich erkannte Geliebte vor, wie eine Wunderblume, aus der Früh-
lingsdämmerung und träumerischen Still seiner frühesten Jugend heraufge-
wachsen. Je länger er hinsah, je mehr schien es ihm, als schlüge es die
seelenvollen Augen langsam auf, als wollten sich die Lippen bewegen zum
Gruße, als blühe Leben wie ein lieblicher Gesang erwärmend durch die
schönen Glieder herauf. (17)

---

[11] Cf. Wietölter. Pp. 173ff.

The scene describes the "moving image" of the statue, yet it also illustrates the various literary traditions Eichendorff evokes in his text, for it merges the Pygmalion and Narcissus motifs with the Venus and Diana myths. This literal and metaphorical emphasis on (inter-)textual movement is critical for the interpretation of Eichendorff's text and indeed deserves a closer look.

The function of the Diana myth for the story as a whole is all too obvious: it represents the pagan realm of dark, seductive forces and thus again serves to highlight the already-mentioned juxtaposition of Christianity and heathendom that pervades the entire text. Although the Pygmalion and Narcissus motifs also partake in that static binary scheme, they raise more complex issues. For the depiction of the Venus statue as a Narcissus-like figure admiring its own image in the water remains ambiguously suspended between a three-dimensional body and a plain reflection devoid of spatial depth. It is left unclear which "Bild" is circled by the swans, the reflection or the statue proper. This moment of uncertainty already marks the beginning of a perceptual crisis that is prompted by Florio's long, contemplative gaze and ultimately culminates in the apparent movements of the statue. Yet the scene not only serves to introduce the Pygmalion motif by animating Venus, it also evokes the 18th-century aesthetic controversy regarding the hierarchy among the visual arts, in particular between classical sculpture, idealized by German Classicism, and medieval and Renaissance painting, favored by the Romantics. [12] To simplify the debate, one might state that sculpture and painting represent idealized notions of aesthetic paradigms, contrasting Classicism's belief in the static portrayal of harmony and autonomous form with Romanticism's hope in the dynamic representation of eternal movement and fulfillment. The popularity of the Pygmalion motif in late 18th-century literature may thus be based on its negotiation of stasis and movement as aesthetic principles which allows readers to focus on one of the major artistic concerns at the time. Florio's encounter with the Venus statue thus literally mobilizes a highly complex and indeed confusing array of interrelated aesthetic topoi, many of which themselves focus on the representation of movement in the arts. The intertextual mobility of the novella in turn corresponds to the

[12] Katharina Weisrock interprets Eichendorff's *Das Marmorbild* in this context. Katharina Weisrock: *Götterblick und Zaubermacht. Auge, Blick und Wahrnehmung in Aufklärung und Romantik.* Opladen 1990.

multiplicity of all kinds of "moving images" encountered throughout the narration itself.

My goal at this point is not to attempt to disentangle this inter-textual nexus of aesthetic themes any further, but to accept its complexity as one of the major achievements of Eichendorff's text. Pushing the argument further, one might regard the *Marmorbild* as a form of literary arabesque which successfully fuses the imaginary and the real, creating an amalgamation of sensory impressions that defies the reader's attempt to separate them, as one critic has argued.[13] The complexity in Eichendorff's text thus mirrors or pictures the confusion of its protagonist on its own structural level so as to increase the efficiency of the story it tells. Such an interpretation of the *Marmorbild* implicitly leads us back to the ekphrastic tradition, with the decisive difference, however, that the "ekphrastic principle" tried to "freeze" the text, whereas the reading of it as literary arabesque attempts to "mobilize" it in the context of Romantic aesthetic theory. In other words: my interpretation first tried to picture the *Marmorbild* in relation to the spatial properties of the visual arts, whereas my second approach attempts to read Eichendorff's novella as an ultimately insoluble nexus of moving images. To ascertain the validity of such a reading, we ought to provide a more specific historical and theoretical context of the literary arabesque in which to situate Eichendorff's text.

In Islamic art, the term "arabesque" generally denotes abstract depictions of various motifs and patterns such as flowers, geometri-

---

[13] Cf. Weisrock. Pp. 115-38; especially p. 128: "Eichendorff entwirft im *Marmorbild* einen arabesken Bilderreigen, in den er Motive und Kunstgattungen des Rokoko integriert und zugleich romantisiert [...]. Das arabeske Prinzip – im Feenmärchen stets rational auflösbar – verschließt sich hermetisch dem analytischen Zugriff; die Verknüpfung der Bildbereiche bleibt rätselhaft". Similarly, Wietölter, p. 180: "Gleichgültig also, wo man hier ansetzt, ob man sich auf die männlichen oder die weiblichen Figuren oder schliesslich den Text selbst, seinen Sprachbestand und seine innere Ökonomie, konzentriert: Überall zeigt sich Doppeldeutiges, zeigen sich unklare Grenzverläufe und Mischgebilde, die man ohne Substanzverlust aus ihrer angestammten Umgebung nicht herauslösen und schon gar nicht auseinandernehmen kann". Beller tries to prove the opposite, providing a psychological reading that strictly distinguishes between real and imagined imagery in Eichendorff's text. Manfred Beller: Narziß und Venus. Klassische Mythologie und romantische Allegorie in Eichendorff's Novelle *Das Marmorbild*. In: *Euphorion* 62 (1968). Pp. 117-42.

cal figures or other non-referential forms of ornamentation. [14] For Kant, these forms derive their beauty from the free play of human imagination. Since they cannot be conceptualized intellectually, they do not serve as mere illustrations to signify something other than themselves; they simply *are*. Kant regards as the major characteristic of the arabesque its inherent ability for constant change and movement, the inability of the human eye ultimately to fix and perceive the image in its entirety. The arabesque thus defies Lessing's definition of the essential characteristics of the visual arts simply because our "attention oscillates; movement appears as an alternation of perception between various elements" (Behnke, p. 103). [15] In his *Brief über den Roman*, Friedrich Schlegel advances a similar understanding of the arabesque in the literary realm as "a very specific and essential form or expression of poetry" ("denn ich halte die Arabeske für eine ganz bestimmte und wesentliche Form oder Äußerungsart der Poesie"). [16] For Schlegel, the literary arabesque alludes to the aesthetic ideal of the Absolute, i.e, that which cannot, by definition, be signified or become manifest before our eyes. Given its inherent mutability and multiplicity, the arabesque emerges as a means to express those "Zauberworte der Poesie" ("magical words of poetry" [334]) which function as indirect signifiers of "the higher, the infinite, hieroglyph of the one, true love and the holy multitude of life in creative nature" ("[...] Hindeutung auf das Höhere, Unendliche, Hieroglyphe der Einen, ewigen Liebe und der heiligen Lebensfülle der bildenden Natur" [334]). [17]

[14] The following remarks on the history of the arabesque are indebted to the essay by Kerstin Behnke: Romantische Arabesken. In: Hans-Ulrich Gumbrecht and K. Ludwig Pfeiffer (eds): *Schrift*. Munich 1993. Pp. 101-23.

[15] Goethe disagrees with Kant's high estimation of the arabesque, which he, like Karl Philip Moritz and other writers and artists of the 18th century, regards as a "subordinated form of art" ("subordinierte Kunst"). Johann Wolfgang v. Goethe: Von Arabesken. In: *Gesamtausgabe der Werke und Schriften in 22 Bänden*. Ed. Wolfgang Frhr. v. Löhneysen. Vol. 17. Stuttgart n.y. P. 77. Yet, in spite of their differentaesthetic judgments, they, too, agree on movement and multiplicity as the essential characteristics of the arabesque, which they condemn precisely because it cannot be subsumed under the structuring principle of rational thought and philosophical language.

[16] Friedrich Schlegel: *Gespräch über die Poesie*. Stuttgart 1969. P. 331. For a comprehensive, yet complicated analysis of Schlegel's concept of the arabesque, see Karl Konrad Polheim: *Die Arabeske. Ansichten und Ideen aus Friedrich Schlegels Poetik*. Munich 1966.

[17] See also Polheim. P. 56ff.

Any serious attempt to apply Schlegel's theory of the arabesque to literary texts poses several problems, not only because the theory itself remains highly abstract and necessarily fragmentary, as it must, for otherwise it would contradict its own premise. The major difficulty lies in isolating formal characteristics in literary texts that would serve as stylistic equivalents to pictorial representations of the arabesque. One possibility consists in visually conjuring the literary arabesque on the page itself, i.e., on the material level of the signifier rather than on the level of the signified. Florio's horrifying visions towards the end of the *Marmorbild* provide a striking example of Eichendorff's disregard for this option. On the one hand, the following scene is full of arabesque imagery and may be seen as a literary "picture" of arabesque movement:

> Denn auch die hohen Blumen in den Gefäßen fingen an, sich wie buntge-
> fleckte bäumende Schlangen gräßlich durcheinander zu winden, alle Ritter
> auf den Wandtapeten sahen auf einmal aus wie er und lachten ihn hämisch
> an; die beiden Arme, welche die Kerzen hielten, rangen und reckten sich
> immer länger, als wolle ein ungeheurer Mann aus der Wand sich hervorar-
> beiten, der Saal füllte sich mehr und mehr, die Flammen des Blitzes warfen
> gräßliche Scheine zwischen die Gestalten, durch deren Gewimmel Florio
> die steinernen Bilder mit solcher Gewalt auf sich losdringen sah, daß ihm
> alle Haare zu Berge standen. (41)

On the other hand, the passage merely evokes these arabesque forms without actually translating them into the literary medium either formally or structurally, which could have been achieved through poetic means such as ellipses, redundancies, more alliterations like "rangen und reckten" or repetitive phrases, and so forth. The text certainly narrates Florio's horror caused by the overload of visual stimuli he perceives, but fails to visualize this chaos on the level of its syntax. Since Eichendorff neglects the material quality of language in favor of its signifying power, this passage is not arabesque itself, but serves to describe its mere appearance.

One might, nonetheless, pursue the argument on a meta-discursive level by pointing to the intertextuality in Eichendorff's text as an arabesque form. In other words, any kind of structural hybridity, such as framing stories, direct or indirect quotations and the fusion of various literary genres, could be regarded as virtual incarnations of the literary arabesque on the compositional level of the text. [18] However, this approach, too, remains questionable both

[18] Cf. Behnke. P. 119.

with regard to Schlegel's aesthetic theory and to the analytical value of the interpretation itself. To call Eichendorff's depiction of movement or even his variation of Romantic motifs and imagery "arabesque" hardly satisfies Schlegel's understanding of the arabesque as an undecipherable hieroglyph meant to allude to the Absolute or what he calls "infinite multiplicity". On the contrary, the arabesque in this context simply figures as yet another metaphor for intertextuality. This substitution, however, does not provide a framework for further investigating the alleged homology between literature and the visual arts.

Moreover, such a reading is undermined by Eichendorff's limited theoretical engagement of Romantic aesthetic philosophy. Although Eichendorff's personal acquaintance with Friedrich Schlegel and the increased social contact between them after 1811 may lead one to believe that he also gained some knowledge of Schlegel's theoretical writings, I have found only one entry (1807) in Eichendorff's diaries on the subject: "Arabesken. Unendliche Deutung" is all it says,[19] obviously referring to the work of Otto Philipp Runge, whose paintings were often cited as primary examples of the arabesque in the arts. Thus, there is no specific mention of Schlegel's theory of the arabesque and it remains doubtful whether it directly influenced Eichendorff's literary work. This skepticism is further supported by the seductive and dangerous power the *Marmorbild* ascribes to the inherent multiplicity of the arabesque. Whereas Schlegel highly praises the arabesque for its potential to allude to the Infinite or Absolute beyond representation, Eichendorff, on the contrary, pictures his version of arabesque movement as pure chaos, a kind of mental confusion and reverie engendered by the lingering spell of pagan myths and legends.

Finally, in their efforts to highlight the complexity of the novella, recent critics are forced to repress the presence of static imagery and binary oppositions which nonetheless pervade the entire text (Christianity and Paganism, night and day, etc.) and which are evident in the similarity and redundancy of Eichendorff's rhetoric, i.e., his descriptions of places, characters and visual impressions. Eichendorff employs various techniques to emphasize this simultaneity of stasis and motion, one of which consists of describing scenes with both moving and static imagery. The Greek girl whom Florio meets during the costume party, for example, appears first and foremost as an inanimate painting in the middle of other

[19] Diary entry 9. July 1807. In: Gerhard Baumann (ed): *Eichendorff. Werke und Schriften.* Vol. 3. Stuttgart 1964. P. 195.

moving images: "Das schöne Bild schien unverwandt auf ihn hin-
zusehen und stand fortwährend still im Schwarme der nun überall
zerstreuten Tänzer [...]" (28). At times, Florio himself is presented
"as a graceful picture standing blinded in between the fanciful moving images" ("Florio stand noch still geblendet, selber wie ein anmutiges Bild, zwischen den schönen schweifenden Bildern" [27]).

Another way in which Eichendorff highlights the interdependence
of movement and stasis in his text is to mobilize both principles in
opposite directions: whereas Florio's childhood memories literally
"come alive", as they move from representational stasis towards
actual mobility, the dazzling pictures Florio perceives during times
of social gatherings reduce reality itself to its own representation.
Similarly, the animation of paintings and statues during Florio's final
stay at the Venus palace is contrasted with the solidification of the
Venus figure itself, whose features turn "paler and paler" (41), indicating her final regression towards the lifeless marble from which she
originally emerged.

It follows that the text constantly oscillates between the presentation of moving and static imagery on both the diegetic and the
structural level and thus subverts readers' attempts to fix its meaning
in a final reading. While earlier critics emphasized the alleged rigidity of the *Marmorbild*, thus neglecting its diegetic and intertextual
mobility, later ones simply reverse the process but, in doing so,
display mechanisms of exclusion similar to those they criticized.
Both readings are unsatisfactory: although Eichendorff's text focuses on the depiction of movement, it employs the same literary
means and verbatim expressions over and over again to do so; although the text delights in the lifelike presentation of various kinds
of "moving images", it also issues a warning about the disastrous
psychological effects these pictures can cause in the mind of the
naive beholder. And although the *Marmorbild* constantly evokes a
complex nexus of interrelated Romantic imagery and literary topoi,
it nonetheless advances a static scheme of binary oppositions which
seem to structure the text.

II

In the following section I want to suggest that the reason for this
peculiar oscillation within the text is the loss of a mediating faculty
able to function as a bridge between the two poles of movement and
stasis. Classical as well as early Romantic theory had insisted on the
necessity of such a mediator to provide an anchor for any true
aesthetic experience that was within the power of human imagina-

tion. The second half of the 18th century already had introduced a new aesthetic discourse that replaced the critical evaluation of art with statements of empathic experience resonating within the individual beholder. Essays by Winckelmann, Rousseau, Füssli, and Herder, among others, attest to a growing concern for the documentation of a highly subjective and emotional response supposed to complement the work of art so that it may come alive and lose its objective status as a mere point of discursive reference. Several critics have pointed to the transgressive and transformative nature of such discourse, its fusion of stasis and mobility, living and dead, that already anticipates early Romanticism's hope of overcoming the subject/object dichotomy through the bridging power of the poet's imagination.[20]

In turn, early Romantic philosophy relied on the imaginative power of the poet to allude to and ultimately express the harmonious balance between "Ich" and "Welt" in the work of art. The latter is thus reduced to a mere signifier of artistic genius, a necessary, but transitory moment of solidification in an ongoing creative process that originates and returns to the immateriality of human "Einbildungskraft" as the locus proper of true art. The work of E.T.A. Hoffmann provides a pertinent example, in particular his fairy tale *Der Goldne Topf*, which describes the history of its own genesis and reception as a work of art, as the German media theorist Friedrich Kittler has argued.[21] In other words, *Der Goldne Topf* illustrates the birth of poetic language (and thus its own birth) out of a series of hallucinatory visions which it attempts to recreate in the minds of its readers who, in turn, are then encouraged to become the authors of a similar text.

Without doubt, Eichendorff's text remains highly skeptical of such idealist hopes of artistic production, emphasizing instead the concomitant danger of social seclusion and reverie. Florio certainly reacts emotionally to any work of art he encounters, including the marble statue of Venus, yet he does not succeed in harmoniously uniting self and world during this process. Instead, he either becomes distracted or self-absorbed, and often is presented as changing from one extreme to the other, for example in the following passage: "Florio stand in blühende Träume *versunken*, es war ihm, als hätte er

---

[20] Cf. Oskar Bätschmann: Pygmalion als Betrachter. Die Rezeption von Plastik und Malerei in der zweiten Hälfte des 18. Jahrhunderts. In: Wolfgang Kemp (ed.). *Der Betrachter ist im Bild*. Berlin 1992. Pp. 237-78. Also Weisrock. Pp. 79-97.

[21] See Friedrich Kittler: *Aufschreibesysteme 1800/1900*. Munich 1985.

die schöne Lautenspielerin schon lange gekannt und nur in der *Zerstreuung* seines Lebens wieder vergessen und verloren [...]" (22, my emphasis).[22] Florio's psychological instability is recognized not only by fictional characters such as Bianca, who despairs over her impression that "everything was a lie, for he [Florio] was so distracted, so cold and strange" ("Nun war alles Lüge, er war ja so zerstreut, so kalt und fremde!" [35]), but is referred to by contemporaneous critics as well, who lament a sense of distraction after reading the text.[23]

In contrast to Classical and early Romantic theory, Florio's aesthetic experience opens up an abyss of confusion and madness. Florio completely loses himself in his emotional response to art; his lapses into the moods of "Versenkung" and "Zerstreuung" indeed threaten to dissolve the very notion of identity that the aesthetic discourse during Classicism and early Romanticism had hoped to develop via artistic (self-)expression. As a consequence and unlike other Romantic heroes such as Hoffmann's protagonist Anselmus or Novalis' Heinrich von Ofterdingen, Florio is not at all encouraged to become a poet. The text repeatedly exposes his limited artistic talents, which merely suffice for a merry drinking song in the company of friends. His more serious poetic aspirations, however, are presented ironically and with considerable skepticism, particularly by Fortunato, the already established poet, who continuously ridicules Florio's nocturnal songs and the "tender emotions" ("sanfte Empfindungen") he seeks to express.

The novella thus juxtaposes two different kinds of artistic creation: Fortunato's cheerful, vigorous, and lucid praise of God is compared to Florio's dark, brooding and seductive fantasies about ancient myths and legends. Although the latter provide the fertile ground for Hoffmann's heroes (and readers) to explore and develop

---

[22] Richter notes that the word "Versenkung" appears at least 23 times in the text, usually referring "to a dangerous, ruined, finally abandoned world" (p. 61). "Zerstreuung" appears almost as frequently.

[23] In 1818, for example, one critic writes: "Dem *Marmorbilde* von Jos. Freiherrn von Eichendorff konnten wir wenig Geschmack abgewinnen. Uns scheint hier eine blühende Phantasie, die leicht etwas Befriedigendes hätte schaffen können, an einem undankbaren Stoff verschwendet. Man fühlt sich einfach nur zerstreut und betäubt nach dem Lesen; weil der Gedanke den Schmuck nicht zusammenhält und beseelt". Qtd. in: *Joseph von Eichendorff. Das Marmorbild. Erläuterungen und Dokumente.* P. 59. Another critic emphasizes that Eichendorff will fully develop his artistic potential "wenn er erst mit sich selber ins Reine gekommen, dem Fluge seines Genius keine Irrlichter zum Ziel stellt". Ibid. P. 60.

their own creative powers, they are dismissed by Eichendorff as dangerous reveries and delusions of a melancholic mind which inhibit rather than sustain true art. Because of this rejection, the *Marmorbild* faces a peculiar void, a lack of creative power that would be able to bridge and reconcile the binary oppositions throughout the text. Since any attempts made by Florio to creatively engage art or other "pictures" of the world are denounced as mere illusions that must be avoided, Eichendorff, in contrast to Hoffmann, cannot appeal to his reader to engage his own text in an empathetic, imaginative fashion. In other words, by reducing the mediating power of human imagination itself to just one of the conflicting poles within the text, the *Marmorbild* cannot but continuously rehearse simple variations of the very same religious and aesthetic predicament which I have traced during this essay. Even Fortunato's poetry, which Eichendorff presents as the "right" kind of art, does not transcend, but simply repeats the binary structure of the text. His initial song contrasts the merry joy of social life with the somber awareness of death growing in the single individual, a juxtaposition that again mainly relies on the conflict between moving and static imagery.

The seemingly contradictory reactions of critics lamenting either the simplicity or the obscurity of Eichendorff's text thus describe the same phenomenon, namely the text's oscillation between binary structures, a kind of "moving standstill" which remains confined to the story proper without any hope of finding a "higher" resolution either in the mind of the hero or the reader. This lack of dialectical movement in the *Marmorbild* becomes most obvious at the very end of the story. Once again the master of his own visual apparatus, Florio magically overcomes the "strange delusions" that clouded his eyes "like a magical fog" ("Eine seltsame Verblendung hatte bisher seine Augen wie mit einem Zaubernebel umfangen" [48]) and sees things as they really are: "Nun erstaunte er recht ordentlich, wie schön sie [Bianca] war" (48). This abrupt ending attempts to neutralize the exhilarating multiplicity of conflicting images and motifs hitherto explored in the text within the peaceful and harmonic picture of a typical Italian vista, the very symbol of the ideals of German Classicism. Nonetheless, Florio's idyllic ride into the Italian sunrise remains utterly unconvincing, for it produces a "deus ex machina" effect that simply asserts the self-evident clarity of a "truthful" vision whose existence nonetheless has been the major point of contention throughout the entire narrative. Eichendorff's ending does not actually advance a "solution" for the Romantic quandary of artistic creation and aesthetic reception, but instead tries to suspend the entire problematic as such.

In the last part of this essay, I want to argue that Eichendorff's text is symptomatic of a larger crisis of Romanticism in which the authority of vision is increasingly challenged by new concepts and theories about the subjective nature of human perception. In other words, Eichendorff's skepticism towards early Romantic aesthetic theory was not merely rooted in philosophical weariness, but was in fact supported by specific artistic and scientific practices that became increasingly popular at the time, most of which served the double purpose of both social amusement and edification. One of these practices consisted in watching sculptures that were illuminated by torches or large candles, a practice also referred to by Karl Philip Moritz and Goethe in the late 18th century. The ever-changing contrast of light and darkness not only let sculptures appear more painterly but also bestowed upon these figures a semblance of life. A British critic in 1811 remarks that "the improved effect of the marble [thus achieved] amounted [...] almost to animation [...]. To a mind replete with classical imagery the illusion was perfect".[24]

Perfect illusion was also the main attraction of the phantasmagoria, a term coined in 1802 with reference to spectral illusions evoked by magical lanterns and projected onto an invisible screen. The effect was a luminous appearance inexplicably hovering in thin air, an apparition used to frighten spectators or enlighten them about the technological nature of ghost-sightings and similar unfathomable visions. However, as Terry Castle has pointed out, such rational denunciation of external spectral phenomena was bought at the expense of a ghostification of internal mental space, such that thought itself was now conceived of in terms of "seeing images".[25] "The true 'Phantasmagoria'", Castle writes, "is the human brain itself".[26] It follows that 19th-century discourse on phantasmagoria not only anticipates the Freudian theory of projection; it also points to the history of pre-cinematic devices as the material basis for the genesis of projection-theory and the Romantic exploration of the

---

[24] Qtd. in Bätschmann. P. 274, footnote 48.

[25] Terry Castle: Phantasmagoria: Spectral Technology and the Metaphorics of Modern Reverie. In: *Critical Inquiry* 15 (Autumn 1988). Pp. 26-61.

[26] Castle. P. 46. There exists, of course, a much longer tradition linking "idea" and "image" going back as far as the Greek verb "eidolon". See W.J.T. Mitchell: *Iconology. Image, Text, Ideology*. Chicago 1986. Phantasmagoria, however, insisted on only a marginal distinction separating "normal" mental imagery from the hallucinatory visions of an overwrought imagination. According to this model, reverie and madness literally "realize" (i.e., make real) the images they envision.

dark realm of the human unconscious. The phantasmagoria served both rational and irrational imperatives. It enlightened the public about the technological apparatuses it employed in order to demystify the genesis of optical illusions, but at the same time succeeded in mystifying the entire interior apparatus of human perception itself. It helped to "subjectivize" vision by means of "objective" proof about the inherently deceptive nature of human perception.

According to Jonathan Crary, the phantasmagoria was merely one of many "scientific" devices emerging around 1820 that challenged traditionally-held views about the nature of vision. The stereoscope, the kaleidoscope, the zootrope, etc., were all based on a physical engagement of the observer with the apparatus and thus emphasized the physiological conditions of human perception. For Crary, the development of these apparatuses marked a decisive rupture in visual theory at the beginning of the 19th century. While the 17th and 18th centuries suppressed subjectivity in vision as they presupposed a unified, autonomous space of universal order, vision after 1820, by contrast, depends on the "possibility of the observing subject who is both the historical product and the site of certain practices, techniques, institutions, and procedures of subjectification". [27] Vision becomes subjective; it is rooted in the body of the individual observer who himself is deeply affected or even constructed by the social mechanisms and apparatuses he confronts. In other words, there emerges around 1820 an increasing awareness about the subjective nature of vision, giving rise to the necessity of social intervention in the form of scientific discourses that interprets and secures the validity of visual paradigms.

Without further examining the Foucaultian dimension of Crary's argument, I merely want to stress the obvious difference between those theories of the early 19th century that openly problematize the subjectivity of vision demonstrated by modern phantasmagoria on the one hand, and early Romanticism's idealization of the imaginative power of the creative, autonomous individual on the other. Whereas subjective vision in the former emerges as a crisis in the history of human perception, Romantic theory still struggles to uphold the unquestioned authority of visual imagery precisely because it is subjective and purely imaginative. The latter, however, becomes increasingly problematic in light of proto-cinematic devices that both question the previously-assumed stability of the visual field and declare the mind as the source not of artistic inspira-

---

[27] Jonathan Crary: *Techniques of the Observer. On Vision and Modernity in the Nineteenth Century*. Cambridge 1990. P. 5.

tion, but of potential madness. The lifelike projections of the laterna magica thus emerge as cultural manifestations that challenged the representational system of the traditional arts in a similar way as did the rise of modern media at the beginning of the 20th century. To clarify this point we need to once again refer to the work of Friedrich Kittler. and his juxtaposition of the 19th and 20th centuries' modes of representations.

Kittler discerns the exploration of the visual quality of language as the pervasive goal of what he calls the discursive network around 1800. He situates Romantic aesthetic philosophy within the institutional context of educational programs and cultural politics at the time. The period around 1800, according to Kittler, gave birth to the very idea of the hermeneutic process understood as a kind of holistic approach towards reading whose explicit goal it is to dissolve language into the imagery it describes. Correct reading no longer consists of the painful effort of deciphering letters and spelling words; on the contrary, the goal is to recognize and understand the essence of the word, to use language as the mere vehicle for the creation of phantasmagoria in the mind of the reader. However, owing to the lack of technological media at the time (i.e., a lack of competition for saving and reproducing analogue data), Kittler argues, writing remained the only reliable means to inspire poetic imagination. When Novalis defines the latter as precisely "that magical sense able to substitute for all others" ("der wunderbare Sinn, der uns alle Sinne ersetzen kann"),[28] he points to a receptive mechanism that literally requires the "over-looking" of linguistic signifiers so that they may transform into their own signified: black marks on the page reemerge as phantasmagoria in the minds of millions of readers.

While I agree with Kittler's major thesis that Romantic theory is constituted in the alphabetization of society and particular form of institutional discourses that produce educated readers, I want to highlight the importance of the phantasmagoria as pre-modern media events that foreshadow the arrival of the "moving images" of film. Most phantasmagoria, for example, emphasized the sensation of movement by enlarging a tiny image to a huge figure, a procedure that suggests an inherent connection to the traumatic "birth-scene" of Lumière's cinema in Paris, which presented an oncoming locomotive that allegedly frightened the spectators and caused them to run for cover. Although Kittler repeatedly refers to the visionary

[28] Qtd. in Kittler. P. 122.

power of poetic imagination as phantasmagoria that give rise to what he calls "a multimedia show" or a "talking movie avant la lettre", [29] his definition of media as technological means for saving and reproducing data necessarily excludes the primitive predecessors of film. Kittler's theory thus relegates proto-cinematic devices to the periphery since their show is always life and cannot be recorded. For him, phantasmagoria merely function as incentives for the production of more literary texts, since literature still remains the only means to repeat the very same experience over and over again – not in the form of an actual public performance, of course, but in the mind of the individual reader. This distinction serves to validate Kittler's main thesis concerning the fundamental rupture between 19th-century aesthetics and modern 20th-century media: "Media define what is real", he claims, "they are thus always already beyond traditional aesthetics". [30]

My objection to Kittler concerns this easy dismissal of proto-cinematic devices, whose specular forms of entertainment, I argue, anticipated the psychological impact of modern media in spite of the fundamental technological differences that separate them. Eichendorff's *Marmorbild* serves as a pertinent example to illustrate the different perspective I want to emphasize vis-à-vis Kittler's theory, which does not account for the particularities of the *Marmorbild*. On the one hand, the novella remains unconcerned with the particularities of the signifying process itself and thus differs fundamentally from those meta-discursive and self-reflexive texts Kittler often refers to, i.e., texts such as E.T.A. Hoffmann's that are primarily concerned with their own genesis as they examine the dynamic unconscious power governing the process of artistic creation. On the other hand, the *Marmorbild* advances the distinction between hallucinatory projections of the mind and factual projections of quasi-technological apparatuses. The text contrasts Florio's subjective impressions of the Venus statue with the narrator's objective descriptions of what happens in her palace. While the animation of the statue is always presented in the subjunctive mode and from the viewpoint of Florio, to whom "it seemed as if" she had opened her eyes, etc. (17, 40), the animation of the other statues during Florio's final stay in the palace is presented in the indicative, introducing it as a factual event that really happened. Even if we

[29] Kittler. P. 123ff.
[30] "Medien definieren, was wirklich ist, über Ästhetik sind sie immer schon hinaus". Friedrich Kittler: *Grammophon, Film, Tyewriter*. Munich 1986. P. 10. Similarly, p. 226.

concede to most critics that this scene could be read as a metaphor for Florio's confused state of mind, there still remains a factual difference between these two modes of presentation in the text. It signifies a change in perspective that illustrates very well the distinction between inner and outer forms of projection that I advanced above.

Similarly, one might consider the following scene in Eichendorff's *Marmorbild* as one of many that do not simply function as some form of literary image, but could be read as a detailed description of "real" phantasmagoria and the ghostly figures illuminated by flickering lights:

> Es begann nun ein wunderliches Gewimmel von Wagen, Pferden, Dienern und hohen Windlichtern, die seltsame Scheine auf das nahe Wasser, zwischen die Bäume und die schönen wirrenden Gestalten umherwarfen. Donati erschien bei dieser wilden Beleuchtung noch viel bleicher und schauerlicher als vorher. [...] Alles war unterdessen reisefertig, [...] und bald war die ganze schimmernde Erscheinung in der Nacht verschwunden. (13)[31]

In light of such a reading, a new juxtaposition of artistic media emerges in Eichendorff's text. To paraphrase Kittler, one might say that the "Marmorbild" illustrates the rivalry between static forms of representation in the traditional arts, whose animation or "coming to life" depends entirely on the imaginative power of the spectator (or reader) as opposed to the lifelike, audio-visual immediacy engendered by proto-cinematic devices such as the magic lantern. The latter simply do not owe their factual existence to the active participation of their audience; its images are "real" in the sense that they are undeniably perceived from the outside of human imagination. These new apparatuses thus dispense with the need for literary texts as the production site of lifelike images, which in turn eliminates the need for the creative power of poetic imagination to bring these images to life. In other words, once the creation of moving images has been secured outside the purely imaginative realm of the mind, the latter can then be denounced by scientific discourse as the source of delusion and madness rather than true art.

I want to suggest that Eichendorff's *Marmorbild* is situated at the juncture of this epistemological break regarding the validity of visual paradigms and artistic creation. The anti-dialectical nature of the

---

[31] The strangeness of similar scenarios and their impression on Florio's mind is also referred to as "gaukelnde Zauberei" (12) or "seltsame Erscheinung" (32), in which lamps appear as "Irrlichter" in the wind, etc. (33).

novella mirrors the new mode of perception inaugurated by specular forms of entertainment: both reject the dynamic, dialectic power of imagination and expose the fallacy of subjective vision as ghostly projections of the mind. With the decisive difference, of course, that Eichendorff's *Marmorbild* remains a literary text after all. In order to be understood, i.e., read, his text depends on the very hermeneutic principle of imaginative power it so vigorously denounces as delusional and dangerous, which in turn leaves the actual readers of Eichendorff's novella bewildered and confused. Eichendorff's text falls prey to the imagery it conjures, yet cannot control; following the discourse of phantasmagoria at the time, Eichendorff's "solution" at the end of the novella tries to contain these specters through a process of interiorization as it relocates them in the mind of its protagonist.

The problems raised by Eichendorff's novella as a whole, however, transcend the simplicity of its ending. The *Marmorbild* continuously reduces life itself to a series of moving images, thus merging the danger of reverie (the aesthetic mode of "Versenkung") with public forms of "Zerstreuung", a fusion that acknowledges the increasing difficulty of distinguishing between private hallucinations and public spectacles. Situated between Romanticism and Modernism, Eichendorff's *Marmorbild* duplicates the discursive history of phantasmagoria, both unveiling and disavowing the mechanisms of visual projection. As the text problematizes vision, it uses language as the seemingly inconspicuous medium to illustrate and resolve the paradoxes created by the nascent visual media of modernity. This attempt is bound to fail, for it is based on the undoing of the poetic imagination necessary to guarantee the literary success of the text, leaving the *Marmorbild* to oscillate between stasis and mobility, inside and outside, subject and object. The problems raised by Eichendorff's text will later be solved through the click of a shutter and the cranking of a shaft. Photography and film will finally finish what the phantasmagoria had already started earlier: the elimination of the Romantic mode of artistic production.

Jürgen H. Petersen

Wilhelm Meisters Wanderjahre – ein "romantisches Buch"

This essay demonstrates the connections between Goethe's late novel Wilhelm Meisters Wanderjahre *and Romantic aesthetics and art history. Against the backdrop of the novel's reception history, the present analysis considers in detail structural, thematic, and conceptual components of the text that shatter traditional narrative paradigms of unity and totality. Goethe's novel is thus informed by an aesthetic comparable to the Romantic program formulated above all by Friedrich Schlegel and Novalis: an all-inclusive, comprehensive "universal poesy" that combines all kinds of thought and all poetic genres, that mixes narrative, song, and other forms; Novalis even speaks of "narratives without cohesion". Schlegel's emphasis on the "poet's caprice" is mirrored in the novel's compositional structure; and the tale "Die neue Melusine" clearly exhibits Romantic features. Goethe, perhaps unintentionally, realizes the basic tenets of the Romantic conception of art in his novel, and, quite naturally, follows the aesthetic inclinations of the era.*

Denkt man an die Resonanz, die dem *Werther*, die *Wilhelm Meisters Lehrjahren* zuteil wurde, so muß man jene, die *Wilhelm Meisters Wanderjahre* erfuhren, als mäßig, ja sogar als eher kläglich bezeichnen. Das gilt für die erste Fassung von 1821 nicht weniger als für die zweite von 1829. Erich Trunz, der verdiente Goethe-Forscher, glaubt auch den Grund dafür zu kennen: "Der Roman mußte zu seiner Zeit befremdend wirken, teils durch seinen Gehalt, teils durch die damit zusammenhängende Form".[1] In der Tat meinte der zeitgenössische Kritiker Karl Förster, schon bei der Lektüre der *Lehrjahre* habe man erkennen müssen, "daß der Roman als Ganzes unbefriedigend sei, daß ungewiß und rätselhaft bleibt, was Goethe eigentlich damit gewollt, daß nur eins mit völliger Gewißheit hervortrete, nämlich daß Wilhelm Meister noch kein Meister geworden". Aufschlüsse über das eigentliche Ziel des Romans habe man sich daher von der Fortsetzung erhofft, indes: "Nun ist der

---

[1] Erich Trunz: Nachwort zu *Wilhelm Meisters Wanderjahre oder die Entsagenden*. In: *Goethes Werke*. Hamburger Ausgabe. Bd. 8. Zehnte, neubearbeitete Auflage. München 1981. S. 526-554, hier: S. 552.

erste Teil jener *Wanderjahre* erschienen; aber man hat sich seitdem vom erwünschten Aufschluß über das Werk viel mehr entfernt gefunden, als ihm näher gerückt gesehen".[2] Es hängt dies offensichtlich auch mit dem zusammen, was Förster als irritierend, weil ungewöhnlich hervorhebt: Es ist nämlich "nötig, keineswegs die aus den gewöhnlichen Romanen entlehnte Vorstellung von einem Helden mit hinüber zu bringen. Eine Fülle unendlicher Beziehungen und Stoff für unermüdliches Nachdenken wird dem Leser die Reihe der objektiven Erscheinungen gewähren, welche Wilhelms Wandertage bereichern".[3] Aber eine geschlossene Kunstpräsentation mit einem Helden im Zentrum liegt eben nicht vor. Es ist diese offenbar als ästhetische Inkohärenz empfundene Offenheit der Darstellung, die den zeitgenössischen Lesern schon bei der Lektüre der ersten Fassung auffällt, weshalb Achim von Arnim auch bündig von "jener Novellensammlung"[4] spricht, die *Wilhelm Meisters Wanderjahre* darstelle. Auch er sieht in Goethes spätem Roman also ebenfalls kein in sich geschlossenes Kunstgebilde.

Theodor Mundt, ein Jungdeutscher, hatte im Gegensatz zu diesen beiden Kritikern, die über die Erstfassung urteilten, bereits die Fassung von 1829 vor sich. Doch nach seiner Ansicht hat Goethe auch in dieser Version "wieder nur unausgearbeitete Fragmente des Romans zusammengestellt":[5]

Das aufgespeicherte Material möglichst zu ordnen, scheint das Hauptgeschäft des Dichters bei der nochmaligen Zusammenstellung gewesen zu sein, und er nennt sich daher im Verfolg des Romans selbst ganz passend den *Redakteur* des Werkes; denn nur als solcher, nicht als schaffender und weiterbildender Dichter, hat er die letzte Hand an die *Wanderjahre* gelegt. Der Stil ist daher auch meist nur der Stil eines Kompilators, und nach der schönen Prosa der *Lehrjahre* sehnen wir uns hier vergeblich.[6]

Das Mißlingen des Romans führt Mundt auf Goethes Vorliebe fürs

---

[2] Karl Förster: Goethe-Artikel in Brockhaus' Conversationslexikon (anonym erschienen). In: *Goethe im Urteil seiner Kritiker. Dokumente zur Wirkungsgeschichte Goethes in Deutschland.* Teil I, 1773-1832. Hg. v. Karl Robert Mandelkow. München 1975. S. 368-376, hier: S. 369.
[3] Ebd. S. 373.
[4] Ludwig Achim von Arnim: Einleitung zu "Wunder über Wunder". Ebd. S. 379-383, hier: S. 379.
[5] Theodor Mundt: Rezension über die "Wanderjahre". Ebd. S. 452-462, hier: S. 454.
[6] Ebd. S. 455.

Belehrende zurück:

> Da es dem Dichter nur immer hauptsächlich darum zu tun gewesen,
> didaktische Ansichten, Lebensweisheit und Sentenzen in diesem Roman
> geltend zu machen, so ist er damit so bequem verfahren, daß er auf Kosten
> aller poetischen Gestaltung selbst solchen Personen sibyllinische
> Aussprüche und Paradoxen in langen Reden in den Mund legt, die durch
> sich selbst gar nicht berufen sind, auf dergleichen zu kommen und es auszu-
> sprechen, z. B. Frauen, wie der Angela, diesem Unding von Unpersönlich-
> keit [...].[7]

Aber nicht nur die Sentenzen und die mißlungenen Frauengestalten,
sondern auch "die zahlreich eingelegten Novellen, welche als Episoden
einen großen Teil des Werkes einnehmen" und "Den Mangel an
eigentlichem Romanstoff, an Fülle lebendiger Gestalten" notdürftig "zu
ersetzen"[8] suchen, sprengen jede ästhetische Einheitlichkeit und Ganzheit des Romans. Denn: "Diese Episodennovellen sind [...] unsymme-
trisch durch das Ganze des Werkes verteilt, besonders indem sie in die
Kapitel des Romans selbst hinübergreifen und auch oft mit den Ro-
manverhältnissen des Ganzen, ehe man es sich versieht, wunderlich wie
Wolkenbilder zusammen – und durcheinanderlaufen".[9]

Unabhängig davon, ob man Mundts Werturteil folgen mag oder
nicht, ist kaum zu bestreiten, daß er die textualen Fakten treffsicher
beschreibt. Einerseits handelt es sich um einen Text, in dem beinahe
alle literarischen Gattungen und Ausdrucksformen Verwendung finden,
so etwa das Märchen, die Novelle, der Brief, Gedichtstrophen, Tage-
buchaufzeichnungen usf. Sogar der Dialog und insofern eine
dramatische Reminiszenz fehlt nicht, denn in "Wer ist der Verräter"
findet sich eine Reihe von Passagen, die – durchaus nicht zeituntypisch
– ohne zwischengeschaltete *inquit*-Formel, also ohne eine Vermittlung
durch den Erzähler auskommen und gelegentlich sogar mit Regiebe-
merkungen versehen sind: "*Lucidor* (aufspringend)" oder "*Julie* (aufge-
standen ihm folgend)".[10] Dazu kommen die Sammlungen von Sentenzen "Betrachtungen im Sinne der Wanderer" sowie "Aus Makariens
Archiv". Und durchaus hat Mundt auch mit der Beobachtung recht, daß
sich die eingeblendeten Erzählungen, an sich mit eigener Personnage
arbeitend, gelegentlich in die Haupthandlung drängen, etwa wenn Hila-

---

[7] Ebd. S. 461.
[8] Ebd. S. 461f.
[9] Ebd. S. 462.
[10] *Wilhelm Meisters Wanderjahre* (Anm. 1). S. 111.

rie und die schöne Witwe aus "Der Mann von fünfzig Jahren" plötzlich
Wilhelm begegnen und auch am Ende des Romans wieder auftauchen.
Und es kann auch keine Frage sein, daß bei der Verteilung der Novellen so wenig eine Symmetrie waltet wie bei deren epischer Behandlung: Wilhelms Erzählung von seinen Anatomie-Erlebnissen wird in
die Haupthandlung integriert, erhält daher keine eigene Überschrift, das
Kapitel, in dem Lenardos Erinnerungen ausgebreitet werden, erhält
hingegen – noch bevor diese Erinnerungen überhaupt zur Sprache
kommen – die Überschrift "Das nußbraune Mädchen". Auch der Bericht Sankt Josephs des zweiten bekommt an zwei Stellen eine Überschrift ("Die Heimsuchung", "Der Lilienstengel"). Aber warum? Man
erfährt es nicht. Oder anders gefragt: Wieso erhalten andere Sequenzen
keine Überschrift? Auch dies erfährt man keineswegs. Der Leser ist
gefordert, er selbst muß sich auf alles einen Reim machen. Das erste
und das zweite Kapitel der Haupthandlung tragen Titel ("Die Flucht
nach Ägypten" und "Sankt Joseph der zweite"), sämtliche anderen
nicht. Wieso? Steckt dahinter eine Absicht, hat dergleichen eine Bedeutung? "Der Mann von fünfzig Jahren" zieht sich über drei Kapitel,
dieweil die anderen Erzählungen in einem Kapitel Platz finden. Die
Länge allein kann nicht ausschlaggebend sein, sonst müßte man auch
"Die neue Melusine" in Kapitel unterteilen usw. usf. Und es läßt sich
einfach nicht leugnen, daß diese tektonischen Elemente nicht binden-
den, sondern diffundierenden Charakters sind: sie fördern nicht die
Einheitlichkeit des Ganzen, sondern dessen Zergliederung, sie brechen
es auf. Würden alle Kapitel Überschriften tragen, könnte man ebenso
von einer die Geschlossenheit fördernden Parallelität sprechen, wie
wenn alle Kapitel ohne Überschrift blieben. "Der Mann von fünfzig
Jahren" wirkte kohärenter, zerstückelte die Kapiteleinteilung nicht das
Textganze, die Erzählung von Joseph dem zweiten wird durch die
Gliederung in mit Titeln versehene Abschnitte deutlich seiner Einheitlichkeit beraubt, der Bericht Lenardos wird in Teile zerlegt, weil eine
Partie, "Das nußbraune Mädchen", zwar zunächst noch der Haupter-
zählung zugehört, dann aber zu einem eigenen Text gebunden und insofern ausgegliedert erscheint. Wie immer man dergleichen bewertet – es
kann keine Frage sein, daß dieses Erzählverfahren den Text öffnet und
tektonisch segmentiert, keineswegs hingegen die Einheitlichkeit und
Geschlossenheit fördert. Die Inkohärenzen reichen noch weiter, und
Mundt wendet sich denn auch entschieden gegen die große Bespre-
chung von Heinrich Gustav Hotho[11], einem Hegelianer, der die *Wan-*

---

[11] In: *Berliner Jahrbücher für wissenschaftliche Kritik* 1829 (Nr. 108-112) und

derjahre – mit den Worten Mundts – "ein *vollendetes*, überaus tiefsinniges und in jeder Hinsicht bedeutendes *Kunstwerk*"[12] genannt hatte. Hotho war indes nur einer der ersten, die diese Ganzheitlichkeit auch in Goethes spätem Roman glaubten wahrnehmen zu können. Viel nachdrücklicher geschah dies in unserem Jahrhundert. Als Beispiel soll die Interpretation von Erich Trunz dienen, dem schon genannten Goetheforscher und Herausgeber der Hamburger Goethe-Ausgabe.

Trunz sieht die Ganzheitlichkeit des Romans zunächst schon dadurch gewahrt, daß es sich um eine Rahmenform handele, die die einzelnen Textsegmente, d. h. die eingeschalteten Märchen, Novellen, Briefe, Tagebuchpartien, Gedichte und Spruchsammlungen stets auf sich, also die Rahmenhandlung beziehe, und die daher – umgekehrt – von dieser ihren Sinn erhielten, entweder durch Parallelität oder durch Konterkarierung oder durch Spiegelung. Indes handelt es sich bei den *Wanderjahren* überhaupt nicht um eine Rahmenform, was Volker Neuhaus schon 1968 in seinem Aufsatz "Die Archivfiktion in *Wilhelm Meisters Wanderjahren*"[13] gezeigt hat. Bei einer Rahmenform müßten sich sämtliche Binnenerzählungen aus der Rahmenhandlung ergeben. Das ist zwar bei einigen auch durchaus der Fall – etwa bei der "Pilgernden Törin" oder auch bei "Wer ist der Verräter?" , aber eben keineswegs bei allen. "Der Mann von fünfzig Jahren" wird vom Erzähler selbst und direkt in den Roman integriert und ebenso "Die gefährliche Wette". Und auch die Haupthandlung, also das Geschehen um Wilhelm, ist keineswegs autonom, sondern ebenso abhängig vom Erzähler-Redakteur wie die Binnenerzählungen und wird wie diese vom epischen Medium willkürlich unterbrochen, kommentierend fortgesetzt usw. Über allem also schwebt der Archivar und Redakteur, der das Textmaterial arrangiert, und diesem ist es keineswegs um Kohärenz und Einheitlichkeit zu tun.

Vielmehr handelt es sich um einen höchst willkürlich schaltenden und waltenden Narrator. Er bricht eher Handlungsstränge ab und Verständniszusammenhänge auf, als daß er sie stiftete. Als Wilhelm "etwas aus dem Busen", zieht, "das halb wie eine Brieftasche, halb wie ein Besteck aussah", da klärt er die Angelegenheit nicht, sondern etabliert ein Geheimnis: "Was es aber gewesen, dürfen wir an dieser Stelle dem

---

1830 (41-48).
[12] Theodor Mundt (Anm. 5). S. 455.
[13] Volker Neuhaus: Die Archivfiktion in *Wilhelm Meisters Wanderjahren*. In: *Euphorion* 62 (1968). S. 13-27.

Leser noch nicht vertrauen".[14] Unsinn: es handelt sich um Wilhelms Arztbesteck, und daß er den Beruf des Wundarztes erlernen will, wird gleich anschließend angedeutet und eignet sich wahrhaftig nicht für ein poetisches Rätsel. Geheimniskrämerei liegt vor, kein Tiefsinn. Der Hausfreund Makariens will etwas vortragen, was offenbar mit Mathematik zusammenhängt, und damit er sich nicht verheddert, will er aus seinen Unterlagen vorlesen. Es heißt da:

> Er fing nunmehr nach erhaltener Erlaubnis folgendermaßen zu lesen an. – Wenn wir aber uns bewogen finden, diesen werten Mann nicht lesen zu lassen, so werden es unsere Gönner wahrscheinlich geneigt aufnehmen [...]. Unsere Freunde haben einen Roman in die Hand genommen, und wenn dieser hie und da schon mehr als billig didaktisch geworden, so finden wir doch geraten, die Geduld unserer Wohlwollenden nicht noch weiter auf die Probe zu stellen. Die Papiere, die uns vorliegen, gedenken wir an einem anderen Ort abdrucken zu lassen, und fahren diesmal im Geschichtlichen ohne weiteres fort [...].[15]

Ja, will uns der Erzähler auf den Arm nehmen? Schon daß er uns auf irgendwo anders Abgedrucktes vertröstet, kann man nur als einen Jux betrachten, mit dem er alles offen, nämlich unbekannt läßt. Aber die Mitteilung "Er fing nunmehr [...] folgendermaßen zu lesen an" durch den Hinweis zu unterbrechen, daß er das "folgendermaßen" Vorgelesene nicht wiedergeben werde, ist doch nichts als eine willkürliche Dupierung des Lesers. – Das dritte Kapitel des zweiten Buches beginnt so: "Der Angewöhnung des werten Publikums zu schmeicheln, welches seit geraumer Zeit Gefallen findet, sich stückweise unterhalten zu lassen, gedachten wir erst, nachstehende Erzählung in mehreren Abteilungen vorzulegen. Der innere Zusammenhang jedoch, nach Gesinnungen, Empfindungen und Ereignissen betrachtet, veranlaßte einen fortlaufenden Vortrag".[16] Es folgt "Der Mann von fünfzig Jahren". Doch gerade diese Erzählung ist in Kapitel unterteilt. Und auch wenn sich hinter der dann aufgegebenen Überlegung, dergleichen nur in Stückchen nach und nach zu präsentieren, lediglich eine Spielerei verbirgt, so handelt es sich doch um eine Spielerei mit der Absicht, Ganzheitlichkeit aufzubrechen. Ohnehin betont ja der Eingangssatz ganz ausdrücklich, daß *Wilhelm Meisters Wanderjahre* dem Prinzip folgt, "stückweise" erzählt zu werden und mithin Kohärenzen zu tilgen. "Hier aber finden wir uns in

---

[14] *Wilhelm Meisters Wanderjahre* (Anm. 1). S. 40.
[15] Ebd. S. 118.
[16] Ebd. S. 167.

dem Falle, dem Leser eine Pause und zwar von einigen Jahren anzukündigen"[17], lesen wir in einer "Zwischenrede", und abgesehen von solcher Willkürlichkeit, alles zwischenzeitlich Geschehene hintanzuhalten, zerstört die ausdrückliche Betonung dieses Erzählsprungs erst recht die Illusion, wir hätten ein geschlossenes Gebilde vor uns. Dergleichen rückt auch die folgende Einleitung zur Wiedergabe von "Die gefährliche Wette" ins Abseits: "Unter den Papieren, die uns zur Redaktion vorliegen, finden wir einen Schwank, den wir ohne weitere Vorbereitung hier einschalten, weil unsere Angelegenheiten immer ernsthafter werden und wir für dergleichen Unregelmäßigkeiten fernerhin keine Stelle finden möchten".[18] Abgesehen davon, daß der Hinweis auf die ernster werdenden Angelegenheiten wohl eher ein Scherz ist, ließe sich ein solcher Schwank ja auch verschweigen. Er muß nicht erzählt werden, doch dem Erzähler ist es ersichtlich gerade um die von ihm hervorgehobenen "Unregelmäßigkeiten" zu tun. Der Versuch von Erich Trunz, solche Willkür als bloßen Schein zu qualifizieren, nämlich aus Goethes Vorliebe für einfache Erklärungen allertiefster Zusammenhänge abzuleiten, zieht nicht: Was immer mit dem Autor sein mag, der Erzähler läßt keinen Tiefsinn erkennen, sondern einen recht willkürlich schaltenden Redakteur.

Keineswegs sind Trunz die Abweichungen von einem Einheitlichkeitsparadigma entgangen: "Von einem Roman im alten Sinne ist nur geblieben, daß sich eine lose verbindende Handlung durch das ganze Werk hindurchzieht. Vielfach löst die Erzählung sich in eine Reihe von Einzelbildern auf, aber es ist keine beliebige Reihe, sondern ein Zyklus".[19] Wie der neue Roman sich im Gegensatz zum alten ausnimmt, das steht hier tatsächlich zur Diskussion. Um einen Zyklus indes handelt es sich nicht, dafür verbindet die Erzählungen zu wenig miteinander, genauer: dafür sind die Beziehungen zu gegensätzlich und mithin beliebig. Denn auch wenn hier nicht unbedingt eine "beliebige Reihe" von Novellen vorliegen mag, so ist doch zumindest *auch* Beliebigkeit im Spiel. "Das Tiefste wurde erst ganz zum Schluß gefunden und formuliert: die Makarien-Kapitel",[20] meint Trunz. Das mag wohl sein, doch zeigt die Editionsgeschichte gerade der Schlußpartie "Aus Makariens Archiv", wieviel Beliebigkeit bei allem angeblichen Tiefsinn auch

---

[17] Ebd. S. 244.
[18] Ebd. S. 378.
[19] Erich Trunz: Nachwort zu *Wilhelm Meisters Wanderjahren* (Anm. 1). S. 527.
[20] Ebd. S. 549.

hier mitspielte und wie offen also die Komposition des Romans sein
muß, wenn er dergleichen verkraftet, ohne Schaden zu nehmen. Denn
durch die Ausdehnung der *Wanderjahre* in der Fassung von 1821 um
ein Buch auf drei Bücher in der Fassung von 1829 waren die einzelnen
Partien zu schmal geworden, und Goethe sann folgendermaßen auf
Abhilfe, wie Eckermann berichtet:

"In diesen beiden Paketen", sagte er, "werden Sie verschiedene bisher un-
gedruckte Schriften finden, Einzelnheiten, vollendete und unvollendete Sachen, Aussprüche über Naturforschung, Kunst, Literatur und Leben, alles
durcheinander. Wie wäre es nun, wenn Sie davon sechs bis acht gedruckte
Bogen zusammenredigierten, um damit vorläufig die Lücke der *Wanderjahre* zu füllen. Genau genommen gehört es zwar nicht dahin, allein es läßt
sich damit rechtfertigen, daß bei Makarien von einem Archiv gesprochen
wird, worin sich dergleichen Einzelnheiten befinden. Wir kommen dadurch
für den Augenblick über eine große Verlegenheit hinaus und haben zugleich
den Vorteil, durch dieses Vehikel eine Masse sehr bedeutender Dinge
schicklich in die Welt zu bringen". [21]

Ja, mit dem Tiefsinn ist es so eine Sache, und jedenfalls ist der Erinnerung Eckermanns zu entnehmen, daß Goethe das Archiv Makariens
nicht einmal selbst zusammenstellte, daß er es nur als Füllsel betrach-
tete, daß er es als dem Text gar nicht zugehörig erklärte. Er war sich
offensichtlich durchaus der Beliebigkeit bewußt, die hier waltete, und
aus Eckermanns Notiz, an deren Realitätsgehalt zu zweifeln kein Grund
vorliegt, geht deutlich hervor, daß Goethe die Zufälligkeit der Ro-
man-Komposition ebenso gezielt wie notdürftig kaschierte, indem er
den Titel "Aus Makariens Archiv" über das Sentenzen – "durcheinander" stülpte, um ihm den Anstrich des ästhetisch Funktionalen zu geben. Schlimmer noch. Eckermann erledigte die Aufgabe, "und da
Goethe gerade zu dieser Zeit zwei bedeutende Gedichte vollendet hatte,
eins 'Auf Schillers Schädel', und ein anderes: 'Kein Wesen kann zu
nichts zerfallen', so hatte er den Wunsch, auch diese Gedichte sogleich
in die Welt zu bringen, und wir fügten sie also dem Schlusse der beiden
Abteilungen an"[22] Trunz hat in seiner berühmten Hamburger Ausgabe
diese ästhetische Zufälligkeit beseitigt; sie schien ihm denn doch wohl
allzu peinlich zu sein, zumal sie Tiefsinn und ästhetische Kohärenz
ohne Umwege und unzweideutig außer Kurs setzt: Er hat deshalb zwar

[21] Johann Peter Eckermann: *Gespräche mit Goethe in den letzten Jahren
seines Lebens*. Hg. v. Fritz Bergemann. München 1981. S. 467 (15. Mai 1831).
[22] Ebd. S. 468.

die "Betrachtungen im Sinne der Wanderer" und "Aus Makariens Archiv" abgedruckt, aber jeweils ohne das am Schluß von Goethe eingefügte Gedicht – editorische Skrupel hat er dabei nicht gezeigt. Sein Vorgehen war ihm keine Anmerkung wert, obgleich er damit zwei vom Autor ausdrücklich als zugehörig qualifizierte Texte entfernte und damit eindeutig gegen den Verfasserwillen verstieß.

Doch ist auch dies noch nicht genug der Beliebigkeit. Denn an sich hatte Goethe das Archiv als Ergänzung des *ersten* Buches gedacht, doch war dieses schon ausgedruckt, als er seine Sentenzen an den Verlag schickte, so daß er, da ja auch das dritte Buch nicht wirklich umfangreich ist, sogleich und herzlich dem Vorschlag zustimmte, die Archiv-Sprüche kurzerhand dort abzudrucken.[23] Sie bilden nicht aus Tiefsinn und nicht aus Gründen ästhetischen Kalküls und epischer Ganzheitlichkeit den Schluß des Romans, wie Trunz mutmaßt, sondern aus reinem Zufall. Doch auch damit noch immer nicht genug der Beliebigkeit. Denn Eckermann erzählt: "Als nun aber die *Wanderjahre* erschienen, wußte niemand, wie ihm geschah. Den Gang des Romans sah man durch eine Menge rätselhafter Sprüche unterbrochen [...]. Auch wurden die beiden Gedichte so wenig verstanden, als es geahnet werden konnte, wie sie nur möchten an solche Stellen gekommen sein".[24] Was soll man da nur machen? – Der Dichter wußte sich auch diesmal auf pragmatische Weise aus der Affäre zu ziehen, denn Eckermann berichtet:

Goethe lachte dazu. "Es ist nun einmal geschehen", sagte er heute, "und es bleibt jetzt weiter nichts, als daß Sie bei Herausgabe meines Nachlasses diese einzelnen Sachen dahin stellen, wohin sie gehören; damit sie, bei einem abermaligen Abdruck meiner Werke, schon an ihrem Orte verteilt stehen, und die *Wanderjahre* sodann ohne die Einzelnheiten und die beiden Gedichte, in zwei Bänden zusammenrücken mögen, wie anfänglich die Intention war".[25]

Ob mit oder ohne die "Betrachtungen im Sinne der Wanderer" und "Aus Makariens Archiv" – Goethe war es offenbar einerlei. Jedenfalls waltete hier weder Tiefsinn noch das Bedürfnis nach ästhetischer Einheitlichkeit, und die Hamburger Ausgabe bietet an dieser Stelle keinen authentischen Text: Entweder müßte sie auf die beiden Partien ganz

[23] Vgl. den Brief an Reichel. In: *Wilhelm Meisters Wanderjahre* (Anm. 1). S. 525.
[24] Johann Peter Eckermann (Anm. 21). S. 468 (15. Mai 1831).
[25] Ebd.

verzichten oder die beiden Gedichte mit abdrucken. *Tertium non datur.* So haben es denn auch alle anderen namhaften Goethe-Ausgaben gehalten: Die Weimarer Ausgabe und die Jubiläumsausgabe verzichten auf die "Betrachtungen" und das "Archiv", die Ausgabe Beutlers, die des Klassiker Verlages, auch die des Aufbau Verlages und die Münchener Hanser-Ausgabe drucken beide Sammlungen einschließlich der beiden Gedichte. Trunz' Hamburger Ausgabe präsentiert sich mit einem schweren, ersichtlich von dem Einheitlichkeitsparadigma hervorgerufenen editorischen Fehler, den der Herausgeber zu verantworten hat.

Ich wende mich nun der eigentlich entscheidenden Frage zu, ob es denn nicht jenseits solcher textualen Zufälle, jenseits auch der Willkürlichkeiten des Erzählers, der Behandlung der Binnenerzählungen usw. nicht doch jene Spiegelungen und symbolischen Beziehungen gibt, von denen wie viele andere auch Erich Trunz spricht und die in ihrem Zusammenspiel ein "einheitliches Bild des Menschen, das von verschiedenen Beispielen aus erschlossen wird"[26], konstituieren. Und da zeigt sich schnell, daß weniger Einheitlichkeit, wohl aber Ganzheitlichkeit im Sinne einer gedanklichen Totalität *Wilhelm Meisters Wanderjahre* prägt. Einheitlichkeit bringt alles Gesagte auf einen Zentralsinn und tilgt letztlich die Differenzen durch Aufhebung. Totalität hingegen läßt die Gegensätze gerade zu, tilgt die Inkohärenzen nicht und spielt auch mit Diffusionen und Widersprüchen. Wenn dem Auswandern als dem eigentlichen Gipfelpunkt des Wandermotivs das Bleiben als gleichberechtigtes Verhalten des Menschen entgegengesetzt wird, wie es am Ende der *Wanderjahre* geschieht, dann haben wir eine solche Totalität vor uns, die Widersprüche umschließt und auf Einheitlichkeit verzichtet. Die Entsagenden, so wird man leicht übereinkommen, repräsentieren das hier scheinbar nachdrücklich postulierte, im Untertitel signalisierte eigentlich menschliche Verhalten; indes wird man durchaus eines gänzlich anderen belehrt, wenn man berücksichtigt, daß Hersilie und Juliette die Welt des Oheims und letztlich sogar die Makariens als Gegenwelten schildern. Am Ende ihrer Beschreibung jenes Lebensraums, den der Oheim prägt, heißt es: "Sie sehen hieraus, daß wir alle Sorgfalt anwenden, um nicht in Ihren Orden, nicht in die Gemeinschaft der Entsagenden aufgenommen zu werden"[27] Es gibt also das eine *und* das andere, Alternativen sind durchaus gleichberechtigt, so sehr sie sich widersprechen mögen. Die weisen Sentenzen, die sich überall im Haus

---

[26] Erich Trunz (Anm. 1). S. 527.
[27] Ebd. S. 84.

des Oheims finden, haben ihre hohe Berechtigung. Indes meint Hersilie: "ich aber finde, daß man sie alle umkehren kann und daß sie alsdann ebenso wahr sind, und vielleicht noch mehr".[28] Und selbst der Oheim läßt sich auf solche Widersprüche zu seinen Merksätzen ein. Wilhelm übernimmt Hersiliens Überlegung: "'Kurzgefaßte Sprüche jeder Art weiß ich zu ehren, besonders wenn sie mich anregen, das Entgegengesetzte zu überschauen und in Übereinstimmung zu bringen.' – 'Ganz richtig', erwiderte der Oheim, 'hat doch der vernünftige Mann in seinem ganzen Leben noch keine andere Beschäftigung gehabt'".[29] Sankt Joseph der zweite lebt ebenso ein entsagendes Leben wie Montan, Nachodine und die vielen verwandten Gestalten. Aber die schöne Witwe mit ihrem Major, Hilarie und Flavio denken gar nicht daran und präsentieren sich dennoch nicht als Außenseiter. Die Beispiele mögen genügen, um zu zeigen: Nicht das Einheitliche, Geschlossene bildet das eigentliche thematische Element dieses Werks, sondern das Universelle und eben deshalb Offene, das Widersprüchliche prägt den Text. Und dem entspricht offenbar die textuale Vielfalt, der willkürliche Umgang mit den eingebauten Novellen, Schwänken, Märchen, die Segmentierung und Pluralisierung der Erzählgegenstände und der Erzählstrukturen, so daß auch hier Bewegung und Inkohärenz, nicht indes Geschlossenheit und Einheitlichkeit zu konstatieren sind. Daß es in der Poesie aber um eine Universalität der Gegenstände und Wirkungen gehen muß und daß diese nur durch die Überschreitung alles ganzheitlich Einheitlichen auf die Offenheit und inkohärente Pluralität in der Darbietung hin gewonnen werden kann, – dies ist ein Gedanke, nein: dies ist *der* Gedanke der frühromantischen Literaturtheoretiker und Ästheten.

Natürlich habe ich nicht vor, die vernichtenden Äußerungen Goethes über die Romantik und die Romantiker zu unterdrücken. "Das Klassische nenne ich das Gesunde, und das Romantische das Kranke".[30] Diese und viele andere Verurteilungen des Romantischen sollen nicht beiseitegeschoben werden. Doch was zählt dergleichen? Es existieren ja auch gänzlich andere Äußerungen. Nicht einmal ein Jahr nach der eben zitierten niederschmetternden Diagnose des Romantischen als des Kranken notiert Eckermann das Folgende: "'Der Begriff von klassischer und romantischer Poesie, der jetzt über die ganze Welt geht und so viel Streit und Spaltungen verursacht', fuhr Goethe fort, 'ist ursprünglich

---

[28] Ebd. S. 68.
[29] Ebd. S. 70.
[30] Johann Peter Eckermann (Anm. 21). S. 310 (2. April 1829).

von mir und Schiller ausgegangen'".[31] Ja, mitunter kommt man aus dem Staunen wirklich nicht heraus! Wie nennt Goethe die in die *Wanderjahre* integrierten Novellen? – "Erst diktierte ich kleine romantische Erzählungen",[32] heißt es in einem Brief an Charlotte von Stein aus Karlsbad über die Arbeit an den *Wanderjahren* . Gewiß: Goethe dürfte den Begriff des Romantischen nicht in eng literaturwissenschaftlichem Sinne verstanden haben, er meint eher das Unterhaltsame, Wunderliche, ja Wunderbare an seinen kleinen Geschichten; aber es scheint ihm wie auch anderen das romantisch Diffundierende seines Romans nicht gänzlich verborgen geblieben zu sein. Goethe an Zauber: "ist es nicht aus Einem Stück, so ist es doch aus Einem Sinn".[33] "Dem einsichtigen Leser", so Goethe ersichtlich besorgt um die Wirkung der Diffusionen, "Dem einsichtigen Leser bleibt Ernst und Sorgfalt nicht verborgen, womit ich diesen zweiten Versuch, so disparate Elemente zu vereinigen, angefaßt und durchgeführt, und ich muß mich glücklich schätzen, wenn Ihnen ein so bedenkliches Unternehmen einigermaßen gelungen erscheint". Er weiß offenbar ganz genau, wie stark das Werk von den "disparaten Elementen" geprägt erscheint, und er weiß auch, daß die lockere, die inkohärente Form in Zusammenhang mit dem universellen Reichtum des Inhalts steht: "An Stoff und Gehalt fehlt es nicht, und ich kann froh sein, daß Sie für die Form ein so rühmliches Gleichnis gefunden haben".[34] Boisserée, der Adressat dieses Briefes, hatte die *Wanderjahre* mit dem *Rasenden Roland* des Ariost verglichen und dabei die "Umschaffung des Werks in die scheinbar unzusammenhängenden Teile desselben"[35] durch die zweite Fassung hervorgehoben. Mit dieser Analyse betont Boisserée indes nicht weniger als durch den Vergleich der *Wanderjahre* mit Ariosts *Orlando furioso* die Inkohärenzen von Goethes Roman, denn Ariosts Epos galt beispielsweise Tasso und manchen Zeitgenossen als obsolet, nicht zuletzt seiner lockeren Form wegen. Goethe bleibt denn auch offensichtlich angesichts ihrer disparaten Elemente um die Form des Werkes besorgt. Indes hatte sich zur Entstehungszeit der *Wanderjahre* das ästhetische Einheitlichkeits- und Ganzheitsparadigma nun einmal verwandelt und einem Modell ästhetischer Universalität Platz gemacht, dem Goethes Roman durchaus ent-

---

[31] Ebd. S. 379 (21. März 1830).
[32] *Wilhelm Meisters Wanderjahre* (Anm. 1). S. 519 (Brief vom 10. August 1807).
[33] Ebd. S. 521 (Brief vom 7. September 1821).
[34] Ebd. S. 525f. (Brief an Sulpiz Boisserée vom 2. September 1829).
[35] Brief an Goethe vom 25. August 1829 In: *Briefe an Goethe*. Hamburger Ausgabe. Hg. v. Karl Robert Mandelkow. Bd. 2. München 1988. S. 515f.

spricht. Insofern folgt er den ästhetischen Prinzipien, die in der Zeit seiner Abfassung herrschten – einerlei, wie absichtlich Goethe in dieser Hinsicht verfuhr.

Es waren, wie gesagt, die jungen Romantiker, an ihrer Spitze Friedrich Schlegel und Novalis, die diese neuen ästhetischen Vorstellungen entwickelt und mit großer Wirkung in der Literatur etabliert haben; bis auf den heutigen Tag, bis in die Moderne hinein sind sie prägend geblieben. Am bekanntesten ist Friedrich Schlegels Äußerung zu dem, was er Universalpoesie nennt:

> Die romantische Poesie ist eine progressive Universalpoesie. Ihre Bestimmung ist nicht bloß, alle getrennten Gattungen der Poesie wieder zu vereinigen und die Poesie mit der Philosophie, der Rhetorik in Berührung zu setzen. Sie will und soll auch Poesie und Prosa, Genialität und Kritik, Kunstpoesie und Naturpoesie bald mischen, bald verschmelzen [...]. Andere Dichtarten sind fertig und können nun vollständig zergliedert werden. Die romantische Dichtart ist noch im Werden, ja das ist ihr eigentliches Wesen, daß sie ewig nur werden, nie vollendet sein kann [...]. Sie allein ist unendlich, wie sie allein frei ist und als ihr erstes Gesetz anerkennt, daß die Willkür des Dichters kein Gesetz über sich leide.[36]

Ich behaupte hier nicht, Goethes *Wanderjahre* habe man als durch und durch romantisches Kunstwerk zu qualifizieren. Es handelt sich zwar schon der fehlenden Geschlossenheit wegen gewiß nicht um einen Roman der deutschen Klassik, aber um einen, der den Altersstil Goethes deutlich repräsentiert, ähnlich wie *Faust II*. Doch was Schlegel hier über das Wesen der romantischen Dichtung sagt, trifft zu einem guten Teil auf Goethes späten Roman zu, auch wenn dies seinem Autor nicht bewußt gewesen sein dürfte, und auch wenn durchaus die spezifisch Goethische Handschrift, seine individuellen poetischen Präferenzen und Stilmerkmale deutlich genug hervortreten. Aber die Vorstellung von einer Universalpoesie, die mithin alles umschließt und insonderheit das Philosophische, das Kritische, das Reflektierende (Prosa) wie das Poetische (Vers) miteinander verknüpft, zudem aber auch "alle getrennten Gattungen der Poesie zu vereinen" trachtet, beschreibt so genau, was es mit der Textur der *Wanderjahre* auf sich hat, daß man nur verblüfft sein kann. In der Tat hat Schlegel kein Werk bestimmter Gattung im Sinn, sondern ein sprachliches Gebilde beliebigen Zuschnitts, das alle Elemente inhaltlicher wie formaler Art miteinander verknüpft

---

[36] Friedrich Schlegel: *Kritische Schriften*. Hg. v. Wolfdietrich Rasch. 3. erw. Aufl. München 1971. S. 38f.

und insofern als 'Textur' am besten zu fassen ist. Auch das Unabge-
schlossene, das Schlegel unter den Begriffen 'progressiv', 'unendlich'
und 'Werden' als Spezifikum romantischer Poesie zu fassen sucht,
zeichnet – wie gleich noch genauer zu sehen ist – das späte Erzählwerk
Goethes in nicht geringem Maße aus. Und selbst die "Willkür des
Dichters", die "kein Gesetz über sich leidet", scheint bei Goethe wirksam zu sein, wie am freien Schalten und Walten des Archiv-Redakteurs
erkennbar ist.

Bei Schlegel wird zum erstenmal in der Geschichte der Poetik und
Ästhetik der Gedanke kunstvoller Ganzheit im Sinne von Einheit und
Geschlossenheit zugunsten der Vorstellung von ästhetischer Totalität
im Sinne eines allumfassenden Konglomerats aufgegeben, das sowohl
einander Zugehöriges wie einander Unzugehöriges, also auch Inkohä-
rentes und Diffundierendes – mit dem Wort Goethes: Disparates – zu-
sammenzwingt. Dementsprechend betont Schlegel in seinem *Gespräch
über die Poesie* den Gedanken, daß Dichtung in ihrem Wesen hinsichtlich der Gattungen grenzüberschreitend sei. Zu Beginn darf Marcus,
einer der Diskutanten, noch "mehr Rücksicht auf die Dichtarten" ein-
fordern, doch hält ihm wenig später Amalia entgegen: "Mich schau-
dert's immer, wenn ich ein Buch aufschlage, wo die Phantasie und ihre
Werke rubrikenweise klassifiziert werden".[37] Am Ende jenes Teils, der
die Überschrift "Brief über den Roman" trägt, heißt es dann: "Ja, ich
kann mir einen Roman kaum anders denken, als gemischt aus
Erzählung, Gesang und andern Formen".[38] Da kann es dann kaum noch
überraschen, daß die Romanpoetik Schlegels schließlich in Antonios
Satz gipfelt: "Ein Roman ist ein romantisches Buch".[39] Mehr Gattungs-
poetik im Sinn einer Gegenüberstellung von Formen und Funktionen
der Dichtarten existiert nicht.

Nimmt man Schlegels Äußerung, der Roman sei ein romantisches
Buch, als die Beschreibung einer poetischen Textur, die als universal in
Hinsicht auf ihre Inhalte wie auf ihre Darbietungsformen bezeichnet
werden muß, dann stellt Goethes *Wilhelm Meisters Wanderjahre* ohne
Zweifel ein "romantisches Buch" dar. Eine solche Bestimmung ist kein
literaturwissenschaftliches Taschenspielerkunststück und auch kein
gattungspoetologischer Gag, sondern weist auf die ästhetischen
Grundlagen dieses Werkes hin, die auch dann gelten, wenn sich der
Autor ihrer gar nicht bewußt ist. Gewiß gehört zum Romantischen

---

[37] Ebd. S. 492.
[38] Ebd. S. 515.
[39] Ebd.

mehr als die ästhetische und gattungsüberschreitende Totalität des poetischen Textes. Aber Goethe folgt bei allen charakteristischen Merkmalen, die er seiner Dichtkunst bewahrt und die, wie z.B. das Didaktische, keineswegs romantisch sind, doch einem ästhetischen Prinzip, das von den Frühromantikern entdeckt, entfaltet und im Bewußtsein der Zeit etabliert wurde.

Zugegeben: Auch Brentanos *Godwi*, von seinem Dichter im Untertitel als "verwilderter Roman" bezeichnet, spielt mit unterschiedlichen poetischen Gattungen, E.T.A. Hoffmanns *Kater Murr* ist ein Montageroman, der es in der Verschränkung höchst differenter Textstränge unter den genuin romantischen Romanen am weitesten gebracht hat, und auch Tiecks *William Lovell* mag man hier einordnen. Aber eine derartige textuale Freiheit, wie sie sich Goethe in den *Wanderjahren* herausnimmt, eine solche Weiträumigkeit, eine solche Universalität hinsichtlich des Gedanklichen, des So-und-auch-anders einerseits und der Darbietungsvarianten, Textkombinationen und damit eben auch der textualen Grenzüberschreitungen andererseits sucht im 19. Jahrhundert ihresgleichen. Erst mit dem modernen Montageroman rückt Goethes *Wanderjahren* etwas Ähnliches an die Seite. Nimmt man Äußerungen des jungen Novalis hinzu, rundet sich das Bild. Über das Wesen eines wirklich gelungenen poetischen Produktes sagt er: "Äußerst simpler Stil, aber höchst kühne [...] Übergänge, Folgen – bald Gespräch – dann Rede – dann Erzählung, dann Reflexion, dann Bild und so fort".[40] Welcher Text hätte ein solches Programm eher erfüllt als der der *Wanderjahre*? – "Erzählungen ohne Zusammenhang, jedoch mit Assoziation wie *Träume*":[41] auch diese Einlassung des Novalis stellt eine Bestimmung dar, welcher Goethes später Roman am nächsten kommt. Dabei mag man sich streiten, ob der Begriff der Assoziation nicht der Forderung nach Zusammenhanglosigkeit widerspricht. Denn entscheidend bleibt doch, daß Novalis Gewicht auf die Segmentierung textualer Phasen legt und auf diese Weise einen größeren Bedeutungsspielraum öffnet, als es jene epischen Techniken tun, die mit genauen Spiegelungen oder präzisen Konterkarierungen arbeiten und auf diesem Wege keine Bedeutungsvielfalt, sondern Bedeutungs- und Sinneinheit konstituieren.

In der Romantik dient dem Ziel, die Poesie mit Bedeutungsvielfalt

---

[40] *Novalis Werke*. Hg. u. kommentiert v. Gerhard Schulz. Zweite, neubearbeitete Aufl. München 1981. S. 551 ("Fragmente und Studien 1799-1800").
[41] Ebd. S. 535.

und Sinnvarianten anzureichern, bekanntlich auch das Element des Wunderbaren, des Verrätselns und des Märchenhaften. So bildet die Weiterung der Dichtung zur Universalpoesie den Grund für die Entwicklung des Kunstmärchens in der Romantik, und wir müßten blind sein, wenn uns Goethes in die *Wanderjahre* integriertes Kunstmärchen "Die neue Melusine" nicht als erzromantisches Element auffiele. Es gibt aber noch andere Verrätselungsversuche Goethes in dieser Textur. Nur zwei seien herangezogen. Da ist zum einen das Täfelchen mit den Grüßen von Felix:

> "Felix
> liebt
> Hersilien.
> Der Stallmeister
> kommt bald".[42]

Es wird von einem hausierenden Jungen überbracht, der offensichtlich in der Pädagogischen Provinz war und nun den Gegengruß Hersiliens mitnimmt:

> "Hersiliens
> Gruß
> an Felix.
> Der Stallmeister
> halte sich gut".[43]

Manches ist rätselhaft: die weiterhin nicht geklärte halbe Doppelliebe Hersiliens zu Wilhelm und zu Felix, die Verfremdung durch die Er-Form anstelle der Ich-Form des Grußes, der Nachricht, des Briefes, und die ungeklärte Identität des Überbringers der Täfelchen erscheint zusammen mit den anderen Merkwürdigkeiten auch Hersilie selbst als ein Element des Romantischen:

> Ich habe mir Zeit genommen, nachdem ich Vorstehendes geschrieben; was ich aber auch darüber denke, will immer nicht fördern. Allerdings etwas Geheimnisvolles war in der Figur; dergleichen sind jetzt im Roman nicht zu entbehren, sollten sie uns denn auch im Leben begegnen? Angenehm, doch verdächtig, fremdartig, doch Vertrauen erregend; warum schied er auch vor aufgelöster Verwirrung?[44]

---

[42] *Wilhelm Meisters Wanderjahre* (Anm. 1). S. 265.
[43] Ebd. S. 266.
[44] Ebd. S. 267.

Goethe ist es also keineswegs verborgen geblieben, wie romantisch sein
Verfahren war, Verrätseltes, Verwirrendes, Ungelöstes in seine Textur
zu verweben. Hersiliens Bemerkung, daß das Geheimnisvolle "jetzt im
Roman", also in der zeitgenössischen Erzählliteratur gang und gäbe sei,
läßt daran keinen Zweifel. Und denkt man an das Kästchen, um das
man so viel Aufhebens macht, so ist das Element des romantisch Ver-
dunkelnden und Unaufgelösten erst recht nicht zu übersehen. Da wan-
dert das seltsame Ding von Hand zu Hand, ein Schlüssel wird auf wunderbare Weise entdeckt und vom Erzähler doch tatsächlich abgebbildet,
so wichtig scheint er zu sein, beim Öffnen indes bricht das kleine Gerät
ab, dann stellt sich heraus, daß da nur eine Sollbruchstelle wirksam war
und ein geheimnisvoller Magnetismus die beiden Teile zusammenhält,
und als dann endlich der alte Goldschmied in das Kästchen hinein-
blickt, bleibt dennoch alles beim alten, nämlich beim Rätselhaften und
Ungeklärten, weil er das Dingelchen gleich wieder verschließt: "an
solche Geheimnisse sei nicht gut rühren, meinte er".[45] Sind wir nun
enttäuscht oder innerlich erschüttert, waltet hier rätseltiefer Sinn oder
bloße Spielerei? – Jeder muß das wohl selbst entscheiden.

Denn der Text gibt seinerseits keine Verständnis- und
Rezeptionsanweisung. Ja, darin besteht das Wunderbare und Rätsel-
hafte, das Ungeklärte und Offene, daß es das Verständnis freigibt und
damit Rezeptionsvarianten weckt und weite Rezeptionsspielräume öffnet. Erst dies führt zu jenem Universalverständnis der Universalpoesie,
das die Aufnahme traditioneller Texte übersteigt. So wie ein guter Teil
der Personnage der *Wanderjahre* auftritt und wieder im Dunkeln verschwindet, ohne daß man erfährt, was mit den Personen weiter geschieht – etwa mit Sankt Joseph und seiner Familie, dem Knaben Fitz,
der pilgernden Törin, der Gattin Odoardos und seiner unbewußt ange-
beteten Aurora usw., – so dient auch der Umkreis des Rätselhaften und
Ungeklärten einer Erweiterung des Rezeptionsraums. Denn wo alles
ungeklärt bleibt, da erscheint alles möglich, und jeder Rezipient mag
sich das Seine denken – der Text lenkt das Verständnis nicht, sondern
gibt es frei. Insofern dasselbe für das widersprüchliche Mit- und Ge-
geneinander aller Binnentexte, der Märchen, Novellen, Briefe, Tagebücher usw. gilt, löst die Textur von Goethes *Wanderjahren* auf kühnere
Weise und in höherem Grade die ästhetisch-poetologischen
Forderungen der jungen romantischen Theoretiker ein, als es die Romantiker selbst vermochten, und sie löst diese Forderungen ein, ohne

---

[45] Ebd. S. 458.

ein im eigentlichen Sinne romantisches Werk zu sein. Wie gesagt: Der Goethesche Altersstil, seine didaktische Tendenz und manches andere bewahren sie davor. Aber Montage unterschiedlicher Texte und Textsorten mit dem Ziel, die Verständnisräume zu erweitern, und der Rückgriff auf Elemente des Rätselhaften und Wunderbaren sind durchaus von romantischer Art.

Ob aus dem Element des Wunderbaren in der Moderne das Absurde und Surreale wird, möchte ich dahingestellt sein lassen. Indes läßt sich kaum bezweifeln, daß der moderne Montage-roman an den romantischen Vorstellungen von einer universalpoetischen Textur anknüpft. Über seinen Roman *Die Aufzeichnungen des Malte Laurids Brigge*, der Tagebuchnotizen, Zitate, Prosa-Lyrik, Erzählungen usw. bündelt und zusammenmontiert, sagt Rilke beispielsweise: "was nun das Buch ausmacht, ist durchaus nichts Vollzähliges. Es ist nur so, als fände man in einem Schubfach ungeordnete Papiere und fände eben vorderhand nicht mehr und müßte sich begnügen". Das ist genau jene textuale Beliebigkeit, von der ich im Zusammenhang mit der Entstehung von *Wilhelm Meisters Wanderjahren* gesprochen habe. Und auch die folgende Äußerung Rilkes paßt genau in diesen Zusammenhang: "es hätten immer noch Aufzeichnungen hinzukommen können".[46] Denn ein festumrissener Sinn soll nicht präsentiert werden. Man sagt deshalb wohl nicht zuviel, wenn man behauptet, Goethes *Wanderjahre* stellten ein exzeptionelles Beispiel für ein "romantisches Buch" im Sinne Schlegels dar und bildeten damit zugleich einen bemerkenswerten Vorläufer des Montageromans der Moderne.

[46] Rainer Maria Rilke: Brief an Gräfin Manon zu Solms-Laubach v. 11. April 1910. In: *Rilkes "Aufzeichnungen des Malte Laurids Brigge"*. Hg. v. Hartmut Engelhardt. Frankfurt a.M. 1984. S. 81-83, hier: S. 82.

GERMAN-SPEAKING EXILES
IN GREAT BRITAIN

Ed. by Ian Wallace

Amsterdam/Atlanta, GA 1999. VIII,277 pp.
(The Yearbook of the Research Centre for German and Austrian Exile Studies 1)
ISBN: 90-420-0415-0   Hfl. 90,-/US-$ 49.50

Contents: Ian WALLACE: Preface. Anthony GRENVILLE: The Integration of Aliens: The Early Years of the *Association of Jewish Refugees Information*, 1946-1950. Dorothea McEWAN: A Tale of One Institute and Two Cities: The Warburg Institute. Jennifer TAYLOR: The 'Endsieg' as Ever-Receding Goal. Literary Propaganda by Bruno Adler and Robert Lucas for BBC Radio. J.M. RITCHIE: The *Thomas Mann Newsletter* in London 1940-1942. Jörg THUNECKE: 'Characterology', not 'Ideology': Sebastian Haffner's Refutation of Daniel Goldhagen in *Germany: Jekyll and Hyde* (1940). Jonathan ROSS: 'Grenzüberschreitungen'. The Life and Works of Werner Ilberg (1896-1978). Charmian BRINSON/N.A. FURNESS†: 'Im politischen Niemandsland der Heimatlosen, Staatenlosen, Konfessionslosen, Portemonnaielosen...': Otto Lehmann-Russbueldt in British Exile. Steven W. LAWRIE: Erich Fried - Language and *Heimat*. Axel GOODBODY: 'Eine Synthese deutscher und englischer Dichtungstraditionen': Erich Fried and Michael Hamburger as translators and poets. Ursula SEEBER: Wo andere Leute wohnen. Kinder- und Jugendliteratur des österreichischen Exils in Großbritannien. Charmian BRINSON and Richard DOVE: Free Austrian Books: The Austrian Centre and its Publications 1939-1946. William ABBEY: 'Mit freundlichen Grüßen aus der Ferne': Exile Holdings at the Institute of Germanic Studies. J.M. RITCHIE, Richard DOVE, Marian MALET: The Research Centre for German and Austrian Exile Studies. Index.

------------------------------   *Editions Rodopi B.V.*
USA/Canada: 2015 South Park Place, Atlanta, GA 30339, Tel. (770) 933-0027, *Call toll-free* (U.S.only) 1-800-225-3998, Fax (770) 933-9644

All Other Countries: Tijnmuiden 7, 1046 AK Amsterdam, The Netherlands. Tel. ++ 31 (0)20 6114821, Fax ++ 31 (0)20 4472979
orders-queries@rodopi.nl —— http://www.rodopi.nl

SUBJECTIVITY

Ed. by Willem van Reijen and Willem G. Weststeijn

Amsterdam/Atlanta, GA 1999. VI,330 pp.
(Avant Garde Critical Studies 12)
ISBN: 90-420-0738-9   Bound Hfl. 140,-/US-$ 77.50
ISBN: 90-420-0728-1   Paper Hfl. 50,-/US-$ 27.50

Contents: Introduction
Mario MORONI: Dynamics of Subjectivity in the Historical Avant-Garde
Hubert van den BERG: Dadaist Subjectivity and the Politics of Indifference. On Some Contrasts and Correspondences between Dada in Zürich and Berlin
Christine van BOHEEMEN: Subjectivity in a Post-Colonial Symbolic. The Anxiety of Joyce
Annelies SCHULTE NORDHOLT: Proust and Subjectivity
Matthijs ENGELBERTS: A Glimpse of the Self. Defence of Subjectivity in Beckett and his Later Theatre
Willem G. WESTSTEIJN: The Subject in Modern Russian Poetry
Manfred FRANK: Self-Awareness and Self-Knowledge. Mental Familiarity and Epistemic Self-Ascription
Willem van REIJEN: Tested to the Breaking Point: Postmodernity in Modernity
Boris GROYS: The Russian Novel as a Serial Murder or The Poetics of Bureaucracy
Albrecht von MASSOW: Subjectivity as a Basic Presupposition of Modernity in Music
Patricia PISTERS: New Subjectivity in Cinema. The Vertigo of Strange Days
Saskia KERSENBOOM: It Takes Three to Epistemology

-------------------------------   *Editions Rodopi B.V.*
USA/Canada: 2015 South Park Place, Atlanta, GA 30339, Tel. (770) 933-0027, *Call toll-free* (U.S.only) 1-800-225-3998, Fax (770) 933-9644

All Other Countries: Tijnmuiden 7, 1046 AK Amsterdam, The Netherlands.
Tel. + + 31 (0)20 6114821, Fax + + 31 (0)20 4472979
          orders-queries@rodopi.nl —— http://www.rodopi.nl

JOHN P. WIECZOREK

Between Sarmatia and Socialism: The Life and Works of Johannes Bobrowski

Amsterdam/Atlanta, GA 1999. XII,269 pp.
(Amsterdamer Publikationen zur Sprache und Literatur 139)
ISBN: 90-420-0756-7   Hfl. 85,-/US-$ 47.-

Interest in Johannes Bobrowski (1917-1965) has suffered from an impression of the complexity of his works and of the narrowness of his focus: on 'the Germans and their Eastern European neighbours'. The current study re-examines aspects of Bobrowski's 'Sarmatian' works, especially their chronological development, but places them within the wider context of the whole of his oeuvre. It looks at the long period of development before he discovered his 'theme' in the early 1950s and examines his development after *Sarmatische Zeit* and *Schattenland Ströme*, seeing the volume *Wetterzeichen* as moving increasingly away from the past and towards more contemporary issues. His short stories and novels are related to the issues confronting him in East Germany and develop increasingly into responses to immediate poetic and social problems.
Far from being a remote and backward orientated 'Sarmatian', Bobrowski emerges as a writer attempting to communicate with a society which, he felt, threatened to ignore basic human needs and aspirations. The study makes use of material from Bobrowski's *Nachlaß* to present a figure looking for and offering patterns for orientation in his East German society, but with renewed relevance for post-unification Germany.

-------------------------------   *Editions Rodopi B.V.*

USA/Canada: 2015 South Park Place, Atlanta, GA 30339, Tel. (770) 933-0027, *Call toll-free* (U.S.only) 1-800-225-3998, Fax (770) 933-9644

All Other Countries: Tijnmuiden 7, 1046 AK Amsterdam, The Netherlands. Tel. ++ 31 (0)20 6114821, Fax ++ 31 (0)20 4472979
orders-queries@rodopi.nl ⸺ http://www.rodopi.nl

ALAN MUSGRAVE:

Essays on Realism and Rationalism

Amsterdam/Atlanta, GA 1999. XIII,373 pp.
(Series in the Philosophy of Karl R. Popper and Critical Rationalism 12)
ISBN: 90-420-0418-5   Hfl. 150,-/US-$ 83.-

The book's essays represent an important contribution to the contemporary philosophical debate concerning Realism and Rationalism. The author defends in a clear and consistent fashion a fallibilist, realistic, and rationalist position in opposition to the idealistic and relativistic viewpoint characteristic of present postmodern philosophy.

Hans Albert

Contents: Preface. Part I: REALISM
1: Explanation, Description and Scientific Realism
2: The Myth of Astronomical Instrumentalism
3: The Ultimate Argument for Scientific Realism
4: Wittgensteinian Instrumentalism
5: Realism Versus Constructive Empiricism
6: Realism and Idealisation
7: Unreal Assumptions in Economic Theory: The F-twist untwisted
8: NOA's Ark - Fine For Realism
9: Conceptual Idealism and Stove's Gem
10: The T-Scheme Plus Epistemic Truth Equals Idealism
Part II: RATIONALISM
11: Falsification and its Critics
12: Logical versus Historical Theories of Confirmation
13: Facts and Values in Science Studies
14: Deductivism versus Psychologism
15: Deductive Heuristics
16: Critical Rationalism. References. Index of names

-------------------------------- *Editions Rodopi B.V.*
USA/Canada: 2015 South Park Place, Atlanta, GA 30339, Tel. (770) 933-0027, *Call toll-free* (U.S.only) 1-800-225-3998, Fax (770) 933-9644

All Other Countries: Tijnmuiden 7, 1046 AK Amsterdam, The Netherlands. Tel. + + 31 (0)20 6114821, Fax + + 31 (0)20 4472979
orders-queries@rodopi.nl —— http://www.rodopi.nl

ORATIO FUNEBRIS

Die katholische Leichenpredigt der frühen Neuzeit. Zwölf Studien. Mit einem Katalog deutschsprachiger katholischer Leichenpredigten in Einzeldrucken 1576-1799 aus den Beständen der Stiftsbibliothek Klosterneuburg und der Universitätsbibliothek Eichstätt

Hrsg. von Birgit Boge und Ralf Georg Bogner

Amsterdam/Atlanta, GA 1999. XI,845 pp.
(Chloe 30)
ISBN: 90-420-0748-6   Bound Hfl. 360,-/US-$ 198.-

Inhalt: Vorwort und Danksagung. TEIL A Die katholische Leichenpredigt der frühen Neuzeit. Zwölf Studien. Birgit BOGE und Ralf Georg BOGNER: Leichenpredigtforschung auf Abwegen? Zu den Gründen für die bisherige Ignoranz gegenüber einer Gattung frühneuzeitlicher katholischer Gebrauchsliteratur. Statt einer Einleitung. Liselotte POPELKA: Trauer-Prunk und Rede-Prunk. Der frühneuzeitliche Trauerapparat als rhetorische Leistung auf dem Weg zur virtuellen Realität. Birgit BOGE: Der teure Tod. Die frühneuzeitlichen Bestattungskosten am Beispiel der Bestimmungen in der Land- und Policeyordnung für Bayern von 1616. Johann Anselm STEIGER: *Oratio panegyrica* versus *homilia consolatoria*. Ein exemplarischer Vergleich zwischen einer römisch-katholischen Trauerrede (Wolfgang Fuchs) und einer lutherischen Leichenpredigt (Johann Gerhard). Birgit BOGE: Nekrolog als Handlungsanleitung für weibliches Wohlverhalten. Zur Leichenpredigt auf Maria Catharina Manz aus dem Jahr 1654. Ralf Georg BOGNER: Mord unter Ordensbrüdern. Die Leichenpredigt von Wolfgang Haas auf den vergifteten Lambacher Abt Plazidus Hieber aus dem Jahr 1678. László JÓNÁCSIK: *"Verus Israëlita, in quo dolus non est"*. Zur allegorischen Naturdeutung, zur Emblematikrezeption und zur *applicatio sensuum* bei Abraham a Sancta Clara am Beispiel der Schwanenallegorese in der *laudatio funebris* auf Johannes von Eilers. Ralf Georg BOGNER: Polemische Leichenpredigt. Die Augsburger Kontroverse um Franz Xaver Pfyffers Schmachrede auf Gottfried Lomer. Stephan MAUELSHAGEN: Trauer und politisches Kalkül. Zwei Leichenpredigten für Damian Hugo von Schönborn (1676-1743). Andreas BRANDTNER: Zu einer Rhetorik des Herzens. Pater Maurus Lindemayrs Leichenpredigten auf den Schwanenstädter Pfarrer Johann Ferdinand Gessl und den Baumgartenberger Abt Eugen Schickmayr. Christian v. ZIMMERMANN: "Mit allen seinen Saiten schlaff geweint?" Zur poetischen Form und politischen Funktion der dichterischen Denkmäler auf den Tod Maria Theresias. Birgit BOGE und Ralf Georg BOGNER: Katholische Leichenpredigten des 16. bis 18. Jahrhunderts. Einige vorläufige Thesen zur Geschichte von Produktion und Distribution einer Gattung der religiösen Gebrauchsliteratur der frühen Neuzeit. Personenregister TEIL B Katalog deutschsprachiger katholischer Leichenpredigten in Einzeldrucken 1576-1799 aus den Beständen der Stiftsbibliothek Klosterneuburg und der Universitätsbibliothek Eichstätt. Birgit BOGE und Ralf Georg BOGNER: Zu den bearbeiteten Beständen und den Prinzipien ihrer bibliographischen Erfassung. Katalog. Register

----------------------------- *Editions Rodopi B.V.*

USA/Canada: 2015 South Park Place, Atlanta, GA 30339, Tel. (770) 933-0027, *Call toll-free* (U.S.only) 1-800-225-3998, Fax (770) 933-9644

All Other Countries: Tijnmuiden 7, 1046 AK Amsterdam, The Netherlands. Tel. + + 31 (0)20 6114821, Fax + + 31 (0)20 4472979

orders-queries@rodopi.nl —— http://www.rodopi.nl

MARTINA SCHERBEL

Phänomenologie als absolute Wissenschaft Die systembildende Funktion des Zuschauers in Eugen Finks VI. Cartesianischer Meditation

Amsterdam/Atlanta, GA 1999. 223 pp.
(Elementa 75)
ISBN: 90-420-0538-6   Hfl. 70,-/US-$ 38.50

Editions Rodopi B.V.

USA/Canada: 2015 South Park Place, Atlanta, GA 30339, Tel. (770) 933-0027, *Call toll-free* (U.S.only) 1-800-225-3998, Fax (770) 933-9644

All Other Countries: Tijnmuiden 7, 1046 AK Amsterdam, The Netherlands. Tel. ++ 31 (0)20 6114821, Fax ++ 31 (0)20 4472979
E-mail: orders-queries@rodopi.nl — http://www.rodopi.nl

GERMANY AND EASTERN EUROPE: CULTURAL IDENTITIES AND CULTURAL DIFFERENCES

Ed. by Keith Bullivant, Geoffrey Giles and Walter Pape

Amsterdam/Atlanta, GA 1999. VI,366 pp.
(Yearbook for European Studies/Annuaire d'Études Europeennes 13)
ISBN: 90-420-0688-9   Bound Hfl. 175,-/US-$ 97.-
ISBN: 90-420-0678-1   Paper Hfl. 55,-/US-$ 30.50

The opening up, and subsequent tearing down, of the Berlin Wall in 1989 effectively ended a historically unique period for Europe that had drastically changed its face over a period of fifty years and redefined, in all sorts of ways, what was meant by East and West. For Germany in particular this radical change meant much more than unification of the divided country, although initially this process seemed to consume all of the country's energies and emotions. While the period of the Cold War saw the emergence of a Federal Republic distinctly Western in orientation, the coming down of the Iron Curtain meant that Germany's relationship with its traditional neighbours to the East and the South-East, which had been essentially frozen or redefined in different ways for the two German states by the Cold War, had to be rediscovered. This volume, which brings together scholars in German Studies from the United States, Germany and other European countries, examines the history of the relationship between Germany and Eastern Europe and the opportunities presented by the changes of the 1990's, drawing particular attention to the interaction between the willingness of German and its Eastern neighbours to work for political and economic integration, on the one hand, and the cultural and social problems that stem from old prejudices and unresolved disputes left over from the Second World War, on the other.

-------------------------------   *Editions Rodopi B.V.*
USA/Canada: 2015 South Park Place, Atlanta, GA 30339, Tel. (770) 933-0027, *Call toll-free* (U.S.only) 1-800-225-3998, Fax (770) 933-9644

All Other Countries: Tijnmuiden 7, 1046 AK Amsterdam, The Netherlands. Tel. + + 31 (0)20 6114821, Fax + + 31 (0)20 4472979
orders-queries@rodopi.nl — http://www.rodopi.nl

ANNE FUCHS

A Space of Anxiety
Dislocation and Abjection
in Modern German-Jewish Literature

Amsterdam/Atlanta, GA 1999. VII,200 pp.
(Amsterdamer Publikationen zur Sprache und Literatur 138)
ISBN: 90-420-0797-4   Hfl. 70,-/US-$ 38.50

A Space of Anxiety engages with a body of German-Jewish literature
that, from the beginning of the century onwards, explores notions of
identity and kinship in the context of migration, exile and
persecution. The study offers an engaging analysis of how Freud,
Kafka, Roth, Drach and Hilsenrath employ, to varying degrees, the
travel paradigm to question those borders and boundaries that define
the space between the self and the other. *A Space of Anxiety* argues
that from Freud to Hilsenrath, German-Jewish literature emerges
from an ambivalent space of enunciation which challenges the great
narrative of an historical identity authenticated by an "originary"
past. Inspired by postcolonial and psychoanalytic theories, the author
shows that modern German-Jewish writers inhabit a "Third Space"
which poses an alternative to an understanding of culture as a
homogeneous tradition based on (national) unity.
By endeavouring to explore this "third space" in examples of
modern German-Jewish literature, the volume also aims to contribute
to recent efforts to rewriting literary history. In retracing the inherent
ambivalence in how German-Jewish literature situates itself in
cultural discourse, this study focuses on how this literature subverts
received notions of identity and racial boundaries. The study is of
interest to students of German literature, German-Jewish literature
and Cultural Studies.

Editions Rodopi B.V.
USA/Canada: 2015 South Park Place, Atlanta, GA 30339, Tel.
(770) 933-0027, *Call toll-free* (U.S.only) 1-800-225-3998, Fax (770)
933-9644

All Other Countries: Tijnmuiden 7, 1046 AK Amsterdam, The
Netherlands. Tel. + + 31 (0)20 6114821, Fax + + 31 (0)20 4472979
     E-mail: orders-queries@rodopi.nl — http://www.rodopi.nl

THE GRUPPE 47 FIFTY YEARS ON A RE-APPRAISAL OF ITS LITERARY AND POLITICAL SIGNIFICANCE

Ed. by Stuart Parkes and John J. White

Amsterdam/Atlanta, GA 1999. 296 pp.
(German Monitor 45)
ISBN: 90-420-0687-0   Hfl. 150,-/US-$ 83.-
ISBN: 90-420-0677-3   Hfl. 50,-/US-$ 27.50

Fifty years after its inception the Gruppe 47 remains a controversial part of the intellectual history of Germany. Particularly in the light of new material that has become available in recent years, this volume takes stock of both the overall significance of the Group and of the roles of individual writers within it. It contains general essays on the beginnings of the Group and the short-lived periodical *Der Ruf*, the situation of the Group in the 1950s and 1960s, its image as seen by others as well as its self-image and an overall assessment of the Group in literary-sociological terms. Among authors dealt with in detail in relation to the Group are Ilse Aichinger, Alfred Andersch, Ingeborg Bachmann, Johannes Bobrowski, Heinrich Böll, Hubert Fichte, Peter Rühmkorf and Martin Walser. This volume will be of interest to all those with an interest in German literature. It breaks away from traditionally held views of the Group to present an incisive re-appraisal of the one of the most significant phenomena of German post-war cultural development.

Editions Rodopi B.V.

USA/Canada: 2015 South Park Place, Atlanta, GA 30339, Tel. (770) 933-0027, *Call toll-free* (U.S.only) 1-800-225-3998, Fax (770) 933-9644

All Other Countries: Tijnmuiden 7, 1046 AK Amsterdam, The Netherlands. Tel. ++ 31 (0)20 6114821, Fax ++ 31 (0)20 4472979

E-mail: orders-queries@rodopi.nl —— http://www.rodopi.nl

NATION BUILDING AND WRITING LITERARY HISTORY

Ed. by Menno Spiering

Amsterdam/Atlanta, GA 1999. XV,220 pp.
(Yearbook of European Studies/Annuaire d'Etudes Europeennes 12)
ISBN: 90-420-0627-7   Hfl. 110,-/US-$ 61.-

Contents: Authors in this volume. Introduction. Annelies van HEES: N.M. Petersen and the Case of Denmark. Egil TÖRNQVIST: Henrik Schück as Historiographer of Swedish Literature. Klaus F. GILLE: *Germanistik* und Nation in the 19th Century. George VIS: Literary Historiography in the Northern and Southern Netherlands between 1800 and 1830. D. van der HORST: Jan Frans Willems: A Literary History for a new Nation. Joep LEERSSEN: A la recherche d'une littérature perdue: Literary History, Irish Identity and Douglas Hyde. Ton HOENSELAARS: A Taste of George Saintsbury: *A Short History of English Literature* (1898). Menno SPIERING: The Englishness of English Literature and Literary History: The Lectures of Sir Arthur Quiller-Couch. Ruud MEIJER: Travailler Pour La Patrie: Gustave Lanson, The Founder of French Academic Literary History I. Manet van MONTFRANS: Travailler Pour La Patrie: Gustave Lanson, The Founder of Academic Literary History in France II. Lily COENEN: M. Menendez Pelayo: Literary History in the Context of a Religious Question. Fernando VENÂNCIO: 'Quick Fleeting Sketches': Literary History in Portugal in the 19th Century. Lucas BRUYNING: From Tiraboschi to Francesco De Sanctis: Italian Literary History as a Legitimation of National Unity. Dina ARISTODEMO: National Values and Literary Form in De Sanctis' *History of Italian Literature*.

Editions Rodopi B.V.

USA/Canada: 2015 South Park Place, Atlanta, GA 30339, Tel. (770) 933-0027, *Call toll-free* (U.S.only) 1-800-225-3998, Fax (770) 933-9644

All Other Countries: Tijnmuiden 7, 1046 AK Amsterdam, The Netherlands. Tel. + + 31 (0)20 6114821, Fax + + 31 (0)20 4472979 *E-mail:* orders-queries@rodopi.nl —— http://www.rodopi.nl